"This second edition is a must for any inclusive perspective on working with persons struggling with substance use. The additions, namely, the expansion of family diversity to include sexual and gender minorities, the neurobiology of addictions, motivational interviewing, ethics, expansion of treatment models and case application, offer a comprehensive text relevant for therapists-in-training and seasoned therapists seeking continuing education. Dr. Reiter's years of wisdom as a therapist and academic is evident throughout the book and especially in the self-of-the family therapist chapter that addresses issues crucial for growth and sustenance. Highly recommended!"

Joyce Baptist, PhD, LCMFT, Certified EMDR Therapist,
Associate Professor, Kansas State University

"Down-to-earth and comprehensive, *Substance Abuse and the Family* (2nd Ed.) allows you to grasp the nuts and bolts of assessing and treating individuals and families dealing with substance abuse issues. In this second edition, Reiter takes us to the crossroads of neurophysiological, genetic, cultural, ethical, relational, and risks factors of addiction. Providing hands on information for clinicians and students, Reiter exemplifies various family therapy approaches that might contribute to the process of recovery. One of the useful tools this book provides is applying each chapter's concepts to a standard case, which helped bring the concepts to life."

Jimena Castro, PhD, Assistant Professor, Our Lady of
the Lake University

SUBSTANCE ABUSE AND THE FAMILY

In this updated edition of *Substance Abuse and the Family*, Michael D. Reiter examines addiction through a family systems lens which considers a range of interconnected contexts, such as biology and genetics, family relationships, and larger systems.

Chapters are organized around two sections: Assessment and Treatment. Examining how the family system organizes around substance use and abuse, the first section includes contributions on the neurobiology and genetics of addiction, as well as chapters on family diversity, issues in substance-using families, and working in a culturally sensitive way. The second half of the book explores various treatment options for individuals and families presenting with substance abuse issues, providing an overview of the major family therapy theories, and chapters on self-help groups and the process of family recovery.

The second edition has many useful additions including a revision of the family diversity chapter to consider sexual and gender minorities, brand new chapters on behavioral addictions such as sex and gambling, and a chapter on ethical implications in substance abuse work with families. Additional sections include information on Multisystemic Therapy, Behavioral Couples Therapy, Motivational Interviewing, and Twelve-Step Facilitation. Each chapter now contains a case application to help demonstrate treatment strategies in practice.

Intended for undergraduate and graduate students, as well as beginning practitioners, *Substance Abuse and the Family, 2nd Ed.* remains one of the most penetrating and in-depth examinations of the topic available.

Michael D. Reiter, PhD, is Professor of Family Therapy in the Department of Family Therapy of the College of Arts, Humanities, and Social Sciences at Nova Southeastern University. Michael is a licensed marriage and family therapist and has authored eight previous textbooks, 18 peer-reviewed journal articles, and has presented at national and international conferences on various aspects of family therapy.

SUBSTANCE ABUSE AND THE FAMILY

Assessment and Treatment

Second Edition

Michael D. Reiter

Routledge
Taylor & Francis Group

NEW YORK AND LONDON

Second edition published 2019
by Routledge
52 Vanderbilt Avenue, New York, NY 10017

and by Routledge
2 Park Square, Milton Park, Abingdon, Oxon, OX14 4RN

Routledge is an imprint of the Taylor & Francis Group, an informa business

First edition published by Routledge 2014

Library of Congress Cataloging-in-Publication Data
A catalog record has been requested for this book

ISBN: 978-1-138-62587-7 (hbk)
ISBN: 978-1-138-62597-6 (pbk)
ISBN: 978-0-429-45957-3 (ebk)

Typeset in Sabon
by Swales & Willis Ltd, Exeter, Devon, UK

This book is dedicated to my siblings: Alyssa, Sean, Howard, and David

Contents

About the Contributors

Myron J. Burns, PhD, is an Associate Professor at Nova Southeastern University (Fort Lauderdale, FL). He received his doctoral degree in Counseling Psychology from Tennessee State University. Before attending Tennessee State University, Dr. Burns graduated from Howard University. He has worked in many roles at the University of Miami Center for Family Studies as a counselor, supervisor, and project director. Dr. Burns' research interests are in the areas of health, drug use, and the interplay of personality and stress process variables.

Christina M. Gobin, MS, is a PhD candidate at the University of Florida. She received her Master's degree at Nova Southeastern University where she investigated the effect of sleep quality on cognitive function and emotion processing. Currently, she is studying the neurobiology of cocaine addiction. Her research focuses on identifying neurobiological substrates underlying post-cocaine cognitive function and drug seeking.

Paul J. Kiser, PhD, is an Associate Professor of Biology at Bellarmine University (Louisville, KY). He has been involved for nearly two decades at the local and state level studying and advocating for health policy initiatives and preventive efforts to reduce the health and economic burdens that the use of alcohol, illicit drugs, tobacco and tobacco-related products place on our society. He was a certified prevention specialist who served on numerous local, regional, and state executive boards and committees, and he has consulted on health policies for numerous private businesses and organizations as well as at city council, fiscal court, and state legislative levels. Currently, Dr. Kiser is researching the pervasiveness of alternative nicotine delivery systems in his community and the implications of this on the perceptions and use rates by college students in the region.

Joshua Leblang, Ed.S, is a Senior Lecturer in the Department of Psychiatry at the University of Washington (Seattle, WA). He has been a clinician, supervisor, and consultant for the past 18 years, working with teams in Washington, New Mexico, Illinois, Connecticut, and New York, as well as with teams internationally in the UK and New Zealand. He has been working on the MST-FIT (Family Integrated Transitions) adaptation for the past 13 years, transitioning youth from out-of-home placement back to their natural environment.

Michael D. Reiter, PhD, is Professor of Family Therapy at Nova Southeastern University in the Department of Family Therapy of the College of Arts, Humanities, and Social Sciences. He is the author of eight previous books including *Systems Theories for Psychotherapists* (2019), *Family Therapy: An Introduction to Process, Practice, and Theory* (2018), *Case Conceptualization in Family Therapy* (2014), and *The Craft of Family Therapy* (2014), written with Dr. Salvador Minuchin, one of the founders of family therapy. Dr. Reiter has authored 18 peer-reviewed articles and presented at numerous local, state, national, and international conferences on family therapy. He served as Coordinator of the Substance Abuse Specialty Program in the Division of Social and Behavioral Sciences at Nova Southeastern University and was a Certified Addictions Professional. He is a licensed marriage and family therapist and approved supervisor of the American Association of Marriage and Family Therapy.

Jaime L. Tartar, PhD, is a Professor of Behavioral Neuroscience at Nova Southeastern University (Fort Lauderdale, FL). She earned her PhD in the Behavioral Neuroscience program at the University of Florida where the focus of her research involved discovering long-term changes that occur in neurobiological pathways involved in stress responses and developing animal models of chronic stress. Dr. Tartar completed postdoctoral training at Harvard Medical School, where she studied neurological consequences of sleep perturbations using in vitro electrophysiological recording techniques. She earned a certificate in Sleep Medicine from Harvard Medical School Division of Sleep Medicine. Dr. Tartar's current research is focused on stress, sleep, and human athletic performance.

Julius Thomas played for seven years in the NFL. He retired from football to pursue a doctoral degree in clinical psychology to help others. He is currently pursuing post-graduate work at Nova Southeastern University (Fort Lauderdale, FL), working in the neuroscience lab with Jaime Tartar where they are researching the comprehensive effects of participating in contact sports.

Preface

This book was born over 20 years of teaching family therapy and substance abuse courses. At my university, I taught a course specifically designed to explore understanding addictions through a family systems lens. Throughout that time I struggled to find the right textbooks that were broad enough to give the reader an overview of the field with enough depth to allow them to use the information effectively. While I was able to use a lot of good textbooks, none satisfactorily accomplished my objectives for the course. Either they were based on one specific theoretical lens or too focused on a specific perspective of addictions. Thus, I decided to write the first edition of *Substance Abuse and the Family*.

That book was quite well received as many training programs utilized the book in their Addictions and Family Therapy course. While I was very pleased with the initial book, over the last five years I saw several areas that could be enhanced and thus the second edition of the book developed. My intent for this book is to provide the beginning practitioner with enough information to be able to conceptualize substance abuse through a family systems lens. Hopefully after reading the book, you will not be able to just see an individual, but will understand that the individual acts based on interconnected contexts—which include biology and genetics, family relationships, and larger systems.

The book is divided into two parts: Assessment and Treatment. In the first half of the book we explore how to assess the various aspects of clients when they present with substance abuse. Chapter 1 conceptualizes addiction, providing the basis of understanding the terms in the field as well as different models of addiction. Chapter 2 explores the neuroscience of addiction, explaining how substances impact brain chemistry and thus human behavior. Chapter 3 describes the genetics of addiction and how genes may predispose some people to be more susceptible to substances. Chapter 4 explains how a family may go through a process of becoming an addicted family. Chapter 5 presents information on family diversity, particularly as it relates to substance abuse. Chapter 6 presents several different models of roles that members in addicted families may adopt. Chapter 7 describes the family life cycle, focusing on children of alcoholics and adult children of alcoholics. Chapter 8 identifies several issues in substance-abusing families including domestic violence, dual diagnosis, and readiness for change. Chapter 9 focuses on behavioral addictions, such as sex, gambling, and internet addiction.

The second half of the book explores various treatment options for individuals and families presenting with substance abuse issues. Chapter 10 focuses on working with partial systems, as many times the person abusing substances does not want to enter therapy. This chapter explores various self-help groups as well as various programs designed to work with the family to help get the substance abuser into treatment. Chapter 11 is a brief overview of ethical issues involved when conducting substance abuse therapy with families. Chapter 12 provides an overview of systems theory as these ideas form the basis for most family therapy theories. Chapter 13 presents five of the prominent family therapy theories, involving intergenerational, experiential, and communication approaches. Chapter 14 presents five other family therapy theories involving strategic, systemic, and postmodern models. Chapter 15 presents four specific treatment approaches based on family therapy principles for working with families dealing with substance abuse. Chapter 16 describes the process of family recovery and how families change over time throughout their growth, as well as a brief discussion of family prevention. Chapter 17 concludes the book with a focus on the substance abuse family therapist.

The second edition has many additions including a section on the family-disease perspective (Chapter 1), a complete revision of the family diversity and the family chapter with the inclusion of a new section on sexual and gender minorities (Chapter 5), enhancing motivation/motivational interviewing (Chapter 8), criminality and addictions (Chapter 8), a new chapter describing the behavioral addictions (Chapter 9), expansion of the CRAFT section (Chapter 10), the addition of a section on Multisystemic Therapy (Chapter 10), the addition of a section on Twelve-Step Facilitation (Chapter 10), a new chapter exploring some of the ethical issues involved in substance abuse and family therapy (Chapter 11), the addition of information pertaining to family-based substance abuse prevention (Chapter 16), and a new section at the end of every chapter called Case Application where the material from the chapter is applied to the case that was presented in Chapter 1. The Case Application section helps solidify the learning of the information by applying it to a case family struggling with addictions.

My hope is that after reading this book you will never view an individual the same way again! The family systems viewpoint is just one of many, but one that I think is very useful as it not only pertains to the individual but to the larger spheres of influence (their family and the society they live in).

This book spans almost all of my life as I was able to work with friends from almost all stages of my career. Paul Kiser, who has been a friend since high school, was able to help out with his expertise in substance abuse prevention. Joshua Leblang, a friend from my Masters program at the University of Florida, contributed with his expertise as a trainer/supervisor in Multisystemic Therapy. Christopher Burnett, one of my original family therapy teachers, mentors, colleagues, and friends, provided the cover photo. My colleague and good friend Jaime Tartar was my office next-door neighbor for almost ten years—consistently yelling at me that my being in my office made her office cold. For years Jaime would ask me when we were going to collaborate on a project. Most of my work was in the application of family therapy theories which did not mesh with her pursuits in neuroscience. Fortunately, this project allowed us to see how our two interests intersected. Jaime was kind enough to write the neuroscience of addiction chapter and the genetics of addiction chapter with Christina Gobin, a graduate student she was advising and a past student of mine. Thanks to Christina for agreeing to help out on the project. I also want to thank Dalis Arismendi, one of my former graduate students, who helped me on Chapter 5 for the first edition of this book. Myron Burns, a colleague for the last five years, had wanted to collaborate on a project and this second edition fit nicely into his wheelhouse. Lastly, my newest friend, Julius Thomas, who was fortunate to get connected to Jaime Tartar to help him in his pursuit of utilizing clinical psychology to help athletes, as well as to work with her on revision of "The Neurobiology of Addiction" chapter. April Brown, my Graduate Assistant, aided me in a variety of ways including figure and genogram development, updating statistics, reference procurement, as well as a variety of other helpful acts. I also want to thank Clare Ashworth, editor at Routledge, who helped bring this second edition to fruition.

PART I

ASSESSMENT

ONE

Conceptualizing Addictions

On Monday morning you enter your agency, ready for another day of providing counseling to your clients. Mondays at your agency are always intriguing since this is the day that you conduct new client intakes. Today you have several new clients on your schedule. You do not know anything about them or what the issues are that bring them to see you.

At the appointed time you walk to the waiting room and greet your first client. As you introduce yourself, you look him over, making initial impressions based on his age, height, weight, clothing choices, and hygiene. Walking with him back to your office, you make small talk about the current weather, finding the office, or something that recently happened in the news. Upon sitting down, you talk with the client about informed consent and make sure all the proper paperwork is signed. Then you let him know that you will need to gather a lot of information from him, as is required from the agency, since the first meeting is designed for you to develop a biopsychosocial assessment. You start to talk with him about his history and current situation, all the while trying to figure out how you will understand what is happening for him and, most importantly, what you will be able to do to help him, regardless of what the "problem" may be.

After a few minutes of small talk and joining, you ask the client the all-important question, "What brings you in to therapy?" (or "How can I help you," "What would you like different in your life," "etc."). The client responds that he has been addicted to alcohol and drugs for the last two years and that he wants to stop.

You now have a dilemma. Based on how you conceptualize problems, you will not only ask different questions, but will pay attention to some material more than others, leading you to develop a theory of problem formation and an associated theory of problem resolution (Reiter, 2014, 2019). When the client says that he is abusing drugs, how do you view this? Do you see this as strictly a biological problem? Do you believe that there is something mentally wrong with your client—that he has a psychological disorder? Do you think that the addiction is housed within a web of relationships and view it from a systemic perspective? Or do you expand a systemic view to see that biology, psychology, and social factors all contribute to the client's experience?

Your answer to these questions is anything but insignificant. How you answer each question informs how you conceptualize why the client developed the problem, how it is currently maintained, and what you might do in therapy to help him. Your view of why people develop addictions and how they continue to use guides the whole of the treatment.

While there is validity to many different conceptualizations, this book attempts to help therapists view substance abuse problems from a systemic perspective. This includes an understanding of how the individual is impacted by the drug compounds, their susceptibility based on their genetics, as well as how past and current family and relational functioning impacts use of the substance. This systemic orientation can help individuals to move beyond their abuse of drugs. We will come back to our client later in this chapter, but first we should focus on knowing some of the most prominent terms in the substance abuse arena so that we are clear on what we are talking about.

Defining Addiction

Perhaps we should start our exploration of the field of substance abuse and the family through defining some of the key concepts. It is important, especially when interacting with other mental health professionals, to be on the same page when we are discussing what is occurring for our clients. While various substance abuse professionals may have differing views on the etiology of addiction or the most efficacious treatment, we can usually agree on the basic terms that we use when we are explaining the situations clients find themselves in.

In the field of mental health the definitive source for criteria of mental disorders is the *Diagnostic and Statistical Manual of Mental Disorders* (DSM), which is currently in its fifth edition (American Psychiatric Association, 2013). The DSM does not provide a definition of addiction but does provide criteria for which various types of substance (and primarily mental health) issues can be categorized. What might be viewed as addiction-related issues are housed under the title of **substance-related disorders**, which encompass 10 classes of drugs: alcohol; caffeine; cannabis; hallucinogens; inhalants; opioids; sedatives, hypnotics, and anxiolytics; stimulants; tobacco; and other (or unknown) substances.

These 10 classes of drugs were chosen because they all have very similar processes in how they impact people physiologically. The primary process focuses on a direct activation of the brain reward system (which we will talk about more in Chapter 2). This activation impacts the reinforcement of the drug use behavior. While these drugs will show differential effects on people—for instance, it may take more or less of the drug to produce the same effects in two different individuals—they each demonstrate some type of impact on brain functioning.

Within the category of substance-related disorders the DSM-V makes a distinction between substance use disorders and substance-induced disorders. **Substance use disorders** are a cluster of cognitive, behavioral, and physiological symptoms, which impact the individual's functioning, even after problems develop. What this means is that once the person's use of drugs begins to impair their functioning in a variety of areas (i.e., perhaps they are not able to maintain a job or they find that they need much more of the drug to attain the effects) the person continues to use. Criteria include impaired control, social impairment, risky use, and pharmacological criteria (including tolerance and withdrawal).

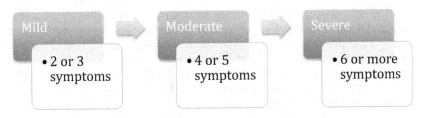

Figure 1.1 The severity classification for substance use disorders according to the
Diagnostic and Statistical Manual-V

Substance use disorders are viewed on a continuum from mild to severe. This designation depends on how many symptoms are present. Mild substance use disorder is based upon the presence of two or three symptoms, the moderate designation has four or five symptoms and the severe criteria is determined by six or more symptoms (see Figure 1.1).

Substance-induced disorders are secondary disorders that occur from the use of the drugs. Some examples of these include intoxication, sleep disorders, sexual dysfunctions, and anxiety disorders. The symptoms from substance-induced disorders are reversible, coinciding with a reduction or abstinence from the specific drug being used. A key component here is that the symptoms cannot be associated with a medical condition or other mental disorder. As an example, substance-induced disorders may demonstrate themselves in a relationship where the male may not be able to get or maintain an erection—not because of physiological problems, but because of the use of a specific drug. Once they stop using the drug, they are able to have erections again.

In the substance abuse field, there are many overlapping concepts and terms. Perhaps the most prominent one is the notion of addiction. What is addiction? What comprises someone who is addicted? The answer to this is highly debated, as part of the answer to this question relates to the hypothesized etiology of drug abuse. While there may be alternative definitions to the terms/concepts that are presented here, we will use these definitions throughout the book to help us develop a common language.

Addiction: The American Society of Addiction Medicine (ASAM, 2014) defined addiction as "a primary, chronic disease of brain reward, motivation, memory and related circuitry." The ASAM holds that it is the dysfunction of brain circuitry which leads to problems in the biological, psychological, social, and spiritual realms. They promote an A-B-C-D-E acronym for the characteristics of addiction:

a. Inability to consistently **A**bstain;
b. Impairment in **B**ehavioral control;
c. **C**raving; or increased "hunger" for drugs or rewarding experiences;
d. **D**iminished recognition of significant problems with one's behaviors and interpersonal relationships; and
e. A dysfunctional **E**motional response.

This definition provides a medical perspective to addiction where the action occurs within the individual but also has external consequences.

While this is one of many definitions and criteria, overall, definitions of addiction and substance-related concepts have been changing over time. As more information about drug science and brain functioning comes forth, newer and more accurate understandings of addiction can be developed. Given this, the definition of dependence in the DSM and *International Statistical Classification of Diseases and Related Health Problems* (ICD) has changed over time (Nielsen, Hansen, & Gotzsche, 2012).

The following are many of the primary terms in the substance abuse and addiction field.

Abstinence: Abstinence is the complete disuse of a substance. The person does not put in their body the drug that they were using. If someone were addicted to alcohol and consumed 20 beers per week, but cut down to 10, they would not be abstinent. They would need to not ingest any type of alcohol for us to be able to utilize this term.

Craving: Craving is an intense or heightened desire for a substance. While almost all of us have had what we might call a "craving" at some point (for instance, on Thursday I was really craving peanut butter and chocolate ice cream), in the substance abuse field craving refers to a desire for the substance, which becomes a primary motivating factor to obtain that substance.

Drugs: Drugs are usually considered to be a substance (outside of things such as food) that impacts the physiology of the body. While foods, nutrients, and vitamins do have physiological results, they are necessary for survival. Drugs, as used in substance abuse, are not. A person can easily live a healthy life never having consumed alcohol, nicotine, cocaine, heroin, etc.

Drug of choice: Drug of choice is the preferred drug that a person uses. While they may use multiple drugs, such as alcohol, tobacco, and cocaine, the drug of choice is the one the person would use if given the choice.

Dual diagnosis: Dual diagnosis is a term used when a person has more than one recognized diagnosis (as determined by fitting the criteria of either the DSM-V or the ICD-11). Usually this term is in reference to having a psychological diagnosis in conjunction with a substance abuse diagnosis. Other terms for this condition are co-occurring disorders or co-morbid disorders.

Psychotropic drugs: Psychotropic drugs are those that are prescribed by medical professionals usually for the purpose of treating mental disorders. Although these are prescribed and are legal, they can be misused by the person (i.e., taking more of the pill than prescribed) or may even become addictive for the individual. For instance, a woman who was prescribed Xanax for anxiety episodes begins to take a pill every day rather than as necessitated by the occasional onslaught of a panic attack. After some time, her behavior becomes organized around the daily taking of the Xanax rather than being able to function without the drug.

Recovery: Recovery is the process of a person reducing or abstaining from a drug that they were dependent on. Usually, recovery is more connected with the notion of abstinence, where the recovery process is focused on the person not using the substance. However, recovery can also refer to a moderated management of use. In this instance, instead of drinking and getting inebriated, which was the normal pattern, the person is able to drink only one or two drinks and not experience becoming drunk.

Relapse: Relapse is a worsening of the problem after some time of improvement. The use of the substance does not have to go back to when it was at its worst to be considered a relapse, but it is usually a movement back into problematic actions and patterns. Relapses might be a one-time occurrence or can last many years.

Slip: A slip is similar to a relapse but not as severe. It is a brief use of the substance after a period of reduction or abstinence from the drug. However, there is usually a quick return to a more functional state. For instance, if someone who had smoked two packs of cigarettes per day for three years had completely stopped smoking, but then found themselves smoking one cigarette and then did not smoke again after that, this would be considered a slip. The main difference between a slip and a relapse is that a slip is just use of the substance while relapse involves a return to negative patterns of behavior.

Substance abuse: Substance abuse occurs when a person uses a drug beyond its normal purpose or when they develop a pattern of use that necessitates further use and/or difficulties in various areas of their life. Prescription medications can be abused when they are used for symptoms for which they were not intended or in amounts not prescribed. An estimated 54 million people (more than 20% of those aged 12 and older) have used prescription medications for nonmedical reasons at least once in their lifetime. The most misused prescription drugs are pain relievers, followed by tranquilizers, stimulants, and then sedatives (Center for Behavioral Health Statistics and Quality, 2016). For instance, a doctor may have prescribed Vicodin for someone who was recovering from an accident. If the person began to take more pills each day than the recommended dosage then they would be abusing the substance. This has been a growing trend, with opioids, central nervous system depressants, and stimulants being the three classes of medications that are most misused.

Substance dependence: Substance dependence occurs when a person needs an increased amount of the drug to feel the effects of that drug. This process is known as **tolerance**. Further, dependence happens when the person experiences withdrawal symptoms when they do not use that substance. We might see this in someone who uses cocaine, where each time they use, they need just a little more of the drug to achieve their normal high. When they do not use cocaine they may experience cravings for it, fatigue, and tremors or chills, among other possible withdrawal symptoms.

Substance use: Substance use is when a person comes into contact with a substance that is deemed a drug. There are many instances when

(continued)

(continued)

someone uses a substance and it is legal and not problematic for the individual. Going to a pub with friends and having one or two beers once a week (drinking within recommended limits) can be a physiologically (Mukamal, 2010) and socially beneficial endeavor. It is when the use of the substance begins to impair the person that substance use shifts to abuse or dependence.

Tolerance: Tolerance is the diminishing physiological impact of a substance upon repeated usage. In essence, we need to use more of the drug to obtain previous results. As an example, one year ago it might have taken three vodka tonics for the person to feel inebriated, but, having consumed much alcohol over the past year, today it takes five vodka tonics to have the same feeling.

Withdrawal: Withdrawal is the physiological and psychological reactions when the person reduces usage of the drug. Each drug has its own physiological consequence when a person begins to lessen their connection to the substance. For some drugs, such as marijuana, the obvious withdrawal symptoms are minimal. For other drugs, such as heroin, the body's physiological reactions are severely debilitating to the individual. There are even some drugs that if a person attempts to stop using by going "**cold turkey**" (stopping total use rather than engaging in a controlled reduction of use) may lead to death. These include benzodiazepines, opiates, and even alcohol (if the person has chronically used for a long time).

Addiction

Substance use/abuse is a wide field covering a myriad of different drugs. It may include legal substances, such as caffeine, nicotine, or alcohol, as well as common illegal drugs such as opium, cocaine, and heroin. Then there are drugs that, in some states and in some situations, are legal but are otherwise illegal, such as marijuana (which in some states was legal for medical purposes, but has recently become legal for any adult to use recreationally). When discussing the substance abuse field we are talking about some type of substance that gains entrance into the body. This can happen through several means such as ingestion (e.g., consuming psychedelic mushrooms or alcohol), inhalation (e.g., smoking cigarettes or marijuana), injection (e.g., heroin), and absorption (e.g., LSD).

Over the last 20 years there has been a generalizing of the term addiction to refer to non-substance-related behaviors in which the person seems to have a compulsion to engage in that activity, such as gambling addiction, sexual addiction, or internet addiction (see Chapter 9). Although in this book we will be primarily talking about alcohol and drug addiction, any of these other ideas can be systemically conceptualized as well since they all contribute to redistributing how the family of the person engaging in that behavior is organized. However, there is still debate if these non-drug addictions should be considered in the same class as alcohol/drug addiction or even if they should be classified as a disease.

Addiction as a Serious Social Problem

Before we explore the various models of addiction, let's take a minute to focus on the prevalence and impact that addiction has on society. According to the National Institute on Drug Abuse (2014), the abuse of tobacco, alcohol, and illicit drugs, in the United States alone, costs over $600 billion annually. This includes costs related to health care, lost productivity at work, and crime. In 2016, the harmful use of alcohol resulted in some 3 million deaths (5.3% of all deaths) worldwide and 132.6 million disability-adjusted life years (DALYs), which accounted for 5.1% of all DALYs in that year (WHO, 2018). The World Health Organization states that tobacco use accounts for almost 9% of all deaths worldwide and 4% of disability-adjusted life years. These authors hold that alcohol consumption is one of the most significant *avoidable* risk factors, where reduction of alcohol use can prevent disability and/or death. The 2017 World Drug Report, from the United Nations Office on Drugs and Crime, holds that almost 30 million people globally suffer from drug-use disorders. Of all drugs used, opioids were associated with the highest level of negative health outcomes. Other potential serious health issues as a consequence of drug use include hepatitis C and HIV.

While the rates of substance use for middle and high school students have been reducing slightly, they are still significant. Based on data presented by the National Institute on Drug Abuse, in 2017 for 12th graders, 61.5% had used alcohol over their lifespan, 50.3% illicit drugs, 45% marijuana, 26.6% cigarettes, 16.5% any prescription drug, 11% smokeless tobacco, 9.2% amphetamines, 6.8% narcotics other than heroin, 7.5% tranquilizers, 6.7% hallucinogens, 4.9% inhalants, and 4.2% cocaine (Johnston et al., 2018). Thus, by 18 years of age, a significant proportion of United States adolescents had engaged in some type of drug use. This does not mean that they will develop substance abuse disorders, but it opens the possibility for some type of negative consequences of drug use to occur (not to mention possible involvement with the juvenile justice system).

These trends in what substance is used tend to continue into adulthood. While 34% of adults do not use any type of alcohol or drug, 65% use alcohol, 6.2% use any type of drug, and 5.6% use both alcohol and drugs (Falk, Yi, & Hiller-Sturmhofel, 2008). According to the National Institute on Drug Abuse, in 2013, an estimated 24.6 million Americans aged 12 or older—9.4% of the population—had used an illicit drug in the past month. This number is up from 8.3% in 2002. The increase mostly reflects a recent rise in use of marijuana, which is the most commonly used illicit drug. The primary drug used was marijuana (19.8%), followed by prescription drugs, cocaine, hallucinogens, inhalants, and heroin. In terms of alcohol, there has been a reduction in use by people between the ages of 12–20. Current alcohol use by this age group declined from 28.8% to 22.7% between 2002 and 2013, while binge drinking declined from 19.3% to 14.2% and the rate of heavy drinking went from 6.2% to 3.7%. This decline in substance use can also be seen in smoking cigarettes, where fewer Americans are smoking. In 2013, an estimated 55.8 million Americans aged 12 or older, or 21.3% of the population, were current cigarette smokers. This reflects a continual but slow downward trend from 2002, when the rate was 26%.

What was just presented focused on drug and alcohol *use*, rather than *dependence*. As we have talked about already, there is a distinction between the two. The two most prominent abused substances are alcohol and marijuana. According to the National Institute on Drug Abuse, in 2013, 17.3 million Americans (6.6% of the population) were dependent on alcohol or had problems related to their alcohol use (abuse). In 2013, 4.2 million Americans met clinical criteria for dependence or abuse of marijuana in the past year. Further, in 2013, an estimated 22.7 million Americans (8.6%) needed treatment for a problem related to drugs or alcohol, but only about 2.5 million people (0.9%) received treatment at a specialty facility. This lets us know that there is a strong need for programs to help get people into treatment. These statistics are only focusing on the individual and do not account for the impact that one person's use has on those in the family.

Models of Addiction

Now that we have an understanding of what the terms in the field mean, we can start to explore how people view the etiology of addiction. We have begun talking about how a therapist conceptualizes what is happening for the client. This conceptualization is based on a model of what impacts people. On a more zoomed level, "**model**" in therapy refers to the theoretical orientation of the therapist. This could be, for instance, person-centered, cognitive-behavioral, or psychodynamic. If we expand this view, the model can be an individual lens versus a family/systemic lens. Zooming back into the family lens we can look at a variety of family therapy approaches such as Structural, Solution-focused, or Bowenian (see Chapters 13, 14, & 15).

In the field of substance abuse there are many different views of how and why people become addicted. In this section we will cover three of the primary models

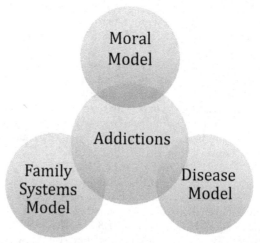

Figure 1.2 The three main models of addiction: The moral, disease, and family systems models

of addiction: the moral model, the disease model, and the family systems models (see Figure 1.2). Although this book primarily focuses on a family systems model, that does not mean that the other models are incongruent with the family systems model. In this section we will cover each of the standard models of addiction to provide you with a general understanding of the differences between each.

Moral Model

The moral model was perhaps the first major model of addictions, being prominent in the early part of the 20th century. However, it has grown out of favor and is perhaps currently the least championed of the three models of addiction. This is because it had its roots in religion rather than being supported by empirical evidence. In this model people abuse alcohol (or other drugs) not because of physiological reasons (as will be seen in the disease model) but because the person lacks the willpower to choose otherwise. Thus, addiction is not a disease but is rather faulty choice making. The person is most likely not choosing to become an addict, but their choices lead them into a particular lifestyle and destructive behavioral patterns. Having roots in religious doctrine, the moral model proposed that people could easily choose to be abstinent if they were psychologically strong enough.

Based on choice rather than disease, proponents of the moral model believed that the user should be punished, rather than be provided with the possibility of rehabilitation. Based upon this viewpoint, alcoholics were grouped in with criminals, sinners, and others who were "lazy" and did not want to abide by society's rules. Since the decision to drink was based on a moral/characterological defect, alcoholics were put in jails or asylums rather than provided with alternative services that might have helped them. This model can be seen in the United States government's "War on Drugs" where the focus is on the indictment and incarceration of people who use and sell illegal drugs.

For the general public, the moral model makes sense. Especially in Western societies, where personal responsibility is emphasized, there is an expectation that people are in full control of what they do. The scientific community has moved away from accepting the moral model as issues such as genetics, neurobiology, and environmental factors gain widespread empirical support. However, many people still believe that the individual has a choice of picking up that first drink or smoking that first pipe. While this is the case, what happens afterward is dynamically involved.

Disease Model

The predominant view of addictions has been through the disease model (also known as the medical model). The disease model is perhaps the most known of all models of addictions, having been popularized through media and twelve-step programs. Originally developed to explain alcoholism, it has been used to understand other types of drug addiction as well as food addiction, sexual addiction, compulsive gambling and other behavioral addictions. Given that it was developed and has been primarily utilized in viewing alcoholism, we will primarily explore it through that lens. The disease model holds that alcohol is a primary problem and should be its own focus of treatment. What this means is that alcoholism is not a secondary symptom of some other problem (such as family dysfunction or a psychiatric disorder). As such, treatment focuses specifically on the addiction. Whereas the moral model views the addict as being *at fault*, the disease model views them as being *at risk*—since they initially had a choice whether to use the drug or not, but once they did use it to whatever extent it overwhelmed their ability to choose (Wilbanks, 1989).

Adopting the disease model of addiction changes how the therapist views the course of the problem. As such, there are several characteristics of the addiction (Johnson, 1986). First, it can be described. The disease impacts many people in very similar ways—just like chicken pox has the same symptoms, course, and treatment for a widespread population. Second, the disease is primary—rather than being a symptom of something else. Third, the disease follows a predictable course, which is progressive. As will be explained in the next several paragraphs, addiction flows through four phases. Fourth, the disease is permanent (chronic). People will always need to be on guard to prevent the disease from taking over (thus, they must maintain abstinence). Fifth, the disease is fatal. If people do not get treatment, they will die. Lastly, and most importantly for this model, the disease is treatable.

The two clinical features of substance abuse that are associated with the disease model are tolerance and withdrawal (Thombs & Osborn, 2013). Tolerance to a drug means that over time it requires more of the substance to obtain effects that were previously reached with lower doses. So the person progressively uses more while receiving the same outcome. Withdrawal is a physiological effect that occurs from reduced use of the substance. Depending on the drug, the amount of previous use, and the person's physiological makeup, withdrawal symptoms could be insomnia, delirium tremens, or, in severe cases, even death.

Species of Alcoholism

The disease model was proposed by E. M. Jellinek and has been greatly expanded since this first introduction. In this section we will discuss Jellinek's (1983) original classification of four species of alcoholism. These designate various levels of severity and functioning of someone who is considered alcoholic. Jellinek used Greek letters to provide a more neutral approach to discussing the concepts.

The first type is **alpha alcoholism**, which is a psychological phenomenon. Here, instead of a physiological dependence, the person has a psychological dependence on alcohol to help relieve stress, anxiety, or pain. At this point, the individual is still most likely in control of the drinking and, if they decide to quit, they may not have that many withdrawal symptoms. Yet the person continues to drink as a way to mute psychological and emotional pain. In this condition, there is not a progressive process. However, there is the possibility that someone who is classified as an alpha alcoholic may shift into a different species of alcoholism.

Beta alcoholism has many of the physiological effects of drinking (such as cirrhosis of the liver) but without the psychological or physical dependence. Thus, the person has the opportunity to stop their heavy drinking, which they do quite often—perhaps every day. The people who fall into this category might be called "social drinkers," where they drink when they have the opportunity (such as at parties, on New Year's Eve, etc.) but do not feel the need to have to drink.

Gamma alcoholism contains both a physiological dependence as well as psychological impacts. For instance, not only does a person develop a bodily tolerance for alcohol, they also lose control of their use. Jellinek (1983) explained that for those with this species of alcoholism there is the greatest damage. Not only do they find that their interpersonal relationships suffer, as well as work, economics, etc., their physical health is also at the most severe risk. This is probably the most predominating type of alcoholism in Western cultures.

The last type of alcoholism is called **delta alcoholism.** Delta and gamma alcoholism are very similar yet the delta species does not include the individual losing control. Thus, they are able to function well in their personal, business, and social lives. This type of alcoholism would occur in countries, such as France or Italy, where drinking (such as wine) is legal and ritualistic and forms a primary role in social life.

Phases of Alcoholism

Jellinek (1983) delineated a four-phase progression of alcoholism. The first phase is the **pre-alcoholic phase** where the person drinks mainly for social reasons. It is at this point that a connection between drinking and stress reduction occurs. Depending on genetics and social conditions, the pre-alcoholic phase may last a couple of months to several years.

The second phase is the **prodromal phase.** Here, a person's use of alcohol has shifted from being a social endeavor to a primary means of stress reduction. During this period the person is usually in control of most of their actions but begins to develop problematic patterns such as sneaking drinks and having **blackouts** (where the person cannot remember what occurred during the time they were drinking).

The third phase is the **crucial phase** wherein the person has little control of their actions, especially around consumption of alcohol. At this point they have changed their normal patterns of behavior so that they can consume alcohol more frequently. Their tolerance has increased to where they need more alcohol to feel the effects and they need it more often. The person has likely attempted to control the use of alcohol with little success.

The last phase is the **chronic phase** where the person experiences a necessity to drink. They may go on **benders** (extended periods of time being drunk), suffer serious withdrawal symptoms if they do not drink in a given period of time, and have experienced major difficulties in their work, social, and family relationships.

Life-Long Addiction

The disease model holds that addiction is not a disease that can ever be cured. The individual is currently and will always be battling this disease. Thus, words such as "cured" or "recovered" are not used. Instead, people who have currently stopped their drug use are seen as being "in recovery." This is an ongoing process where the person needs to be vigilant each and every day for the rest of their lives.

In the disease model, one use of the drug can trigger a recapitulation of where the person was when they were at their worst in the throes of the disease; what is considered a relapse. To counter this, the model espouses that abstinence should be the goal of someone dealing with addiction. When understanding an individual, the disease model holds that the person will likely develop the same symptoms if they discontinue use of one drug and begin using another drug (Fisher, 2011). Thus, they are encouraged to be abstinent from all psychoactive drugs.

While the disease model is currently the most widespread model, it has come under fire. Wilbanks (1989) explained that there is not a way to determine whether the compulsion to use the drug is uncontrollable or uncontrolled. How we figure this out is through self-report of the addict. A second critique is that not everyone that engages in the behavior (drug use—or sex, gambling, shopping) becomes "addicted" (Fisher & Harrison, 2018; Wilbanks, 1989). Wilbanks warns that if people do view addiction as an inevitability, once drinking/drug use happens, they may develop a sense of learned helplessness. He encourages a shift from viewing the addict as a helpless victim to one that is not actively trying to control the drug use.

The disease model, in many ways, holds addiction to be a medical illness. McLellan, Lewis, O'Brien, and Kleber (2000) supported this view as they conducted an extensive literature review comparing the diagnoses, heritability, etiology, pathophysiology, and response to treatments of drug dependence versus type 2 diabetes mellitus, hypertension, and asthma. They found that genetic heritability, personal choice, environmental factors, medication adherence, and relapse rates were similar for all of the disorders. They recommended viewing drug dependence as a chronic mental illness, which necessitates long-term care.

Regardless of the challenges to the disease model of addiction, one of the primary benefits that has come from this viewpoint is the destigmatization of addiction. Fisher and Harrison (2018) explained, "Perhaps the greatest advantage to the articulation that addiction is a disease has been to remove the moral stigma attached to addiction and to replace it with an emphasis on treatment of an illness" (p. 43). This has led away from attempting to punish people who are dealing with addiction to trying to help and treat them. These viewpoints have led to more people dealing with substance abuse seeking out treatment.

While addiction is referred to as a disease, many current researchers talk more specifically in terms of the **brain disease model of addiction** (BDMA) (Bell et al., 2014). This is because, based on genetics of addiction research as well as neurobiological research of animals and humans, the brain is impacted through substance use. In essence, repeated drug use leads to changes in the brain that are difficult to reverse. This makes it difficult for the individual to refrain from the use of the substance and remain abstinent. Besides the neurological impact that drugs have on people, vulnerability to and recovery from substances is also tied to social environments, developmental stages, and genetics (Volkow, Koob, & McLellan, 2016).

Family-Disease Perspective

It wasn't until the 1980s that people in the field began talking about addiction as a family disease, being popularized by the work of Wegscheider-Cruse (1989).

The **family-disease perspective** is based on the disease model of addiction (Lemieux, 2009, 2014; Thombs & Osborn, 2013). It expands the view of just the individual substance abuser to include the dysfunctional relationships that maintain the substance use. This model is primarily utilized with families dealing with alcoholism and sees these families as being inherently dysfunctional.

While the disease model focuses on how the alcoholic/substance abuser is biologically, physically, emotionally, socially, and behaviorally impacted by use of the substance, the family-disease model expands this to view how family members are impacted as well. Perhaps the most visible member in this is the codependent. The family-disease model views codependency as a disease (McCrady, Ladd, & Hallgren, 2012). The codependent engages in enabling behavior, which helps perpetuate the substance abuser's use and continued dysfunction. However, there has not yet been clear empirical evidence to substantiate the notion of codependency (Lemieux, 2009, 2014; McCrady et al., 2012).

The family-disease model highlights the interpersonal impact that addiction has in the family system. This is evidenced by the family rules and family roles (see Chapter 6). These include the enabler, hero, scapegoat, lost child, and mascot (Wegscheider-Cruse, 1989). Along with the substance abuser, family members function in unique ways to try to survive the pain of addiction. This family illness can also be viewed as occurring across generations (Nowinski & Baker, 2018). This is because interactional rules and processes are passed down and learned from parents to children to grandchildren.

Therapists operating from the family-disease perspective usually take the position that family members should separate themselves from the addict and work on themselves for personal recovery (Lemieux, 2009, 2014; O'Farrell & Fals-Stewart, 2006). This is why many therapists with a family-disease perspective utilize family support groups such as Al-Anon and Nar-Anon as well as psychoeducation and individual therapy. O'Farrell and Fals-Stewart (2006) explained that, based on the family-disease model, treatment for the substance abuser's partner and/or family members usually includes psychoeducation about addiction as a family disease, individual and/or group therapy, and referral to a family support group.

Family Systems Model

The **family systems model** of addiction views addiction as a symptom that signifies a larger issue within the user's family and relational world. This may be a local issue, involving only the members of the nuclear family, or a multigenerational process, having developed over many generations in how individuals in the family are able to cope with the anxiety and stressors of being an individual while also being part of a social group.

The person who is abusing the substance is considered the **Identified Patient** (IP). They are the focal point of the family dysfunction, yet are not isolated in the problem. Given that human beings are interdependent entities, the IP is the manifestation of many factors at work within the relational web of the family. This goes along with one of the primary tenets of a systems view in that change in one part of the system leads to change in the whole system. This widening of focus from the individual to the family, from part to whole, is one of the aspects that separate the family systems model from the other models of addiction.

A family-systems perspective is perhaps best known for the saying, "The whole is greater than the sum of its parts." What this means is that if we only look at each individual in the family, we would not understand the dynamic interaction that occurs when those members come together. Another way of expressing this is with a mathematical formula: $1 + 1 = 3$. In this equation each 1 refers to an individual. The sum is 3 rather than 2 because not only do we need to understand each individual (their developmental stage, intellectual–emotional–psychological capacities, previous experience, gender, age, culture, etc.) but, and perhaps most importantly, how those two individuals come together—their relationship. If we substituted one of these 1s out of the equation and put someone else in, we would see a different dynamic between the two. For instance, think about you as a person. We would see a different "you" when you are in relationship with one of your parents, your significant other, your child, your boss, a police officer, or your last significant other who broke up with you a year ago! The same would be true for the other 1 in the equation. Thus, when we put you two together, you each simultaneously impact and are impacted by the other.

The family systems model is a conglomerate of many ideas, and thus is difficult to specify, as there are various models of family functioning. In this book we will present some of the basic and overarching ideas as well as some of the specific models of family therapy. However, many of the family-centered interventions view substance abuse through a biopsychosocial perspective—where there is a combination of biological, psychological, and social components (Lemieux, 2014). For now, we will explore this model in terms of how these three components connect through concentric circles. Bronfenbrenner (1979) proposed the notion of an ecological systems theory, also known as a bio-ecological systems theory. This theory helps to describe how an individual is impacted by others in his relational field as well as larger systems. There are four ecological systems in this model. The first, the **microsystem**, is the innermost system. This is where the individual is connected to those closest to him; for instance, a spouse, relational partner, or close family members. The next outer subsystem is the **mesosystem**. This includes systems that directly impact the individuals in the microsystem. For instance, the addict's job is part of the mesosystem; or the spouse's family. The third ecosystem is the **exosystem**. Here, various aspects of the structure of individual/family functioning occur such as finances or socio-economic status. The last system is the **macrosystem**, which refers to the social and cultural milieu in which the individual is housed. Housing all of these ecological systems is the chronosystem. That is, these systems are dynamic and change over time.

If we look at this framework we can see the individual in the center, with close friends and family around him, with larger systems such as work, school, or church containing them, and then a larger circle that has aspects of culture and national citizenship. All of these various systems are at play at all times. However, usually there is greater influence from outside in rather than inside out. For instance, the culture that a person is born and raised in inserts more influence on how the individual functions than the individual can impose on

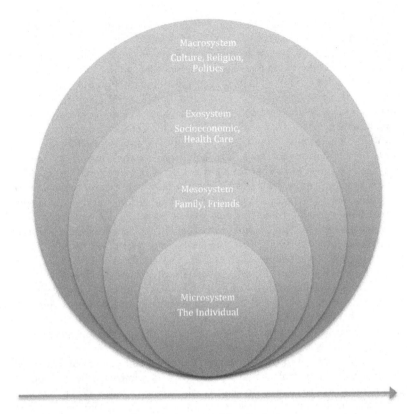

Figure 1.3 Representation of Bronfenbrenner's bioecological systems approach

the overarching culture. This is just one model that helps us to understand that an individual does not operate in isolation, but is influenced not only by the people they are in contact with but the larger systems that define the context for how we understand the world. Figure 1.3 represents these concentric circles.

There are many different theories within the family therapy model. Throughout this book, and especially in Part II, we will briefly present an overview of the major theories of family therapy. Some specifically focus on family systems and addiction while others explore how all symptoms are created by and impact the family. When examining the specific field of substance abuse treatment, three main models are useful to be aware of: family disease model, family systems models, and behavioral models (McCrady et al., 2012). As explained, family disease models highlight the notion of addiction as a disease, codependency, and how family members can change themselves. Family systems models hold to the notion that addiction serves a function in the family. Therapy, from this orientation, focuses on family rules, roles, and boundaries. Behavioral models explore the antecedents and consequences to substance use and the role the family plays in these events. Throughout this book we will explore aspects of these three models, as well as additional ideas that help locate addictions within the context of relationships and families.

To end this section, I want to highlight the importance of why we should study the family and view an issue like addictions through the lens of the family. Gruber and Taylor (2006) explained, "substance abuse is a problem for families because (1) It *occurs* in families, (2) It *harms* families, (3) Families both participate in and can *perpetuate active* addiction, and (4) Families are a potential *treatment and recovery resource*" (p. 3, italics in original). For every individual who has a substance abuse problem, the lives of four other individuals are impacted (van Wormer & Davis, 2013). Individuals are not born as isolates; they come into the world as part of a physiological and emotional system. Who we are is a combination of our DNA and genetics (we are primed to display certain traits based on our genes, such as height, skin/hair/eye color, temperament, and other such components), our past experiences, and our current choices. These choices are based on our values and beliefs, which were primarily forged within the iron of our family (which were mainly determined by the cultural contexts in which that family was housed). The family is our first classroom; learning how to be, think, and feel. Problematically, people tend to view people as individuals—devoid of their context. This has the possibility of leading to attributional errors. Gruber and Taylor (2006) called "for researchers and treatment providers to increase their recognition of the role that family and family functioning has for understanding the incidence and impact of substance abuse" (p. 1). This book is an attempt to do so.

As we will discuss through the course of this book, substance abuse does not only impact the individual; the family impacts and is impacted by addiction as well. From parents, to spouses, to children, the family organizes differently when addiction is involved; usually in ways that we would call "dysfunctional" where members are negatively affected by the transactions. Thus, viewing addiction as a "family problem" helps the clinician to include the genetic predisposition that children have based upon their parents' use, as well as the environmental factors prevalent within the relationships of the family.

McCrady et al., (2012) described several advantages for utilizing a family-based approach when working with clients dealing with substance abuse issues. These include strong empirical support for the models, the focus on the environmental context, and an exploration of factors that might maintain the substance use outside of the individual. Further, these authors explained that family-based approaches are connected to better engagement with treatment as well as better treatment outcomes. In comparison with other treatment modalities, family therapy seems to be at least equally effective (Hawkins & Hawkins, 2012).

However, there are disadvantages to using family-based approaches (McCrady et al., 2012). These include these models' heightened complexity of theory and practice, the therapist's need to focus on multiple relationships simultaneously, the difficulty of arranging for all parties to be together in a session, and their sometimes-discrepant views to disease-based models in which the individual is responsible for change. These challenges lead to necessary education and training for family-based therapists to be able to successfully navigate these unique demands of practice.

Case History

Now that we have an understanding of the various terms and models of addiction, we will come back to our client that we met at the beginning of the chapter. The following section provides information that would have been obtained through conducting a biopsychosocial with a new client. We will refer back to this case at the end of each chapter of the book as a way to apply the ideas presented. Our client, Mark Rothers, has come to a social service agency seeking help. The case study is presented here to be used as a template for how a family systems view can be used, even if an individual enters into the therapy room.

Presenting Problem and Past Problem History

Mark Rothers was born on March 13, 1979 in Gainesville, Florida. He is currently remarried for 15 years to Hannah, and they have three children together: Steve, 14; Kayleigh, 12; and Pete, 11. Mark was previously married for two years to Angelina. He has one child with Angelina, a daughter Nina, who is 17 years old.

Mark often drinks alcohol, frequently uses marijuana, and occasionally uses cocaine. He has been very upset with life for the past six months. He is having difficulty sleeping, has been having difficulties at work, as well as some thoughts of death, stating, "It would be easier if I were dead."

Mark went for couples counseling with his first wife, Angelina. They went for four sessions, but found that things only got worse. He also went to individual therapy to deal with his substance use. This occurred seven years ago and lasted for seven sessions. Mark reduced his drinking and drug use at that time and maintained this for six months. Then he returned to his prior usage. At the time, he did not engage in any self-help groups. Mark is taking over-the-counter aspirin and ibuprofen when he senses a migraine attack is going to occur, which he occasionally gets—perhaps five times per year. He does not take any other medications.

Mark first used substances starting at 12 years old. At that time, he would take various hard liquors from his father's supply. He also started to smoke cigarettes when he was 14. At 16 he began to smoke marijuana. In his freshman year of college, he experimented with hallucinogens; specifically LSD. During his senior year of college he began using cocaine, having been introduced to it through friends. Mark's primary drug is alcohol, drinking approximately four beers per day. He smokes marijuana approximately two times per week, usually when he is stressed out. He infrequently uses cocaine. This is usually when he is with a certain group of friends who use that as their primary drug of choice. Mark smokes approximately one pack of cigarettes per day.

Client's Family History

Mark's maternal grandmother was schizophrenic and many members on his paternal side have issues with addiction; primarily with alcohol. His grandfather, father, and two uncles all, in his estimation, had serious addiction issues. On his mother's side there is a history of depression as his grandmother and, he believes, his mother, suffered from occasional bouts.

Mark is the second of three children of Ian and Des. The family was a lower-class family as Ian worked as a custodial staff-person at the local university and Des worked as a behavioral tech at a group home for developmentally disabled adults. The oldest child, Mick, is three years older than Mark. The youngest child, Judy, is two years younger. Currently, Judy is married, has one child—age 9—and works as an accounts administrator. Before that child was born she had a miscarriage. Mick graduated college with a degree in engineering and moved out of the state. He is remarried and has a 16-year-old daughter. Mark and Mick had a falling out when they had gone out together one night and Mick had berated Mark for being alcoholic. At that point, Mick had been in recovery from alcohol for five years. The two came to physical blows and do not talk to one another anymore. Mark also has conflict with his father, Ian. This is usually when either of them has been drinking. Ian usually expresses his disappointment in how Mark's life turned out and Mark explains how he thinks Ian was a bad father and is a bad grandfather.

Mark completed high school and college with a degree in business. During both high school and college he tended to be a "B" student. He is a manager for a national rental car agency and has been with the company for 12 years, beginning soon after he graduated from college. In high school he worked in a fast food restaurant as his family was not wealthy. Throughout his college career, he worked various jobs including fast food, restaurant server, and in the college bookstore.

Mark was involved with the legal system when he and his first wife divorced. He was arrested for domestic violence against his first wife. The two had argued and Mark pushed Angelina to the ground. This was the only instance of physical violence in the marriage. He was drunk at the time. He spent two days in jail and received probation. At the time of the divorce he was made to pay alimony and child support, which continue to be garnished from his wages.

Mark married Angelina, his college girlfriend, when he was 23 years old. The couple were married for two years and had one child, Nina, a daughter who was born in the first year of marriage. After Nina was born, things deteriorated quickly between Mark and Angelina. He was arrested once for domestic violence. When the couple divorced his ex-wife received full custody of their daughter. Mark sees Nina infrequently; approximately three times per year. They talk on the telephone perhaps one time per month. Nina is very close with her mother.

Mark met his current wife, Hannah, one year after his divorce. They dated for six months and then were married. They have three children, Steve, Kayleigh, and Pete. Hannah does not utilize any substances and is concerned with the amount of alcohol Mark consumes. Steve is in eighth grade and is having difficulties in school, getting into fights and struggling academically. Kayleigh is in seventh grade and is excelling. She is in the gifted program and is at the top of her class. Pete, in sixth grade, is the closest with his mother and seems to be a fun-loving child.

Genograms: A Family Picture

We have taken in a lot of information from our client and can display this through the narrative of a biopsychosocial. We also have enough data to begin making a pictorial depiction of the family. In family therapy, the primary way we do this is through the use of a **genogram**. There are many layers to the genogram. These include who is in the family (usually exploring three generations), the relationships between each of them, history of medical, psychiatric, and substance issues, as well as any other particular developmental changes. One of the main purposes of creating a genogram with the family is to start· to explore potential patterns that have been occurring within the family. A subsequent benefit of using genograms in clinical work is as a summary for self or others on the status of the case (McGoldrick, Gerson, & Petry, 2008).

When constructing a genogram there tends to be information that is sought that may not be explored in-depth when conducting a typical intake assessment.

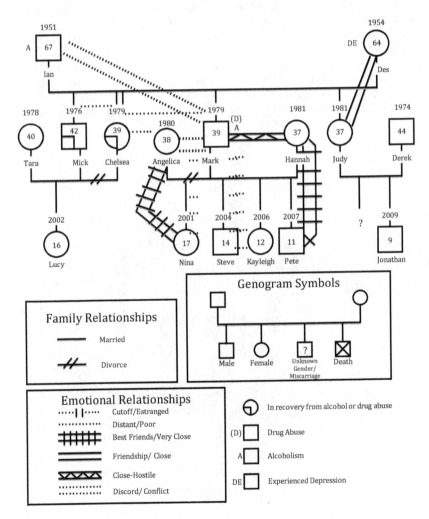

Figure 1.4 A genogram of the Rothers family

This usually comes in the form of interviewing the client regarding the two or three generations previous, which would include the client's parents, siblings, and grandparents, and may also involve aunts, uncles, cousins, close friends, great grandparents and pets. Family therapists can use a genogram to provide many varied layers of a family's functioning. The first layer is who is in the family. This may include the person's gender, age, or name. A second layer is demographics—which may include year in school, employment, relationship status, past/current medical issues, psychiatric history, substance abuse, and other unique identifiers. A third layer, and perhaps the most important layer, is distinguishing the relational dynamics between people. These include who is close with whom, who has conflict with whom, who is cutoff, distant, or overly close.

While the genogram seems to be a current snapshot, it is actually a longitudinal view of the family. The family therapist can explore major family transitions such as moves, deaths, financial hardships, and the impact of one or more members' substance abuse. Figure 1.4 presents a genogram of the Rothers family that we met in the previous section.

Genograms can be expanded to include not only the nuclear and extended family, but also the larger systems the family comes into contact with. These might be the legal, medical, educational, social, religious, cultural, and community systems. McGoldrick et al. (2008) refer to this as a **genogram within community context.**

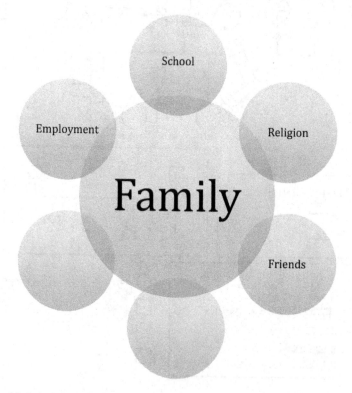

Figure 1.5 A depiction of a generic family ecomap

Other therapists create a picture called a **family ecomap**. An ecomap usually houses the nuclear family within a center circle, displaying that family's connections to larger systems. An example of an ecomap can be seen in Figure 1.5.

One of the benefits of using a genogram (or ecomap) is that it is model neutral and can be adjusted—where the therapist brings forth some information more than others depending on their approach. Although the genogram has roots in intergenerational approaches, such as Bowen Family Systems Theory, it has also been used with Narrative family therapy (Chrzastowski, 2011), Solution-focused therapy (Kuehl, 1996), Reality therapy family counseling (Duba, Graham, Britzman, & Minatrea, 2009), and in training family therapists (Hardy & Laszloffy, 1995). Regardless of the reason to develop the genogram, it should be done through a process of joining with whoever is providing the information, as it is usually constructed during the first meeting(s) with the client.

Summary

After finishing the biopsychosocial and the genogram, you now must decide how to approach your work with Mark. Do you work with him individually? Do you try to get his family to come to treatment? If so, do you try to get his parents and siblings into therapy? His wife? His ex-wife and child? Everyone? How much should self-help groups be a part of the therapeutic process? Is abstinence the goal of therapy or reduction of use? Are there other goals that are pertinent? In the following chapters we will explore these questions, as well as various issues of assessment when dealing with clients and their families who are having issues with substances. The second half of the book will focus on treatment from a family systems lens.

We will start our journey of exploring how a client coming into therapy dealing with substance use issues can be viewed from a wide lens through focusing first on a smaller zoomed lens. When people think about addiction, they may view it from a physiological dependence issue. Drugs, including caffeine, nicotine, alcohol, prescription medication, and harder drugs do have a chemical and biological impact on the human body. This is something that cannot and should not be discounted. The following chapter explains the physiological impact of drugs on the brain.

Key Words

Diagnostic and Statistical Manual	drugs
substance-related disorders	psychotropic drugs
substance use disorders	substance use
substance-induced disorders	substance abuse
addiction	substance dependence
	craving

(continued)

(continued)

tolerance
abstinence
withdrawal
cold turkey
relapse
slip
recovery
dual-diagnosis
model
moral model of addiction
disease model of addiction
alpha alcoholism
beta alcoholism
gamma alcoholism
delta alcoholism
pre-alcoholic phase
prodromal phase

blackouts
crucial phase
chronic phase
benders
brain disease model of addiction
family-disease model
family systems model of
    addiction
identified patient
microsystem
mesosystem
exosystem
macrosystem
genogram
genogram within community
    context
family ecomap

Reflection Questions

1. What are the distinguishing factors of addiction, according to the DSM-V?
2. How can a mental health professional determine whether substance use has moved into substance abuse or dependence?
3. What is the relationship between tolerance, withdrawal, and relapse?
4. How do the moral model, disease model, and family systems models of addiction differ?
5. What benefits does creating and utilizing a genogram have in addictions treatment?

TWO

The Neurobiology of Addiction

Jaime L. Tartar, Christina M. Gobin, and Julius Thomas

As presented in Chapter 1, this book is designed to help you shift your orientation from viewing addictions as an individual phenomenon to a more systemic epistemology. However, within any system are individual parts. This chapter narrows the lens of focus to the more microlevel—seeing the physiological impact that substances have on people. We cannot deny that drugs impact people—emotionally, behaviorally, and physiologically. Accordingly, the goal of this chapter is to present information on how and where drugs act in the brain as well as how they can temporarily or permanently change brain function. We will also briefly review the particular neurobiological effects of commonly abused substances. Here, we focus on a special classification of drugs— **psychoactive drugs**, which are drugs that alter mental functioning. Because of their ability to alter mood, psychoactive substances are developed and widely used to treat mental disorders (such as depression). However, because of these same properties, psychoactive drugs are also commonly abused and can be biologically addictive.

In neurobiological terms, *addiction* can be distinguished from *dependence—* addiction is reserved for the process through which a drug changes the brain's natural reward circuitry in the mesocorticolimbic dopamine system (discussed in detail below). **Behavioral addictions**, sometimes referred to as **process addictions**, share common features with drug addictions such as impairment in self-regulation, impulsivity, and demonstrations of relapsing behavior despite mental and physical consequences. Examples of behavioral addictions include compulsive buying, sex addiction, pathological gambling, binge-eating disorder, and internet addiction disorder (Smith, 2012). Moreover, there is a high degree of comorbidity between drug addiction and behavioral addiction and between drug abuse and psychological disorders; especially affective disorders. In this view, not all drugs that result in dependency are biologically addictive. The changes that occur with addiction require continued use of the drug in order for an individual to feel "normal." However, all psychoactive substances (for medical purposes or abuse) are used for their ability to alter thoughts and behavior. It is interesting to note that the use and abuse of psychoactive substances is not a new human phenomenon—records of psychoactive drug use by humans date back to the chewing of the betel nut 13,000 years ago (y.a.), with psychoactive effects on attention and well being similar to those of caffeine or nicotine. The opium poppy (*Papaver somniferum*), whose seed extract can produce morphine (which can be converted to heroin), is a psychoactive drug with a particularly extensive history of human use with records dating back to Mesopotamia 7,000 y.a. (Sullivan & Hagen, 2002).

Psychoactive Drug Action in the Brain

Routes of Administration and Entry into the Central Nervous System

In order for a psychoactive drug to influence behavior, it must first reach the central nervous system (CNS). There are many routes through which a drug can reach the CNS, but the most common routes are through inhalation, oral administration, and injection (intramuscular, IM, intravenous, IV, or subcutaneous, SC). In general terms, the different routes of administration offer a trade-off between safety and efficacy. Intravenous injection offers the fastest route to the brain; however, it is also the most dangerous route since the speed of action offers little time to counter an overdose. The oral route is the slowest since the drug experiences more barriers (e.g., the stomach) before reaching the bloodstream, but it is also the safest route in terms of overdose prevention. For these reasons, the oral route requires the greatest concentration of drugs and IV the least—making IV administration the fastest and cheapest, but most dangerous, route. Whether they do it quickly or slowly, all psychoactive drugs ultimately reach the CNS through crossing the blood–brain barrier in order to affect thoughts and behavior.

The **blood–brain barrier** is made up of a very tightly knit group of cells called endothelial cells, which serve to isolate the brain from the circulating blood in the rest of the body. In doing this, the brain is considered to be "immunologically privileged" since infectious or other dangerous compounds in the body are not able to cross into the brain. Because psychoactive drugs are very fat-soluble, though, they are able to cross the blood–brain barrier and the rate of entry for any particular drug is dependent on its particular lipid solubility. For example, heroin can cross the blood–brain barrier 100 times faster than morphine because it is much more lipid soluble—this gives heroin its powerful "rush." Of note, too, is that stress can potentiate the effect of drugs since stress makes the blood–brain barrier more porous (Butt, Buehler, & D'Agnillo, 2011; Skultétyová, Tokarev, & Jezová, 1998). This increase in permeability will allow psychoactive drugs to cross the blood–brain barrier more readily. In other words, when drugs are taken during times of stress, their effect on the brain will be greatly increased. In fact, chemicals that do not normally even cross the blood–brain barrier can gain access to the brain during times of stress. For example, pyridostigmine, a chemical that causes an overabundance of the neurotransmitter acetylcholine (ACh), can only cross the blood–brain barrier in times of stress. Beyond the direct effects on increased ACh concentrations, increased pyridostigmine itself increases the permeability of the blood–brain barrier to other chemicals (Amourette et al., 2009; Friedman et al., 1996). For recreational drug use this means that during stress there is a greater risk for drug toxicity and overdose.

Receptors: Mechanisms of Drug Action in the Brain

All psychoactive drugs affect brain function by directly or indirectly influencing the activity of specific sites on neurons called **receptors**. Receptors are proteins that span the membrane of a cell and can bind a particular molecule—this molecule can be the internal (endogenous) neurotransmitter or a drug. Once activated by a particular molecule, neuron receptors can alter brain function through changing the voltage of a neuron, activating chemical cascades, or changing gene transcription. An important concept here is that **neurotransmitters** are the naturally occurring, endogenous chemicals in the brain that activate their specific receptors. The effect of any neurotransmitter depends on the function of the receptor to which it binds. This means that the same neurotransmitter can have different effects in different regions of the brain due to the properties of the receptors in those regions. The ability of a neurotransmitter to bind to a receptor is determined by the specific shape and size of the neurotransmitter. A good analogy here is to think of the receptor as a lock and the neurotransmitter as a key—a dopamine key can only fit the dopamine lock. However, when psychoactive drugs are used they usurp the process of neurotransmitter and receptor activity that influences brain processing. For example, a non-natural chemical (drug) can "look like" a dopamine key and activate the receptor. This means that by activating neurotransmitter systems, chemicals can directly cause people to not function as they normally would. With drug use the brain adapts by increasing dopamine receptors, which makes everyday activities less "rewarding." Indeed, the person will rely on the drug in order to feel normal—at a physiological level interpersonal relationships no longer activate motivation and reward networks.

So here we want to take note of the fact that psychoactive drugs work through their influence on naturally occurring neurotransmitter systems. There is not a place in the brain that is intrinsically and uniquely sensitive to any psychoactive drug, but rather, naturally occurring neurotransmitter systems are able to be usurped and influenced by these drugs. There are many ways through which psychoactive drugs can influence receptor behavior, but the two main classification systems to describe their activity are as either an **agonist** or as an **antagonist**. In simple terms, **an antagonistic drug** behaves much as its name implies—it antagonizes the receptor by decreasing its activity. It can decrease (or antagonize) receptor function by and large through two means, (1) by decreasing the amount of the neurotransmitter that naturally binds to a receptor (there are many specific pathways through which it can do this) or (2) by binding to and blocking the receptor to which the neurotransmitter binds—this is essentially like putting gum in the keyhole!

A **drug agonist** is effectively the opposite of a drug antagonist—it works to increase the activity of a receptor. The same general understanding as the antagonist works here, but in the opposite direction. Agonists increase receptor activity by (1) increasing the amount of the neurotransmitter that naturally binds to a receptor (again, there are many specific pathways through which it can do this) or (2) by binding to and *activating* the receptor to which the neurotransmitter binds. As an example of how drug agonists can change behavior we can look at how the drug nicotine, found in cigarettes, is an agonist for a type of acetylcholine (Ach) receptor that is associated with physiological arousal. In fact, these receptors bind nicotine so well that they are referred to as nicotinic acetyl-choline receptors. Accordingly, smoking cigarettes (nicotine) mimics the effect of acetylcholine and causes an increase in behavioral activity/arousal. Nicotine directly affects muscle activity because all skeletal muscles function through acti-vation of nicotinic acetylcholine receptors. Not surprisingly, then, antagonists for the nicotinic acetylcholine receptors will decrease behavior and muscle activity. These drugs are not used recreationally—their main function is to induce muscle paralysis during surgery.

The classification of antidepressant psychoactive drugs known as selective serotonin reuptake inhibitors, or SSRIs, provide another good example of a drug agonist. The SSRIs, such as Fluoxetine (Prozac), work as agonists to increase the amount of serotonin that will bind to its receptor by inhibiting the ability of serotonin from being taken back into the neuron (reuptake) by the seroto-nin transporter (SERT) once it is released. This ultimately leaves more serotonin (5-hydroxytryptamine; 5-HT) in the synapse to bind to the receptor and the mood changes that occur from this increase can combat major depression. One interesting feature of SSRIs in particular, though, is that behavioral/mood changes do not occur until weeks after the initial increase in serotonin at the syn-apse, which may indicate a different mechanism of action through which SSRIs like Fluoxetine exert their anti-depressant effects. In fact, research has indicated that Fluoxetine increases levels of a certain microRNA within serotonergic raphe nuclei which are involved in suppression of the SERT (Baudry, Mouillet-Richard, Schneider, Launay, & Kellermann, 2010). Thus, a delay in the antidepressant effects may be partially attributed to the time it takes for suppression of this transporter to regulate serotonin levels in the brain.

Most drugs of addiction work as an agonist to a neurotransmitter system; however, caffeine is one drug that has effects through working as an antagonist. Although caffeine increases arousal through working on several neurotransmitter system pathways, its primary behavioral effects occur through its ability to work as an antagonist to the adenosine system. The neurotransmitter adenosine serves as a biological signal to increase sleepiness throughout the day—adenosine levels "build up" during the day to promote sleepiness. By working as an antagonist to the adenosine system, caffeine can counteract sleepiness.

Mesocorticolimbic Reinforcement System

The addictive properties of any psychoactive substance stem principally from their ability to modulate the brain's innate reward network. This pathway, the **mesocorticolimbic dopaminergic pathway**, is composed of the connection from the ventral tegmental area (VTA) of the midbrain to the nucleus accumbens (NAc), prefrontal cortex (PFC) and on into the limbic (emotional) system. This system is depicted in Figure 2.1 and is thought of as "the reward pathway." In fact, this pathway has such a profound ability to make the organism feel good that rats are willing to cross a painful electrified grid in order to obtain electrical stimulation to this pathway (Carlezon & Chartoff, 2007; Olds, 1958). Before we outline how this pathway works, it helps to appreciate that addictive sub-stances can be so powerful because this pathway evolved and serves to "reward" humans and other animals when they engage in behaviors that are beneficial for survival (O'Connell & Hofmann, 2011). The hedonic responses experienced by the organism from natural reinforcers such as food and sex are accompanied by a release of the neurotransmitter dopamine (DA) from VTA neurons released onto the NAc. Dopaminergic transmission within this pathway may be involved in the subjective "feel good" experience as well as learning to "want" or seek that pleasurable stimulus again by ascribing incentive salience to that reward (Berridge & Robinson, 1998; Kelley & Berridge, 2002). This dopamine modulated reward-related learning for natural reinforcers is evolutionarily advantageous to keep us (or our species) alive. However, drugs of abuse can result in a profoundly greater release of dopamine along this pathway compared with these natural reinforcers, thereby "hijacking" this reward pathway. Maladaptive reward-related learning can occur in which valuation for these drugs is greater than for natural reinforcers or other pleasure-associated stimuli. Indeed, human cocaine users exhibit greater brain activation when watching a film with cocaine-associated cues compared with a non-drug evocative film, and less brain activation compared with non-drug users in response to the evocative film (Garavan et al., 2000). Because most psychoactive drugs are able to stimulate this pathway and cause the release of dopamine onto the NAc, we can begin to appreciate why these drugs can have such profound impacts on behavior and social functioning. These effects are mediated through known brain changes that occur from addiction and give rise to poor judgment, impaired decision making, and a loss of behavior control (Robinson & Berridge, 2003). It is easy to see how these impairments can lead to a massive disruption of proper day-to-day functioning. Indeed, when rats are allowed to press a lever that will cause cocaine to stimulate this pathway, they will lever-press to the exclusion of all other behaviors—even to the point of starvation (Wise, 1989).

The mesocorticolimbic system is responsible for determining motivation and drive and is necessary for the processing of natural rewards (e.g., food, sex, and social interaction). Two of the key players involved in reward processing within

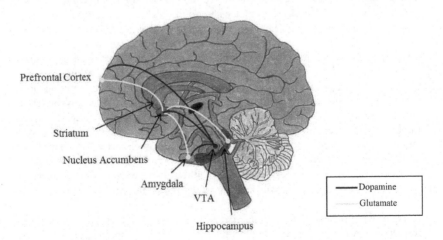

Figure 2.1 The mesocorticolimbic system

this system are the neurotransmitters dopamine and glutamate. Dopaminergic transmission along this pathway underlies hedonic responses and reward-related learning while glutamatergic transmission mediates learning and memory. Dopaminergic neurons in the ventral tegmental area (VTA) send axonal projections to the nucleus accumbens (NAc), the prefrontal cortex (PFC), and the amygdala, and release dopamine. Additionally, glutamatergic projections from the PFC, amygdala, and hippocampus project to the NAc. The NAc is implicated in reward and motivation. The PFC is the main region involved in higher order cognitive function such as inhibition of inappropriate responses, planning, and mediating goal-directed behavior. The mesocorticolimbic amygdala is implicated in emotion processing of a stimulus as well as establishing conditioned associations between cues and rewarding or aversive experiences. The hippocampus underlies context-specific memory under which a rewarding or aversive stimulus was experienced.

The **mesocorticolimbic system** involves a series of feedback loops with parts of the brain to control internal balance, or homeostasis. Physiological homeostasis involves maintaining biological "balance" within the body by ongoing compensation for perturbations or chemical fluctuations (e.g., hormone changes). It is important not to confuse physiological homeostasis with the idea of family homeostasis, which concerns how family members come together and regulate their functioning. In this book, we will primarily be focusing on family homeostasis. Physiological homeostasis helps us respond when a basic need is detected. In response to a need, the mesocorticolimbic dopamine system will feed forward into motor control areas and memory systems in order to respond to the body's need. These other areas include the learning and memory systems (the PFC, hippocampus and amygdala) as well as sensory and motor input (i.e., the basal ganglia, thalamus) (Söderpalm & Ericson, 2013). These areas, combined with cortical integration, serve as the "motivation control system" of the body to ensure that we engage in behaviors that keep us (or our species) alive. For example, homeostatic signals which communicate hunger to the brain will activate the mesocorticolimbic and ancillary systems to motivate humans and other animals to start searching for food, remember where food was found, and recognize areas where food was previously found (Söderpalm & Ericson, 2013). Essentially, the mesocorticolimbic system drives us to get motivated and get moving in a goal-directed manner. Psychoactive drugs that activate the mesocorticolimbic system will be treated as intrinsically rewarding (just like food, sex, or other naturally pleasurable stimuli). Indeed, this pathway appears to serve as a common neurobiological vulnerability that underlies behavioral as well as psychoactive addictions. With repeated use of chemical substances, the body learns to treat the drug as part of the homeostatic drive—in the absence of the drug the system activates to seek out the drug (Wise, 1989). All psychoactive drugs that are addictive either directly or indirectly activate the mesocorticolimbic system. The pharmacological properties of these drugs allow their activation of this system to be quite powerful—even usurping the strength of other natural reinforcers to activate this system.

To provide an example of the impact that these processes have on human functioning, we can look at one reason why addicts may not engage in normal processes like eating and sex. They may find that activities that they used to find pleasurable, such as having sexual intercourse with their partner, are no longer as physiologically gratifying as they used to be. They may even need to get "high" to enjoy sex with their partner. While this physiological process is in play, there are also relational impacts that the reduction of pleasure has, which we will discuss throughout the remainder of this book.

Psychoactive Drug Classifications and Brain Actions

Inhalation Drugs: Marijuana and Cigarettes

Marijuana is a widely used psychotropic drug whose active psychoactive substance is the **tetrahydrocannabinol (THC)** chemical that is produced by the cannabis plant. As we reviewed above, psychotropic drugs have their effect in the CNS by serving as agonists or antagonists for naturally occurring neurotransmitters. Tetrahydrocannabinol is an agonist for the receptors that naturally bind the neurotransmitter anandamide. Interestingly, though, in this case the effects of THC were well known before the endogenous neurotransmitter was discovered. For that reason, anandamide took its name from the Sanskrit word for "bliss."

There are two known receptors to which THC binds in the brain—cannabinoid receptors 1 and 2 (CB1 and CB2). Anandamide activation of the cannabinoid receptors can impair working memory (Kunos & Bátkai, 2001) and increase feeding behavior.[1] Unsurprisingly, then, marijuana (i.e., THC) use is also associated with decreases in working memory and increases in appetite (a reason why people seem to get the "munchies" after smoking or ingesting marijuana). The potential effect of THC on psychotic behavior is less clear. Although there is a well-described association between psychotic disorders (such as schizophrenia) with ongoing cannabis use (Chadwick, Miller, & Hurd, 2013), it is not certain if marijuana use precedes the behavior changes or is a response to it (e.g., in an effort to "self-medicate"). As reviewed at the beginning of this chapter, the mesocorticolimbic system is the final common pathway whose activation mediates the addictive properties of all psychotropic drugs. Tetrahydrocannabinol activates this system, and, accordingly, can also have addictive effects. In fact, THC can activate dopamine release in the NAc even at relatively low doses (Chen, Paredes, Lowinson, & Gardner, 1990). There is also a probable role for THC in potentiating alcohol use since a drug that antagonizes the CB1 receptor also reduces ethanol intake in rats (Colombo et al., 1998). This means that marijuana *is* biologically addictive and, in fact, 9% of marijuana users become dependent on it (Danovitch & Gorelick, 2012). However, this rate is much lower compared with all other addictive substances (Lopez-Quintero et al., 2011). Like other drugs, when the person stops using marijuana, there may be physiological and psychological withdrawal issues. The most common withdrawal symptoms include marijuana cravings, mood-swings, and sleep disruption.

The use of cannabidiol (CBD) alone is becoming increasingly popular. Although marijuana contains THC and cannabinoid, CBD alone is not psychoactive. Cannabidiol has a low affinity for the CB1 receptors and CB2 receptors, but can increase the production of endogenous cannabinoids (Hayakawa et al., 2008). Recent evidence points to the use of CBD as an anti-inflammatory agent and as a possible therapeutic agent in the treatment of anxiety, depression, and addiction (Zlebnik & Cheer, 2016).

Cigarettes, like marijuana, are a common inhalation drug; however, cigarette use is legal and regulated across the U.S. Cigarette smoking is the most common use of the tobacco plant whose chemical, **nicotine**, gives tobacco its reinforcing and addictive properties. Nicotine influences behavior through binding to the previously described nicotinic acetylcholine receptors (nAChRs) on neurons in the mesocorticolimbic pathway. When nicotine binds to the nAChRs on the VTA neurons it causes them to release more dopamine onto the NAc neurons. Nicotinic acetylcholine receptors are also located on neurons in the VTA that indirectly modulate dopamine activity (Koob & Volkow, 2010). Compared with marijuana, and even other psychotropic drugs, nicotine is extremely addictive (Kandel, Chen, Warner, Kessler, & Grant, 1997). Although there is not a clear consensus on what constitutes "addiction" to nicotine, it can be clearly characterized by persistence of use and withdrawal symptoms. There is also a larger degree of individual variability on the likelihood to become addicted to nicotine and the ability to quit nicotine use. Clear genetic factors have emerged that point to individual risk for nicotine use and are discussed in the next chapter.

Antianxiety and Sedative Hypnotics: Barbiturates, Benzodiazepines, and Alcohol

The general classification of **antianxiety and sedative hypnotics** refers to drugs that have **anxiolytic** (anxiety-reducing) and **sedative** (sleep-inducing) properties. Here we will focus on the sedative hypnotics alcohol and barbiturates (derivatives of barbituric acid) and the antianxiety benzodiazepines. All of these drugs affect behavior by essentially decreasing brain function (which is one reason why, when prescribed, individuals are warned not to operate heavy machinery or drive motor vehicles while taking the drug). Importantly, these drugs decrease brain function in a **dose-dependent** manner, meaning that as the drug dose increases, brain activity decreases. This dose-dependent property translates into reduced feelings of anxiety at low doses, loss of inhibition followed by sleepiness at medium doses, and, at the highest doses, coma and even death can occur.

A critical feature of all of these drugs is that they have **cross-tolerance** for each other; tolerance for one of these drugs will increase tolerance for another. For example, if a person develops a tolerance to alcohol, they will also develop a tolerance for antianxiety medication. Cross-tolerance is possible because antianxiety and sedative hypnotic drugs all work as agonists at the same brain receptor—the **GABA$_A$ receptor**. The GABA$_A$ receptors are widely distributed throughout the brain and function as one of the "workhorses" of the brain to inhibit neuron activity. When activated, the GABA$_A$ receptor will open up and allow chloride (Cl-), a negatively charged ion, into the neuron, thus reducing the excitability of that neuron (Olsen & DeLorey, 1999). The GABA$_A$ receptor has a binding site for the endogenous neurotransmitter, GABA. There are two additional binding sites on this receptor to which other endogenous chemicals bind in order to modulate the effects of GABA on the receptor. It is these other binding sites that can also bind benzodiazepines, alcohol, or barbiturates.

Activation of the benzodiazepine binding site modulates the receptor so that GABA binds to it much more easily (increases the affinity for GABA). In other words, benzodiazepines reduce anxiety by allowing GABA to more easily bind to its receptor, which decreases neuron excitability. Barbiturates, on the other hand, do not function by changing the ability of GABA to bind to its receptor, but rather, increase the amount of time the channel is open so that more Cl- ions can pass into the neuron and reduce the excitability of the neuron. Although these benzodiazepines and barbiturates seem to have similar enough effects on the GABA$_A$ receptor, barbiturates are much more dangerous since prolonged increases of Cl- into the cell can cause the brain to rapidly shut down through a decrease in neuron activity. In addition, they can further decrease brain activity by binding to sodium (Na+) channels on neurons and preventing the flow of sodium ions (which also decreases neuron excitability). The combined effect of barbiturates on prolonged Cl- influx and decreased Na+ influx into cells causes neurons to essentially "shut down." While this can aid in increasing sleepiness at normal doses, this effect can result in a loss of consciousness or even death minutes after a barbiturate overdose.

Alcohol is lipid (fat) soluble and, as such, can easily cross the blood–brain barrier inducing widespread effects on the CNS. Alcohol has two major binding sites in the brain—one is the GABA$_A$ receptor and the other is the N-methyl-D-aspartate receptor (NMDA) receptor. Alcohol enhances the inhibitory effects of GABA at the GABA$_A$ receptor, which accounts for the sedative effects of alcohol. The NMDA receptor naturally binds the neurotransmitter glutamate and acts as a coincidence detector (the binding of glutamate along with post-synaptic depolarization) to allow for memory formation in the brain (through a process called long-term potentiation, or LTP). Since alcohol decreases glutamate's ability to bind to the NMDA receptor it can decrease memory formation (possibly related to the "black out" effects of alcohol) in addition to a decrease in overall brain excitation (since NMDA receptors have an excitatory effect of neurons). Behavioral consequences to this reduced excitation include a loss of higher cortical (especially frontal lobe) functions and loss of motor control. Examples of frontal lobe impairments can include an inability to think clearly, a change in personality, difficulty with emotional control, and difficulty with rational thought. This is one reason that there are so many motor vehicle accidents when the person who is driving has alcohol in their system since the individual has a loss of cerebellar control. Damage to the cerebellum with alcohol use or injury results in difficulty with the timing and coordination of intended movements. This means the intentional mouth and tongue movements (which can cause slurring), standing up from a sitting position, walking, or even swerving in time to avoid a collision when driving, are hampered.

These physiological impacts of alcohol use are also a major factor in the change of a person's functioning in interpersonal relationships—especially when they are drunk. Given that their ability to think and emotional control are depressed, they have a tendency to act in ways that are not "normal" for them. This may come in the form of someone who is usually quiet and non-violent becoming boisterous and physically abusive.

Long-term alcohol use causes NMDA receptors to increase in number in response to the ongoing antagonistic effects of alcohol on these receptors. As a consequence, the abrupt cessation of alcohol intake in chronic users can cause NMDA-receptor-mediated seizure activity 6–48 hours later (Hughes, 2009). The up-regulation of NMDA receptors that occurs with chronic alcohol use is also associated with **delirium tremens** (DTs), which include tremors, increased blood pressure/racing heart, and hallucinations (Hughes, 2009). It is uncertain in humans how long it takes for these consequences to occur—the prevailing view is that these effects begin after at least a few years of heavy drinking. However, other findings show that heavy use for a short period can bring about seizures and DTs (Ng, Hauser, Brust, & Susser, 1988).

Alcohol is a very addictive substance. In the next chapter we will review various biological factors that contribute to individual differences in the sensitivity to alcohol's addictive properties. In general, though, the addictive properties of alcohol are mediated through the mesocorticolimbic dopamine system. Like other addictive drugs, alcohol increases the release of dopamine in the NAc. Experiments in rats support the idea that it is alcohol's activation of the mesocorticolimbic dopamine system that gives alcohol its addictive properties. In particular, the intake of alcohol can be reduced by injecting a dopamine antagonist directly into the NAc (Samson, Hodge, Tolliver, & Haraguchi, 1993). The reinforcing effects of alcohol are also mediated through its ability to release endogenous opioids (Davidson, Swift, & Fitz, 1996). Endogenous opioids, binding to opioid receptors, cause feelings of pleasure and euphoria in humans and other animals. Thus, a person may seek out alcohol, outside of the taste, to attain the physiological effects.

Stimulants: Caffeine, Amphetamine, and Cocaine

In general, the classification "**stimulants**" are a class of drugs that increase energy and alertness and also create a sense of well-being. These drugs increase energy through an increase in sympathetic nervous system (SNS) activity. This causes the same types of physiological and behavioral effects to stimulants that the body naturally produces during a "fight or flight response." The physiological changes include an increase in heart rate, increased respiration, pupil dilation, increased sweating, and elevated blood pressure. Behaviorally, activation of the SNS causes an increase in alertness and attention. However, continued stimulant use can result in paranoia and hostility. Due to the role of stimulants in increasing energy, alertness, focus, and concentration this classification of drugs is used therapeutically in different forms for the management of attention disorders (e.g., ADD/ADHD) and severe daytime sleepiness (e.g., narcolepsy). Of note, though, is that these prescription stimulants are also commonly used to increase academic or professional performance. Attention-enhancing drugs such as Modafinil, Adderal, and Ritalin are also referred to as "smart drugs" for their ability to boost academic performance.

By far, the most widely used general stimulant is caffeine (in fact I wager that many reading this chapter are doing so with the help of this drug!). Above, we discussed the role of caffeine as an antagonist for the adenosine system and here we clarify how caffeine can directly increase energy production in the body. Caffeine readily crosses the blood–brain barrier and inhibits an enzyme called phosphodiesterase (PDE), which breaks down a chemical called cyclic adenosine monophosphate (cAMP). Without PDE putting on the brakes, cAMP levels increase, which results in an increase in glucose production in the cell (which results in more energy). The rise in cAMP also prolongs the effects of epinephrine (adrenaline) or drugs that have adrenaline-like activities such as amphetamines.

Caffeine use is not considered biologically addictive. While caffeine use *can* cause physical withdrawal symptoms (such as headaches), withdrawal symptoms do not always mean that there is physical dependence. The main reason that caffeine is not considered biologically addictive is that (at doses that reflect human use) it does not alter the mesocorticolimbic pathway (Nehlig, Armspach, & Namer, 2010). However, there are possible withdrawal symptoms, such as jitteriness and mood instability.

Like caffeine use, amphetamine and cocaine use cause an increase in SNS activity, but, unlike caffeine, they are both highly addictive. Amphetamine and cocaine have similar behavioral effects to each other, but they have distinct modes of action in the brain. Behaviorally, both of these drugs can produce an increased sense of euphoria, increased focus and concentration, an increase in energy, and decreased appetite. In the mesocorticolimbic system amphetamine and cocaine are both "extreme" dopamine agonists.

Amphetamine[2] use causes the direct release of dopamine from neurons and blocks dopamine reuptake (going back into the neuron after it is released), while cocaine mainly works by blocking the reuptake of dopamine. Another difference is that amphetamine is also an agonist for the neurotransmitter noradrenaline (A.K.A norepinephrine). The neurobiological differences between the two also cause amphetamines to have longer-lasting effects compared with cocaine (Barr et al., 2006). These longer-lasting effects, however, are also the reason why amphetamines are also more likely to result in behavioral psychosis. Importantly, both of these stimulants result in profound and irreparable brain damage by causing lesions in the neurotransmitter systems (at axon terminals) that they activate (Gouzoulis-Mayfrank & Daumann, 2009; Yamamoto, Moszczynska, & Gudelsky, 2010).

Psychedelic Drugs: LSD and MDMA

Hallucinogenic drugs have their effects through actions on the serotonin (5-HT) neurotransmitter system. These drugs are not biologically addictive and their reinforcing effects are derived from their ability to alter perceptual experiences. The drug **lysergic acid diethylamide (LSD)** works as an agonist for the serotonin receptor 5-HT$_{2A}$. The activation of this receptor by LSD produces visual hallucinations and perceptual distortions. While some people find these experiences to be rewarding and exciting, others find the hallucinations and perceptual distortions to be frightening. LSD was originally created as a blood stimulant in Switzerland in 1938. The hallucinogenic properties of LSD were discovered when its discoverer, Albert Hoffman, accidently spilled some of it on himself. After this, Sandoz Pharmaceuticals distributed the drug for psychiatric research (Dyck, 2005). Recently, a Phase 2 pilot study conducted by the Multidisciplinary Association for Psychedelic Studies (MAPS) has demonstrated that LSD-assisted psychotherapy for anxiety associated with a life-threatening illness can be safely administered to patients. A positive trend in the reduction of anxiety was noted and warrants further research.

Another commonly abused hallucinogenic is the drug **MDMA** (3,4-methylenedioxy-N-methylamphetamine)—commonly known as "Ecstasy." MDMA works as an agonist of serotonin and norepinephrine systems. MDMA was originally manufactured by the German drug company, Merk. MDMA was used clinically to help patients "open up" during psychotherapy (Bernschneider-Reif, Oxler, & Freudenmann, 2006). Indeed, the behavioral effects of MDMA create an increased sense of euphoria and empathy and also produce hallucinations. While MDMA is not biologically addictive, its neurobiological effects are nevertheless devastating to its users through selective lesions on the same serotonin neurons that are activated by its use; this results in memory problems and declines in cognitive processing (Gouzoulis-Mayfrank & Daumann, 2009; Yamamoto, Moszczynska, & Gudelsky, 2010). MDMA is currently being used again during psychotherapy and especially for posttraumatic stress disorder (PTSD) due to the ability of MDMA to assist with reprocessing of traumatic memories (Feduccia & Mithoefer, 2018).

Psilocybin is another frequently used hallucinogenic drug. Psilocybin is produced by over 100 species of psilocybin mushrooms and has low addictive risk and toxicity. The behavioral effects of Psilocybin are similar to the other psychedelics and are mediated (at least partly) through the 5-hydroxytryptamine (HT)2A receptor. Psilocybin is also sometimes used as an adjunct in psychotherapy and has shown some benefits for the treatment of anxiety, depression, and drug addiction (Johnson & Griffiths, 2017).

Case Application

Addiction adds a significant amount of strain on the Rothers' family environment. A family therapist would benefit from understanding and exploring the neurobiological basis of Mark's addiction in treating Mark and the Rothers family. Understanding the biological basis of the addiction can allow the family to form a basis for appreciating the future intrapersonal and interpersonal difficulties as Mark works through reducing or abstaining in substance use. In particular, Mark and his family will need to understand that his brain is currently biologically addicted to alcohol. Recognizing the biological changes in the brain that occur with addiction can assist in the recovery process.

Like all chemical addictions, the natural motivation and reward centers of Mark's brain have experienced "hard-wired" changes. The pathway through which Mark, or any addict, progresses from casual drinking to dependence involves a complex interplay between psychological, biological (including genetic, see Chapter 3), and environmental variables. It is possible that Mark had a natural vulnerability for alcohol addiction since individuals who naturally have decreased DA signaling (through decreased DA D2 receptor density and function) in the mesolimbic pathways appear to be at an increased risk for dependence (Tupala & Tiihonen, 2004). In the brain of any addict, increased use of alcohol will result in a reduction in the release of DA in the NAc and in limbic pathways, which will create withdrawal symptoms and craving (e.g., restlessness, irritability, anxiety, and insomnia). For Mark, alcohol use during withdrawal is reinforcing since it will restore DA levels (Hui & Gang, 2014).

Many areas of the brain that are important for emotion and memory processing have been altered as a result of the addiction to alcohol and possibly through the comorbid use of other substances. Critically, environmental experiences and exposures can create a state of neurological vulnerability for relapse. In particular, even a single drink after Mark quits can prime his brain for continued use through the role of dopamine in "priming" the brain for drinking behavior. Mark's brain will also be in a vulnerable state for relapse when he is around cues that were part of his routine alcohol use. These cues can be people, places, or even objects. This is because drug abuse can sensitize the mesolimbic system (see the "Mesocorticolimbic Reinforcement System" section in this chapter) so that the experience of the drug is intertwined with the environment in which it is taken. Of note is that there is a significant amount of strain on Mark's family environment. One useful possibility will be for Mark to obtain stress management techniques as part of the therapeutic process. Stress commonly works as an antecedent for addiction relapse. In particular, the stress hormone cortisol crosses the blood–brain barrier and can bind directly to receptors in the VTA, ultimately increasing the drive for substance use (Adinoff, 2004).

The family therapist can consider incorporating education about the neural circuits of addiction in order to help Mark and his family understand that chemical addiction presents unique challenges relative to other behaviors. One avenue of approach would be to explain that, at a neurological level, we are all motivated to engage in particular behaviors based on the natural reward the brain receives from successfully completing motivated behavior. At birth, we are hard-wired to engage in certain activities necessary for sustaining our survival (the canonical "4 Fs" of motivation: fight, flight, food, and sex). This basic reward circuitry has been significantly altered in Mark—the motivation to engage in adaptive and healthy human behavior is decreased in the addicted individual. With consistent exposure of brain receptors to an addictive substance, the substance can easily become the most desirable thing in life to the addict. In Mark's case, he has decreased motivation to pursue the healthy behaviors in which we expect non-addict adults to engage. His body is now motivating him to seek out alcohol for pleasure and punishes him for not using alcohol. When he does not use alcohol, he will experience physiological withdrawal symptoms. Summarily, Mark's body may now be receiving signals from his brain that alcohol is more important to the system than food, sex, or relationships. As an addict, his role and interactions in his family environment are severely altered. His desire to maintain and engage in his interpersonal relationships is no longer as imperative as it once may have been. It is difficult to accurately predict the complete behavioral consequences of his alcohol use. There are many biological and social factors that will contribute to the withdrawal symptoms experienced by each individual. As the reward network has been altered we can expect varied levels of motivation based on the re-wiring of neural networks.

The family should also understand how alcohol has, and will continue to, affect his life. The most common behavioral consequences of alcohol's long-term effects on the brain are the loss of frontal lobe function and motor control. This creates an inability to think clearly, personality changes, and difficulty with emotion control, and these effects can take place slowly over time. With continued chronic use of alcohol the individual tends to slowly suffer more severe decreased function. The rate and extent of impairment that someone experiences is individual and has many contributing factors. This is important for Mark's family to understand since this information may allow the family to interact with him better knowing the limitations in his cognitive ability. Due to the effects that the substance abuse has had on his brain, he is now hard-wired to value alcohol over other aspects of life. His dopaminergic pathway has been hijacked by his dependency on alcohol and is now, in essence, taking over his thinking. Motivation on a neurological level is the sequential events that lead from our brain to our body in order to complete a desired action. Because of his dependence on alcohol, and its effects of reducing psychological pain and providing pleasure, Mark is now no longer functioning in a cognitively normal way. It will be challenging for him to be motivated to enjoy or engage in healthy behaviors.

Perhaps most importantly, it is critical for the client or therapist to know that not all hope is lost for an addicted brain and that meaningful changes in brain plasticity can come about with strenuous and consistent therapy. With addiction recovery the brain shows increased pre-frontal cortex (PFC) activity and some recovery of executive control and general cognitive functioning. Notably, if the inhibitory control networks of the client can be strengthened, the ability to withstand the drive to use will be concomitantly strengthened. Mindfulness training techniques have also been associated with overcoming strong drug cravings through increasing inhibitory control (Adinoff, 2004). In addition, over time, changes in the DA pathways in the mesolimbic pathway can become at least partially restored (Charlet, Rosenthal, Lohoff, Heinz, & Beck, 2018).

Summary

In this chapter we have presented some of the basics of the neuroscience of how addiction happens. The processes that we have discussed impact people differentially. For instance, it may take four alcoholic drinks for the person to begin to experience some of the effects while others may need only one or two drinks. Regardless of how much, or how little, of the drug is needed to activate the various receptors in the brain, the individual effects affect the person's relational world.

The physiological brain changes that occur for people who use and abuse substances may be the frustrating aspect for family and friends, and probably also for the individual, as to why they cannot just stop, cold turkey, in using. While drug use is a choice, there are more factors in play, such as dependence and withdrawal mechanisms. Thus, having an understanding of how drugs impact the body should help in conceptualizing what is happening for the individual while the individual is engaged in the relational networks of their life.

Key Words

psychoactive drugs
behavioral addiction
process addiction
blood–brain barrier
receptors
neurotransmitters
antagonistic drug
agonist drug
mesocorticolimbic pathway
mesocorticolimbic system
marijuana
tetrahydrocannabinol (THC)

antianxiety and sedative
  hypnotics
anxiolytic
sedative
dose-dependent
cross-tolerance
delirium tremens
stimulants
hallucinogenic drugs
lysergic acid diethylamide (LSD)
MDMA
Psilocybin

Discussion Questions

1. Explain the relationship between psychoactive drugs and their impact on the brain.
2. What are the differences between antagonistic and agonist drugs?
3. How do stimulants and sedatives differ in their impact on the body?
4. Why are some drugs cross-tolerant?
5. How might the physiological impact of different drugs impact a person's familial relationships?

Notes

1 An interesting aside here is that chocolate contains anandamide-like substances—this might explain why so many people find chocolate so scrumptious and difficult to deny!
2 Methamphetamine is a common variant of amphetamine. The only difference between them is that methamphetamine is double methylated. The process of double methylation causes methamphetamine to have faster, stronger, and more dangerous effects in the body. Methamphetamine breaks down into amphetamine once metabolized in the body.

THREE

The Genetics of Addiction

Jaime L. Tartar and Christina M. Gobin

In the last chapter, we reviewed the basic concepts surrounding how psychotropic drugs can be biologically addictive through their ability to activate and modulate the mesocorticolimbic dopaminergic system. In this chapter, we will focus on how specific natural variations in genes can make individuals more susceptible to the effects of drugs and biological addiction. In reviewing the effects of genes on any behavior, including addiction, the most important concept to understand is that genes do not code for *any* behavior. In other words, it is a common misconception to think that genes control behavior.

In recent years, we have seen headline-grabbing reports of behavior-controlling genes. These include the so-called smart gene, the happiness gene, the aggression gene, the athletic gene, and the addiction gene. This is a misunderstanding of what genes actually do. While genes *contribute* to different aspects of behavior, no individual gene is *responsible* for a single behavior. In other words, when we describe a particular gene as one that contributes to the development of a behavioral characteristic, such as alcoholism, we are not saying that the trait is "genetically-determined." There are certainly genes that contribute to drug sensitivity and to drug addiction, but there can never be an "addiction-gene." This is a very important distinction and one that is commonly confused in the media and in everyday conversation. It is likely that individuals seeking therapy will be equally confused about this. In order to better understand why this can never be the case, let's first review what it is that genes actually do.

Genes: The Basic Units of Heredity

Genes are the basic units of heredity and are located within strands of **deoxyribonucleic acid (DNA)**. DNA is made up of two strands of four repeating **nucleotides:** adenine (A), thymine (T), cytosine (C), and guanine (G). The two strands of DNA fit perfectly together in such a way that an A on one strand always pairs with a T on the other strand, and a C on one strand always pairs with a G on the other strand. For example, if one strand contained the base sequence C-A-T-G, the corresponding strand would be G-T-A-C. The chain of these matching nucleotide bases are held in place by a backbone of sugar and phosphate running along each side of the paired nucleotides. These two side backbones are strong and flexible structures that coil around each other giving DNA its famous double-helix shape. Humans have 23 pairs of very long strands of DNA—these are the chromosomes and they are stored in the nucleus of each cell. Each parent contributes 23 chromosomes to their offspring, and, altogether on these chromosomes, the human genome contains about 3.2 billion base pairs (matching pairs of nucleotides). Interestingly, *most* of the nucleotide sequence in the DNA does not code for genes—these sections occur within and between genes and are collectively called **non-coding DNA** (sometimes referred to as "junk" DNA).

The relevant or **coding DNA** consists of a series of nucleotides that code for a specific amino acid. When the DNA sequence is set to be "read," it is unwound and a molecule very similar to DNA called ribonucleic acid (RNA) is copied from one of the DNA strands (one strand is specifically designated for this purpose). When RNA is produced, it carries its own matching nucleotide sequence (except here Thymine is substituted for Uracil so, in RNA, A pairs with U, in place of T). The production of RNA from the DNA strand is called **transcription**. This is just like when you transcribe a recorded lecture—you copy exactly what was said in the same language. Transcription does exactly this—it transcribes, or copies, the information from the language of nucleotides (DNA) into a matching language of nucleotides (RNA). This RNA will then carry the matching nucleotide code out of the nucleus—by doing this it serves as a messenger and is appropriately called messenger RNA (mRNA). The mRNA then reaches protein-making factories called **ribosomes** in the cell. The ribosomes read the mRNA as part of **translation**—the process of making proteins from the mRNA code. Here, the mRNA is translated from the language of nucleotides (RNA) into the new language of proteins. In particular, every 3 nucleotides that are read by the ribosomes represents one **codon**. From the 4 aforementioned nucleotides, 64 combinations of these nucleotide triplets or codons can be generated. Each codon will tell the ribosome to make one of 20 possible **amino acids**. These chains of amino acids will then combine to make a **protein** with a unique 3-D structure and specific function such as executing enzymatic reactions, providing structure, or signaling communication within and between cells. Some of these proteins may include receptor proteins, which are involved in the neurochemical cascades that result in certain physiological or behavioral responses. This whole process through which DNA makes RNA, which then makes proteins, is a fundamental principle in understanding how genes work. It is so fundamental, in fact, that **"DNA makes RNA makes protein"** is known as the central dogma of biology. Altogether, the human genome contains 20,000–25,000 distinct protein-coding genes.

So now that we have an appreciation that a gene is only a strand of DNA that codes for a specific protein, we can better appreciate *why* it is inappropriate to think of genes as controlling behavior. It would never make sense to think that one protein determines your cheerful disposition! In sum, genes code for proteins and proteins can *contribute* to behavior, but they do not *determine* behavior.

Polymorphisms

Within a population, there can be differences in the genes that lead to differences in the expressed proteins. These differences are known as **polymorphisms** and are described by how many times a number of the nucleotides repeat. **Variable number tandem repeats (VNTRs)** have a core repeat sequence that ranges from 500–30,000 nucleotides. **Short tandem repeats (STRs)**, on the other hand, have a much shorter core repeat sequence that ranges from 50–300 nucleotides. Single nucleotide polymorphisms (SNPs, pronounced "snips") consist of only a single nucleotide difference in the sequence of the DNA. These types of polymorphisms are inherited and lead to differences in protein or enzyme activity between individuals. Later in the chapter we will confront specific polymorphisms that are associated with addiction. Since each person has two copies of a gene (**alleles**), they can be heterozygous or homozygous for polymorphism—they could have inherited two different alleles (heterozygous) or two of the same alleles (homozygous).

Genetic Vulnerability to Addiction

Susceptibility vs Inevitability

Like other behaviors, the genetic vulnerability to addiction is complex. Having a genetic susceptibility for addiction does not determine someone's fate—it only affects the way the body responds to drugs. For example, one set of genetic polymorphisms can make it harder to quit using and increase withdrawal symptoms. Conversely, other polymorphisms can make it harder for someone to become an addict (for example, if unpleasant symptoms are experienced from using a drug that typically induces pleasant feelings). Later in this chapter we will review some of the genetic factors that are shown to increase addiction susceptibility. For therapists, it is important to appreciate that some individuals can be biologically predisposed to drug sensitivity. These biological differences in how the body processes and responds to drugs can help to explain why addiction is much harder to control in some individuals compared with others. In other words, two people can "try" just as hard and be equally motivated to overcome addiction, but a biological predisposition can make it physiologically more difficult for one of them to get better. With advances in "personalized medicine," it might soon become practical to genotype addicted populations in order to better treat them. **Genotyping** is a technique of identifying an individual's genetic code (genotype). In other words, it is the process of determining the genetic make up (genotype) and identifying the specific alleles that an individual has inherited from his/her parents. Finding differences in drug sensitivity at a physiological level means that addiction treatment can be aided by *customized* therapy and treatment strategies. In the field of psychopharmacogenetics, research is currently underway to customize addiction treatment based on individual genotypes (reviewed in Heilig, Goldman, Berrettini, & O'Brien, 2011). The idea of customized treatment has already shown promise in addiction treatment. For example, in the finding that naltrexone hydrochloride is significantly more effective in alcoholics with a specific opioid receptor gene polymorphism (Asp40), compared with alcoholics without the polymorphism (48% vs 26%, respectively; Anton et al., 2008).

Patterns of Inheritance: Pedigree Studies

Gene polymorphisms are passed down from parents to children through specific patterns of inheritance. However, the pattern of inheritance in families does not follow the classic "Mendelien" transmission pattern where one allele is dominant or recessive and only one trait is expressed. Drug abuse and addiction involves multiple genes and is susceptible to environmental influences (Enoch & Goldman, 1999). Investigations in the genetics of addiction and substance abuse are thought to follow **a gene–environment interaction (G x E) model**. The GxE model assumes that both genetics and environment play a role in addiction susceptibility (Hesselbrock & Hesselbrock, 1990). For this reason, analyses of families with substance-use disorders are helpful in uncovering the inheritance pattern and environmental influences on addiction development. Figure 3.1 portrays the complex gene x environment interaction.

An important note to make here is that heritability estimates are sometimes misinterpreted as estimates of genetic contribution to a particular trait in an individual. Heritability estimates do not refer to individuals, but rather, to variation within groups of people (i.e., a population). **Heritability** is the proportion of the total variation of a certain trait in a population that is due to genetic variation. With this in mind, pedigree studies on addiction provide overwhelming evidence that addiction to alcohol and other psychoactive substances have

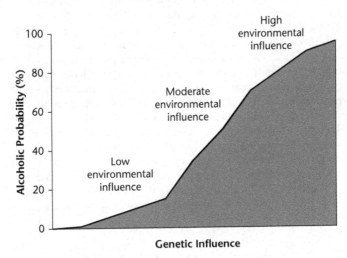

Figure 3.1 Environmental and genetic factors play a combined role in addiction. In this figure alcoholism susceptibility is shown as a function of a G x E model. Addiction probabilities are low when there is little genetic susceptibility and little environmental influence towards alcohol use. The highest probabilities of alcoholism arise with a high genetic influence and strong environmental influence towards alcohol use. Figure adapted from Dick and Kendler (2012)

strong heritability estimates. For example, first-degree relatives (mother, father, sibling) of people who use opiates are significantly more likely to have drug or alcohol addiction (Rounsaville et al., 1991). Of note here is that there is also a family-linked association between alcoholism, opiate use, and depression— suggesting a common genetic link between these conditions (Kosten, Rounsaville, Kosten, & Merikangas, 1991). In addition, pedigree studies find that, compared with the general population, the potential for alcoholism is increased in people who are biologically-related to someone with alcoholism. Moreover, this risk is increased up to seven-fold for first-degree relatives of an alcoholic (Cotton, 1979; Merikangas, 1990). The specificity of inheritance for specific substances is not clear. The reason for this uncertainty is that drug users tend to use more than one substance and the availability and popularity of specific substances changes with time. In other words, it is difficult to pinpoint the inheritance for one drug in particular since many drug users also use other common substances (e.g., alcohol), and the availability of any particular drug may wax and wane over the years while other substances become more readily available.

Genome-Wide Association Studies (GWAS): Polymorphism Identification in Addiction

In addition to looking at inheritance patterns in families, there is also a goal of genotyping individuals in order to better understand addiction and improve treatment. Findings in this area stem largely from **genome-wide association studies (GWAS)**. GWAS identify genetic markers of disease, mental illness, or behavioral differences by comparing the variation in DNA between people. Family-based GWAS on addiction and substance use behavior have shown many genes involved in these behaviors. These studies typically look at the entire genome (all of the DNA) in a group of people with substance addiction and compare their genome to a group of people who do not have substance addiction. Gene sequencing machines can "read" the entire nucleotide sequence for each person. Polymorphisms (VTTRs, STRs, and SNPs) in genes that are found to be more common in the addicted compared with the non-addicted group are further investigated as genes that are associated with addiction. These identified polymorphisms require further investigation since genes are often inherited in linkage groups. Therefore, a polymorphism that is shown to be commonly found in addicted individuals might just be "tagging along" with another gene or group of genes that is actually affecting drug or alcohol sensitivity. Results from GWAS have found various genetic markers that are associated with substance use and abuse.

From Mice to Men: Animal Studies

Once a gene is identified as playing a role in the vulnerability to substance-abuse disorders, animal models are widely employed to test the function of the gene at a level of analysis that isn't possible in humans. Specifically, the mouse and rat are particularly useful in showing the role of genes in addiction since humans and rodents share many of the same genes and their reward pathways function similarly.

Researchers commonly use knockout (KO) mice to model the genes involved in substance abuse. **Knockout mice** are laboratory mice in which an existing gene is inactivated and replaced with an artificial piece of DNA. By doing this, the gene will no longer express certain proteins. To construct knockout mice, embryonic stem cells are first collected from mouse embryos four days after fertilization. Embryonic stem cells are used because they have the ability to differentiate into almost any type of adult cell. Thus, the effects of inactivating a gene in an embryonic stem cell can be detected in any tissue of an adult mouse. Next, researchers insert artificial DNA into the chromosomes within the nuclei of embryonic stem cells by utilizing either gene targeting or gene trapping.

Gene targeting, also known as homologous recombination, involves manipulating a gene contained in an embryonic stem cell's nucleus. An artificial piece of DNA that shares a homologous (identical) sequence of the genes is added. The homologous sequence borders the existing DNA sequences for a particular gene both upstream and downstream of the gene's location on the chromosome. The identical patterns of DNA sequence are readily recognized by the cell's specific mechanisms; subsequently, the existing gene is exchanged with the artificial piece of DNA, which eliminates the function of the existing gene since the artificial DNA piece is inactive. This artificial piece of DNA contains a reporter gene which serves as a genetic tag used for tracking.

Gene trapping is similar to gene targeting in the sense that researchers once again manipulate a gene in an embryonic cell. Rather than direct targeting of a particular gene, however, a random process is utilized instead in which an artificial DNA piece with a reporter gene is organized to attach itself randomly into any gene. With this method, the cell's RNA splicing mechanisms are inhibited from functioning properly. As a result, the existing gene's function is inactivated and the existing gene is precluded from producing its specific protein.

Employing these methods to produce knockout mice can help researchers determine the function of genes within the context of drug addiction. Particularly, researchers may inactivate a gene that codes for a specific receptor protein and then test the animal's physiological and behavioral responses to a particular drug of abuse. For example, the conditioned place preference test (CPP) may be used to measure how rewarding or aversive the drug is to the animal. This test uses an apparatus containing three chambers to test an animal's preference for a drug-conditioned chamber versus a vehicle-conditioned chamber. On alternating days, the animals receive injections of a drug in one chamber, or injections of a vehicle solution in the other chamber. These chambers are designed to have distinct visual, olfactory, and/or tactile sensations. On testing day, the animal is placed in the neutral center camber which contains gates that are opened to access each chamber. If the animal spends significantly more time in the drug-paired chamber versus the vehicle-paired chamber, a conditioned place preference is found, suggesting the drug is rewarding to the animal. On the other hand, significantly more time spent in the vehicle-paired chamber versus the drug-paired chamber suggests a conditioned place aversion. Using this test, a gene targeting study found that KO mice lacking the mu-opioid receptor gene (MOR) (which codes for the mu-opioid receptor) no longer demonstrated a conditioned place preference after being injected with morphine. This implicated the mu-opioid receptor as playing a role in the rewarding properties of morphine (Matthes et al., 1996).

Other behavioral models such as *self-administration* were designed to answer different questions about the rewarding properties of a drug by considering an animal's voluntary choice to take the drug. In a classical version of this model, an animal is implanted with a jugular catheter, which exits through a subcutaneous excision on the back and connects to a tether within an operant chamber. The rat is presented with two levers throughout a two-hour session. Pressing the "active" lever results in an infusion of the drug through the jugular vein paired with light and tone cues, while pressing the other "inactive" lever provides no programmed consequences. With drugs that are rewarding to the animal, the animal will choose to continuously press the active lever over the inactive lever. This paradigm combined with targeting a particular gene has elucidated the role of some key receptors that may underlie the behavioral responses of voluntary drug taking and persistent drug seeking. As mentioned in the previous chapter, releases of dopamine following administration of drugs of abuse subserve some of the rewarding effects of the drug. So too have increases in the neurotransmitter glutamate been noted within areas implicated in reward following administration of psychostimulants such as cocaine. One particular receptor that modulates glutamate release, the metabotropic glutamate receptor 5 (mGlu5), is highly expressed within the nucleus accumbens (the region implicated in reward) (Tallaksen-Greene, Kaatz, Romano & Albin, 1998), and repeated cocaine administration has been shown to result in increases in mGlu5 mRNA within this region (Ghasemzadeh, Nelson, Lu, & Kalivas, 1999). How this related to the behavioral aspects of cocaine addiction were unknown. Using KO mice lacking the GRM5 gene that codes for mGlu5, the functional role of this receptor was able to be investigated within the context of cocaine addiction. It was found that mGlu5 KO mutant mice, when compared with the wild-type (WT, typical form) mice, do not self-administer cocaine, despite both the mutant and WT mice showing similar cocaine-induced increases in dopamine (Chiamulera et al., 2001). This shifted research to investigate a more complex neurocircuitry of addiction implicating alterations in dopaminergic and glutamatergic transmission within the mesocorticolimbic pathway. Understanding how these genes function and how their respective receptor proteins are expressed within specific brain regions of non-human animals, modeled throughout the addiction cycle (repeated voluntary use, withdrawal, and relapse), pharmacotherapies to target those same receptors in humans can be utilized to help treat addiction.

Genes and the Environment

While GWAS and animal models offer objective evidence for the heritability of addiction, it is also commonly accepted that addiction sensitivity "runs in families." However, the extent to which these traits are expressed also depends largely on the environment. It is very difficult to untangle the distinct contribution of genes from the distinct contribution of the environment to behavior— especially given that most families share a similar environment. Researchers have tried to better pinpoint the genetic contribution to behavior through adoption studies in order to compare "genetic" siblings with "environmental" siblings. In addition, twin studies are used to quantify behavior in twins (identical and fraternal) who are reared apart vs reared together. Findings from these methods provide heritability factors for many behaviors and these numbers are often reported (and accepted) as percentages (e.g., the heritability of religiosity is ~27%; Button, Stallings, Rhee, Corley, & Hewitt, 2011). However, an important factor to consider here is that within each study, there is not a large amount of environmental variation in the test subjects; people who adopt children tend to be a pretty homogenous group. This underscores an important point in heritability factors in general, and one that is particularly critical for addiction therapy: **Greater environmental differences lead to less genetic contributions to behavior, and, conversely, greater environmental similarities lead to greater genetic contributions to behavior.** We can use a thought experiment to solidify this idea. Imagine that there were 100 genetic clones of Einstein. Now imagine 50 of the cloned baby Einsteins were raised in families in extreme poverty with limited access to educational, social, and nutritional resources (the "impoverished" group), and 50 baby Einsteins were raised in affluent families with easy access to many intellectual, social, and nutritional resources (the "enriched" group). Even though our Einsteins are all genetic clones, there is little doubt that when these Einsteins are grown, we will see *marked* differences in intelligence between the impoverished and enriched group but only *marginal* differences in intelligence when we compare the Einsteins within the groups. In other words, the genetic contribution to intelligence would be overwhelmed by the vast environmental differences between the enriched and impoverished group, while the slight differences in environment within each group barely impacts intelligence when comparing members of each group with each other.

With addiction counseling and research these ideas are pronounced because the genetic contribution to addiction is quite high compared with other factors: 40–50% of a person's susceptibility to drug addiction can be linked to genetic factors (Uhl, 2004). The effect of home environment on addictive behaviors shows that parents have much *less* of an influence on substance use and abuse than do peers and same-sex siblings (Grant et al., 2007). During adolescence the heritability of substance abuse is thought to be 40%; however, this likelihood of addiction increases when there is an association with delinquent peers or same-sex siblings who use addictive substances (Button, Stallings, Rhee, Corley, Boardman, & Hewitt, 2009). Thus, someone whose genes may predispose a predilection for substance abuse may not become addicted if they are around people who do not use (or only use occasionally), while another person whose genes do *not* predispose a predilection for substance abuse may become addicted if they spend a lot of time with their friends who are using.

However, as with all behaviors, genes and environment combine to influence substance use and the likelihood of addiction. In particular, several environmental factors have been identified which appear to decrease heritability estimates of substance use and addiction. These include factors that indicate a less "permissive" environment such as: late-age of first substance use (Agrawal et al., 2009), being married (Heath, Jardine, & Martin, 1989), being raised in a religious household (Koopmans et al., 1999), being raised in a family that is strict or cohesive (Miles, Silberg, Pickens, & Eaves, 2005), and having non-deviant peer-groups (Kendler, Gardner, & Dick, 2011). Combined, these findings underscore the idea that the heritability of substance use and abuse is not static, but, rather, is moved by the environment. An individual with the strongest genetic risk imaginable for alcohol addiction will not become an addict if they never drink. In this extreme case the environmental contribution to alcoholism has become 100%! That same individual, though, who is raised in an environment that is very permissive with alcoholic family members and peers, will be at extreme risk for alcoholism.

What we are talking about here is the move away from the nature-or-nurture debate. We have reviewed how the GxE model can show gene–environment probabilities; however, perhaps this is not the most productive way of viewing this problem. Perhaps, instead, we can explore it as nature-via-nurture. We have already made note of the fact that life events and environmental factors work in concert with genetic predispositions to shape the likelihood of substance abuse and addiction. However, not all environmental effects have the same impact on addiction. One way to overcome this is to calculate how environmental "weights" combine with genetic predisposition to explain the percentage of the variance each factor holds and the overall likelihood of addiction in any one individual. This idea—that gene polymorphisms and environmental factors each have small individual effects, but can combine to have profound effects on the likelihood of addiction, is the next stage of addiction research. One way that researchers are beginning to look at this is through **Genetic Risk Scores (GRS)**. Unlike GWAS, where you look gene by gene for polymorphic effects, with GRS you can compare one total score against a factor of interest (genetic or biological). Strategies for mathematically incorporating environmental or biological factors into genetic polymorphism studies provide a valuable tool for therapists. For example, these findings can shed light on when therapists should focus on stress reduction intervention vs impulse control training. Before genetically-tailored addiction counseling can be fully realized, however, several hurdles in testing efficiency, understanding, and interpretation need to be overcome. The mutagenic nature of addiction (involving the expression of several hundred genes) will also require more basic research in order to develop a genetic profile for patients in therapy.

Epigenetics: How the Environment Changes the Genome

There are some heritable genetic factors that are strongly influenced by the environment, but do not cause modification to the DNA sequence. These changes, and the study of them, are known as **epigenetics**. Unlike polymorphisms in the nucleotide sequence, these changes involve DNA methylation and the modification of histones; changing either of these will alter how genes are expressed. Heritable epigenetic changes are probably more related to methylation, since histone modification is not thought to be heritable. DNA methylation is a tool that cells use to prevent genes from being expressed; it essentially locks genes in the "off" position. Unlike methylation changes, histone modification doesn't directly "turn off" genes. Since the DNA is wrapped around histone cores, their modification can indirectly influence which genes are expressed. In general, epigenetic changes or the "epigenetic landscape" explains the effect of the environment on gene expression—it explains how identical genotypes (i.e., identical twins) can show variation based on individual environmental experiences. Perhaps unsurprisingly, epigenetic modifications have been shown to play a crucial role in substance abuse and addiction behaviors. Since epigenetic changes can affect long-term and heritable changes in gene expression, it serves as an attractive mechanism for the heritable and persistent factors that characterize drug addiction. Research into the epigenetics of addiction shows that stress during childhood and adolescence increases the risk of addiction, independent of one's genotype (Zhang et al., 2013). These changes in drug sensitivity and addiction probability are now thought to come about through epigenetic changes in gene transcription that can make the brain more sensitive or vulnerable to addictive substances (Robison & Nestler, 2011). In addition, the behavioral changes seen with substance abuse are also thought to be a product of epigenetic changes. For example, the "hyperactivity" changes that are commonly seen with cocaine use are associated with histone modification in the NAc (Kennedy et al., 2013).

In addition to the canonical epigenetic pathways of methylation and histone modification, **MicroRNAs (miRNAs)** are also shown to play an important role in addiction susceptibility. These miRNAs are small RNA molecules (~22 nucleotides long) that are non-protein coding RNAs whose main function is to downregulate or "turn-off" gene expression. There is an emerging role for the miRNAs in addiction. In particular, there is strong evidence to support a critical role of miRNAs in alcohol (Pietrzykowski, 2010), cocaine (Eipper-Mains, Kiraly, Palakodeti, Mains, Eipper, & Graveley, 2011), and nicotine (Lippi et al., 2011) addiction. In general, miRNAs are emerging as crucial regulators in addiction behavior, and, as such, hold the promise of serving as potential targets for adjuvant medical treatment during addiction therapy (Dreyer, 2010; Jonkman & Kenny, 2013).

"Risky" Genes

In this section we review some of the prominent polymorphisms that have been linked to drug addiction; this list is not meant to be exhaustive, but rather, to provide a general idea of how genetic differences can increase addiction susceptibility. Most of the polymorphisms are not drug-specific—meaning that they are associated with addiction to more than one substance. For that reason, we will talk about the genes themselves and how addiction works through different pathways to influence drug sensitivity. As shown in Figure 3.2, we will see that one common final pathway in addiction appears to be a left-shift in the dose-effect curve.

Polymorphisms in the Alcohol Metabolic Pathway

The heritability for alcoholism is shown to be strongly associated with genes that affect the enzyme family of **alcohol dehydrogenases (ADHs)**. ADHs are enzymes that convert ethanol to acetate and the genes that produce these enzymes are clustered together on the short arm of chromosome 4 (Foroud et al., 2000). In particular, ADH converts alcohol to acetaldehyde, which is then converted to acetate by aldehyde dehydrogenase. A genetic change that slows the rate at which acetaldehyde is converted to acetate causes unpleasant effects of alcohol such as facial and neck flushing, increased heart rate, headache, and nausea. Perhaps unsurprisingly, individuals who experience these effects with alcohol tend not to

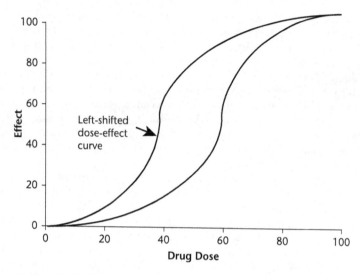

Figure 3.2 The left shift in drug effects means that for those individuals who have a genetic predisposition for drug abuse, feelings of reward from a drug occur at lower doses. For substitution therapy (e.g., methadone) this also implies that the dose should match those that are most sensitive in the primary substance of abuse (see Li et al., 2008)

consume alcohol often. The genetic basis for this change in alcohol metabolism has been found in the ADH gene. This gene is located in a cluster in a **linkage region,** meaning that these genes are inherited together. Polymorphisms in the ADH gene and the aldehyde dehydrogenase (ALDH2) gene are associated with alcohol abuse. In particular, a SNP in the ALDH2 allele renders one copy of the ALDH2 gene useless (thus leaving only one functional copy). This SNP is referred to as rs671 and ALDH*2. This results in a smaller production of a key enzyme needed for alcohol metabolism. Individuals with this polymorphism are much more sensitive to the above-mentioned unpleasant effects of alcohol, and, as a consequence, have extremely low risk for alcohol abuse (Higuchi et al., 2004). Approximately 18% of individuals are heterozygous for this SNP and approximately another 2% are homozygotes (HapMap data release #28). These are the biological principles on which the drug disulfiram (Antabuse) are based to assist with alcohol therapy.

Polymorphisms in the Opioid Pathway

The endogenous opioids are important for reward perceptions and pain reduction (Vaccarino & Kastin, 2000). **Endogenous chemicals** are those that are naturally produced by the body. The endogenous opioids such as endorphin, enkephalin, and dynorphin are produced and released to aid in decreased pain and/or increased pleasure. A polymorphism in one of the receptors for the opioid system, the μ-opioid receptor (MOPR), is associated with increased addiction susceptibility.

This polymorphism is a SNP where one nucleotide change causes the amino acid adenine to be substituted for guanine (the SNP is referred to as rs1799971 or A118G). When the endogenous opioid, β-endorphin, or an exogenous drug (e.g., morphine) binds to the MOPR on interneurons in the mesocorticolimbic dopaminergic pathway, there will be an increase in dopamine in the nucleus accumbens (NAc). The MOPR adenine to guanine (A118G) SNP results in an increase in MOPR binding and activity which is thought to make individuals have stronger cravings for alcohol and become more physically dependent on the exogenous drugs (Bond et al., 1998).

Exogenous chemicals are those that are produced outside of the body, but have physiological effects on the system. As reviewed in the last chapter, drugs of addiction trigger an increase in dopamine activity in the mesocorticolimbic dopaminergic pathway. Activation of this pathway appears to be the mechanism through which stimulants and other psychoactive drugs result in addiction. Increased risk for addiction (especially alcohol addiction) occurs if an individual carries at least one copy of the MOPR A118G SNP (van den Wildenburg et al., 2007). Approximately 25% of individuals are heterozygous for this SNP and approximately another 5% are homozygous (HapMap data release #28).

Polymorphisms in the Dopamine System

Whereas a SNP polymorphism in the MOPR indirectly affects dopamine activity, another polymorphism in a dopamine receptor is also associated with increased risk for addiction. Specifically, one allele type (the TaqI A minor, A1 allele, rs2283265) of the dopamine 2 receptor gene (DRD2) is associated with alcoholism and addiction to cocaine, opioids, and nicotine (Le Foll et al., 2009). There is also a smaller, but still significant, role for this polymorphism in alcoholism risk (Munafò, Matheson, and Flint, 2007). The dopamine receptor D2 (DRD2) TaqI A polymorphism is associated with a decreased amount of available receptors, which decreases the receptor density in the synapse (Noble et al., 1991). In the NAc, the DRD2 A1 polymorphism can lead to 40% fewer dopamine receptors (Ritchie & Noble, 2003). Approximately 40% of individuals are heterozygous for this SNP and another 10% are homozygous (HapMap data release #27). Functionally, this change is thought to lead to a "reward deficiency syndrome," which is thought to increase thrill-seeking behavior and drug use in order to increase feelings of pleasure (Blum et al., 2010).

Racial Frequencies in Addiction Sensitivity

There are well-documented genetic differences in race for substance abuse risk. Overall, people of European descent (i.e., "Whites") have higher rates of substance use and abuse compared with other racial groups (McCabe et al., 2007). In young adults, 38.2% of illicit substance users self-report as White, with self-reported Blacks and Hispanics following, at 30.6% and 27.5%, respectively (Substance Abuse and Mental Health Services Administration, 2005). Differences in racial frequencies, beyond cultural mores, are likely related to the racial frequency differences found among specific polymorphisms' associations with substance use and addiction. For example, there is a racial difference in the ALDH2 polymorphism frequencies with approximately 50% of Northeast Asians carrying the mutant ALDH2 SNP. In addition, the MOPR A118G SNP is most common in people with European (15–30%) or Asian (40–50%) ancestry and less common in people of African American and Hispanic ancestry (1–3%) (Tan, Tan, Karupathivan & Yap, 2003). The Dopamine D2 A1 allele polymorphism is associated with severe substance dependence in Whites and non-White groups, but the A1 allele polymorphism is far more frequent in Whites (18%) compared with Blacks (7%) (Moyer et al., 2011).

Specific polymorphisms tend to be carried within races only because, historically, people of certain geographic regions in the world would mate with each other and, accordingly, share common polymorphism or mutations. Polymorphism frequency differences among races, however, do not imply a genetic basis for race. In fact at a genetic level race does not exist—it is a sociocultural construct. In human DNA 85% of the genetic variation is due to individual variation, while only 15% can be identified as racial variation. In other words, the overwhelming majority of genetic variation among humans is individual, not racial, variation. Underscoring this point is the finding that Europeans and sub-Saharan Africans are more genetically similar than sub-Saharan Africans are to Melanesians (Pacific Islanders). This is in spite of the fact that both sub-Saharan Africans and Melanesians share "African" features such as dark skin, curly hair texture, and similar cranial-facial features. Racial traits that are readily observable and easily classify people into groups only account for the minority of genetic variation (Templeton, 1998). Accordingly, racial frequency differences in addiction biology exist primarily due to "in-group" mating. These differences can be useful in understanding and treating addicted populations. For example, the strong genetic link to problems with alcohol metabolism can explain why this group is much less likely to show alcoholism even in risky environmental circumstances.

Case Application

In Mark's case it can assist the family therapist to be familiar with the idea that genetic differences between individuals can contribute to the way someone responds to drugs and how easily that person can become addicted to drugs. Genetic differences between people can also change how easily treatment might be for that person. In Mark's case, his environment contributed to his alcohol use and we can surmise that there was a likely gene-by-environment interaction in his pathway to addiction—nature-via-nurture.

Earlier in this chapter we introduced the concept that it might become practical to genotype addicted populations in order to develop customized therapy and treatment strategies. While the genetic contribution to his addiction can't be known through interviewing Mark and his family, there has been a recent surge in personalized treatment options in order to apply genetic information to better treat patients. While it is helpful for the family therapist to be aware of potential genetic contributions to addiction, it is not expected that the therapist will offer genetic counseling or carry out complex genotyping of patients. This type of personalized treatment might occur within a treatment center or hospital. For example, if Mark entered a treatment center, it might be discovered that, based on his genotype, naltrexone hydrochloride will not be very effective for him. In this case, extra emphasis on behavioral strategies might be critical to his recovery.

As the field of behavioral genetics grows, continued gene mapping of "risky genes" can also shed light on gene polymorphisms that are associated with co-morbid disorders such as depression and addiction. These findings can help the family therapist consider possible co-occurring disorders or risks that the client might be experiencing.

Finally, a critical consideration for the family therapist is to consider the likeli-hood for addiction risk in other family members. Mark's brother Mick struggled with alcoholism and Mark and his father do not have a healthy relationship when alcohol is involved. As we reviewed in this chapter, there is a genetic contribution to addiction risk and first-degree relatives of addicts are at risk for addiction with a seven-fold increase in risk for first-degree relatives of an alcoholic.

Summary

Whether or not a person will become an addict—and how fast and strongly—depends on many things, including his or her surroundings and personal history, what types of drugs are involved, and the way that person's body and brain respond to drugs. Individuals are impacted by their genetic makeup, having predispositions to react to certain chemicals. However, this is not a one-to-one relationship. Rather, there is a connec-tion between genes and environment. People behave and react based on the interplay between predisposition and experience—which can best be viewed through the notion of nature-via-nurture. Thus, whether someone becomes addicted to drugs or alcohol is partially explained by their genetic predisposition and partly by their environmental history.

Key Words

genes
Deoxyribonucleic Acid (DNA)
nucleotides
non-coding DNA
coding DNA
transcription
ribosomes
translation
codon
amino acids
protein

polymorphisms
Variable Number Tandem
    Repeats (VNTRs)
Short Tandem Repeats (STRs)
alleles
genotyping
gene–environment interaction
    model
heritability
Genome-Wide Association
    Studies (GWAS)

(continued)

(continued)

knockout mice
gene targeting
gene trapping
Genetic Risk Scores (GRS)
epigenetics
microRNAs (miRNAs)

Alcohol Dehydrogenases
(ADHs)
linkage region
endogenous chemicals
exogenous chemicals

Discussion Questions

1. Explain why we do not refer to genes controlling behavior.
2. Describe the relationship between polymorphisms and addiction.
3. How is addiction best viewed as susceptibility rather than inevitability?
4. Describe the gene–environment interaction model.
5. Discuss the genetic implications for racial differences in addiction.

FOUR

The Addicted Family

In this chapter we will be talking about families—and more specifically about those that have one or more members addicted to alcohol or drugs. However, there is debate about what constitutes a family. Some people view it as a traditional nuclear family, with a husband and wife and their children. Others view it as either married or non-married partners. Some view it to include three generations; children, parents, and grandparents. Others may hold a wider lens to include the extended family, which will include aunts, uncles, cousins, and great-grandparents. Some may include close friends who are viewed by family members as kin (i.e., a parent's good friend is called "Aunt Debbie" or "Uncle Brian" by the child).

In this book we will be using a wide definition of family, which includes people who are in committed relationships, either by choice or circumstance, who come to function as an organized unit. This may include partners who do not have children, step-families (which also includes the non-residential parent/siblings), same-sex couples, or a variety of other family configurations. While we discussed in Chapter 3 the impact that genetics has on substance abuse, what we will be talking about from this point forward in the book is how the transactional patterns that develop in a family (as well as whatever genetic and biological processes are in play) not only impact one or more member's use of substances, but their psychological and emotional well-being as well.

While all families are idiosyncratic, they also are universal. Universally, they all function based on family rules and roles, with various types of boundaries, which lead them to develop a level of homeostasis—a stable state—at which they function (see Chapter 12 for a more in-depth explanation of these concepts). All families experience this. These components are what make the family a system and allow it to function (however, we would then label that unique way of being as "functional" or "dysfunctional"). What is idiosyncratic is what the level of homeostasis is; the specific family process.

Because people and families operate based on patterned behavior, it is these patterns that lead us to understand how that specific family functions. For instance, we would classify a family as being paternal if we see that the male is the head of the household. This would not come from a one-time observation but from many observations over an extended period. That the family has rules to maintain the male as the head of the household (such as wife deferring to husband and children needing to ask father rather than mother for privileges), and consequences when this does not occur (the children getting in trouble for going to mother after father has said "no" to a request), keeps it functioning as it is. This is what we would call their **homeostasis**—a steady state.

Once established, families then engage in behaviors that maintain the homeostasis. However, these rules and patterns change over time, usually at family life cycle transitions (such as having a baby, a child becoming an adolescent, or when a family is launching a child—see Chapter 7 for a more in-depth description of the family life cycle). When substance abuse is involved in a family, there are usually disruptions to the family's normal routines and rituals. For instance, in families in which the father is abusing alcohol, there are daily disruptions (such as waking, food, and bedtime rituals) but also to annual celebrations and holidays. The father's engagement usually becomes reduced during these events, which forces the family system to change how it might normally function at these times. Extended family members may not invite this nuclear family, or perhaps just not the alcoholic, to family events, or the spouse may have to take over most of the caretaking duties because the other person is incapable (physically or emotionally).

While the physiological impact of using substances is primarily an individual occurrence (besides second-hand smoke of cigarettes or marijuana), the abuse of the substance permeates the individual, family, and social system. As such we can view addiction as a family issue—some would say a family disease. We know that addiction runs in families (see Chapter 3). Each individual in a family is predisposed, to certain levels, to engage in substance use themselves. In families where past generations had issues with substances, the next generation is more likely to use than in those families with no overuse issues. Also, given what we know from systems theory, all components of a whole are interconnected to develop and maintain a symptom. In the case of the families we are talking about in this book, this means that the symptom is addiction. This symptom demonstrates that there is some type of dysfunction within the interactions of the family members. Addiction can also be viewed as a family disease in that the addict's behaviors have deleterious consequences on the other family members. Not only does the partner have to, at times, physically care-take for the addicted individual (i.e., when they are drunk, under the influence, or dealing with the consequences of a recent use), but they have to also keep the family afloat. Grandparents may be needed to lend a hand or children may be recruited to take on more adult roles. These are just a few of the possible ways that family members have to change to accommodate the addiction. We will cover more of these changes throughout the course of this book.

For addicted families, several patterns and processes may be in place (Ruiz, Strain & Langrod, 2007). First, if the adults in the house abuse substances, they may inadvertently model problematic drug use. This is in contrast to socially sanctioned use, especially with moderate levels of alcohol consumption. Given the recent rise in legalized recreational use of marijuana, children and teens are more likely to be exposed to its use. The question comes as to the difference between use and abuse. Second, the family's homeostasis may be maintained and centered on drug use. Third, family members may have adapted to the substance use and inadvertently function in ways that enable the current level of drug use as well as the progression of use and familial dysfunction.

Families in which drug use/addiction plays a key factor tend to have rigid boundaries between the family system and other larger systems (Lawson & Lawson, 1998). Rigid boundaries, as will be talked about further in Chapter 12, do not allow much information to flow from one system or subsystem to another. Thus, people become closed off from letting others know what is happening within the system. These families tend to engage in keeping many secrets. As Lawson and Lawson explained: "The rules in these families are: (1) do not talk about the alcoholism, (2) do not confront the drinking behavior, and (3) protect and shelter the alcoholic so that things don't become worse" (p. 58).

For addicted families, much effort is spent in not allowing the outside world know what is occurring within the family system. The rules to prevent talking about the family's situation can be overt or covert. **Overt rules** are those that are easily known, where there was a direct statement that someone is to do or not to do something. For instance, a family may develop "Mommy's 'Relaxation Time'" where she cannot be disturbed, which allows her to take a bottle of wine into the den and drink without having to engage the other members of the family. **Covert rules** have to be assumed based on people's actions surrounding that issue. We might view covert rules in an addicted family by seeing how children back off from engaging their father when he comes home from the bar in fear of him having a blow-up, which has happened in the past when he has come home drunk. No one in the family has ever said anything about this (such as, "Mom, I am scared when Dad comes home drunk because I don't want him to yell at me"), but they operate in ways to keep this rule maintained.

Addicted families, particularly those operating from rigid boundaries, will usually not let the school, work, or friend systems know that there is discord in the house; discord due to excessive drug use. This is why sometimes it is a shock to those who know the family when the system becomes overwhelmed and the secret can no longer be hidden. This might be when there was an explosion and some type of domestic violence occurred or perhaps the person abusing drugs was fired from his or her job.

Further, the consequences of substance abuse tend to be progressive, where over time the use and the negative consequences from it get worse. McCrady, Ladd, and Hallgren (2012) explained, "Reciprocal interactions between the drinker [substance abuser] and his or her social environment typically tend to worsen drinking and drinking-related consequences over time, and dysfunctional patterns of individual and family interactions become overlearned and 'automatic' through repetition" (p. 235). That is, the family's homeostasis changes over time to where dysfunction and distressing interactions become the family's primary way of engaging one another.

This may make it seem strange that the family can hide the chaos for as long as they do. However, if we look below the surface we can understand better as to why they may be able to keep the addiction—and the consequences of the addiction—a secret. As a whole, the family tends to adopt certain beliefs that help to maintain their problematic interactions. Wegscheider-Cruse (1989) provided several of these alcoholic family rules, which include:

- The alcoholic/drug user's intake of the substance becomes the central focus of the family.
- The family's problems are not because of the alcohol/drug use.
- The addict is not responsible for the family problems.
- Everyone must maintain stability of the family.
- Family members do not talk about the family problems with people outside of the family.
- People are not allowed, even within the family, to talk about their feelings.
- If people stop doing what they are doing to maintain the system, things will get worse.

As family members engage in these rules, they maintain the functioning level of the family. Hoping that they do not rock the boat to make things worse, family members paradoxically allow things to get incrementally worse. Because members are not allowed to talk to each other or the outside world about the problems happening in the family, this becomes the homeostasis, with an incremental deterioration in how people engage one another. It is like the family is a ship that has scraped an iceberg. There has been a breach in the hull that every crewmember is ignoring. However, to keep the ship afloat, each member starts to bail water. But by not acknowledging the breach, more water enters the ship and requires more time to try to deal with. Eventually, everyone drowns.

Characteristics of Addicted Families

While all families are idiosyncratic, there are characteristics that tend to occur in families that are experiencing one or more members dealing with substance abuse. However, I want to be clear that not all families will fit into these; yet, some semblance of them will be pertinent for most families dealing with addictions. How many and to what degree these characteristics fit a particular family is based upon a multitude of factors which include how many members are in the family, the family's culture, how severe the addiction is, the type of substance that is abused, and the amount of time the family has been organized around addiction, as well as many other factors.

Reilly (1985) provided three primary characteristics of addicted families: negativism, parental inconsistency, and parental denial (see Figure 4.1). Addicted families tend to experience **negativism**. While most families have an ideal of harmony and happiness, addicted families are usually not content with love and excitement flowing throughout their days. People tend not to be supportive of one another; usually seeing the negative in themselves and others. In many ways the "life" of the family has been sucked out. To offset this, family members may unconsciously help to promote various types of crises as ways to imbue some type of excitement into the family. This is not done on a conscious level, but has become an expected and habitual way of living. Although this life is painful, it may be viewed as more favorable than the bland and dull life they are otherwise experiencing.

A second major characteristic of substance-abusing families is that of **parental inconsistency** (Reilly, 1985). If there are two parents in the household, they tend

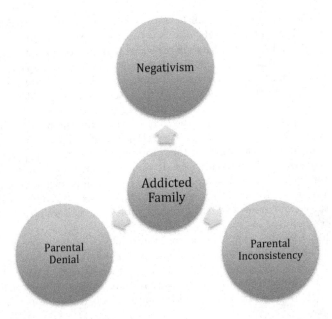

Figure 4.1 Addicted families tend to engage in negativism, parental inconsistency, and parental denial

not to be aligned with one another. Thus, children receive mixed messages which one parent promotes while the other negates. The rules in these families tend to become blurry, where one day they are arbitrarily enforced while on another day they are ignored. Children are unsure of what they are or are not allowed to do in the family. This confusion leads children to try to seek some type of clarity and consistency; even sometimes through acting out as an attempt to get the parents to engage in a more consistent form of parenting. For instance, a child may be allowed freedom by one parent, such as being able to have a friend over, but not by the other parent. This can become extremely confusing to the child when they are following the directives of one parent yet the other parent tells them they cannot—such as mother agreeing to allow a friend come over for a play date and then have the father, who is alcoholic, tell the daughter once the friend comes over that the friend has to leave.

Addicted families also tend to engage in **parental denial** (Reilly, 1985). Usually in these families, one or more children tend to have symptoms—these might be emotional, such as depression or anxiety, or they might be behavioral, such as getting into fights, not listening to directions, or even using substances themselves. As the child's problematic behavior escalates, the parent attempts to deny that there is a problem. Perhaps they try to justify the misbehaviors as "a phase" or "a reaction to a crisis." This denial is family-wide. The parents may use this strategy in regards to their child's substance use or to their partner's. While they look away and fail to recognize the signs of distress in the person and the family system, the problematic behavior and interactions increase.

As we have seen, one person's behavior not only impacts that individual but others within their relational web (and are conversely impacted by others' behaviors). In an alcoholic family, there are problems that impact the individual (i.e., the physical consequence of drug use) but more importantly impact multiple people. These can be seen in the marital, parental, and parent–child subsystems (Lawson, 2011). In the marital subsystem, these relational problems include the partners having conflict, abuse, instability, and separation or divorce. The two partners usually do not have the same view on the use of the substance. For the parental subsystem, relational problems include difficulties parenting, where one or both parents may not fulfill their parental duties, the parents may not agree on what or how to care-take, leading to a potential chaos in terms of the structure of the family. In the parent–child relationship, problems may come in the form of physical or sexual abuse, an influx of secrets, communicational problems, role reversal—including parentification—and issues of trust and conflict in the family.

In addicted families, it may be one or more adults or one or more children—or both an adult and a minor—who is addicted. For substance-abusing families where the adolescent or adult child is addicted, they typically have one parent who becomes overinvolved while the other is more punitive toward the abuser (Stanton, 1985). The one who is more punitive tends to be the parent of the opposite sex.

So far we have been talking about how addicted families tend to organize and some of the rules that develop that maintain the dysfunctional family system. If we look specifically at the use of alcohol, we can see some repetitive ways of being for these families. Middleton-Moz and Dwinell (2010) provided the common characteristics of alcoholic families (p. 3). These include:

- Focus on alcohol by all family members.
- All family members operate based on shame.
- Inconsistency and insecurity: Parental responses, discipline, and rules change depending on the stage of alcohol intoxication and/or the codependent's response.
- Denial of feelings and/or addictions.
- Looped, indirect communication and double messages.
- Repetitive emotional cycles of family members.
- Chaotic interaction or no interaction.
- Hypervigilance and hypersensitivity.
- Unspoken rules.
- Doubting own perceptions.
- Fear of normal conflict.
- Broken promises.
- Family members develop survival roles and coping mechanisms.

Not all families will engage in these characteristics; however, many families will have many of these traits. The more of these characteristics that are present, the more the family will likely spiral out of control and lead to multiple members displaying symptoms.

Alcoholic Family Types

As presented in Chapter 1, there are varying categories of alcoholism (e.g., alpha, beta, gamma, and delta alcoholism). Conversely, there are also varying categories of families in which alcohol plays an organizational function. This is because there is an interaction between family dynamics and the dynamics of alcoholism (Kaufman, 1984, 1985). These categories are played out through the patterns of relating that family members engage in over time.

Edward Kaufman (1984, 1985) is one of the primary theorists of how families develop various constellations around abuse. He illuminated four different types of families that are dealing with addiction (he was specifically talking about alcohol, but these conceptualizations may be appropriate for families where one or more members are having serious issues with other drugs). These are the functional, neurotic enmeshed, disintegrated, and absent family systems.

The functional family system is one in which all of the various family members, for the most part, are able to successfully navigate the challenges of intrafamilial and external relationships. Families will usually be in this stage during the very early part of the addictions process. In these families, one member may drink, but it is usually controlled and in specific contexts (such as just on a "boy's night out" or at dinner). Members tend to be able to get along well with one another and can function at school, work, and other social systems.

Over time, stressors may increase and biological functions may kick in, such as tolerance for the drug, so that the individual who is using develops a psychological and physiological dependence on the substance. As the person's need for the drug changes over time, so do the rules of the family system. When this happens, the functional family system may eventually shift into the neurotic enmeshed family system. This is when the system can be considered an alcoholic family.

In the neurotic enmeshed family system the behavior of the person who is using will interrupt normal family processes. Based on this, conflict tends to arise and family members have to shift previous functional roles to help to maintain homeostasis in the family. For the person dependent on the substance, their physiological, psychological, behavioral, and emotional functioning is usually hampered (for instance, they develop physical illness or sexual dysfunction). Because of this underfunctioning in various areas of personal and family life, other members must take up the cause and overfunction.

The ambiguity and confusion surrounding the loss of stability leads the various members to attempt to gain some type of control. This may come in the non-dependent spouse trying to control the alcoholic's drinking (i.e., "Honey, don't you think you've had enough drinks tonight") or children may attempt to hide the liquor so their parent does not drink. The alcoholic's behavior may start to become disorganized, where they may engage in yelling and screaming or even physical abuse toward their spouse or children. Within the family, shifts start to happen within the subsystems and between individuals. The adults may close off their ranks and become more rigid in how they handle the children. Most likely, the alcoholic is beginning to feel isolated from other members—perhaps experiencing the family members ganging up on them (usually in an attempt to get them to stop drinking, which they take as a personal assault).

Toward the end of this phase of the alcoholic family's development, the system will change into the **disintegrated family system**. At this point, the actions of the addicted individual have gotten so severe and negatively impacted the family to such a degree that the family has separated. Some of the possible problems that might have arisen in the family include physical or sexual abuse, economic loss, or the loss of close connections with larger systems such as religious organizations, work, or extended family members. In the disintegrated family system, the situation has spiraled out of control and led to such chaos that the addicted individual has usually been made to leave the house, but still probably has contact with family members. Perhaps they have supervised visits with children or may be invited for a family event, such as a graduation or Thanksgiving dinner.

The final type of family is the **absent family system**. If the addiction has become so severe and endemic that others have lost hope of change, after time they will give up on the individual. Family members most likely have tried for years to help the addicted individual only to be let down over and over with the person perhaps saying they would get treatment and not following through, hurting members in the family (physically or emotionally), and overall being a major burden on the family. The addiction, whether to alcohol or other substances, may have led to the addicted individual making many poor economic choices (i.e., gambling, poor business decisions, or not using money to pay for needs such as mortgages). Family members have probably given second, third, and fourth chances—more realistically countless chances—and have been continuously let down. They have been told that the person was going to change, and perhaps they did for a very short time, only to quickly enter back into drug use and chaotic behavior. In the absent family system, members have come to disown the addicted individual. Kaufman (1985) states that for many in this type of family stage, even after sobriety is gained, a reconnection to their family of origin is unlikely, and they may need to develop a new nuclear family. Figure 4.2 presents Kaufman's four categories of addicted families.

Kaufman (1984, 1985) provided suggestions for working therapeutically with each family system, as families in each structure are in a different functional state and thus will need different approaches to work with them effectively. When working with the functional family system, which is doing fairly well, they may be able to better utilize family educative approaches. This may cover concepts such as drug interactions and recovery processes, which may help them to be able to make changes. Therapists might also explore family rules and roles in order to determine dysfunctional role behavior and develop new, more effective, rules and roles.

Figure 4.2 Kaufman's four categories of addicted families

For the neurotic enmeshed family system, the psychoeducational techniques will probably be useful but not sufficiently effective. They will most likely need more formal psychotherapy. Therapy for families in this category is difficult as members will likely try to stay in the past rather than focus on and deal with the present (Kaufman, 1984). Since these families usually have significant levels of enmeshment, therapists might focus on engaging in boundary-making to help people and subsystems to define their roles. Helping the alcoholic to engage a support group is useful as well as helping family members to connect with their own support groups, such as Al-Anon or Alateen.

In the disintegrated family system, trying to engage in family therapy from the get-go may be difficult as members are very hesitant to engage the alcoholic. Thus, Kaufman suggests that in these cases, individual work with the alcoholic to help them to stabilize and become sober will most likely need to happen before a reconnection to the larger family system occurs. However, therapists may explore what role family members might play in treatment for the possibility that a new foundation for familial relationships can take shape. Kaufman (1984) suggests that after prolonged abstinence of several months, if family members are willing to support themselves and the alcoholic, family definitional sessions might be used to help people develop new roles and identities in relation to one another.

Therapy with the absent family system tends to be quite different than with the other three types of family systems. With each of the previous three family systems, the goal is a reconstitution of the family system. With the absent family member those connections have been severed. What is most likely required here in therapy is a focus on developing a new nuclear family.

Phases of the Alcoholic Family

As we have seen in the previous section, we can classify addicted families based on the severity of the substance abuse and the impact it has had on the family. The movement from one type of family to another is a gradual rather than instantaneous process. As such, we can look at how the addicted family changes through a sequence of stages. The developmental phase of alcoholism is based upon the user's mode, which is either wet (in active use) or dry (in abstinence). This is connected to the status of the phase, which can be stable or unstable. Steinglass (1985) and Steinglass, Bennett, Wolin, and Reiss (1987) delineated three phases in the development of the alcoholic family; the early phase, the middle phase, and the late phase (see Figure 4.3).

In the **early phase of alcoholism** the family begins to develop an alcoholic identity. What this means is that when alcohol is introduced into the family it becomes a major organizing principle, overriding the normal family development. The focus in the family shifts from normal family processes such as values, rules, and boundaries to a lens of values, rules, and boundaries (internal and external of the family system) around alcohol.

One of the determining factors in how the family addresses the introduction of alcohol as a major factor in the system is each of the adults' families-of-origin. For those that came from an alcoholic family, they might fall into the patterns that they know so well. Part of what happens at this stage is the negotiation,

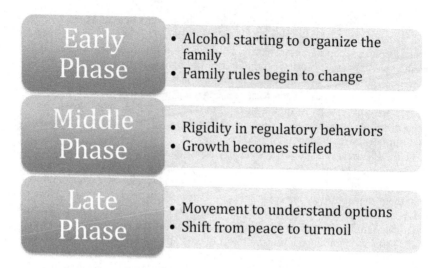

Figure 4.3 Three phases of development for the alcoholic family

usually unconsciously between partners, of whose family of origin will be used as the guide for the current nuclear family.

The early phase of the alcoholic family might not have anyone using alcohol to the degree that might be considered addicted or dependent. However, it is at this point that the rules of the system are laid down as a foundation for how people are going to be in various areas of their lives; one of these areas being the use of alcohol. For those who came from alcoholic families, an acceptance of alcohol with family rules about not talking about use or abuse could become the groundwork for later alcoholism.

The **middle-phase alcoholic family** occurs when the regulatory behaviors of the family enable whatever use of alcohol is occurring (whether it be daily, weekly, or monthly abuses). Family members alter their behavior to try to maintain a calm in the family. However, there is usually some type of developmental hindrance as family members tend to become more rigid in their regulatory behaviors. For instance, having more expectations of members not to talk about the abuser's behaviors; especially to anyone outside of the family system.

In this phase the focus of growth becomes stifled as members work toward just trying to maintain the status quo. It is at this point that both individual and family development does not move as it should. Instead of having a solid foundation for people to grow in healthy ways, people are restricted in how they can act and how they view themselves.

During the middle phase, family members have come to adopt certain roles that help to maintain the family's homeostasis around substance use (see Chapter 6 for a more in-depth explanation of family roles). The family usually goes through **the sobriety-intoxication cycle** (Steinglass et al., 1987). Here, there are periods of use and non-use; each having constraints and pressures on the family. And during these two ends—sobriety and intoxication—the family will display different patterns of interactional behavior. This can make it difficult for the family therapist to have a wide view of the family as they may only be seeing a very limited behavioral repertoire of the family—depending on which cycle the family is currently exhibiting.

When the family is in the intoxicated interactional state, they may be able to engage in strategies of short-term problem-solving that they weren't able to in the sobriety state. The family adopts a perception that they can perform some behaviors during use and others during non-use. In each part of the cycle, there are interactional sequences that are predictable. And although alcohol is seen as the primary problem of the family, there are certain constructive—at least in the immediate context—aspects of being in the intoxicated state. This may be that the family more readily cooperates with one another during this period rather than being more autonomous when in the sobriety state.

The middle phase of the alcoholic family is characterized by stability and regularity. This is not the case in the early or late phases, which find the family engaging in significant systemic reorganization. In many ways, these two phases are mirror images of one another, in which the family experiences shifts in their functioning. Issues to be addressed include delineating family boundaries, determining who is inside and outside the family system, identifying life themes, and protecting the family from implosion, and these tend to dominate the family's life.

In **the late phase of development of the alcoholic family**, the family tries to defend the family themes that have been developed, primarily in the productive moments of the middle phase. While, for the most part, the alcoholic family had difficulty in finding a purpose and identity, there is now a movement toward understanding the options available to them. However, this can be felt by the family as a shift from a more peaceful position to that of turmoil. This is because in the late phase there is a shifting of the family rules—which is usually experienced as anxiety-provoking since most families attempt to maintain stability (homeostasis).

In the early phase of the alcoholic family there was an attempt by the adult partners to separate from their families-of-origin. The middle phase found the family focusing within, figuring out how to stay together. Now, during the late phase, the children in the family will begin to launch and potentially develop families of their own. Thus, the family begins to develop a future orientation to explore issues of family values and family heritage.

To summarize the exploration of phases of the alcoholic family, we can look at the developmental tasks of the family at each phase of the family's development. While these tasks play a role during each phase, they become more prominent at specific phases in the family's life. In the early phase, perhaps the key task is to determine family member configurations. This is figuring out who is in and who is out of the family. To complete this task, the family will develop boundaries to demarcate itself from larger systems, such as extended family. At times, the early phase alcoholic family will procure rigid boundaries to ensure that what happens in their family stays there and other people do not get involved. During the middle phase, the family's developmental task is to focus on major life themes. Here, the family is determining where to place their focus and construct a way of organizing itself—usually around alcohol. In the late phase, the family shifts to an exploration of family values and heritage.

Family Typology of Addiction

In this chapter we have looked at some of the general characteristics of addicted families, alcoholic family types, as well as the developmental phases an alcoholic family may go through. Now, we switch our focus to exploring addicted families based on the use of a family typology.

Haugland (2005) delineated a four-tier family typology based on paternal drinking: protective families, emotional disruptive families, exposing families, and chaotic families. **Protective families** are perhaps the most functional. These families have the lowest level of drinking by the adults, with fewer comorbid symptoms (such as depression or anxiety). The protective aspect of the families is that the parents are able to shield the children from the alcohol use and whatever consequences are present. This happens by the drinking partner being able to still engage in being a parent. As such, these families have only minor disruptions in their rituals and routines; perhaps only happening during the drinking phase. We might look at the substance abuser as a functional user, where they can maintain control of their actions. The use of the substance is not widely known and people outside of the family—and perhaps even the children—would be very surprised to learn the extent of the use.

In the **emotional disruptive family**, the non-drinking partner actively maintains the rituals and routines of the family when the other spouse is involved in a drinking phase. When the substance-abusing spouse does drink, the family rituals and routines are fraught with conflict and negative emotions. This plays out in the abusing spouse having less of a parenting role and the non-abusing spouse having a more difficult time taking on the brunt of the parenting responsibilities. Whereas in the protective family the children were shielded by any conflict between the parents and the consequences of the drinking, this is no longer the case. They may witness the alcoholic when drunk, experiencing hangovers, and when the parents are arguing with one another. Members of the family may experience other difficulties such as anxiety, depression, or other types of disruptive behaviors.

The third typology of family is the **exposing family**, which finds itself having more severe disruptions in its normal rituals and routines. When the person is drinking the family atmosphere changes substantially, usually with a heightened tension and increased conflict. The children tend to be exposed to a lot of the drinking behavior and consequences, viewing their parent underfunction and decompensate. Arguments, heated exchanges, and perhaps even violence occur between the adult partners. This leads to the children interfering in the conflict between the parents or trying to get the alcoholic to stop their drinking. At this point in the family's life, most likely every member will be displaying some type of emotional or psychological problem.

The last type of family is the **chaotic family**, which displays the most severe type of dysfunction in family process. The normal family routines and rituals have been severely disrupted. The alcoholic parent has most likely given up parental responsibility and the non-abusing spouse is not able to compensate for this abdication. There is a high level of stress and conflict between the adults, leading to perhaps emotional and physical abuse. In these families, there is a high likelihood that one child will become parentified; which has negative

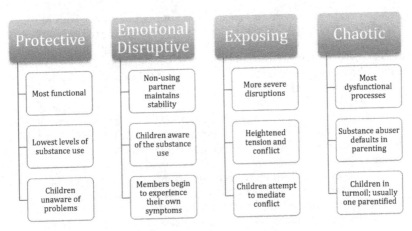

Figure 4.4 Haugland's (2005) four-tier family typology based upon paternal drinking

consequences on all members. The drinking of the alcoholic is at its height and members' emotional and psychological functioning is quite negatively impacted.

Case Application

The Rothers family is finding itself in a difficult place where alcohol is becoming more of an organizing principle in family life. While Mark is the identified patient, the ripples of discord are emanating to all reaches of the family. They have become an addicted family. Rigid boundaries have become the primary demarcation between subsystems. Rigid boundaries usually lead to disengagement. This can be seen in the cutoff between Mark and his brother Mick as well as between Mark and his ex-wife Angelina and daughter Nina. The rules in the Rothers family have allowed drinking to organize family life, where Mark is allowed to keep his "stash" in the refrigerator in the garage. Overt rules were developed between Mark and Hannah where Mark is allowed two beers before dinner and one after. This is why Hannah is quite upset as Mark goes over the allotted amount of beers just about every day. Other overt rules of the family include everyone having dinner together without being on any electronic device. Covert rules include the children going to Hannah for all of their emotional and psychological needs as Mark is usually in a bad mood if he is disturbed when in his man cave, which is where he does most of his drinking.

While there has been conflict and discord within the family, the Rothers have not fully articulated their concerns to one another. Mark and Steve have had several verbal altercations where they have cursed at each other, especially surrounding Mark trying to discipline Steve when the school lets them know of Steve's misbehaviors. Mark and Hannah rationalized that Steve was just a teenager and was in a phase. This demonstrates one aspect of them being an addicted family; that they are engaged in parental denial. They have not asked Steve yet whether he has tried alcohol or marijuana, but both Mark and Hannah are concerned that this is a possibility, especially given Mark's family history of substance use and abuse. The Rothers also engage in parental inconsistency, where rules are transitory, usually depending on Mark's mood. He tends to be in a better mood early on the weekends but can be quite angry later in the afternoon, after who knows how many beers and if his favorite sports teams have lost. There is also rampant negativism in the family, with members not fully trusting other members. Mark, Hannah, and Steve are currently displaying the most overt negativism, mainly toward each other, but Steve is also negatively viewing his sister (as a goody-two-shoes) and his brother (as a momma's boy).

The Rothers family has most likely moved into the category of the neurotic enmeshed family system. Mark's need for alcohol has increased over the last several months and the rules of the family have shifted to allow this continued use. Mark is beginning to underfunction, having called in to work several times when he was not feeling well, and Hannah has had to do even more around the house and with the children, although she was already the primary care taker for the children. The animosity between husband and wife has increased and is beginning to shroud many of the interactions occurring in the home. At this point, Mark feels an outsider, both within his nuclear family as well as in his family-of-origin. While they are still a ways away from moving into the disintegrated family system, the seeds have been sown. We can look at Mark's first marriage and family as having moved into that category, where there was physical, emotional, and psychological separation. While that family never became an absent family system, there is a lack of trust and respect between Mark and Angelina and Nina, who are very close. For the therapist working with the current iteration of the Rothers family, it will be important to talk about the intra-familial patterns where Mark is feeling ever-increasingly the outsider. Ways to incorporate him back into the family may help to increase his sense of desire for change. The therapist will likely suggest a self-help group, such as Alcoholics Anonymous, for Mark. Groups such as Al-Anon and Alateen might be useful for Hannah as well as the children.

The Rothers are also most likely in the middle phase of development for an alcoholic family. Mark has likely fallen into the patterns that he experienced growing up in his own family, where addiction was a common presence, especially with his father Ian as well as his brother Mick and sister Chelsea. It used to be a bit charming when Mark would go into his den and have a drink after work and watch television or play video games. However, the family discovered that these times became more frequent and longer in duration, to the point where they are currently spending very little time with him. No one yet has really confronted him as to his drinking behaviors as well as his disengagement from the family. The Rothers family does not seem to be currently growing. Rather, they are in a survival mode, trying not to let the undercurrents of hostility and resentment seep to the surface. However, this is not always the case as Steve seems to be experiencing his pain in negative ways both at home and at school. The family does engage in the sobriety-intoxication cycle, but the sobriety periods are become more infrequent and of lesser duration. These usually happen when there is a family event that everyone must attend.

The Rothers may be classified as an emotional disruptive family. Hannah is actively engaged in keeping the family on its normal routines, such as eating dinner together every night as well as Sunday Fun Day. Previously, the children just thought their father enjoyed a beer or two while watching sports. However, they pretty much now consistently see him with a beer in his hand. This is when he is watching television, playing video games, and at the dinner table. They have also seen more tension and disagreement between their parents. Family members are finding that they are experiencing their own symptoms, with Mark thinking that life would be better for all if he wasn't on this Earth, Hannah angry and confused, Steve acting out at home and school, and Pete becoming more clinging to Hannah. On the surface it seems as if Kayleigh is doing quite well. However, she is feeling a lot of pain without showing it.

Summary

Families function as a unit, developing patterns of interaction that determine how people are supposed to be with one another. In families dealing with substance abuse, these interactions tend to become restricted as the family organizes around the use of the substance. This usually comes in the form of protecting the family from outside systems—by having rules about not talking to others, or even themselves, about the drug use. Over time, the family adapts and changes by the severity of the drug use and its impact on various family members. As this is happening, the family reconfigures the rules of the system to develop a new homeostasis so that it can function—however well or poorly that might be.

Key Terms

homeostasis
covert rules
overt rules
negativism
parental inconsistency
parental denial
functional family system
neurotic enmeshed family
   system
disintegrated family system

absent family system
early phase of alcoholism
middle phase of alcoholism
the sobriety-intoxication cycle
late phase of alcoholism
protective families
emotional disruptive families
exposing family
chaotic family

Discussion Questions

1. Describe some of the overt and covert rules of addicted families.
2. What are some of the common characteristics of addicted families?

(continued)

(continued)

3. What are the differences between the functional, neurotic-enmeshed, disintegrated, and absent family systems?
4. How does a family move through the early, middle, and late phases of alcoholism?
5. What are the developmental tasks at each phase of the alcoholic family's development?
6. Describe the distinctions between protective, emotional disruptive, exposing, and chaotic families.

FIVE

Family Diversity and Substance Abuse

For the last quarter century, the notion of diversity has been an ever-increasing topic in the field of counseling and therapy. There is not enough space in this book to do a thorough review of the importance of understanding diversity when working with clients. However, this chapter provides an overview of some of the main topics specifically exploring the intersection of ethnicity and substance use.

Diversity is a very wide term referring to difference. People are diverse entities; we are not all the same. However, based on various factors such as age, gender, sexual orientation, race, and culture we learn how to be who we are (how to think, feel, and behave). These classifications of people can in some ways be arbitrary, but they help inform the therapist about possible factors impacting the client. Yet even within a cultural group there can be significant variations based on age, gender, economics, sexual orientation, etc. As it relates to substance abuse, one's country of origin, culture, and religion play a significant role in the individual's beliefs and values as well as their views on the use of substances.

When exploring diversity and substance abuse, we need to explore what has been the "normal" way of viewing addiction and recovery. This has been from a White European-American culture (Cable, 2000). For instance, the founders of Alcoholics Anonymous (Bill W. and Dr. Bob) were both White heterosexual males, one of which worked on Wall Street while the other was a physician, who developed a view of power in addiction based on a Western view (Krestan, 2000). This view is a "power over" rather than a "power to." Based on this Western view, the first principle of AA was developed—we admitted we were powerless over alcohol—that our lives had become unmanageable. However, people from non-Western societies may not adhere to this basic premise of AA.

This chapter explores the intersection of diversity issues, most notably ethnicity, culture, and addiction. It is important for the therapist to understand the role that substance use and abuse has in various cultural groups and its impact on therapy. This is especially so since the United States is projected to soon become a "minority White" country in that Whites are projected to comprise only 49.9% of the population in 2045, whereas Hispanics are projected to comprise 24.6%, African Americans 13.1%, Asians 7.8%, and multiracial groups 3.8% (Frey, 2018). The K–12 enrollment is also changing where, by 2025, it is predicted that Whites will comprise 46%, Hispanics 29%, Blacks 15%, Asian/Pacific Islanders 6%, American Indian/Alaska Natives 1%, and those of two or more races 4%.

According to the U.S. Census Bureau, the percentage of foreign-born individuals in the U.S. is projected to rise from 13.3% in 2014 to 14.3% in 2020, 15.8% in 2030, 17.1% in 2040, 18.2% in 2050, and 18.8% in 2060.

Culture and Ethnic Diversity

Elements of **culture** primarily involve beliefs and traditions that families teach over generations in explicit and implicit ways. Some traditions, such as the way women should dress and holiday celebrations, are taught directly by family or community members to their children. However, elements of culture are also expressed through family roles, family dynamics, communication patterns, affective behaviors, and levels of support, attachment, and connectedness (Szapocznik et al., 2007). Cultural transmission occurs through **enculturation,** a process of social learning by which there is exposure of new generations to particular and different social contexts depending on their place of origin.

While individual and familial factors are important, many patterns of behavior within a given culture are collective in nature. The group establishes norms of acceptable behavior and most of the individuals tend to follow them; sometimes even without noticing. Cultural patterns work in the same way. While individuals and families live in a specific location, they follow behaviors, thoughts, attitudes, and trends that come from those geographical and cultural locations. In that way, conflicts may emerge when individuals and families from other countries migrate to the U.S. and adapt to new cultural patterns while trying to maintain elements from their original culture.

This is the battle between ethnic identity and acculturation issues. **Ethnic identity** refers to the identification of the individual with his or her ethnic group based on shared social experience or ancestry. It is a sense of collective identity based on the perception that the individual shares a common heritage with his or her ethnic group. This can be observed in the way people dress, eat, and behave according to their culture of origin. **Acculturation** refers to the process of psychological, interpersonal, and behavioral changes that result following interaction between different cultures. Acculturation includes changes in food, clothing, language, and the rules of interaction. However, changes in psychosocial patterns occur as well. For instance, a parent moving from a Caribbean country to the U.S. may change the way she disciplines her children as a natural process in the way to adapt to the new culture.

The ethnic groups presented in this chapter are Hispanic Americans, African Americans, American Indians, Asian Americans, and Caucasians. This is not exhaustive of the variety of ethnic groups that can be explored, but they are the most prominent in the United States. Sexual and gender minority individuals and families will also be presented. This chapter presents generalities and not all families that come from these ethnic groups will be reflected in the explanations. Further, what is presented is about homogamous ethnic families. This does not take into consideration the increase in the United States of interethnic couples and families. According to the Pew Research Center, in 2015, 29% of Asian, 27% of Hispanic, 18% of Black, and 11% of White newlyweds were intermarried. These numbers are higher for U.S.-born individuals (i.e., 46% of

U.S.-born Asians and 39% of U.S.-born Hispanics). This is leading to a change in the demographic of the youth of the United States, where 14% of U.S. infants are multiracial or multiethnic.

We will explore some of the risk and protective factors for each cultural group. These include risk and protective factors in the individual, peer, school, community, and family domains. However, while these are general patterns for people from certain cultural groups, an individual assessment for that person/family is needed to ensure you understand the uniqueness of each client. **Risk** relates to the factors that may lead people to engage in problematic substance use and/or drinking. Regardless of culture, family risk factors for substance use include family conflict, parental attitudes that allow substance use and antisocial behavior, family history of substance abuse, lack of parental supervision, and poor family management and supervision (Montgomery & Springer, 2012). **Protective factors** lead the person or family to either not use or be able to recover from problematic use. In many ways, protective factors are related to the resiliencies that people and families utilize to make it through difficult times. Family protective factors against substance use include close family attachment and family engagement in pro-social activities (Montgomery & Springer, 2012). Each section ends with ideas about treatment for that specific group, since there are treatment implications for each group. As Fisher and Harrison (2018) explained, "Without sensitivity to cultural differences and cultural competency, providers will likely be ineffective from the outset because attempts to assess alcohol and other drug involvement will be met with both cultural and therapeutic resistance" (p. 48).

Treatment considerations when working with clients dealing with substance abuse have traditionally focused on majority populations. However, there have been many recent advances when working with underserved populations in the area of substance abuse therapy (Blume, 2016). Also, therapists should adapt their engagement and strategies for clients depending on the setting, presenting problem, and **intersectionality** of the client. Figure 5.1 presents some of the primary factors that impact intersectionality. Keep in mind that this is quite limited and there are many other factors of intersectionality including weight, ability, intelligence, etc.

Hispanics/Latin American Families

Hispanics and/or Latinos, which include Mexican American, Central and South American, Puerto Rican, Cuban, Dominican, and "other Hispanics," represent the largest and fastest growing minority group in the U.S. Census, comprising just over 18% of the population in the United States (56.7 million people). This accounts for the second largest group behind Whites (non-Hispanic). According to Frey (2018), it is estimated that by 2045 Hispanics will comprise 24.6% of the U.S. population.

According to data from the 2016 U.S. Census, Hispanic families have a household median income on the lower end of the continuum, earning $47,675 in 2016. As a comparison, White non-Hispanics had a median income of $65,041. About 19.4% of Hispanic families lived below the poverty line. Although Hispanics have the highest dropout rate of high schoolers of any race, they have also had

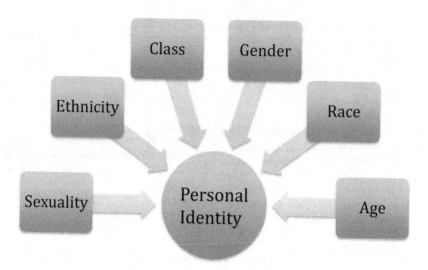

Figure 5.1 Personal identity is based upon an intersectional perspective where people form a sense of self due to the variety of domains of their lives

the highest reduction in dropouts. In 1996, 34% of Hispanic high schoolers dropped out, while, just 20 years later in 2016, 10% did so. Hispanic Americans had the highest percentage increase of any ethnic group of enrollment in K–12 schools and colleges. This was an 80% increase from 9.9 million to 17.9 million. Approximately 47% of Hispanic high school graduates were enrolled in college, which was tied with White Americans, just above Black, and significantly under Asian enrollments. Around 67.8% of Hispanic households contain a married couple while 22.6% are female households with no husband present.

Issues of migration play a significant role for many Hispanic families. Some individuals and families migrate willingly while others do so involuntarily, perhaps to escape serious economic and dangerous unrest in their home country. For those forced to leave their country because of these reasons, they may experience various levels of trauma (Falicov, 2014). Latino immigrants may differ based on the circumstances of immigration, reasons for coming to the U.S., the relationship between the U.S. and their home country when they immigrated, and cultural aspects of where they settled in the U.S. (Marano & Roman, 2017).

Hispanic families tend to operate based on **familismo**, an attitudinal and behavioral set of values and expectations that underpin a strong family network of support, connection between nuclear and extended family, and living in close proximity, where loyalty across the lifespan is valued (Hernandez & Moreno, 2018). Familismo reflects cultural values of collectivism and interdependence (Falicov, 2014). Hispanic families have strong nuclear family units. Children play a central role as they tend to connect husband and wife in marriage (Fisher & Harrison, 2018). Filial love, that is, the love of a parent for a child, tends to be viewed as more important than romantic love. Children, especially females, tend to live at home until they get married.

Hispanic families also tend to engage in patriarchy and marianism (Eshleman & Bulcroft, 2010). **Patriarchy** is when the authority members in the family are men, who tend to have dominance over the women and children. This is seen in many Hispanic families through males operating from a place of **machismo**; where the male tries to be strong, aggressive, and authoritarian. **Marianism** is a focus on the mother as being cherished and the focal point of the family. This leads to an interesting dynamic in Hispanic families where the mother tends to keep everything in order yet the father has ultimate say-so.

Hispanic American Families and Substance Abuse

Hispanics have reported the highest lifetime prevalence rates of alcohol, cigarette, licit, and illicit drug use (except for amphetamines) of any racial group (Delva et al., 2005; Johnston et al., 2018). Hispanics initiate their drug use earlier than other racial groups. The annual prevalence rate of any illicit drug use is 14.6 for African Americans, 14.9 for Caucasian, and 20.9 for Hispanics (Szapocznik et al., 2007). The National Household Surveys on Substance Abuse revealed that Latino drug use has increased progressively since 2002 (SAMHSA, 2009).

Cuban Americans had the highest rates of marijuana, cocaine, and alcohol use compared with Mexican American, Puerto Rican, and other Latin American adolescents living in the U.S. (Delva et al., 2005; Turner et al., 2006). American-born Hispanic adolescents reported higher drug use rates than foreign-born Hispanics (Szapocznik et al., 2007). Among Hispanic groups, Mexican Americans tend to show the highest levels of alcohol abuse (Carvajal & Young, 2009). At the same time, another vulnerability for substance abuse as a risk factor for Hispanics is the higher level of other factors such as low socioeconomic status, lower levels of education, poor access to healthcare, and language barriers (Ramirez & De La Cruz, 2002; Stevenson et al., 2004). Along with African Americans, the Hispanic population, as compared with other cultural groups, experiences more negative consequences, such as homelessness, HIV, partner and family violence, and incarceration (Amaro et al., 2006).

As previously explained, familismo is an important aspect of Hispanic families and plays a role in substance use. Some authors have found that familismo is a protective factor against substance use (Ma et al., 2017), while others found that it actually is a risk factor for addiction (Applewhite et al., 2017; Escobedo, Allem, Baezconde-Garbanati, & Unger, 2018). As a protective factor, familismo may connect the Hispanic youth with family support that provides self-efficacy to be able to avoid negative peer group influence (Ma et al., 2017). As a risk factor, familismo and the push for interdependence may lead Hispanic emerging adults to stay at home, which may lead them to continue to associate with peers who engage in substance misuse (Escobedo et al., 2018).

Hispanic Youth

Hispanic adolescents tend to use drugs at higher rates than White and African American adolescents (Cardoso, Goldback, Cervantes, & Swank, 2016). This is especially so for marijuana use, leading to a rise in Hispanic youths being admitted to substance abuse treatment programs (Marzell, Sahker, Pro, & Arndt, 2017). This increase is likely for those aged 15–17 living in dependent situations and who were most likely referred through the school system. However, Latino youth may be quite vulnerable to moving from general use to abuse or dependence on substances (Hernandez & Moreno, 2018). This is especially important since Latinos tend to underutilize mental health services. One reason for this is a potential language barrier, given the youth's acculturation status and the availability of Spanish-speaking therapists in that locale.

There is a relationship between Hispanic youth's cultural orientation and that of their perceived parents' cultural expectations (Unger et al., 2009). Those who experienced higher levels of parental expectations to adhere to a Hispanic lifestyle had higher risk of cigarette, marijuana, and alcohol use. Youth with higher levels of Hispanicism (i.e., those who held more closely to Hispanic cultural values and beliefs) had lower levels of recent substance use and peer drug use as well as higher levels of family functioning and school bonding (Martinez et al., 2017). However, the protective effects of Hispanicism were reduced as levels of Americanism were increased.

Hispanic youth and emerging adults had increased substance use when experiencing several role transitions (Allem et al., 2016). More specifically, when they entered a new relationship, they had increased use of cigarettes, marijuana, and binge drinking. When they experienced a breakup of a relationship, they had increases in binge drinking, marijuana, and hard drug use. For those starting a new job, they had increases in binge drinking and marijuana use. Thus, Hispanic youth may experience use and/or abuse of a variety of substances depending on their levels of acculturation, family cohesiveness, and specific transition they are experiencing at that point in their lives.

Risk and Protective Factors

For Hispanics, family network is a source of emotional social support and familismo is an integral part of the culture. Familismo has been shown to be a protective factor among Latinos against negative behaviors including drug use and abuse. At the same time, lack of family, family dysfunction, and family disorganization have been shown to be related to more drug and alcohol use (Griffin et al., 2000). This connection to family, in the form of high parental presence and high parent–family connectedness, is also a protective factor against the initiation of the youth engaging in smoking (Mahabee-Gittens et al., 2011). This leads to the consideration of the family as being the ideal realm of intervention for Latinos (Hernandez & Moreno, 2018).

Identification with and pride in the individual's culture is also beneficial and related to lower substance and alcohol use (Vega et al., 2002). Latino self-identification is a protective factor for Latin American substance use (De La Rosa et al., 2005). Adolescents with high levels of acculturation, represented by preference for English language use and endorsement of interests and values of the U.S., show higher rates of substance use (Gil et al., 2000; Turner et al., 2006). Discrepancies in acculturation between adolescents and their parents in the way that adolescents from immigrant families born in the U.S. master English and adopt host country behaviors more than their parents, have been found to be related to drug use in adolescents. This is because differential acculturation creates an additional familial conflict that affects adolescent bonding to the family and parental authority (De la Rosa et al., 2005; Szapocznik et al., 2007).

Substance abuse tends to increase as Hispanics acculturate to the U.S. (Alegría et al., 2006). One of the key cultural Hispanic values is that of respect, which is sometimes referred to as **respeto** or **simpati'a**. Ma et al. (2017) found that higher levels of simpati'a were associated with reduced levels of drug use. They explained, "Simpati'a, a construct that encourages respectful, smooth, and pleasant interpersonal relationships, is inconsistent with deviant behaviors" (p. 329).

Hispanic adolescents who experience family economic stress, acculturative gap stress, community and gang exposure, and family and drug stress were at higher risk of substance use than those without these stressors (Cardoso et al., 2016).

King, Vidourek, Merianos, and Bartsch (2017) found that Hispanic youth at highest risk for alcohol use had authoritarian parents, poor school experiences, legal problems, and perceived alcohol use by peers. Perceived discrimination also plays a role as a risk factor in increased substance use. For instance, Unger, Soto, and Baezconde-Garbanati (2016) found that Hispanics who experienced higher levels of discrimination were at greater risk for cigarette, alcohol, marijuana, and hard drug use. However, respeto is a protective factor against binge drinking, marijuana, and hard drug use (Escobedo et al., 2018). Moreover, being male, unmarried, young, and under/unemployed are risk factors for alcohol and substance abuse for Latin Americans. Concomitantly, being female and employed can be protective factors against drug consumption (Carvajal & Young, 2009).

Treatment Implications

Barriers for Hispanic Americans to receiving mental health care include language issues, lack of insurance, cultural beliefs against psychotherapy, tendencies to keep things within families, and a reluctance to take medications (Falicov, 2014). Sparks, Tisch, and Gardner (2013) held that there are not many treatment programs that gear themselves toward the Hispanic culture. This can be problematic as there are several issues that seem to be unique to this population and adherence to Hispanic culture may be a protective factor to reduce the risk of substance use. For instance, therapists should consider acculturation issues when working with Hispanic clients as there is a relationship between Hispanicism, Americanism, and substance use and abuse (Martinez et al., 2017).

Ma et al. (2017) suggested that substance abuse treatment for Hispanic adolescents include components that strengthen the sense of familismo and simpati'a. Escobedo et al. (2018) concurred, promoting treatment programs that addressed familismo and respeto, which are core Hispanic cultural values. This leads to the recommendation of the inclusion and/or integration of parents, school, and peers in substance abuse treatment for Hispanic adolescents (King et al., 2017). Further, treatment that targets and reduces stress from a variety of contexts (i.e., family, work, and school) is encouraged (Cardoso et al., 2016). For instance, therapists can be aware of the relationship between particular role transitions (such as dating, employment, or moving) and specific substance use (Allem et al., 2016).

Given the relationship between perceived discrimination and increased substance use, therapists might consider helping Hispanic clients to find ways other than substance use to cope with discrimination (Unger et al., 2009; Unger et al., 2016). Not only might Hispanic Americans experience discrimination in their lives outside of therapy, they may experience it within the mental health system as well. Latinos were twice as likely as other groups to experience perceived discrimination in health care/mental health substance abuse treatment (Mays et al., 2017). This leads to a greater likelihood of premature termination of treatment.

Falicov (2014) suggested that treatment for Hispanic Americans include therapists who are culturally aware, have cultural competence, maintain flexibility in the therapeutic process to accommodate to more specific cultural practices (i.e., temporality, gift giving, kisses as greetings, or advice giving), are focused on trust-building practices (successive engagement over time of a meaningful relationship), are strength-based, and are able to decrease system barriers and stigma (i.e., finding culturally appropriate services or using a translator). Marano and Roman (2017) concurred, stating that therapists working with Latino families should follow cultural expectations, cultural variables, and be flexible and adaptable in their interventions.

Therapeutic intervention should focus on both substance-use factors as well as fit culturally for Latino families. Hernandez and Moreno (2018, p. 276) provided several suggestions for effective interventions when working with Latino substance-using youth:

1. Assessing acculturation, potential acculturation gaps between parents and adolescents, and cultural orientation to capture the heterogeneity among Latino subgroups and generate information that may offer guidance on what therapeutic approaches may offer the best "fit" for any given family.
2. Working with parents and adolescents to restore the protective factors of familismo and respeto by improving communication, particularly in situations where acculturation gaps exist.
3. Strengthening parenting practices (increasing monitoring and supervision) and parenting self-efficacy among Latino parents, who may feel they have lost control over the lives of their adolescents since arriving in the United States.
4. Educating parents on the various cultural perspectives their adolescents may be identifying with so that they understand and offer their adolescents culture-specific guidance.
5. Increasing access for Latino families by taking linguistically competent interventions out into the communities in which they live or socialize.
6. Including explicit protocols for addressing culturally based attitudinal stigmas and misconceptions regarding the therapy and the treatment process.
7. Stressing the importance of interpersonal connections with families, not only during the treatment process but also during recruitment and follow-up methods.

While these are general ideas for working with Latino families, therapists are encouraged to be flexible and make sure their assessment is idiosyncratic for that particular family.

African American Families

African Americans are a distinct cultural group, but one that has tremendous cultural diversity (Boyd-Franklin, 2003; Williams, 2016). African Americans constitute a wide array of national origins, including Africa, the Caribbean, and South and North America. African Americans—those who in the U.S. Census identified as Black alone or as a combination—comprise approximately 14% of the U.S. population (42 million people). This accounts for the third largest group behind Whites and Hispanics.

African Americans are unique as an ethnic group in three main areas: the African legacy, the history of slavery, and racism and discrimination (Boyd-Franklin, 2003). African Americans have a long connection to Africa, the continent from which they or their ancestors come and for which there are associations with customs and ideas that are not mainstream in the United States. One of the primary lasting vestiges of this African legacy is the importance of kinship ties. Additionally, African culture is associated with the importance of religious and spiritual beliefs. The period of slavery in the U.S. led to a strained relationship between the African American community and that of mainstream U.S. culture. The racism and discrimination that occurred during and after slavery, through segregation, and up until the present day, has had a severe impact on African Americans in a multitude of areas including education, employment, and economics. Boyd-Franklin stated, "Both [racism and discrimination] affect an African American from birth until death and have an impact on every aspect of family life, from childrearing practices, courtship, and marriage, to male-female roles, self-esteem, and cultural and racial identity" (2003, p. 9).

African American families tend to have one of the lowest median incomes, averaging about $39,490 in 2016. Around 22% live below the poverty line, which is the highest rate among the four largest ethnic groups. Approximately 7% of African American youth drop out of high school; this is the second highest rate of the four major ethnic groups. In 2016, 43% of Black high school graduates enrolled in college and 18.5% graduate college. One of the distinguishing characteristics of African American families is the prominence of motherhood, whether it is the child's biological mother, grandparent, or community mothering (Pellebon, 2012).

While a typical two-parent family is part of the African American community (46.6%), there is a high number of single-parent families; specifically female-led (44.8%). This pattern is known as the **matricentric female-headed family pattern**, leading to a possibility of African American families being "multi-problemed" as they tend to fall below the poverty line, have young mothers, and have members with low levels of education (Eshleman & Bulcroft, 2010). There is also a high proportion of cohabitation and nonmarital births for African Americans, partly due to economic barriers (Kelly & Hudson, 2017). These factors lead to the possibility of eventual relationship dissolution. While African American families tend to be matricentric, they also tend to give high value to extended family (Kelly & Hudson, 2017). Households may have multiple generations living together, with grandparents helping to raise grandchildren. African Americans also espouse both individualistic and collectivistic values and have very strong religious and spiritual beliefs.

African American Families and Substance Abuse

Wright (2001) provided several explanations for substance abuse patterns in African American families:

- Using and abusing substances on the weekend which may be reminiscent of the times immediately following slavery when ex-slaves were given their paycheck on Friday and would use the money to drink on the weekend.
- The proliferation of liquor stores and drug availability in predominantly Black neighborhoods.
- Economic instability and frustrations of not being able to fully provide for the economic welfare of the families.
- Attempts to deal with social environments ripe with racism and discrimination.

Compared with Caucasian and Hispanic populations, African Americans have reported the lowest rates for use of alcohol, cigarettes, and illicit drugs (Nasim et al., 2011). However, the biggest social, economic, and public health problem for this group is drug addiction (Dei, 2002). Mortality rates for alcohol-related diseases are 10% higher in African Americans than in other populations in the U.S. Wright (2001) explained that many African Americans use drugs and alcohol as a way to cope with the stress of living in an oppressive environment. Blacks who experienced racial discrimination were more likely to engage in weekend and problematic alcohol use (Thompson, Goodman, & Kwate, 2016).

African Americans tend to view substance abuse as a secondary problem to the social context of racism and poverty. Drug use may be a method of trying to cope with racism for some African Americans, using drugs for relief from oppressive social problems over which they have no control (Nasim et al., 2011). Substance use and abuse for African Americans may be related to the inability to cope with social exclusion, rather than directly related with drug and alcohol consumption. African Americans experience racism in all aspects of their lives, including drug treatment and incarceration, as Blacks experience higher rates of incarceration for drug offences (Nicosia, MacDonald, & Pacula, 2017).

A second factor influencing African American drug and alcohol use is peer influence. There is solid evidence demonstrating the negative effect of peer influence on African American youth alcohol behaviors (Epstein, Williams & Botvin, 2002). As a consequence of racism and social exclusion, African Americans tend to interact more with other individuals from the same racial group and are more vulnerable to being influenced by social pressure from other African Americans. Nasim et al. (2007) found that **peer group affiliation**, defined as the sense of belonging to a particular social group, influences early alcohol initiation, which is related to current use, heavy use, and lifetime use.

The national differences for African Americans have implications for cultural beliefs, values, and practices. For instance, substance abuse is higher for Blacks from the United States as compared with those from the Caribbean (Lacey et al., 2016). This may be due to acculturative stress, where the longer time in a country being exposed to negative social conditions (i.e., economic stress and discrimination) may lead to increased substance use. However, there are also likely differing views of what is drug or substance use/abuse based on culture and religious views.

African American Youth

Overall, African American adolescents use alcohol less than their counterparts from other ethnicities while using marijuana at approximately the same amount (Clark, Nguyen, & Belgrave, 2011). African American teens use alcohol more than any other drug (Scott et al., 2011). Annual drug use among African American youth is lower than that of Hispanic youth and slightly higher than that of Caucasian youth. However, the consequences of drug use in African American youth are more severe than for Caucasians and Hispanics in terms of HIV/AIDS contraction (especially for women) and criminal justice involvement (especially for men) (Szapocznik et al., 2007). Black females tend to engage in earlier sexual onset and, when using alcohol, have increased rates of sexually risky behavior (Chung et al., 2017). At the same time, alcohol is the primary contributor to accidents and suicides for African American adolescents (Centers for Disease Control, 2003). There are also psychological consequences, such as low self-esteem and depression, due to alcohol use among African American youth (Maag & Irvin, 2005).

African American college students, when compared with their White peers, are less likely to engage in heavy alcohol use and more likely to abstain from alcohol consumption (Wade & Peralta, 2017). One reason for this is perceived race-based police bias, where African American students experience unsolicited policing more than their White counterparts. This may lead them to be more cautious when the possibility of drinking presents itself. While Blacks, Whites, and Hispanics had similar risks for adolescent and early adulthood drinking issues, Blacks were at greater risk of developing alcohol problems after young adulthood (Lui & Mulia, 2018).

Risk and Protective Factors

Cho and Kogan (2016) viewed the risk and protective factors for African American males from a developmental perspective, where there is a possible cascading effect for young African American men who have had harsh, unresponsive parenting while they were growing up. This environment influences precocious transitions in adolescence (having to engage in adult roles prematurely), which was related to economic instability in young adulthood. Further, economic instability was related to a poor sense of future orientation, which was associated with increased substance abuse. A risk factor in this process was when the individual grew up in a disadvantaged community as this increased the risk of substance abuse. However, a protective factor for these African American men was being in a supportive romantic relationship. Zemore et al. (2016) found similar results in that risk factors for heavy drinking for African Americans included being poor, experiencing prejudice, being young, and being unmarried.

While harsh, unresponsive parenting is a risk factor associated with increased substance use, positive parenting behaviors, such as authoritative parenting, helping with schoolwork, limiting television time, and giving of praise, have been found to be protective factors against substance use (Vidourek, King, Burbage, & Okuley, 2018). African American youth whose parents did not engage in positive parenting behaviors were one-and-a-half to three times more likely to recently use alcohol than those whose parents engaged in positive parenting behaviors.

Religious involvement and spirituality may also be protective factors for African Americans. Higher levels of spirituality and a sense of purpose in life, for African-American substance abuse clients, were related to higher physical and psychological well-being (Blakey, 2016; Stewart, Koeske, & Pringle, 2017). Further, engaging in religious services and experiencing self as religious and spiritual were associated with lower levels of alcohol-use disorders, especially so for African American females (Ransome & Gilman, 2016).

Ethnic identity can be a protective factor as it is associated with better outcomes in drug use for African American adolescents (Chavous et al., 2003). African American adolescents who had positive attitudes towards being African American had lower tendencies of drug use (Belgrave, 2002; Caldwell et al., 2006). Adolescents expressing a strong ethnic group affiliation have low susceptibility to heavy drinking, even as peer risk behaviors increased (Nasim et al., 2007). **Africentrism**, which refers to the values, beliefs, and behaviors deriving from an African cultural heritage and religiosity, has also been found to be a protective factor from drug use in the African American community. Nasim et al. (2007) concluded that youth with higher Africentric beliefs started consuming alcohol at a later age than other racial groups. At the same time, Africentrism promotes a concern for significant others, which reduces the rate of alcohol consumption. Additionally, susceptibility for alcohol use is low for highly religious adolescents where moral and social judgment plays an important role when engaging in activities out of church.

Social support has been shown to be another protective factor for substance abuse behaviors for African Americans. However, Nasim et al. (2011) found that social support is significantly different for Caucasians and African Americans in that Caucasians reported more family support and African Americans reported social support from church members and other religious-related networks. Conversely, those individuals with less family support were most at risk because they had fewer resources to cope with adversity.

Treatment Implications

Given the importance of protective factors as well as the understanding of the familial and cultural impact for African Americans, counselors and therapists who work in the area of substance abuse should be promoting and incorporating the identified protective factors during prevention and treatment processes. One means to do this is to enhance the client's racial identity by including family members and important role models such as teachers, relatives, friends, and the community in the treatment plans.

Since spirituality is extremely important to the African American community, as well as its association to positive gains in psychological well-being, incorporating spirituality into treatment should be a possible avenue, depending on the particular client's beliefs (Nasim et al., 2011; Stewart et al., 2017). Cheney, Booth, Borders, and Curran (2016) encouraged treatment providers for African American substance abusers to help connect them to social capital. This included connecting clients to religious and spiritual activities, non-drug-using friends and family, abstinence-supporting networks, and engagement in conventional activities (i.e., "normal" activities, such as leisure, church, and play). Kelly and Hudson (2017) recommended that therapists working with African American clients address the following five areas: joining (being warm and authentic); stressors, traumas, socioeconomic concerns, and a lack of role models; racial stigma and shame; identifying and supporting cultural values; and therapist self-awareness.

African Americans tend to exhibit unique treatment barriers, including treatment location, perceptions for treatment necessity, and treatment stigma (Fisher & Harrison, 2018). Scott et al. (2011) explained that African Americans tend to lack access to treatment, usually because of socioeconomic factors. Compared with other racial groups, African Americans are less likely to enter and complete outpatient substance abuse treatment (Mennis & Stahler, 2016; Montgomery, Burlew, & Korte, 2017). Another reason for this, besides economics, may be people's readiness for change (see Chapter 8). To help substance abuse treatment retention, therapists should consider focusing on increasing client motivation and improving their readiness for change.

African Americans may also engage in early treatment termination because of perceived experiences of discrimination when receiving health care (Mays et al., 2017). Patient discrimination may increase for those individuals who are uninsured and/or racial/ethnic minority patients. With these potentials, as well as cultural suspicion and mistrust of the mental health field as a backdrop, it is especially important for therapists to be able to join with and develop a positive therapeutic relationship with African American families (Boyd-Franklin, 2003).

Asian American Families

Asian Americans were the fastest growing ethnic group in the United States between 2000 and 2010, increasing by 43% (U.S. Census, 2012). They now account for approximately 5% of the total population (18.2 million people). This is the fourth largest group behind Whites, Hispanics, and African Americans. Asian American families tend to earn more than any other ethnic group. In 2016, their annual median income was $81,431. However, approximately 10% live below the poverty line. They also have the highest percentage of completion of high school (approximately 97%) and college (52%). Only 3% of Asian Americans drop out of high school, which is the lowest amount of any of the primary ethnic groups. Out of all the ethnic groups presented in this chapter, Asian Americans have the highest rate of married couples (80.4%). Only 11.8% of families are female only with no husband.

Asian American families tend to operate from a patriarchal perspective, with children showing a lot of respect for their elders. Asian American parents have many expectations for success and high achievement of their children, which may lead to children feeling self-blame or feelings of isolation if they do not meet those expectations (Fisher & Harrison, 2018). Asian American families have a strong respect for elders, filial history, and authority, leading them to function more collectivistically than individually. Yet, the family structure is geared more toward the nuclear rather than the extended family (Suzuki et al., 2017). Thus, family pride tends to be more important than individual pride and individual feelings tend to be kept in and not discussed. One means of social control in Asian American families and communities is through shame and "saving face" to avoid embarrassment. However, the more acculturated the child, the less the sense of family obligation, which would lead to not engaging in as many family face-saving behaviors.

Asian culture tends to favor perfectionism, which is associated with values such as filial loyalty, collectivism, and adhering to social norms (Fisher & Harrison, 2018). This leads to clarity in role functions so that families are strongly structured, with children deferring to parents, and wives usually deferring to husbands. Asian American males tend to be the breadwinners while females are in charge of the home and disciplining the children. Acculturation has serious implications for Asian American families, especially since they are, more than other ethnic groups, likely to intermarry (Suzuki et al., 2017).

Asian American Families and Substance Abuse

Asian Americans are considered a low-risk group in the substance abuse literature (Iwamoto, Grivel, Cheng, & Zamboanga, 2016a) and have been under-researched (Iwamoto, Kaya, Grivel, & Clinton, 2016b; Sahker et al., 2017). Substance use rates are generally lower for Asian Americans than for other U.S. ethnic groups, although there are variations among Asian subgroups. They tend to avoid activities that could be potentially embarrassing to themselves or their family members. Asian American women, compared with men, start drug use later, have less education, and have lower employment rates (Han et al., 2016).

Lo and Cheng (2012) found that racial discrimination towards Asian Americans increases the individual's likelihood of having a substance abuse disorder. They also found that income moderates the relationship between discrimination and substance use disorders in that low income was related to more discrimination and more substance abuse. Yoo, Gee, and Lowthrop (2010) found that many Asian Americans reported racial discrimination in various aspects of their lives, including being passed over for a promotion, treated like "not an American," and viewed with suspicion, which led to them using substances when trying to cope with racial stressors, especially discrimination. However, Asian Americans perceive less discrimination than African Americans. Since Asian Americans tend to be high achievers, increased education inhibits the levels of discrimination compared with African Americans (Lo & Cheng, 2012).

Asian American and Caucasian families tend to have differences in parenting styles, with Caucasian families displaying more parental warmth, which tends to be a protective factor for those families (Luk, Patock-Peckham, & King, 2015). However, lack of maternal warmth was not associated with substance use for Asian Americans, which may be because this is seen as more normative. Further, Caucasian families tend to operate more from a position of individuality while Asian Americans do so from a more collectivistic orientation. This leads Caucasians to tend to engage in increased substance use if their individuality is violated whereas Asian Americans may be exposed more to parental denial of their individuality.

Asian American parents are likely to maintain the traditional values and practices of their home country; however, the children, much more quickly than the parents, are able to connect to the new dominant culture (Fang & Schinke, 2011). This leads to a potential increased generation gap between parents and children. As such, those adolescents who have acculturated to the U.S. culture are at higher risk of alcohol use than peers with more traditional beliefs (Hahm, Lahiff, & Guterman, 2003). However, a protective factor is the strong sense of familial connection as the more attached the adolescents are to their parents, the lower their risk of alcohol use. Parental attachment is such an important mediating factor that those Asian American adolescents who were highly acculturated and had low parental attachment were 11 times more likely to use alcohol than those low in acculturation.

Asian American Youths

Rates of substance use among Asian American youth have been increasing during the past decades, putting Asian American adolescents as likely as youth of other racial groups to be at risk of substance abuse (Hong, Huang, Sabri, & Kim, 2011). As Asian Americans become more acculturated, problems in behavior such as substance abuse increase (Ryabov, 2015). As immigrants, especially adolescents, become more acculturated they are more likely to relate with American peers who may influence their behavior towards substance use. Asian American adolescents who spend more time with non-Asian peers are more likely to drink than Asians who socialized with other Asian Americans (Thai, Connell, & Tebes, 2010). This pattern of increased substance use by successive immigrant generations is called **second generation decline** and may be due to initial immigrants not engaging in substance use as much because of a protective culture, lack of inter-generational conflict, and resiliency (Ryabov, 2015). That is, first-generation immigrants are more acculturated into Asian culture, have more respect for generational roles, and come to the U.S. with resiliencies. Each of these protective factors may decrease for each subsequent generation that is born in the U.S.

Although family is the first of the social influences that has primary impact on Asian Americans' behavior, peer use is one of the most robust predictive factors of substance use and abuse among Asian American youth (Le, Goebert & Wallen, 2009; Liu & Iwamoto, 2007). In Liu and Iwamoto's (2007) study, Asian Americans who had peers using substances were twice as likely to drink and use illicit drugs and four times more likely to use marijuana. Further, masculine norms are related to more substance use in Asian American men than women. Males tend to drink to have power over women and to display risk-taking behaviors.

For Asian American emerging adults, heavy episode drinking and associated alcohol-related problems are increasing (Iwamoto et al., 2016a, 2016b). These researchers found that, for college students, the rates of alcohol-related problems are similar for Asian American and White males. Asian Americans have traditionally been viewed as a model minority, especially regarding substance use and risky sexual behavior (Sabato, 2016; Sahker et al., 2017). However, this may not necessarily be the case. While past 30-day drug use was lower for Asian American youth than for other groups, they are more likely to use cigarettes, pipes, and cigars (Sabato, 2016). Further, there is a high level of association between substance use and risky sexual behavior.

Risk and Protective Factors

Family relationships are a primary protective factor for Asian Americans (Fang & Schinke, 2011). Family represents an integral socialization source, which can influence or inhibit risky and negative behaviors (Hahm et al., 2003). Asians that perceived higher negativity from parents and/or friends toward drinking are less likely to relate with peers that use substances or alcohol and therefore are less likely to engage in drinking behaviors (Thai et al., 2010; Luk et al., 2013).

Higher levels of acculturation, family conflict, and discrimination are risk factors for alcohol and drug use disorders for Asian Americans (Savage & Mezuk, 2014). Wang, Kviz, and Miller (2012) explained that "while the cultural context unique among Asian American adolescents may multiply their vulnerability to alcohol use and abuse, parent-child bonding may be sufficiently protective to mediate this risk" (p. 833). Asians with high levels of attachment and cohesion with their parents are less likely to use drugs (Savage & Mezuk, 2014). Additional protective factors against substance use for Asian Americans include neighborhood safety (Savage & Mezuk, 2014) and high academic achievement (Luk et al., 2013). Religiosity is another protective factor for Asian Americans against alcohol and marijuana abuse among acculturated Asian Americans. Religiosity in Asian Americans is related to perceiving alcohol and substance use/abuse as a negative behavior that goes against the family. The higher the level of acculturation, the more religiosity serves as a protective factor (Luk et al. 2013).

Asian parenting styles are predominantly authoritarian (Chuang & Su, 2009). In that way, acculturation gaps start to develop between parents and children leading to parent–child separation through intergenerational conflict or intergenerational cultural dissonance. As a good relationship with parents is a protective factor, parenting style could influence children's behaviors in positive or negative ways. Asians' collectivistic values, which include the notion that children should think of their family first and obey their parents, can be in conflict with the individualism that Asian American children born and raised in the U.S. are likely to espouse. This potentially leads to conflict with their parents who have the expectation of teaching Asian values to the new generations.

While Asian Americans are more likely than their White counterparts to binge drink when they experience psychological distress (Woo, Wang, & Tran, 2017), they may be at risk the more they take on U.S. beliefs, values, and behaviors since acculturation to the United States may be a risk factor for substance abuse for Asian Americans. For instance, those who were born in the U.S. reported higher levels of drug use in the past year than those born outside the U.S. (Bersamira, Lin, Park, & Marsh, 2017). These authors found that predictors of past-year drug use for Asian Americans included acculturation (those being born in the U.S. and better English proficiency with higher rates), gender (men higher than women), ethnic subgroup, age, lifetime prevalence of a major depressive episode, and drinking behavior.

Treatment Implications

Asian Americans (and Pacific Islanders) have had a higher trend of substance abuse treatment admissions than other ethnic groups (Sahker et al., 2017).

More Asian Americans are seeking out treatment, possibly as a result of Asian American families having an increased acceptance of psychotherapy than they traditionally had. Those seeking services tended to have much lower levels of income or were at that time homeless. Those that did go to treatment were primarily forced by their family, legal, or work systems to go. This may relate to the stigma for substance abuse among Asian Americans, not only for the individual, but for the entire family (Han, Lin, Wu, & Hser, 2016).

As described, all Asian Americans are not the same, depending on country of origin and history of immigration. Therapists should be aware of the various subgroups to ensure they are utilizing appropriate interventions that address culturally appropriate stress coping strategies (Woo et al., 2017). Barriers for treatment for Asian Americans tend to include peer pressure, family influences, and face-loss concerns (Masson et al., 2013). Han et al. (2016) recommended providing culturally competent treatment for Asian Americans, focusing on mental health issues and communication between therapist and client. These authors found that Asian American women had lower levels of treatment satisfaction, especially concerning their perceptions of therapist empathy and the agreement about treatment goals.

Since Asian Americans are likely to come from families where going to therapy is associated with stigma, therapists are encouraged to provide clients with information as to the therapeutic process and the collaborative nature of the therapeutic relationship (Suzuki et al., 2017). Luk et al. (2015) explained, "Given the collectivistic nature of Asian cultures, it is reasonable to assume family factors are critical points of intervention" (p. 1367). Fisher and Harrison (2018) recommended that the therapist keep in mind that the father or elder of the family may be the gatekeeper for treatment.

Wang, Kviz, and Miller (2012) recommended that when working with Asian American families, prevention programs need to be designed to deal with acculturation effects and should incorporate culture-specific strategies. These strategies can shorten the divide between generations, especially for newly immigrated families where the children are being raised in the United States but with parents who are maintaining values and practices from their home country.

American Indian Families

The U.S. Census Bureau combines data for American Indians and Alaska Natives (AI/ANs). There are approximately 5.2 million American Indian and Alaska Natives, which comprise between 1–2% of the population in the United States. In the United States, there are 567 federally recognized tribes, with 100 state-recognized tribes. While many AIs belong to tribes, not all do. Based on the National Survey on Drug Use and Health (NSDUH) data collected from 2005 to 2014, approximately 22% of American Indians/Alaska Natives live on reservations or trust lands (Center for Behavioral Health Statistics and Quality, 2016). Those AI/ANs living on tribal lands have the same or less mental and behavioral health issues as AI/ANs that don't live on tribal lands. Sixty percent of AI/ANs live in metropolitan areas, which accounts for the lowest percentage for the major ethnic groups. American Indians are one of the fastest growing and one of the youngest ethnic groups in the U.S. (John, 2012). This growth rate may be four times that of the national average (Eshleman & Bulcroft, 2010).

While the iconic view of American Indians is living on reservations, only about 22% do (U.S. Census, 2012). Approximately 58% of households are run by married partners, which is a higher level than African American families but lower than Caucasian, Asian, and Hispanic families. However, the configuration of these couples is changing, as American Indians tend to have a high rate of intermarriage—marrying outside of their ethnic group, usually to a White partner.

There tends to be a wide economic disparity between American Indians and their White counterparts. In 2015, the median family income for American Indians was $38,530 while for the nation as a whole it was $55,775. Part of the reason for this disparity is that American Indians tend to live in rural environments, as well as their ethic for sharing (John, 2012). The poverty rate for AIs is over 30% (Robbins et al., 2017). Further, they tend to not achieve high levels of education, with a dropout rate that is twice that of African Americans and Hispanics and three times as much as Whites (Schaefer, 2010).

One of the distinguishing features of American Indian families is the importance placed on kinship as they tend to be collectivistic, where self identity happens in relation to family, clan, and tribe (Robbins et al., 2017). Elders play a special role in the family, with children learning from an early age to respect the older generation (Eshleman & Bulcroft, 2010). Given that American Indian women tend to start having children at an earlier age than other ethnic groups, the disparity in age between a grandparent and grandchild tends to be smaller than in other ethnic groups (John, 2012).

American Indian Families and Substance Abuse

American Indians and Alaska Natives have higher rates of substance abuse compared with the larger population (Fish, Osberg, & Syed, 2017). There are several possible reasons for this disparity as AI/ANs have experienced the effects of colonialism and serious historical trauma, such as massacres, removal from tribal land, and family separations (Myhra & Wieling, 2014). Ehlers et al. (2013) found that a majority of AIs occasionally think about historical losses, which is associated with substance dependence. Other negative outcomes of the historical trauma AIs have experienced are economic difficulties and overcrowded housing.

While American Indians are impacted by abuse of many substances, alcohol has been the most dominant and detrimental (Greene, Eitle, & Eitle, 2014). About 10.5% of U.S.-born AI/AN adults, in the past year, exhibited an alcohol use disorder while 13% had a substance use disorder (NSDUH). Lifetime prevalence rates for alcohol use showed that American Indians had 5% to 15% more alcohol consumption than non-American Indians. One potential reason for this is that American Indians start drinking earlier than other ethnic groups.

Drinking represents a double-edged sword for American Indians, with both socially reinforced and socially destructive behaviors (Fish et al., 2017). Problem drinking is associated with reduced transmission of traditional values and practices through generations. But at the same time alcohol use is viewed as a part of native life and identity. Because Indians were colonized by White men who used alcohol to control and destroy Indian communities, some American Indians perceive drinking as a way of not letting non-American Indians or "Whites" control them. American Indians also may view drinking as a social shared activity. On the other hand, most see alcohol as an enemy that separates people from their family members. In this way, alcohol has been perceived in ambiguous ways; weakening or strengthening American Indian life and promoting social connectedness or fragmenting Native communities (Yuan et al., 2010).

Elders play a significant role in AI/AN families. For those families where a grandparent is raising the grandchildren, 36% had either a child, parent, or grandparent experiencing an alcohol or drug problem (Mignon & Holmes, 2013). In these families, grandparents typically face financial issues as well as lack of support from extended family and various human service organizations.

Besides the cultural aspects that may predispose AI/AN individuals to engage in substance use, there is also a genetic component (Ehlers & Gizer, 2013). These authors explained that high levels of substance dependence in AI tribes may be based on lack of genetic protective factors, genetically mediated risk factors (drug sensitivity, externalizing traits, and consumption drive), as well as environmental factors. According to the NSDUH survey data, approximately 36% of AI/AN adults used tobacco products in the past month, with 63% smoking cigarettes daily. Almost 50% used alcohol in the past month while 26% binge drank and 8% drank heavily. Those living on tribal lands drank significantly less (39.7% vs 53%) than those living off tribal lands. In the past year, 10.5% of AI/AN adults were diagnosed with an alcohol use disorder, 13.1% with a substance use disorder, and 4.5% with an illicit drug use disorder. Almost 14% of AI/AN adults needed substance abuse treatment in the past year.

American Indian Youth

American Indian and Alaska Native youth have many similarities to youth from any cultural group while also having some distinct challenges. American Indian and Alaska Native youth may have different experiences with substance use, culture, and trauma that other ethnic groups do not (Paul, Lusk, Becton, & Glade, 2017). Patterns of increases in drug use over time have proven to be very similar in American Indian adolescents to those seen among youth from other cultural groups (Beauvais, Jumper-Thurman & Burnside, 2008). However, research has also found that American Indian adolescents tend to engage in the use of alcohol and tobacco more than youth from other ethnic groups (Lowe, Liang, Riggs, & Henson, 2012). King, Vidourek, and Hill (2014) found that one in three AI youth reported recent alcohol use. This was significantly lower than their White or Hispanic counterparts who reported recent alcohol use at approximately one in two. Compared with adolescents of other ethnic groups, American Indians suffer more social consequences from alcohol consumption such as sexually transmitted diseases and health problems such as chronic liver disease and cirrhosis.

For AI/AN youth, increased drinking is related to lower engagement in school, lower community norms against drinking and drugs, lower perceived police enforcement and higher neighborhood disorganization (Friese, Grube, & Seninger, 2015). Tingey et al. (2017) also found that AI adolescents who used alcohol were likely not bonded to school or engaged in structured extracurricular activities.

The more acculturated American Indians are with non-American Indian values, the higher the rates of alcohol use (Fish et al., 2017).

One of the most serious issues for AI/AN adolescents is suicide. Leavitt et al. (2018) provided evidence that AI/ANs, of all ages, are 3.5 times more likely to die by suicide than those from racial and ethnic groups that had the lowest rates of suicide. Seventy percent of AI/ANs who died by suicide lived in rural areas and were likely to have used alcohol and marijuana in the hours before death. They were almost two times more likely to have had a reported alcohol problem. Gray and McCullagh (2014) found alcohol/substance abuse, bullying, poverty, friends and family who attempted and completed suicide, and mental health problems to be risk factors for American Indian suicide.

Risk and Protective Factors

Risk factors for American Indian alcohol consumption are primarily related to demographic variables such as low income, gender, family history, and geographic location. Poverty, being male, and a family history of alcohol are associated with higher levels of alcohol and drug consumption among American Indians (Lieb et al., 2002). American Indians and Alaska Natives tend to have early exposure to drinking and drug use by their parents and grandparents, which leads to early onset of drinking and drugging, usually in early adulthood (Myhra & Wieling, 2014). One of the messages they may receive is that substance use is acceptable and maybe even desirable. This is important since early onset of drinking is a significant predictor of the person developing an alcohol use disorder (Stanley et al., 2014).

Morrell, Hilton, and Rugless (2018) found that peer and family substance use, favorable attitudes toward substance use, easier access to substances, higher levels of sensation-seeking, and poor school performance were potential risk factors for AI/AN youth substance use. Whitesell et al. (2014) explained that risk factors for AI youth substance misuse included exposure to stress, early puberty, and deviant peer relationships. For AIs living in urban settings, externalizing behaviors, family conflict, and not liking school were all predictors of later alcohol use disorder (Stanley et al., 2014). These results have serious consequences as AI youth who have a substance use disorder or conduct disorder have higher arrest rates, with over 50% of AI youth arrested having one or both of these disorders (Hartshorn, Whitbeck, & Prentice, 2015).

Peer attitudes may be a risk or protective factor for this population. Peer groups tend to include more relatives (i.e., cousins, siblings) than unrelated friends, because American Indians tend to have bigger families and relate more to family members than with individuals from other racial groups. American Indian youth with prosocial peer relationships tend to have low or no substance use (Whitesell et al., 2014). Concomitantly, positive engagement in extracurricular activities is associated with lower levels of substance use (Moilanen, Markstrom, & Jones, 2014).

American Indian youth who have a strong sense of spirituality and religious involvement engage in lower levels of substance use (Kulis et al., 2012). Connection to the American Indian church or Christianity is associated with lower substance use while connection to AI beliefs is associated with antidrug attitudes, norms, and expectancies. Tribal beliefs encourage togetherness and prohibit violence and related behaviors. Those individuals who identify with tribal values have less orientation towards alcohol use (Kulis et al., 2012). Pride in being American Indian and religious affiliation is associated with lower levels of alcohol use. American Indians with a low orientation toward traditional culture are more than 4.4 times as likely to use alcohol compared with those who are more traditionally oriented (Yu & Stiffman, 2007). While American Indians tend to have the highest rates of abstinence among all racial groups, when they do engage in substance use they experience more related health disparities (Spillane & Venner, 2018).

Treatment Implications

For AI youth, early substance use intervention is extremely important since exposure to stress and problematic peer and family relationships are associated with high substance use (Whitesell et al., 2014). These prevention programs should be aimed at decreasing the youth's exposure to stress, enhancing prosocial peer relationships, and increasing positive parental influence and relationships.

Myhra, Wieling, and Grant (2015) found that AI families have several resources that can be accessed by therapists. These include grandparents as a source of stability, intergenerational communication regarding substance use, forgiveness and healing, and healing through cultural means. For many, grandparents help to raise the grandchildren, being both parent and teachers of the culture. Grandparent injunctive norms against substance use can be significant protective factors (Martinez, Ayers, Kulis, & Brown, 2015). American Indian families are encouraged to talk about alcohol's individual and intergenerational use in an attempt to break negative intergenerational patterns of substance use and abuse. One way that AI individuals have healed in their own sobriety is through forgiveness and/or making amends. For many AI/AN individuals who have abused substances, healing can come through cultural means. Various cultural, spiritual, and language practices bring strength and help connect them to important values.

When working therapeutically with American Indian adolescents, Spillane and Venner (2018) provided some general cultural considerations for therapists. These include the client's cultural identity and acculturation, religiosity and spirituality, collectivism and conceptions of family, history of discrimination, experienced microaggressions, and negative stereotypes of American Indians. Therapists are recommended to be culturally sensitive to these aspects, which have impact on the risk and protective factors of the person and family. In order to engage in culturally sensitive interventions, therapists and agencies need to be flexible while incorporating evidence-based treatments, as well as developing original means of working that take into consideration the client's traditional and cultural worldview (Croff, Rieckmann, & Spence, 2014). Incorporating Alcoholics Anonymous may be useful as AA's focus on a higher power in many ways relates to the spiritualism that many AI/ANs espouse (Myhra & Wieling, 2014) and has been shown to assist in increased abstinence for this population (Muñoz & Tonigan, 2017).

Interventions that incorporate culturally relevant health beliefs tend to have the best outcomes (Lewis & Myhra, 2017). Thus, interventions should connect the AI/AN client with cultural activities and positive cultural constructs (Brown, Dickerson, & D'Amico, 2016). One way of doing this is to bring in cultural experts when conceptualizing intervention and treatment programs. Chen, Balan, and Price (2012) suggested that therapists include tribe leaders and elders when developing treatment programs for American Indians. Legha, Raleigh-Cohn, Fickenscher, and Novins (2014) recommended that substance abuse treatment for AI/ANs should be integrated, individualized, comprehensive, and long term. The use of peer recovery support is an effective means of reducing substance use as members of the culture work together for sobriety (Kelley, Bingham, Brown, & Pepion, 2017).

Sexual and Gender Minority Individuals

This chapter has primarily presented brief overviews on how families function differently based on their primary culture. However, the notion of diversity has expanded beyond concepts such as ethnicity to that of intersectionality. This includes notions of sexual orientation, ability, education, social class, attractiveness, weight, age, etc. All of these aspects of privilege and oppression lead to individuals developing a sense of identity. In this section we will explore two aspects of self that may impact substance use and family functioning, sexual and gender identities.

Lesbian, Gay, Bisexual, Transgender, Queer/Questioning (LGBTQ) awareness has significantly increased during the 21st century. We will use the phrase **sexual and gender minority** (SGM) communities to refer to those individuals who experience either same-sex attractions or behaviors (**sexual minority**) and those whose **gender identity** does not match with their sex assigned at birth (Mereish, Gamarel, & Operario, 2018). Anderson (2009) explained, "Gender identity is a person's internal sense of being male or female, regardless of his or her genitals" (p. 9).

SGM Families

While there are many similar processes between SGM and non-SGM families, there are some issues that are specific to SGM families. One of these is the family-of-origin issue, which usually centers around issues of sexuality and gender identity (Shelton, 2017). Sexual and gender minority individuals and couples may not be out to their family and must hide their sexual orientation or gender identity. Or, if they are out, there may be tension or even emotional and physical cut-off from the family.

For those who do come out, there may be community implications (Shelton, 2017). These can include homophobic reactions, prejudice, discrimination, and the possibility of hate crimes. Physical safety and emotional abuse, such as online bullying for SGM teens, become significant daily concerns. These are dependent on the locale of the individual/family as some communities are more open for diverse individuals, as well as having better resources.

Sexual and gender minority families, when the person is out, go through developmental stages of coming out (Anderson, 2009). This is an internal and external process where family members adjust to the notion of having an LGBTQ family member, disclosing internally to family members as well as those outside of the family, and accepting a new family identity.

SGM Individuals and Substance Use

Similar to heterosexual and cisgender youth, SGM youth might use substances to deal with stress, conform to peer pressure, deal with family difficulties, and for experimentation (Mereish et al., 2018). However, SGM youth may have additional factors that could contribute to substance use. They tend to have an experience of social oppression (Anderson, 2009). Additionally, they may have difficulty in dealing with the process of sexual or gender identity development. This is significant since there is a higher rate of suicidality for SGM individuals. Substance use and misuse may be a means of trying to cope with potential victimization (Anderson, 2009; Mereish, O'Cleirigh, & Bradford, 2014). Sexual and gender minority individuals have unique health concerns such as perceived or overt stigma, increased emotional problems, and increased substance use problems (Davila & Safren, 2017).

There are varying findings on the differences in substance use between SGM and heterosexual individuals. Marshal et al. (2008) found that SGM youth were, on average, 190% more likely to engage in substance use. This finding was even higher for those who were bisexual (340% higher) and female (400% higher). However, Senreich and Vairo (2014) noted that the difference in substance use between SGM and heterosexual youth is not as much as originally believed.

Yet, SGM youth have higher reported use of emerging drugs than their heterosexual counterparts (Goldbach, Mereish, & Burgess, 2017). These **emerging drugs** include cigarettes, smokeless tobacco, e-cigarettes, alcohol, marijuana, synesthetic marijuana, and prescription drugs. Hatzenbuehler, McLaughlin, and Xuan (2015) also found that SGM adolescents were more likely to smoke, drink, and misuse alcohol. Compared with their heterosexual counterparts, sexual-minority women have a larger difference in their reported levels of alcohol and drug use than sexual-minority males (Hughes, Wilsnack, & Kantor, 2016).

Risk and Protective Factors

The coming out process can be related to the person's substance use (Senreich & Vairo, 2014). First, SGM individuals might self-medicate due to feelings of shame and guilt. Second, the person might be using substances to deal with the fear of how family, friends, and community will react once they come out. Third, the person may be increasing their substance use based upon their peer network and social environment. That is, coming out may lead to a sense of liberation, which might encourage increased substance use.

One of the primary stressors for SGM youth is acceptance by family members. When family members reject the SGM youth, health problems increase.

Ryan, Huebner, Diaz, and Sanchez (2009) found that SGM individuals who experienced higher levels of family rejection during adolescence were 8.4 times more likely to have attempted suicide, 5.9 times more likely to report depression, 3.4 times more likely to use illegal drugs, and 3.4 times more likely to have engaged in unprotected sex.

Because there is a higher likelihood that SGM individuals may be rejected by family members after coming out, they may not experience a traditional family configuration. Thus, they tend to place more import on what are called "families of choice" or **elected families**. These elected families might include family members, supportive friends, and romantic partners who support the SGM individual in their identity. Elected families may be more important for the SGM individual than biological families (Anderson, 2009; Shelton, 2017).

Peer networks also play a significant role in the risk factors for SGM adolescent use. For SGM adolescents, substances tend to play a significant role in their social environments (Senreich & Vairo, 2014). For instance, Hatzenbuehler et al. (2015) found that SGM youth have increased rates of tobacco use in their peer networks. Further, gay bars and clubs tend to play a significant role in peer relations for SGM young adults, where **club drugs** are popular (Adam & Gutierrez, 2011; Anderson, 2009). Some of the primary club drugs are ecstasy, Ketamine (Special K), Gamma Hydroxybutyrate (GBH), and LSD.

The socioeconomic status (SES) that youth come from also plays a role in their risk or resiliency. Sexual and gender minority youth that come from higher SES are more likely to have the support of family, peers, and significant others (McConnell, Birkett, & Mustanski, 2015). This is important since more family support is related to higher levels of mental health. Conversely, lower levels of family support is related to lower levels of mental health. However, even if family support is low, SGM youth may have better outcomes when their peer and social supports are in place. Yet, when family, peer, and social supports are all lacking, SGM youth tend to have the worst outcomes. Sexual and gender minority youth of color may be even more at risk of substance abuse as well as suicidal ideation and attempts, homelessness, sexually transmitted diseases, sexual victimization, and trauma (Murphy & Hardaway, 2017). This could be due to these individuals being at risk for discrimination because of their sexual orientation as well as their race.

Treatment Implications

Sexual and gender minority substance abuse clients will likely find themselves in heterosexual-dominated treatment (van Wormer & Davis, 2013). Thus, it is important that therapists working with SGM clients utilize a **gay affirmative practice** (Crisp & DiNitto, 2012; Senreich & Vairo, 2014; van Wormer & Davis, 2013). This includes the therapist's knowledge, attitudes, and behaviors when working with the SGM population. Therapists should have knowledge about SGM terminology, the impact of oppression, social policies impacting SGM individuals, the coming out process, and community resources. Attitudinally, therapists should have positive attitudes in working with the SGM population. This takes self-reflection to assess for any internalized homophobia or denial of people's gender identities. Behaviorally, therapists working with SGM individuals should be able to create a safe environment, focus on the substance abuse as the problem rather than the client's sexual orientation or gender identity, explore the substance abuse within the person's interpersonal and social contexts, support clients in their perspectives of self, include significant others in treatment (i.e., family members or friends), and obtain supervision when necessary.

Because SGM individuals are impacted by a variety of individual, familial, and social factors, Mereish et al. (2018) encouraged interventions to focus on the individual, familial, and structural levels. Senreich and Vairo (2014) explained, "The impact of the client's sexual orientation on the relationship with his or her family and how it will affect recovery, particularly if it is a source of tension and secrecy, needs to be explored" (p. 475). On the macro-level, therapists and others working with SGM individuals can help to change norms, policies, and societal discourses to reduce potential stigma and victimization.

Therapy of SGM families may involve aspects of psychoeducation of both LGBTQ issues and substance abuse (Senreich & Vairo, 2014). This is important since issues of acceptance are a prevalent risk factor for SGM adolescents and young adults. Hicks (2000) recommended that when working with LGBTQ substance abusers, the therapist might consider connecting the client to specialized addiction treatment programs. These specialized programs allow a space for inclusivity and acceptance and can focus on SGM considerations, such as coming out, homophobia, discrimination, self-acceptance, socialization, family issues, and spirituality. Murphy and Hardaway (2017) expressed a need for community-based outreach programs that would assist LGBTQ youth of color. These programs would focus on the interpersonal, social, and community intersections that would enhance racial, ethnic, and LGBTQ pride.

Case Application

Regardless of culture and ethnicity, the Rothers family has both risk and protective factors in relation to various members' usage of drugs and alcohol. Family members are at risk for alcohol use and abuse. This is especially so based on the paternal intergenerational alcoholism. Mark grew up being exposed to frequent alcohol use in his home. Further, he was exposed to and involved in a family that had organized around alcohol. These same experiences and patterns are occurring in the present family, where Steve, Kayleigh, and Pete are each living in a house where frequent alcohol use, and now dependence and abuse, is happening on a daily basis. Other risk factors include the increase in family conflict and discord between the parents where family rules may be inconsistent.

The therapist working with Mark, and potentially his family, should assess what culture each member identifies with. While someone may be raised in one cultural group, they might identify more closely with another group's beliefs and values. Further, not all members of a family may identify with the same cultural group. Even if they do, they might have differences in beliefs, values, and behavioral processes based on other factors such as socioeconomic status, immigration, or geographic location.

Working with the Rothers, the therapist should not just assume their ethnicity based upon family name, looks, or color of their skin. Instead, the therapist can ask them about their ethnic and cultural history and how that currently informs their actions and viewpoints. Further, the therapist should be aware of potential ethnic and cultural differences between themself and the Rothers family members as these may play a role in the therapeutic process. This is enhanced by the therapist being aware of his or her own **social location**—the various contexts that influence the person's identity, such as race, social class, ethnicity, sexual orientation, gender identity, age, ability status, etc. The therapist can then engage in the process of **location of self** where the therapist has a dialogue with the clients about the intersection of their identities and how these may facilitate or limit what occurs in therapy (Watts-Jones, 2010). This dialogue is enhanced when the therapist is able to engage in self-reflection, empathically connect with the client as two human beings, as well as to the client's social location and community context (Aponte & Nelson, 2018).

Summary

This chapter presented issues of family diversity; especially in regard to ethnicity of families. It presented general characteristics, adolescent drug use, risk and protective factors, and various aspects of treatment for Hispanic American, African American, Asian American, American Indian, and SGM families. I encourage you to engage in further exploration of the various ethnic groups that you work with in therapy. What was presented were some of the common risk and protective factors in relation to substance abuse. However, these are generics. You can use them as a foundation for what might possibly be in play for the individual and family in front of you. Yet, keep in mind the idiosyncratic way that that family fits—and does not fit—in relation to what is commonly known about that ethnic group.

Key Terms

diversity
culture
enculturation
ethnic identity
acculturation
risk factors
protective factors
familismo
patriarchy
machismo
marianism
simpati'a
matricentric female-headed
    family pattern

peer group affiliation
Africentrism
second generation decline
intermarriage
intersectionality
sexual and gender minority
sexual minority
gender identity
emerging drugs
elected families
club drugs
gay affirmative practice
social location
location of self

Discussion Questions

1. Discuss why it is important to understand the culture of the family when working with them in therapy.
2. What are some of the unique risk and protective factors for the various ethnic groups?
3. How do the various ethnic groups differ in their relationship to substance abuse?
4. What is the relationship between ethnic youth, peers, and family?
5. Describe how family ethnicity and culture play a role in substance use and abuse.

SIX

Roles in the Addicted Family

When substance abuse is present, perhaps the most visible person in the family—because they tend to be the one having the most difficulties—is the person abusing drugs or alcohol. We would call this person the **dependent**. However, the dependent is not alone in the sea of troubles the family is experiencing. Others in the family impact and are impacted by the effects of the substance use. For those most central to the substance abuser, they have been labeled enabler, co-alcoholic, or codependent.

Whether it was as a child growing up in a house where one or both parents utilized drugs or alcohol, or in their current family, people's behavior is integrally linked to that of their parents, spouse, siblings, and children. For instance, adolescents with substance-using parents use substances three times as often as adolescents who come from non-drug-using parents (Horigian et al., 2015). Each person comes together, accommodating to others, influencing others, and being a participant, in a unique dance of the family. While each family dances in their own unique way, family members tend to adopt one or more roles to ensure that the dance continues—even if the music is a bit discordant—as that dance is more familiar and safe than the myriad of possibilities they have not yet explored. Gruber and Taylor (2006) explained, "Family role structures and role assignments can be barriers to facing substance use and abuse issues" (p. 5).

We know that families are a system—a unit—and that systems are comprised of many differing parts. These parts all come together to lead the family to function in its current manner. For families where substance abuse is involved, relationships are usually inundated with resentments, fears, frustration, anger, hopelessness, and helplessness (Wallace, 2012). The family's specific functioning will change over time depending on the life cycle stage of the family, as well as current stressors such as job loss, addiction, or divorce. Families are organized to maintain the status quo—the family homeostasis—where the current functioning level is maintained by family members taking on one or more primary roles in the family.

Family members usually do not consciously try to fulfill a role, but tend to do so as a way to accommodate the current situation in the family. Some people, depending on family configuration, will need to take on multiple roles. These roles are based on the rules of the family. In this chapter we will explore several conceptualizations of the various roles that family members adopt and what individual members, as well as the family as a whole, gain or lose through taking on these roles.

Rules in Substance-Abusing Families

While all families function based on a myriad of overt and covert family rules, alcoholic families tend to have distinct rules which they abide by (Wegscheider-Cruse, 1989). The first rule is that the dependent's alcohol use becomes the primary organizing principle and focus of the family. The family believes that alcohol is not at the core of whatever problems they are having. There is something else, perhaps unruly bosses, bad teachers, over-demanding extended family, or a bad economic situation, which is leading to the tumult in the family.

The alcoholic family tends to absolve the dependent of blame on having become addicted, putting that responsibility on someone or something else. For these families, they believe that they need to maintain consistency; even at the cost of the pain they are currently feeling. And what is interesting is that it is not just one member doing this, but the recruitment, to some degree, of each member. Everyone in these families is expected to help; in essence, to become an "enabler." For instance, the Rothers family may say that Mark's drinking is because of his family-of-origin; him having been born into a family of drinkers and that is just how it is with "Rothers men."

Another rule of alcoholic families is in the realm of communication. Members are not allowed to talk about what is occurring in the house to people outside of the family. This prevents others from knowing about the family pain and disconnects family members from possible support systems. People from the larger system may suspect that something is not quite right in the family, but are not given enough of an opening to understand or to help. For instance, a child who has one or both parents abusing substances, with the family having significant tension, may begin to do poorly in school—academically and behaviorally. The teacher might inquire of the student as to what is going on, wherein the child says, "Nothing. Everything is fine." But said in a tone that clearly says that everything is definitely not fine. The teacher, hearing the **metamessage**—the message within the message—explores a little more with the student as to whether there is anything going on at home. The child, knowing that they should not talk about what is happening in the house, holds to their position and loses a potential resource for individual and perhaps systemic change.

One of the other primary rules in the alcoholic family deals with honesty. Members cannot be open and honest with one another; they must provide a false face of strength. When a child approaches the non-addicted parent and asks how come their father is acting differently, the parent may chastise the child, saying that there is nothing wrong or it is none of their business. Each person now pretends that there is not a problem in the family and all is as it should be. Yet what is happening is that people begin to restrict themselves. They do not allow themselves, or each other, to "be"—to say and do what they think and feel. Dishonesty and lying begins to become an operating principle, where the individual becomes closed off from others while the family system closes itself off from the outside world. People learn how to be incongruent and lose the connection between their thoughts, feelings, and behaviors.

This next section describes some of the primary roles that are seen in alcoholic and other drug-using families. While substance-abusing and non-substance-abusing family members adopt roles within the family, these roles have an added dimension in addicted families (Hawkins & Hawkins, 2012). Family roles are multiple, that is, someone is not only in one role. We are all son or daughter, partner, parents, friend, etc. Further, the roles that are given to people, and that people take on, change and adapt over time. This coincides with how the family's homeostasis changes as the family moves through the family life cycle. In addicted families, it also coincides with the progressive changes that substance abuse has on the individuals, interpersonal processes, and family identity.

The family roles presented here for those in addicted families are the most popular constructions in the United States regarding family roles (Vernig, 2011). Keep in mind that an individual may, depending on the structure of the family, occupy one or more roles. This usually happens in smaller families. In larger families, one or more individuals may demonstrate the same role. Whenever a person takes on one of these roles—what are called **survival roles**—they are not able to access their full self (Satir, Banmen, Gerber, & Gomori, 1991). This prevents them from engaging in a positive growth process. The more they rely on their survival role, the less they are able to experience their own thoughts and feelings.

Wegscheider-Cruse's Family Roles

Sharon Wegscheider-Cruse was one of the first substance abuse therapists to talk about the various ways that family members adapt and conform to living life in an alcoholic family. Originally a student of Virginia Satir (see Chapter 13), Wegscheider-Cruse opened people's eyes to the notion that the family is one entity but is comprised of many individuals who are impacted differentially to what is happening in the family—but that they all work in conjunction with one another (see Figure 6.1).

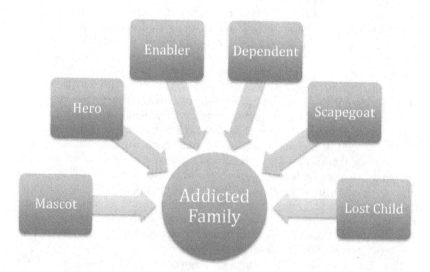

Figure 6.1 Wegscheider-Cruse's roles in an addicted family

Dependent

The **dependent** individual is the person who uses the substance. From a family system's perspective, their behavior is a symptom of underlying issues in the family—usually centering on unresolved conflict between people based on how the family has organized. This conflict may be between spouses or intergenerationally between children and parents (even if the children are now adult). The dependent person tends to move away from responsibilities in various contexts (i.e., career, parenting, emotional). The dependent incrementally shifts from the family being the central organizing feature of their life to the drug of choice being their main focus.

The dependent's primary motivating feeling is that of shame. They feel bad about themselves but do not know how to change. We can tell the dependent's symptoms through their use of whatever substance(s) they overuse. While we might think that there are no benefits for their actions, people who use substances overwhelmingly talk about how it reduces or numbs their pain. Although this might only be in the short run, there at least is a temporary barrier between the pain of their life, their shame, and experiencing that pain. For the family there is really no payoff, yet the dependent is so caught up in their own experience that they have difficulty connecting their actions with those of their loved ones. If they stay in this role too long (depending on what substance they are overusing) there is a possibility that they can become addicted. Severe addiction may lead to many physical problems (such as cirrhosis of the liver, brain malfunction or even death).

Enabler

In a family there may be one or more **enablers**—people who inadvertently help to maintain the family function that supports the dependent's usage. While there may be several enablers in a family, there is usually one person who is the **chief enabler**—the person who tries to help the dependent, but in a way that maintains the problem cycle. The chief enabler is usually the spouse of the addicted person.

The enabler tries to protect the dependent from having to face the full consequences of their actions. This protection, in the short run, diverts social and financial consequences, yet does not protect the dependent from the emotional pain they are experiencing. Just as addiction is a process that usually begins without awareness, enabling follows the same course. Without conscious awareness, the enabler does not realize the depth of the addiction and attempts to save the person, a little at first and then greater over time.

The primary motivating feeling for the enabler is that of anger. We can tell the enabler has been caught in the web of the family process through their sense of powerlessness. Regardless of all of their attempts to try and help, things do not get better. Slowly, the family's situation becomes even worse. So why do they stay in this role? The enabler gains a sense of importance and self-righteousness. Further, since they are trying to keep things together for the family, they take on most of the responsibility and make sure that things keep on running. However, having the weight of the world on your shoulders is back-breaking. Eventually, the enabler may develop physical illness and a sense of martyrdom.

The enabler tends to be the person closest to the dependent and the person who takes their mental, emotional, and physical abuse. Instead of focusing on themself, the dependent tends to criticize the enabler. This leads into a downward spiral where the enabler tries to help because if the substance abuser could just get past this point they would be able to show love again. The enabler then takes on more of the dependent's responsibilities, but also more of the criticism.

Many people use the terms enabler and codependent interchangeably. However, the two are not quite the same. While the codependent does enable, they do it differently than many other people in the dependent's circle (Curtis, 1999). A lot of people in the dependent's relational field tend to enable their behavior (i.e., a boss not inquiring about them being late for work, a coworker covering for the absent dependent who left work early to go to the bar, or a friend who does not tell the dependent's wife how drunk the person got). Yet it is usually only one person, the person closest to the dependent, whose identity becomes intertwined with their connection and role in trying to help the substance abuser—this would be the codependent.

Hero

The **hero** is usually the oldest child, who tries to help the family in its pursuit of success. They may do really well at school, sports, music, or other such endeavors. Their primary motivation is from inadequacy and guilt. They feel bad about themselves as well as their family. In order to try to show themself, their family, and the community that the family is not problematic, they try to pull everyone up through their own success. Although others may see it in a positive vein, their identifying symptom is that of overachievement.

As we've discussed, the roles of the family are intertwined. While the dependent individual shifts their focus from the family to the drug and begins to abdicate their parental power, the enabler makes excuses for this behavior and tends to overcompensate for the dependent's inactions. The family hero also steps into some of the responsibilities that were given up by the addict. For instance, since the hero is likely to be the oldest child, they are likely to take on some of the parental duties that the dependent is no longer doing. Thus, they are very likely to become **parentified**.

The hero takes this role for several reasons. First they gain positive attention from those within and outside of the family. Second, they bring some sense of self-worth to the family in a time when they are beginning to fall apart. The hero's behavior gives the family a sense of pride and something to focus on during the chaos they are experiencing. However, if they take on this role too much they can develop a compulsive drive that will eventually catch up with them.

The hero tends to be the overachiever in the family. They try to control their own behavior by doing "well" while also attempting to control those around them and the situation. For some, they may exhibit signs of perfectionism. Glover (1994) recommended that therapists help the hero shift from an external locus of evaluation and acceptance to an internal locus. This will allow the individual to increase their own sense of self-worth. In this process, the therapists can work to increase the person's self-esteem and development of their self-concept from internal conceptualizations of who they are.

Scapegoat

In family systems terms, the **scapegoat** is the identified patient. This is the person who will most likely be presented as the problem in the family; the person who needs therapy. They are most likely to be engaged in some type of delinquency, be it stealing, lying, behavior problems, or their own potential drug use. Their motivating feeling is that of hurt. The scapegoat is likely to be the second oldest child (Thombs, 1999).

We might look at people and wonder why they continue to engage in behaviors that others deem inappropriate and suffer the consequences for those actions. While the hero is getting attention through praise, the scapegoat also receives attention, just negative. However, attention is attention. And this attention focuses the drama away from the dependent person. So the misbehaving actions can be seen as a way to protect the family by the individual becoming the lightening rod of the family. But staying in this role too long can lead to severe consequences as the person may engage in self-destructive activities that might lead to their own addiction, incarceration, or even death.

There is a dialectic happening with the scapegoat. They seem weak as they cannot keep things together and succeed. Part of this is based on seeing all of the attempts by the codependent and the hero to try to save the family—only to see each attempt fail. In some ways they may develop a sense of learned helplessness; where they do not try to make things better—and why would they if others couldn't?

On the other side of the coin is that the scapegoat—the identified patient—has power in that the system must organize around them (Reiter, 2016). Their actions get results. Part of this power comes in the form of defiance. They are able to stand up to others, showing strength, but these actions hide their weakness. The scapegoat feels inadequate and tends to feel self-pity and hostility.

Lost Child

In families that are having some type of crisis, some children such as the hero or the scapegoat tend to draw the attention away from the crisis and the dependent and onto themselves. Other children try to deflect any attention away from themselves. They do not want to be involved in any type of conflict. This is the plight of the **lost child**, who tends to demonstrate a heightened sense of shyness and engages in solitariness. They operate from a primary feeling of loneliness.

Whereas the hero escapes into success, the scapegoat into destruction, the lost child escapes into themself. This provides a sense of relief for the family as they do not need to put much energy into them as they do not take up much of their resources. Yet if the lost child takes this escape too far they may become socially isolated. Their engagements with other people are severely limited, even extending into adulthood. They might also think that if they were no longer in the family, things would be better for everyone—and thus they may have suicidal ideation.

Mascot

The ambience of families dealing with substance abuse is one of caution, fear, pain, and restraint. If these were the only possibilities, the family would quickly sink.

However, the **mascot** helps bring some type of amusement into the family through their clowning around. They tend to be hyperactive and try to joke as much as they can. This is problematic because it is coming from a motivating feeling of fear. The mascot tends to be the youngest child in the family (Thombs, 1999).

The mascot gets attention through smiles from others and brings a sense of fun to the family. Yet this is done to try to cover up the distress of everyone in the family. When they take this to extremes they maintain an immaturity that does not allow them to grow. They might also develop some type of emotional illness. Family members tend to view the mascot as the most fragile person in the family and may try to protect them (Thombs, 1999).

Some have suggested that the mascot is the last role to be developed in an alcoholic family (Veronie & Fruehstorfer, 2001). These authors believed that when both parents were alcoholic there was a lower likelihood that one of the children would grow into the mascot role. Further, families that do not have a functioning adult would most likely not develop a mascot as this role would take too much energy from the family system.

These roles—the dependent, enabler, hero, scapegoat, lost child, and mascot—all work together to try to keep the family ship afloat throughout a storm of pain and distress (see Figure 6.2). Each member has their own way of trying to make things better; by taking focus off the addiction and the pain and onto something else—be it achievement, misconduct, humor, or invisibility.

Black's Survival Roles

Claudia Black (2001), along with Wegscheider-Cruse, is one of the most influential proponents in working with families dealing with substance abuse. She proposed

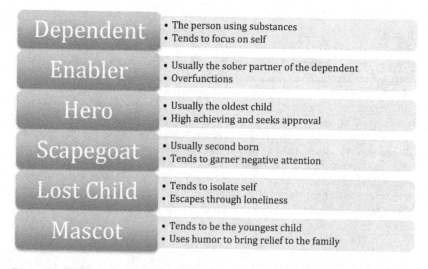

Figure 6.2 The various family roles that work together to maintain an addicted family's problematic homeostasis

similar roles that family members tend to take on in addicted families. While there are many overlapping ideas between her conceptualization and Wegscheider-Cruse's, an understanding of Black's roles may help to broaden the notion that individuals in a family tend to become restricted in certain ways of being in the family.

Codependent

As we have seen, the dependent does not use in isolation. Although the actual consumption of the drug might occur when the individual is alone, the emotional field surrounding the drug use happens in a relational field. The person who is closest to the dependent, usually their spouse/partner, tends to unconsciously enter into a dance of destruction with the dependent where their own identity becomes obscured—a process known as **codependency** (see Figure 6.3). Black (2001) describes how this happens, "It now encompasses the dynamics of giving up a sense of self, or experiencing a diminished sense of self in reaction to an addictive system" (p. 3).

The codependent's experience is one of giving up focus on the self to focus on the other—in this case the person whose drug use has become out of control. Black (2001) explained some of these processes: They tend to lose a sense of self; of what they want and what they need. They become so focused on another person whose needs are ever increasing that they do not focus on their own life. They tend to be reactive to someone else rather than thoughtful of what and why they are behaving as they are. Codependents focus more on the dependent's needs rather than on their own priorities. While doing this they take responsibility for the other person; doing for them instead of letting the addicted individual do for themselves. Problematically, the codependent tends to utilize denial as a key theme in their lives.

The Responsible Child

At least one child in the family tends to become more responsible than the other children. Usually this is the oldest or only child (Black, 2001). Their behavior is designed to help calm the storms that are present in the family. Black explained, "This child takes responsibility for the environmental structure in the home and provides consistency for others" (p. 17). **The responsible child** helps to provide a semblance of normalcy in an otherwise potentially chaotic family.

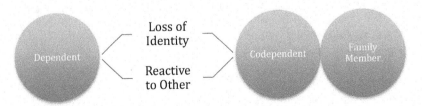

Figure 6.3 The codependent loses a sense of identity and becomes reactive to the dependent's emotions and behaviors

They exhibit good organization skills, responsibility, and are able to set and achieve goals. When they engage in these types of behaviors, they are rewarded. This occurs at both home and school. For those who come into contact with a family only through the responsible child, they might think that the family is functioning quite well.

On the surface the family seems to be functioning, as the individual is succeeding. However, while they are being responsible they are also learning about distrust. The responsible child has learned that his or her parents cannot be relied upon; thus, the responsible child has to become very independent and learn how to fend for themselves if they want to ensure that things get accomplished. This can have serious consequences for their future relationships with adults.

Because the responsible child is so focused on acting more mature than they really are, they tend to lose out on their childhood. Instead of being able to be a child/adolescent they have to be an adult. This leads to them being more serious in social situations and not being able to let go and have fun.

The Adjuster

The adults in the family (usually the dependent and codependent), as well as the responsible child, tend to be the main players to organize and structure the family. This structure is chaotic but manageable, especially by the responsible child who learns to forge their own path. Not all children develop this type of navigation. Black (2001) described this alternative role, "The child called the adjuster finds it much easier to exist in this increasingly chaotic family situation by simply adjusting to whatever happens" (p. 20). **The adjuster** tends to be a younger child who does not try to impose their will on the situation. Rather, they roll with the flow, going along with what is happening. One of the reasons for this is that they have developed a belief system that, regardless of what they might try, they wouldn't make a difference. In essence, they have developed a sense of learned helplessness.

In looking in from the outside of this family, the adjuster would seem to be the loner of the family. They are more detached, physically and emotionally. During conflicts in the home, the adjuster might sneak away to their room and not put themselves into the center of attention. The parents in the family may provide more attention to other children, as they seem more present in the family.

One of the difficulties of adopting the adjuster position is not coming in contact with one's true thoughts and feelings. The person may just behave rather than have a sense of what or why they are acting in the way they are. As adults they continue to not take control of their situation and just go with the flow. While they may be more flexible and spontaneous than the responsible child, they have a reduced sense of control, lacking a sense of power or direction.

The Placater

Whereas the adjuster has a fairly flat affect and does not become emotionally reactive, there is usually one child in the house who does; this is the most sensitive child. Black (2001) explained, "In the addicted family the placating child is not necessarily the only sensitive child in the home, but is the one perceived as the 'most sensitive'" (p. 22). **The placater** experiences a lot of pain due to their heightened sensitivity. Whereas the responsible child overcomes their pain through achievement and order, and the adjuster blunts their pain, the placater attempts to lessen their own and others' pain. They tend to try to be the "fixer" in the family. When they grow up, this child might go into the mental health field as they are attuned to knowing people's pain and trying to reduce it.

While it may seem that this attunedness to another's pain and being empathic is a positive trait, it can become problematic. The placater has a tendency to not disagree with others. In this case, the person may lose a sense of self, not being able to stand up for his own rights. In the family, the parents tend to like the placater because the child does not put up an argument. They get along with others and do not bring more drama to a play that is full of discord. Further, if there is conflict, they are usually the first to apologize.

As adults, the placater still attempts to care-take for others. They will tend to find jobs where they can help others. However, they may have a tendency to develop symptoms such as depression (Black, 2001), as internally their experience is one of loneliness. Although they are in connection to others, the relationship is usually lopsided where they are giving and the other person is taking. Placaters tend to not receive the gifts of due concern that others may be able to give.

The Acting-Out Child

The roles of the various children in drug-using families that Black has proposed have so far all been ways for the members to deal with the chaos of the family without making things any worse. Members either try to provide stability, fade into the woodwork, or make others feel better. However, there is usually one member who deals with the pain and chaos of the family by taking the focus off of the dependent person and onto himself. This is **the acting-out child**. Black (2001) explained this role, "They will cause disruption in their own lives and in the lives of other family members. In doing so, they will often provide distraction from the real issues" (p. 25).

The acting-out child tends to produce conflict through confrontation within and outside of the family. The more that the parents can focus on this child's negative behavior the less they have to focus on what is happening in other areas of the home—especially as it relates to drug use. Although not done intentionally, the child attempts to save the family by offering themself up as a scapegoat. This tends to have deleterious effects on the child's self-esteem. They may think of themselves as worthless and troublesome.

This low level of self-esteem follows the acting-out child into adulthood. They have most likely entered into peer systems where they can cause trouble with others. Out of all of the children in the house, the acting-out child has the highest probability of developing their own addiction. However, alcohol and/or drugs can serve a purpose for a person displaying any of these roles. For instance, alcohol may loosen up the rigidity of the responsible child. The adjuster may develop a heightened sense of power when under the influence. For the placater, alcohol might give them the courage to stand up for themselves and become more assertive. Figure 6.4 presents Black's roles for people in an addicted family.

Figure 6.4 Claudia Black's classification of roles in an addicted family

Overlap of Wegscheider-Cruse's and Black's Family Roles

As can be seen, there are many similarities between the family roles proposed by Wegscheider-Cruse and Black (see Figure 6.5). The responsible child is similar to the hero. The scapegoat is similar to the acting-out child. The adjuster is similar to the lost child. The placater is similar to the mascot. Whatever term is used, if treatment is not sought at some point in the individual's life, the person will most likely develop future symptoms in school, work, relationships, and health and emotions; usually based on which family role they had adopted (Middleton-Moz & Dwinell, 2010).

The hero/responsible child seems to be doing very well during their childhood as they tend to succeed in various areas of their life, providing a positive focus for the family. However, without intervention, they may try too hard to succeed, perhaps becoming a workaholic. They have learned that it is their responsibility to *do*, as they could not rely on others in their families. As adults, they may tend to not trust others and not be a team player. They could also develop symptoms of perfectionism, where they punish themselves for making mistakes. In their relationships, they may try to take over and control the other person, operating from a need to be right. They tend to have difficulty forming very intimate relationships and may find a partner who needs them to continue to be responsible. In the areas of health and emotions, these individuals may not be able to express

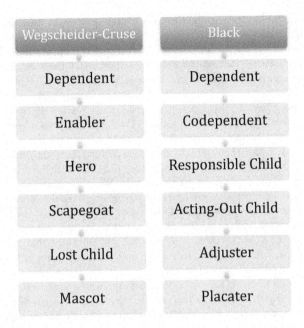

Wegscheider-Cruse	Black
Dependent	Dependent
Enabler	Codependent
Hero	Responsible Child
Scapegoat	Acting-Out Child
Lost Child	Adjuster
Mascot	Placater

Figure 6.5 Comparison of Wegscheider-Cruse and Black's roles in an addicted family

their emotions well, keeping things inside. This pain may come out in the form of physical illnesses. The hero/responsible child tends to deny their pain and anger, and is not happy when they complete projects.

The acting-out child/scapegoat helps to channel the family's energy away from the addicted individual by sacrificing themselves as being the family's problem. In school and work this person tends to get into trouble, perhaps getting detentions and suspensions, or often getting fired. They tend to go against authority and the rules of the system they are operating in at the moment. In relationships, they create conflict. During adolescence this may manifest itself in running away from home. As an adult, they may find a partner who is codependent, takes care of them, and allows them to continue to act out. They tend to find ways to hurt their partner and create chaos in their lives, perhaps by having unplanned pregnancies or getting into frequent verbal and physical altercations. In terms of health and emotions, they are likely to engage in their own substance use and possibly abuse. Instead of being able to talk with others about what is going on for them, they display their emotions behaviorally—usually focusing on pain and anger. Because they have adopted this role of the "tough guy" they are not able to show their softer and more loving side.

The adjuster/lost child tends to meld into the background where they do not bring focus on themselves—either good or bad. This person will tend to isolate from not only their family members, but from people at school or later at work. They tend not to be able to take much initiative in their lives—instead finding themselves not engaging others. Because they are trying to stay in the background, they stifle their abilities so they do not shine. In relationships, when they do engage with someone, they take the backseat in the relationship—finding a partner who can take the focus off them. As regards their health and emotions, they tend to have low self-esteem and low self-worth. Others would view them as shy and may try to control them. These individuals feel helpless and may use substances as a way to control a very small aspect of their lives.

The placater/mascot tries to engage others to make them feel good about themselves and take focus off the family pain. This individual would most likely be the "class clown," where others may laugh when around them but may not take them seriously. Even when they do well in something, they may allow someone else to take credit for it. In relationships they may lose their identity and do for others rather than standing up for themselves. When conflict happens they will either try to avoid it through joking about it or giving in to the other. When in an authority position, they may not follow through on discipline or consequences. Instead of standing up for their needs and wants they may become dependent on the other person. When it comes to their health and emotions, they do not do well handling stress. Substance use may help them to dissipate some of their feelings, as they tend to internalize their emotions.

There may also be role reversal where someone who adopted one of the family roles later gives up that role and adopts a different role. For instance, the family hero, who has been succeeding in various areas of life (i.e., school) may eventually become the scapegoat (i.e., they begin abusing substances and develop an addiction). This reversal is not something that happens quickly, but over time as the person gives up one role for another. However, I want to make it clear that a person does not develop a family role on their own. It is only when other family members allow them to take it on and all family members engage one another in ways that maintain everyone's roles that people are able to function as they do.

The problems the people have based on the family roles they have adopted may (or may not) develop if intervention does not occur. However, with therapy and/or self-exploration, this does not need to be the case. People who adopt any of these roles can change their lives so that they are able to function well in school, work, relationships, and with their physical and emotional health.

Support for the Family Roles

There has been considerable debate regarding the various family roles put forth by Wegscheider-Cruse and Black. While empirical attempts have been made to validate these proposed family roles, there has not been enough testing and support to validate them (Vernig, 2011). Potter and Williams (1991) developed the Children's Roles Inventory (CRI) as a means of measuring the various roles that children may play in alcoholic families. This measure was based on Black's construction of family roles and was found to have good internal consistency. However, these authors believe that alcoholic as well as non-alcoholic families all have these same roles. Using the CRI, Alford (1998) found that people from dysfunctional families showed greater agreement with the lost child and scapegoat roles, but less strong agreement with the hero role. Factoring out adult children of alcoholic participants, people from dysfunctional families were three times more likely to be in the lost child role and less likely in the mascot role. Alford concluded that, irrespective of parents' substance use, family dysfunction had the greatest impact on which role a member identified with. Fischer et al. (2005) found that in families with high parental drinking and family dysfunction, oldest children tended to take on the hero role, especially in relation to their younger siblings, who tended to adopt the lost child role. Yet, those older siblings in the hero role were buffered from the family of origin whereas siblings in the lost child and scapegoat roles had higher levels of vulnerability to the family of origin (Fischer & Wampler, 1994). These researchers held that males in the mascot role were buffered from family dysfunction much more than those in the lost child or scapegoat roles. Thus, there are differential impacts on children in substance-abusing families based on gender and which role they take on.

There has been a lot of controversy surrounding whether Wegscheider-Cruse's or Black's family roles can be empirically substantiated. Rhodes and Blackham (1987) developed scales to determine Black's roles of placater, acting-out child, adjuster, and responsible child. In their study they compared children from alcoholic and non-alcoholic families to determine whether there were any differences on these scales. They found that there were not any significant differences except for the acting out scale. Devine and Braithwaite (1993) developed alternative scales that represented the placater, acting out, lost child, and mascot. These researchers found that their scales helped support the various family roles developed by Wegscheider-Cruse and Black. Although there was support, their scales did not endorse all of the various behaviors hypothesized with these roles. As added evidence of the usefulness of using the family role typologies, these scales were effective in differentiating children from alcoholic and non-alcoholic homes.

While Wegscheider-Cruse and Black's family roles tend to be the predominate models proposed about how family members cope with what is occurring in the addicted family, other therapists and theorists have also proposed their own typologies. We will end this chapter by discussing one more model of family roles—that of Vernon Johnson.

Johnson's Family Roles

Johnson (1986) explained that in families dealing with alcohol, family members take on one or multiple roles, depending on the family configuration and what is occurring in the family. These roles include the protector, the controller, the blamer, the loner, the co-dependent, and the intervener (see Figure 6.6). Many of these roles overlap with the roles that Wegscheider-Cruse and Black endorsed.

The Protector

The protector role will usually demonstrate itself during the beginning of the family's encounter with addiction. At this point, the drinking/drug use is only infrequently impacting the family functioning. The protector tends to become defensive of the addict and the family. This comes in the form of apologizing for

Figure 6.6 Vernon Johnson's typology of family roles in an addicted family

the addict's behavior (i.e., not showing up, anger outbursts, disregard), contacting the addict's employer to provide excuses for being late or missing work, and agreeing with the addict's rationalization for the drug use.

As the protector begins to engage in each of these actions, their sense of self diminishes. They do not feel as good about themselves and find that they are using rationalizations for their own actions like the addict uses for theirs. The addict will tend to project their anger and frustration onto the protector who takes this on and feels increasingly inadequate. The commonality between the protector and addict is that they are both deceiving themselves and others as to what is happening.

The Controller

As the addiction process progresses, family members' sense of self wears away to where they feel out of control. They may believe that they are at fault for what is happening in the family. To gain some type of continuity and equilibrium, a person may adopt the role of **the controller**. Here, the person tries to be active in trying to change the addict's behaviors.

The controller engages in many different behaviors to reduce the drug use and its consequences. They might take over the buying and procurement of the substances so that they have control over what type and how much is present. As a more extreme aspect of this, the controller may engage in drinking/drug use with the addict in the hopes that if they do it together the addict will not use as much as they do on their own or with their substance-use cohorts. Some more subtle behaviors they might engage in include pouring out alcohol or disposing of drugs, not agreeing to go to events where the person may use, and pleading with the addict to stop (for self, spouse, and/or children). However, there is a paradoxical process that happens where the more the person tries to control the addict's use, the more the addict uses.

The Blamer

When feelings of low self-worth grow, the individual's self-deception takes over and they project their feelings of anger, hurt, and failure on others; most likely the addict. Active conflict becomes more prominent in these families as **the blamer** begins to covertly and overtly go after others. Covertly they may give the silent treatment to the other person when they do not like what the other person did. Overtly, they may bring up, in an aggressive manner, actions the other person just did (or did in the past) that they did not like, such as not getting along with their parents or being late for an event.

One of the interesting aspects of the blamer is their fluctuations, where at some points they seem to be quite depressed and at other points they are demonstrating outbursts. These seem to be related to quite trivial events. However it might be, the person is so focused on blaming the other that they are not in touch with their own feelings of uncontrollability, unrest, and self-delusions.

The Loner

As the ability to control one's surroundings slips away, the individual may shift from an external focus to an individual focus. The person's self-worth and self-esteem are most likely extremely low. Their interactions with others have become strained and they tend to isolate themselves; eventually adopting **the loner** role. Here, the person has become increasingly defensive, leaving friends and family members to feel uncomfortable in their presence and likely to disengage from them. The loner feels alone in their misery, floating on a raft in an ocean with the current flowing away from land.

The Enabler

Over time, the addicted person progressively underfunctions, and one or more family members tries to compensate for this and overfunction. They become responsible for the addict. At this point they may take on **the enabler** role. This is perhaps one of the most famous roles, as the enabler's behavior allows the addict to not have to face the consequences of his actions. As the enabler tries to control the chaos, the addict is able to continue to use, and the family continues to spiral into dysfunction.

The Co-Dependent

The co-dependent is, in essence, the next stage of the addiction process from the enabler. The person is clearly not able to see how their own behavior is deteriorating and is tied to the addict's behavior. The person increasingly has aspects of each of the roles presented here; they become more protective, more controlling, and more blaming. Their sense of reality is distorted and they are not able to see how they are falling into a morass of progressive and chronic pain. Co-dependents tend to exhibit poor self-esteem, a need to be needed, a strong urge to control and change others, a willingness to suffer, a resistance to change, as well as a fear of change (Thombs, 1999).

The Intervener

The roles that were previously described present a dysfunctional way of trying to deal with the chaos occurring in a family dealing with addiction. Johnson (1986) provides a role that is more productive; that of **the intervener**. This happens when the person understands addiction and the process that happens for not only the user but those in his relational field. The intervener will have engaged in a self-exploration to understand how he or she may have adopted the role(s) of protector, blamer, controller, enabler, and/or co-dependent. The person is able to make a distinction between self and addict and not take the responsibility for change totally onto themselves.

Case Application

Mark is the dependent in the Rothers family. He is drinking enough that he is considered an alcoholic, where there is both abuse and dependence. If he stopped drinking there would be withdrawal. On initial assessment of the family, Mark would be the first concern, as he is isolating himself, increasing the amount of his alcohol consumption, and has made statements about wanting to be dead. However, there are concerns throughout the family as individuals have developed survival strategies of various roles to help them cope with being an addicted family.

The Rothers family find themselves organized by alcohol, but don't quite know it. They have come under the spell of the first rule of addicted families; that substance use is the primary organizing principle of the family. They realize that they are having problems, but have not put the focus on substance use and abuse. Rather, they are looking at Mark as being depressed and Steve as acting out. While they might think that alcohol does not help Mark's discontent, they view it as an accomplice rather than as the mastermind of the disharmony. Since they do not know whether Steve is using any drugs or alcohol, the family views his acting out at home and school through a developmental lens, as a rebellious teenager rather than as symptomatic of being raised in an alcoholic family. People may be seen in isolation rather than connected in a web of intergenerational patterns and relationships.

The Rothers family also find themselves abiding by the rule of not talking about how alcohol is now running their lives. There may be times when Hannah suggests to Mark that he not take another beer, but after being rebuked several times for this intrusion in his drinking, she keeps it to herself. The children also do not talk about Mark going off into his den to watch television and drink by himself and have accepted this as just how their family is. Steve may be the first to bring the drinking to the forefront, but it would likely occur during a huge confrontation where all parties involved are angry. This would devalue his concern for the amount of Mark's drinking. Hannah has not yet said anything to her family about her concerns for Mark's drinking and how the family seems to be slowly unraveling. There are rigid boundaries between the Rothers and other systems, such as extended family, religious, and school systems.

While Mark is the dependent in the family, he is not the only member to take on a role that maintains the family's current homeostasis. Hannah is the chief enabler. While she does not like Mark drinking, and his associated foul mood and disconnection from the family, her actions inadvertently keep the family functioning in their current state, which allows Mark to continue his pattern of usage. She serves as a buffer between the children and Mark, ensuring that no one upsets him. She can feel the tension underneath the surface of the family's interactions and does what she can to keep that at bay. She may have explored possibilities for Mark, such as therapists, self-help groups, or treatment programs, but hasn't approached him about it in fear of rocking the boat too much. She at first covered for Mark in terms of calling in sick for him at his work, or taking care of their children when he was drunk. However, she is also one of the most vocal about him changing, not realizing how some of her past actions had contributed to maintain the substance abuse.

The hero in an addicted family is usually the oldest child, but not so in the Rothers family. Kayleigh is the hero as she is overachieving at school. While on the surface it would seem that she is the most "healthy" person in the family, her striving to do well is likely in reaction to the tension and discord in the family. She may believe that if she does everything right, everything will be fixed in the family. However, she is likely to learn about her own inadequacy as the harder she tries to take the weight of the family on her shoulders, the more the family negatively spirals. This could eventually lead to a sense of guilt that she could not help the family.

Steve has taken on the role of scapegoat in the family. He is acting out in school and at home. In all likelihood, the Rothers family will come to therapy with Steve as the identified patient, most likely through a referral from the school system. Steve's negative behaviors bring him attention both inside and outside the house. Whenever he argues at home, his parents interact with him. While that may be through yelling and argument, it shows that he is important and has some type of power. His feelings of weakness, fear, and inadequacy become hidden when he defies authority and attempts to show strength and power.

Pete likely fills both the role of lost child and mascot. There are times when he will be alone in his room to get away from the cloud of misery that has been hovering over the family. In these moments, he is the lost child as no one in the family has to worry about him. They have a reprieve for wondering, "What next?" At other times, Pete may act in the role of the mascot as he can be the most playful person in the family.

Summary

As can be seen from each of the models presented in this chapter, families in which there is addiction tend to have members who engage in various coping strategies to survive what is currently happening in the family. It is important to remember that the adoption of these roles is relational, expressing both individual and familial coping responses. When people adopt a role in the family, they and the other members restrict the behavioral, psychological, and emotional experience of that person. If the role becomes their identity, there is a greater likelihood that some type of symptom (physical, emotional, or psychological) will be present. However, it is important to keep in mind that people adopt these roles, and allow others to take on their role, as a way to survive the chaos and pain that is living in the addicted family.

Key Words

metamessage
survival roles
dependent
enabler
chief enabler
hero
parentified
scapegoat
lost child
mascot

codependency
the responsible child
the adjuster
the placater
the acting-out child
the protector
the controller
the blamer
the intervener

Discussion Questions

1. Explain the differences between each of Wegscheider-Cruse's family roles. How do they all interweave with one another?
2. Describe each of the survival roles that Claudia Black proposes.
3. Discuss Johnson's family roles.
4. How are Wegscheider-Cruse's, Black's, and Johnson's family roles similar?
5. In what ways are the development of family roles both individual and relational?

SEVEN

Family Life Cycle

This chapter discusses how a family changes over time. Families are not static entities. Not only do the individuals in them follow normative developmental patterns (i.e., Erik Erikson's stages of individual development), but the family as a whole does as well. The chapter starts by exploring the typical stages a family goes through and then will narrow in on the individuals in the family by first talking about children growing up in alcoholic families and then exploring adult children of alcoholics. The chapter ends by focusing on the concept of resiliency and how children growing up in addicted families might gain and utilize strengths and resources to help them through the chaos.

Normal Family Development

We have described the family as a system; a group of interacting parts that come together to function as a whole. As an organized unit the family develops rules to help it navigate various transitions of living. While not all families go through the same transitions, they all change over time. This section focuses on the "typical" North American family life cycle, which entails a heterosexual couple that has one or more children. These stages may change based on various factors such as not having children, premature death of a member, divorce, or other such issues. To be clear, these are the generic transitions for what has become the "standard" North American family. However, the configuration of families has changed to some degree as two-income families, stepfamilies, same-sex couples, and having children out of wedlock alters the timing and fluidity of the stages. But having this knowledge as a foundational understanding of family development can assist in understanding these other family configurations.

A family's life cycle can be seen as being comprised of six stages (Carter & McGoldrick, 1999). These include: leaving home—single young adults; the new couple; families with young children; families with adolescents; launching children; and families in later life. At each of these stages there are emotional processes based on the transitions from one stage to another as the family has to accommodate the introduction or departure of one or more members. Further, the family system needs to change—shifting various boundaries and rules—at the end of each stage to be able to function well when moving into the next stage.

We can look at the beginning of a family life cycle as starting with a **single young adult**. In previous years this may have been when the adolescent became an adult—around 18 years of age. Due to various circumstances including economics and culture, the age of launching may be being pushed back. For the individual who is starting their adult life, there are many challenges that must be faced. Perhaps foremost in this is taking on the responsibility for one's own life. This comes in the form of economic, social, and emotional ownership of one's self. The individual must differentiate from their family, developing their own life while also still being connected to the family. At this stage in the life span, a shift tends to happen from the importance of nuclear family relationships to peer relationships. The young adult will also need to establish themselves financially, usually through the beginning of their career. At this stage the person is also looking for a potential romantic partner, which leads into the next stage of the family life cycle. However, the single young adult stage has been increasing in length as more men and women have been gaining a post-secondary education as well as beginning their work career before marrying. According to the U.S. Census Bureau, median age at first marriage has increased from around 20 years old for women and 23 years old for men in 1950 to 27 years old for women and 29 years old for men in 2017.

At some point two individuals who are in the young adult stage meet one another and decide to enter into some type of committed relationship (i.e., marriage). **The new couple** isn't only the joining of two individuals, but two family systems. Although some of these connections of in-laws are very close, others are more distant. Yet the projections of these family systems—the two people in the new couple—interact with one another based on patterns and understandings from each of their family of origins. At this point, each individual needs to commit to the new family system requiring a readjustment of how they operate to include more time, energy, and loyalty to their new partner and a reduction of energy in relationships with peers and other family members. This can be a very discordant time, especially if one or both members of the couple were extremely close to their family of origin. If so, the person may feel split loyalties, where they are caught in a tug of war between wanting to do for their original family and doing for their partner (Boszormenyi-Nagy & Krasner, 1986).

The third stage of most families occurs when they have their first child. In **families with young children**, the two individuals who have adapted to become a couple now must adapt again to allow the entry of another member into the family. This requires a change in the rules of the family system. Many families experience difficulties at this stage as they are unsure of how to negotiate time and energy into the couple and as well as their parental responsibilities. In traditional sex role families, the wife exerts much of her focus on the new child while the husband feels excluded to some degree. Besides the parents having to negotiate with one another around financial and child-caring issues, they also must open the boundaries of their new family to include the role of grandparents and extended family. For some families where there are more diffuse boundaries between the couple system and the grandparent system, there may be role confusion as the grandparents try to take over the executive functioning of parenting. Depending on how many children the couple has, there may be multiple adjustments of new members into the family, which would lead to this stage lasting longer.

The next stage is that of **the family with adolescents**. The major systems change that needs to occur is the parents' increasing flexibility to allow more independence for the adolescent in the preparation of the adolescent developing into a young adult. The adolescent tests boundaries to try to begin the differentiation process from the family. Also at this stage, the parents' parents may begin to need more assistance in their own lives due to illness. For those adults who must take care of their own children while taking care of their aging parents a new term has recently been put forth—**the sandwich generation**—as they are sandwiched between having to care-take for those generationally above and below them (their children and their parents). While the adolescent is beginning to move away from the family, husband and wife now must put focus back on the marital relationship.

Once the adolescent becomes a young adult, the family moves into the fifth stage; **launching children** and moving on. Here the family allows the departure of the young adult and must renegotiate from three or more people to now only two. Parents have the difficulty of letting go their primary parenting responsibilities to allow their child, who is now an adult, to make their own choices. This requires a shift from parenting to more of a consulting or even a friendship role with the child as they now are having an adult–adult relationship with their children. At some point after the launching, the young adult will have found their partner and the parents will have to allow for the entrance of new family members (son-in-laws or daughter-in-laws) as well as the possibility of grandchildren. The parents' parents are likely to be ailing at this point and the possibility of their deaths play a major role in the family. The launching stage is also a significant time for marital discord as the empty nest syndrome happens. If the couple has not kept engaged with one another as a romantic dyad, they may find at this point, with no one in the house besides themselves to focus on, that they have grown apart.

The last stage of the family life cycle is **families in later life**. The two adults must deal with each of their own frailties. A generational role shift occurs where instead of being caretakers for others, the elderly individuals find that others are beginning to take care of them. Retirement has occurred, which can be a significant loss of identity to those who had seen a close connection between themselves and their careers. Spouses must adjust to the loss of their partner by death and shifting their role from primary to secondary in their children and grandchildren's lives.

As has been hinted at in this explanation of the family life cycle, there are usually four family subsystems operating at the same time in this developmental process. The launching stage is a fork in the family's life where the parents take one road—moving closer to later life—and the child, who is now a young adult, taking the other road. When a new couple forms, we can see three families in play: (1) the couple; (2) one partner's parents, who are in the launching or recently launched stage; and (3) the other partner's parents, who are also in the launching or recently launched stage. As the new couple has a child and that child matures into an adolescent, each of the original families-of-origin begins to move into the families at later life stage. When the adolescent matures enough to enter into the single adult stage (and enters the fork of single adulthood—launching), their two sets of grandparents may be at the latter end of their lives.

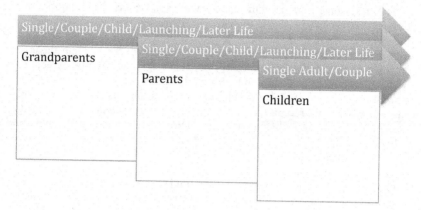

Figure 7.1 The generational overlapping of family systems during each family's
developmental life stage progress

Thus, at one time we may see three or more different generations operating
separately, yet intertwined. Figure 7.1 presents a visualization of these overlapping family systems.

What was just presented is based on a family life cycle where there is not a
major change in the family, such as divorce, early death of a partner and/or
remarriage. However, approximately 50% of couples do divorce and the divorce
rate is even higher for second marriages. When remarriage happens, there is now
a joining of multiple family systems where the integration of three or more family systems needs to occur. Also, the parental subsystem attempts to negotiate
parenting duties; determining whether the step-parent will play a primary role in
disciplining non-biological children.

The family system is impacted when substance abuse is involved. As discussed
in Chapter 4, families dealing with addiction tend to have boundaries that are
either too rigid or too diffuse. Since clearer boundaries usually help the system
function more effectively, families that hold onto rigid or diffuse boundaries will
tend to not be able to adapt when they transition into new life stages. These transitions between family developmental stages are a likely time for the development
of symptoms if the family cannot adjust to deal with the current situation. For
instance, families in the launching stage may have an adult engage in increased
substance use as a way to negotiate the loneliness and disengagement they feel
from their partner and the family.

The understanding of life stage needs to be housed within a multicontextual
perspective where individual, family, and larger systems all influence and are
influenced by each other (Carter & McGoldrick, 1999). The family therapist
should be able to assess the individual in terms of their own developmental process (perhaps through an understanding of Piaget's perspective or Erikson's life
tasks). The therapist must then understand how the various individuals come
together to form the family system. This nuclear family is housed within the context of the extended family. The extended family is housed within the community

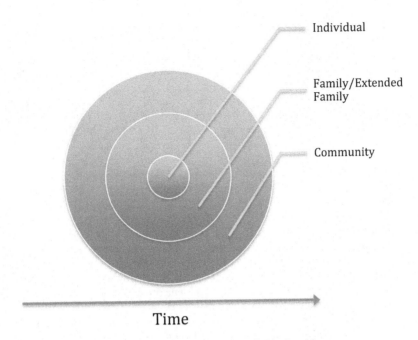

Figure 7.2 The embedded connections between the individual and larger systems over time

and the social connections the family has with others. Lastly, the community can be viewed within larger frames of social structure that include issues of hierarchy and power inequality. Figure 7.2 provides a visualization of these embedded connections and that they change over time.

Addiction and the Family Life Stages

In families dealing with addiction, members have difficulty in being able to differentiate from one another (Hudak, Krestan, & Bepko, 1999). One of the reasons for this is that the more ingrained and organized around the addiction the system becomes, the more isolated it becomes from extended family and larger systems. Family members have probably developed rigid boundaries with outside systems and either rigid and/or diffuse boundaries within. Further, they are most likely engaging in the use of secrets; not letting others outside the family, or even within the family, know about the addiction, violence, abuse, and discord.

Family therapists must be able to see the interacting process of individual and family development to help put into perspective the development and maintenance of the symptoms (i.e., the substance abuse or acting out) that one or more members display. Hudak et al. (1999) explained, "Two interacting sequences occur simultaneously: the progression of the alcoholism within the individual and the developmental progression within the family itself. Alcoholism both influences and is influenced by the movement through the family life cycle" (p. 459).

During the single young adult stage, the individual—whether abusing substances themselves or coming from a family dealing with addiction—may not be able to separate from the family system. Alternatively, if the young adult is the addict, the family may emotionally cutoff, leaving the individual with a reduced support system. These and other factors may hamper the substance abuser's ability to engage with others in the future. There may also be conflict where the addicted young adult tries to delay the launching stage, as they are not financially or emotionally stable. At the same time, the parents try to separate from their child, wanting to decrease their already exhausted attempts to help. Ruiz, Strain, and Langrod (2007) reported that 60–80% of adult substance abusers live with their parents or have regular contact with them, and 75–95% of adult substance abusers have weekly contact with at least one parent. Thus, adult substance abusers tend to come into frequent contact with their parents, where dysfunctional patterns of interaction will likely increase as the severity of the substance use increases.

For the new couple, if addiction is present at the beginning of the relationship, many of the key patterns will be forged around the maintenance of the addiction. This can negatively impact the development of a solid foundation upon which to grow the relationship. These may come in the form of inability to handle differences between the partners, dynamics of power, and issues of intimacy (Hudak et al., 1999). Couples where addiction plays a key role tend to have intense conflict and experience one member overfunctioning while the other partner underfunctions. This puts strain on an already stressed system where some partners may not be willing to continue to invest the amount of energy needed to maintain the relationship. There is also the possibility that having addiction present in the relationship between the couple will lead to them disconnecting from their own families-of-origin to maintain the secrets that are developing around the substance use.

Once the parents have children, addiction plays a significant role in how the family members interact with one another. There is an increased risk of physiological problems if the mother was using during pregnancy (see Chapter 8 for a discussion of fetal alcohol syndrome) as well as emotional and behavioral difficulties for children of alcoholics (see the section below). The more that addiction impacts one or both adults, the greater the chance that their parenting will be distorted. This may come through in one or both parents neglecting or even abusing the children. Depending on the severity of the addiction, the family has most likely isolated itself from extended family and larger systems, thus losing potential support.

When launching children, addiction can have a serious negative effect in that the couple must reengage one another, as much of their time has been spent centered on the children. If addiction is present, it may not allow the two adults to reconnect to one another, increasing the possibility that conflict and divorce may occur at this stage. There may also be issues surrounding economics if money was diverted to pay for the substances or the addicted person was not able to maintain employment. The launched children, now single young adults, may use this opportunity to leave home and emotionally disengage from their addicted parent.

For families in later life, addiction may change from illegal drugs such as cocaine and heroin to prescribed drugs. One of the problems of drug use in later life is the difficulty in assessment (Hudak et al., 1999). Symptoms such as memory loss, disorientation, and impaired body functioning may be viewed as a result of old age rather than because of drug use. This stage can be especially difficult if there was divorce and the individual did not remarry or enter into another committed relationship. They can feel very isolated, which may increase the cycle of substance use.

While we have explored the family life cycle and some of the risk factors for substance abuse at each stage, we can also look at a smaller process specific for substance-abusing families called the **family addiction cycle** (Ruiz et al., 2007). These authors explained this process, "A cyclical, homeostatic pattern has been described in families of addicts in which, when the addict improves in some way, the parents begin to fight and to separate emotionally from each other" (p. 275). This separation occurs until the substance-abusing individual relapses or has serious difficulties in other areas of his or her life (i.e., getting fired from a job, failing at school, or having a relationship end). Once this happens the parents focus their attention on the substance abuser rather than on each other. That is, the substance abuse serves a function in the family for togetherness. This cycle continues once the substance abuser improves, leading to increased couple conflict (see Figure 7.3).

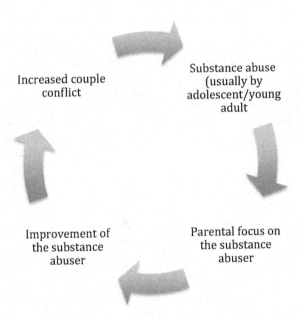

Increased couple conflict

Substance abuse (usually by adolescent/young adult

Improvement of the substance abuser

Parental focus on the substance abuser

Figure 7.3 The family addiction cycle happens when the substance abuser improves. Conflict happens in other relations until increased substance use diffuses that conflict

Children of Alcoholics (COAs)

Once adults enter into the families with young children stage, they must negotiate their own individual growth as well as caring for the well-being of another person; one who cannot take care of themselves (at least for several years). This task is hard enough on its own, but becomes even more complex when the adults are dealing with addiction in the system. In the previous chapter, we discussed the various roles that members tend to adopt in addicted families. In this section, we will spotlight specifically on the children, as growing up in a family where addiction is present can have serious consequences for the child, even when they mature into adulthood.

Children of alcoholics (COAs) are any people under 18 living in a house with one or more alcoholic parent(s). Based on data from the combined 2009 to 2014 National Survey on Drug Use and Health, about 1 in 8 children, or 8.7 million children aged 17 or younger, lived in households with at least one parent who had a substance use disorder in the last year. That represents about 12.3% of children aged 17 or younger in the U.S. Most of the children lived in families where the parent abused alcohol while others had a parent abusing illicit drugs.

Perhaps a disturbing finding that the NSDUH survey uncovered was that younger children were more likely to have a parent abusing substances. An annual average of 1.5 million children aged 0 to 2 (12.8% of this age group), 1.4 million children aged 3 to 5 (12.1% of this age group), 2.8 million children aged 6 to 11 (11.8% of this age group), and 3 million children aged 12 to 17 (12.5% of this age group) lived with at least one parent who had an SUD.

There was a clear difference by gender in terms of which parent abused substances. Of children living in a family with a substance-abusing parent, a much larger portion of the substance-abusing adults were the fathers rather than the mothers (5.4 million for the former and 3.4 million for the latter). Approximately 7 million children aged 17 or younger resided in a two-parent household where at least one parent had a SUD in the past year. Among the 1.7 million children residing in single-parent households with a parent who had a past year SUD, about 344,000 lived with their fathers and 1.4 million lived with their mothers.

In this section, I present many of the adverse impacts of growing up in a family where one or more adults are abusing substances. However, this is not the case for all COAs. Hawkins and Hawkins (2012) explained, "Children of alcoholics often show remarkable resiliency in the face of potentially detrimental effects of parental alcoholism and grow into well-functioning adults" (p. 265). While many COAs can foster their resiliencies to live healthy lives, living in a family with a substance-abusing parent can have serious consequences.

One of the potential problems for children growing up in a family with one or more drug-abusing parents is that they may become parentified. **Parentification** is when a child is placed into a parental role in the family. This is usually due to the adults in the family being unable, for various durations, to fulfill that role. This may be because the adult is a single parent and must work one or more jobs, leaves the house in search of the substance, or that they are intoxicated and are not psychologically present. In two-parent families, parentification usually happens when one or both parents are impaired, such as having a chronic illness (i.e., Parkinson's, cancer) or is battling drug use.

Children may become parentified not only when there is parental alcoholism, but also when there is unpredictability in the family (Burnett, Jones, Bliwise, & Ross, 2006). In drug-using families, there tends to be a higher prevalence of unpredictability. As such, some children may find the need to try to control the situation; in this case, attempting to take over for the underfunctioning parent. The child can feel the anxiety in the system and see that there are jobs and functions that are being neglected; such as bathing, feeding, and overseeing young children.

The parentified child will usually be the oldest child. This would most likely be the responsible child or the hero. They will try to raise the younger children, providing rules and punishments in an attempt to get the family to function better. The parentified child will also tend to be female, adapting more quickly to a care-taking function in the family (Burnett et al., 2006). In the short run the parentified child helps the family as the other children are taken care of, having their immediate needs met. This is important so that larger systems, such as child welfare agencies, do not get involved with the family. However, the parentified child enables the addicted adult to continue to abdicate their responsibilities.

Through this abdication, there is a greater chance of attachment difficulties. In family therapy, **attachment** can be conceived as the child's connection to one or more adult caregivers. The better the attachment to one's caregivers, the more the child's emotional and psychological well-being develops. One of the issues that happens in addicted families is that positive attachments can be hampered when one or both parents is addicted. Buelow and Buelow (1998) explained that COAs might exhibit two ends of a continuum; being overly dependent or severely independent. These issues of too much dependency or too much self-reliance will last into later life. For instance, children may grow up to enter relationships where they find themselves engaging in co-dependent behaviors; needing someone else so much that their own identity becomes obscured. Or alternatively, they might quickly end relationships at the first sign of conflict, not being able to stay engaged during times of distress.

The problems that children in alcoholic families experience can be classified into four realms (Lawson, 2011). The first is physical neglect or abuse. When abuse happens, the child is physically harmed. This may result in bruises, cuts, and marks. More severe abuse can lead to broken bones, damage to internal organs, or, in severe cases, to death. Physical neglect leads to the possibilities of isolation, potential illness, and accidents. The second classification of problems is acting-out behaviors. These include the child engaging in problematic behaviors such as fighting and aggression or even their own substance use, which may be severe enough to bring in the police and legal system. The third realm of problems in alcoholic families is emotional reactions, which include a variety of fears, low self-esteem and confidence, a repression of emotions, depression, or even suicidal desires. The last realm of problems living in alcoholic families includes social and interpersonal difficulties. These include peer and family interactional problems. Children of alcoholics tend to feel different from other children, leading to a sense of embarrassment, not being loved or connected, and adjustment problems.

Children of alcoholics tend to exhibit behavioral problems as they get older, where the type of problem varies based on age. Younger children tend to engage in more externalizing problem behaviors while older children engage in more internalizing problem behaviors (Puttler et al., 1998). **Externalizing behavior problems** are symptoms the child displays to the external world in a negative manner. These tend to be in the areas of aggression, delinquency, and hyperactivity. **Internalizing behavior problems** impact the internal world of the child. These may include being withdrawn, anxious, or depressed. Some of the coping strategies that COAs use, such as suppressing their feelings, may seem adaptive in the present, but can become maladaptive at some point in the future (Hawkins & Hawkins, 2012). There is also a difference in problem manifestation based on gender, where boys display more behavior problems than girls. Externalizing behaviors increase when one or both parents is experiencing alcohol-related symptoms (Hussong et al., 2010). So, while any child who is growing up in a house where there has been alcohol abuse is more likely to have higher levels of externalizing behavior problems than those from non-alcoholic families, these behavior problems are heightened when the parent is actively experiencing negative effects of problem drinking.

Depending on the substance of choice, there are differential impacts upon the children. For instance, children who come from families where their fathers abused illicit drugs rather than alcohol had significantly more negative child behaviors, such as irritability, fighting, anger, fear of new situations, and worrying (Cooke, Kelley, Fals-Stewart, & Golden, 2004). Whether a child displays symptoms, and which type of symptoms, is related to the organization of the family, the severity of the addiction, how open the family is in talking about their experience—with each other and outside systems—as well as the various resiliencies the child may have available.

Children of alcoholics grow up in an environment that in many ways is very different than their non-COA peers. The chaos that they tend to live in impacts them emotionally and psychologically. This is most likely based on them having a less healthy lifestyle and more mental health difficulties than non-COAs (Serec et al., 2012). While the child may not demonstrate symptoms right away, living in an addicted family can take a toll in various ways. When children grow up in a house where at least one parent has a long-standing alcohol disorder, they are more prone as adolescents to engage in alcohol, marijuana, and illicit drug use (Hussong, Huang, Serrano, Curran, & Chassin, 2012). This may be based on the interplay of their genetic predispositions as well as the environment they are living in (see Chapter 2 for the gene–environment hypothesis). Further, COAs who came from chaotic families, especially during preschool and middle school, had increased risk for dating violence in late adolescence (Livingston et al., 2018).

The problems of COAs can start from when the child is very young. In attachment theory, young children may not develop positive attachments to their parents (or whoever is their primary caregiver) when addiction is present. This can have very deleterious effects on the child. Fitzgerald, Puttler, Refior, and Zucker (2007) explained that preschool children growing up in families where there is an alcoholic "have organized a system of dysfunctional behaviors, cognitions, and self-concepts that are symptomatic of psychopathology and that are embedded within the maintenance structures of poor parenting, poor family relationships and poor socioeconomic resources" (p. 19).

It is extremely important to keep in mind the impact that substance use in a family has on the children throughout the course of the addiction. Even after the adult(s) in the family have ceased substance use, the balance of the family is still usually out of kilter (Lawson, 2011). This can be seen in the children maintaining the roles that they developed to cope with the chaotic family functioning. As the family's homeostasis had organized around the addiction, it takes time and energy for the rules of the system to change so that a more functional arrangement is developed. Even then, there has already been psychological ramifications for each member of the family.

We have presented many issues that COAs may face; however, these are dependent based on several factors (Middleton-Moz & Dwinell, 2010), which include:

- the degree to which the parent or parents focus on the developmental needs of their children rather than on the addiction or the effects of addiction;
- delayed grief and/or trauma that has not been resolved in the parent(s);
- which parent is alcoholic and the other parent's response to the addiction;
- the stage of alcoholism the parent is experiencing, and how the alcoholism or addiction is manifested;
- the amount of energy that is available to the child rather than expended on repression and denial of unfinished business left over from the parent's childhood;
- the presence or absence of a caring adult caregiver who is not in denial;
- the birth order and personality of the child (p. 58).

The family therapist will need to assess each of these areas, as well as other aspects of family functioning, to gain a more comprehensive perspective of the coping of children in addicted families.

It would seem that it is imperative to locate and provide intervention for COAs since there are so many possible negative consequences of growing up in a family where there is significant drug use. However, addicted families tend to develop rigid boundaries with outside systems, keeping what is happening in the family a secret. Although they may know that something is not right within the family, COAs tend to be very hesitant when it comes to disclosing to non-parental adults about the family situation, usually engaging in an internal risk assessment to try to determine what might happen after the disclosure (Tinnfalt, Eriksson, & Brunnberg, 2011). Children of alcoholics are more likely to disclose the substance abuse happening in the family to outside parties when the parent has self-identified as being alcoholic and is receiving treatment, as well as when they believe they can trust the adult to whom they would potentially disclose. One of the primary reasons for not telling adults about the substance abuse is the fear of what may happen to the family; for instance, would child welfare try to take the COA and his or her siblings out of the family, or would the drug-abusing adult be arrested.

For younger COAs, the therapist might consider helping them enter into group therapy as a way to increase peer support and reduce isolation, as many substance-abusing families have rules that isolate people and diminish their voices (Markowitz, 2014). One aspect of treatment for younger COAs is to help them deal with the denial of their parent(s)' difficulties. This prevents the COA's anger from seeping out and boiling over. Given that COAs tend to receive messages from their parents that deny and invalidate their feelings, therapists should actively validate the COA's beliefs and feelings.

Adult Children of Alcoholics (ACOAs)

We have seen that while children are growing up in a house where one or both parents engages in drug and alcohol abuse they might experience internal and external problems. They may act out in school or develop issues such as anxiety and depression. But what happens when these individuals grow up?

When children who grew up in alcoholic families become adults we refer to them as **adult children of alcoholics** (ACOAs). While some are able to engage in healthy and meaningful relationships with their family of origin, as well as being able to establish their own families, many are not. There are many factors that go into how well an ACOA copes as they develop. For instance, ACOAs who had a mother who was alcoholic showed less positive relationship with their parents and peers as opposed to non-ACOAs (Kelley et al., 2010).

While it seems to go against logic that someone who was negatively impacted by parental alcoholism would use alcohol and become addicted themselves, this is a common pattern. Adult children of alcoholics tend to start using alcohol earlier than children who did not grow up in alcoholic families (Braitman et al., 2009). When they get into college, they drink as much and as often as non-ACOAs. However, they have a tendency to engage in more drug use than their counterparts.

As they get older, ACOAs tend to have more relational difficulties than non-ACOAs. For instance, ACOAs have a higher need for control (Beesley & Stoltenberg, 2002). Given that when they were children there was a lot of unpredictability in their addicted family, as adults they may try to ensure not only that they are stable and behaving appropriately, but that their partner, children, and business associates are as well. This leads the individual to have difficulty forming trusting relationships, which impacts their relationships, as ACOAs tend to report lower relationship satisfaction than non-ACOAs.

Adult children of alcoholics have a higher likelihood of developing depressive symptoms as they enter young adulthood (Kelley et al., 2010). This may come from internalizing behavior problems where they were not able to openly express their pain and now find it bottled up. By having no outlet for their distress, and having a low sense of efficacy in control, they may find their sadness escalating into depression.

Adult children of alcoholics tend to experience some type of stigma associated with their parent's substance abuse, dependent on the child's gender. Female ACOAs tend to experience stigma when their parent had high levels of alcoholism and the family avoided talk about it (Haverfield & Theiss, 2016). Male ACOAs usually feel stigma when the family avoided talk of alcoholism. For both groups, experiencing stigma was associated with increased symptoms of depression and decreased self-esteem and resilience. Thus, work with ACOAs might focus on helping to increase self-esteem and decrease various issues of shame.

Wegscheider-Cruse and Cruse (2012) suggest that many ACOAs become "addicted" to trying to seek relief from their pain. Not only do the substances one uses impact brain chemistry, but the actions that we engage in also impact our brain's functioning. Individuals who do not use substances, but who attempt to deal with the pain of living in or having grown up in a dependent house, tend to engage in medicating behaviors. These behaviors become addictive for the person because, when they engage in them, their brain releases chemicals that temporarily medicates and reduces their emotional pain. The person, unknowingly, may become addicted to this sensation.

In this process, there are some medicating behaviors that occur more often than others (Wegscheider-Cruse & Cruse, 2012). These include, "workaholism; compulsive eating; which is different from sugar addiction; compulsive controlling of eating, such as anorexia, a highly medicating behavior; compulsive caretaking and controlling others; seduction; sexual acting out; spending and gambling; excessive exercise; and 'guru chasing'" (p. 28). Guru chasing is when the individual continuously seeks the latest fad of help (such as a new group, therapist, or method of treatment).

Adult children of alcoholics tend to have several common characteristics (Middleton-Moz & Dwinell, 2010), which include: fear of trusting, debilitating guilt, loyalty to a fault, hyperresponsibility or chronic irresponsibility, a need to be perfect, counterdependency/fear of dependency, a need to be in control as well as a difficulty with spontaneity, a guess at what is normal, difficulty hearing positives and difficulty with criticism, a desire to please or defy others, overachievement or underachievement, poor self-worth or shame, compulsive behaviors, continual trigger responses, addictions, living in anxiety and fear, a need to be right, denial, fear of conflict and normal anger, being chaos junkies, a fear of feeling, frequent periods of depression, fear of intimacy, repetitive relationship patterns (usually negative), fears of incompetence, hypersensitivity to the needs of others, a fatalistic outlook, difficulty relaxing or having fun, discounting and minimizing pain, as well as resiliency strengths. Not all of these characteristics are present; however, they tend to be more prominent in adults who grew up in families where one or both parents were alcoholic.

Adult children of alcoholics may narrate their lives differently than non-ACOAs (McCoy & Dunlop, 2017). The ACOAs story their lives with less agency, meaning that they did not view themselves as able to influence their lives in positive ways. While having the same amount of redemptive imagery in their life stories, they experienced them differently than non-ACOAs. The redemptive and agentic stories of ACOAs were related to poorer emotional functioning.

Growing up in an alcoholic family may also impact later occupational choice. This is because ACOAs tended to have expectations placed on them as children/adolescents to assume adult roles and have responsibilities to be caregivers either to the underfunctioning parents or their younger siblings (Vaught & Wittman, 2011). Because of these early responsibilities, ACOAs may not have engaged in normal child play like non-ACOAs, which can have a role in how they interact with peers and employers.

Perhaps one of the most lasting and negative consequences of growing up in an addicted family is the residue of unstable relationships. Adult children of alcoholics tend to be attracted to people who espouse the emotional qualities they were not able to demonstrate in their family of origin (Middleton-Moz & Dwinell, 2010). These qualities may later become points of contention when the ACOA, based on their desire to control the situation, tries to change them in the other person.

Adult children of alcoholics that present for treatment are likely to experience one or more of the following issues: guilt, shame, poor sense of self, fear of anger, denial, and likely use of substances and/or compulsive behavior (Markowitz, 2014). Therapists might assess for each of these to ensure a wide lens in which to understand the potential difficulties for a COA. One way of helping ACOAs is for them to develop a **cognitive life raft**. Middleton-Moz and Dwinell (2010) defined this as "an intellectual understanding of the emotional impact of growing up in an alcoholic and/or addicted family" (p. 99). In many ways, understanding the patterns and legacy of the past allows people to come to terms with their previous experience and to prevent it from taking such an unconscious hold on their current functioning. In the following section we will discuss another concept that enables ACOAs to survive and overcome their situation.

Resiliency

So far, we have talked about how children can be negatively impacted while growing up in an addicted family as well as in their life away from the family as adults. However, I want to end the chapter on a more positive note. While children growing up in families dealing with substance abuse are at risk for a variety of emotional and behavioral difficulties, not all experience these. Many children (and later when they become adults) come out of these families and succeed. Perhaps the distinguishing feature of this is having resilience. **Resilience** can be defined as "being able to overcome adverse situations and develop a positive self-image despite a difficult situation" (Mignon, Faiia, Myers, & Rubington, 2009, p. 194). As we have seen, children growing up in addicted families face the challenges that all children face, and they also deal with the excesses of stress, anger, disappointment, fear, and chaos that others who were raised in non-addicted families may not. Developing various means of resiliency is a key strategy for survival for many of these children.

In exploring a variety of studies focused on resiliencies for children who grew up in families where one or both parents had a substance use disorder, Wlodarczyk et al. (2017) categorized them into child-related, family and parental, and environmental factors. Child-related resiliencies and protective factors included both psychological and biological factors. Those who could positively engage adults, use coping strategies, and had certain biological responses had better mental health outcomes than those who did not have these conditions. Family and parental factors included strong family cohesion and adaptability, secure parent–child attachment, low parenting stress, and high parental support. Environmental factors that functioned as protective factors against later mental health negative outcomes included positive social support.

Wolin and Wolin (1993) listed seven resiliencies that can help children living in troubled families: insight, independence, relationships, initiative, creativity,

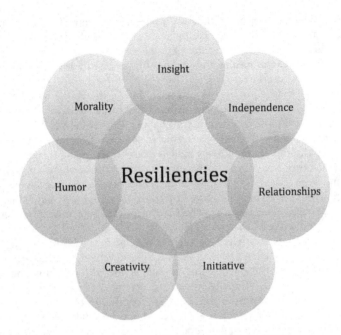

Figure 7.4 The seven resiliencies proposed by Wolin and Wolin (1993)

humor, and morality (see Figure 7.4). **Insight** is the ability of the person to explore and be honest with themselves. It includes sensing, knowing, and understanding. The child can *sense* danger in the family based on people straying from the safe norm. Sensing then shifts into *knowing*, where the child takes in the larger picture of what is happening in the family and how that is impacting them. As the child becomes an adult they develop *understanding*—of who they are and their relationships with others.

The resiliency of **independence** includes straying, disengaging, and separating. In troubled families there is a pull for togetherness that can be overwhelming. Children who are able to engage in some type of independence have the potential for more successful functioning. This happens first in terms of the child *straying* from the family conflict, where they remove themselves from the center of chaos. The further they stray, the more the child feels comfortable and can begin to *disengage* emotionally from the family. As adults they are able to *separate* themselves from the family—by being able to choose their own path rather than getting swept away in the family's troubles.

Relationships—positive relationships—connect us to other people in meaningful ways. They allow people to be affirmed as a unique individual; one who can love and is worthy of love. The resiliency of relationships grows over time from connecting, to recruiting, and then to attaching. As children, resiliency is aided by the child finding and *connecting* to meaningful adults. These early connections tend to be somewhat sporadic, but help to establish a foundation of inner worthiness. This foundation allows the child to actively seek out and *recruit* people to engage in a relationship, many times as a parent substitute. This adult may be a neighbor, teacher, or extended family member. As the child moves into adulthood, recruitment changes into *attaching*, where the individual is able to hold and maintain long-term meaningful relationships where there is a balanced give and take of due concern.

Resilient individuals are also skilled at **initiative**; the ability to take control of their environment. This happens through exploring, working, and generating. Growing up in addicted families is chaotic. The resilient child will engage in *exploring*, finding very small ways to have some control in the environment. This may be through keeping items hidden from others, going through parents' drawers, or other small experiments of initiative. During this time they start developing self-efficacy. Once they enter school, this exploring changes into *working*; perhaps in trying to achieve in school. As adults, these individuals tend to be able to engage in *generating*, where they are developing projects of personal satisfaction and self-growth.

The resiliencies of **creativity** and **humor** are related to each other. They each start with the child playing and then shaping. The development of creativity then moves through composing while that of humor goes through laughing. These resiliencies are located internally, where the person uses her imagination as a safe place to move away from the chaos and conflict in the family. Creativity and humor begin with *playing*, where the child imagines themself to be someone else; perhaps a superhero, princess, doctor, or firefighter. In adolescence, playing becomes *shaping*, where the individual engages in some form of art. This may be painting, music, poetry, or dance. In adulthood, the resiliency of creativity is developed through a shift from shaping to *composing*, producing an active product, where their art has become a skill. For the resilience of humor, shaping becomes *laughing*, where the person is able to take misery and absurdity and find a way to laugh at what happened.

The last resilience we will talk about is **morality**, which occurs through the person's life through judging, valuing, and serving. Morality is the process of trying to be good—to one's self and to others. As children, individuals may feel wronged and try to figure out and *judge* the rights and wrongs of what occurred. When the child grows into an adolescent, they then engage in *valuing* various principles to live by; such as honesty, caring, and helping. This leads them to focus on helping other people; especially those who have been wronged. In adulthood, this resiliency comes out via *serving*, where the person devotes time and energy to others, such as volunteering—perhaps working in a soup kitchen, homeless shelter, or other such community-based organizations.

People who survive troubled families may have one, several, or all of these resiliencies working for them. Depending on how chaotic the family is, the same level of resilience in one person may not help to prevent trouble as it might in someone else whose family situation was a little more stable. These resiliencies can be enhanced, with parents or adult mentors helping to build them throughout the child's development. Further, those children who receive professional interventions (i.e., parenting skills training, individual and group interventions) are more likely to connect to the various resiliencies available to them (VanDeMark et al., 2005).

Case Application

The Rothers family is a remarried family that is somewhat unique in that all of the children who live in the home are the biological children of the two adults. While technically the family is a step-family, they do not function as one since there is extremely minimal interaction between Nina, Mark's biological child from his first marriage, and Mark and the other children. So, in many ways, the Rothers family life cycle conforms to that of the typical North American family. Although this is a second marriage for Mark, and a first marriage for Hannah, they still married earlier than the median age of men and women for first marriage in the United States.

The family currently finds themselves in the stage of families with adolescents. This is the point in the family life cycle where parents usually begin to allow more autonomy for the adolescent, preparing him or her for being able to function independently in the single young adult stage. However, this process may be hampered in the Rothers family as addicted families usually maintain more rigid boundaries both within the family and between the family and larger systems. In order to provide more autonomy, boundaries need to become clearer, allowing more flexibility and negotiation between subsystems. Further, Mark and Hannah may not be as likely to allow Steve, the oldest of the children, increasing levels of freedom since he is frequently acting out and getting into trouble at both home and school. Steve's acting out would likely lead the parents to try to develop more rigid boundaries, where they are better able to assert their parental authority rather than allowing him more say in his development. Thus, we might expect that there will be quite a delay in the Rothers family in their transition from a family with young children to a family with adolescents where boundary flexibility might be stunted. This may lead to later difficulties for one or more of the children when they move into the single young adult stage, in that they might not be able to handle well the challenges of individual choice making and autonomy.

While we do not know much about Hannah's family of origin, we would need to consider whether Mark and Hannah find themselves in the sandwich generation. We know they are caring for their own children and there is the likelihood that each of their parents has either retired or is close to retirement. Depending on their physical and psychological health, Mark and Hannah may need to put energy into thinking about and caring for their aging parents.

We can hypothesize that the Rothers family finds itself in the family addiction cycle. In all likelihood, there are times when Mark does not drink as much and begins to interact with the family. When this happens, Hannah may find that the tension is not as severe and she might let her frustration and anger out at him around non-drinking issues, such as his cleanliness around the house or his disciplining of the children. We would then likely see Mark increasing his drinking and Hannah backing off on her criticisms of him. Instead, Mark and Hannah would likely focus their attention on Steve's misbehaviors.

Steve, Kayleigh, and Pete can be considered to be children of alcoholics. This is a family experience that is multigenerational in the Rothers family as there is alcoholism for several generations on the paternal side of the family. While it is usually the oldest child who becomes parentified, that is not the case in this family.

If anyone is parentified, it would be Kayleigh, helping Hannah to look after Pete. Out of the four primary problems that COAs experience, the Rothers are dealing with acting-out behaviors, difficult emotional reactions, and some social and interpersonal difficulties. Each of the children may be experiencing various aspects of low self-esteem, manifesting differently in each person. While Steve is the only child currently engaging in externalizing behavior problems, all may be internalizing their pain, which will likely have a serious negative impact at some point in their lives, whether it be depression, lack of confidence, or poor interpersonal relationships.

While things may seem grim for the members of the Rothers family, all hope is not lost as they likely have various resiliencies that can help them weather the storm of addiction. Kayleigh seems to have the ability to positively engage adults while Kayleigh and Pete both have a secure parent–child attachment with Hannah. The more that all of the children utilize their various resiliencies, such as creativity, humor, and positive relationships, the greater the likelihood that they will be able to overcome the risk factors of growing up in an addicted family.

Summary

This chapter presented a way to view the developmental growth of the family and how that growth can be hampered when addiction is involved. As children, living in an addicted family can have many deleterious effects. Children of alcoholics face a range of behavioral, psychological, and emotional challenges that non-COAs usually do not come across. As adults, the legacy of the addicted family will usually still be present. Adult COAs find challenges in employment and their own adult relationships. However, the more resiliencies present, especially from when the person is young, the better able the person is to survive and to grow into a well-functioning person.

Key Words

single young adult
the new couple
families with young children
the sandwich generation
launching children
families in later life
children of alcoholics (COA)
parentification
attachment
externalizing behavior problems
internalizing behavior problems

adult children of alcoholics
   (ACOA)
cognitive life raft
resilience
insight
independence
relationships
initiative
creativity
humor
morality

Discussion Questions

1. How might families adhere to the typical progression in the family life cycle?
2. What are some factors that would lead families not to follow the standard family life cycle?
3. How does addiction impact each stage of the family life cycle?
4. What are some of the main factors when exploring children of alcoholics?
5. What are some of the main factors when exploring adult children of alcoholics?
6. Discuss the seven types of resiliency. What impact do they have for a person living within an addicted family?

EIGHT

Issues in Substance-Abusing Families

We previously talked about how families are both universal and idiosyncratic. The processes that form and maintain a family happen in all families (thus, families are universal); however, how these processes happen is unique to each family (thus, families are idiosyncratic). In substance-abusing families, there are many issues that tend to be present. Yet not all of these difficulties are present in every family. In this chapter we will cover some of the common issues, outside the actual addiction, that you may need to assess when you know that one or more family members is dealing with some type of substance abuse.

The chapter starts with perhaps the most common of these issues, that of domestic violence. While many families where alcohol is not involved have some type of domestic violence, it tends to be more prevalent the more severe the substance abuse. We then move to a more severe form of violence, that of child sexual abuse. The chapter then shifts to a potential issue when the pregnant mother drinks alcohol, leading to the possibility of fetal alcohol syndrome disorder. In many ways this can be considered a form of child abuse. Next, we cover the prevalence of the association between substance abuse and criminal behavior. The chapter then provides a widening of the assessment lens by exploring the phenomenon of people tending to not only have a substance abuse disorder but also having a mental health disorder—what is called dual diagnosis. We then end the chapter focusing on how we can view how ready individuals and families are for change, as well as ways of enhancing motivation.

Domestic Violence

Domestic violence is an extremely serious issue for families around the world. The abuse can be from a parent to a child—what we will call **child abuse**—or from an adult to an adult—what we will call **intimate partner violence** (IPV). According to the National Coalition Against Domestic Violence (2014), in the United States approximately 20 people experience intimate partner violence every minute. Annually, this accounts for 10 million victims of abuse per year. One in four women and one in nine men experience IPV. Thirty-three percent of women and 25% of men have been the victims of IPV over the course of their lives. When one or more members in a family is abusing substances there is an increased risk of domestic violence occurring in the family. The American Society of Addiction Medicine reported that 40–60% of domestic violence incidents also involve substance abuse. Although the use of alcohol and other drugs does not necessitate that IPV will happen, addiction is one of the causal agents of violence in the family (Flanzer, 2005; Leonard & Quigley, 2017). Flanzer provided some of the intervening variables when examining the role of alcohol/drugs and IPV:

- alcohol as an instigator of violence;
- alcohol as a disinhibitor of social control;
- alcohol's destruction of the normal growth and development of the individual and the family system;
- alcohol as a rationalization for violence;
- alcohol's alteration of brain functioning (p. 170).

Taken individually or together, these factors set the stage for an increased risk that families dealing with addiction will come in contact with IPV.

While not all IPV occurs with the male being the perpetrator and the female the victim (in heterosexual relationships), this is the most reported type of dynamic and will be used as the framework to discuss this issue. However, I want to be clear that domestic violence can take any combination: male-to-female, male-to-male, female-to-male, and female-to-female. It can be from adult-to-adult, adult-to-child, child-to-child, child-to-adult, child-to-elder adult, or adult-to-elder adult. Whichever form it takes, violence in a family has the potential for very deleterious effects—to the point of incarceration and death.

There are many forms of domestic violence. For purposes of clarity in this section, we will focus primarily on adult–adult violence (see the next section for a discussion on child abuse). Patterson et al. (2009) estimate that violence of some type is prevalent in 15–20% of all families. In families with some type of substance abuse, this percentage will be higher as there is a significant relationship between IPV and substance use and abuse (Cafferky, Mendez, Anderson, & Stith, 2018). In general, we can look at five forms of domestic violence: physical, sexual, psychological, emotional, and economic.

Power and Control

Many people have looked at domestic violence through the lens of power and control. One way of viewing this is looking at the Power and Control Wheel (see Figure 8.1), developed at the Domestic Abuse Intervention Project. Through their work with women who had been abused, they developed a model of how male batterers utilize various tactics to try to control their female partners.

At the heart of the wheel is power and control. These are the spokes of the wheel and are the main intention of the abuser. On the outside of the wheel is physical and sexual violence. Inside the wheel are eight pathways that the abuser utilizes to maintain power and control: using intimidation; using emotional abuse; using isolation, minimizing, denying and blaming; using children; using male privilege; using economic abuse; and using coercion and threats.

The **physical form of domestic violence** is the most recognizable of the types. It is the most visual, as it tends to leave bruises and scars. In IPV, one person

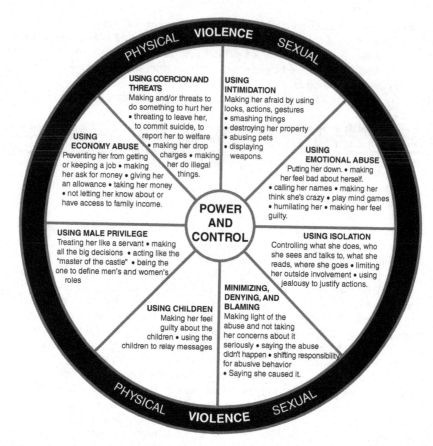

Figure 8.1 The Power and Control Wheel

attempts to inflict bodily harm on another person. This may be in the form of hitting, slapping, biting, kicking, or using an object against the other person such as hitting the other with a piece of electrical cord, stabbing them with a knife, etc. The consequences of this type of abuse are visual and may result in the victim needing medical attention. Perhaps a broken bone or severe lacerations lead them to seek emergency room treatment, which can cause a major conflict as the victim may try to protect the abuser through developing a false story as to how they incurred their injuries. However, only about 34% of victims of IPV seek out medical treatment.

Sexual domestic violence mainly occurs when one person attempts to engage in any type of sexual contact with another without that person's consent. A common misconception is that rape is usually committed by a stranger to the victim. According to the National Health and Social Life Survey, most rape is committed by someone the victim is in love with (46%), knows well (22%), or who is a spouse (9%) rather than a stranger (4%). It has only been in the last few decades that there has been an awareness that rape can happen within a marital relationship. Relational rape also occurs in same-sex relationships, although that accounts for only 1% of all statutory rape incidents (Chaffin, Chenoweth, & Letourneau, 2016).

The **psychological type of domestic violence** occurs when a partner tries to instill fear in the other. This may happen through threats of violence or breaking household items. For instance, a husband may break plates on the floor while screaming at his wife. Although he never laid a finger on his wife, he still promoted an atmosphere of aggression. A second type of psychological abuse is when the partner attempts to isolate the victim. Here, the victim is told not to talk with friends, co-workers, or even family members.

Emotional violence is when one partner belittles the other partner. This is usually through name-calling, cursing at, and insulting the person. In this situation, as a means to keep her in the relationship, a husband may frequently tell his wife that she is stupid and ugly and that no one would ever want her. The intent is to lower the victim's self-esteem and assert control over them.

The fifth type of domestic violence is **economic abuse**. In this situation, the abuser is in command of the finances. Even if the victim works, the abuser will gain control of the money in the house. The partner would then have to go through them to get any money to use. The abuser may then only provide a small allowance for the victim, thus asserting greater control over the person and making it more difficult for the victim to leave the relationship since they do not have access to money.

While drugs and alcohol play one role in the etiology of domestic violence, there are many other possible causes. These include views on gender roles, cultural upbringing, psychological well-being, and other situational variables. Any or some of these (and other) factors converge to present a possibility for violence in the home. However, there may be differing motivation for the violence. Greene and Bogo (2002) distinguish between two types of violence; patriarchal terrorism and common couple violence. **Patriarchal terrorism** is about control. The perpetrator of the violence is using it as a means to wield authority and control over the victim. It is usually engaged in as a coping mechanism to ensure some type of stability for the individual. **Common couple violence**, on the other hand, is not about control, but is part of an escalation of conflict. In this type, either partner may initiate the violence.

Just as addiction starts slow and builds up, violence does as well. Intimate partner violence is a process; it does not start the minute that the two adults first meet. It occurs slowly over time, building up to where the abuser shifts from a subtle to more overt form of abuse. This leads to confusion for the victim as the beginning of their relationship most likely did not contain the severity of abuse that happens later. By slowly asserting power and control in the relationship, the victim has usually developed caring feelings and dependence on the abuser.

While there may only be one cycle of abuse between members of a couple, usually there are many cycles that connect over time with one another. As each cycle happens, the abuse tends to escalate so that the abuse in the first cycle between the couple is not as severe as the most recent episode. For instance, two months into the relationship the couple may have a fight and the man calls the woman a degrading name. Several months later he may begin to try to isolate her from friends and family. Perhaps a few months later he may slap her during a verbal conflict. Each incident becomes a stepping-stone leading to heightened escalation of abusive behavior as the abuser still does not feel like they have power and control in the relationship.

The cycle of abuse begins with what might be considered normal behavior. The couple is able to interact in what seems to be a peaceful environment. At some point in time the abuser believes his partner has wronged him in some fashion (perhaps by not listening to what he has told her to do or engaging with people outside of the relationship such as friends or family). The cycle then moves into the fantasy and planning phase where the abuser develops a scenario of how he will let the person know of their offense. The third phase is the setting-up of the plan. Fourth, the abuse, in whatever fashion (physical, emotional, etc.) occurs. The next phase is guilt, where the abuser feels guilty, usually to reduce the chance of the victim reporting the offense or leaving. This is where the abuser would probably apologize. The next phase is one of excuses, where the person rationalizes why the abuse happened, usually blaming the victim for putting them in a position where they had to do what they did. Lastly is a honeymoon stage where the relationship seems to be calm, which is also the first stage of the next cycle that may come in a few days, weeks, or months. This process is visualized in Figure 8.2.

This process can also be viewed within three phases: tension building, abuse, and honeymoon. In the **tension building phase** the abuser feels tension and begins to escalate insults and threats. The victim at this time minimizes the tension.

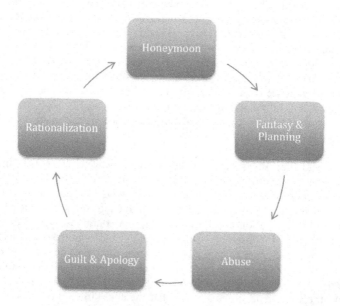

Figure 8.2 The cycle of abuse where each subsequent cycle escalates in severity of the abuse

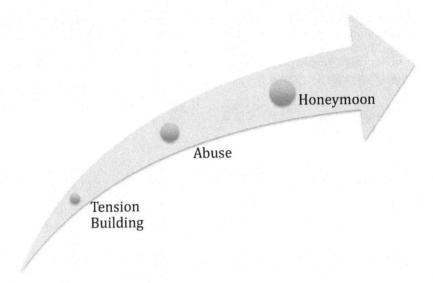

Figure 8.3 The tension building process of domestic violence

During the second phase, called **abuse**, the abuser reacts to a sense of losing control by increasing the intensity of threats to the victim. The victim is unsure of what to do and does not know how to reduce the tension or leave the environment. At this point the abuse incident occurs. Lastly is the **honeymoon phase**. Here the abuser becomes very apologetic and loving. The victim is confused as she was just hurt (physically and emotionally) yet she sees before her the potential of what the person might be if they did not exhibit the controlling/violent side of their actions. This three phase model is presented in Figure 8.3.

When assessing for domestic violence, clients are usually hesitant to disclose on first inquiry. This is especially the case in couples or family sessions. Because one of the main aspects of domestic violence is intimidation, the victim may be very reticent to openly acknowledge the abuse in front of the abusing partner. As such, one possibility in sessions is to see members separately, at least for the assessment interview or first session.

Child Abuse

So far we have primarily focused on adult-to-adult violence. However, children are also in the line of fire of violence when alcohol and other drugs are involved in a family system. Children in drug-using homes are at risk for physical and/or sexual abuse, as 25% of child abuse victims had adults who engaged in substance abuse (www.acf.hhs.gov). This subset of the family is referred to as **children of alcoholics** (see Chapter 7 for an in-depth discussion of COAs).

Data from the National Child Abuse and Neglect Data Systems showed that in 2016 there were approximately 7.4 million children involved in allegations of child maltreatment, which included abuse or neglect. Of these investigations, 676,000 were substantiated or indicated as maltreatment with over 388,000 victims receiving postresponse services. Younger children are at higher risk of maltreatment as each year of life the number of children abused decreased.

98,393 < 1

47,583 – 1 year old

44,800 – 2

42,045 – 3

40,312 – 4

39,773 – 5

39,990 – 6

38,900 – 7

36,776 – 8

33,848 – 9

30,529 – 10

28,155 – 11

27,544 – 12

27,560 – 13

26,784 – 14

23,303 – 15

15,334 – 16

2,493 – 17

671,622 – Total

Of these children 27.1% were 2 years old or younger, 19.6% 3–5, 16.4% 6–8, 13.7% 9–11, 12.9% 12–14, and 10.3% 15–17. There was also a distinction on who was abused based on race (44.9% White, 22% Hispanic, and 20.7% African-American). Although the total number is lower than other ethnic groups, American Indian or Alaska Native children had the highest rate of victimization. There does not seem to be a difference in child abuse as a whole in reference to gender (48.6% were boys and 51.1% girls—the gender was not reported for the remaining percentage). While a majority of abuse cases came under the subset of neglect, 17.6% of these children were physically abused while 9.1% were sexually abused. Of child maltreatment cases, 74.8% were categorized as neglect while 18.2% were physical abuse. It is estimated that in 2016, 1,750 children died from abuse or neglect.

While not all child abuse is perpetrated by the parents, an overwhelming percentage is (81%). Over 83% of perpetrators of child maltreatment were between the ages of 18 and 44. Further, over 53% were women and just over 45% were men (the other 1% were of unknown sex). Ethnically, Whites accounted for almost 50% of perpetrators, African-Americans 20%, and Hispanics almost 19%. Of victims of child maltreatment, 11.5% had a caregiver suffering from alcohol abuse and 28.5% had a caregiver dealing with drug abuse.

Even if the abuse is not directed at the child, witnessing IPV and being exposed to the various incidents of domestic conflict has serious implications (Jaffe, Wolfe, & Campbell, 2012). Witnessing IPV may be almost or as damaging emotionally to a child as being the actual victim. According to the NCADV, each year, 1 in 15 children are exposed to IPV, with 90% of these children being an eyewitness to the violence. Eiden et al. (2009) found that children living in a house with alcoholic fathers who engaged in marital aggression with their wives had higher levels of anxiety and depression than children who did not witness IPV. While externalizing their problems (acting out and getting in trouble at home or at school) is more common for children in conflictual alcoholic families, they may internalize problems resulting in psychological and/or emotional difficulties such as anxiety and depression.

As discussed in Chapter 5, the substance-dependent adult will most likely begin to abdicate their parenting responsibilities. This leaves the possibility that the children in the family may become neglected. Since alcoholics tend to have a low frustration tolerance, becoming autocratic and blaming others (Flanzer, 2005), they may utilize corporal punishment and violence as response mechanisms when dealing with their children.

Child Sexual Abuse

Witnessing the violence of adults has negative impacts on the child during childhood, which can endure into adulthood. When the child is the victim of the abuse, and specifically when the abuse moves from being emotional or physical to sexual, there may be more severe consequences. When the familial abuse becomes sexual it is considered **incest**.

Incest can take many forms in a family, such as father–daughter, father–son, mother–daughter, mother–son, sibling–sibling, grandparent–grandchild, or other configurations (i.e., uncle–niece). The most common of these is the father–daughter form of incest. According to the U.S. Department of Health and Human Services, in 2011 there were over 61,000 cases of child sexual abuse. Of these, 48% of the children were 12 or older.

The harm of child sexual abuse occurs not only in the present but in the future as well. People who were sexually abused as children have a higher likelihood than those who did not, when they are older, of problematic drinking, the potential for sexual revictimization, and riskier sexual practices (Sartor et al., 2008). Having been a victim of sexual abuse as a child, the person is more at risk for the use of cigarettes and cannabis as well as the abuse being a strong predictor of early drinking of alcohol (Sartor et al., 2013).

Therapist Responsibility

As a therapist you are ethically obligated to report suspected abuse or neglect of children or elders. Given that children living in addicted homes are at greater risk for being abused (this includes neglect and psychological or physical maltreatment), therapists should pay special attention to this possibility. Assessment is critical at an early stage, as well as being clear with family members about your role and your obligations regarding confidentiality and reporting (see Chapter 11 for a more in-depth discussion of therapeutic ethics and confidentiality).

The most important thing for the therapist to keep in mind is family members' safety. This can be difficult in some families since the abuse has become part of the family's homeostasis and an accepted way of being. Although it shifts the therapist's position from service provider to more of a control agent, the welfare of family members, especially children, takes precedence. The therapist can be very overt about the assessment, asking family members if violence is present in the family. Some possible questions to ask include:

- Has there been any type of violence in the family?
- When you become very angry, how do you tend to engage others in the family?
- Are there any weapons in the house?

However, therapists need to be ready to act on the information they receive—be it calling the child protection services in the area if there is abuse present or developing a safety plan if one or more members feel fearful.

Given that addicted families tend to operate based on secrets, the family therapist may consider, especially in the first session, to meet with each member separately and then the family as a whole. Being alone with the therapist may allow a family member to discuss what is going on in the house without fear of the abuser while they are saying this. Separated sessions may also be used in addicted families to try to counteract some of the underlying rules of maintaining secrets.

Fetal Alcohol Abuse Syndrome

As discussed in Chapter 2, the substances that we utilize have direct impact on our brain. Whatever consequences they have for us, there is the possibility that they can also effect a fetus if the substance user is pregnant. For pregnant women who are abusing alcohol, they run the risk of giving birth to a child with **fetal alcohol abuse syndrome (FAS)**. Originally called fetal alcohol syndrome, it was later referred to as fetal alcohol abuse syndrome to reflect that it was not alcohol but the abuse of alcohol that causes the pattern of abnormalities the fetuses acquire (Abel, 1998). Thus, a pregnant woman who drinks one glass of alcohol will not cause FAS. It takes a pattern of heavy episodic consumption. However, heightened use of alcohol in the last trimester of pregnancy may have the most severe effects. One area of optimism is that FAS does not need to occur as FAS is the most preventable cause of birth defect and developmental disabilities (Mohammad, 2016).

Fetal Alcohol Syndrome Disorder (FASD) can be broken down into three types, depending on the symptoms of the individual. The primary type is Fetal Alcohol Syndrome. This is the most severe of the FASD types—and the most severe outcome of this is fetal death. The second FASD type is Alcohol-Related Neurodevelopmental Disorder where the individual has some type of intellectual disability. This usually leads to the child having learning and behavior problems in school. The third FASD type is Alcohol-Related Birth Defects. Here, the newborn may have physiological problems with their heart, lungs, kidneys, or other organ or bodily systems.

There is usually a major change in women's consumption of alcohol once they become pregnant (Armstrong, 2003). Before becoming pregnant, 61% of women do not drink alcohol at all, 29% engage in low consumption (fewer than three drinks per week), 9% have medium use (3 to 13 drinks per week), and 1% engage in high alcohol consumption (14 or more drinks). However, once pregnant, these percentages change drastically; 83% of women have no alcohol use, 15% low consumption, 2% medium, and 0.5% high consumption. While these are very positive data, where 83% of women do not drink during pregnancy, 2.5% still engage in medium to high usage.

The good news is that FASD and FAS do not occur that often. The bad news is that they occur. According to the Centers for Disease Control and Prevention (www.cdc.gov), FAS occurs in approximately 0.2 to 1.5 cases per 1,000 live births. Since FASD has a somewhat wider catchment, it is estimated that there are three times as many FASD cases than FAS cases. There is not a direct correspondence between the amount of alcohol consumption and a specific impact on the fetus. As Pagliaro and Pagliaro (2012) explained, **teratogenesis** (the process of embryonic or fetal congential malformations) occurs through a multitude of factors including drug/substance factors, maternal factors, placental factors, time factors, environmental factors, and fetal factors (see Figure 8.4). This is why

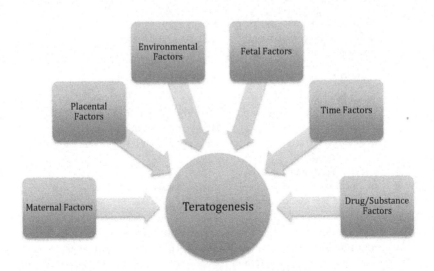

Figure 8.4 The various factors that impact the level of teratogenesis

the same amount of repeated consumption by two different pregnant women can lead to very different results.

Fetal Alcohol Syndrome Disorder requires that the mother drinks heavily during pregnancy. There are many factors that lead to a woman drinking at high risk factors during pregnancy (Armstrong, 2003). For instance, Black women have the highest odds of high-risk drinking (2%), then all other races (1.4%), with White women having odds of 1%. Those who have not finished their high school degree have higher odds of risky drinking. However, as women get older, the odds of high-risk drinking during pregnancy increases (with women over 35 at 1.7%, whereas women under 20 are just below 0.5%). Married and single women have just about the same odds of high-risk drinking, but the biggest difference comes in family income. The lower the family income the higher the risk of drinking during pregnancy (3.1% for those under $10,000; 2.25% for family income between $10,000–$19,000; 1.6% for income between $20,000–$34,000; and 1% for family income over $35,000).

In 1996 the Institute of Medicine developed diagnostic criteria for FAS Category 1. These included:

A. Confirmed maternal alcohol consumption:

- excessive drinking characterized by considerable, regular, or heavy episodic consumption.

B. Characteristic facial features include:

- short palpebral fissures;
- characteristic premaxillary features, e.g., flat upper lip, flattened philtrum, flat midface.

C. Growth retardation:

- decreased birth weight for gestational age;
- failure to thrive postnatally not related to nutrition;
- disproportionate ratio of weight to height.

D. CNS abnormalities, including at least one of the following:

- small head size;
- structural abnormalities, e.g., small brain, partial or complete absence of corpus callosum, decreased size of cerebellum;
- neurological hard or soft signs (age appropriate), such as impairment of fine motor skills;
- neurosensory hearing loss;
- incoordination;
- impaired eye–hand coordination.

Not all of these characteristics will be present in a child born with FAS, which makes diagnosing it difficult as there is not a specific test that can be given but a confluence of symptoms. To reiterate, these symptoms are prenatal exposure to alcohol, abnormal facial features, lower-than-average birth weight and/or height, and central nervous system problems.

Children with FASD are born into a situation that is extremely complex, as they must face individual difficulties (such as learning, motor skills, social skills, and attention deficits) as well as social difficulties. Their development is also hampered by being born with physiological impairments (e.g., low birth weight or depressed immune function). However, what makes these symptoms even more problematic is that the FASD child is likely born into a family that is currently dysfunctional.

One of the distinguishing features of FAS is growth retardation. This may happen at two points in the individual's life; prenatally or postnatally. Prenatally, these growth anomalies will be visible at birth including low birth weight (less than the 10th percentile). However, symptoms of growth retardation can also begin displaying themselves after birth—postnatally. These symptoms include reduced height or weight at any point in the person's development. When there is heavy prenatal alcohol exposure, the child, when born, may experience severe damage to the central nervous system—which will include the cerebellum, basal ganglia, and cerebral cortex (Nguyen et al., 2012). One deficit of this damage will come in the form of difficulties in fine motor activity.

Unfortunately there is no "cure" for FASD. However, the earlier the child receives intervention, the greater the chance to improve the child's development. The Center for Disease Control suggests possible treatment options including medications for various symptoms, parent training, and behavior and education therapy. The child will most likely need the inclusion of various social services and special education access as well as frequent medical care. Children with FASD can have better outcomes when there are family-focused interventions in place (Reid et al., 2017). These interventions may include focusing on self-regulatory skills of the child with FASD, incorporation of mindfulness-based techniques, and improvement of the parent–child relationship. Wilhoit, Scott, and Simecka (2017) concurred, stating that children with FASD have the best outcomes when their family collaborates with school, therapists, and medical professionals.

Criminality and Substance Abuse

There is a high correlation between substance use and criminal behavior (Diehl et al., 2016; Nam, Matejkowski, & Lee, 2016; Newbury-Birch et al., 2016). Diehl et al. found that approximately 27% of people in treatment for substance abuse had engaged in criminal behavior. These crimes were more against people rather than property. Newbury-Birch et al. found much higher rates, with rates of over 64% of those in police custody, 53% in probation settings, 60% in the prison system, and 64% of young people in the criminal justice system having an alcohol use disorder.

Much work with substance abusers, especially adolescents, is geared toward reducing their substance use as well as reducing the risk for criminal activity to prevent their involvement in the juvenile justice system. However, youth do find themselves involved in the juvenile justice system. There are many evidence-based programs for youth who are in the juvenile justice system to help them reduce substance use as well as reduce criminal behavior. These include several that will be presented in Chapter 15, including Brief strategic family therapy, Multidimensional family therapy, and Multisystemic therapy. Other programs include Alcohol Treatment Targeting Adolescents In Need (ATTAIN), Adolescent Contingency Management (Adol CM), Familias Unidas, and Motivational Enhancement Therapy + Cognitive-Behavioral Therapy (MET-CBT). Each of these programs have juvenile justice youth as their target population, but they may have different inclusion criteria based on age, severity of substance use and criminal issues, as well as ethnicity. The programs also differ based on the number of sessions and treatment aims. For example, Multidimensional therapy typically lasts three to six months while MET-CBT typically lasts five to seven sessions. Dauria, McWilliams, and Tolou-Shams (2018) summarized some of the key elements for empirically supported interventions when working with substance-abusing juvenile justice clients, which included cultural consideration, motivation enhancement, family involvement, and a focus on co-occuring disorders.

For adults who engage in illegal activity, they may find themselves involved in the criminal justice system and perhaps even incarcerated, leading to physical separation from the family. Miller and Miller (2016) explained that a majority of inmates in state and federal prisons have substance abuse histories. Some criminal offenders engage in diversionary programs where they take part in substance abuse treatment as a way to avoid prison time or reduce the amount of time served. Depending on the correctional institution, treatment programs for substance abuse may or may not be available. These programs occur within the correctional institution, which may make it difficult to include family. Lemieux (2009) explained that families of criminal offenders with substance abuse issues have been underutilized as a resource for change. This is unfortunate since a focus on the family is in line with the principles of correctional systems.

Approximately 3–11% of jail and prison inmates have a dual diagnosis (see the next section), where they have both a substance abuse issue and a mental disorder (Ruiz et al., 2007). Usually there are more programs in prisons than in jails as prisons have more resources and have the inmate incarcerated for longer periods of time. Peters, Wexler, and Lurigio (2015) explained that incarceration for those with dual diagnosis tends not to be effective. Rather than incarceration, they suggested that this population would be better served through community-level treatment.

Lemieux (2009) provided six levels of involvement when matching family-based interventions to correctional settings (see Figure 8.5). Each level builds on the strategies of the previous level, based on the correctional institute's resources and access to the families. Level 1 includes staff awareness and education. Level 2 focuses on client education. Level 3 addresses education of the family. Level 4 provides referral, usually to family support groups. Level 5 involves family collaboration, helping the family with crisis intervention and problem solving. Level 6 integrates family therapy into the treatment.

Treatment for substance abusers in the criminal justice system is designed to reduce or eliminate problematic substance use as well as to prevent recidivism. Substance abuse treatment seems to be more effective for older rather than younger individuals, and for females rather than for males in preventing a subsequent arrest (Kopak et al., 2016). These authors found that risk of re-arrest was higher for young males who continued to engage in drug use. These authors suggested that treatment considerations include helping this population to gain employment and move toward abstinence.

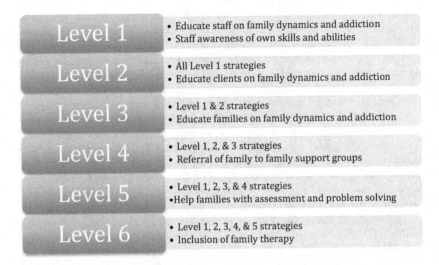

Level 1
- Educate staff on family dynamics and addiction
- Staff awareness of own skills and abilities

Level 2
- All Level 1 strategies
- Educate clients on family dynamics and addiction

Level 3
- Level 1 & 2 strategies
- Educate families on family dynamics and addiction

Level 4
- Level 1, 2, & 3 strategies
- Referral of family to family support groups

Level 5
- Level 1, 2, 3, & 4 strategies
- Help families with assessment and problem solving

Level 6
- Level 1, 2, 3, 4, & 5 strategies
- Inclusion of family therapy

Figure 8.5 The six levels of involvement for family-based interventions in correctional settings

Dual Diagnosis

Dual diagnosis—also called *co-occurring disorders* or *comorbidity*—is when two mental disorders are present at the same time. When two or more disorders occur simultaneously, they are considered to be **comorbid**. The presence of a substance abuse disorder along with a mental health disorder is quite high. According to the 2016 National Survey on Drug Use and Health, 43% of adults who experienced a substance abuse disorder in the past year had a co-occurring disorder. This worked out to 8.2 million people. Only 16% of adults without a diagnosed substance disorder in the past year had any mental illness. For those with co-occurring disorders, most fall within the 18 to 25 year old range. The percentage decreases significantly for people over 50 years of age. Mason et al. (2016) noted that 1.4% of adolescents in the U.S. had a dual diagnosis in the past year. However, that number jumps to over 50% for those involved in substance abuse treatment. For these adolescents, the co-occurring psychiatric disorder tends to be externalizing disorders such as conduct disorder or attention deficit hyperactivity disorder. Yet, there are still a significant number with internalizing disorders such as depression and anxiety disorders.

Comorbidity does not mean that one disorder causes another. However, they usually interact with one another in some fashion. For instance, someone might have a diagnosis of major depression while also having a diagnosis of cocaine addiction. Neither caused the other, however they happen to be occurring at the same time. Yet, when there is comorbidity, there is usually a higher impairment for both disorders (Mason et al., 2016). Substance abuse disorder is the most prominent disorder involved in dual diagnosis. When alcohol use disorder is one of the dual diagnostic disorders, the other comorbid disorders tend to be attention deficit hyperactivity disorder, post traumatic stress disorder, anxiety disorders and mood disorders (Mulsow, 2007).

The two (or more) disorders that are involved in dual diagnosis can be viewed as being primary or secondary disorders. The distinction is which disorder had the earliest onset and whether they are independent of one another. For instance, if a client comes in with cocaine addiction and delusional disorder, the therapist would need to determine which of these two came first. Further, a primary disorder should not be based on the effects of the drugs that are being abused.

When working with a client who is dually diagnosed, the therapist will need to decide whether to address either diagnosis separately or at the same time. Many people believe that it is important to focus on the substance disorder first as that is the one that is more amenable to change. Someone can go cold turkey with the substance they are using (depending on the drug and their usage level) yet cannot do the same with a diagnosis such as bipolar disorder or panic attacks. According to the 2016 NSDUH survey, just over 48% of adults with a dual diagnosis received either substance abuse or mental health treatment. Almost 7% received both substance abuse and mental health care. While these data seem promising, it is still concerning that a majority of those with dual diagnosis received no treatment.

When looking at treatment, we can distinguish between partial, sequential, and parallel treatment (see Figure 8.6). **Partial treatment** focuses only on the diagnosis that the therapist believes is more imperative. **Sequential treatment** first focuses on the primary diagnosis and then, once that is addressed, on the secondary diagnosis. **Parallel treatment** targets both (or more) diagnoses at the same time. This has also been called integrated treatment. Some of the possible key features of integrated treatment include medication management, family work, self-help programs, psychoeducation, enhancing motivation, and relapse prevention (Scheffler, 2014).

For those clients who have a dual diagnosis, the therapist should be aware that things can quickly deteriorate. Watkins, Lewellen, and Barrett (2001) explained,

> Regardless of which disorder came first, dual disorders are difficult to treat because of the vicious cycle of the substance abuse worsening the coexisting disorder, which in turn increases the client's tendency to use drugs to relieve the discomfort of the coexisting disorder. (p. 137)

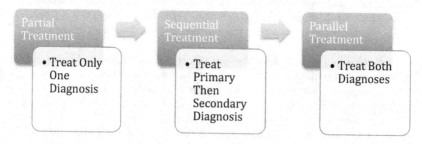

Figure 8.6 Treatment for dual diagnosis can be partial, sequential, or parallel

Thus, co-existing disorders are more problematic than either disorder separately. Further risk factors for this population are that they have low treatment attendance and high dropout rates (Thombs & Osborn, 2013). When a client does have a comorbid disorder, the likelihood that they complete treatment is reduced as compared with having only one disorder (Mulsow, 2007). They also have a greater chance of relapsing. One of the reasons for this is that their social support system—their family—experiences greater levels of stress, perhaps to the point of engaging in a cut-off with the addicted individual, which puts greater levels of stress on the substance abuser.

Family-based interventions for dual diagnosis have been found to be more effective than individual-based treatment (Mason et al., 2016). Scheffler (2014) explained that family involvement is important since families likely provide emotional, physical, and financial support for the client. The more the families of those with dual diagnosis are unsupportive and critical, the greater risk of relapse (Daley, Salloum, & Thase, 2003). When working with the family, the therapist will likely provide psychoeducation about both the substance abuse and the psychiatric diagnosis.

Despite understanding the impact that dual diagnosis has for the client and client's family, we also need to consider the role of the therapist. Pinderup (2017) stated that therapists have tended to have counterproductive attitudes toward clients with dual diagnosis. Pinderup found that therapists' attitudes changed considerably for the better when they were trained in areas surrounding dual diagnosis. This suggests that therapists working in the substance abuse field get additional training on the implications of treatment for those with dual diagnosis so that they can be the most effective.

Readiness for Change

When working with any client, but especially with those dealing with substance abuse, having an understanding of where they are on a continuum of acceptance of problems and desire of change is extremely important. Not all clients who enter therapy are at the same point of motivation for change. By understanding the client's perspective of whether and to what degree a problem exists, as well as their motivation in changing their own behavior, the therapist can more readily join the client where the client is at. This sets up a more collaborative therapeutic relationship.

There have been many different models for understanding a client's position in therapy. In this book we will present two models. In this chapter, we present the stages of readiness for change model that was originally developed by Prochaska and DiClemente and then further elaborated upon (Connors, Donovan, & DiClemente, 2001; DiClemente, 2003). In Chapter 15, you will read about a solution-focused view of client relationship types. At that point we will discuss how these two models overlap.

The **stages of readiness for change model** has changed over the years. When originally developed, Prochaska and DiClemente (1986) proposed a four-stage model that included precontemplation, contemplation, action, and maintenance. A fifth stage, called preparation, occurring before the action stage, was inserted

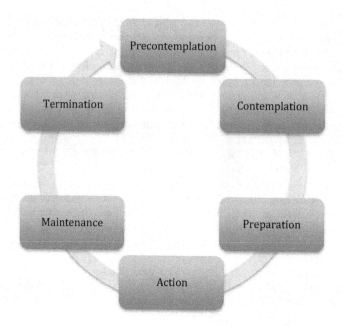

Figure 8.7 The circular process of the stages of readiness for change

to highlight how people get ready to make changes. A sixth stage was then added to the end of the process; termination (see Figure 8.7). However, many times when you come across this model in the literature you will not see this last stage.

The **Precontemplation** stage is when the individual does not think that they have a problem, and, as a consequence, they do not intend to change. For substance abusers this is usually toward the beginning and middle of their addiction. Although things have not completely deteriorated, the problems that have been occurring have been managed to some degree. Since this person does not view their drug use as being problematic, the therapist should not target behavioral change, as this will not make sense for the client (DiClemente, 2003). If the therapist pushed for the client to do something different, a rift would most likely be created between the client and therapist. Instead, therapists might consider using motivational strategies. To move from the precontemplation to the contemplation stage the person must first acknowledge that there is a problem and understand the negative consequences associated with it.

In the **contemplation** stage, the individual realizes that there is a problem yet they are not ready to make any proactive changes. In this stage, the person is doing a lot of thinking around their role in the problem and what the problem has brought to their life and what life will be like without it. They tend to try to find out more information, such as the course of the drug or what therapy might entail. While they are thinking about what change might look like, they are not yet prepared to engage in different behaviors. Therapists working with clients in the contemplation stage help clients in **consciousness raising**. To do this, the therapist might present educational information to the client about the effects of the drug of choice. The therapist may also encourage the client to reevaluate their connection to the drug and the associated consequences. This includes when, where, and with whom they use and the impact to self and others from this use. To move to the preparation stage, the client will need to get off the fence and decide that it is in their (and perhaps others') best interest to make a change.

People in the **preparation** stage are in a place in their life where they want change because there is an issue that they want different in their life. However, they have been unable to make changes in the last year (Prochaska, DiClemente, & Norcross, 1992). They do intend to begin taking action in the next month. This stage was originally called the decision-making stage because the individual has to come to grips with the problem as well as actually deciding to change their behaviors. There may be some very small changes made during this stage. The therapist helps the client to increase their commitment to moving toward a goal (usually a decrease or cessation of the drug use). Before moving into the action stage the client needs to set clear goals and develop a plan of action to get there.

The **action** stage is the implementation of the decision to change that occurred in the preparation stage. Here, individuals are actively altering their behaviors to address whatever problem they were encountering in their lives. Besides moving toward some goal, the person is also learning how to ensure that the problem does not return. The therapist working with a client in this stage is able to give direct action tasks, since the client is ready and motivated to move toward change. Before moving to the maintenance stage, the person will most likely have made and sustained the changes; approximately for six months (DiClemente, 2003). While therapists would likely prefer their clients to be in the action stage (or even maintenance and termination), most people dealing with addictions are not in the action stage (Prochaska et al., 1992).

In the **maintenance** stage, the individual has made positive changes and is now working to maintain those changes. This does not mean they do not actively work on keeping these changes going. The individual is attempting to prevent relapses and engaging in other activities to keep on the positive path they developed in the action stage. The therapist can focus on the resources the client has exhibited in the action stage to move from problem to non-problem. Further, the client moves beyond the addiction to see what other areas of their life they can improve upon to ensure their continued stability (DiClemente, 2003).

Termination is the sixth and final stage of the change process. At this point the person has made productive changes and has been able to maintain them. They have increased their ability to cope with life and do not have to actively try to change anything (they are not focused on what was the problem but on the resources and aspects of their life that are working). At this stage, they do not have temptation to use and have increased their self-efficacy.

There is not a set amount of time that someone will stay in one stage, although there are some averages (such as from three to six months in the action stage). There is also the possibility that when a person moves from one stage to another, they may then move back to a previous stage. Prochaska et al. (1992) explained that people usually move through a spiral pattern where they go through several cycles of these stages until the point they get to termination (see Figure 8.8). Included in this spiral is the possibility of relapse where the person uses and then readjusts their view of how their use is impacting their life.

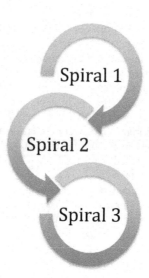

Figure 8.8 People tend to spiral through the stages of readiness several times before entering into the maintenance/termination stage

While we can look at these stages of readiness for change as an individual model, we can also see it as a family process as well. This tends to be a parallel process where both the individual and the family follow similar courses (Connors, Donovan, & DiClemente, 2001). The family may not see that the way they have organized is problematic and deny that there is a problem with the individual as well as themselves (precontemplation). Over time, they realize that there are problems, but they may not be sure what they are exactly or what they could do differently (contemplation). The family may then want their family functioning to be different and might talk about going to therapy (preparation). Family members may take small actions to try to fix things or they may search out possible avenues of change—such as gathering names of therapists. They also might try to encourage the abuser into therapy. As a whole the family could make changes of how they interact with one another (action). At this point, the substance abuser has most likely refused to go into treatment or perhaps has agreed to go into treatment and sabotaged it somehow. However, family members have decided to work on themselves. After making these changes, they engage in ways of being, not only to prevent the problem behaviors, but to enhance other areas of their lives (maintenance). After many months of actively ensuring that they are functioning well, this behavior becomes their homeostasis and they will not have to even think about how to be; they just will be with one another (termination).

Therapists are encouraged to alter their treatment and interventions based on the current stage of the client (Prochaska et al., 1992). For those in the precontemplation stage, the therapist will likely not push too much as the person is the least motivated to change. For those in the contemplation stage, the therapist will likely use consciousness raising and self-reevaluation activities as clients are better able to use the cognitive, affective, and evaluative processes of change. During the preparation stage, the therapist might include some counterconditioning and stimulus control interventions as the client is taking the first steps toward change. In the action stage, the therapist taps into the client's self-liberation and willpower, building on the client's renewed sense of agency and autonomy. In the maintenance stage, besides using all of the previous interventions, the therapist also highlights how the person is becoming who he or she wants to be. This might be through reinforcement management and the therapeutic benefits of the helping relationship.

Enhancing Motivation

In the previous section we discussed how substance abuse therapists assess how ready individuals, couples, or families are for change. This readiness is related to the person's motivation to engage in treatment. One of the therapeutic tasks is to help enhance this motivation. Miller and Rollnick (2012) provided five areas that therapists can keep in mind which help influence engagement or disengagement in therapy as well as potential questions to ask clients:

1. *Desires or goals.* What did you want or hope for in going? What is it that you're looking for?
2. *Importance.* How important is what you're looking for? How much of a priority is it?
3. *Positivity.* Did you feel good about the experience? Did you feel welcomed, valued, and respected? Were you treated in a warm and friendly manner?
4. *Expectations.* What did you think would happen? How did the experience fit with what you expected? Did it live up to (or even exceed) your expectations?
5. *Hope.* Do you think that this situation helps people like you to get what you're seeking? Do you believe that it would help you? (p. 46, italics in original)

The answers to these questions help connect the therapist to the client's perspective.

These five areas lead to five therapist actions that can build engagement between therapist and client, which will likely lead to increased motivation for change.

1. Asking the client why they are coming to therapy at this point in time.
2. Thinking about how significant the person thinks his or her goals are.
3. Figuring out how to join with the person, providing an accepting atmosphere.
4. Explain the process of therapy and see how much this overlaps with the client's expectations.
5. Explain how you think therapy can be helpful to build the client's sense of hope for change.

These actions put the client in a more respected position. This is important since motivation can be viewed as purposeful behavior (Thombs & Osborn, 2013). These authors explained,

> Learning the purpose or function of a behavior requires direct interaction with, and listening to, an individual with substance use problems or persons from a targeted population at risk for developing addiction (e.g., low-income adolescents who have been exposed to repeated trauma). (p. 277)

A person's motivation for change changes over time and is based on the situation in which they currently find themselves (Hanson & El-Bassel, 2014). Motivation is based upon the person's level of distress, goals, outcome expectancies, perceived self-efficacy, environmental resources, and personal skills. Given that each of these elements changes as people experience themselves and life differently, people's motivation also changes.

Thus, therapists working with substance-abusing clients are encouraged to listen to and assess the client's current motivation, finding out what they want from therapy. This can be done for therapy of any length or intensity level. Bien, Miller, & Tonigan (1993) reviewed 32 controlled trials of therapy for addiction issues and found brief interventions for problem drinking to be more effective than no treatment and similar in effectiveness to more intense interventions. These researchers also suggested six common components of effective brief therapies, which are found in the acronym **FRAMES**: Feedback, Responsibility, Advice, Menu, Empathy, and Self-efficacy (Miller & Sanchez, 1994) (see Figure 8.9).

Feedback
• Providing client with personalized feedback

Responsibility
• Client drinking and sobriety is solely the responsibility of the person

Advice
• Therapist provides possible pathways to reduce or stop drinking

Menu
• Multiple strategies for reduced drinking

Empathy
• Therapist is warm, accepting, and understanding

Self-efficacy
• Focus on client's strengths & resources to change

Figure 8.9 FRAMES is an acronym used to explain six common components of brief therapies

Motivational Interviewing

One of the leading approaches in working with people dealing with substance abuse to enhance their engagement and motivation for change is **motivational interviewing** (MI). Motivational interviewing is an evidence-based approach that is client-centered and is usually used when a substance abuser is ambivalent for change. Miller and Rollnick (2012) provided a definition of this approach, "Motivational interviewing is a collaborative conversation style for strengthening a person's own motivation and commitment to change" (p. 12). The therapist mainly engages in guiding the client, while at times utilizing elements of directing and following. This leads the therapist to not try to persuade the substance abuser to change, as more directing therapist styles are associated with the client having opposing arguments.

The spirit of MI is based upon four interrelated elements: partnership, acceptance, compassion, and evocation (Miller & Rollnick, 2012) (see Figure 8.10). **Partnership** means that the therapist is not the expert who works with a passive recipient. Rather, the client is viewed as the expert on who they are as a person. Motivational interviewing is not done "to" someone, but rather is done "with" and "for" them. This is important since change needs to come from the client's own motivation and resources.

Acceptance involves respecting and appreciating what the client brings with him or her to therapy. Acceptance in MI has four aspects: absolute worth, autonomy, accurate empathy, and affirmation. **Absolute worth** is related to Carl Rogers' (1961) notion of unconditional positive regard where the therapist does not have to like or even approve of a person's actions, but believes in the worth of the client as a person. **Accurate empathy** is an attempt by the therapist to understand the inner world of the client. **Autonomy** means that it is the client's position to choose the direction for his or her life. **Affirmation** relates to the therapist acknowledging the client's strengths and efforts.

Figure 8.10 The spirit of motivation interviewing consists of partnership, acceptance, compassion, and evocation

The third key spirit of MI is **compassion**. Miller and Rollnick (2012) explained, "To be compassionate is to actively promote the other's welfare, to give priority to the other's needs" (p. 20). Therapy is all about the client, rather than being in the therapist's self-interest.

The last key spirit of MI is **evocation**. This means that the therapist utilizes a strength-based approach, focusing on the client's strengths and resources rather than deficits and failings. What is evoked is the client's expertise on their own self, beliefs, values, and actions.

Motivational interviewing is based upon four overlapping processes that guide the client's decision making: engaging, focusing, evoking, and planning (Miller & Rollnick, 2012). **Engaging** is about developing a positive working relationship with the client. Motivational interviewing holds that therapeutic relationships should be collaborative, where both therapist and client are honored in terms of ideas for therapy and are both working together for the same purpose. **Focusing** relates to therapy's agenda and goals. What to focus on is based on the client, setting, and therapist, with the client's focus being the most common source of direction. The setting in which therapy happens may have an agenda for what services are available and appropriate. The therapist is also able to bring forth potential foci for therapy; however, it should be done in a way that has the client's buy in. **Evoking** in MI consists of the therapist listening for and enhancing the client's motivation for change. **Planning**, the last process in MI, involves developing a specific change plan that the client is willing to work toward. Therapists can pay attention to several signs to let them know there is readiness to move from evoking to planning (Miller & Rollnick, 2012). These include increased change talk, the person has taken steps in the direction of change, diminished sustain talk (the person reduces their arguments against change), increased resolve, envisioning a changed future, as well as the client asking questions about change. Figure 8.11 presents a pictorial representation of the four aspects of client decision-making in MI.

Based upon the four key interrelated elements that form the spirit of MI—partnership, acceptance, compassion, evocation—and the four primary processes—engaging, focusing, evoking, and planning—there are many strategies used to help enhance clients' motivations for change (Hanson & El-Bassel, 2014). These microskills can be summarized with the acronym **OARS**: open-ended questions, affirmations, reflections, and summaries (Tooley & Moyers, 2012). A MI therapist uses a lot of *open-ended questions*, as these help to elicit the client's thoughts and beliefs, allowing them to present their story in their own way. Additionally, with a foundation of Rogerian therapy, MI therapists use *reflective listening*. Instead of telling clients "what is," reflective listening attempts to bring forth the client's meanings. Another MI strategy is *affirming clients' concerns*. This is done as a means of acceptance and working with the client's goals. Motivational interviewing therapists also use a lot of *summarizing*, where the therapist ties together the client's statements and concerns. Lastly, a major MI tactic is *eliciting change talk*. This helps to address the client's ambivalence and brings forth the direction of the sessions.

While MI has been primarily used with individuals, it has also been used with couples, families, and groups. However, the therapist should first make an assessment that includes the client's desire for family member involvement and

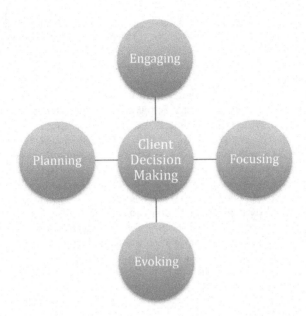

Figure 8.11 Client decision making in motivational interviewing includes engaging, focusing, evoking, and planning

investment in them as well as the significant other's support of and ability to engage in the treatment process (Hanson & El-Bassel, 2014). In use with families, MI may be able to support a strong therapeutic alliance between therapist and family as well as between family members (Lloyd-Hazlett, Honderich, & Heyward, 2016). The use of MI in family therapy provides an opportunity for family members to pause in trying to change each other and instead to listen to one another. This allows them to hear what each person deems as important and what change and goals they have that might overlap. This leads to the possibility of second-order change (a change in the rules of the system) rather than first-order change attempts (change within the existing rules), since family members stop trying to get the substance abuser to stop using, leading to new interactional processes.

When using MI with families, the same four primary processes of MI can still be used (Belmontes, 2018). The therapist needs to figure out how to engage the family, developing a positive therapeutic alliance with multiple members. In focusing with the family, the therapist follows various family members' goals while also seeing if the family is open to discussing substance-related issues. Next, the therapist evokes the multiple motivations to change from the various family members. Lastly, the MI therapist works collaboratively with the family to plan for change and develop a treatment plan.

In work with couples, the MI therapist might engage partners in one of three ways for the purpose of therapeutic intent (Burke, Vassilev, Kantchelov, & Zweben, 2002). The first is including the partner in the session for the substance abuser's benefit. Second, MI might be used with both partners, usually if both see themselves as clients, if the partner is dealing with some issues that hinder him or her in supporting the substance abuser, or if the partner is ambivalent about his or her actions in maintaining the partner's substance use. Lastly, the MI therapist might work with partners when focusing on the couple's interactions that maintain the problem.

Miller and Rollnick (2012) recommended that when utilizing MI with the substance abuser and a significant other, the therapist should establish ground rules with the partners to ensure that sessions do not include blaming and instead focus on positive change. However, when a significant other is involved in the MI session, the therapist might be able to gain additional information that will help to enact the four key principles of expressing empathy, developing discrepancy, rolling with resistance, and supporting self-efficacy (Burke et al., 2002). A further benefit of working with couples is that the therapist can teach the couple how to engage in effective listening and communication skills.

Motivational interviewing has been found to be effective with a wide range of presenting problems, various abused substances, treatment lengths, and client populations including adolescent substance abusers (Jensen et al., 2011). Motivational interviewing has been found efficacious with those trying to reduce their use of alcohol, tobacco, and marijuana, as well as, to a lesser extent, cocaine (DiClemente et al., 2017), and may have more positive effects early in treatment (Carroll et al., 2006).

Steinglass (2008) integrated notions from family systems with motivation enhancement to develop the **systemic-motivational model** (SMM). The SMM assists families dealing with chronic alcoholism in accessing their strengths and resources in an effort to develop their own solutions. Based on a "both/and" perspective, the therapist brings forth the multiple perspectives of all family members as well as the therapist's position. This model utilizes three phases: assessment/consultation, family-level treatment, and aftercare and relapse prevention. Steinglass explained the overlap between family systems and motivational interviewing principles:

> As explicated by Miller and Rollnick, MI has five basic principles that underscore the approach to be taken by the therapist treating a patient with a substance abuse problem: (1) *express empathy* about the patient's condition; (2) *develop discrepancy* regarding the patient's beliefs about his/her behavior; (3) *avoid argumentation* with the patient about continued alcohol use; (4) *roll with the patient's resistance* to change; and (5) *support patient self-efficacy* regarding decisions about behavior change. It would be our contention that every one of these principles is compatible with a family therapy approach to alcoholism treatment. (p. 21, italics in original)

The SMM model utilizes a harm reduction approach to help educate family members of the possible pathways to change and works with them to develop pros and cons for each change option.

Another adaptation of motivational interviewing is **Motivational Enhancement Therapy** (MET). This brief intervention, using principles and strategies of MI, was developed for Project MATCH (1993) and provides personalized feedback to the participant that compares their drug and alcohol use with that of peers and national standards of use. It is this feedback component that separates MET from MI (Thombs & Osborn, 2013). Motivational enhancement therapy is a brief manualized intervention that has been found to be effective across populations and with most abused substances (Lenz, Rosenbaum, & Sheperis, 2016). Motivational enhancement therapy is benefitted when the client's significant other (SO) is involved. The client's change talk is significantly increased when the SO engages in pro-change talk (Bourke, Magill, & Apodaca, 2016).

Case Application

The Rothers family find that they are experiencing some of the issues for families dealing with addiction, but not all of them. Fortunately, as far as we know, there has not been any issue of congenital problems because of drug or alcohol use during pregnancy and no report of child physical or sexual abuse. However, Mark has a history of violent episodes in close relationships. This includes having a fist-fight with his brother Mick, centering around Mark's use of alcohol. This fight occurred while Mark was drunk one night. Since then Mark and Mick have not talked with one another. Mark also was arrested for physically assaulting his first wife Angelina, when they were going through the process of divorce. At that time, Mark was at one of his highest points of alcohol consumption. While this was an isolated instance of physical violence, we might hypothesize the potentiality for other means of power and control that have been used by Mark in his relationships with Angelina and Hannah. The Rothers' therapist might explore whether Mark has used male privilege, minimized and blamed, or engaged in emotional abuse in his current relationships. At this point Hannah has not expressed that Mark has threatened, intimidated, or isolated her emotionally or economically.

Criminality has not had a major role in the Rothers' family life besides the domestic violence arrest that Mark had over 15 years ago when he pushed his then wife Angelina. However, there is cause for concern that Steve may find himself involved in the juvenile justice system. His externalizing behaviors seem to be increasing, where he is engaging in more disruptions outside of the house. While Steve is currently not part of the juvenile justice system, he seems to be at serious risk for escalation of problematic behaviors, including the potential for drug and alcohol abuse as well as criminal mischief. The Rothers' therapist should keep these possibilities in mind and focus on prevention issues.

At the current moment there is no one in the Rothers family that has been diagnosed by a mental health professional. However, we can hypothesize that Mark and Steve would likely be diagnosed if they were to present for assessment and treatment. In all likelihood, Mark would receive a diagnosis of alcohol use disorder. Further, given some of his other behaviors, such as isolating himself and suicidal ideation, there may be a co-existing psychological disorder. If so, the therapist would need to consider how to work with this dual diagnosis. While we do not know the specifics of Steve's problematic behaviors at school, we might consider whether any of the patterns of behavior falls within the category of conduct disorder.

Mark is most likely currently either in the precontemplation or contemplation stage. From what we know, he does not believe that his drinking is problematic. However, he is likely aware of some of the interpersonal discord in the family and that his drinking plays a role in these problematic interactions. If he is aware of this, then he may be in the early part of the contemplation stage. Hannah is likely in the preparation stage, viewing her own behavior as not doing enough to change Mark but still aware that she has likely been allowing his drinking and disengagement. Steve seems to be in the precontemplation stage as he likely views any problems he is experiencing as the result of others, such as his parents, friends, or teachers. We do not have enough information to determine what stage of readiness Kayleigh or Pete are currently in.

Summary

Addicted families have many issues that may or may not be present in non-addicted families. Given that members tend to feel like their own lives and the family as a whole are becoming chaotic, they have a tendency to try to control others. This may lead to domestic violence. Children in domestic violence families are at greater risk for being physically and sexually abused. Toward the extreme end of consequences of coming from an addicted family is developing fetal alcohol syndrome, depending on the severity of drug use by the mother during pregnancy. Therapists must also consider assessing for multiple disorders, as there is a heightened probability of dual diagnosis. Yet, whatever substance is being used, therapists can assess for how ready the individual and/or family is to make changes in their lives. One means of enhancing the client's motivation is through motivational interviewing, a model of working with clients that is collaborative, focusing on the client's desired changes.

Key Words

child abuse
intimate partner violence
physical domestic violence
sexual domestic violence
psychological domestic violence
emotional violence
economic abuse
patriarchal terrorism
common couple violence
tension building phase
abuse
honeymoon phase
children of alcoholics
incest
fetal alcohol abuse syndrome
fetal alcohol syndrome disorder

teratogenesis
dual diagnosis
comorbid
partial treatment
sequential treatment
parallel treatment
stages of readiness for change
   model
precontemplation
contemplation
consciousness raising
preparation
action
maintenance
termination

Discussion Questions

1. Discuss the relationship between domestic violence and power/control.
2. What are the differences between the various types of domestic violence?
3. What implications are there for the family system when child abuse is present?
4. Discuss how fetal alcohol syndrome disorder impacts the child as well as the family.
5. Why should the therapist consider assessing for dual diagnosis?
6. Explain how a client (and a family) can proceed through the stages of readiness for change.

NINE

Behavioral Addictions

Myron Burns

As human beings we seek relief and pleasure in our lives, whether that is having a drink and a bite to eat after a long hard day of work or enjoying family and friends during a night on the town. However, as the old saying goes, "Too much of anything is not good for you." Historically, people have excessively engaged in addictive behaviors like drinking, gambling, sex, and shopping. Behavioral addictions can lead to problematic behaviors that put the individual at risk or in danger and possibly lead to other psychological disorders.

The *Diagnostic and Statistical Manual of Mental Disorders* (DSM) recently added a category of Substance-Related Addictive Disorders (APA, 2013). Gambling is the only non-substance-related disorder included in this diagnostic section. However, in Section III, Internet Gaming Disorder has been proposed as a diagnosis for future study. There are neurobiological similarities between behavioral addictions and substance use disorder. For example, serotonin, which helps prevent excitability and the rapid firing of nerve cells that leads to anxious feelings, and dopamine, involved with seeking pleasure and rewards, motivation, and impulse control, may contribute to both disorders (Potenza, 2008). Brain imaging studies suggest that the dopaminergic mesolimbic pathway may be involved in substance use disorders and pathological gambling (Reuter et al., 2005; Wrase et al., 2007). The American Society of Addiction Medicine (ASAM) (2014) and the American Psychiatric Association (2013) have acknowledged the similarities between the brain pathways of substance use disorders and behavioral addictions.

In this chapter non-substance-related disorders and behavioral addictions will be discussed. This chapter provides an overview of the prevalence rates, general criteria for diagnosis, relationship to substance use, and family dynamics of behavioral disorders. The specific criteria for the DSM-5 diagnosis of gambling disorder will be discussed. Although they have no formal diagnosis in the DSM-5, compulsive buying, internet, and sex addiction have been identified in the mental health field and will be discussed. Because of a void in research related to substance abuse and the family with exercise addiction, this disorder is not covered. Disorders related to eating are also not discussed as they are listed in the DSM-5 under Feeding and Eating Disorders.

Definition of Behavioral Addiction

Behavioral addictions are difficult to define. One of the reasons is because behavioral addictions involve "normal" activities (sex, food, etc.) and the other reason entails behavioral addictions being dismissed as habits. **Behavioral addictions are typically defined as compulsive and impulsive behaviors where an individual persistently and repetitively engages in actions without it necessarily leading to a reward or pleasure, nor does the individual reflect about the consequences of their actions** (Stevens & Smith, 2018).

Like substance abuse, the individual with a behavioral addiction will continue to engage in these behaviors despite the consequences of endangering one's health, and the loss of one's job and loved ones or spouse. Moreover, if we use gambling as an example, like those with substance use disorders, the individual will lie to cover up their behavior and/or engage in increasing the risk of the stake to feel "alive" or excitement. Other similarities between behavioral addictions and substance abuse include spending a considerable amount of time on the activity or behavior, having cravings and urges, and producing a conditioned response (e.g., use drugs or gamble to feel good or when stressed).

Mental health care professionals trained in addiction are careful not to label people based on their behaviors alone. For example, there are professional gamblers who know how to manage their money or recreational gamblers who do not gamble to excess. Also, many mental health professionals are concerned that these behaviors may be used to excuse actions like compulsive buying or infidelity. Nevertheless, valid diagnoses should involve detailed structured interviews, psychological testing and assessments, and the use of the DSM-5.

Previous editions of the DSM only referred to the misuse of substances; however, the current edition (DSM-5) lists gambling disorder as the only behavioral addiction alongside substance use disorders. The other addictions (sex, compulsive buying, and internet) discussed in this chapter have no DSM-5 criteria. Sex addiction, while not an official diagnosis in the DSM-5, has been included in previous editions and still merits attention. Compulsive buying disorder shares similar processes to substance use disorders. Internet addiction disorder could entail shopping, sex, and gambling, and internet gaming disorder is a form of internet addiction and has been listed in section III of the DSM 5 for future study.

Gambling Disorder

About 1.5 million Americans experience severe gambling disorders and between 3 to 6 million fall in the "mild to moderate" category (Kessler et al., 2008). African Americans have the highest prevalence rates (0.9%), in comparison with Caucasians (0.4%), and Hispanics (0.3%). Men gamble at a higher rate than women. Someone with a gambling disorder is obsessed with gambling and rarely refuses a bet. Despite the loss of money, the gambler will continue to bet and "double down" (i.e., double or increase the amount of their previous wager to try and regain lost funds) until no more funding options are available. A person diagnosed with a gambling disorder may be preoccupied in thoughts of past winnings or future ventures and will repeatedly engage in the behavior despite the negative consequences it may cause to their finances and intimate relationships. These individuals may gamble when stressed or depressed and find it difficult to cut back or stop their gambling. Like those diagnosed with a substance use disorder, those with a gambling disorder will lie to cover up their behavior or excitement and engage in increasing the risk of the stake to feel "alive."

It is important to note, as Griffiths (2014) and Marjot (2006) state, that problem gambling should not be confused with a gambling addiction or disorder. Those with a gambling addiction or disorder can be problem gamblers, but problem gamblers are not necessarily gambling addicts. Addictions rely on constant reward expectations and frequency of the behavior. So, while placing a bet or buying a lottery ticket once or twice a week can be problematic, particularly when it causes a financial burden, the frequency and reward expectation is much lower in comparison with someone who gambles every day or pulls the slot machine lever 11 times in a 1-minute interval.

Gambling and Substance Abuse

"Whatever happens in Vegas stays in Vegas." This is a phrase synonymous with vacations in Las Vegas. Also synonymous with Vegas are gambling, drinking, smoking, drug use, and sex. Some of these behaviors will often occur simultaneously. It is not uncommon for a gambler to be given a free drink in the casino or smoke cigarettes while at the slot machines, blackjack, and "craps" table. These behaviors can become an engrained conditioned habit (cannot do one without the other, or while engaging in one behavior will automatically engage in the other).

Given its role in drug addiction and rewarding behavior, dopamine has been heavily investigated in the neurochemical abnormalities of pathological gamblers (Clark et al., 2013). Patients with Parkinson's disease display sudden onset gambling as a side effect of dopamine agonist medications (Ambermoon, Carter, Hall, Dissanayaka, & O'Sullivan, 2011). Higher levels of dopamine release are also correlated with greater subjective excitement (Linnet, Møller, Peterson, Gjedde, & Doudet, 2011) and gambling severity (Joutsa et al., 2012). Campbell-Meiklejohn et al. (2011) found that serotonin and dopamine appear to play separate roles in the tendency of individuals to gamble to recover, or to judge whether previous losses are worth chasing. Based on their findings, lowering of brain serotonin by acute tryptophan depletion was associated with a reduced number of decisions made to chase losses and the number of consecutive decisions to chase losses in which participants completed a computerized loss-chasing game following treatment. D2/D3 receptor activity was found to produce changes in the value of loss chasing. Pramipexole, which is a dopamine agonist, was significantly related to placing a high value on loss chasing and being associated with valuing losses less.

Meta-analysis has revealed that substance abusers engage in gambling at higher rates than the general population (Shaffer, Hall, & Vander Bilt, 1999). Welte, Barnes, Wieczorek, Tidwell, and Parker (2001) reported that 25% of pathological gamblers met the diagnoses for alcohol dependence, compared with 1.4% of non-gamblers. Not surprisingly, Maccallum and Blaszczynski (2002) found nicotine dependence to be highly related to gambling. In their investigation of treatment-seeking poker players, 65.3% smoked cigarettes and 37% met the nicotine dependence criteria. If we look at methadone specifically, rates of pathological gambling have ranged from 7% to 18% in comparison with the general population (0.4% to 2%) (Petry, 2007).

Gamblers with a substance use disorder also have significantly more mental health problems than gamblers without a substance use diagnosis. In a nationally representative sample of 43,093 households aged 18 years and older, Petry, Stinson, and Grant (2005) collected data on lifetime prevalence and comorbidity of pathological gambling with other psychiatric disorders. Results revealed pathological gambling was significantly associated with having a mood disorder (49.6%), anxiety disorder (41.3%), and personality disorder (60.8%). Gamblers with a substance use disorder also have more severe legal, employment, and family difficulties than those without a substance use disorder (Ladd & Petry, 2003).

For cocaine-dependent patients, those with a gambling problem were more likely to be unemployed, involved in illegal activities, have more legal problems, and spend more time in prison than cocaine-dependent patients without a history of a gambling problem (Hall et al., 2000). In relation to sexual behavior, which will be discussed in more detail later in this chapter, gambling problems in substance abusers are also related to risky sexual behaviors. In a sample of 134 substance abusers, Petry (2000) reported that high severity of gambling problems in substance abusers significantly predicted more sex partners, and less frequent use of condoms with casual and paid sex partners, in comparison with non-problem gamblers. When looking at the relationship between gambling and substance abuse, both behaviors together could be more problematic than either behavior alone.

Gambling and Family Dynamics

Like substance use disorders, the etiology for gambling disorders is similar (e.g., biological, genetics, environment, conditioning, and social/cultural factors). Most of the studies which have looked at the relationship between gambling and the family have investigated the development of the disorder beginning in adolescence. Vachon, Vitaro, Wanner, and Tremblay (2004) found that adolescent gambling was related to parents' gambling (primarily that of the father), low levels of parental monitoring, and lack of discipline. In a study of 2,336 students, Grades 7–13, Hardoon, Gupta, and Derevensky (2004) investigated the impact of adolescent gambling. In their sample, 4.9% of adolescents met the criteria for pathological gambling and 8% were found to be at risk. Problematic gambling predicted substance use (primarily alcohol and tobacco), conduct problems, and strained family relationships.

Adults who were diagnosed as being problematic gamblers were more likely to have first-degree relatives (parents, siblings, and children) who were problematic gamblers than control families (Black, Monahan, Temkit, & Shaw, 2006). Moreover, these relatives were also more likely to have significantly higher lifetime rates of substance use disorders and antisocial personality disorder. The adult gambler will often isolate themselves from the family and pay little attention to family needs and concerns. As inattention to family and preoccupation with gambling increases, so does family strife. The individual will lie to hide losses and increased debts, and relationships with spouses deteriorate. This puts a financial strain and burden on the entire family.

Gambling addiction is related to a lower quality of life. Using a health utility index, Kohler (2014) compared the Health-Related Quality of Life costs of pathological gamblers recruited from treatment centers in Western Switzerland with the general population. Pathological gambling was shown to be associated with a significant loss of quality of life in comparison with the general population. This loss is then transferred to both the gambler's family and society.

Treatment Possibilities for Gambling Addiction

Some of the same practices used to treat substance use disorders are also applicable in treating gambling disorder. For example, motivational interviewing, cognitive behavioral therapy (CBT), and 12-step programs appear to be effective in treating gambling addiction. According to Gooding and Tarrier (2009), CBT is considered the widely recognized evidence-based treatment for gambling addiction. In their meta-analysis, Gooding and Tarrier found that various forms of CBT were effective in reducing pathological gambling. These treatment approaches encourage individuals to identify use patterns, learn how to recognize and avoid triggers, and identify lifestyle changes to avoid high-risk situations. Topf, Yip, and Potenza (2009) found similar approaches were beneficial in relapse prevention strategies.

The FDA has no approved medication for specifically treating gambling disorder; however, Naltrexone, which is an opioid antagonist, has shown some positive results. Grant, Kim, and Hartman (2008) found that a treatment group which received Naltrexone reported a 40% abstinence rate post one-month follow up in comparison with a placebo group. Other medications that have shown to be effective in treating gambling disorder includes Nalmefene, N-acetylcysteine (NAC), and antidepressants (Stevens & Smith, 2018).

Engaging family members in the treatment process is also highly important. Families may feel distrust over the gambler's lies, and possible legal and employment issues. This can lead to increased stress on the family system. Steinberg (1993) highlighted the importance of including the family in treatment and stated that, typically, the spouse of the gambler initiates therapy. In addition, Steinberg further stated that including the family in therapy can offer an accurate picture of the gambling problem, prepare the family for involvement in the treatment process, and provide a clearer understanding of the family dynamics. Families need to be able to communicate financial concerns, issues of power and control, and role reversal. Gamblers Anonymous for families (GAM-ANON) can provide support and education for family members.

Makarchuk, Hodgins, and Peden (2002) modified the Community Reinforcement and Family Training (CRAFT) program (see Chapter 10) to address problem gambling and the specific needs and issues of the family. Community Reinforcement and Family Training places an emphasis on three aspects: (1) Persuading the gambler to enter treatment, (2) helping to reduce gambling, and (3) encouraging family members to take care of themselves. In this modified version of CRAFT, a self-help manual was used rather than the traditional face-to-face format commonly used in the treatment of alcohol and drug addiction.

The manual included topics such as: Motivation to help, self-care and help, awareness and knowledge of the gambling problem, and helping the gambler. Makarchuk et al. (2002) noted that the self-help manual provides a private treatment option where family members are actively involved in addressing their issues surrounding the addiction.

In Makarchuk et al.'s study, 31 significant others were randomly assigned to receive either CRAFT or a control package. Post three-month follow up showed that CRAFT participants' gambling members had significantly decreased gambling and that participants felt the program met their needs. There were no adverse consequences for either group related to gambling (e.g., financial, legal, employment), which might suggest that any treatment is better than no treatment at all. However, for the control group, some participants sought additional treatment and reported separating from the gambler, something that did not happen in the treatment group. Those who were in the CRAFT intervention reported utilizing various coping strategies they had learned in treatment (e.g., managing finances, open communication, understanding enabling behaviors, and finding activities to do outside of gambling). Participants in CRAFT reported that the self-help manual helped them understand the severity of the problem, reduced their guilt, and they reported feeling better about their situation.

Sex Addiction

The adage that "sex sells" has never been more popular than today. What was once a taboo topic is now seen almost daily in advertisements, T.V., film, and media coverage. The adult entertainment industry generates close to 4 billion dollars a year (Stevens & Smith, 2018). Patrons gain access through films and videos sold in retail stores, on the internet (for purchase and free), and cable providers (both home and in hotels). Strip clubs and/or escort services are also available in almost every city worldwide. Given the access to sexual material and content, defining sex addiction can be tricky.

Sex addiction was deleted from the DSM-IV and is not included in diagnoses for future research in the DSM-5. The difficulty in defining sex addiction lies in what constitutes it, as many experts in the field cannot agree on a definition. Part of the problem lies with sex being a normal behavior that, while many people may engage in it, some may not be as forthcoming in describing their sexual habits. Also, there is such a wide variety in sexual behaviors in terms of gender, age, sexual orientation, race, ethnicity, etc., that what may be abnormal to one person may be totally normal to others. Despite the limitation in defining sex addiction, it is possible to look at the consequences of sexual behavior. **Sex addiction** involves hypersexual and compulsive behaviors. The individual may spend considerable time engaging in recurrent and intense sexual fantasies, sexual urges, and/or sexual behaviors. These behaviors lead to repeated engagement and psychological distress, despite the danger to one's health and strain in social, family, and work life.

Similar to defining sex addiction, it is difficult to determine the prevalence rates. Estimates indicate that between 3% and 6% of Americans suffer from some type of sex addiction (Kuzma & Black, 2008). Sex addiction is more common among middle-aged Caucasian males who are primarily in the middle-to upper-class income bracket. Sex addiction is also more common among gay and bisexual men, with studies reporting close to 60% of them displaying behaviors like compulsive sexual behaviors. Sexual addiction has comorbidity with substance use disorders, personality disorders, depression, and anxiety (Rosenberg & Feder, 2014).

Sex Addiction and Substance Abuse

"Sex & Drugs & Rock & Roll" is a song by Ian Dury from the late 1970s and a popular phrase that has been used in our society since its release. The use of alcohol and sexual activity often occur together. Alcohol and drugs can lower one's inhibitions, distort thinking, and lead to risky sexual behavior (Rawson, Washton, Domier, & Reiber, 2002; Washton, 1989). Some individuals report that stimulants like cocaine and methamphetamine increase their interest, desire, and arousal for enhanced sexual fantasies (Washton & Zweben, 2006). Moreover, Washton and Zweben (2006) report that drug users with increased sexual desire will often display impulsive behaviors such as seeking out prostitutes and hooking up with strangers. The use of drugs and engaging in sex can become a conditioned habit in which one behavior often triggers the other.

Some studies identifying compulsive sexual behaviors have found that a comorbid diagnosis of substance abuse ranges from 39% to 71%, with alcohol being the primary drug (Black, Kehrberg, Flumerfelt, & Schlosser, 1997; Kafka, 2010). Raymond, Coleman, and Miner (2003) found that 38% of sex addicts met the criteria for a lifetime cannabis substance use disorder. For more severe and illicit drugs, Reid et al. (2012) found that those meeting the criteria for methamphetamine dependence reported using drugs so that they could act out sexually. Among homosexual men, results from Benotsch, Kalichman, and Kelly (1999) indicated that men scoring high on sexual compulsivity reported engaging in more frequent unprotected sexual acts with more partners, greater cocaine use by self and partner in conjunction with sexual activity, rated high-risk sexual acts as more pleasurable, and reported lower self-esteem.

Sex Addiction and Family Dynamics

According to the Augustine Fellowship (1986), most individuals with compulsive sexual behaviors come from disengaged and rigid families. Early childhood trauma and poor attachment styles play a major role. They often grow up in families with neglect, abuse, poor boundaries, and the absence of healthy courtship modeling (Turner, 2009). Turner further states that children in these families may experience emotional incest and have emotional boundaries violated in which the child is labeled as being "special" to a parent. The child then assumes responsibility for the emotional well-being of the parent. When the original caregiver is also an abuser, this sets the stage where future relationships often become one of abuse.

For women who have a sexual addiction, childhood trauma and sexual abuse are major contributing factors. Women with broken relationships with their mother and men with their father were reported to be at a higher risk for sexual addiction (Rosenberg & Feder, 2014). Shame from early childhood trauma can develop into sexual addiction. As a result, the behavior of the sex addict can put a strain on a relationship, marriage, or family.

The sex addict may unconsciously use adult sexuality and sex as a means for coping with traumatic childhood events and trying to escape and numb feelings (Kasl, 1989; Turner, 2009). This type of behavior may become maladaptive in adulthood, which could destroy and exploit future relationships (Carnes, 1991). The partners of sex addicts may get caught up in this process and lose their sense of identity by worrying about the sex addict's behavior and putting the addict's needs and issues first. Healthy dating relationships are usually not possible for someone with a sex addiction without receiving proper treatment. Dysfunctional attachment styles obtained from parents can become generational legacies for children. As adults, the sex addict's dating relationships often lack true intimacy and respect. Ultimately the sex addict feels flawed.

Treatment Issues for Sex Addiction

Like substance use and gambling disorder, treatment for sexual addiction uses some of the same clinical practices. Group therapy has been identified as the primary mode for treatment (Hook, Hook, & Hines, 2008). Group therapy can help with shame, relapse prevention, and developing ways for healthy intimacy. Treatment programs are often supplemented by 12-step groups, such as Sex Anonymous, Sexaholics Anonymous, Sex Addicts Anonymous, and Sex and Love Anonymous. Additionally, psychoeducational groups and Sex-Anon family groups can help family members understand the nature of sexual addiction and the recovery process.

Many partners of sex addicts may also have a history of addiction (i.e., sex and drugs) and dysfunctional intimacy patterns from their family of origin (Turner, 2009). Therefore, it is imperative that treatment should include the spouse. For those sex addicts whose partner does not have a history of sexual addiction, the sex addict's recovery can be seen as a sign of rejection (i.e., sex addicts are instructed to not engage in sex until the root cause of addiction is uncovered and treated). Because couples' behaviors have become engrained, partners are helped not only to overcome their own problems, but to maximize and repair their relationships. It is crucial that the recovering sex addict learns and discovers how to engage in sex in a loving, caring, and healthy manner. Because of the addict's past struggles, couples are faced with the challenge of overcoming issues of trust and consistency. Feelings of anxiety, guilt, remorse, and forgiveness will need to be explored in a safe, nonjudgmental, and caring environment.

Sexual genograms maybe useful for exploring generational issues (Berman, 1999). According to Berman (1999) the therapist should assess for abuse, neglect, and family attitudes towards sex. Bibliotherapy is also useful to help in the recovery process (Hastings, 2000). Through this process the couple is helped with understanding mutually satisfying sex and the relationship can begin to grow from there. As an adjunctive therapy, Eye Movement and Desensitization and Reprocessing (EMDR) is a commonly used alternative therapy for sexual addiction (Weiss, 2004). This form of therapy can help with a patient's defenses by working to unblock emotional states. According to Weiss (2004), EMDR is most helpful in dealing with traumatic memories and pent-up emotional experiences.

As with gambling addiction, there is no FDA-approved medication for sex addiction. However, the same drugs that were mentioned for treating gambling disorder could also be used to treat sexual addiction. Naltrexone and selective serotonin uptake inhibitors (SSRIs) have shown promising results (Stevens & Smith, 2018), and Citalopram has been associated with a reduction in masturbation to pornography (Tosto, Talarico, Lenzi, & Bruno, 2008). As was previously mentioned, a co-occurring diagnosis of substance use disorder is common and may also need to be treated. For example, the addict when engaging in one behavior (sex) may automatically engage in the other (drug use) or vice versa.

Compulsive Buying Disorder

The role of advertisement and the internet was briefly mentioned in the selling of sex, and for compulsive buying disorder it is no different. Consumers are constantly exposed to commercials or ads promoting products that often emphasize *wants* as opposed to actual *needs* for goods. The increased availability of goods and ease of access in purchasing have contributed to compulsive buying disorders.

Like sex addiction, it is difficult to define **compulsive buying disorder**. Potenza, Koran, and Pallanti (2009) have considered this behavior to involve impulses (continued urge to purchase even after the behavior has been acted upon) and compulsions (inability to resist the urge to purchase). The individual may engage in this behavior more so to reduce anxiety than receive pleasure. As with substance use, when the buying starts to disrupt and effect the individual's personal, social, work, and finances, these behaviors can be defined as an addiction or disorder. A key characteristic is that the compulsive buying will continue despite negative feedback from others (Sohn & Choi, 2014).

In the United States, estimates of compulsive buying range between 1% and 10%, primarily by those with a low income (Benson & Eisenach, 2013; Black, 2007; Hartston, 2012). Most buyers are under the age of 30, and the general age of onset of the buying compulsion is from late teens to early 20s (Black, 2012). The behavior is seen more in developed Western countries, with the rates being equal for men and women (5.5% vs 6% respectively; Koran, Faber, Aboujaoude, Large, & Serpe, 2006). Men tend to purchase functional, technology, and collector items, whereas women purchase items more tied to identity and appearance (e.g., clothing, shoes, jewelry, cosmetics, and household items) (Mueller et al., 2011). The compulsive shopper experiences the negative consequences of increased debts, not being able to pay off debts, criminal activity, and legal ramifications. While there is no formal diagnosis in the DSM-5, Rosenberg and Feder (2014) proposed three criteria: (1) "the act of buying is irrepressible (the urge)"; (2) "one's buying tendencies are uncontrollable (the behavior)", and (3) "one's behavior continues regardless of the negative consequences" (p. 288).

Compulsive Buying Disorder and Substance Abuse

Limited research is available with respect to compulsive buying and substance abuse. However, individuals with compulsive buying disorder do present with substance use disorders diagnoses. Between 21%–46% of patients presenting with a compulsive buying disorder met the diagnosis for a substance use disorder (Black, Repertinger, Gaffney, & Gabel, 1998; Christenson, Faber, & de Zwann, 1994). In another example, Roberts and Tanner (2000) investigated compulsive buying and risky behaviors among teenagers aged 12–19 and found that self-report measures of illegal drug use were significantly associated with compulsive buying. What's still not clear from research is if substance use triggers compulsive buying behaviors or vice versa (Zhang, Brook, Leukefeld, & Brook, 2016).

Compulsive buyers are more likely to have first-degree relatives who suffer from mood and personality disorders, and 20% suffered from severe alcohol disorders (Black et al., 1998). Like substance use and gambling disorders, compulsive buying shares similar neurocircuitry (e.g., decreased serotonin) and activates the same brain reward mechanisms (dopamine) (Raab, Elger, Neuner, & Weber, 2011). As a result, the etiology for compulsive buying has the same biological, genetic, environmental, conditioning, and family social/cultural explanations as other addictions.

Compulsive Buying Disorder and Family Dynamics

There is also limited research with compulsive buying and family dynamics. Compulsive buying was related to families emphasizing materialism, and children whose parents went through a divorce were more likely to engage in compulsive buying as a means of coping (Rindfleisch, Burroughs, & Denton, 1997). Roberts, Manolis, and Tanner (2003) found similar results, except that divorce was not supported as a determining factor. They speculate that the age of the child when the divorce happens is a more important factor, as previous research suggests that divorces which happen when children are between the ages of 11–16 may be more detrimental than when children are between the ages of 7–11 (Chase-Lansdale, Cherlin, & Kiernan, 1995). Baker, Moschis, Rigdon, and Mathur (2011) state that the previous studies mentioned focused only on the stressful experiences of disruptive family events and failed to consider the negative consequences these family events may have had on the child's socialization experiences and psychological development. Their research suggests that compulsive buying is the result of family disruptions experienced early in childhood, which leads to a strain on socioeconomic resources that interferes with the child's socialization practices and leads to ineffective parent–child communications.

Research has shown that compulsive buyers often experience family and marital conflict (Lejoyeux & Weinstein, 2010). Because of the disorder, compulsive buyers find it difficult to provide the attention and care needed by their family. A partner's sense of being neglected increases because of the spending habits of compulsive buyers. This also puts a strain on joint finances. As one of the major sources of family discord, family finances play an important role with respect to marital stability and satisfaction. Financial difficulties and dissatisfaction with one's financial status can lead to marital conflict and divorce (Poduska & Allred, 1990).

Treatment Options for Compulsive Buying Disorder

No one treatment strategy for compulsive buying disorder is more effective than the other. Psychodynamic approaches have been used in the past; however, cognitive behavioral therapy and dialectical behavior therapy are often used now (Black, 2007; Stevens & Smith, 2018). Benson (2006) developed a self-help program that contains a workbook, diary, and CD-ROM program. The overall program contains cognitive-behavioral strategies for self-monitoring. Self-help books and bibliotherapy are also helpful (Arenson, 1991; Catalano & Sonenberg, 1993). Those with compulsive buying disorder may also develop financial problems and can benefit from financial counseling (McCall, 2000).

Group therapy, couple counseling, and 12-step approaches are also effective. Groups can provide support, encouragement, and offer insight on how to live within one's means and abandon compulsive buying disorder traits (Andrews, 2000). Couples counseling may be particularly helpful when the compulsive buyer has disrupted the dyad (Mellan, 2000).

Pharmacological treatments are also beneficial. Antidepressants and mood stabilizers have helped with managing emotions and impulses associated with compulsive buying (Rosenberg & Feder, 2014). Grant (2003) and Kim (1998) have highlighted cases in which those with compulsive buying disorder showed improvement with the opiate antagonist Naltrexone.

Internet Addiction Disorder

With the advancement of technology, the internet may serve as both a blessing and curse. The internet allows for immediate and easy access to education, entertainment, news, banking, social, work, and leisure activities. As with the previously mentioned behavioral addictions, the internet is no different. Contributing factors to **internet addiction** include depression, loneliness, low self-esteem, lack of impulse control, and neurological and brain region deficiencies (Han, Hwang, & Renshaw, 2011; Ko et al., 2009; Rosenberg & Feder, 2014). In fact, internet addiction could entail viewing pornography, usage for shopping, and gambling. While internet addiction is not an official diagnosis in the DSM-5, **internet gaming disorder** (i.e., limited to gaming and does not include problems with general use of the internet, online gambling, use of social media or smartphones) has been included in Section III of the DSM-5 for future research.

Despite the DSM-5 exclusion of internet use in general, constantly checking one's email, phone messages, social media page, and other websites or electronic services can become an obsessive and conditioned habit, where the individual develops a fear of missing out on something which leads to psychological distress. Internet addiction can also indirectly affect one physically. For the chronic user, sleep deprivation contributes to fatigue, impairs mental functioning, and may decrease one's immune system (Young, 1999). Moreover, lack of physical activity outside of computer use may contribute to carpal tunnel, back strain, and eye strain.

Because there are no standard diagnostic criteria for internet addiction, estimates for prevalence rates have ranged from 0.1% to 50% (Hur, 2006; Zhang, Amos, & McDowell, 2008). Prevalence is higher among college-age students. Asian countries have the highest rates with adolescents in Taiwan and South Korea reporting 17.9% and 16% respectively (Rosenberg & Feder, 2014). Rates in China range from 0.6% to 10.2%. Estimates in the U.S range from 0.3% to

12.5% (Aboujaoude, Koran, Gamel, Large, & Serpe, 2006; Christakis, Moreno, Jelenchick, Myaing, & Zhou, 2011; Shaw & Black, 2008).

Internet Addiction and Substance Abuse

Internet addiction is highly related to substance use and substance use disorders. Among the young adult population, studies have reported that the risk of internet addiction is associated with an increased prevalence of substance dependence (i.e., alcohol, marijuana, and other illegal drugs) (Bakken et al., 2009; Padilla-Walker et al., 2010). Recently adolescents have been a focal point in studies because of the high prevalence in internet use. Adolescence is a time period of vulnerability and risk taking. Preoccupation with body image and the internet is common. Adolescents may also display impulsivity and experiment with sex and drugs.

Ko et al. (2006) report that adolescents with internet addiction were more likely to have substance use experience. Lee, Han, Kim, and Renshaw (2013) found that alcohol, smoking, and other drug use predicted internet addiction for adolescents. Logistic regression analysis has found that adolescents' hostility and depression were associated with internet addiction as well as substance use (Yen et al., 2008).

While internet addiction can affect both genders, data suggests that adolescents with internet addiction are more likely to be male and have experienced substance use (Ko et al., 2006). Moreover, these males primarily engage in online gambling and computer gaming (i.e., video games), with problematic computer gaming being associated with cannabis use, and problematic gambling associated with tobacco, alcohol, and cannabis use (Walther, Morgenstern, & Hanewinkel, 2012). The accumulation of these factors can lead to family dissatisfaction and has been related to arguments with one's parents (Rosenberg & Feder, 2014).

Internet Addiction and Family Dynamics

Marriages, dating relationships, parent–child interactions, and friendships can be disrupted by internet addiction. Those addicted to the internet will spend more time alone with the computer and less time with family and friends (Young, 1996). Obsessive internet use interferes with responsibilities and obligations at home, leaving the spouse feeling neglected. Those addicted to the internet will avoid discussing these issues and, like substance abuse, may minimize the problem (e.g., "it's just the internet," "at least I am home") and forget important obligations (e.g., picking up a child from school).

Young (1999) reports that family members will initially rationalize their loved one's internet use as "a phase" in hopes that the behavior will decrease. However, when the addiction continues or increases, arguments develop in which those suffering from internet addiction will deny their issues. For adults addicted to the internet, divorce may be common as marriages deteriorate and are replaced with online activities or companionship.

For adolescents, higher parent–child conflict, habitual alcohol use of siblings, perceived parents' positive attitude to adolescent substance use, and lower family functioning predicted internet addiction (Yen et al., 2007). Habitual alcohol use of siblings, perceived parents' positive attitude to adolescent substance use, and lower family functioning also predicted adolescents' substance use. Park, Kim, and Cho (2009) conducted a study concerning the relationship between family factors and internet addiction among South Korean adolescents. Their results showed that positive parenting attitudes, family communication, and family cohesion served as protector factors against internet addiction, whereas marital violence and parent to child violence were strongly associated with internet addiction. Adolescents who receive more support from parents are less likely to display conduct disorder behaviors, while adolescents whose parents provide insufficient attention and support are more likely to be psychologically distressed, which could lead to overuse of the internet to escape their home environment.

Treatment Issues for Internet Addiction

Treatment for internet addiction is relatively new. Cognitive behavioral treatment strategies have been used (Young, 2011). As with treating other disorders, CBT encourages the individual to identify maladaptive thoughts and triggers related to the addictive behavior. Another treatment strategy suggested by Young (1999) is *Practicing the Opposite*. For example, if the person normally uses the internet first thing in the morning, the therapist might suggest that the individual take a shower or eat breakfast first before logging in.

In addition, abstinence, harm reduction, and moderation strategies could also be used. While the individual may not completely abstain from the internet, the client could be instructed to abstain from certain activities, particularly if they are the most problematic (e.g., chat room). The individual could also be instructed to cut down on the number of hours spent on the internet, for example 20 hours a week instead of 40. This could entail usage from 9:00 pm to 11:00 pm every weeknight, and 12pm to 5pm on Saturday and Sunday. Relapse prevention strategies used in substance abuse could also be employed. For example, "*Think Beyond the High Play the Tape to the End*" (see Washton, 1990; Washton & Stone-Washton, 1990), where the individual might keep reminder cards identifying major problems caused by addiction to the internet.

Many individuals may use the internet because of a lack of tangible social support. Real-life support groups outside of the internet could be employed where alternative activities and hobbies could be explored and developed. Groups based on the 12-Step principles can help address maladaptive thinking which may lead to internet addiction and provide an opportunity to share common concerns, issues, and build a meaningful real-life relationship. These groups can help individuals rely less on the internet for the support, companionship, and communication that may be missing in their lives.

For marriages and families that have been disrupted by internet addiction, family therapy may be helpful and beneficial. Young (1999) identified several areas where interventions should focus: (1) Educating the family about the nature of internet addiction; (2) reduction of blaming the addict for their behavior; (3) opening communication about the problems and issues which may have driven the addict to seek out fulfillment of psychological and emotional needs online; (4) encouraging the family to help in the recovery process by finding new hobbies, taking a vacation, and listening to the addict's feelings. Family support is crucial in order to help the addict in the recovery process.

Lastly, pharmacological treatments have included SSRIs and extended-release methylphenidate, which is a drug used to treat ADHD and OCD (Dell'Osso, Allen, Altamura, Buoli, & Hollander, 2008). A dopamine and norepinephrine inhibitor, Bupropion, which is used in substance abuse treatment, has been associated with a reduction in internet use and depression (Han et al., 2011). As an alternative treatment, electronic acupuncture was associated with a reduction in internet addiction and impulsiveness scores (Yang et al., 2017). Because adolescents who are addicted to the internet are vulnerable to drug use, a comorbid diagnosis with substance abuse should be evaluated and treated if found.

Case Application

Based on the information that we know about the Rothers family, there has not been any stated behavioral addiction. However, during our assessment, it will be very important to ask questions around several of these areas as there is a higher preponderance of behavioral addictions when there is a substance abuse disorder. Thus, the therapist should assess what happens when Mark is alone and whether he is having issues with the internet in regards to online gaming or internet sex. Exploration of his engagement with sports and whether he is involved in sports betting and to what degree would help to determine whether Mark may be a problem gambler. The therapist should assess whether Mark, when he is using drugs and/or alcohol, changes his usage of gambling and the internet.

While Mark may or may not engage in a behavioral addiction, other family members may as well. The therapist should assess all family members for their use of drugs and alcohol as well as for the possibility of someone having a behavioral addiction. Pete is least likely in the family to exhibit symptoms while Kayleigh is also unlikely—both due to their age. Given his age, Steve is likely to frequently engage the internet, which would lead the therapist to assess if his (or anyone's) internet use is problematic. Lastly, the therapist's assessment should also explore Hannah's drug and substance use, as well as possibilities for compulsive buying as well as internet usage and sexual behaviors.

Summary

In this chapter the behavioral addictions of gambling disorder, sex, compulsive buying, and internet were presented along with their relationship to substance abuse and family functioning. It appears there is much overlap between these behavioral addictions and substance use disorders. Behavioral addictions encompass time consumed pursuing the addiction, excessive and repeated use of engaging in the behavior, and lack of ability to stop or change the behavior despite negative consequences.

Therapists should be aware of the behavioral addictions mentioned above, as well as how substance use often accompanies them. Treatment for behavioral disorders includes many evidence-based approaches such

(continued)

(continued)

as 12-step self-help groups, family therapy, cognitive behavioral therapy, dialectical behavior therapy, and pharmacological interventions. Because of the similarities between the brain pathways of substance use disorders and behavioral addictions, and the fact that both disorders often occur together, it is imperative that research is continued in this area to effectively treat these disorders.

Key Words

behavioral addictions
gambling disorder
sex addiction

compulsive buying disorder
internet addiction
internet gaming disorder

Discussion Questions

1. What are behavioral addictions?
2. What are the similarities and differences between gambling disorder, sex addiction, compulsive buying disorder, and internet addiction disorder?
3. What is the relationship between substance use disorders and behavioral addictions?
4. What role does the family play in the development of gambling disorder, sex addiction, compulsive buying disorder, and internet addiction disorder?
5. What is the impact of gambling disorder, sex addiction, compulsive buying disorder, and internet addiction disorder on the family?
6. What are the treatment options for gambling disorder, sex addiction, compulsive buying disorder, and internet addiction disorder?

PART II

TREATMENT

TEN

Working with Partial Systems

The family therapist's job would be substantially easier if every member of the family was fully engaged and committed to moving the family forward. However, this is usually an unrealistic expectation to have when working with families; especially those that are dealing with some type of addiction. As we discussed in Chapter 8, people may be at different stages of readiness for change. We can look at a family, as a whole, being in the precontemplation, contemplation, preparation or action stage, yet there is also each member who may be at varying stages. For instance, the wife may be at the preparation stage, the addicted husband in the precontemplation stage, and the child at the contemplation stage (and this is only talking about their readiness for change in one particular issue—people and families deal with multiple issues at the same time).

Given this, when therapy is started, not all family members may be willing to come to the session. Sometimes the non-addicted family members may think that the fault lies completely with the addicted individual and that they do not need to attend a session. In other families, it may be that the addicted person does not see a problem and refuses to attend therapy. Depending on the therapist's orientation, the level of motivation of each person in the family, and the presenting problems, the therapist may work in a variety of ways with families where one or more member is abusing substances. The Center for Substance Abuse Treatment (2004, p. xxii) provided four levels of therapist involvement when working with families dealing with addiction:

- Level 1: Counselor has little or no involvement with the family.
- Level 2: Counselor provides the family with psychoeducation and advice.
- Level 3: Counselor addresses family members' feelings and provides them with support.
- Level 4: Counselor provides family therapy (when trained at this level of expertise).

Working with the family can be quite daunting for therapists, especially those not trained in family therapy. This can lead to tension between the therapist and the family members, particularly parents of substance-abusing youth (Misouridou & Papadatou, 2017). The rest of this book will focus on concepts and programs that address each of these levels of family engagement in order to better help substance abuse therapists enhance their relationships and better utilize family members in the treatment process. This chapter primarily focuses on level 2, and Chapters 13–15 on levels 3 and 4. This current chapter explores possibilities of working with the family system when you only have a partial family—i.e., where not all of the members agree to engage in therapy.

The primary person who will most likely not engage in treatment is the person dealing with the substance abuse. Of substance abusers, 90–95% in any given year do not seek therapy or self-help (Landau et al., 2000). Usually, once the family members have gotten to the point of not accepting the drinking/drugging behavior (and the associated consequences), they attempt to get the addicted person into treatment. This is usually met with resistance, as the abuser is most likely in the precontemplation stage regarding the issue. Given this, what can family members do to make their situation better? One possibility is that they can attend a self-help support group, find a different way of getting their family member/loved one to engage in treatment, or seek therapy for themselves.

This chapter explores various self-help programs related to substance abuse, primarily 12-step programs. It also focuses on several prominent treatment programs for people in the abuser's social network, which can be beneficial for them, even if the addicted individual never enters treatment. While these programs may be geared specifically for the non-addicted family members, they have the added potential benefit of helping to get the addicted individual to engage in treatment, whether it be individual or family therapy or a self-help group. The use of therapy for a cooperative member, usually for changing the behavior of a uncooperative member, is generally called **unilateral family therapy** (Thomas & Santa, 1982). This chapter presents several programs that can be considered to be under the auspices of unilateral family therapy.

Self-Help Groups

Millions of individuals dealing with various types of addiction, as well as their loved ones, seek help and support through self-help groups. Alcoholics Anonymous, the most famous and largest self-help group for addiction, has a worldwide active membership of over 2 million people. **Self-help groups** occur outside the realm of formal therapy, where individuals who are dealing with a particular substance or issue (alcohol, cocaine, gambling, etc.), or their family members, come together to talk about how they are impacted by the addiction. Self-help is a bit of a misnomer as one of the main benefits of these groups is being supported and helped by others.

One of the benefits of self-help groups comes through the notion of **universality** (Yalom & Leszcz, 2005), where the individual can take solace knowing they are not alone in the problem and that many other people experience the same thing. Further, many of these self-help groups utilize a **sponsor**—a person who is farther along in the process who acts as a guide. Sponsors usually are available any day of the week, at any time, as a first response in case the individual has serious urges to use whatever substance they are trying to stop using.

As a mental health professional you will not, unless you are in active recovery, have any direct involvement in self-help groups. They are not therapist-led. However, it is important to know how they function, as they can be a key component in the change process for clients. Having a thorough understanding of the various groups, as well as how a client can access them, is important in case a client and/or family that you are working with might find benefit from them.

Yet not all self-help groups are the same. Depending on your client and their values, one group might be a better fit than another. For instance, some are more confrontational than others or there might be a spiritual component that a person may or may not appreciate. This chapter provides you with an overview of some of the most significant self-help groups in the substance abuse realm.

Alcoholics Anonymous

The most famous and most popular addictions self-help group is **Alcoholics Anonymous (AA)**. Alcoholics Anonymous began in the 1930s through a confluence of events. Rowland H. sought help for his alcoholism from Carl Jung. Jung believed that Rowland did not need medical help, but, rather, spiritual help. He referred him to the Oxford Group, which was a religious movement that focused on self-improvement through an exploration of one's actions, making amends for wrongs committed, prayer, meditation, and then bringing this message to others. Over time Rowland recruited Ebby T. to the Oxford Group. One of Ebby's drinking buddies was Bill W., a past successful stockbroker who had declined in functioning based on the effects of alcohol. Although he was reluctant at first, Bill W. had a spiritual awakening and dedicated himself to helping others dealing with alcoholism.

Bill W. then joined the Oxford Group and began to attend meetings, providing his voice of hope to others. In 1935, Bill W. was introduced to Dr. Bob. From their first meeting, the two men realized the importance of two alcoholics talking to one another. Dr. Bob's last drink was on June 10, 1935. This date is considered to be the birth date of Alcoholics Anonymous.

Eventually AA developed **The Twelve Steps**. These steps have become one of the most influential guidelines in the substance abuse field. They are that we:

1. Admitted we were powerless over alcohol—that our lives had become unmanageable.
2. Came to believe that a power greater than ourselves could restore us to sanity.
3. Made a decision to turn our will and our lives over to the care of God *as we understood Him.*
4. Made a searching and fearless moral inventory of ourselves.
5. Admitted to God, to ourselves, and to another human being the exact nature of our wrongs.
6. Were entirely ready to have God remove all these defects of character.
7. Humbly asked Him to remove our shortcomings.
8. Made a list of all persons we had harmed, and became willing to make amends to them all.
9. Made direct amends to such people wherever possible, except when to do so would injure them or others.
10. Continued to take personal inventory, and when we were wrong, promptly admitted it.

11. Sought through prayer and meditation to improve our conscious contact with God *as we understood Him*, praying only for knowledge of His will for us and the power to carry that out.
12. Having had a spiritual awakening as the result of these steps, we tried to carry this message to alcoholics, and to practice these principles in all our affairs.

Although Alcoholics Anonymous is strictly a self-help program, where meetings are run by members (some of whom may be mental health professionals, but engaging in their role as someone in recovery rather than in a clinical capacity), many therapists discuss with their clients the benefits of engaging in AA as an auxiliary to more formal therapy. Alcoholics Anonymous can be a useful component of a wider treatment regimen, or can stand on its own for the individual. Usually, if done in conjunction with therapy, the individual continues engaging in AA long after termination with their therapist.

There are three types of AA meetings; Speaker meetings, Discussion meetings, and Step meetings (see Figure 10.1). In **Speaker meetings**, various members, one at a time, self-disclose to the other participants about their own experience with addiction—in essence, they tell their story. There may be some discussion about the person's story afterward. In **Discussion meetings**, members talk about their own experience with addiction yet the meeting centers on a specific topic related to substance abuse. For **Step meetings**, one of the 12 steps will be chosen as the focal point of the conversation wherein members talk about their personal experiences trying to engage that step.

Most AA meetings, especially Speaker meetings, are **open meetings**, meaning that anyone can attend. **Closed meetings** only allow people who are members or prospective members. Alcoholics Anonymous meetings are all free, regardless of meeting type. When someone first begins to attend AA, they are encouraged to attend 90 meetings in 90 days. As the person reaches certain temporal milestones

Speaker Meetings

• Various members tell their stories

Discussion Meetings

• Members tell their stories around a topic

Step Meetings

• Focus on one of the 12 steps

Figure 10.1 Alcoholics Anonymous has three different types of meetings: Speaker, Discussion or Step meetings

of sobriety, they receive a token, called a **sobriety coin**, which is a reminder of their accomplishment. Most people who attend AA will eventually read the *Big Book*, which was written by the founders of AA in 1939 and has become the foundation upon which the groups operate.

Alcoholics Anonymous conducts a triennial survey of its members to obtain demographic data. The 2014 survey found that almost 90% of AA members identified as White, 4% as Black, and 3% as Hispanic. Approximately 50% of members were between 41 and 60 years old. Forty-one percent were married or had a life partner, 32% were single, and 21% were divorced. Fifty-seven percent of AA members were referred by a counselor, medical, or mental health professional. Thirty-two percent were introduced to AA by an AA member, 30% were self-motivated, 27% were introduced by family, and 12% by the judicial system. Approximately 50% of AA members have been sober for five or more years; 22% being sober for over 20 years. On average, members attend 2.5 meetings per week. Fifty-nine percent of members received some type of treatment before beginning AA, with 74% of them finding this treatment useful in helping to get them connected to AA. After going to AA, 58% of members received treatment, with 84% saying this treatment was important for their recovery. Alcoholics Anonymous attendance for those wanting help with alcohol problems leads to short and long-term decreases in alcohol use (Humphreys, Blodgett, & Wagner, 2014). However, for those who already were part of the AA community, increasing attendance may not impact the level of alcohol consumption.

Al-Anon

While AA and similar groups such as Narcotics Anonymous (NA), Cocaine Anonymous (CA), and others are designed for the person who is utilizing the substances, groups such as **Al-Anon** are geared toward the loved ones who are in relationship with the addicted person. However, the two movements are intertwined.

Lois W., the wife of AA cofounder Bill W., was a cofounder of Al-Anon. Having traveled with him across the country to various AA groups, she was able to talk informally with other addicts' family members, and gained benefit from these interactions. Family members realized that when they, as well as the alcoholic, lived by the 12 steps, family relationships improved (although it was still a process of growth in dealing with the continuing changes based on everyone's new contributions to the family). These informal meetings came to be known as **Family Groups**.

Al-Anon began more formally in 1951 when the various Family Groups were unified. Given their belief in the 12 Steps, Al-Anon petitioned AA to use them. Once this was granted, Al-Anon changed only one word of the steps. This was in the last and final step where instead of "carry this message to alcoholics" Al-Anon uses "carry this message to others."

Al-Anon meetings are less about the alcoholic and more about the family members living with the alcoholic. Many of these family members, particularly spouses, view themselves as just as sick or sicker than the alcoholic. Al-Anon is the most utilized support source for family members of someone dealing with problem drinking (O'Farrell & Clements, 2012). Al-Anon is viewed as beneficial because of its philosophy, accessibility, effectiveness, format, and the possibility of having the alcoholic reduce or stop drinking (Young & Timko, 2015).

O'Farrell and Fals-Stewart (2003) found that family members of alcoholics who were referred to Al-Anon or engaged in Al-Anon-facilitated therapy showed increased coping abilities. As we will discuss in systems theory (see Chapter 11), when one part of the system changes, the other parts are perturbed and may change as well. Thinking back to our discussion of family roles, these roles were developed as a means of coping for the current state of the addicted family. When members can cope in other, more functional ways, it changes the rules of the system leading to change from the remaining family members. However, there is a fundamental difference between how 12-step fellowships and traditional family therapies view the role of substance abuse (Nowinski, 1999). Twelve-step fellowships hold that addiction is a primary dysfunction whereas many family therapies view addiction as a symptom of family dysfunction. This is why 12-step programs primarily focus on helping people become sober and maintain sobriety for the rest of their lives.

Just as Alcoholics Anonymous has expanded to cover various drugs such as Narcotics Anonymous and Cocaine Anonymous, Al-Anon has grown as well. Groups such as Alateen (designed specifically for younger members) and Nar-Anon (developed for friends and family of drug addicts) provide a resource for family members living in a house that has drugs and/or alcohol as a primary organizing component.

Twelve-Step Facilitation

The previous 12-step groups are usually not therapist-led and can be used by people alone or in conjunction with psychotherapy. However, for therapists working in the addictions field who support these programs, one of the keys is to help get the substance abuser to actually go to the meetings and then have them become active in working the steps. One way of doing so is through **twelve-step facilitation** (TSF). Twelve-step facilitation, originally developed in the early 1990s for the Project MATCH program, is a means for therapists to encourage their clients to attend and use various 12-step programs (Nowinski, 2006, 2012, 2015; Nowinski & Baker, 2018). Twelve-step facilitation can be used for individuals, couples, families, or in a group setting. One of the benefits of TSF is that the therapist does not have to be an expert on 12-step programs; just that they have the desire to help their clients access this resource. Twelve-step facilitation is considered to be an evidence-based treatment (Nowinski, 2006, 2012; Nowinski & Baker, 2018).

There are two primary goals to TSF: Acceptance and surrender (Nowinski & Baker, 2018). These goals correspond to the first three steps of AA. These authors explained that, "By acceptance, we mean the breakdown of the illusion that the individual, through willpower alone, can effectively and reliably limit or control his/her use of alcohol and/or drugs" (p. 3). **Acceptance** here is viewed in terms of the substance abuser accepting they are dealing with a chronic illness, that their life has become unmanageable, they don't have the willpower alone to fix things, and the only solution is abstinence. Nowinski and Baker continued, "Surrender involves a willingness to reach out beyond oneself and to follow the program laid out in the twelve steps" (p. 3). **Surrender** is related to recovery being only through sustained sobriety, faith that a Higher Power can help them, a belief that fellowship with other addicts is a path to sobriety, and a belief that their best chances for sobriety are through the twelve steps and twelve-step community.

Twelve-step facilitation is organized around three programs: core, elective, and conjoint (Nowinski, 2012; Nowinski & Baker, 2018). The **core** or **basic program** is designed for those in early recovery, where the individual most likely is experiencing ambivalence. It involves an introduction and assessment, focus on acceptance, exploration of people, places, and routines, exploration of surrender, and promotes getting active. The core program is an in-depth conversation between therapist and client that addresses the first three steps of the 12-step program as well as how the person might get active in meetings and seek a sponsor (Nowinski, 2015).

The **elective program** is designed to assist the person in making AA or NA an active lifelong aspect of their recovery (Nowinski & Baker, 2018). This program usually lasts between four to six sessions. It focuses on six topics: genograms, enabling, people-places-routines, emotions, moral inventories, and relationships. Depending on the needs of the client, any of these elective topics might be covered. During this stage of the program, the facilitator might cover areas from both the core and elective programs. Whichever topics are covered, the elective program always is focused on three behavioral objectives: Helping the substance abuser go to meetings, being active in AA or NA, and getting and using a sponsor.

In the **conjoint program,** the facilitator works with the substance abuser and his or her partner. This program lasts for two sessions. The purpose is to help educate the partner/family member about alcoholism and/or addiction as well as inform them about the 12-step model. During this program, the facilitator explores issues such as enabling and detaching. The partner is encouraged to attend at least six Al-Anon or Nar-Anon meetings.

Nowinski (2012) explained that TSF's objectives can be broken down into two categories: (1) active involvement and (2) identification and bonding. For TSF, **active involvement** means that the person who has been abusing drugs or alcohol is going to 12-step meetings. And not just going to meetings, but working the steps. This may necessitate the therapist helping the person to work through issues of resistance. During early recovery when using TSF, the therapist might explore with the person how many meetings they go to, the type of meeting (i.e., Speaker, Step, or Discussion), and how active the person is during the meetings. One means of doing this is through a recovery journal. The **recovery journal** is used by the client to record all of the meetings he or she went to, the type of meeting, as well as their own reactions to the meeting.

The second category of TSF objectives is that of **identification** and **bonding** (Nowinski, 2012). Part of this happens through a process of psychoeducation where therapist and client talk about the various stereotypes the person has about 12-step programs, its members, and the process of what happens at meetings. Then the therapist encourages the person to attend a meeting and further evaluate the stereotypes they had. After having attended at least one meeting, the therapist will likely ask whether there was a person whose story the client identified with and to which they could relate. This is the beginning stage of helping the client in bonding to the 12-step community. Figure 10.2 presents the goals, programs, and objectives of twelve-step facilitation.

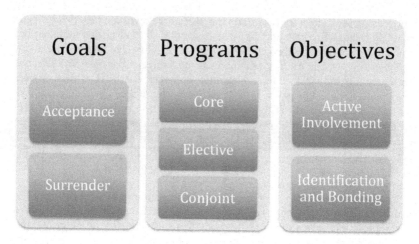

Figure 10.2 Twelve-step facilitation is based on two goals, two objectives, and three different programs to help get the addicted individual to attend a twelve step program

Termination in TSF happens when there is a "turning over" of the person to the 12-step community (Nowinski, 2012). The goal of TSF is to enhance the identification and bonding of the individual to the 12-step program to enhance their active involvement. The belief is that greater bonding to the twelve-step community leads to greater active involvement in it and a higher likelihood of lifelong sobriety.

Moderation Management

The self-help groups that we have discussed thus far all operate from the disease model of addiction and have abstinence from the substance as the goal for the individual. They believe that the person should not use the substance (or similar substances) for the rest of their lives. However, not all groups abide by this philosophy. One such group is **Moderation Management** (MM). Developed in 1994 by Audrey Kishline, Moderation Management is an alternative to AA and other 12-step groups. Rather than a disease model, it is based on a cognitive-behavioral approach. Instead of targeting the alcoholic—someone whose use of the substance is severe—MM is designed for the problem drinker. Since there are many more problem drinkers than alcoholics, MM has a wide catchment of potential participants.

Moderation Management views alcohol abuse as a habit; a pattern of learned behavior rather than as a disease (Kishline, 1994). This distinction between a habit and a disease is a very consequential one. Whereas with a disease the person needs to always be aware of the disease and take steps to keep it in remission, habits are much more temporary. Once the person changes their learned behavior and continues to engage in the new behavior rather than the previous pattern,

Figure 10.3 Moderation Management does not specifically push for abstinence, but instead attempts to help the person reduce the harm of alcohol consumption

they do not need to think about the problem as they used to. This goes counter to the notion that alcoholism is an irreversible progression wherein the individual does not have control over themselves.

In MM, the person is not directed to abstinence (see Figure 10.3). Instead, a treatment matching occurs where the level of treatment coincides with the level of the problem (Kishline, 1994). For those people whose problems are less severe, intervention will be reduced. For those with more severe alcohol problems, more significant self-management tools will be implemented. This goes counter to the AA model where everyone, regardless of severity, is instructed to follow the 12 steps.

To explain this in more depth, if a client came to MM and was in the beginning stages of heavy alcohol consumption, they might be directed to lessen the amount of alcohol consumed, but would not need medical services. However, a heavy alcohol consumer might need more medical supervision to deal with withdrawal symptoms.

Moderation Management groups are free and are led by volunteers. When someone begins in the group they are asked to abstain from alcohol for 30 days. This is to allow them to shift out of their current problematic drinking behavior patterns. During this time they are asked to think about how alcohol has impacted them, what their priorities are, and the conditions of their alcohol use (who, what, where, when). Once the 30-day abstinence period is up, the individual sets moderate drinking limits. They begin to make small steps toward changing their lifestyle. At this point they review their progress and revise their goals, if needed.

Participants in MM tend to be White (98% of participants), female (66% of participants), and educated (94% having attended at least one year of college) (Kosok, 2006). A majority of members utilize MM as their first attempt at help in reducing their drinking (56% of participants). The other 44% had unsuccessfully sought help through AA or therapy. Before starting MM, 61% of members had engaged in daily consumption of alcohol, averaging six drinks per day.

Sanchez-Craig, Wilkinson, and Davila (1995) determined that there is an upper limit of drinking that people who have been problem drinkers should follow. For men, they should drink no more than four standard drinks in a day and no more than 16 in a week. For women, they should drink no more than three standard drinks in a day and no more than 12 in a week. These authors found that their results compared with guidelines from other official bodies and recommended that those who are working toward moderation, rather than abstinence, adhere to these limits.

Moderation Management is not as widely popular or known as Alcoholics Anonymous and other self-help programs. This may be because it is not as publicized as AA, and therapists and other medical professionals base their view of addiction on a disease model rather than the possibility of controlled drinking (Kosok, 2006). However, for some who are dealing with problem drinking, moderation and harm reduction is a viable option.

Working With the Non-Addicted Family Members

Usually in families where there is some type of substance abuse, it is usually the person who is abusing the substance who is the last person who wants to attend therapy sessions. In this case, effective therapy can still occur, even without this person. Marriage and family therapy can be used with the non-addicted individuals. This can be for two purposes (O'Farrell & Clements, 2012). First, the therapy allows the family members to cope with the family situation. Since we know that a change in one part of the system can lead to system-wide change, even if the addicted person never comes to therapy, if other family members change, the repetitive dysfunctional transactions in the family have a higher likelihood of being altered. A second purpose for the non-addicted family members to go to treatment is that it helps to motivate the addicted individual to enter treatment themselves.

When family members go to therapy without the addicted person, they decrease their emotional distress (O'Farrell & Clements, 2012). This is based on unilateral family therapy, which occurs when one or more family members engage in therapy around the substance abuse issue, but where the person who is using is not involved in the therapy (Thomas & Santa, 1982). One of the first tasks when working with the non-using family member is to help them to change their enabling behaviors (Zelvin, 2014). The focus on problem-maintaining interpersonal patterns is important since familial support for all members is integral in the change of family rules and roles.

Various programs/models have been developed to either work with the family alone (regardless of whether the dependent enters treatment) or with the family to bring the abuser into the treatment fold. In this section we will talk about three of the most prominent: ARISE, CRAFT, and the Johnson Intervention.

ARISE

One such program to work with the non-addicted family is ARISE. Initially this acronym stood for the Albany-Rochester Interventional Sequence for Engagement (Garrett et al., 1997); it now stands for A Relational Intervention Sequence for Engagement (Garrett & Landau, 2007; Landau & Garrett, 2008). The **ARISE** model is a manual-driven relational intervention that assists non-substance-abusing family members to get the addicted individual into treatment (Landau & Garrett, 2008). The ARISE model was born from families not using the Johnson Intervention (see below) and based on ideas from systems theory and addictions treatment. However, one of the main factors that sets ARISE apart from typical interventions is that it is an invitational model, where the substance abuser is invited at each stage of the program to participate rather than having a surprise approach. Landau and Garrett (2008) explained, "It draws on the connectedness, interest and commitment of other concerned members of the extended family and support system to motivate the alcoholic or substance abuser to enter treatment" (pp. 148–149).

The ARISE model is rooted in the notion of engagement methods, where the network of the substance abuser is the focus of intervention (Landau et al., 2000). The therapist works with these individuals until the substance abuser enters treatment/self-help. Sometimes the abuser is part of these meetings, but is not yet seeking treatment; many times they are not. As noted, ARISE focuses on engagement of the substance abuser to encourage them to seek therapeutic services. As such, ARISE is not a therapy model but rather a pre-treatment engagement technique (Landau & Garrett, 2008).

The **Family Motivation to Change model** is based on the notion that the family can play a key role in helping in the recovery from alcoholism for a member of the family. These underlying assumptions form the groundwork for the effectiveness of the ARISE model (Landau et al., 2000). The abuser's social network is viewed as being competent and accessible; concerned individuals who are able to help the abuser. Part of the intervention is to get members of the social network to realize their own competencies so that they can be more successful in their interactions with others. This is important since it is the individuals in the abuser's social network who truly care for and love them, and spend a majority of time with them, rather than treatment professionals. The ARISE model helps the support system to utilize honesty in contacting the abuser to establish trust and an implication that a long-term relationship is desired. This investment in the person's recovery is significant since the abuser's social network will most likely have the greatest impact on them.

Family Motivation to Change is based on the multifaceted forces that occur in a family, pushing it toward health during an unhealthy or crisis period (Garrett & Landau, 2007). When disruption happens in a family, one member usually sacrifices him/herself for the protection of the family. This may come in the form of developing a substance abuse disorder. While this may not seem to be useful, they are providing a way for the family to distract themselves from other problems (perhaps loss and grief) and put the focus on them and their newfound problematic behavior instead.

There are three stages to the ARISE program (Garrett & Landau, 2007; Garrett et al., 1997; Landau & Garrett, 2008). The therapist will work with the family members starting at level 1 and will stop at the first level where the person with the drinking problem enters into treatment. As such, it is a brief approach that is focused on efficiency. **Level 1** is when the treatment professional begins to work with one or more concerned individuals in regards to a substance abuser. These may be phone or face-to-face meetings. It is designed to get information on who is involved in the family and encouraging members, including the substance abuser, to come to treatment. The person who contacts the therapist (called the "**First Caller**") is told that they did right by calling, that the ARISE method can help, that they should get as many family members and concerned others to help them as possible, that they should operate with love and respect, and that they do not have to deal with the alcoholic on their own anymore. Through the First Caller's attempt at inviting the alcoholic into treatment, 55% of alcoholics decide to come for the first session (Landau et al., 2004). At this level, the therapist attempts to increase the level of hope in the family.

Level 2 is when the therapist meets with the family, usually for two to five sessions. These sessions may or may not have the alcoholic involved. They are designed to develop motivational strategies for family members; all in the pursuit of getting the substance-dependent into treatment. Most families are able to get the alcoholic into treatment while working at this stage, thus meaning there no need to proceed to level 3.

The third and final stage is **level 3**, to which only 2% of families need to get in order to motivate the alcoholic into treatment (Garrett & Landau, 2007; Landau & Garrett, 2008). This level includes the therapist helping family members to set limits and consequences for the dependent person. This is done in a respectful and supportive way by family members. In a manualized treatment study, the ARISE approach was found to have an 83% success rate of working with the concerned other to help engage a substance abuser into either treatment or some type of self-help (Landau et al., 2004). Figure 10.4 presents the three levels of the ARISE program.

The ARISE model is a cost-efficient approach since the concerned others of the substance abuser take on a lot of responsibility for getting the substance abuser into treatment (Landau & Garrett, 2008). In a National Institute of Drug Abuse (NIDA) study, the average total time per case was 1.5 hours and lasted a median of seven days (Landau et al., 2004). The ARISE model is also an effective method, as, based on the NIDA study, it has helped concerned others get the substance abuser into therapy or self-help groups 83% of the time. Ninety-five percent of people chose treatment while 5% chose self-help. The model has primarily been used for people with a substance-abusing family member, but has also been used for those with online sex addiction (Landau, Garrett, & Webb, 2008).

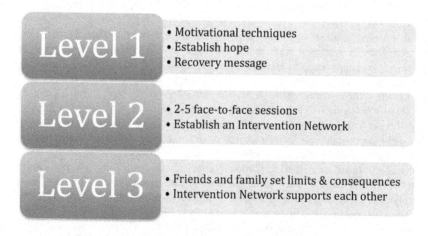

Figure 10.4 The three levels of the ARISE program. Treatment does not move to the next level if the addicted individual enters treatment

CRAFT

Robert J. Meyers developed the **Community Reinforcement And Family Training (CRAFT) program**. Based on learning theory, CRAFT was designed for concerned significant others of individuals with alcohol and/or drug problems who refused to go to treatment. This program is an off-shoot of the Community Reinforcement Approach, developed by Azrin, which was geared toward the alcohol/drug user (Meyers, Roozen, & Smith, 2011). Through the principles of operant conditioning, community reinforcement attempts to shift the drug user from a problematic to pleasurable lifestyle without alcohol or drugs. This new rewarding lifestyle is enhanced through the community of family and employment.

The family members of the addict are referred to as **Concerned Significant Others (CSOs)**. There are three main goals of the program (Smith & Meyers, 2004). The first is to attempt to get the abuser into treatment. While that is occurring the second goal is to get whoever is overusing substances in the family to decrease their use. The last goal focuses on how CSOs can enhance other problematic areas of their lives to move towards a more enjoyable life. This program is viewed as a motivational rather than confrontational style (Smith, Meyers, & Austin, 2008).

The CRAFT program shifts the development of a rewarding non-drug lifestyle from the person who is using the drugs to the significant others of that individual. The program is useful for those whose partner/family member/friend is refusing to go to treatment. Participants in CRAFT are taught how to arrange the home environment so that when the drug-using individual engages in behaviors of sobriety/non-drug use they are rewarded, via operant conditioning principles. Unlike Al-Anon, which does not intentionally try to change the drug user, CRAFT is geared to help not only the concerned significant other but the drug user as well.

Because the focus of CRAFT is on the CSO rather than the substance-abusing individual it is important for the therapist to ensure they are building rapport and motivation with the CSO. This is because CSOs tend to enter the CRAFT program highly enthusiastic and motivated, but to change the behaviors of the substance abuser. As Smith, Meyers, and Austin (2008) explained,

> This enthusiasm sometimes waivers a bit when, in the course of the CRAFT program description, CSOs discover that *they* are the ones who are going to have to do all of the hard work to influence this behavior change [the other's substance use]. (p. 175, italics in original)

Further, CSOs are encouraged in the program through understanding that there will most likely be an enrichment in their own lives.

During the program, the clinician asks the CSOs to conduct a CRAFT **functional analysis**, which looks at the purpose of the drinker's behavior from the perspective of someone other than the substance abuser (Smith, Meyers, and Austin, 2008). It explores the positively and negatively reinforcing behaviors of the person's drinking through exploration of the person's patterns of use, external triggers (i.e., the who, where, and when of drinking), and internal triggers (i.e., the person's thoughts and feelings associated with the initiation of drinking). The analysis then is used to help develop a plan of action.

The CSOs are taught positive communication skills since they usually want to maintain relationships with the problem drinker (Smith, Meyers, and Austin, 2008). The basic rules for positive communication that are taught in the program include: be brief, positive, specific, label one's feelings, provide an understanding statement, accept partial responsibility of non-drinking problems, and offer help. Further, CSOs are taught how to positively reinforce non-drinking behavior. This includes an understanding of what might serve as reinforcers for the drinker. Given that sober behaviors are being rewarded, drinking behaviors are met by withdrawing reinforcers. That is, if the CSO was going to spend quality time with the person if they did not drink, they should not spend that quality time if the person is not sober.

From the beginning of their involvement in the CRAFT program, CSOs are prepared to think about when and how to invite the substance abuser to enter treatment. Usually this comes after the previous interventions of positive communication skills, knowledge and facility of providing positive reinforcement for sober behavior, and withdrawal of positive reinforcement for drinking behavior. The therapist works with the CSO to identify the most promising times and places for the invitation to enter treatment (Smith, Meyers, and Austin, 2008). Suggestions for the CSO to use during the invitation includes telling the drinker they can have their own therapist (and not the CSO's), they can use therapy for issues above and beyond alcohol, they will be a co-collaborator of treatment and treatment goals, and they can go to therapy on a trial basis to see if it is helpful for them. Figure 10.5 presents the pathways to the goal of the CRAFT program—getting the substance abuser into treatment.

Meyers, Miller, Smith, and Tonigan (2002) found that CSOs who participated in 12 sessions of CRAFT or CRAFT plus aftercare had higher rates of partner engagement in therapy than a group that attended Al-Anon and Nar-Anon facilitation therapy. In the CRAFT group, 58.6% of unmotivated drug users engaged in treatment. This engagement percentage increased to 76.7% for the CRAFT plus aftercare group. In the Al-Anon/Nar-Anon facilitation group the unmotivated drug user only engaged in treatment 29% of the time. One potential reason for this discrepancy is that Al-Anon is not designed to attempt to get the using family member into treatment, but as a program to focus on oneself.

These results compared favorably with a previous study focusing on CRAFT's efficacy (Miller, Meyers, & Tonigan, 1999). In this study, the CRAFT program was the most effective in getting previously unmotivated alcohol/drug users into therapy as compared with Al-Anon or the Johnson Intervention (which is a confrontative method of getting a drug-using partner into treatment; discussed next). Sixty-four percent of drug-using partners entered treatment for those in the CRAFT program. This is in contrast to 13% in the Al-Anon group and 30% in the Johnson group. Similar results were found by Roozen, de Waart, and van der Kroft (2010) where drug-user partner engagement was highest in the CRAFT group, second highest in the Johnson Institute Intervention and lowest is the Al-Anon/Nar-Anon condition. The CRAFT program is effective in an individual or group format (Manual et al., 2012).

Figure 10.5 The CRAFT program is designed to get the substance abuser to enter into treatment

Besides getting the substance abuser into treatment, CRAFT is also useful for the concerned others. The CRAFT program has been found to lead to significant reductions in symptoms of depression for CSOs as well as increases in relational happiness and mental health (Bischof, Iwen, Freyer-Adam, & Rumpf, 2016). This is significant since there can be a negative spiral between drug use and relational dysfunction but also a positive spiral between relational happiness and substance-use recovery.

Interventions

Perhaps the most iconic understanding that the lay population has of how families try to get the addicted individual to change is through interventions. There has even been a reality television show that presents families engaged in this process. **Interventions** are meetings, usually as a surprise to the person abusing substances, where family members and friends get together and let the addicted person know their fears for them and their hopes that the person will change.

Interventions, developed by Vernon Johnson in the 1960s, have come to be called either interventions or the Johnson Intervention. The belief behind interventions is that anyone who wants to help the addicted individual, regardless of background or clinical training, can help that person (Johnson, 1986). Interventions are based on the disease model of addiction (see Chapter 1).

This is why people who endorse interventions believe it is so important for those who care about the addicted individual to *do something*. If not, and the person does not get help, they believe the addicted individual will die. As Johnson explained, "Chemical dependency is a disease that kills. It is also a disease from which people can and do recover" (p. ix).

Interventions do not have to happen when a person "hits bottom" but can be enacted at any time that the individual is experiencing a loss of functioning in one or more areas of his or her life. Johnson (1986) defined an intervention as "presenting reality to a person out of touch with it in a receivable way" (p. 61). As we know, most individuals who are dealing with addiction live a life full of secrets, denials, and lies. They engage in many behaviors and beliefs to hide and mask the actual drug use as well as the physical, emotional, and behavioral consequences. Interventions provide a space for friends, family, and loved ones to try to get the substance abuser to move from behind the curtain of their denial to see the impact that their drug use is having on their own lives as well as on the lives of others. In intervention language, this process is called **confrontation**.

Interventions can be informal (not involving a mental health professional) or can be a formal intervention, defined as "a professionally guided, organized response to an individual that is intended, in part or total, to facilitate change in his or her substance using behavior" (Fernandez, Begley, & Marlatt, 2006, p. 207). Interventions are well-planned events that bring together individuals who care about the addicted person to help these individuals to shift from caring *for* the substance abuser. This is an important process as many members of the addicted individual's support system have either become co-dependent or helped to enable and maintain the problem behavior. Interventions not only provide a crisis for the substance abuser—to step up to the plate and deal with the reality of their addiction—but a crisis for the friends and family—to find a different way of caring about the person.

Instead of individuals trying to help one-on-one with the substance abuser, interventions bring the significant people in the abuser's life together so that they cannot be easily dismissed. The more people who are jointly concerned, the bigger the statement to the person that what is occurring is serious. Besides allowing the addicted person to see the enormity and reality of the situation, being a cohesive group helps to support the individuals involved. As a group, each member will more likely hold his or her ground and be honest with the addicted person as to the impact their behaviors are having.

The intervention team (see Figure 10.6) should be people who are meaningful to the addicted individual, have first-hand knowledge of the impact that chemical dependency has had on the person's life, are emotionally stable, and are willing to put their relationship with the person on the line (Johnson, 1986). This last characteristic is a very important point, as members must follow through in whatever it is they lay on the table.

The team members do not go into the intervention blindly, but come prepared with thoughts, ideas, and data that they can clearly provide for the abuser. There are two types of data they should have with them: facts about the individual's drug use and possibilities for treatment (Johnson, 1986). In terms of facts of drug use, they may compile lists of previous drug behavior and the consequences of that behavior. For instance, in the Rothers family, they might approach Mark

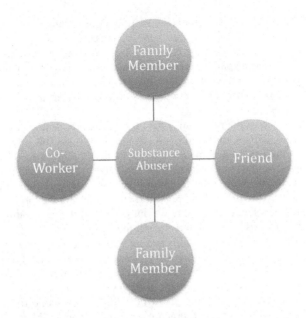

Figure 10.6 The intervention team in an intervention consists of people who are close and meaningful to the substance abuser

and talk about how when he drank on a specific night he forgot to visit his child, Nina, when he was supposed to. Since team members are encouraged to write down their prepared statements, they should do so in the second person: "Last Thursday, you went to the bar after work and had four beers, then you drove home and passed out having forgotten that you had arranged to pick your daughter up and take her out for ice cream." Each team member should have many of these specific incidents that they observed first-hand. It is important to be specific (i.e., "On Thursday you screamed and cursed at your son") rather than general (i.e., "Your drinking is problematic") since the more detailed the account the more difficult it is for the person to deny or rationalize it.

Given that the purpose of the intervention is to help the substance abuser get into some type of treatment, having a sense of these various opportunities is very important. Depending on the severity of the addiction, team members may come up with lists that include private practice therapists, outpatient facilities, inpatient facilities, various self-help groups or other possibilities.

Before the actual intervention, the team should meet to do one or two rehearsals of the intervention (Johnson, 1986). These rehearsals help prepare members for what is to come and help provide the confidence for them to follow through—as they are most likely expected to receive denial and resistance from the substance abuser. Team members can also use these rehearsals as a support system for one another and to help each other prepare better for the actual intervention. For instance, they might suggest to one member to develop a more detailed list of how they saw the person impacted by chemical dependency.

At the rehearsal, the first step for the group will be designating a **chairperson**. This is the person that will help facilitate the process of the intervention. This person's job is to ensure that the rehearsal, but more importantly the intervention, are focused on helping the person rather than turning it into an attack on the person—since the intervention is an attack on the addiction. Thus, those closest and most emotionally connected to the substance abuser may not be the best choice as chairperson.

The second step of the rehearsal is for each person, sequentially, to read their lists and have each item approved by the rest of the group. This helps to prevent an attack on the person and maintains a focus on the impact of the addiction. The list items should demonstrate each person's concern for the individual rather than other emotions such as anger, hostility, pity, or blame. The third step is determining the order of who will present their lists during the intervention. The chairperson makes sure everyone knows this order and that it is followed so that the intervention flows rather than turning into chaos.

The fourth step of the rehearsal is getting someone to role-play the addicted individual. This may be one person throughout or each team member may take a turn, as this step will allow each person to voice possible responses, denials, and reactions that the addicted person will likely have during the intervention. Step five is for team members to think about how they will respond to the abuser's replies. This allows them time to prepare a realistic response. Here, people take an internal audit of what they are willing to do in the situation and to agree to follow through on it. For instance, if Mark's wife, Hannah, threatens to take the kids and leave, she should be prepared to do this if he does not seek help after the intervention. False promises and unfulfilled ultimatums send a message to the abuser that they can continue to provide their excuses without real consequences. The last step is having the actual rehearsal.

At the time of the intervention, the chairperson will begin by trying to set the context that everyone is there because they care about the person and are hoping that something useful and productive comes from the meeting. Johnson (1986) provided a possible opening for the intervention:

> _____ (the name of the chemically dependent person), we're all here because we care about you and want to help. This is going to be difficult for you and for us, but one of the requests I have to start out with is that you give us the chance to talk and promise to listen, however hard that may be. We know it's not going to be easy for the next little while . . . Would you help us by just listening? (p. 81)

The intervention is not intended as a dialogue, as the substance abuser would most likely take it as an opportunity to deny and possibly blame others, but as a chance for the addicted individual to really hear the concern that others have for him.

Interventions may or may not involve a mental health professional. If so, the therapist shifts in their role of therapist to that of the chairperson of the intervention. This is important since this is not an actual therapy session but an attempt to get the substance abuser to recognize that drugs have negatively impacted them and others and that they need to engage treatment in some manner.

However, before the intervention takes place there are some contraindications to its use (Johnson, 1986). These include the substance abuser having a dual diagnosis, there having been violence or abusive behavior, the substance abuser having been depressed for an extended period of time, or that there is a possibility that the person is abusing multiple drugs (but that the team members are not sure what the other drug use is).

To summarize interventions, Johnson (1986) developed the **Five Principles of Intervention:**

1. Meaningful persons in the life of the chemically dependent person are involved.
2. All of the meaningful persons write down specific data about the events and behaviors involving the dependent person's chemical use which legitimatize their concern.
3. All of the meaningful persons tell the dependent person how they feel about what has been happening in their lives, and they do it in a nonjudgmental way.
4. The victim is offered specific choices—*this* treatment center, or *that* hospital.
5. When the victim agrees to accept help, it is made available immediately. (p. 103)

It is important for the treatment team to have set up the treatment options, so that if the addicted individual agrees to enter therapy they can do so immediately. The longer that it takes from the intervention to the availability of a treatment option, the greater the likelihood that the person will renege on their agreement.

One of the critiques of the Johnson Intervention is that it focuses exclusively on getting help for the addicted person and does not target change in the family system (Fernandez, Begley, & Marlatt, 2006). However, this is not necessarily the case. Once the intervention has ended, the team should meet with the therapist to process what happened and to talk about what they each might do to change themselves and their family (Connors, Donovan, & DiClemente, 2001).

According to Johnson (1986), interventions are effective in getting the substance abuser to agree to go for treatment 80% of the time. However, these results have been questioned as other studies have found quite different results. While the Johnson Intervention was found to be more effective than other types of referrals to outpatient therapy (coerced, noncoerced, unrehearsed, and unsupervised) in getting the addicted individual into treatment (Loneck, Garrett, & Banks, 1996a), it also had one of the highest relapse rates (Loneck, Garrett, & Banks, 1996b). The Johnson Intervention had a lower effectiveness (30%) of getting unmotivated problem drinkers into treatment than CRAFT (64%), but a higher rate than Al-Anon (13%) (Miller, Meyers, & Tonigan, 1999). These authors also found that 70% of the concerned significant others that had planned to engage in the family confrontation did not, but, for those that did, 75% were successful in getting the person into treatment.

A Johnson Intervention is perhaps one of the most controversial actions in the whole of the substance abuse field. This is an interesting conundrum since it is also the type of action that is perhaps most expected from the lay population besides attendance at AA. Some of the arguments against this method is that this type of "in your face" confrontation does not keep the individual in treatment. One of the problems with the approach is that if the person refuses treatment the team members are put on the spot to follow through with their ultimatums. Also, since it is a group of people who "surprise" the individual with this intervention, the addicted person may feel ganged up on as if a conspiracy is occurring against them.

Working Only With the Addicted Individual

We are not spending much time in this book discussing how to work only with the addicted individual, as that is the purview of most other substance abuse therapy books. Further, this is a book designed to help contextualize addiction within a family systems lens. As such, we will only use this small space to explain that there are many ways to work with only the addicted individual; however, this is not the preferred way of operating when dealing with addictions.

As we discussed in Chapter 1, family therapy can be done with only one family member. Although it may look like individual therapy (one client talking with one therapist), the content of what is being talked about will be different. Instead of talking about intrapsychic processes (i.e., unconscious conflict, faulty cognition, anxiety, and meaninglessness), the focus of family therapy with an individual will explore interpersonal transactions—what is going on *between* people rather than *within* a person. Although some of the models that we will talk about in the subsequent chapters are amenable to work with only one family member present, most of them are more effective when multiple family members are in session working together to change the family system.

Working with Multiple Systems

In this chapter we have explored therapeutic implications when the clinician is only able to work with a part of the family when there is substance abuse involved. This came in the form of the substance abuser or impacted family member going to a self-help group as well as several programs that are designed to help family members and friends get the substance abuser into treatment. In this last section we switch the focus to explore how therapists might work with multiple systems concurrently.

Multisystemic Therapy:
Joshua Leblang

Multisystemic Therapy (MST) is an evidence-based model designed to work with the caregivers of adolescents who are displaying anti-social behaviors, including substance use (Henggeler & Schaeffer, 2016; Henggeler et al., 2009). Dr. Scott Henggeler created the model after trying to identify a model to work with high-risk youth and finding little empirical evidence for most treatments. Multisystemic Therapy is designed to work with youth engaging in antisocial behavior, who are usually referred by the juvenile justice system (Henggeler &

Schaeffer, 2017). The overarching goal of MST is to empower families to resolve the serious problem behavior of their youth as well as to develop and utilize the resources to handle future potential problems (Sheidow & Henggeler, 2008). While effective for various presenting problems, such as anti-social behavior as well as serious emotional disturbance (Henggeler, Schoenwald, Rowland, & Cunningham, 2002), this section will focus more on MST's application with juveniles who are using and abusing substances. The Pathways to Desistance study (which followed more than 1,300 youths who committed serious offenses for seven years after their court involvement) found that the most common mental health problem was substance use disorder (76%) (Espinosa, Sorensen, & Lopez, 2013). However, the principles and procedures of MST remain the same, regardless of the presenting complaint.

Multisystemic Therapy is built upon the foundation of the **social ecological model** created by Bronfenbrenner (1979). Behaviors that we see are complex and multidetermined (e.g., while the adolescent may be doing the behavior, such as smoking marijuana, this is influenced by the systems around him/her, such as being around peers who smoke, having easy access to money, gaps in supervision, lack of clear expectations, etc.). Thus, an adolescent substance user may be influenced (positively or negatively) by their family, extended family, peers, school, and the greater community in which they reside, while at the same time exerting influence on these other systems (Henggeler et al., 2009).

Research indicates that working primarily on an individual basis with adolescents is challenging (Gearing, Schwalbe, & Short, 2012; Song & Omar, 2009; Sylwestrzak, Overholt, Ristau, & Coker, 2015). Often times, teenagers are not motivated to change their behavior. This creates problems in getting adolescents to appointments, keeping them in treatment as they may engage in stonewalling once in treatment, and little to no lasting changes as change in behavior is often mood- or time-dependent and can fluctuate from moment to moment. Adolescent development is a significant barrier as adolescents tend to have an increase in impulsive/risk-taking behaviors (including substances) (Willoughby et al., 2014). The adolescent brain goes through a period of myelination and pruning, as the prefrontal lobes are being developed (Squeglia, Jacobus, & Tapert, 2009). Additionally, there are often shifts in social groups as well as a pushing away from traditional family values, making it more challenging to manage effectively.

In contrast to the individual approaches listed earlier in this chapter, MST is focused on the ecological aspects that lead to substance use and abuse. Elliott, Huizinga, & Ageton (1985) identified that the greatest predictor of adolescent substance use is prior use. While this is informative, unfortunately no interventions have the ability to go back in time to prevent it from occurring. The second greatest predictor is an adolescent's peer group. The variables that lead to involvement with negative peers include elements from the family (high conflict, low warmth, low monitoring) and school (low academic achievement, poor school involvement). Hence, MST posits that the most effective way to achieve changes in youth behavior is by working with the family (Henggeler & Schaeffer, 2017; Henggeler et al., 2009). By doing so, the family is able to: change the way they interact with their youth; learn how to assist the school to better meet the needs of their child; increase involvement with prosocial peers; and thereby decrease opportunities for substance use.

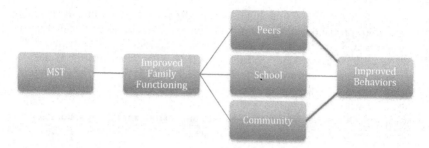

Figure 10.7 Multisystemic Therapy is designed to improve behavior through improved
family functioning as well as coordination through peers, school, and
community resources

Multisystemic Therapy therapists work using a home-based model of service
delivery where master's level therapists work with a caseload of four to six families and are available 24 hours a day/7 days a week (Henggeler & Schaeffer,
2017). An advanced MST practitioner [supervisor] supervises a team of two to
four therapists. The treatment team takes an ecological treatment approach to
help the youth and caregivers first assess and then intervene on the factors leading to the youth's substance use (Figure 10.7). Commonly, these factors include
low structure and monitoring by the youth's family and other adults in the community, limited access to positive activities at school or in the community, family
conflict, school failure, boredom, favorable attitudes toward drug use, and association with substance-using peers. In fact, being with other individuals who use
drugs has been established as the best predictor of adolescent drug use (Farrell &
Danish, 1993). In light of the strong influence of negative peers, MST therapists
work with caregivers to change the people with whom they associate—finding
positive pro-social friends to replace the negative or anti-social peers.

When MST therapists develop interventions for youth drug use, or other problem behaviors, care is taken to follow certain principles (See MST Nine Principles
and Figure 10.8), and these are considered to be key ingredients in MST's success
(Henggeler & Schaeffer, 2017; Henggeler et al., 2009). First, a critical emphasis
is placed on caregiver involvement. Parents know their children best, so these
caregivers play a central role in helping MST therapists assess, plan, and carry
out interventions. Second, MST therapists are comprehensive in their approach;
they work with the multiple individuals and systems in the youth's life that may
contribute to or help solve the youth's problems.

MST Nine Principles

Multisystemic Therapy is based upon nine treatment principles to which all interventions adhere (Henggeler & Schaeffer, 2017; Henggeler et al., 2009; Henggeler
et al., 2002). These principles help determine the treatment specification process,
which connects the causes of problem behavior to actions that manage those
problems (Henggeler et al., 2002).

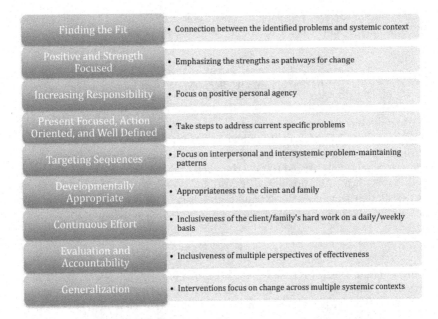

Finding the Fit	• Connection between the identified problems and systemic context
Positive and Strength Focused	• Emphasizing the strengths as pathways for change
Increasing Responsibility	• Focus on positive personal agency
Present Focused, Action Oriented, and Well Defined	• Take steps to address current specific problems
Targeting Sequences	• Focus on interpersonal and intersystemic problem-maintaining patterns
Developmentally Appropriate	• Appropriateness to the client and family
Continuous Effort	• Inclusiveness of the client/family's hard work on a daily/weekly basis
Evaluation and Accountability	• Inclusiveness of multiple perspectives of effectiveness
Generalization	• Interventions focus on change across multiple systemic contexts

Figure 10.8 Multisystemic Therapy is based upon nine principles which inform all treatment decisions

Principle 1: Finding the Fit

Multisystemic Therapy ensures that treatment matches the context of the situation. This happens by first understanding the **fit** that happens between the identified problem and the context. The fit serves to answer the question "why" the behavior occurs or does not occur, looking for reasons (drivers) from the individual, family, peer, school, and community.

Principle 2: Focusing on Positives and Strengths

Problems (weaknesses) are best addressed by using the strengths of the family. If a family was to state that they fought six days a week, looking at what was different on the seventh day highlights a resilience factor on which we can expand. It's far easier to build off a foundation of strength than deal with the flood of problems/reasons that keep a family "stuck."

Principle 3: Increasing Responsibility

Regardless of the identified problem, the youth as well as those in his or her relational field can engage in responsible behavior to more effectively manage the problem. The goal is to ensure that the family/youth have the skills to manage their own behaviors/actions and take accountability for solving their own problems.

Clinicians are constantly looking for opportunities to increase effective behaviors by stakeholders and decrease reliance on the MST therapist for success.

Principle 4: Present-Focused, Action-Oriented and Well-Defined

Clinicians are focused on moving the discussion of problems to the present and future and avoiding (as much as possible) getting pulled into the history of past problems. This prevents both blaming and helplessness, which can hamper positive movement. Given that MST treatment occurs in four to five months, considerable time is needed to take the steps to make changes, rather than just talk about them. Additionally, therapists focus on ensuring that interventions are clear; that is, easily measured and understood, not just from the therapist's perspective but from that of anyone involved with the youth/family.

Principle 5: Targeting Sequences

Multisystemic Therapy is based on the belief that problem behavior is maintained through repeated sequences of interactions that happen on multiple levels, including youth, family, peers, school, neighborhood, and/or community. Treatment then focuses on targeting and stopping these problem-maintaining patterns.

Principle 6: Developmentally Appropriate

While MST is based on these nine principles, treatment is individualized, as each problem situation is housed within a unique context. One aspect of this context is the developmental stage of the individuals as well as the family. Different treatment strategies would be used for someone who is 12 than for someone who is 16, or for someone in foster care, a one-parent or two-parent family. The MST therapist pays attention to each person's social, psychological, intellectual, physical, and emotional needs and incorporates that into the treatment regime.

Principle 7: Continuous Effort

Given that interactions between systems levels maintain problematic behaviors, continued positive interactions between systems levels are needed to maintain prosocial behaviors. Thus, MST is designed to get all stakeholders to continuously engage in behaviors that maintain the gains of treatment. This effort usually occurs on a daily basis or as frequently as possible.

Principle 8: Evaluation and Accountability

Evaluation in MST comes from utilizing multiple perspectives in the assessment process. It is the MST clinician's responsibility to identify possible treatment barriers and develop ways to overcome them. When identified goals are not being met, it is the responsibility of the MST clinician to reconceptualize the drivers for the problematic behavior and modify the intervention strategy accordingly.

Principle 9: Generalization

Multisystemic Therapy is not designed to fix a problem in the here and now, but rather to address systemic issues and have the treatment gains maintained for the long term. By focusing on the strengths of the youth, caregivers, and other stakeholders, MST interventions are designed to assist in the current problem as well as prepare people to address possible future problems.

MST Interventions

Multisystemic Therapy interventions are individualized to the specific case, yet guided by the nine treatment principles listed above, as well as by utilization of the analytical process (Henggeler et al., 2009; Sheidow & Henggeler, 2008). A key factor involved in working effectively is ensuring that the clinician is aligned and engaged not only with the family, but also with all the stakeholders working with or around the family. Multisystemic Therapy's systemic approach is designed to look at problematic behaviors from all the different systems, as well as assuring alignment between the various systems, not only to what the goal is, such as reducing substance use, but also to the specific steps to achieve this goal. This emphasis on engagement/alignment is paramount, as the ability of a caregiver to be successful is highly contingent on the other systems around him/her supporting these changes. If an adolescent hears a mixed message, they are experts in exploiting these loopholes. Multisystemic Therapy clinicians spend a great deal of time and effort to gain engagement/alignment, not only at the beginning of treatment but also throughout the treatment process.

When using MST with substance-abusing adolescents, the addition of **contingency management** (CM; Higgins, Silverman, & Heil, 2008) may be considered (Henggeler et al., 2009; Sheidow & Henggeler, 2012), which has been used effectively in various empirical studies (Henggeler et al., 1999; Henggeler et al., 2008; Schaeffer et al., 2008). While MST on its own can be very effective when dealing with adolescent substance abuse, also incorporating CM may speed the therapeutic process. Multisystemic Therapy and CM are both action oriented, appreciate systemic contexts, goal oriented, use variations of functional analyses, are based on behavioral and cognitive interventions, and are focused on empirical validations (Henggeler et al., 2009).

The Analytic Process

The MST **analytic process**, also called the "**do-loop,**" is used as a broad road map to help the clinician in treatment planning and intervention development (Henggeler & Schaeffer, 2017; Henggeler et al., 2009). It helps the clinician to prioritize youth and family problems that have been targeted for change (Sheidow & Henggeler, 2008). Once there is a referral, the first step in the analytic process is to engage and align with the various stakeholders of the case, which includes the youth, family members, and various individuals in the social ecology. During this step, the clinician obtains the desired goals of each key participant. These are then integrated into about three or four overarching measurable treatment goals. Next comes the "loop" of the analytic process. First, the MST team engages in hypothesis testing by developing a conceptual framework, which is known as finding the "fit" of the problem. The therapist and team prioritize fit factors as targets of intervention. These fit factors are used to develop intermediary goals, whereupon the clinician, with the support of the MST team, supervisor

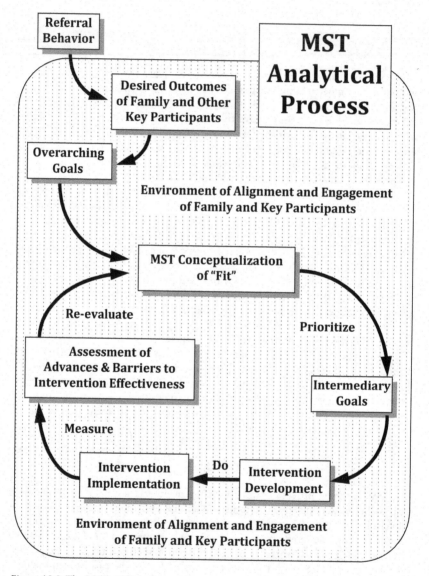

Figure 10.9 The MST analytical process

Henggeler, Schoenwald, Borduin, Rowland, & Cunningham (2009). *Multisystemic therapy for antisocial behavior in children and adolescents* (2nd Ed.). Copyright holder: Guilford. Reprinted with permission of Guilford Press.

and expert/consultant, develops and implements empirically-based interventions. At approximately weekly intervals, the therapist assesses and evaluates the progress and, if needed, repeats the "do-loop" until the treatment goals are obtained.

To illustrate the analytical process, we will hypothesize about the Rothers family and take one behavior (Steve's marijuana use) through the analytical process. It is important to note that substance use is typically one of multiple behaviors that are usually addressed (including school refusal, conflict at home, absconding, stealing, physical aggression, etc.). The referral behavior in this situation is Steve's use of marijuana three times a day, which has occurred for the past 18 months. Key participants could include: Parents Mark and Hannah, who want Steve to stop smoking; Steve, who wants to get off probation and have everyone leave him alone; siblings Kayleigh and Pete, who want better relationships with Steve; the high school football coach, who wants Steve to be able to play again and pass the drug tests; and the probation officer, who wants Steve to stop using.

The next step is the creation of an overarching goal. In this case it would be: Steve will reduce substance use by 90% by the end of treatment as evidenced by parental reports, youth reports, and probation/family urinalysis tests. We now move into following the analytical process. Principle 1 of MST is finding the fit— we want to look at all the systemic drivers that allow/encourage use of marijuana:

Individual: impulsive, enjoys the feeling, assists in dealing with boredom and past traumatic events, access to money.

Family: lack of monitoring, no effective consequences, limited incentives, modeled in the past, lack of awareness of peers.

School: opportunities for use, limited opportunities for prosocial activities.

Peers: peer encouragement, lack of non-using peers.

Community: easy access, modeled in neighborhood, places to use.

Step two is to prioritize, which often focuses on drivers within the family domain, as it may be faster to change a parenting practice than some of the other issues. The clinician may address the lack of monitoring as well as lack of effective consequences as primary drivers (as there is evidence that Steve does not use when well monitored). Unfortunately, things often times are not as easy as they may appear—as efforts to create a monitoring and behavior plan may be stalled due to low follow-through by the caregiver. At this point, the clinician may need to do a subfit to look at the potential barriers of low follow-through by the parent. This assessment may identify drivers such as parental cognitions (I feel bad about what he went through when he was younger, and I don't want to make things harder than they already are), fear of youth (past violence in the caregiver's life by youth), low supports (caregiver may not be around to monitor or hold youth accountable), past negative experiences (youth has made things harder for parents in the past when they tried to change behavior), low skills (caregiver lacks skills/knowledge on how to create and maintain a plan), or others (could even include substance use by the caregiver, caregiver's mental heath or physical health issues).

Clinicians utilize this process to identify the main problems (including substance use), to look at all the reasons for the behavior (Principle 1: finding the fit), prioritize the driver(s) for change, create an intervention, implement it, and measure the outcome (both successes and failures), and then go around the analytical process again and again until the behavior to be addressed is reduced/eliminated.

Empirical Support

Multisystemic Therapy has been researched for over 30 years and has served over 200,000 youth and families. Although developed initially in the United States, MST has been implemented worldwide, being currently active in 15 different countries (see Porter & Nuntavisit, 2016; Schoenwald, Heiblum, Saldana, & Henggeler, 2008; Wells et al., 2010). It currently has the largest body of evidence of successful interventions for high-risk youth and is considered an empirically supported treatment (Henggeler & Schaeffer, 2017). Multisystemic Therapy has been successfully used with adolescents dealing with substance abuse and dependence (Henggeler, Clingempeel, Brondino, & Pickrel, 2002; Henggeler et al., 2009; Sheidow & Henggeler, 2012; Sheidow & Houston, 2013; Wells et al., 2010) as well as with a range of other anti-social youth behaviors.

In a meta-analysis of family-based treatments of drug abuse, the MST effect sizes were among the highest of those reviewed (Stanton & Shadish, 1997). Van der Stouwe et al. (2014), in their meta-analysis of the effectiveness of MST, identified that small but significant treatment effects were found regarding delinquency, substance abuse, family factors, psychopathology, and out-of-home placement and peer factors. In this analysis, MST was most effective for those under 15 years of age and with severe starting conditions. Multisystemic Therapy also improved the outcomes for substance-using youth in their experiences in drug court (Henggeler et al., 2006).

As per the aim of MST, intervention is systemic. Utilizing family therapy rather than individual therapy helps not only with the identified youth's problematic behaviors, but supports those in his/her relational field. Rowland, Chapman, and Henggeler (2008) found that the siblings of juvenile offenders decreased their own substance use. Furthermore, caregivers of youth in which MST was used had 94% fewer felonies and 70% fewer misdemeanors than caregivers of juvenile offenders who received individual therapy (Johnides, Borduin, Wagner, & Dopp, 2017). Use of MST in communities has a serious economic benefit as MST saves $4,600 per youth in the behavioral health domain, $15,000 per youth in the juvenile crime domain, and gives a $3.34 return for every dollar spent (Dopp et al., 2018).

Case Application

As we hypothesized in Chapter 8, Mark Rothers is likely in the late precontemplation or early contemplation stage of readiness for change. Given this, as well as his previous negative experience of couples therapy with his first wife Angelina, we can assume that he is unlikely to quickly seek out or agree to go for therapeutic services. This leads to a high likelihood that the Rothers family will engage in unilateral family therapy, with Hannah being the most likely person to seek assistance in helping the family during their current time of conflict.

At some point in the addiction process, Mark is likely to utilize a self-help group. Given that alcohol is his drug of choice, this may be a group such as Alcoholics Anonymous, Rational Recovery, or SMART Recovery. His participation in this type of program would be most likely to lead to him becoming abstinent in his use of alcohol and other drugs, or perhaps engaging in harm reduction and moderation management principles. Participation in these types of self-help groups attempts to change his relationship to drugs and alcohol, and changes to his relationships with his wife, children, others, and himself will happen as well. The difficulty for the Rothers family will be in getting Mark to attend his first meeting. At this point he probably does not believe he is an alcoholic. While he may have experience with AA through his father or brother Mick, Mark may find a program such as Moderation Management to be more amenable to his view of his behaviors at this point in time. The therapist working with this family may do well in educating the family about the various self-help groups to help each of them determine which would serve their needs the best.

There are several avenues for the other members of the Rothers family to try to get Mark to either attend a self-help group or go to a therapy session. Al-Anon seems to be an appropriate group for Hannah while Alateen may be more useful for Steve, Kayleigh, and Pete. The Rothers family members, if Mark declined to go to therapy or self-help, might find themselves in either the ARISE or CRAFT programs, designed to help them help Mark to agree to treatment. For instance, Hannah would be the First Caller for the ARISE program and she and perhaps one or more of the children would be involved in inviting Mark to engage in treatment. It is likely that it may take the Rothers several sessions and Level 2 to get to when Mark would agree to at least try some type of treatment. If the family was instead to utilize the CRAFT program, we can hypothesize that the person who would make the biggest changes would be Hannah, who would start to reinforce Mark's positive sober behaviors rather than focus on his drunken behaviors. However, the Rothers may be more likely to try having an intervention since interventions are more widely known, having been shown on television shows.

While Mark seems to be a likely focus for who needs therapy, the Rothers may find themselves engaged in the therapeutic system through Steve's increasing problematic behavior. Given the intergenerational use of substances in the family, along with his age and externalizing behaviors, Steve is likely to come to the attention of the juvenile justice system or the school system. A program such as multisystemic therapy might be useful for the Rothers to not only prevent more serious problems such as substance abuse or criminal behavior, but to help change the patterns in the family that are leading to the current tumultuousness.

Summary

In the substance abuse field, self-help groups can play a prominent role in the engagement, treatment, and maintenance of the substance abuser as well as the family members and significant others. The most utilized self-help program is Alcoholics Anonymous. Depending on the person's drug of choice, they may seek out an alternative 12-step program, such as Narcotics Anonymous, Cocaine Anonymous, Gamblers Anonymous, etc. For family members, self-help programs such as Al-Anon or Alateen have been developed so that they can change their own problematic behaviors. Since the substance abuser is likely not to willingly enter treatment, family members may utilize one or more programs to deal with the family situation or to help get the abuser into treatment. Three of the more popular programs in working with the non-addicted family members are ARISE, CRAFT and the Johnson Intervention. For adolescents who are engaged in problematic behavior, a program such as Multisystemic Family Therapy may be useful.

Key Terms

self-help groups
unilateral family therapy
universality
sponsor
Alcoholics Anonymous
The 12 Steps
Speaker meetings
Discussion meetings
Step meetings
open meetings
closed meetings
sobriety coin
Al-Anon
Family Groups
Moderation Management
ARISE
Family Motivation to Change
    model
Level 1
First Caller

Level 2
Level 3
Community Reinforcement And
    Family Training (CRAFT)
    program
Concerned Significant Others
    (CSOs)
functional analysis
interventions
confrontation
chairperson
Five Principles of Intervention
Multisystemic Therapy
social ecological model
fit
Contingency Management
    (CM)
analytic process
do-loop

Discussion Questions

1. Describe the purpose of Alcoholics Anonymous. What is the relationship between AA and the disease model of addiction?

2. How do programs such as Al-Anon help non-addicted family members?

3. What are the differences between ARISE, CRAFT, and the Johnson Intervention?

4. Discuss some of the areas of concern when planning an intervention.

5. How does Multisystemic Therapy utilize the important systems in the adolescent's life to provide effective treatment?

ELEVEN

Ethics in Substance Abuse and the Family

Therapists, regardless of their training (i.e., psychologist, family therapist, or social worker), the population they work with (i.e., substance use, eating disorders, or depression), or the context in which they work (i.e., private practice, university, or agency) must abide by a set of professional standards. These standards, called **ethics**, designate the minimum standards therapists follow when interacting with clients. There are many different ethical codes, depending on the organizing body to which the therapist or agency adheres. This might make needing to know the various differences in ethical codes seem quite overwhelming. However, in most cases, the many ethical codes overlap a lot more than they differ.

In this chapter we explore some of the key ethical concepts to consider when working with an individual or family with the presentation of substance abuse or addictions. This chapter will not be able to do justice to the variety of ethical considerations needed when working with clients, and in particular with clients dealing with substance abuse and family issues. We also will not be able to do a cross comparison of the various organizations' ethical codes. Rather, we will focus on their similarities to provide a foundation to consider when working in the addiction field. However, throughout the chapter, we provide examples from many different organizations' ethical codes to demonstrate the variety of codes along with their particular wording for that ethical principle and guideline.

Core Ethical Principles

Most ethical bodies hold core **ethical principles**, primarily focusing on the therapist's respect for the client as a person who can make his or her own choices. These core ethical principles can be viewed as moral principles focusing on what is good and moral behavior (Kumpf, 2013). These ethical principles are in place to ensure that clients are treated in ways that enhance them as human beings and so that the therapist does not take advantage of them. In this section I present some of these basic principles.

Beneficence

Therapy is about helping another person. This principle is called **beneficence**— seeking to do good. Beneficence is about having some type of benefit for the client based on the therapeutic work. While many therapists view beneficence in terms of enhancing the well-being of the person they are working with, others view this concept on an individual, group, societal, and population level (Campbell & Morris, 2017; Corey, Corey, & Corey, 2019). Corey et al. explained, "Ideally, counseling contributes to the growth and development of clients within their cultural context" (p. 17). The principle of beneficence is so important that if the therapist finds that he or she is not helping the client, then the therapeutic relationship should end.

> The International Association of Marriage and Family Counselors' code of ethics holds that:
>
> > Couple and family counselors withdraw from a counseling relationship if the continuation of the relationship is not in the best interests of the client or would result in a violation of ethical standards.

Nonmaleficence

Conversely, the therapist should not do any harm. This principle is called **nonmaleficence**. Most people know this from the Hippocratic Oath that is used in the medical profession—"first, do no harm." It is the therapist's responsibility to not exploit or intentionally inflict harm on the client, as well as thinking ahead to avoid possible future harm (Corey et al., 2019). The client's life should hopefully be better for coming to therapy, or, at the least, not worse. However, despite the best of intentions from the therapist, some clients experience more difficulties after coming to therapy (Snyder, Castellani, & Whisman, 2006).

Traditionally, therapists who primarily worked in the substance abuse field were themselves in recovery (Bissell & Royce, 1994). Therapists who help others in their recovery while they themselves are going through recovery have unique potential ethical issues, different from those of therapists not in recovery. These include whether to self-disclose to clients about their own recovery, the possibility of encountering clients at self-help groups, appropriate training, and complications from slips or relapses in their own recovery.

Obviously, therapists need to be competent. Historically, in the substance abuse field, many counselors got their training through their own recovery rather than through academic education. This was because, in the mid part of the 20th century, addictions counseling became more prominent and there were not enough trained professionals to work with the large amount of clients. Thus, those who had gained sobriety were recruited to become counselors and given on-the-job training (Doukas & Cullen, 2011). Over time, greater expectations were placed on education so that therapists had to be certified and then licensed. Education does not end when the person gets their degree or license. As in many other health care professions, licensed therapists are required to keep up to date on new developments in the field. One way this happens is through the attainment of continuing education, usually acquired through participation in workshops and conferences.

Based on one's training, therapists can have quite varied scopes of competence. For instance, some therapists might have been trained in being able to assess and work with clients with dual diagnoses. However, another therapist may not have had that education. The first therapist would be working within his or her scope of competence when agreeing to work with a client with a co-occurring disorder, while the second therapist would not. It is the therapist's responsibility to gain the appropriate and necessary training to work in his or her chosen area. Further, when getting trained in an area, the therapist must ensure that no harm is coming to the client. To do so, the therapist should only use new skills after appropriate training and supervision.

Competence also refers to the therapist's ability to be professional and conduct themselves appropriately in their clinical work. Thus, therapists have an ethical obligation to seek appropriate professional assistance if they are experiencing any personal issues that impair them in their professional capacity. For those therapists who are in recovery, one obstacle to competence may be whether the therapist has had a slip or a relapse.

The Commission on Rehabilitation Counselor Certification's ethical code states:

> Rehabilitation counselors are alert to the signs of impairment due to their own health issues or personal circumstances and refrain from offering or providing professional services when such impairment is likely to harm clients or others. They seek assistance for problems that reach the level of professional impairment, and if necessary, they limit, suspend, or terminate their professional responsibilities until it is determined they may safely resume their work. Rehabilitation counselors assist colleagues or supervisors in recognizing their own professional impairment, provide consultation and assistance when colleagues or supervisors show signs of impairment, and intervene as appropriate to prevent harm to clients.

It is imperative for therapists in recovery that find themselves experiencing a slip or a relapse to ensure their own emotional and psychological well-being before continuing to work with clients. The therapist's recovery is of utmost importance to make certain that they are able to be completely focused on helping the client rather than being hampered by their own issues.

Alcoholics Anonymous disseminated guidelines for AA members who work in the addictions field and recommended that therapists in recovery have several years of uninterrupted sobriety before working in the field. Therapists should then be clear which context they are operating in and only function in one role at a specific time. Thus, they should not be sponsors for their clients or have clients as their sponsors. In their role as AA member, it is recommended for them to maintain regular attendance at meetings to have a personal AA life in trying to stay sober. All in all, therapists who are AA members should use common sense and make sure they are following and maintaining the AA traditions.

For all therapists, regardless of their training or the population they work with, self-care is an important component of being competent (Knapp, VandeCreek, & Fingerhut, 2017). **Self-care** is when therapists focus on their own personal welfare, including being physically, mentally, and emotionally sound. Physically, therapists might exercise, eat well, and get regular medical checkups. Mentally, therapists might meditate, engage in thought-provoking conversations with non-clients, and engage in activities that are not therapy-related (giving themselves a moratorium on therapy when they are not working). Emotionally, therapists might connect with loved ones and friends or perhaps seek out their own therapy. When therapists ignore their own self-care, they put themselves at risk of therapeutic burnout or of not being as effective with their clients as they could be.

Autonomy

Therapists are tasked with respecting people's decision-making capabilities—that is, their self-determination—as pertains to that person's social and cultural framework (Corey et al., 2019). This ethical principle is called **autonomy**. Wilcoxon, Remley Jr., and Gladding (2013) explained, "Autonomy proposes that an individual has a right to make his or her own decisions if those decisions do not violate the rights of others" (p. 112). As long as clients are mentally competent and able to make their own choices, while also not harming or potentially harming others to the point where the therapist would need to engage in a duty to warn, therapists need to operate so that clients make their own choices.

The National Association of Social Work code of ethics states the following about autonomy (what they call self-determination):

> Social workers respect and promote the right of clients to self-determination and assist clients in their efforts to identify and clarify their goals. Social workers may limit clients' right to self-determination when, in the social workers' professional judgment, clients' actions or potential actions pose a serious, foreseeable, and imminent risk to themselves or others.

Therapists should not tell clients what to do or that clients *have* to do something, but rather should encourage clients to make their own choices. However, this does not mean that therapists do not inform clients about rules. Many substance abuse clients find themselves in treatment programs, which have rules about behavior. Therapists should be clear and upfront with clients about what those rules are and the consequences of breaking them. For instance, a client might be removed from a treatment program if they use a substance while at the facility. The therapist can inform the client of the rule and encourage the client not to use, however it is the client's choice of whether to use or not.

Another aspect of autonomy is **informed consent**. Therapists need to clearly inform clients as to the nature of the services that the therapist intends to offer. This presentation should be in clear language that the client can understand. This means the therapist may need to alter how the information is presented based on the client's age and/or understanding. For those not legally able to provide consent to treatment (i.e., children or those with mental status difficulties), the therapist procures consent from a legal guardian. However, the therapist should also attempt to obtain **assent** from the client. The AAMFT code of ethics includes five components for informed consent: (1) the client can consent; (2) the therapist informs the client about the treatment process; (3) the therapist informs the client about potential risks and benefits of treatment; (4) the client freely consents to treatment; and (5) the consent is appropriately documented. One issue of informed consent that is more likely to occur in substance abuse treatment than in other settings is that of drug testing. Many addictions facilities will utilize urine testing to ensure client sobriety. If drug screening or testing is a component of the treatment, it is necessary for the client to be informed about this at the beginning of treatment, which should come during the informed consent.

For therapists working in the substance abuse field, there is a high likelihood that they will work with clients who have been mandated to treatment. The therapist is then confronted with attempting to work collaboratively with a client who may feel coerced to engage in the therapeutic process. On the surface, then, mandating clients to therapy would seem to restrict their autonomy.

The American Counseling Association code of ethics states the following when working with mandated clients:

> Counselors discuss the required limitations to confidentiality when working with clients who have been mandated for counseling services. Counselors also explain what type of information and with whom that information is shared prior to the beginning of counseling. The client may choose to refuse services. In this case, counselors will, to the best of their ability, discuss with the client the potential consequences of refusing counseling services.

Given the movement of therapy from therapist-as-expert to client-as-expert, the notion of informed consent has also changed. Most therapists utilize informed consent in terms of a **consent event** (Lidz, Appelbaum, & Meisel, 1988). However, some therapists are moving to a **consent process** wherein the client's motivation for treatment and change is continually considered. This is in line with the stages of readiness for change (see Chapter 8). As such, the treatment regime changes to account for the client's current position. This requires the therapist to update what he or she is doing therapeutically. Basing treatment on a consent process puts the client in a more respected position, wherein the client is continually agreeing to participate in a collaborative treatment plan.

Perhaps the most widely known ethical principle is that of **confidentiality**. For the most part, confidentiality holds that, except based on what is required by law, the therapist will not disclose with anyone what was spoken about in session. The client does have autonomy and could give consent (i.e., by signing a release of information), allowing the therapist to speak to specific people about a specific aspect of therapy. For instance, the client might want the therapist to speak with his or her lawyer about the goals and progress of the therapy. Therapists are required to maintain confidentiality except for a few instances, such as if there is imminent harm to the client or someone else, there is suspected child or elder abuse, an emergency situation, or through a written court order.

> The American Mental Health Counseling Association code of ethics states:
>
> > Confidentiality is a right granted to all clients of mental health counseling services. From the onset of the counseling relationship, mental health counselors inform clients of these rights including legal limitations and exceptions.

While therapists are bound by the limits of confidentiality, clients are not. This becomes a potential issue when there is more than one client in the therapy room, as in family or group therapy. Since many clients dealing with substance abuse disorders may find themselves in family or group therapy, therapists should encourage clients to maintain the confidentiality of the other members. In many groups, this comes in the form of the therapist saying, "What happens in the group stays in the group." For those clients who attend self-help meetings, such as AA or NA, confidentiality is not assured, as there is most likely not a trained therapist who is held to professional ethical standards. However, AA has a tradition of respecting member anonymity. Anonymity is the spiritual foundation of all of the AA traditions so that principles are put before personalities.

Justice

Most therapists will likely come into contact with clients from a variety of cultural groups. It may be the rare therapist in today's society that lives in a remote location with little diversity. Regardless, therapists are ethically accountable to engage in **non-discrimination**. That is, they should provide services to people regardless of the client's race, age, gender, gender identity, ethnicity, religion, national origin, socioeconomic status, sexual orientation, disability, health status, or relationship status. This refers to the ethical concept of **justice**. This does not mean that a therapist cannot specialize, for instance, by working primarily with LGBTQ clients or with religious clients if engaged in pastoral counseling. However, therapists cannot refuse service based on any of these demographic characteristics.

The International Association of Marriage and Family Counselors' code of ethics states:

> Couple and family counselors do not abandon clients and do not withhold treatment to clients for discriminatory reasons such as race, disability, religion, age, sexual orientation or identification, cultural background, national origin, marital status, affiliation or socioeconomic status.

One of the biggest recent movements in psychotherapy is incorporating the notion of **social justice** into therapeutic practice. Becvar (2008) defined this term, "That is, in general, social justice may be understood as the achievement of fairness in terms of the treatment and the sharing of a society's benefits for all of its members" (p. 139). Justice also refers to ensuring that intervention strategies and program formats are relevant to all segments of the population (Corey et al., 2019). For instance, therapists can accommodate those who have transportation, childcare, and poverty issues by making home visits or perhaps through teletherapy. Many therapists view social justice practices on a macrolevel, exploring how to change economic and political policies that marginalize people. However, there are microlevel practices that can enhance a social justice perspective when working with individuals and families. This section briefly discusses both levels of influence.

The American Psychological Association code of ethics states the following about the ethical principle of justice:

> Psychologists recognize that fairness and justice entitle all persons to access to and benefit from the contributions of psychology and to equal quality in the processes, procedures, and services being conducted by psychologists. Psychologists exercise reasonable judgment and take precautions to ensure that their potential biases, the boundaries of their competence, and the limitations of their expertise do not lead to or condone unjust practices.

The National Association of Social Workers takes it a step further and promotes social workers to pursue social change, especially for marginalized populations. This may come at the local level of city or county politics, or perhaps state and national organizations and policies.

Taking a social justice position might be difficult for family therapists who have to utilize categorizing assessments such as the DSM-V or the ICD-11. Sutherland et al. (2015) noted that diagnostic labels have the possibility of objectifying people and limiting the scope of the sociocultural dynamics of dominance and subordination that lead to people experiencing their current problems. One way to move forward is to utilize discursive resources, holding both social justice and medical perspectives together in the therapeutic conversation to see how each might be resourceful for the therapeutic situation. Sutherland et al. explained, "Engaging in critical practice with respect to the DSM can help therapists re-conceptualize clients' concerns with reference to the social context in which dominant norms for being and relating may have constraining or distressing effects on individuals and groups" (p. 95).

Another possibility for therapists operating from a social justice perspective is to engage in activism (D'Arrigo-Patrick, Hoff, Knudson-Martin, & Tuttle, 2017). This might be through challenging larger social discourses that tend to be marginalizing and oppressive. That is, ethically, some therapists believe their work happens both in the therapy room and in larger policy and societal fields. These activities can be considered as consciousness-raising and social education.

In the therapy room, therapists can work more locally with clients to address social justice issues and engage in consciousness-raising activities. Kosutic and McDowell (2008) provided several of these activities:

- Engage in a discourse about the client's social context and impact of various forms of oppression.
- Use cultural genograms to discuss family systems' impact of oppressive forces.
- Deconstruct oppressive family myths and cultural narratives.
- Use externalizing language to offset internalized oppressive social discourses.
- Promote strength-based and resource-focused narratives.
- Promote affirming personal and family narratives.
- Encourage client activism to change social situations.

Each of these activities leads to greater awareness of intrapersonal and interpersonal understandings by individuals, families, and groups.

Fidelity

Fidelity focuses on trust, where the therapist engages in ways that enhance the client's belief in the therapeutic relationships and process. Corey et al. (2019) explained, "Fidelity means that professionals make realistic commitments and do their best to keep these promises" (p. 18). One primary way that therapists can enhance trust in the therapeutic relationship is to ensure that the relationship stays therapeutic. Not only should the therapist not have any type of sexual relationship with the client, but also should take care not to engage in a dual relationship.

The American Psychological Association code of ethics states the following about fidelity:

> Psychologists establish relationships of trust with those with whom they work. They are aware of their

(continued)

(continued)

> professional and scientific responsibilities to society and to the specific communities in which they work. Psychologists uphold professional standards of conduct, clarify their professional roles and obligations, accept appropriate responsibility for their behavior, and seek to manage conflicts of interest that could lead to exploitation or harm. Psychologists consult with, refer to, or cooperate with other professionals and institutions to the extent needed to serve the best interests of those with whom they work. They are concerned about the ethical compliance of their colleagues' scientific and professional conduct. Psychologists strive to contribute a portion of their professional time for little or no compensation or personal advantage.

Dual relationships occur when the therapist has a relationship with the client in a different context; for instance, as a work partner or a known neighbor. Ethical codes attempt to reduce and limit therapists having dual relationships with clients since the therapist may gain knowledge about and power over the client that they would not normally have.

The AAMFT code of ethics holds the following about multiple relationships:

> Marriage and family therapists are aware of their influential positions with respect to clients, and they avoid exploiting the trust and dependency of such persons. Therapists, therefore, make every effort to avoid conditions and multiple relationships with clients that could impair professional judgment or increase the risk of exploitation. Such relationships include, but are not limited to, business or close personal relationships with a client or the client's immediate family. When the risk of impairment or exploitation exists due to conditions or multiple roles, therapists document the appropriate precautions taken.

While some dual relationships cannot be helped, especially in small communities, others are completely unethical and potentially unlawful. These include sexual intimacy with current clients or utilizing a client's career for personal benefits, such as getting stock tips from a stockbroker. Therapeutic organizations such as AAMFT also prohibit the therapist from having sexual intimacy with a client's family members, or with past clients and known family members.

For substance abuse therapists, concerns about dual relationships involve types of self-disclosure, identification with the client, asymmetry of power, clients potentially entering careers in the substance abuse field, risk of relapse, and difficulty of objectivity (Chapman, 1997; Hecksher, 2007). This is because many therapists who work in the substance abuse field have personal experience with addictions. This might be through their own or a family member's past or current use. There has also been a notion by clients that they can only be helped by a therapist who has also experienced addictions. Given this, many clients ask therapists about their own addiction history and recovery. This question, as well as the therapist's own beliefs of treatment, lead to the therapist possibly self-disclosing; usually regarding their own past use and recovery. While many therapists utilize self-disclosure as a means of joining with clients, there is the possibility of the blurring of boundaries and the shift of focus of the session from the client to the therapist. For instance, the client may become inquisitive about the therapist's process of recovery and the possibility of a threat to the therapist's well-being in case there is a slip or a relapse.

Recovering therapists can minimize the potential dangers of dual relationships (see Figure 11.1). The following are several guidelines these therapists can use to more ethically engage in therapeutic relationships (Doyle, 1997; Stevens & Smith, 2018). First, therapists should be up to date and aware of all ethical codes that relate to their work. The better the fluency with the ethical codes, the more knowledge and awareness therapists have to make informed decisions. Second, the therapist should access consultation and/or supervision from experienced colleagues or a supervisor. This protects therapists from narrow thinking, as an outsider will be able to better view the context and provide alternative ways of viewing situations that the therapist may not have been able to do previously. Third, therapists should utilize self-help groups in a thoughtful manner, where there is a reduced chance of interacting with clients. For instance, the therapist might access his or her own self-help group in an area quite a ways away from where they practice to reduce the chances of coming into contact with local clients. Fourth, the therapist should be cautious in how he uses self-disclosure to ensure it is purposeful. Sometimes, if the therapist self-discloses often, with quite personal information, the client may attempt to gain greater amounts of personal information about the therapist, which may blur the therapeutic boundaries. Fifth, the therapist should use common sense when potential dual relationships surface. For many situations, therapists are implicitly aware of what is best to do to ensure ethical standards. Lastly, therapists are encouraged to advocate to organizational bodies for clarification in ethical codes surrounding therapists in recovery.

Veracity

Veracity relates to the therapist being truthful and upholding truth in the therapy context. This comes into play by bringing clarity and honesty into therapeutic relationships. Corey et al. (2019) stated, "Unless practitioners are truthful with their clients, the trust required to form a good working relationship will not develop" (p. 18).

Based on the principle of veracity, therapists working with multiple members of a system tend to implement a no secret policy (Caldwell & Stone, 2016).

Figure 11.1 Guidelines help to minimize the potential harm of dual relationships

When secrets are present between one member of the family and the therapist, the therapist may be engaging in dishonest and disloyal behavior to other members of the family. We present more about dealing with secrets in therapy later in the chapter. Figure 11.2 presents the six core ethical principles that all therapists use as a foundation for being ethical in their work with clients.

Risk Factors and Suicide

According to the 2014 National Survey on Drug Use and Health, suicide was the 10th leading cause of death in the U.S. in 2013. This number was higher for those aged 15 to 54. In 2014, almost 3% of adults in the U.S. had serious thoughts of suicide, which is about 9.4 million people. During the previous year, 2.7 million people had made suicidal plans and 1.1 million made nonfatal suicide attempts. Of these individuals, 0.9 million made suicide plans and 0.2 million made no suicide plans. This works out to 1 out of 9 adults with serious suicidal thoughts making a suicide attempt. Approximately 55% of those who made a suicide attempt received medical help, with almost 43% staying overnight or longer in a hospital.

Individuals with alcohol and/or drug problems are much more likely than the general population to experience lethal or non-lethal overdose, attempt suicide, and complete suicides (Bohnert, Roeder, & Ilgen, 2011). While overdoses

Beneficence

Do Good

Nonmaleficence

Do no harm

Autonomy

Self-determination

Justice

Fairness

Fidelity

Trustworthiness

Veracity

Truthfulness

Figure 11.2 Core ethical principles form the basis of good therapeutic practice regardless of therapeutic role or context

and suicide attempts are distinct behaviors, they each are related to substance use. That is, those who engage in substance use are more likely to overdose or make a suicide attempt. Males complete suicide at a rate of 4 to 1 over females (Yuodelis-Flores & Ries, 2015). Yet, the correlation between substance abuse disorder and suicide is stronger for females. Based on the 2014 NSDUH survey, almost 137 million adults were current alcohol users with 5.6 million having serious thoughts of suicide in the previous year. Suicide plans were made by 1.6 million adults and 658,000 made a suicide attempt. Of those with heavy alcohol use in the past month, 6.2% had serious thoughts of suicide, 1.9% made suicide plans, and 1.2% attempted suicide in the past year. These numbers increase when illicit drug use is included. For instance, almost 12% of adults diagnosed with drug or alcohol dependence or abuse had suicidal thoughts, 4% had suicidal plans, and 2% made suicide attempts. In comparison with those without a substance abuse disorder, 3% had suicidal thoughts, 1% suicide plans, and 0.3% made suicide attempts.

Let's take a second to ensure we are clear about the terms we are using. **Suicidal ideation** refers to thoughts about suicide. Just because someone has ideation does not mean that they are about to attempt to kill themselves. However, it increases the risk of them making an attempt. Most people, at various times in their lives, think about suicide. **Suicidal intent** means that the person has killing themself as a goal. While suicidal ideation may not lead to anything more than thoughts, suicidal intent leads to a much greater level of risk for the person

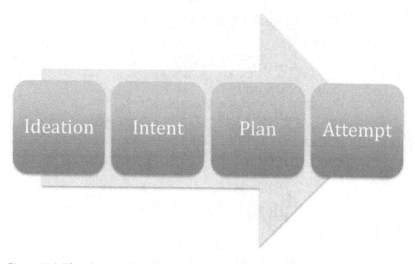

Figure 11.3 The relationship between suicidal ideation, intent, plan, and attempt

engaging in self-harming behaviors. A **suicide threat** is a verbal or nonverbal communication by the person that they may attempt suicide in the near future. This could be hinting at or telling others, through conversation, text, or notes, of wanting to be dead. A **suicide plan** is the person's specific means of killing themselves, such as with a gun, pills, or slitting of one's wrists. The more access that a person has to aspects of the suicide plan, such as a gun or pills, the higher the risk. A **suicide attempt** is behavior taken intended for self-killing. See Figure 11.3 for the relationship between these concepts in levels of severity.

Risk factors for suicide attempts for those dealing with substance use include relationship, financial, and occupational stressors, co-occurring disorders, and previous substance and sexual abuse (Yuodelis-Flores & Ries, 2015). For those with alcohol-use disorder, having interpersonal conflicts, co-occurring disorders, and aggressive behavior are associated with higher rates of suicide (Kõlves, Draper, Snowdon, & De Leo, 2017). Forty percent of primary care patients who had recently used drugs had at least one suicide attempt in their lifetime (Carmel, Ries, West, Bumgardner, & Roy-Byrne, 2016). Those with a high risk of suicide had higher levels of severity in substance use, used more than one substance, and had a co-occurring disorder. Bohnert, Ilgen, Louzon, McCarthy, & Katz (2017) found that, for veterans, there was an increased risk of suicide for those with current diagnoses of alcohol, cocaine, cannabis, opioid, amphetamine or other psychostimulant, and sedative hypnotic or anxiolytic-use disorders. This risk was increased for females; particularly those with only any substance use disorder and opioid use disorder.

Client suicidal intent is a significant ethical factor for therapists as they have a **duty to protect** their clients. It is the therapist's responsibility to assess for suicidality, and, if the therapist has good reason to suspect suicidal behavior, he or she must break confidentiality to ensure the welfare of the client.

The code of ethics for NAADAC, the association for addiction professionals, states:

> Addiction Professionals may reveal client identity or
> confidential information without client consent when
> a client presents a clear and imminent danger to them-
> selves or to other persons, and to emergency person-
> nel who are directly involved in reducing the danger
> or threat. Counselors seek supervision or consultation
> when unsure about the validity of an exception.

When assessing for or working with suicidal clients, it is imperative for the
therapist to document all of the steps he or she has taken to ensure the client's
welfare. Corey, Corey, and Callanan (2007) described these steps:

- Conduct a thorough assessment.
- Obtain a relevant history.
- Obtain previous treatment records.
- Directly evaluate suicidal thoughts.
- Consult with one or more professionals.
- Discuss the limits of confidentiality with the client.
- Implement appropriate suicide interventions.
- Provide resources to the client.
- Contact authorities and family members if a client is at high risk for suicide.
  (p. 238)

While these steps are a guide, the therapist still must decide what represents a
threat that requires a breach of confidentiality.

Flemons and Gralnik (2013) proposed a **relational suicide assessment** (RSA),
which empathically explores risks, resources, and possibilities of people who
have expressed suicidal thoughts. This is different than other suicide assessments, which primarily focus on risks without honoring the client's strengths
and resources. The RSA is an interactive dialog that has three overlapping steps:
empathically explore the intra- and interpersonal world of the client, come to a
safety decision, and develop a safety plan.

Flemons and Gralnik (2013) explained that there are four main areas that
therapists should explore in terms of risk and protective factors: Disruptions
and demands; suffering; troubling behaviors; and desperation (see Figure 11.4).
Therapists can explore both risks and resources of the client and the client's
significant others for each of these areas. For instance, client risks for the area of
disruptions and demands include the ending of a relationship, job, or legal difficulty. Resources could include the ability to problem solve as well as positive
interpersonal relationships. Client significant other risks in this same area might
include separation from, abuse to, and high demands of the client. Resources
would include reasonable expectations and help and support of the client.

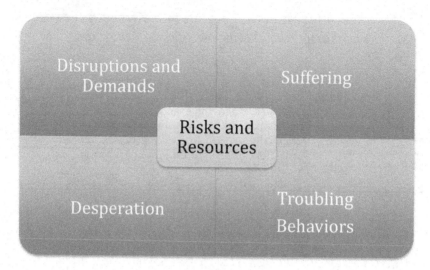

Figure 11.4 The four areas of focus in a relational suicide assessment to determine the intra- and interpersonal risks and resources for clients

If it is determined that the client is at risk but that immediate hospitalization is not necessitated, the therapist should collaboratively develop a safety plan with the client. The safety plan helps the client access various resources to manage the current and near future situation successfully. Flemons and Gralnik (2013) developed an eight-step safety plan guideline which includes identifying resourceful significant others, restricting access to the means of suicide, exploring alternatives to troubling behaviors, establishing safe havens, helping alter demanding schedules, encouraging treatment, mobilizing personal resources, and identifying and employing emergency resources. This safety plan (see Figure 11.5) is not the same as a no-harm or no-suicide contract, which are more so impositions on the client rather than collaborated steps the client chooses and endorses.

Duty to Warn

As we previously discussed when talking about informed consent, there are certain times when the therapist must break confidentiality. One of these relates to the duty to protect, that was just explained, when therapists are working with clients who exhibit suicidal ideation, threats, and behaviors. Another is based on the **duty to warn** if the therapist believes that the client may harm someone else. This is based on the *Tarasoff v Board of Regents of the University of California* court ruling. In that case, a university student, Prosenjit Poddar, had informed his therapist that he wanted to kill Tatiana Tarasoff. The therapist initially contacted campus police, who interviewed Poddar and found him to be rational. No one informed Tarasoff about the threat to her. Poddar eventually killed Tarasoff. Her parents then sued various individuals and organizations that were involved in the situation. Since then, there is a duty to warn; letting the intended target of

Figure 11.5 The eight components of a safety plan for a client who may self-harm

violence know about the threat to their person. The two primary factors for ethical decision making when determining if there is a duty to warn are whether the intended victim is identifiable and if there is imminent danger.

For therapists working with couples where there is intimate partner violence (IPV), they need to determine what responsibility they have to break confidentiality and report. Corey et al. (2019) described the therapist's position, "The therapist's goal is to protect victims from any further harm, including protecting any children the couple may have at home" (p. 415). If the child witnessed the domestic violence, therapists are most likely required to report since there may be negative psychological consequences for the child. However, reporting requirements are dependent on the state in which the therapist is practicing.

If there is domestic violence, couples therapy is not warranted and may even be seen as unethical (Corey et al., 2019). Therapists need to determine what potential physical and emotional danger might be present and the impact that having conjoint sessions could have for the partners. Two important factors to consider are violence history and current violence risk (McLaughlin, 2017). McLaughlin recommended that therapists working with IPV clients become familiar with general IPV issues, assess regularly for IPV, and maintain self-awareness of potential biases as well as their own competence when working with this population. Kress, Protivnak, and Sadlak (2008) explained that therapists should not encourage the IPV victim to leave the relationship, but should instead focus on promoting that person's safety. One reason for this is, when a woman is a victim of IPV, her greatest risk of injury is when she is leaving an abusive relationship. Having a safety plan in place first is extremely important.

Besides clients becoming violent toward others, therapists may have a duty to warn if they suspect someone may be harmed in other ways. Individuals who are dealing with substance abuse disorders may have a higher likelihood of engaging in unprotected sex or sharing infected needles. This leads to higher rates of sexually transmitted diseases. For those with HIV and/or AIDS, therapists are then placed in an ethical situation where they must balance the duty to protect confidentiality versus the duty to warn a potential sexual partner (Alghazo, Upton, & Cioe, 2011). Burkemper (2002) found that family therapists prioritized ethical principles when making ethical decisions regarding therapeutic situations where a client was HIV+. In order of primacy, therapists chose to operate from nonmaleficence, fidelity, justice, autonomy, and beneficence.

Ethics Specific for Marriage and Family Therapy

While all therapists, regardless of whether they work with individuals, couples, families, or groups, are held to the various ethical principles previously described (i.e., informed consent, beneficence, nonmaleficence, confidentiality, etc.), those who work with families have some additional ethical concerns. A few of these will be addressed in this section. Morrison, Layton, and Newman (1982) described four specific ethical concerns for family therapists (see Figure 11.6). The first concerns whose interest the therapist has and how that relates to informed consent.

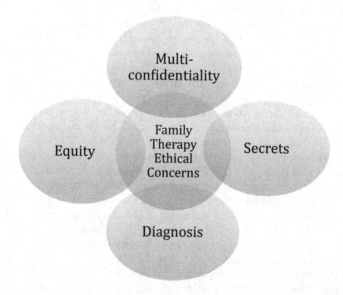

Figure 11.6 Family therapists have ethical concerns that are specific for working with multiple clients simultaneously

Part of this is the issue of multiconfidentiality. Second, therapists must decide on how to handle secrets that will come forth when working with multiple members of a family. Third, therapists should be thoughtful and careful in if and how they label clients and families. In psychotherapy, labeling tends to take place through the process of diagnosing. The fourth specific ethical issue for family therapists is whether the therapist takes one member's side over another member. This relates to the concept of equity.

Multiconfidentiality

Therapists who work with couples and families face an issue that therapists who only work with individuals don't deal with, the issue of **multiconfidentiality**. Therapists have to navigate each person's confidentiality, as well as that of the group as a whole. That is, therapists have to keep clear what was said to them in single session or with others present. Most therapists working with couples and families view the system as the client rather than the individual. As such, their actions are geared toward the well-being of all individuals, but also the family system.

When working with multiple members of a family system, therapists need to be cautious of whom they talk with and what information is divulged regarding treatment. While gaining a release of information is essential before talking with outside parties (excluding crisis situations), the release needs to be given by all adult family members. Corey et al. (2019) explained, "The family therapist and the family members need to agree to the specific limitations of confidentiality mandated by law and also to those the family practitioner may establish for effective treatment" (pp. 402–403).

The American Mental Health Counseling Association code of ethics states:

> In working with families or groups, the rights to confidentiality of each member should be safeguarded. Mental health counselors must make clear that each member of the group has individual rights to confidentiality and that each member of a family, when seen individually, has individual rights to confidentiality within legal limits.

Given that many clients who are dealing with substance abuse are increasingly being referred by the legal system, therapists working with the substance abuser and his or her family need to be clear as to what information should be discussed with the attorney and/or other legal parties and what should not (Gallagher, 2014). For instance, the substance abuser's progress and use or non-use of substances is most likely quite appropriate, while discussion of the non-abusing members' romantic disconnections may be a breach of confidentiality.

An additional issue of confidentiality is when the therapist needs to disclose to the parents of an adolescent client. Health Insurance Portability and Accountability Act of 1996 holds for patient confidentiality. However, depending on the state in which treatment is occurring, the law may or may not require the health care professional to disclose to parents that a minor has sought therapy and the content of those sessions. This becomes even more blurred in that, in most states, adolescents can consent for alcohol and drug treatment and do not need their parents' consent. However, family therapists tend to want to include more rather less family members in treatment. Ruiz and Strain (2014) recommended that, as much as possible, the parents of adolescent substance abusers be involved in all decisions. This is due in part to getting the parents to work together with one another as well as the adolescent and the therapist in a treatment team.

Secrets

In the ethical principle section, you read about the concept of fidelity, where the therapist works from a position of trustworthiness. This ethical principle becomes muddier when multiple family members are seen, especially individually. Further complication comes when working with families dealing with substance abuse, as they tend to have interpersonal rules that support the keeping of secrets.

Therapists are divided on whether to meet with family members separately. On the one hand, meeting individually with members leads to the possibility that people would more likely discuss very important issues, such as domestic violence or marital affairs, in the privacy and safety of a lone session without other family members present. On the other hand, some therapists believe having separate sessions provides the opportunity for the perpetuation of problematic interpersonal interactions that maintain secrets and dysfunctional interactions. These separate sessions may unwittingly provide clients with opportunities to triangulate therapists. Whichever position therapists take, they need to be clear with clients as to the expectations of therapy and whether there will or will not be a secrecy policy. Wilcoxon, Remley Jr., and Gladding (2013) stated, "Unless clients are informed of a nonsecrecy policy when they initiate therapy and are able to adequately consider its consequences, many will seek to influence the therapist using secrets" (p. 75).

One of the primary secrets in families, and particularly couples, is that of infidelity. The disclosure of infidelity by one member outside of the presence of his or her partner leads the therapist into a quandary. They are placed between the ethic of confidentiality and the ethic of equity. Butler, Rodriguez, Roper, & Feinauer (2010) promoted the use of **facilitated disclosure** under most situations, where the therapist assists the client in telling the other member about the infidelity. Exceptions to facilitated disclosure might include if the couple is divorcing or separating, if there is physical or emotional risk if there is disclosure, if the other partner has a serious or terminal illness, or if the infidelity occurred long ago and is not relevant to the current partner issues.

Fall and Lyons (2003) suggest that when dealing with the issue of secrets in family therapy, therapists are clear with clients about informed consent and the benefits and risks of therapy, accurately assess the boundaries in the family, and be clear in how they will assess the impact of the disclosure. For some disclosure of secrets, there may be potential risks in the family system. For instance, the disclosure of a marital affair, a member coming out in terms of their sexuality, or the loss of a significant amount of family money, perhaps due to gambling, may potentially lead to physical or emotional assaults.

An alternative way to view the issue of secrets in family therapy is through the concept of **selective disclosure**. Rober, Walravens, and Versteynen (2012) explained,

> It [selective disclosure] refers to a process of selection as to whom to tell what, how much to tell, when to tell, and so on. Implied in the concept of selective disclosure is the idea that the sharing of secret information would not resolve everything, as it suggests that whatever is said, other things remain unsaid. (p. 538)

Selective disclosure honors the family members' ways of dealing with sensitive issues while also enhancing fidelity in the system. Rather than have a reveal of the secret, disclosure is viewed as a process that occurs over time, with sensitivity and thoughtfulness.

Overall, therapists need to make therapeutic choices as to how they want to handle the notion of secrets. By having a clear understanding of how they want to operate, therapists are better able to, from the start of therapy, be clear with clients as to what will happen in therapy and how the therapist will handle individual disclosures within the family. Southern (2013) provided the following ideas for family therapists as they relate to secrets in therapy:

- Although related, secrecy, privacy, and confidentiality are separate constructs.
- Generally, the more the secret relates to violation of family rules or the more extreme the taboo, the greater is the need for disclosure.
- How the couple and family counselor handles secrets is the issue.
- Counselors should avoid triangulation and other alignments that perpetuate family problems.
- Clients have the right to informed consent regarding how disclosures will be handled.
- Counselors should not harm a client system through the process of disclosure.
- Codes of ethics are biased in favor of reviewing disclosure from the perspective of an individual client's right to confidentiality.
- Disclosure is a process not a discrete event. (p. 252)

Ultimately, it is up to the therapist on how to navigate the dilemma of secrets in sessions.

Diagnosing

For many couples and family therapists who operate from a relational perspective, the notion of an individual having a specific diagnosis might be anathema. This is because diagnosing tends to be based on a linear, pathologizing description of people (Negash & Hecker, 2010). This goes against a circular perspective that many family therapists utilize. Diagnosing based on the DSM primarily focuses on individual psychopathology, which may go against the family therapist's position that problems are housed in relationships rather than individual people. If the therapist does diagnose one member of the family, the likelihood of that person being considered the identified patient by other family members increases.

This situation becomes even more important as many insurance companies require someone to be diagnosed before they will reimburse. Therapists need to be cognizant of potential stigma to clients of being diagnosed. Given this, therapists need to ensure that they do not engage in misrepresentation of diagnosis (Wilcoxon, Remley Jr., & Gladding, 2010). Any diagnosis given must be accurate. Some therapists may believe that providing any diagnosis so that the client receives services is better than not giving a diagnosis and the client is not seen. However, therapists are ethically bound not to "up-code"—to provide a coverable diagnosis. As Corey et al. (2019) explained, "Under no circumstances should clinicians compromise themselves regarding the accuracy of a diagnosis to make it 'fit' criteria accepted by an insurance company" (p. 383).

So what is the way out of this dilemma? DSM-5 is just one type of discourse, whereas many family therapists operate from a different discourse. Family therapy training teaches therapists how to engage in active discourses with multiple perspectives. Strong (2015) suggested that therapists utilize discursive resources, which are ways of understanding that are provided by multiple discourses. This may come in the form of utilizing multiple discourses when working with clients so that both DSM terminology and client-preferred language are used to satisfy administrators, insurance companies, and clients.

Equity

As discussed previously, one of the core ethical principles for therapists is that of equity. Therapists are ethically obligated to consider the welfare of all of their clients. That is, all members of the family are held in equal regard concerning their well-being. This has impact regardless of how many members of the family come to the therapy sessions. One of the key ideas of systems theory (on which family therapies are based) is that one change in the system leads to system-wide change. Thus, therapists need to be conscious of the impact their actions have for the members in the immediate session as well as those people who clients will contact outside of the session.

Boszormenyi-Nagy and Krasner (1986) promoted the therapist stance of **multidirected partiality**. These authors defined this term, "It consists of a set of principles and technical guidelines that require the therapist to be accountable to everybody who is potentially affected by his or her interventions" (p. 418). This accountability is to whoever is coming to sessions as well as those people who clients come in contact with outside of the session. For instance, if the therapist met with the Rothers family, he or she would need to be cognizant that changes made by Mark in his interpersonal relationships will likely impact others, such as Angelina and Nina. By acknowledging all members' positions and merits, the therapist enhances the various resources that are housed in interpersonal relationships. The therapist does not take a juridical role, but instead attempts to help family members to be able to speak and listen to one another.

Another way for ensuring that therapists do not take sides is by being neutral. Palazzoli, Boscolo, Cecchin, and Prata (1980) described **neutrality** as the therapist allying with every member of the family and none of the family members at the same time. What this means is that the therapist, while talking with one member, accepts what that person says in the moment. Then, when talking with the next member, the therapist accepts whatever that person says, regardless of whether it coincides with or contradicts what the first member said. While engaging the family in this manner, the therapist does not approve or disapprove of thoughts, feelings, or behaviors, as this judgment would likely lead to taking sides.

Ethics of Harm Reduction

The primary view in the addictions field is to push for abstinence. This is based on the notion of the disease model of addiction. However, there are alternative models of substance use. One of these is the **harm reduction** model. In this perspective, health care providers attempt to minimize the potential negative impact that drug and/or alcohol use can have on people. Harm reduction also focuses on social justice, holding high the rights of people who use drugs and/or alcohol.

Abstinence-based programs, such as the Just Say No campaign, attempt to eliminate certain behaviors, such as use of illegal drugs or sex before marriage. While this may be effective for some people, the vast majority of people will drink, use some type of licit or illicit drug, and/or have sex before marriage. The harm reduction viewpoint takes into account that abstinence is not the desired modus operandi for all people. As such, it attempts to reduce as much as possible the negative consequences of engaging in these behaviors. Some examples of harm reduction programs include methadone programs (for those dealing with opioid use), needle programs (for those who inject drugs and might engage in needle sharing, which increases the risk of spreading HIV), and free condom programs (for those who are at risk of engaging in unprotected sex).

While harm reduction has become a legitimate viewpoint over the last 20–30 years, therapists may face negative consequences by encouraging this approach. For instance, some of the concepts of harm reduction may go against 12-step or treatment programs that focus exclusively on abstinence. Therapists are held to the ethical mandate of ensuring client autonomy. Thus, it is the client's choice of which decisions to make in their own lives, including whether they want to work toward abstinence or moderation and harm reduction.

Kleinig (2008) provided four ethical challenges when operating from a position of harm reduction. The first ethical challenge is focusing on the bottom line. That is, on the larger macrolevel of harm reduction policies, as many of them are designed to minimize the financial costs rather than focusing on the physical, mental, and emotional benefits of such programs. The second ethical challenge is whether participation in the harm reduction program is voluntary or compulsory. Some programs, such as banning smoking in public places, have become compulsory. Other programs, such as access to free condoms, are voluntary. The implications for whether the harm reduction policies are imposed or offered delve into ethical areas of autonomy. The third ethical challenge is about the permissible strategies; that is, which strategies are ethically legitimate. Given that most mental health fields have been moving toward supporting evidence-based approaches, harm reduction strategies will most likely find themselves legitimized with empirical support. The fourth ethical challenge concerns the delivery conditions. This relates to having a code of ethics when delivering the harm reduction strategies and programs.

Ethical Decision Making

For any situation therapists come across, they will need to make decisions as to the best possible strategy that is both ethical and effective. When attempting to determine the most ethical course of action, there are sometimes no clear-cut guidelines. Therapists must weigh the pros and cons to determine what is in the client's best interests as well as the therapy field and the legal system. While there are times when things are black and white (i.e., therapists should never have any type of sexual contact with their client), other decisions are more difficult, such as when to break confidentiality. To help therapists determine the best pathway, they can utilize a model of **ethical decision making**. "Decision-making models clarify and configure the process of coming to and enacting an ethical decision" (Kumpf, 2013, p. 54).

Knapp, Gottlieb, and Handelsman (2015) and Knapp et al. (2017) utilize a principle-based ethical decision-making model. This model is based on the five-step model developed by Knapp and VandeCreek (2012). Knapp et al. (2017) explained, "Principle-based ethics allows the decision maker to have one more principle trump another if there is good reason to do so. However, an effort should be made to minimize harm to the offended moral principle" (p. 42).

Step one is identifying the problem. Here the therapist determines the most relevant ethical principles involved in the situation and how these may conflict. On the surface this seems like it is an easy step. However, there are times therapists aren't even aware that they are dealing with an ethical issue where they will need to engage in the ethical decision-making process. This step requires therapists to have good working knowledge of the ethical codes that they follow. Further, therapists should be open and connected to their own reactions, as their gut might tell them something is not right and they should more closely analyze whether there are any ethical issues that need to be addressed.

Step two is developing alternatives or hypothesizing solutions. The thought is that the best ethical decisions may come from careful consideration that explores the range of possible pathways. In this step, therapists listen and talk with colleagues to help expand the range of appropriate behaviors. This allows therapists to reflect on which choice seems to be the most appropriate. Therapists might also review overarching ethical principles, ethical codes, and pertinent laws. These actions help move ethical decision making from a solitary endeavor to a social process.

Step three is to analyze, evaluate, and then select the best option from the range of choices of what to do that were brainstormed in step two. The evaluation includes an understanding of the advantages and disadvantages of each ethical choice for a variety of contexts including the practical, clinical, and legal. The best choice may be a combination of different solutions that incorporates the best elements of each.

Step four is for the therapist to act or perform. This is when the therapist puts into practice the strategy that was chosen in step three. At this point, the ethical decision-making process should still be a social process as therapists can consult others about various ways to implement the strategy they've determined seems best for this situation in that context. This may come through both the content of their actions as well as the process of delivering the intervention.

Step five is to look back and evaluate. At this point the therapist may determine that the ethical dilemma has been solved. At other times, further considerations will need to be made. For instance, having gone through these five steps may make the therapist aware of additional ethical dilemmas. If so, the therapist would begin the process again regarding this new dilemma. As such, the five-step model may be more dynamic and circular than linear (see Figure 11.7).

Corey et al. (2019) provided an eight-step ethical decision-making process. These steps include identifying the problem, identifying the potential issues, reviewing relevant ethical codes, knowing applicable laws and regulations, obtaining consultation, considering possible courses of action, considering the possible consequences of those actions, and choosing the seeming best course. Although it seems to be a linear process, this decision making model increases therapists' self-reflection of their own beliefs and actions as well as engaging in further discussions around important issues with clients and colleagues.

Whichever ethical decision making model is used, they all tend to have the following components in common: having the therapist aware of his or her own values, avoid emotional decision-making, and understand the varied possibilities that are available during the decision-making process (Caldwell & Stone, 2016). Therapists that work with couples and/or families have additional complexity in ethical decision making as they must take into account potentially competing needs of family members and subsystems.

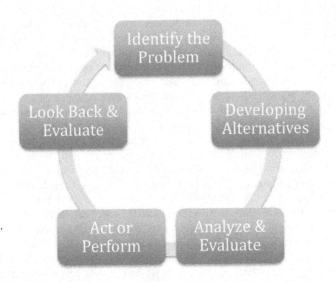

Figure 11.7 Knapp et al.'s five step principle-based ethical decision-making process

Case Application

The therapist working with the Rothers family will need to keep the various ethical principles in mind as he or she engages the family. Beneficence helps the therapist focus on improving the family members' lives; however, the question might be, "Whose opinion of what is 'good' will be used to determine whether the outcome of therapy falls under beneficence or nonmaleficence?" One way to help ensure the therapist is doing good is to focus on the goals the clients bring with them to therapy. This helps support the ethical principle of autonomy, where the family members take the lead in determining what they think will be useful for them and what they want. The therapist might provide suggestions and concerns, but, ultimately, the Rothers will have to lead their own lives.

During the informed consent with the Rothers, the therapist will need to be upfront and clear that, while the intent of therapy is to change their lives to how they wish them to be, therapy may also lead people to view self and others in a different way that may lead to discord in the relationship. This may be likely for Mark and Hannah as they are currently able to live with one another. Depending on the model of therapy being utilized by the therapist, problematic patterns may be brought to the forefront in an effort to reduce or eliminate them. This process may invoke upset and resentment.

Depending on the context of working with the Rothers family, it seems probable that Mark would receive a substance abuse disorder diagnosis. The therapist would then need to consider the implications of this diagnosis, not only for Mark—as it will become part of his client file—but for the therapeutic process as well. This diagnosis, if known by other members of the family, may keep Mark in the identified patient position. If the therapist did not think Mark qualified for a diagnosis, or was just morally opposed to diagnosis, they would need to consider the ramifications for the family to engage in treatment, especially if the family was seeing the therapist through an insurance company. Whatever position the therapist took, he or she would need to ensure that, if a diagnosis was made, the person receiving the diagnosis fits the criteria for that diagnosis.

Like many families dealing with addiction, the Rothers have many secrets that are both internal to the family system and between the family and external larger systems. The therapist working with them will need to determine what type of rules he or she wants to have with the family's surrounding secrets. In order to uphold the ethical principle of veracity, as well as to maintain appropriate confidentiality, the therapist must inform the family, preferably during the informed consent, as to how he or she will handle information told to him or her by family members when other family members are not present. This may be dependent on the type of information disclosed, who it would most likely impact, as well as the age of the other people. For instance, if in an individual session Mark disclosed that he was having an affair, the therapist may be more likely to think about and discuss disclosure of this information to Hannah rather than to Pete.

The therapist working with Mark will need to take extra caution surrounding a suicide assessment. While it seems that Mark has not made a suicide attempt, he has expressed suicidal ideation and the possibility of suicidal intent. Given that he is also a substance abuser, he is at higher risk for making a suicide attempt. Mark's problems sleeping, difficulties at work, and his comment,

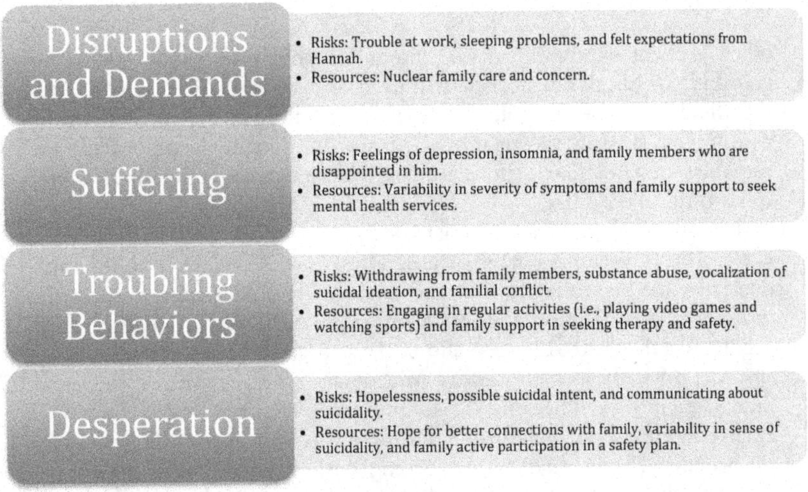

Disruptions and Demands	• Risks: Trouble at work, sleeping problems, and felt expectations from Hannah. • Resources: Nuclear family care and concern.
Suffering	• Risks: Feelings of depression, insomnia, and family members who are disappointed in him. • Resources: Variability in severity of symptoms and family support to seek mental health services.
Troubling Behaviors	• Risks: Withdrawing from family members, substance abuse, vocalization of suicidal ideation, and familial conflict. • Resources: Engaging in regular activities (i.e., playing video games and watching sports) and family support in seeking therapy and safety.
Desperation	• Risks: Hopelessness, possible suicidal intent, and communicating about suicidality. • Resources: Hope for better connections with family, variability in sense of suicidality, and family active participation in a safety plan.

Figure 11.8 Information from a relational suicide assessment with Mark Rothers would provide risks and resources in the four categories of suicidal experience

"It would be easier if I were dead" are all risk factors that should concern the therapist and he or she should make sure that a proper and thorough assessment is conducted. However, the therapist should also pay attention to Mark's resources. If the therapist conducted a relational suicide assessment, the information may be gathered to help the therapist make a determination about client safety (see Figure 11.8).

Summary

All therapists operate from a set of guidelines for proper therapeutic behavior—ethics. These ethics are based on a foundation that puts the client in a respected position to increase their free choice and limit the potential harm that may come from therapy. Therapists attempt to work so that the core ethical principles of beneficence, nonmaleficence, autonomy, justice, fidelity, and veracity inform all of their therapeutic decisions.

While therapists have a duty to protect clients, this is not always possible. However, therapists are in a position where they attempt to keep not only the client safe, but also others in the client's relational world as well. This duty to protect and duty to warn may be at odds with other ethical imperatives, such as confidentiality. Thus, therapists need to make hard ethical decisions. To do so they can follow the steps of one or more ethical decision-making models. One of these serious ethical dilemmas comes

(continued)

(continued)

when a client expresses suicidal intent. All therapists should assess for suicidality with all clients, but will need to take extra precautions when the client is at risk for suicidal behavior. In those cases, engaging in an assessment, such as the relational suicide assessment, helps provide the therapist with necessary information to make a determination on how best to keep the client safe.

For substance abuse therapists working with couples and families, extra ethical dilemmas may surface. These include issues of multiconfidentiality, secrets, diagnosing, and equity. Therapists must respect the individual confidentiality of all members as well as that of the whole family. Further, the therapist should have a clear policy on what he or she will do with secrets that are told outside the presence of the other family members. Therapists also must determine whether they will engage in the use of diagnosing and how this will impact the therapeutic process. Lastly, therapists working with multiple individuals must consider the equity involved in therapy and consider the welfare of all involved. They might do so in a variety of ways including acting from a stance of neutrality or of multidirected partiality.

Key Words

ethics
ethical principles
beneficence
nonmaleficence
competence
self-care
autonomy
informed consent
assent
consent event
consent process
confidentiality
non-discrimination
justice
social justice
fidelity
dual relationships

veracity
suicidal ideation
suicidal intent
suicide threat
suicide plan
suicide attempt
duty to protect
relational suicide assessment
duty to warn
multiconfidentiality
facilitated disclosure
selective disclosure
multidirected partiality
neutrality
harm reduction
ethical decision making

Reflection Questions

1. How might a substance abuse therapist who is working with the family system be able to navigate the primary ethical principles of beneficence, nonmaleficence, autonomy, fidelity, veracity, and equity?

2. What are some of the major implications in the ethical imperatives of the duty to warn and the duty to protect?
3. What are some of the unique ethical quandaries that therapists face when they work with the family system?
4. How does the notion of social justice play a role in therapy with families dealing with substance abuse?
5. What are the key ideas of ethical decision making when working with families?

TWELVE

Systems Theory

Family therapy is predicated on the notion that the family is a system, and, as such, one part of the system impacts some or all of the other parts. The family is also a subsystem of larger systems such as each adult's family of origin, aspects of diversity such as culture, religion, or sexual orientation, as well as societal processes such as social class and education. In this chapter we will explore the various components that make up systems so that you will have a foundation of understanding family process when working with families.

Systems theory was primarily introduced into psychotherapy through the work of Gregory Bateson and his application of cybernetics to humans and families (Bateson, 1972). **Cybernetics** can be considered "the science of pattern and organization" (Keeney, 1983, p. 61). It is based on how systems process feedback to self-regulate. While not all family therapists utilize the cybernetic metaphor, many of the models of family therapy have aspects of cybernetics, or at least systems theory, as foundational concepts. For a more in-depth discussion of the interactional and cybernetic bases of systems theory, as well as other systems theories that undergird various models of psychotherapy (natural systems and language systems), see Reiter (2019).

Systems

Perhaps the place to start in understanding systems theory is to gain clarity on what a system is. A **system** can be defined as a group of parts that come together to function as a whole. When applied to families, this functioning occurs via the transactional patterns of family members. **Patterns** are sequences of interactions that occur repetitively over time. In families, patterns form and are maintained, usually for lengthy periods. When these patterns are to our liking, we say that things are "going well" or therapists might call them "functional." However, when the patterns are not fulfilling, we might explain it as being "in a rut" or "dysfunctional." The patterns, if judged severe, might also become problematic and conflictual. Thus, we can see that patterns are not in and of themselves problematic. Family therapy is geared toward helping families keep patterns they find useful and effective, while changing patterns they believe are problematic to patterns they desire.

While the family is a complete system, it is also a **subsystem** of larger systems. In a family, this comes into play through each partner's family of origin. The nuclear family of husband–wife (or two partners in a same-sex relationship) is a subsystem of two larger family systems, which are subsystems of other extended families. The current nuclear family is also a subsystem of various larger systems such as religion, culture, work, education, etc. The lens that the therapist uses allows either wider or more zoomed views of the larger family system. For instance, if only working with a couple, the therapist may be so zoomed in that they only see two partners and do not see how those individuals are impacted by their children (and thus their parental roles), their parents (and their roles as offspring), their brothers and sisters (and their roles as siblings), as well as their work, friends, and other factors impacting them. This is where creating a genogram (see Chapter 1) with the family may be useful.

In Chapter 1 we discussed the notion that the whole is greater than the sum of its parts through the equation of $1 + 1 = 3$. However, this was a very limited view of the dynamics of systems as two people are not isolated from others. If we look at a family, we can add a child and look at the equation of $1 + 1 + 1 = 7$, or the addition of two children is $1 + 1 + 1 + 1 = 15$, and the addition of a grandparent to this family is $1 + 1 + 1 + 1 + 1 = 30$. Let's take a step back to see how we got to 30 different relational dynamics that we need to look at in a five-person system.

If we changed the numbers that represented people into letters our equation will be as such: $A + B + C + D + E = 30$. Now we can explore all of the two, three, four, and five-person relational permutations that exist.

- *Individual people*: A; B; C; D; E.
- *Two-person relationships*: A + B; A + C; A + D; A + E; B + C; B + D; B + E; C + D; C + E; D + E.
- *Three-person relationships*: A + B + C; A + B + D; A + B + E; A + C + D; A + C + E; A + D + E; B + C + D; B + C + E; B + D + E; C + D + E.
- *Four-person relationships*: A + B + C + D; A + B + C + E; A + C + D + E; B + C + D + E.
- *Five-person relationships*: A + B + C + D + E.

As you can see, the addition of another person exponentially increases the complexity of the relational dynamics of the system. To help give the interpersonal nature of families as well as an understanding of subsystems, we will now substitute the letters for the members of the Rothers family.

- *Individual people*: Mark; Hannah; Steve; Kayleigh; Pete.
- *Two-person relationships*: Mark + Hannah; Mark + Steve; Mark + Kayleigh; Mark + Pete; Hannah + Steve; Hannah + Kayleigh; Hannah + Pete; Steve + Kayleigh; Steve + Pete; Kayleigh + Pete.
- *Three-person relationships*: Mark + Hannah + Steve; Mark + Hannah + Kayleigh; Mark + Hannah + Pete; Mark + Steve + Kayleigh; Mark + Steve + Pete; Mark + Kayleigh + Pete; Hannah + Steve + Kayleigh; Hannah + Steve + Pete; Hannah + Kayleigh + Pete; Steve + Kayleigh + Pete.

- *Four-person relationships*: Mark + Hannah + Steve + Kayleigh; Mark + Hannah + Steve + Pete; Mark + Steve + Kayleigh + Pete; Hannah + Steve + Kayleigh + Pete.
- *Five-person relationships*: Mark + Hannah + Steve + Kayleigh + Pete.

A word of caution here. We will never be seeing the "whole" family. While we might get to the point where we are seeing the five-person family, we know that each person has connections outside of the family system that impact their behaviors and sense of self—which impact how the individual operates within the family. Although not arbitrary, we have to choose to make distinctions as to how wide we see when working with families.

Larger Systems

The family therapist will need to be able to shift back and forth from a very narrow focus on the individual, gradually widening the lens to see the various two-person relationships, three-person relationships, etc., depending on how many people are in the session and in the family. The systems therapist then needs to have the ability to take a very wide focus to be able to see how the individuals who have come together as a system and are now in the therapy room impact and are impacted by larger systems such as culture, religion, socioeconomic status, health, and work (see Figure 12.1). These larger systems influence the various members differentially, which then possibly has a role in determining how the two (or three or four) people find their relationships to be.

For instance, some cultures espouse a paternalistic viewpoint. Understanding this allows the therapist to see how the father is the central arbiter in the family. Other cultures may be more maternalistic. For some families, they may be organized around the medical system where one or more members are dealing with disability or illness (such as a family member having cancer). The families we

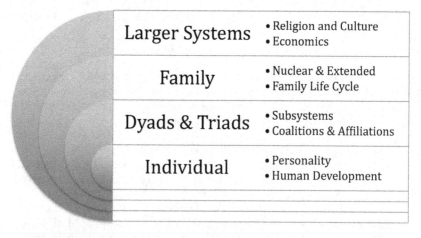

Figure 12.1 The family therapist sees multiple levels at one time and how those levels impact each other

are talking about in this book are organized around addiction. This most likely draws in several larger systems such as the legal system (i.e., the substance abuser may have been arrested for DUI, possession of an illegal substance, or other crimes such as theft), the education system (i.e., when one or more children have difficulty in school), and the therapeutic system (i.e., self-help groups, outpatient or inpatient therapy, or family therapy).

Boundaries

A system may be an individual, a dyad, a family of 20, or a whole country. So how can we distinguish between one system and another? This is where the notion of boundaries comes into play. **Boundaries** are what separate one system from another system. While physical boundaries, like fences between houses, easily demarcate one "thing" from another "thing," the boundaries between the systems we are talking about in this book are a bit more difficult to determine as they can only be seen in transactions. They are determined by who is allowed to do what, where, when, and to whom.

Minuchin (1974) distinguished three types of boundaries: rigid, diffuse, and clear (see Figure 12.2). **Rigid boundaries** do not let a lot of information through from system to system. In families, parents may have a rigid boundary with the child subsystem. Here, parents may restrict the flow of information, making it primarily the parents presenting information and not allowing feedback from the children. In families with rigid boundaries, the parents make and keep the rules and the children are not allowed to challenge them. This is the type of boundary that is prevalent in addicted families. The more rigid the boundaries, the more likely that subsystems are keeping information from one another—which leads to the presence of secrets.

Diffuse boundaries are the opposite of rigid boundaries. Here, too much information flows back and forth. Families with diffuse boundaries might tend to know everyone else's business. For instance, if mother and father get into a fight, one of the parents may go to a child and tell them what is happening to try to get emotional support from the child. In subsystems with diffuse boundaries, members are very connected to one another; usually over-connected in

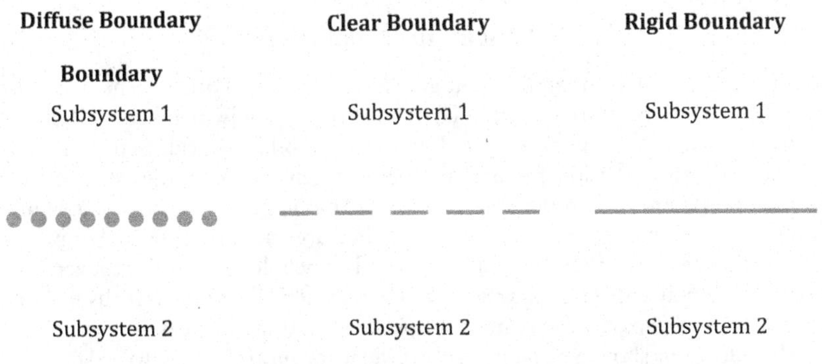

Diffuse Boundary	Clear Boundary	Rigid Boundary
Boundary		
Subsystem 1	Subsystem 1	Subsystem 1
● ● ● ● ● ● ● ●	— — — — — —	▬▬▬▬▬▬▬
Subsystem 2	Subsystem 2	Subsystem 2

Figure 12.2 Family mapping diagram of the three types of boundaries

Figure 12.3 Therapists tend to help families shift from rigid or diffuse boundaries to clear boundaries

inappropriate ways. When this happens we say that the two individuals are experiencing **enmeshment**.

The third type of boundary is a **clear boundary**. Here, information is allowed to move across boundaries, however the information is appropriate for the context. Parents who have clear boundaries with their children will make the rules, yet, depending on the age of the children and the situation, will allow flexibility in those rules. Children would be allowed to talk with the parents and negotiate temporary or permanent changes in interactions. Families usually enter therapy displaying boundaries on the extreme; either diffuse or rigid. Therapy is usually designed to help change the interpersonal rules so that more clear boundaries are present (see Figure 12.3).

The type of boundaries parents have with their children lead to various types of parenting styles. For instance, if we look at the four categories of parenting developed by Baumrind (1967), we can see how these styles may be related to the boundaries between the parental and child subsystems. **Authoritarian parents** tell their children what the rules are and what the child is supposed to do, allowing little to no negotiation and most likely involving a rigid boundary between the parent and child systems. **Indulgent parents** tend to allow their children to do whatever the children want, which may be most indicative of a diffuse boundary between parents and children. **Authoritative parents** provide rules and guidance but are somewhat flexible, allowing potential negotiation. Here, there is most likely a clear boundary between subsystems. The last type of parenting is **negligent** where the focus is not on the children but something else. For addicted families where the addiction has become severe enough, negligent parenting may occur. This style of parenting is likely to utilize rigid or diffuse boundaries.

Alliances and Coalitions

There are individuals in families that get along better than others. There are also times where one or more members go against other family members. When two or more members get along very well with one another we call that **affiliation**. People with an affiliation for one another will tend to hang out together and think and act positively toward one another. At a higher level, these people may form **alliances**, where they make sure that they are supporting the other person in the alliance rather than looking out for other people. At a still stronger position, people may engage in **coalitions** where they actively work to focus negative energy on a third party. There may be coalitions within alliances.

The television show *Survivor* is an excellent forum to be able to see many of the systems processes in action. Strangers are placed together into two teams.

Within each team, members come together and form alliances where they agree to play the game together and help one another through the game. The participants form positive affiliations with one another, where they like the other as a person. They also agree to enter into coalitions where they actively try to vote off someone else. Throughout the course of the show/game, alliances may shift to where someone a player was in a coalition against becomes part of their alliance and someone who was part of their alliance may become the focus of a new coalition. Families also have this shifting of allegiances where members configure with one or more individuals for a time and then shift to connect with others (but fortunately usually not in trying to get a member out of the family!).

Open and Closed Systems

How open or closed a system is depends on the boundaries that have been developed. Systems where the boundaries are looser, where information can more readily move from one system to another, are known as **open systems**. Here, the boundary between the family and a larger system is most likely a diffuse boundary or a clear boundary on the diffuse side of the continuum. This allows the family to more readily adapt to what the outside systems need. For instance, a family in recovery may be open to outside systems such as the legal system, extended family, or the work system as to how the recovery process is going. Conversely, the larger systems are allowed to input information, such as treatment programs or moral support, into the family.

In contrast, **closed systems** are more inflexible where there is a clear distinction between systems. Information does not easily flow from one system to another. Closed systems tend to operate from rigid boundaries and do not readily exchange information. This is where addicted families, especially during the more severe stages of the process, fall. Addicted families usually become more closed over the course of their life-span as long as the addiction is present. Figure 12.4 presents a visual distinction between open and closed systems.

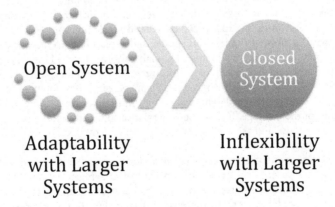

Figure 12.4 Open systems are adaptable in their interactions with larger systems while closed systems maintain a rigidity

Lineal and Circular Epistemologies

One of the biggest components of systems theory is the shift away from a lineal causality model to one that is circular. Viewing action from a **lineal perspective**, A causes B. For instance, your partner yelling at you causes you to become angry. However, that view is severely limited. It does not take into consideration temporality—what occurred prior to this action. Where did your partner's yelling come from? By only looking at the yell–anger transaction, the context of the interchange is lost. Context is perhaps one of the most important concepts in all of systems theory. Without it, behavior may not make sense. **Context** is the situation in which interactions occur. There are times when you have looked at someone's reaction and were quite confused as to why they were happy, sad, conflictual, etc. However, later you found out the context of the situation and then it was clear to you why they acted as they did (for instance, your drinking buddy was very mad at a celebration party, and then you later found out their partner left them that morning).

Another problem with viewing actions from a lineal perspective is where to put the punctuation. **Punctuation** in systems theory explores where to put a starting and ending point. Usually, people punctuate a transaction starting from the other person's action and ending with their response. For instance, I see that my wife did not remember my birthday (the cause) so I am mad with her (the response). Yet, if we expand the punctuation to include the time before this, we might see that I did not recognize our anniversary and she was upset about this. The further back we start punctuating the transaction, the greater the context to understand the situation.

A **circular perspective** takes into consideration the idea that two (or more) people *simultaneously* and *mutually* influence one another (see Figure 12.5). We do not act in vacuums of relationships. When you are having a conversation with your partner, although you may be doing most of the talking, they are being influenced by and influencing you. You, at the same time, are influencing and being influenced by them. During the conversation you are taking in information, both verbal and nonverbal, as to whether they are understanding what you are saying, agreeing or disagreeing with it, as well as metacommunication to tell you to continue to talk or to stop talking. **Metacommunication** is communication about communication (Watzlawick, Bavelas, & Jackson, 1967). This is verbal and nonverbal messages to let each person understand how to make meaning of the communication. As an example, Hannah says to Mark, "Honey, could you please put down the beer and join us for dinner." She is sending several messages. The first, what is known as the **report** of the message, is the content—"Put down the drink, come eat dinner." The second and more important component is the **command** of the message. It describes the relationship between the two people— "I am your spouse and as such I have the right to tell you that I am worried about you and expect you to listen to me."

The punctuation of a circular view includes both individuals over time. For instance, in a parent–child situation, instead of viewing it as child acts out— parent punishes, it can be seen as more of a pattern, over time. Yet this pattern will be punctuated differently by the various players. For the parent, it would most likely be the more the child doesn't follow the rules the more the parent tries to control the child's actions, which leads to the child going against the parent's rules,

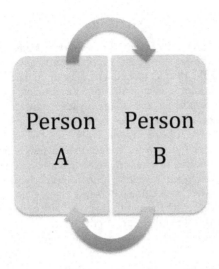

Figure 12.5 Circular causality holds that two people mutually influence one another

which leads to more control attempts from the parent, ad infinitum. However, the child would most likely punctuate it differently. For them, the more the parent tries to control them the more they try to assert their individuality (go against the parent's rules), which leads to the parent trying to control more, which leads to more attempts by the child to be independent (see Figure 12.6).

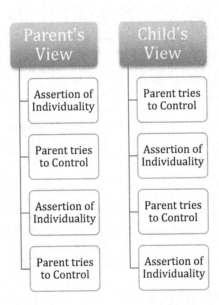

Figure 12.6 People have different punctuations of their patterned relationship

Mutuality

Behind this notion of circularity is that of **mutuality**. Systems theory does not see the individual as separate from the context but an active agent in it. While we can look at the individual as a distinct system with a group of parts (our brains, heart, lungs, blood, etc.) working in conjunction to form a whole (us as a person), the individual is a subsystem of larger systems (dyads, triads, larger families, etc.). Individual parts do not function on their own, but in relation to other parts. For instance, take your heart. It beats in your body, but if we disconnected it from your brain it would not function for longer than a few minutes—and neither would you, unless connected to an alternative life-support system.

People can be seen to function similarly; however, perhaps not to the extreme of separating a person from a relationship (say a divorce) and then not functioning (dying) soon after. Yet, the part—in this case, the person—functions based on *how* it is connected to the other parts in the system. This is why your friends may find it odd when they first interact with you when you are around a person they have never seen you with before (perhaps a new romantic partner, your sibling you haven't seen recently, or your grandparent); they think you are "acting" like a different person. When connected to that other person there are different pushes and pulls for you to act in certain ways.

Homeostasis

The understanding of families as systems occurred through the application of cybernetic principles, which looked at how systems regulated themselves. **Homeostasis** stands for "same state" and holds that systems attempt to maintain a steady state of functioning through the use of feedback processes. This occurs through the combination of two opposing but necessary processes—stability and change (see Figure 12.7).

Perhaps the easiest example of a homeostatic process is that of an air conditioner. Think about what temperature you set your thermostat on. Let's say it is at 74 degrees Fahrenheit. Your HVAC system continually takes in information from the home air, registering the current temperature. When this information confirms that it is at the 74 degree mark, the system does not activate. In systems terminology, we call this **negative feedback**. Negative feedback helps to maintain the status quo (see Figure 12.8). However, if the sun comes out and shines through the windows, the indoor temperature quickly rises. Your HVAC system

Figure 12.7 Homeostasis is the combination of two interlocked processes; stability and change

brings in this hotter air and registers that it has exceeded a certain threshold, which activates the system to turn on and cool the system. This process is called **positive feedback**. Thus, positive feedback is an attempt by the system to bring components back into the standard acceptable way of operating (see Figure 12.9). Once the HVAC system registers that the air temperature is back to 74 degrees it shuts off—or, as we would now call it, negative feedback occurs.

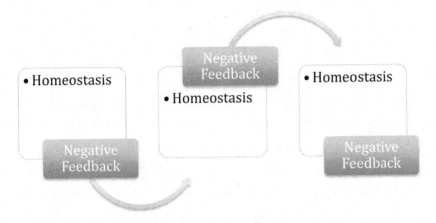

Figure 12.8 A visual representation of how negative feedback maintains the current homeostasis level

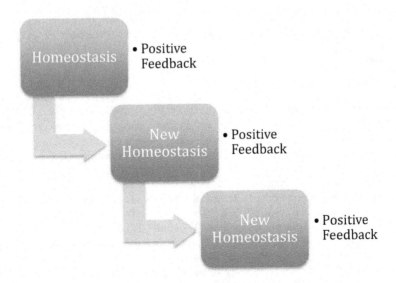

Figure 12.9 A visual representation of how positive feedback maintains the current homeostasis level

This is how homeostasis happens in a mechanic system. How might it occur in a family system? Let's use the Rothers family as an example. The family, consisting of mother, father, and three children—15, 12, and 9 years old. In this family, there are rules in place for everyone to get along with each other. The 15 year old, Steve, has started to try to gain a sense of independence and is hanging out with a new crowd, one that tends to engage in delinquent activities such as skipping school and smoking marijuana. Slowly, Steve begins to argue more with Kayleigh and Pete and to challenge the parents. One or two small challenges to harmony (such as refusing one night to eat dinner with the family or calling Pete a curse word) do not get the system to change—they are still within the realms of the steady state and lead to negative feedback. However, Steve has been told he cannot smoke marijuana, but he does so anyway. When confronted by Mark and Hannah, Steve states, "You do not control me. I can do what I want." This offense to getting along is past the boundaries of acceptability and becomes positive feedback—information that the system needs to put something in place to get back to the original steady state. Thus, the parents begin to put restrictions in place, such as grounding and taking away of privileges, all in the attempt to get Steve to be more harmonious in the house.

However, if a family maintained the same homeostasis for the course of its life it would cause serious difficulties as families must reorganize along various points of their life to help accommodate the requirements of that life stage (see Chapter 7 for the explanation of family life cycle). Systems theorists hold that families are more vulnerable to symptoms during these transition phases between life stages when they have not reorganized to be able to better navigate the new requirements. In the Rothers family, the family is moving from the family with children/adolescents to the family with a young adult. This transition requires the parents to be less rigid in their boundaries with Steve so that he can learn to be able to gain a sense of independence, since he will soon be involved in launching away from the family and needing to be able to function on his own (we use this phrase liberally—as the person is not literally on their own but also not under the direct auspices of their parents).

Patterns

Almost all family therapists pay attention to the patterns of transactions that occur between people. These come in many different forms, yet we can look at three in particular: symmetrical, complementary, and parallel. **Symmetrical relationships** are when each person matches what the other person does; in essence, it is a more of the same. In an **escalating symmetrical relationship** (sometimes called a competitive symmetrical relationship) the more person A engages in a behavior the more person B engages in that behavior (see Figure 12.10). For instance, Mark comes home and starts yelling at Hannah. As he does this Hannah yells back, which leads to more yelling by Mark and more yelling by Hannah. This is just one punctuation of the pattern. We could also say that the more Hannah yells at Mark the more Mark yells at Hannah. In a **deescalating symmetrical relationship** the less Person A does a behavior the less Person B does that behavior (see Figure 12.11). The less Mark opens up emotionally to Hannah the less she opens up to him and vice-versa; the less Hannah opens up to Mark the less he opens up to her.

Instead of matching the other person's behavior, two people may engage in alternate or opposite behavior; what we would call a **complementary relationship**. Here, the more person A engages in a behavior, the less person B does that behavior. We can see this in pursuer–distancer relationships where the more

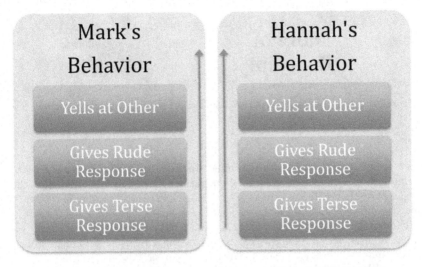

Figure 12.10 Escalating symmetrical relationship between Mark and Hannah where each person attempts to engage in the same or one-up behaviors of the other person

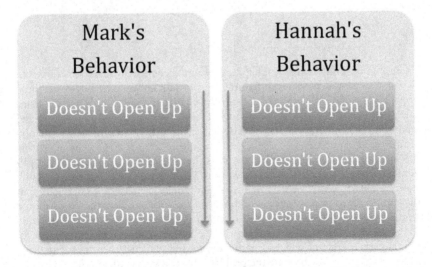

Figure 12.11 Deescalating symmetrical relationship between Mark and Hannah where each person attempts to engage in the same or one-down behaviors of the other person

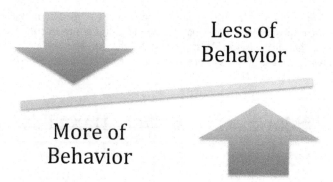

Figure 12.12 Complementary relationships involve the two people in interaction engaging in opposite yet connected behaviors

one person pursues the more the other distances. It is also the main type of relationship in families where one of the partners underfunctions leading to the other partner overfunctioning (see Figure 12.12). In the Rothers family, as Mark begins to find his life being chaotic and is not taking care of his home responsibilities like child care or cleaning, Hannah tends to overfunction and take on more of these duties. Again, we can punctuate this differently as Hannah taking over caretaking duties and Mark giving up his parental duties.

Parallel relationships occur when there is a back-and-forth give-and-take between the two people. There is a negotiation between the people where they are able to swap roles. For instance, the husband may engage in primary caretaking duties three days a week while the wife caretakes for three other days. The seventh day they might both caretake together.

First-Order Change

There are many different ways that families might change how they function. The two general classes of change attempts we will talk about in this book are first-order and second-order change. **First-order change** is change within the existing rule structure of the system. Sometimes first-order change attempts work, and whatever the people wanted to be different changes after they make the attempt. However, when it does not work, families tend to keep trying to change within this class of attempt. First-order change is the type of change that most people/ families attempt as it fits within a Western perspective of "If at first you don't succeed, try try again." The difficulty is that family members are not aware that they are engaged in this process of "more of the same" where they try solution strategies that, although different, maintain the current structure and function of the family. However, the family believes they are trying many different solution attempts; none of which seem to be working. Further, these failed solution attempts may actually become the problem (Watzlawick et al., 1974).

For instance, the Rothers family members may be very frustrated with Mark's substance abuse and subsequent related behavioral problems (i.e., not engaging with the family in a positive manner). Each member attempts solutions to try to fix the situation. Hannah sits down with Mark and tells him she is very concerned about him and that he needs to get his act together. Steve yells at him when Mark forgets his birthday. His mother tells him that she is disappointed in him and he needs to clean up his life. Each of these solution attempts, while different, all fall under the family rules that it is the family members' responsibility to help one another. The members may change what they do (i.e., Hannah may write a letter to Mark on how he is not the man she married or she may even threaten to leave or actually leave), yet it usually does not work because it is a continuation of a class of events that hasn't been useful. A change of change attempts is what is necessitated.

Second-Order Change

Second-order change is when there is a change of the rules of the system. Here, the Rothers family members might change the rule of them being responsible for each other's behaviors. They might do this by stating, "Mark, although we are your family, we cannot decide what you do. We care about you, but the choice of what you do is up to you." They have changed the system from being dominated by responsibility for others to people having to take responsibility for their own actions.

A common way of understanding the difference between first- and second-order change is through the nine dot problem. Look at Figure 12.13.

Here are the rules to solve this problem. Using only four straight lines, connect all nine dots. Once you put your pen down on the paper you cannot lift it up until you finish. See how many times it takes you to solve this before reading any further than this!

Did you solve it? Most people cannot because they work within the given rules, as well as one extra rule that they added; that you cannot go outside of the boundary of what looks like a box. And if you use this additional rule, the puzzle cannot be solved. However, if you change the rule of staying within the box (and follow the old dictum to "think outside the box") to be able to draw your line anywhere you want, the puzzle is more readily solved. Most likely your initial attempts to solve the nine-dot problem, by staying within the confines of the box, were all first-order change attempts; change within the existing rule structure. Once you changed the rules—that you could draw anywhere—you were operating via second-order change. Figure 12.14 presents a three-line and four-line solution for the nine-dot problem.

Figure 12.13 The nine-dot problem

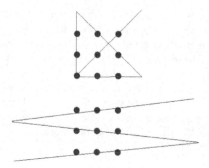

Figure 12.14 The three-line and four-line solutions to the nine-dot problem

Second-Order Cybernetics

In this chapter we have presented the primary principles of viewing the family as a system. However, when a therapist comes in contact with a family, they are not seeing the family as the family is, but as the family is *in relation to* someone (a therapist in this case). While the family is most likely similar to how they operate at home, there may be differences based on family members either trying to look more favorably to the newcomer, an attempt to make someone else look worse, or an attempt to get the therapist on someone's side.

This new combination—of the family and the therapist—is known as **the therapeutic system** (see Figure 12.15). And this new system operates by all of the principles that were discussed within this chapter; rules, roles, boundaries, etc. Looking at this in a different way, we can talk about it as the observer

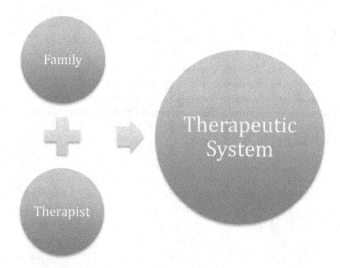

Figure 12.15 The therapeutic system is comprised of the client and the therapist who mutually influence one another

becoming part of the observed system. This viewpoint is known as the cybernetics of cybernetics—or **second-order cybernetics** (Keeney, 1983).

Because the observer is part of what is being observed, the notion of objectivity is questioned. Instead, therapists understand the recursive nature of interactions; the mutuality that happens between family members as well as the dynamics in play between clients and therapist. Each part of the system perturbs the other. So, instead of a therapist being able to sit in a session and provide an objective diagnosis of the client, the therapist has to be self-referential—understanding how the knowledge they have is biased on their own perspective as well as how the clients present themselves.

When family therapists work with a family, they must keep in mind how they enter the system. There are several positions they can take, such as an expert, a control agent, or a one-down position. For instance, if a family enters with an IP who is abusing substances, they are making demands to the therapist. In essence, they are saying, "We are concerned about person X who is addicted and making our lives miserable and we expect you to help us do this." This demand has the potential of putting the therapist in an untenable position. If agreed upon, the therapist will be operating from the expectations and anxiety of others instead of their own therapeutic principles. Family therapists must challenge the family's certainty; that the family knows what the problem is (or more specifically who the problem is) and that the therapist can help them fix this person (Minuchin, Reiter, & Borda, 2014). This is because families tend to view an individual as the problem rather than the interpersonal transactions. To do this the therapist must be aware of his function in the therapeutic system.

Systems Theory in Practice

We have been talking about how families function, yet that understanding needs to be connected to what the family therapist does while working with the family. By understanding that "the problem" the person/family brings to therapy is just a symptom of an underlying organizational issue in the family, the therapist is less focused on the content of what the family is talking about and more concerned about the process of interactions occurring between the family members.

This is perhaps one of the most difficult skills for the family therapist as therapists tend to be trained to examine *what* the problem is, *when* the problem happens, and *what* the person thinks and feels about the problem. To get away from this mindset, the family therapist adopts a relational perspective, focusing on how one person's actions impact another person. Here are several relational questions and their individual question relatives:

Individual: When you drink, what do you think about?
Relational: When you drink, what happens with your wife?
Individual: What type of drunk is your wife?
Relational: Who is most impacted by your wife's drinking?
Individual: How do you feel when you are drugging?
Relational: How do your children react when you are drugging?

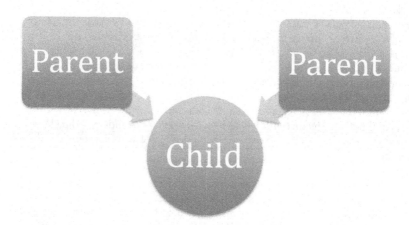

Figure 12.16 Detouring triangulation happens when two people focus on another instead of addressing the underlying conflict between themselves

Symptoms

Symptoms that family members develop usually serve some type of function in the family. For instance, an adolescent who is acting out may unconsciously be doing so as a way to divert attention away from a mother and father who are having marital difficulties. By focusing on the adolescent's problematic behaviors, husband and wife do not have to address their own anger, upset, or disappointment with one another. This is called a **detouring triangulation** (see Figure 12.16). As another example, a husband's drinking may seem isolated from the larger family. However, in looking closer, we may see that his father has recently passed away, and, through his underfunctioning via drinking, his mother is helping out more with the raising of his children. This prevents her from experiencing the grief of the loss of her husband.

Given that families tend to enter therapy offering up an identified patient (IP)—the person in the family who is most demonstrating the symptoms of the family—one of the first steps for a family therapist is to deconstruct the symptom (Minuchin et al., 2014). The family therapist should be able to hear the family's presenting concern yet expand the scope of the problem—externalizing the problem from a trait of an individual to a transactional pattern between several people. Minuchin et al. describe this process as that of a detective uncovering a mystery:

> Knowing that the symptom is but one piece of a larger puzzle that, when put into the context of relationships, uncovers the mosaic of the family, the therapist begins with the symptoms but searches underneath for the relational rules in place that maintain the symptom (p. 11)

Thus, the therapist enters the family transactions via the presenting problem (and the associated IP), with the understanding that family transactions are maintaining that symptom. Thus, the symptom is usually not the focus of therapy but how family members engage one another.

Case Application

The Rothers family can be viewed as a system. They are five individuals that function as a whole. However, they are also a subsystem of larger systems, such as Mark's family of origin, Hannah's family of origin, and Mark's previous marriage and first child. They are also a subsystem of families in the United States. They maintain themselves as a family by engaging in patterned relationships, where there are typical ways that they interact with one another. These repetitive interactions, such as the kids going to Hannah rather than Mark when they are asking for privileges, or Mark and Hannah going to what is called "our bedroom" at night, help distinguish the family in their unique way of being.

There are various boundaries at play in the Rothers family. Between husband and wife seems to be a boundary somewhere between clear and rigid. There is a rigid boundary between Mark and the children. Hannah seems to have a somewhat rigid boundary with Steve, a clear to diffuse boundary with Kayleigh, and diffuse boundary with Pete. There is likely a rigid boundary between the Rothers family and larger systems such as extended family and the school system. Thus, the Rothers tend to function as a closed system. A family map of the Rothers is presented in Figure 12.17. We can hypothesize that Mark attempts to use an authoritarian parenting style while Hannah uses an authoritative parenting style.

There are several affiliations, alliances, and coalitions in the Rothers family. For instance, there is a coalition of Hannah and the children against Mark. While they may not engage in open conflict with him, there is a sense of an "us against him" mentality. Hannah and Pete have a strong affiliation with one another. Kayleigh has an affiliation with both Hannah and Pete. Mark likely feels an outsider in the family as does Steve, who is finding affiliations and alliances more important with those outside of his family and in his peer group.

There are many patterns in the Rothers family that maintain their current way of function—their homeostasis. Each person punctuates these patterns, sometimes with overlap, other times not. If we looked at one small difference in punctuation between Mark and Hannah (see Figure 12.18) we can see that they are each reacting off of the other person's behavior in what will likely be a game without end (Watzlawick, Weakland, & Fisch, 1974).

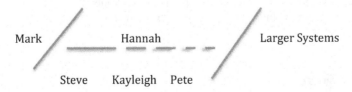

Mark   Hannah   Larger Systems

Steve   Kayleigh   Pete

Figure 12.17 Family map of the Rothers family's boundaries where rigid boundaries separate the family from larger systems and Mark from the rest of the family

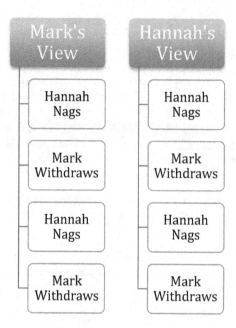

Figure 12.18 Mark and Hannah punctuate their patterned relationship differently

Summary

Systems theory is the foundation for many family therapy approaches. Based on a model of information processing and feedback, families try to maintain stability—homeostasis. The family's functioning level is predicated on the patterned relationships that have developed over time that determine who is in which subsystem and the associated boundaries between those subsystems. These boundaries are determined by the family's rules; overt and covert rules that let people know how they are allowed to be with one another and with those outside of the family. When family members stray too far from the family's homeostasis, various processes become enacted to try to regulate the members' behaviors so that they shift back into the standard way of being. These processes are best seen using a circular epistemology where mutuality between members demonstrates the interconnectedness of people and the development and maintenance of symptoms.

Key Words

cybernetics

system

patterns

subsystem

boundaries

rigid boundary

diffuse boundary
enmeshment
clear boundary
authoritarian parents
indulgent parents
authoritative parents
negligent parents
affiliation
alliance
coalition
open system
closed system
lineal perspective
context
punctuation
circular perspective
metacommunication
report

command
mutuality
homeostasis
negative feedback
positive feedback
symmetrical relationship
escalating symmetrical
    relationship
deescalating symmetrical
    relationship
complementary relationship
parallel relationship
first-order change
second-order change
the therapeutic system
second-order cybernetics
detouring triangulation

Discussion Questions

1. Discuss how a family can be viewed as a system.
2. Explain the notion that 1 + 1 = 3.
3. How do interactional processes such as alliances, coalitions, and affiliations impact the family homeostasis?
4. Provide several examples of symmetrical, complementary, and parallel relationships.
5. What are the differences between first-order and second-order change?
6. Describe some of the implications of using a systems view when working with a family.

THIRTEEN

Family Therapy Overview I

Psychotherapy, as a field, has been around for just over 100 years. Yet family therapy has only been present for approximately half of that time. For various reasons, the beginning of counseling and psychotherapy focused on the individual. It wasn't until the mid-1950s, in which a confluence of events occurred, when therapists brought forth the understanding that person-in-context, specifically family involvement in therapy, was imperative for effective change (although the notion of social systems' involvement in people's lives was present previously).

Today, there are approximately 400 different types/methods of psychotherapy, depending on how one distinguishes between approaches. Of these, perhaps 50 are couples/family therapy theories. Studies have found that no one approach is better than any other (Lambert & Bergin, 1994); however, having an approach, even if it is an integrated/eclectic approach, is imperative. As such, being grounded in the various family therapies is necessary for someone to be able to have the flexibility to work systemically with individuals, couples, and families.

The primary goal of psychotherapy is change, in whatever form that may come (which depends on the client's goals as well as the theory of problem resolution of the approach the therapist is working from). Change comes for a client, generically, in the form of having more response options when they leave therapy than from when they entered (Reiter, 2018). To do this, the therapist must increase his or her response options. The more that you, as a therapist, can operate from multiple theories and multiple positions via the client (at one point being warm and supportive and at another being challenging), the greater chance you have of being able to navigate the unknown of the therapeutic encounter.

In this and the next chapter you will read about some of the most influential family therapy approaches. These are not the only therapies available to you; however, they are perhaps the most prominent. While they each have their idiosyncratic ways of viewing family functioning, they all focus on the dialectic of how people can be individuals while still being a functioning member of the family system (see Figure 13.1). Problems tend to occur when people move to either side of this continuum. Either they try so hard to be an autonomous individual that they lose the sense of togetherness and do not respect other people's autonomy, or they try to become part of the system and lose their sense of self.

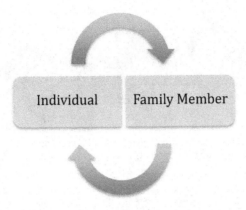

Figure 13.1 Family therapies focus on the ability of people to be unique while also staying connected to their family

Although there are varying ways to classify the different family therapies, in this book we will distinguish them based on their main focus. We can look at the various family therapies based on six categories: intergenerational approaches, experiential approaches, communication approaches, strategic approaches, systemic approaches, and postmodern approaches. The current chapter explores the intergenerational, experiential, and communication approaches. Chapter 14 covers the strategic, systemic, and postmodern approaches. We understand that this will only be an introduction to these various family therapies and highly encourage you to go to the writings of the founders and the second and third generation theorists to gain a more in-depth understanding of each model.

Intergenerational Approaches

Intergenerational approaches examine how family processes occur within and across generations. They explore how the current nuclear family is impacted by what occurred in the nuclear families (the **families of origin**) of the adults in the family. This exploration might be one, two, or three generations previous. Through these models, family members pass on behavior patterns, family values, expectations, and cultural ways of thinking. In this section we will discuss two of these approaches: Murray Bowen's Natural Systems Theory and Ivan Boszormenyi-Nagy's Contextual Therapy.

Natural Systems Theory

Murray Bowen developed one of the most comprehensive theories of family functioning. His approach is rooted in **Natural Systems Theory**, which holds that there are certain, predictable forces, which act on and shape the behaviors of all living systems. One of these crucial forces in shaping human relationship systems is the counterbalancing forces of individuality and togetherness (see Figure 13.2).

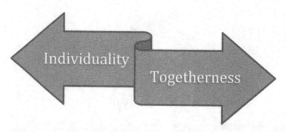

Figure 13.2 People experience two co-equal forces of nature; the push to be oneself while also being connected to others

Bowen Family Systems Theory rests on the premise that there is a relationship in families between the overall level of anxiety and the level of differentiation individual members display. All families demonstrate what Bowen calls disturbances of their **"emotional system,"** and these are most easily thought of in terms of the interplay of anxiety and differentiation among members (Kerr & Bowen, 1988). For families with lower overall levels of differentiation, not much anxiety is needed in the system to lead to one or more members becoming symptomatic (i.e., depression, anxiety, addiction). Families who function at the higher end of the differentiation scale may still become symptomatic, but such expressions are seen in the face of progressively increasing levels of anxiety. Regardless of how well members are differentiated, if chronic and situational anxiety become high enough, members may become symptomatic. Thus, alcoholism happens when family anxiety rises (Bowen, 1992). It is important to understand that the excessive drinking is a symptom of intergenerational family processes.

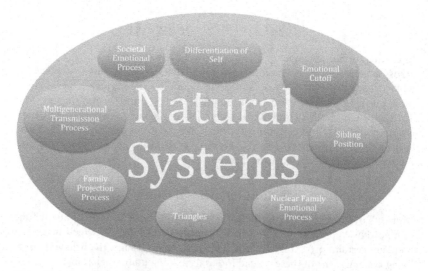

Figure 13.3 Bowen proposed eight interlocking concepts that form the basis for Natural Systems Theory

These concepts perhaps can be best explained using Bowen's eight interlocking concepts: differentiation of self, triangles, nuclear family emotional process, multigenerational transmission process, family projection process, emotional cutoff, sibling position, and societal emotional process (see Figure 13.3).

Bowen's Eight Interlocking Concepts

Differentiation of Self

Bowen's most recognized concept is that of **differentiation of self**. Differentiation is the innate tendency of the person to grow to be an emotionally separate person (Kerr & Bowen, 1988). When we are born we are completely dependent on others. However, as we develop, two life forces weigh upon us; the push to think, feel, and act as a distinct individual as well as a push toward togetherness—to stay emotionally connected to others.

Along this continuum, people can function too autonomously or too connected to others. Bowen thought of either extreme as two sides of the same coin, and people in such positions are vulnerable to problems in their overall functioning. The ideal is for one to be able to be connected to others while at the same time maintaining one's autonomy. When we are too together, we lose ourselves, through a process Bowen called **fusion** (Kerr & Bowen, 1988). This poorly differentiated position does not allow us to use our own thinking processes. When we are on the other extreme of trying to be totally independent we are also functioning from a poorly differentiated position as our "self" is not a real self but operates in isolation of others.

What distinguishes people along the continuum of differentiation is their ability to distinguish between their feeling system and thinking system (Kerr & Bowen, 1988). Those who are better able to choose which process they are operating from tend to function higher on the scale of differentiation. Those who cannot choose and are governed by their feeling process rather than their own thinking process are considered to be functioning toward the lower end of the differentiation scale.

Triangles

The notion of **triangles** highlights how people are connected to multiple individuals. For Bowen, the smallest stable unit of the emotional system is the three-person system (Bowen 1992). The two-person system is stable when anxiety is low. However, once the anxiety in the relationship increases and the individuals are not able to resolve it between themselves they recruit (triangulate) a third person to offset that anxiety (see Figure 13.4). However, alcohol/drugs could become the third part of a triangle. For instance, if Mark and Hannah are having conflict, Mark may go drinking to reduce the anxiety in the system. This is a useful temporary maneuver, but creates more anxiety in the long haul.

In Bowen therapy, the therapist attempts to help people to **de-triangle**. This comes in two main forms. The first is working with people so that they understand how they become triangled by others as well as how they try to triangulate

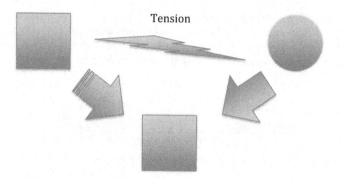

Figure 13.4 Triangulation occurs when two people are unable to handle the anxiety in their own relationship and incorporate a third person to help offset the anxiety

others (Kerr & Bowen, 1988). The second way is that the therapist enters into a triangle with family members (usually a couple) as a nonreactive third person. This is important since people, especially couples, come to therapy expecting the therapist to take their side against one or more other people (i.e., "See how wrong and bad my husband is being to me by drinking all the time"). By being connected but not being reactive, the therapist can serve the function of lowering the overall level of anxiety in the system. Doing this may allow the couple to figure out a way to address what is happening between them in a more thoughtful, less reactive manner.

Nuclear Family Emotional System

The **nuclear family emotional system** refers to how a family—in this case looking at two generations (parents and children)—come together and impact one another. There are four basic relationship patterns, or categories, of dysfunction (Kerr & Bowen, 1988). Based on which patterns the family operates from will lead to symptoms developing in a particular person or relationship. The four categories are illness in a spouse, marital conflict, impairment of one or more children, and emotional distance (see Figure 13.5).

Illness in a spouse is when one of the adult partners (in a two-parent family) underfunctions. This may be due to a physical or psychological ailment such as major depression, addiction, social anxiety, or any other of a multitude of problems. In this situation, the partners engage in a dance where the functioning partner accommodates to the underfunctioning partner to provide harmony in the relationship. However, if chronic anxiety rises enough, symptoms will occur in one or more members. Usually, this will be with the person who makes the most adjustments in their own thoughts and behaviors.

This over/underfunctioning complementarity plays itself out in unique ways in substance-abusing families. As the drinking escalates, social, emotional, and physiological consequences occur. Physically and neurologically, the person may

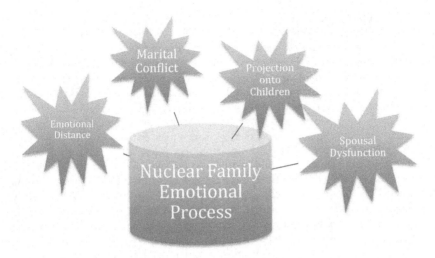

Figure 13.5 Couples bind their anxiety through the nuclear family emotional process

experience blackouts and memory loss, sexual dysfunction, and cirrhosis of the liver. Further, the person is not able to think and be as goal-directed as they once were (McKnight, 1998). These factors not only impact the substance abuser, but permeate the multitude of relationships within and without the family.

Marital conflict occurs when both partners sense the tension increasing and, instead of looking inwardly at their own process, tend to focus externally on what their partner is doing that they think is wrong. Both individuals tend to believe this and try to control what the other person does. They each then try not to be controlled by the other. This escalation perpetuates itself. As emotional reactivity increases, the more fixed each person gets into how they view who needs to change, instead of looking at themselves as part of the process.

A third category in the nuclear family emotional system is that of **impairment in one or more of the children**. Here, children are at risk of developing symptoms when their level of differentiation is low. The lower the differentiation level, the less chronic anxiety is needed to develop symptoms. Once a child does develop symptoms (which may be physical, psychological, or social) the parents tend to focus their energy and anxieties on that child. This increases the anxiety level in the system.

The last category is **emotional distance**. When the pull for togetherness is too great, and people are not able to figure out how to extricate themselves from this pull while still being engaged, they push away to the point of distancing themselves. If they push too much they will isolate themselves. This is problematic as other people, and especially our family members, are social supports.

Family Projection Process

Problems do not just form in an individual, even if that is where the symptoms reside. They are inextricably wrapped within the dynamics of relationships.

The **family projection process** describes how parents transmit their level of differentiation onto one or more children (Kerr & Bowen, 1988). This process has three steps. The first occurs when the parents focus on a child, believing that there is something wrong (psychologically, emotionally, and/or physically) with the child. Second, whatever the child does, the parent views this as confirmation of their fear for the child. Lastly, the parent then behaves toward the child as if their fear for the child was actually real. This process increases the anxiety in the symptom and targets it primarily on one child.

The family projection process can be seen as a triangle in which two parents triangulate a child to offset their anxiety (see Figure 13.6). By focusing so much attention on the child in trying to get the child "better" they do not have to address whatever issues may be present in their own relationship. As a child, the alcoholic usually experienced one of two extremes in their early attachment with their parents (Bowen, 1992). On one extreme is where the individual attempted to deny the attachment. Instead, they utilized a super-independent posture wherein they operated from a stance of saying, "I am a completely separate entity from you and I can handle everything on my own." Most likely, as an adult, they utilize this posture in their career and new nuclear family. In their career, they try to do all job tasks on their own rather than through collaboration. In their new family, with their spouse and perhaps children, they may attempt to overfunction. The other type of emotional attachment that potentially leads to alcoholism is the person who had an over-attachment to their parents. In this case, the person becomes emotionally fused with their parent. They do not become a distinct "self." While their counterpart was able, at least for a while, to function quite well in life (i.e., holding jobs, getting promoted, developing a family), this individual tends not to be able to function well. They may find themselves being a type of social outcast; having a need for connection yet a denial of it. Alcohol may fill a void of connection.

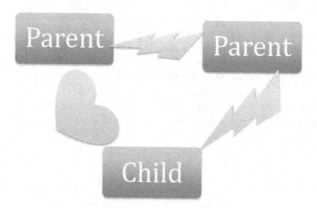

Figure 13.6 The family projection process occurs when parents attempt to bind their anxiety by overfocusing on a child

Multigenerational Transmission Process

Bowen's theory is an intergenerational one, where the functioning of people today is closely tied to the functioning of their ancestors (and will be connected to the children and grandchildren who are yet to be born). This is because of the **multigenerational transmission process.** This concept explains how, over time, there comes to be small differences in individuals and nuclear family differentiation levels.

People tend to marry and find partners at roughly the same level of differentiation that they are at (Kerr & Bowen, 1988). When they have children, the children are born into an emotional system and tend to function at the level of their parents. However, as was seen with the family projection process, one or more children can become the focus of the parents' anxiety, and will tend to develop a slightly lower level of differentiation. One or more other children might be able to function slightly more effectively and develop a slightly higher level of differentiation (see Figure 13.7). Over generations, one branch of the family can be functioning at a much lower level of differentiation than another branch. But keep in mind that someone at a higher level of differentiation may show symptoms before someone at a lower level. This is because it is the combination of self-differentiation and chronic anxiety that determines whether someone experiences symptoms. If anxiety becomes too high, anyone is potentially symptomatic.

Emotional Cutoff

At times, the pull for togetherness becomes so strong that individuals fear the loss of self. At that point they may engage in **emotional cutoff** (Kerr & Bowen, 1988).

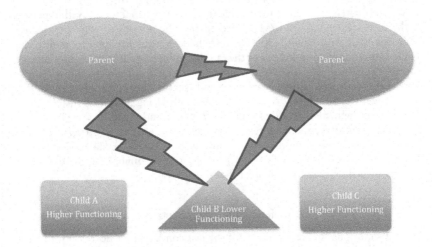

Figure 13.7 The multigenerational transmission process occurs when, over succeeding generations, one child is the focus of the family projection process and develops lower levels of differentiation and then does the same in their own children later in life—with this repeating itself over multiple generations

This may come in a physical form by the person moving away from their family and not having contact with them. Or it may be a psychological cutoff where they can be around family members but not engage them emotionally. Either way is problematic.

When a person engages in emotional cutoffs they are still operating based on the unresolved push and pull of individuality and togetherness. Their response is part of the emotional reactivity of the family. Instead of getting involved in what is going on in the family and potentially getting swept up in the family anxiety, they back out. Yet it is an emotional reaction based on their feeling system rather than a chosen response from their intellectual system.

Many times what happens when people cutoff from their family is that the anxiety and tension they are trying to get away from appear in their new relationships. For instance, in starting a new romantic relationship the individual may become overinvested in how the partner thinks, feels, and behaves. They also have not learned how to maintain connection within conflict. Thus, they may be quick to exit the relationship if the partner brings up issues they are having in the relationship.

Sibling Position

Bowen, based on the work of Walter Toman, found importance in **sibling position**. Bowen explained, "An individual's personality is shaped, to some extent, by being in a certain functioning position in the family" (Kerr & Bowen, 1988, p. 315). As used here, the notion of sibling position is more about *functional position* than birth order, as the two are many times the same but not necessarily so.

For instance, suppose in a family there are two children. The first child, who is two years older, was born with autism. Growing up, the younger child had to develop caretaking skills for his older brother. Chronologically this person is the youngest sibling. However, if we applied the notions of what personality characteristics are attributed to youngest children (i.e., they tend to want to be babied, are usually the jokesters of the family, and tend not to feel the pressure of having to succeed like their older siblings), we would not understand what was happening. This child's functional position is that of the older sibling. With this knowledge, we would look to them as potentially being more responsible, caretaking, with higher expectations on them from self and others.

Sibling position can also be related to the family projection process. Perhaps in the previous generation there was a strong focus on oldest males. This would lead us to suspect that in the current generation there might be more focus and anxiety placed on the oldest male of the sibling group.

Societal Emotional Process

Societal emotional process was one of the last concepts that Bowen introduced. This concept describes the notion that everything that has been presented so far about Natural Systems Theory happens in systems other than the family. Here, instead of just focusing on a nuclear family or three-generational family, issues of differentiation, culture, and transmission process occur at a societal level.

What may have been seen as family emotional system shifts can be seen as cultural forces at play, not only upon the few members of the family but also upon the millions of people in that society.

The Process of Therapy

Bowen therapy helps family members to explore the patterns that have happened in past generations and that are displaying themselves in the present. The therapist acts a coach, helping family members to gain insight into their reactions in the family. By helping members to take an I-position, the therapist works to increase each member's differentiation. The more differentiated the person can become the more they can engage other family members in a non-reactive manner. This may happen through the use of developing a genogram (see Chapter 1) and discussing the family patterns that have occurred over generations. There are not many techniques in Bowen therapy, but rather it is more an intellectual exploration of the client's family's emotional system, which will lead to the client being able to stay connected to family members while also holding to their own position.

Contextual Therapy

Contextual Therapy is a multigenerational therapy approach developed by Ivan Boszormenyi-Nagy. The model focuses on how the past issues of relational ethics (what may be considered fairness) impact current transactions, which, when placed in balance, aid future generations in having more trustworthy interactions (Boszormenyi-Nagy, 1987). As such, although it may help to relieve existing difficulties, it is also a preventative approach, assisting family members to discontinue problematic patterns of engagement so that those who come later can have more effective family legacies.

Boszormenyi-Nagy originally developed four dimensions of relational reality: facts, individual psychology, systemic transactions, and relational ethics (Boszormenyi-Nagy & Krasner, 1986). Before his death he made overt a fifth dimension; the ontic (Ducommon-Nagy & Reiter, 2014). Each of these dimensions can be talked about on their own, however they operate in conjunction with one another, with relational ethics being at the core. The family therapist must understand how they all come together to help highlight the individual's and the family's current context. Figure 13.8 presents the five dimensions of relational reality.

Facts are the components of ourselves and our lives. These include our gender, birth order, race, past physical history, socioeconomic status, ethnicity, etc. That you were born in the United States to parents who divorced when you were two, wherein your mother was an alcoholic, and that you had asthma as a child, are all facts of your life. These are components that you cannot change. Some facts lead to us engaging others productively, while others have the potential for us to expect to be repaid. For instance, someone who grew up in an addicted and chaotic family may expect that they are owed by society for their situation since they were not given a fair deal growing up.

The relational reality of individual psychology takes into account how the person functions as a distinct entity. This would include the person's intelligence,

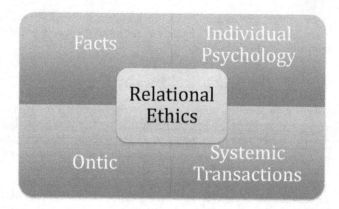

Figure 13.8 The five dimensions of relational reality in Contextual Family Therapy

developmental capabilities, life goals, motivations, and other aspects of person-hood. In this component are various facets of psychodynamic understandings; a focus on ego defense mechanisms, individual desires, and how each person understands themselves. When therapists explore this dimension, they are paying attention to the basic needs of each person in the family.

The third dimension of relational reality is **systems of transactional patterns**. Here, the therapist understands how the conglomeration of members of the family, with their own facts and individual psychology, come together and form a system. The components that we covered in Chapter 12 are all understood here; boundaries, rules, roles, etc. While the previous two dimensions place attention on the internal aspects that make a person distinct, this level of understanding helps the therapist to conceptualize the external aspects that regulate behavior. This dimension is used in contextual therapy for guidelines on tactics, while the fourth dimension, that of relational ethics, is mainly used for designing interventions (Boszormenyi-Nagy & Krasner, 1986).

The fourth dimension of relational reality is **relational ethics**. This focus sets Contextual Therapy apart from most other approaches of therapy. Ethics here is not the ethics that we think about in terms of guidelines by organizing bodies (see Chapter 11), but rather what is needed to earn credit—what is called **merit**. Here, the focus is on how trustworthy people's relationships are, including how they view what they have given to others and what they have received. This dimension is based on the interweaving of the previous three dimensions. Boszormenyi-Nagy and Krasner (1986) explained, "A consideration of the overall fairness (Dimension IV) of the interpersonal ledger requires weighing factual, psychological, and transactional circumstances from each partner's vantage point" (p. 58). Thus, a person has an internal sense of whether they have been treated with due concern by others that they have shown concern for; in essence, have they given more than they received or received more than they've given.

The fifth dimension is the **ontic**. This is the self in relation; describing ourselves as unique beings, based on not being someone else. This comes from an I–Thou relationship where each person understands that they are a distinct being, with different thoughts and viewpoints than the other. However, we develop our identity by distinguishing ourselves from the other person. In the Rothers family, Steve may grow up always assessing whether he is a better or worse person/father than his own father, Mark. Thus, his sense of self is based on "not being" someone else. This process would be utilized with a multitude of people in the individual's relational web.

The Development of Debt and Credit

As Contextual therapists view human transactions, problems are predicated on imbalances of people's relational **ledgers** (Boszormenyi-Nagy & Krasner, 1986). Each person keeps a subconscious accounting of what they have given to others and what they have received from others. This ledger is based upon our **indebtedness**—what we owe to others—and our **entitlement**—what we are owed.

We earn merit when we provide consideration for others. The debt that is accrued in this process can only be repaid by the person to whom the consideration was given. For instance, if you help out a friend who went through a loss by being there for them to talk to, at some later point in time, only that person can repay that debt. Their giving to you should be in proportion to what you gave to them. It does not have to be a one-for-one process where you give them a ride and then they have to give you a ride. Perhaps they look after your cat while you are on vacation or they set you up on a date if you were in the market.

When our indebtedness and our entitlement are in alignment—when we have a balanced ledger—we engage others in trustworthy relationships. We are more open and accepting. However, if we give due caring to someone and do not receive the due caring back that we gave, or, conversely, when we receive from others but do not give them back due concern, problems may develop.

These imbalances can come, over time, from vertical loyalties or horizontal loyalties. **Loyalty** regards placing the interests of those who have shown us concern over those who have not (Boszormenyi-Nagy & Krasner, 1986). **Vertical loyalties** happen between generations. These invisible loyalties occur when a child tries to pay a debt to his parents. **Horizontal loyalties** usually happen in the nuclear family; such as between spouses. Loyalty is not problematic unless the person is caught between two people with competing loyalty pressures (Boszormenyi-Nagy & Krasner, 1986). One of the most destructive forms of loyalty conflict is **split loyalty**. This is when a child is placed in a position of having to choose between parents; giving loyalty to one parent at the expense of loyalty to the other. This may be the case for Nina in the Rothers family where she may feel disloyal to Angelina if she shows love and affection to her father, Mark.

When people have given due consideration to someone and not received in kind from that person, **destructive entitlement** may develop. When this happens, the person who is owed looks toward others to repay a debt that that person did not accrue. Boszormenyi-Nagy and Krasner (1986) hold that substance abuse is usually based in destructive entitlement. Remember that people only owe when they are given. If they give due consideration to someone who is owed by someone else, after a certain amount of time, they will expect to be given back in kind. The first person who is caught up in destructive entitlement will not think they

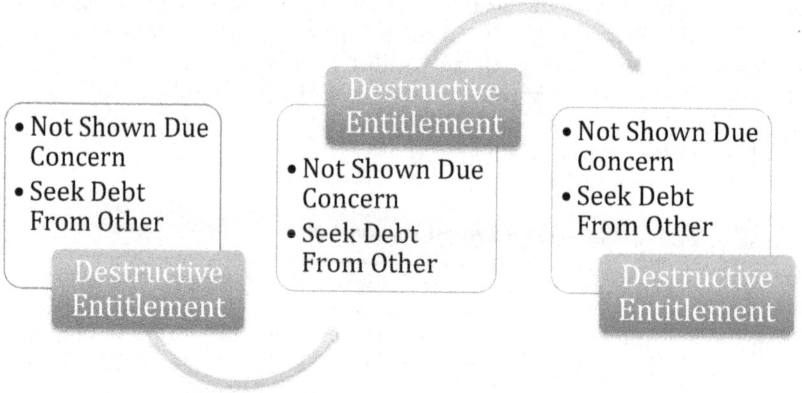

Figure 13.9 Destructive entitlement happens when one person seeks repayment from another who does not owe them. This process can lead the second person to seek recompense from a third person who did not accrue the original debt

owe since they view that they were owed and did not have to give to this new person reciprocally. This process can keep going ad infinitum where one person pays a debt not owed to them and then looks to someone else to repay them (see Figure 13.9). Contextual therapists will attempt to stop this process and help people to balance their ledgers with the people who they owe or are owed.

The Process of Therapy

One of the main therapist attitudes and positions Contextual therapists take is that of **multidirected partiality** (Boszormenyi-Nagy & Krasner, 1986). This is when the therapist helps family members to explore the position of each person who is connected to what is happening in the therapy room. The therapist, in engaging in multidirected partiality, demonstrates inclusiveness by siding with each person sequentially, discovering what credit the person can be given. This acknowledgment, first by the therapist and then by each family member, helps to humanize people, demonstrating that people behave based on their situation.

One of the outcomes of multidirected partiality is that of **exoneration**. In families, there is usually at least one, but sometimes more, family member(s) who seem to bear the brunt of the ire of the family. The process of exoneration explores how family members may be able to understand the context in which the other person acted. This is important since they usually only view what the person did (the offense) rather than how that person's actions made sense given their situation. Exoneration allows people to shift from a stance of blame to an appreciation that the other person was limited in what they could do based on the context of their life. In addicted families that are in a state of despair, the Contextual therapist will have a good chance to establish a therapeutic contract by exploring the past and how the addicted individual had previously contributed positively to the family (Boszormenyi-Nagy & Krasner, 1986).

The overarching goal of Contextual Therapy is stabilization of trust and positive initiatives by people. This occurs by a therapeutic focus on due and fair resources. The therapist helps family members to view their own and each other's relational resources; how they are capable of giving and receiving with one another. This happens when members are able to acknowledge how, in their own way, others have attempted to give them due concern. The following case example by Boszormenyi-Nagy (1987) is a good summary of how a Contextual therapist may work with someone dealing with the impact of substance abuse:

> A case in point is the situation of the daughter of an alcoholic father. Bearing the weight of her father's former behavior and apparent failure, she may press her son toward perfection to make up for her filial shame. Overburdened by unfair legacy expectations, her son is faced with the unacceptable choices of abandoning his mother physically or emotionally or of submitting to her impossible demands. More realistically, contextual therapy offers him still another choice: he can help free himself and his mother for a new balance of trust and fairness in their relationship. Overcoming the mistrust, resentment, and stagnation that have accrued from his mother's undue substitutive and compensatory expectations of him, her son can find ways to discover aspects of his grandfather's behavior, which serve to exonerate his life. Through active strategic work he can also determine and implement his own terms for accountably fulfilling his legacy rather than becoming entrapped into deferring to his mother's terms or simply learning to evade them. (pp. 220–221)

Experiential Approaches

Experiential family therapies focus on the in-session interactions of family members where the therapist helps individuals come in touch with their own experiences as well as the other members of the family. Experiential therapies tend to be focused on the **here and now**, looking at what is occurring, in the moment, in the therapy room. This does not mean that they are devoid of exploring the past, but they do so with a focus on how the past is manifesting itself at the present time. Experiential approaches became popular in North America during the 1950s and 1960s and are known as the "third force"—as an alternative to psychodynamic and behavioral approaches (Pos, Greenberg, & Elliot, 2008).

While many Experiential therapies, in some ways, eschew theory, they are predicated on many similar assumptions. Personal growth is the hallmark for positive therapeutic work as family members' individualism has been stifled by the family process. Rather than attempt to have members gain intellectual insight into what is happening in their lives, Experiential therapists connect with clients on a person-to-person basis for them to have an experience, in the session, that is growth-producing (Pos et al., 2008). This may come through a myriad of techniques, none of which are planned before the start of the session.

In many ways, the Experiential therapies can be viewed as humanistic approaches, where the self of the person is key. While it may seem that these theories are mainly focused on the individual, an understanding of the person does not occur outside of the realm of the family and the constraints the family makes on the person; leading each individual to adopt rigid roles and find insufficient coping mechanisms. As such, family members are not provided with an environment in which they can self-actualize.

Experiential models are based on the notion that individuals develop symptoms because of emotional suppression. The rules of the family do not allow them to have free range of their emotional experience. They may not be able to acknowledge their enjoyment, or others may restrict family members from expressing pain or disapproval. This suppression disconnects people from themselves, which disconnects them from each other. What happens in the therapy room then is about reconnecting people to aspects of self that they disavowed, while getting them to allow other people to be unique as well. This process can be viewed as working from the inside out where people understand and accept their own feelings and then develop more honest and genuine relationships with one another. What becomes important in the therapy room is engagement and communication, which is the medium in which people will risk being true to themselves and real with each other.

Two of the main Experiential approaches are Virginia Satir's Human Validation Process Movement and Carl Whitaker's Symbolic-Experiential Family Therapy. We will discuss each of these in this chapter to provide you an overview of how they understand how families function, the development of symptoms in individuals, the resolution of symptoms, and the process of change.

Satir's Human Validation Process Movement

Virginia Satir was one of the most iconic of the originators of family therapy. She was a huge figure, both in stature and in influence. Her approach stretched across several areas of therapy including communications theory, systemic therapy, and Experiential approaches. I have included it in the latter since, perhaps more than anyone (besides Carl Whitaker), Satir's approach focuses on getting family members to engage one another and have a new and unique experience within the therapeutic session that they will then keep with them as they leave the session and enter their home context.

Satir's approach has been called many things, but here we will use a name she developed, the **Human Validation Process Movement**. This is because her work was intended to help people move toward a progressive validating of not only other people, but of themselves as well. This comes through an appreciation of the uniqueness that each person brings to an encounter (Satir, Banmen, Gerber, & Gomori, 1991). When people feel validated, they can more easily be themselves and accept others. Thus, the therapist helps people to take self-responsibility, a valuing of the self and other, and a movement toward congruent communication.

The approach is not the elimination of problems, as all families have problems. The main issue is how the family copes with these problems. If the family tightens up, living by more rigid rules, with a foundation of low self-esteem, one or more members will most likely become symptomatic. Although one person is likely to be the identified patient, all family members feel the pain of the situation.

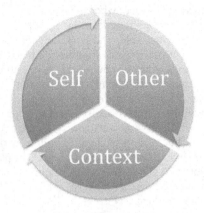

Figure 13.10 Virginia Satir viewed people as being connected in relationships based on the concepts of self, other, and context

For Satir, humans move naturally toward growth. At times, based on various issues such as low self-esteem, they are not in unison with themselves, others, and the world. This is where Satir viewed humans engaging others based on three concepts: the self, the other, and the context (Satir et al., 1991). These need to be in unison with one another for the person to be congruent within themselves as well as in their interactions with others (see Figure 13.10). When we do not honor any of these three aspects, we tend to engage the world problematically.

We learn about our connection to self, other, and context via our connection with others; usually in our family of origin. Satir called this the **primary family triad**, which usually consists of mother, father, and child (but, based on family configuration, could be mother-mother-child in a same-sex family or father-grandmother-child in a family where extended family plays an integral role) (Satir & Baldwin, 1983).

When the marital partners respect each other as unique beings, they then allow the child to develop a unique self. This situation leads to a **functional family triangle** (Satir, 1983). Conversely, a **dysfunctional family triangle** occurs when the partners have low self-esteem and are not honest in their communications. They then do not allow themselves or others to be real in their transactions. As an example, think back to growing up in your family. Were you allowed to let your parents know that you were mad at them? I am not talking here about cursing at them, but that you were disappointed in them. Did you experience yourself as knowing that you couldn't reach out to them, hug them, and tell them that you loved them? If so, a dysfunctional family triangle may have been present in your family as people were not able to have productive communication with one another.

Communication Stances

Productive communication, which leads to each party honoring each other, comes when the communication actors focus on all three aspects of experience;

self, other, and context. However, when people engage each other through low self-esteem they tend to communicate in one of four incongruent ways: placating, blaming, superreasonable, and irrelevant (Satir et al., 1991). These stances are not permanent and people are able to engage in the multitude of stances during the course of their day, but usually with different people.

The person who operates from the **placating** position focuses on the other person and the context yet discounts the self (see Figure 13.11). Placaters will quickly give in to the other person, usually in an attempt to appease them. In doing so they do not get their own wants and needs met. For a time this might please the other person, but, after a while, they will want the placater to make their own decisions and hold firm to their convictions. The placater also feels bad that they are not stepping up and getting their position across. In many ways the placater feels weak and could potentially develop a type of learned helplessness where they do not believe in themselves.

Unlike the placater, the **blamer** does focus on self, but to the exclusion of the other (see Figure 13.12). The self sits at the forefront for the blamer, but they do not honor the personhood of the person they are in contact with. When conflict happens, they find fault in the other person instead of themselves. This is usually done so that they do not have to accept their own faults. If energy and attention is focused on where the other person is wrong, that attention is not focused on what they may be doing wrong. Thus, the blamer comes across as very strong, but underneath they are quite scared.

The **superreasonable** places their focus on the context and discounts the self and the other (see Figure 13.13). This person tends to talk about facts and concepts, using them to prevent a focus on inner feelings. Instead of being personal, using pronouns such as "I" and "you," the superreasonable (also sometimes called the computer) tends to use impersonal pronouns such as "one" or "a person." For instance, a parent upset with their child might say, "One wouldn't want to talk

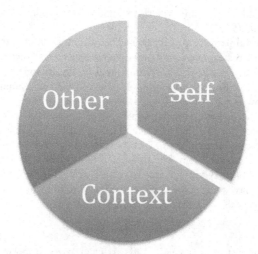

Figure 13.11 Placaters discount the self in favor of the other and the context.

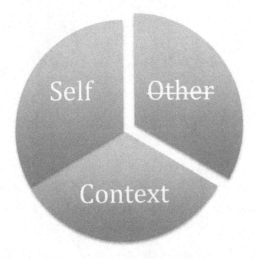

Figure 13.12 Blamers discount the other in favor of the self

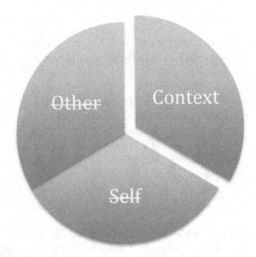

Figure 13.13 Superreasonables discount the self and other in favor of the context

to one's parent like that if one wanted to get along." The superreasonable comes across as intellectual, yet cold and distant. This emotional distance protects them from the possibility of connection, disappointment, and anger.

The fourth incongruent stance is the **irrelevant**. This person discounts the self, other, and context (see Figure 13.14). Instead of keeping the focus on whatever is being discussed, the person operating from the irrelevant stance attempts to change the topic. The intent is that if the conversation does not continue, they do not have to experience the initial topic because the other person may forget about it or give up trying to get their idea (usually disappointment in the person) across.

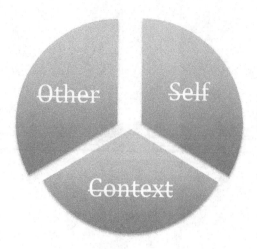

Figure 13.14 The irrelevant communication stance discounts the self, other, and context

For others, the irrelevant might be enjoyable for short periods, usually until they have something serious to discuss with the person, and then they feel very disconnected from the person.

There is a fifth communication stance; that of the **congruent** or the **leveler**. This person honors the self, other, and context. They are able to express their ideas and feelings honestly, while also being open to hearing the other person's ideas and feelings. The person operating from the congruent communication stance is able to stay involved in a transaction, even if there is conflict. What is happening on the inside for this person is coming across on the outside. While taking into account other people's feelings, the congruent communicator connects to them through an honest and genuine means of relating. Thus, the therapist will try to help all members function more from the congruent position.

Drugs and alcohol, as well as many other symptoms, are dysfunctional means of coping (Satir et al., 1991). They occur when the individual has unmet needs or has unfulfilled expectations. They are ways for people to feel better, after experiencing frequent and perhaps long-standing discomfort. Satir et al. explained this process:

> When a family system comes to the stage of unbearable pain, some members might try to cope through extensive use of alcohol or drugs, for example. After some time of alcohol abuse, that becomes the new problem. And when the family finally goes for therapy, the alcohol abuse is often the focus, while the original systemic family pain has gone underground. In the Satir model, the therapeutic task is to find the thread that leads back to the original systemic crisis. (pp. 100–101)

What is usually present in families dealing with addiction is a process of protection. This may be through denials, excuses, or presenting some other symptom (i.e., child misbehavior).

The Process of Therapy

Satir therapy has three stages (Satir & Baldwin, 1983) in which the therapist connects with the family, helps them to experience their situation differently, and then to integrate their learning into their everyday lives. The first stage is the **making contact** stage, where the therapist connects with each family member that is present. This is important since it highlights how each and every individual is unique and distinct, yet connected to one another. Usually, families coming to therapy are not valuing one another; perhaps feeling left out of the family process. The second stage is that of **chaos**, wherein family members are challenged to experience themselves and others in a different way than they have in the past. There is a movement from surface understanding to a deeper level of knowing oneself and other. The therapist also helps family members move from a focus on the past to the present; to the here and now of their contact with one another. The last stage is called **integration**. Here, family members take their new experiences from the chaos stage and integrate them into their lives for a more hopeful, trusting, honest way of being with self and others.

In therapy, the therapist helps family members to learn how to engage one another in congruent means of communication. This comes in the form of clear communication, where members are honest with one another while being respectful of the other person's thoughts and feelings. People are able to get across their message while being willing to receive what the other person is trying to get across to them. To do so, the therapist has to be clear and honest; engaging in congruent communication. This modeling of positive communication opens the door for family members to learn how to be clear communicators—checking with other members whether they understand the person correctly and if the other person understands them (Satir, 1983).

One means of doing this is to have people experience each other in new and unique ways. This comes in the form of interactive techniques, where the therapist gets family members to interact in a very different manner. For instance, one of the most famous techniques that Satir utilized is known as **family sculpting** (Satir & Baldwin, 1983). Here, the therapist gets one member of the family to move other family members into physical and spatial positions, including themselves, that represent what it is like to be in the family. For instance, in the Rothers family, Mark's picture of his family may be with Hannah standing over him, pointing her finger down on him. He may place Kayleigh with her hands over her ears, Pete clinging tightly to Hannah, Steve looking angry with his fists up ready to fight, and himself down on the ground with his hands up in a pleading tone. Family sculpting may allow the family to bypass their normal conflictual ways of dealing with each other and be more open to appreciate another person's position. People can only do this when they develop an awareness of their own deeper level of experiencing, which allows them to understand another person's deeper level of experiencing.

Satir's therapy brought drama into the therapy room, actively engaging people. Sessions are not static entities with people sitting in the same spot for one hour and *talking about* their problems. Rather, people *engage* one another to encounter self and other in new and more genuine ways. Another technique Satir developed was the family reconstruction. A **family reconstruction** is a technique "in which a person relives formative experiences that were influenced by three or more generations of his or her family" (Satir et al., 1991, p. 121). Usually, this occurs in four acts: sculpting the family of origin; sculpting the family of origins of the Star's parents; sculpting the meeting and courtship of the Star's parents; and then resculpting the Star's family of origin. Thus, the historical past is reconstituted into the present where the person can tune into themselves and resolve unfinished business.

Whatever technique is used in the Human Process Validation Movement, it is designed to have people access their inner self and be able to raise their self-esteem. Techniques are a movement away from content and toward intrapersonal self-growth, which will translate into interpersonal growth. When a person can trust themselves to be real, they are more willing to allow and trust the people to whom they are connected to live genuinely as well. This results in a transformation of each individual as well as the family system. Satir et al. (1991) explained this process when working with those dealing with addictions:

> With alcohol dependency, the transformational approach quickly moves to the inner yearnings and then helps individuals and families examine their survival patterns. Replacing survival patterns with coping patterns and coping patterns with healthy self-care patterns brings about major transformations instead of changing some simple behavioral pattern. (p. 165)

Symbolic-Experiential Family Therapy

Carl Whitaker was another iconic figure in the history of family therapy. Playful, provocative, serious, and spontaneous, Whitaker brought drama into the therapy room, where family members experienced each other as they previously had not, allowing them to move away from the restricted roles they were living. He called his approach **Symbolic-Experiential Family Therapy** to highlight the notion that people create symbolism to their experiences (Whitaker & Bumberry, 1988).

The Person of the Therapist

Although Whitaker viewed his approach through a non-theoretical lens, there are some common aspects of his approach that help us understand it better. We will discuss these aspects here, however this approach is very difficult to manualize as a lot of what happens in the room rests upon the person of the therapist. The goal of therapy is to get the family members to engage one another in more genuine ways, and to do this the therapist needs to be able to have a human encounter with the family. Whitaker explained this process, "Your willingness to bring more and more of yourself to the sessions is the catalytic ingredient that can trigger the family's growth experience" (Whitaker & Bumberry, 1988, p. 39). Since the therapist expects family members to be present and engage each other, the therapist must be willing to be present, evoking interaction and being impacted by those he or she is in contact with in the therapy session. In many ways, the therapist grows as much as the family—although perhaps in different ways.

Whitaker (1975) sometimes called his approach the "psychotherapy of the absurd." He embraced **craziness**, as being crazy meant that you were not tied down by the rules of the system but had the full spectrum of your creativity, emotionality, and behaviors. Whitaker explained, "I believe craziness is where life is. Personal confrontation, like accented fantasy, and sharing my own irrational free associative and symbolic experiences, is a stimulus for the other to expand his own model and mode of operating" (Neill & Kniskern, 1982, p. 34). As such, the primary tool in Symbolic-Experiential Family Therapy is the therapist.

However, the therapist is usually not a lone entity. Whitaker believed that co-therapy was an important process as each therapist could agree, disagree, counteract, and augment the other (Whitaker & Bumberry, 1988). This is an important point since the therapist is not supposed to be a cold and technical worker but an emotionally engaged individual—provoking and being provoked by the people with whom he or she is in contact.

The Battles of Therapy

There are two battles that happen in therapy. The first is the **battle for structure**. The therapist must set the stage for what is going to happen in therapy. This includes who comes to therapy. At one point in time, Whitaker demanded that three generations of a family must come to the session if he was going to work with the family, which would be much more difficult in today's migratory culture where adult children may live very far from their parents, who live far away from their own parents. The battle for structure also deals with who the therapist addresses first, what definition of the problem the therapist accepts, and what techniques are to be used (Whitaker & Bumberry, 1988). In this part of therapy, the therapist demonstrates an "I" position, signaling that the family will not be able to control the therapy—and beginning to introduce the notion to the family that they cannot control each other—once they each develop their unique "I" positions. The therapist must win the battle for structure as it is a statement to the family that they will have to play by someone else's rules and cannot use their normal coping strategies to survive in the session.

The second battle is the **battle for initiative**, which the family must win (see Figure 13.15). They must make the choice of how to live their lives. After the therapist has won the battle for structure, the family may try to capitulate to the therapist and do as they say. This can be very problematic as they will continue to be stifled if they are basing their behaviors on other people's demands. Thus, the therapist gets the family members to take responsibility for their own living. They must trust themselves to decide how to be a person instead of being told by the therapist exactly what they should do.

Once these battles have been played out in the session, therapist and family members will then be more free to challenge each other (Neill & Kniskern, 1982). The therapist will push the clients, even when they begin to feel pain, as Whitaker believed that growth necessitates pain. Yet the therapist also expects the family members to challenge him, as he needs to be a spontaneous being in

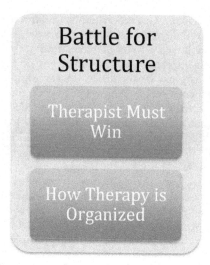

Figure 13.15 The battle of structure is won by the therapist while the battle for initiative is won by the family

the room. By engaging each other in this unique manner, therapist and family members become a team, developing a symbolic togetherness.

The Process of Therapy

The beginning portions of therapy usually center around a history-taking. Understanding the intergenerational patterns helps the therapist to understand what may be situated below the surface in the current family members. Further, this process suggests to the family that the therapist does not accept their offering up of a scapegoat, but that a larger family systems view is important (Whitaker & Bumberry, 1988). The identified patient's problems are explored within the multitude of interactions that have happened within the nuclear family as well as between generations.

For Whitaker, people live in a symbolic world, where our emotional life happens outside of our view and awareness (Whitaker & Bumberry, 1988). These symbols become the way that we take in life and make sense of ourselves and our connections to others. This is one of the main reasons why Whitaker did not think that education should happen in the therapy room, because people cannot process these understandings cognitively, but needed to do so experientially. Thus, techniques in Symbolic-Experiential Family Therapy are engaged to have family members interact with one another. For instance, Whitaker would give batacas (foam bats) to a husband and wife who had not been able to tell each other how disappointed or angry they are with one another. He would inform them that they are able to hit one another since they are soft bats and do not hurt. However, the importance of this technique is getting people in touch with their upset so they can have the symbolic experience of pummeling their partner. Whitaker explained the importance of an experience such as this, "But ordinary people are so afraid of their own fantasies that if you can help them have their fantasies in a justified, nonterrifying way, then they don't have to worry about the behavior" (Whitaker & Bumberry, 1988, p. 187). This expansion of the client's fantasies to absurd ends is a hallmark of Whitaker's work with families.

In order to push family members beyond their comfort zones, the therapist joins with the family and listens and watches for various bits and pieces of the symbolic world of each individual as well as how those individuals have come into contact with one another. These bits are usually outside of the family members' awareness, so the therapist brings them to the forefront; in a way making the unconscious family process conscious.

The Symbolic-Experiential family therapist is not problem-focused. Although the talk in the room might be on a specific issue the family brings, that is usually just a pathway to something deeper—how the family members have constructed a symbolic experience with one another. Usually, this way of viewing each other has been limiting. For instance, family members may have taken on various roles such as the Black Sheep, White Knight, Dutiful Mother, or the Disengaged Father. Once these roles are developed, people restrict what they expect out of self and others. Therapy, then, challenges people to move beyond their constructed roles and to shift their viewpoints of other people's roles so that they can have access to the full range of their being.

One of the main keys for the therapist is to be able to move back and forth, from being joined and connected to the family to backing out and individuating (Whitaker & Bumberry, 1988). It is an isomorphic process that the family members will need to learn as well. Family members are having trouble being a unique individual while still being engaged in the togetherness of the family. By the therapist demonstrating this freedom to join and individuate, that we are individual people who are involved in relationships, family members may more actively be themselves and stay connected.

Communication Approaches

Communication models of family therapy are based primarily upon the communication research led by Gregory Bateson, the renowned anthropologist.

These approaches are very problem-focused, where the therapist addresses patterns of interaction centered around the problem behavior—or the attempts to solve the problem. These approaches hold a general systems theory/cybernetic philosophical approach (see Reiter, 2019).

Mental Research Institute: Brief Therapy

In our current therapeutic culture, the notion of brief therapy is commonplace. However, 50 years ago when family therapy was developing, psychoanalysis was still the prominent approach, which had a long-term focus (i.e., several sessions per week for several years). The therapists who developed the Brief Therapy

Project of the Mental Research Institute (MRI) were perhaps some of the first brief therapists. This model was based on the cybernetic and communication work led by Gregory Bateson, and developed and adapted to family therapy by Don Jackson, John Weakland, Paul Watzlawick, Richard Fisch, and others.

The MRI therapists believe that families try to maintain homeostasis. For all families normal life problems happen. These are not problematic in themselves. It is how the individual/family attempts to solve this problem that leads to a maintenance of problems. This is why MRI therapists say that "the solution is the problem." We can differentiate between difficulties and problems (Watzlawick, Weakland, & Fisch, 1974). **Difficulties** are undesirable states that people can fix based on first-order change strategies (change that happens within the existing rule structure). **Problems** happen when people mishandle difficulties; that is, how they try to fix the difficulty creates more of a problem.

Given that it is the failed solution attempts that are actually the problem, the MRI therapist will target these solution attempts as the avenue of intervention. Getting people to find a different way of trying to solve the problem can solve the problem of incorrectly trying to solve the problem. This usually entails a shift from first-order change strategies to second-order change strategies.

First-order change is a change attempt within the existing rule structure of the family. For instance, families may operate from a rule that the parents are in charge of the family and have a responsibility to try to ensure that the children are doing what the parents think is right for them to do. When a child misbehaves, the parents will act in ways that provide a message (a metamessage) that they are in charge and the child needs to listen to them. They might do this through lecturing, rewarding, or punishing the child. If the child stayed out past curfew, the parent might ground the child for the next week. This is a first-order strategy, where the rule of the parent being in charge is maintained.

However, some difficulties that have become problems require a second-order change strategy. This is a change outside of the existing rule structure. For instance, parents who have a 17-year-old child who is failing at school have probably lectured the child, pleaded with them, punished them (i.e., taken away car privileges), etc., all in attempts to get the child to do well. These were all first-order change attempts. **Second-order change** would be the parents apologizing to the son stating, "We are sorry we were not better parents for you and did not prepare you as well to handle these types of things." Here, the parents have moved out of the rule system of the parents being responsible for the child's behavior. By not engaging in the same strategies of past attempts, they move out of the **game without end** (Watzlawick et al., 1974), where the more one party engages in a behavior the more the other engages in a behavior (i.e., the more the parent attempts to get the child to do well at school, the more the child does poorly at school, and the more the child does poorly at school, the more the parent attempts to get the child to do well at school). This dynamic is known as a symmetrical escalating relationship.

In the addictions field, treatment professionals may also engage in failed solution attempts by focusing on first-order change rather than second-order change. For instance, methadone treatments may become "addictive" for the person dealing with heroin addiction, where the methadone becomes the next addictive substance (Watzlawick et al., 1974). Instead of viewing addictions in terms of a physiological basis, these authors suggest viewing them as behavioral problems.

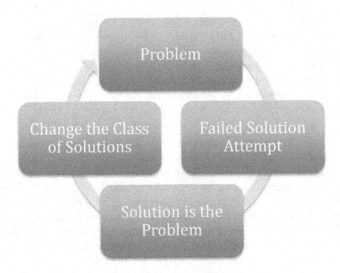

Figure 13.16 The MRI Brief Therapy targets the failed solution attempts that have been perpetuating the problem

Perhaps the most important component for the MRI therapist is exploring where one or more individuals have unsuccessfully attempted to change the behavior (Fisch, Weakland & Segal, 1982). In essence, people are using "more of the same" solution attempts; attempts that not only are not fixing the problem, but are creating more of a problem (i.e., people getting more frustrated, angry, disappointed, etc.). The therapist will focus on interrupting these failed solution attempts in the expectation that once they are no longer happening the problem will solve itself (see Figure 13.16).

The MRI therapists view the mishandling of problems in one of three ways (Watzlawick et al., 1974). The first is when people deny that there is a problem. Here, change is needed but not taken. The second mishandling of problems happens when people try to change something that does not need changing or is unchangeable. Change is made when it should not have been made. The last, and perhaps most important, is when change is made at one level when it needs to be made at a higher level (first-order change is attempted when second-order change is necessitated).

The Process of Therapy

Therapy consists of six stages (Weakland et al., 1974): (1) introduction to the treatment setup; (2) inquiry into the nature of the problem; (3) past solution attempts; (4) setting goals of treatment; (5) selection and implementation of interventions; and (6) termination. To work effectively, the therapist must have a conceptualization of what to look for when working with clients. Segal (1991) provided the following five questions that are useful in gathering adequate information:

1. What is the attempted solution? 2. What would be a 180-degree shift from the attempted solution? 3. What specific behavior would operationalize the shift? 4. Given the client's position, how can the therapist frame the behavior in a way that the client will accept and take action? 5. What might the client report that would signal that the intervention has been successful and the case is ready for termination? (p. 182)

There are two classes of interventions MRI therapists tend to use (Segal, 1991). The first is getting the clients to do something different. This is usually in the form of something that is the opposite of the failed solution attempts. The second class is to get clients to do "more of the same." Here, clients are asked to continue to engage the problem as they have been. This paradoxical intervention has a twofold possibility. If the clients agree to "go slow" and not change, they are going along with the therapist and their behavior becomes controlled rather than spontaneous. On the other hand, if the clients go against the therapist and do not continue the solution sequence, they are then doing something different; something that might get them out of the game without end.

Whichever class of intervention is chosen, it will target one of three change areas: the problem behavior; the attempted solution; and/or the client's definition of the problem (Fisch et al., 1982). In changing the definition of the problem the therapist can utilize a reframe. **Reframing** is when the therapist provides an alternative explanation for a behavior from the client's explanation (see Figure 13.17). For instance, Hannah might say, "Mark keeps using drugs, which shows that he doesn't love me." The therapist might reframe this by saying, "It seems the more Mark uses drugs the more he's telling you, I need you—to help me."

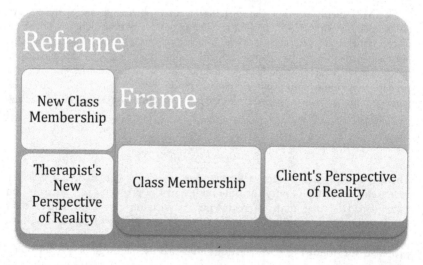

Figure 13.17 Reframes are the therapist's altering of how a client understands a situation

For a family where the parents are taking care of an adolescent child, when the adolescent refuses to take care of themselves, they may be asked to engage in **benevolent sabotage** (Fisch et al., 1982). This intervention has the parents intentionally making mistakes but apologizing for them. As an example, the parents of an adolescent who will not make their own food may be told by the therapist to make the adolescent's food but to burn it and then say to the adolescent, "I apologize for burning your food. I have been so stressed out lately I haven't been able to concentrate well." The intent is for the adolescent to take control of their own food preparation. This technique can be used with an adult, where the spouse makes mistakes in caretaking (i.e., food preparation, cleaning, bill paying), which may force the underfunctioning, adult (perhaps dealing with substance abuse) to increase their functioning.

The MRI approach was one of the first brief therapy approaches as, from the get-go, they contracted with the client for a maximum of 10 sessions. On average, therapy lasts for six sessions (Ray & Brasher, 2010). Termination occurs when the client states that the complaint they came in for is gone or at a level that is no longer problematic. For the therapist, there are three criteria of termination (Segal, 1991). The first is that a small but significant change in the problem has happened. The second is that this change will most likely last. The third criteria is that the client expresses they can maintain these changes without the therapist's help.

Case Application

A Bowenian therapist working with the Rothers family would likely only meet with the adults in the family. Given what we know about the family, Hannah is the most likely person to be able to work at differentiating herself. Thus, therapy would likely be with only Hannah or with Hannah and Mark. However, it would be important for the therapist to let the couple know from the beginning that therapy would not be a place for blaming, but rather as a place to reflect on and explore the intergenerational patterns that are impacting them in the present. While people tend to find partners at similar levels of differentiation, there seems to be a gap between husband and wife's levels of differentiation. Mark experiences greater levels of both chronic and situational anxiety. The chronic anxiety comes from his family of origin, having grown up in an alcoholic family with high demands made on its members. This led people to not be able to take I-positions and instead they try to force others to be in certain ways. This can be seen in the emotional cutoff between Mark and his brother Mick. Mark is also experiencing high levels of situational anxiety, especially surrounding his job, Steve's troubles at school, and underlying tension in the marriage. These all would make it more likely for him to become symptomatic, such as his having sleep disturbance, increased substance use, and suicidal ideation.

There are multiple interlocking triangles in the Rothers family. Perhaps the primary one at this point in time is between Mark, Hannah, and Steve. It is likely that during the family projection process, Steve was focused upon by the parents, leading to that relationship being fraught with anxiety. This may be because of his birth order as the oldest child. Further, when exploring the nuclear family emotional process, it seems that the way the Rothers bind their anxiety is through problems in a child—Steve. Mark may also, when in conflict with Hannah, bind his anxiety through his use of alcohol. The Bowenian therapist will need to be aware of the likelihood during sessions of the couple trying to triangulate him or her into their emotional systems and will need to stay connected to them but not get caught up in their anxiety. This process of de-triangulation will help them to take an I-position and better handle their anxiety.

While a Bowenian therapist is likely only to meet with Mark and Hannah, a Contextual therapist would invite as many members of the family as possible. The Contextual therapist will consider the five dimensions of relational reality for all members in the therapy room. Although this is not a formal assessment, these dimensions help to contextualize the family's current situation and lead to pathways for growth and more trustworthy interactions with one another. If we just take Mark to focus upon, we can see that some of the facts of his life include being born into an alcoholic family, having an older brother and a younger sister, and having had a divorce where his ex-wife gained custody of their daughter. The dimension of individual psychology helps us to see that he is an intelligent person, which allowed him to go to and graduate college, approaching middle age, and a bit lost as to goals for himself. When viewing the dimension of transactional patterns, we can see the various triangles in Mark's life including Mark/Mick/Ian, Mark/Hannah/Steve, and Mark/Angelina/Nina. Focus on relational ethics would help the therapist view how Mark's ledger is balanced and whether he is living by constructive or destructive entitlement. Given his growing up in an addicted family, the dissolution of his first marriage, semi-estrangement from his first child, and his current job difficulties, we can hypothesize that he is operating from a sense of destructive entitlement where he thinks he is owed by people and society. This is leading him to not engage others, especially those in his current nuclear family, in trustworthy ways. Mark likely feels that he has given more to others than he has received back. Unfortunately, it seems Hannah is showing Mark due concern, yet he may be expecting retribution from her for other people's past transgressions against him. Therapy would then focus on helping him to balance his ledger with the people who owe him or whom he owes.

The Contextual therapist will maintain a position and attitude of multidirected partiality. In this, all people who come in contact with members of the Rothers family are given acknowledgment and concern. This would include all five members of the Rothers nuclear family as well as extended family such as Nina, Angelina, Ian, and Mick. One primary technique that will likely be used by the therapist is exoneration. Given the cutoff between Mark and Mick, the therapist may help Mark to exonerate Mick, exploring how Mick was trying to show his concern for Mark, but in a way that, at that time, Mark was not wanting to receive. The therapist may also help the children and Hannah to exonerate Mark, which may lead them to engage him differently and offer him due concern in a manner he is more readily able to acknowledge and receive.

An Experiential therapist working from a Satir-based approach would probably meet with the whole family, helping them to be with one another in a more genuine manner during the session. It is likely that none of the members of the Rothers family feels secure enough that they can be themselves while still being accepted in the family. As such, each is operating from a primary survival stance, which decreases their own and the others' ability to grow as human beings. The Rothers have most likely been engaging each other through several dysfunctional family triangles, where people have felt a low sense of self-esteem and have not interacted with one another in honest ways. This can most clearly be seen in the primary family triangle of Mark/Hannah/Steve where anger and blame is the primary communicational medium rather than love, disappointment, and concern.

We can speculate on the various communication stances of each member of the family. Mark tends to communicate from a blaming stance, holding others accountable for the misery in his life. This may be that the discord with his brother is all Mick's fault, problems at work are because of a jerk of a boss, and problems at home are because Steve is out of control. Hannah seems to move back and forth from a placating to a blaming stance, sometimes trying to appease Mark so things do not spiral out of control while at other times getting on his case for him to change. Steve, like Mark, operates primarily from a blaming stance, holding his parents, teachers, or society at large as the antagonists for his struggles. Kayleigh may function primarily from the superreasonable position, where she focuses on the facts and thus does quite well at school, but may not be able to have strong emotional connections with people. Pete likely has qualities of the irrelevant communication stance, where, regardless of the situation that is happening, he tries to make a joke and have people laugh. One of the goals of therapy would be to help each member become more congruent.

A Symbolic-Experiential family therapist working with the Rothers family would meet with all five members of the nuclear family and might even push for other extended family members to attend, such as Mick and Ian or even Angelina and Nina. This would be part of the Battle for Structure, where the therapist would attempt to organize the sessions in a way that disorganizes the family around their view that the problem is the identified patient. Rather, it would send a message that the problem rests in the interpersonal relations in the family.

Mark finds himself stuck in the role of the disengaged father while Hannah is the dutiful mother. Steve is finding that he has become the black sheep, Kayleigh the perfect student, and Pete the loving son. Each of these roles is only partial, as each of the members has the full range of their experience at their disposal but are not able to access this in the current configuration of the family. Therapy will involve talk and techniques that raise the anxiety in the room so that the members' normal ways of dealing with the anxiety are not effective. This will lead to them expanding their range of experiences, feelings, and behaviors. Therapy with the Rothers will be successful not just when Mark stops drinking so much, but when each member is able to be more real and have a fuller range of their emotional and behavioral repertoire.

The MRI therapists tend to work with customers rather than the identified patient or window shoppers. In all likelihood, Hannah would be the person who would attend sessions. An MRI therapist would enter the first session with the Rothers ready to hear what their complaint is, but with a focus on how the family members have tried to solve the problem. It is these failed solution attempts that will be the target of change. Most likely the family will discuss Mark's isolation from the family as the problem and would explain various ways that they have tried to include him or recruit him to participate more in family life. These attempts all have the same thing in common—family members believing that the way to show care is to push the other person into connection. Thus, they are mishandling the problem by trying first-order change attempts rather than second-order attempts. Intervention would come by getting family members to do something 180 degrees different than the theme of the failed solution attempts. That is, they would do something that did not push Mark into connection. This may be by saying something like, "We are going to the park. You most likely would not like to come and it would probably be better for everyone if you didn't as you wouldn't have to worry about us."

Summary

This chapter provided an overview of five of the most prominent family therapy approaches available. Bowen's Natural Systems Theory is perhaps the most comprehensive theory of individual and family functioning, utilizing an evolutionary perspective to discuss how differentiation of self is related to anxiety and symptom expression. Contextual therapy highlights the relational ethics that people hold; the ledger of our earned merit and debts. Satir's Human Process Validation Movement addresses how family members cope with crises through problematic communicational stances. Symbolic-Experiential Family Therapy attempts to challenge family members to shed their prescribed roles and to gain access to the full continuum of their humanness. The MRI Brief Therapy Model focuses on the failed solution attempts of families; ways in which they tried to solve an initial problem, which only perpetuated and maintained the symptom.

Key Words

intergenerational approaches
family of origin
Natural Systems Theory
emotional system
differentiation of self
triangles
de-triangle
nuclear family emotional system
illness in a spouse
marital conflict
impairment in one or more of
   the children
emotional distance
family projection process
multigenerational transmission
   process
emotional cutoff

sibling position
societal emotional process
Contextual Therapy
facts
individual psychology
systems of transactional
   patterns
relational ethics
merit
ontic
ledgers
indebtedness
entitlement
loyalty
vertical loyalty
horizontal loyalty
split loyalty

destructive entitlement
multidirected partiality
exoneration
Experiential family therapies
here and now
Human Validation Process
    Movement
primary family triad
functional family triangle
dysfunctional family triangle
placating
blamer
superreasonable
irrelevant
congruent
leveler
making contact

chaos
integration
family sculpting
family reconstruction
critical impact reconstruction
Symbolic-Experiential Family
    Therapy
craziness
battle for structure
battle for initiative
difficulties
problems
first-order change
second-order change
game without end
reframing
benevolent sabotage

Discussion Questions

1. Describe how Bowen Theory views the interplay of anxiety and differentiation.
2. How do Bowen's eight interlocking concepts work in unison to determine a family's functioning?
3. What is the theory of problem formation and problem resolution based on Bowen Theory?
4. What is the theory of problem formation and problem resolution based on Contextual Therapy?
5. How do the five dimensions of relational reality in Contextual Therapy help the family therapist understand what is happening in the family?
6. What are some of the core tenets of Experiential family therapies?
7. In Experiential therapies, what is the relationship between the individual and the family?
8. How does the Human Process Validation Movement understand the connection between self-esteem and communication?
9. How does the notion of craziness play a role in Symbolic-Experiential Family Therapy?
10. In what ways does the Human Process Validation Movement and Symbolic-Experiential Family Therapy overlap?
11. Explain how MRI: Brief Therapy is problem focused.

FOURTEEN

Family Therapy Overview II

In the previous chapter we covered some of the intergenerational, experiential, and communications approaches to family therapy. In this chapter we will explore the strategic, systemic, and postmodern models. While there is a connection between these models (for instance, the Strategic, Milan, and Solution-Focused models were heavily influenced by MRI's Brief Therapy, and Strategic and Structural Therapy were, for a time, viewed as one integrated model), they each have their own unique perspective on family function and intervention. In this chapter we will cover Jay Haley's Strategic Therapy, the systemic approaches of the Milan Associates and Minuchin's Structural Family Therapy, as well as Solution-Focused Brief Therapy and Narrative Therapy from the postmodern orientation.

Strategic Approaches

As with the MRI: Brief Therapy, strategic approaches were founded on the notions of cybernetics promoted by Gregory Bateson, as well as the therapeutic techniques of Milton Erickson, the world-famous hypnotherapist. Strategic approaches were very popular during the 1970s and 1980s. However, the advent of the postmodern collaborative approaches (see below) saw a shift from the directive strategies (what some people might view as manipulative) in these models to a focus on language, meaning, and a hesitancy of the therapist pushing for change. Yet these approaches developed some of the seminal and foundational ideas of family therapy. Here, we will discuss Strategic Family Therapy.

Strategic Family Therapy

Strategic Family Therapy was developed primarily by Jay Haley, as well as Cloe Madanes, who for a time were husband and wife and developed the Family Therapy Institute in Washington, DC. Haley was one of the pioneers of the Palo Alto group along with Gregory Bateson. The Bateson group studied communication—and more specifically paradox in communication. Haley primarily explored paradox in hypnosis. To do so, Bateson connected Haley with Milton Erickson, at that time the world's foremost hypnotherapist. After working with Bateson, Erickson, and the pioneers of the MRI: Brief Therapy (Weakland, Jackson, Watzlawick, etc.), Haley moved to Philadelphia to work with Salvador Minuchin (see later in this chapter for a description of Minuchin's Structural Family Therapy). Through this collaboration, he incorporated the notion of hierarchy and family structure into his directive model. Toward the end of his life Haley was calling his approach Directive Therapy, as he saw the responsibility of therapy on the therapist to provide appropriate directives for the family to change (Haley & Richeport-Haley, 2007).

Haley's approach combines the symptom focus of the MRI group, the structural view of Minuchin, as well as the strategic emphasis on directives as related to Erickson. Families tend to have difficulties at family life cycle transitions (i.e., moving from a family with young children to a family with an adolescent) based on a faulty organization (Haley, 1987). Perhaps the family did not adjust their rules to allow more autonomy for the adolescent. The family then continues to operate in their previous patterns that are not useful in the new family context. They maintain their current homeostasis rather than making changes in the rules of the family to develop a newer and more functional state.

The strategic therapist, like the MRI therapist, is less interested in the past but more focused on the present. Problems are occurring in the family not because they happened in the past but because they are continuing in the present. They are repetitive behavioral sequences involving more than one person, which are maintained by the people's continued actions (Haley, 1987). The Strategic therapist's interventions are designed to not only disrupt the sequences of interactions around the problem behavior, but also to change the structure of the family.

The problems that people have are often associated with a failure to adapt to a change in the family life cycle. These stages include: birth, infancy, childhood, school, adolescence, leaving home, being a parent, being a grandparent, and dealing with old age (Haley, 1993; Haley & Richeport-Haley, 2007). The symptoms that people have are signals that the family organization has not changed and that the family is operating from a previous level of homeostasis which is not functioning at this new life cycle; one which requires a reorganization of the family system to develop new rules to function more effectively (see Figure 14.1).

Given that families are systems that organize hierarchically, problems can be viewed through the interplay of three generations (Haley, 1987). Symptoms may develop when there are violations of boundaries across the generations; for instance, if a grandmother tries to usurp her child and take over parenting of her grandchild rather than letting her daughter, the grandchild's mother, have the

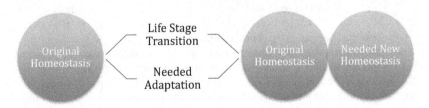

Figure 14.1 Families tend to have symptoms at life-cycle transitions when they maintain a homeostasis that was functional at the previous life stage

primary caretaking duties. Conversely, a child may try to take over leadership from the parent. This is problematic as parents should be on top of the hierarchy.

The Strategic therapist views the problem as a symptom of underlying family discord. Haley described the story of a husband and wife coming to therapy because the wife believed the husband's drinking had ruined their marriage (Richeport-Haley & Carlson, 2010). The husband complained that if he was to stop drinking she should stop smoking. After discussion with the therapist they both agreed. By the next session the husband had stopped drinking and the wife stopped smoking. However, there was a lot of tension between them. The following week the husband entered the session inebriated and the wife was smoking. Haley explains that in this case the couple was saving their unhappy marriage through smoking and drinking.

The Process of Therapy

When Haley was working at the Philadelphia Child Guidance Clinic, he developed a format for the first session to help new therapists (this was for lay professionals who were being trained to be family therapists). There are five stages for the first session: social, problem, interaction, goal-setting, and task-setting (Haley, 1987). The social stage only lasts a few minutes, but the therapist makes a connection to each member of the family. In therapy, we call this process joining. In the problem stage, the therapist asks every member their perception of what is occurring in the family. In the third stage, the interaction stage, the therapist gets family members to engage one another. This can be seen to be an enactment (see below in the Structural Family Therapy section), wherein the therapist gets family members to interact with one another, usually around the problem, which allows the therapist to take a step back and think about his or her position vis-à-vis the family as well as assessing the family organization and process. For the goal-setting stage, the therapist gets the family to come up with a consensus of what it is they want to work on in therapy. Based on everything that was discussed during the session, the therapist ends the first session with a task, a directive that helps to shift the problem sequences and the family organization to something that is more functional. Figure 14.2 provides a visualization of Haley's five stages of a first session.

This last stage is the hallmark of the strategic approach. Madanes (1991) is famous for saying, "The directive is to strategic therapy what the interpretation is to psychoanalysis. It is the basic tool of the approach" (p. 397). Haley believed that it was the therapist's responsibility to develop an effective directive, and that if the family did not change it was on the therapist and not on the family. In that case, the therapist had not developed a directive that made sense in the context of the family. There are three purposes for directives (Haley, 1987). The first is that they function to get the family to do something different. Second, directives help connect therapist and family in a therapeutic relationship. Third, whatever the outcome of the directive, there is information for the therapist to understand the family dynamics and develop another intervention that will move the family one step closer to their goals.

One of Madanes' primary directives was the pretend technique (Madanes, 1981). They are mainly used in families where there is a loving and helpful

Figure 14.2 Haley's five stages of a first session

relationship between family members. They are not encouraged in families dealing with violence and abuse. **Pretend techniques** are when the clients are told to pretend to have the symptom. One of the reasons for this is that when the person is pretending to have the symptom they cannot actually have the symptom. Further, it makes what is usually thought of as an uncontrolled event (the symptom) into something that can be controlled.

Based on Milton Erickson's work, Haley would occasionally utilize an ordeal (Haley, 1984). **Ordeals** are tasks given to clients where if they engage in the symptom then they have to do the task—and that doing the task is more severe than having the symptom, although it is something that will be beneficial to the person.

There are two types of ordeals that can be developed; straightforward and paradoxical. A **straightforward task** is where the therapist provides the specifics of what the client or family is to do if the symptom occurs. The second type of ordeal is a **paradoxical ordeal**. This will most likely come in the form of symptom prescription, where the person is told to engage in the symptom if the symptom happens, but even more so.

The directive a therapist develops is an attempt to move the client one step closer to the goal. Whatever the outcome, or even if the family did not do the given task, there is information for the therapist to utilize in creating the next directive. Each time, the directive is focused on changing the structural organization of the family as well as the interactional sequence around the problem.

Systemic Approaches

Systemic approaches in family therapy focus not only on the interdynamics between members of a nuclear family, but the connections between that family and larger systems, which may include their families of origin as well as social institutions such as the medical, legal, socioeconomic, and psychiatric systems. While the therapist may work with only one part of this equation, the therapist keeps in mind that the problem-maintaining interactions are occurring on multiple levels with various subsystems involved.

Milan Systemic Family Therapy

Milan Systemic Family Therapy was developed by Mara Selvini Palazzoli, Luigi Boscolo, Gianfranco Cecchin, and Guiliana Prata. These Italian therapists were originally psychoanalysts who were working individually with schizophrenic patients. Realizing that this was not as effective as they would have hoped, they decided to take a family systems lens in working with clients. They consulted with members of the Mental Research Institute and based a lot of their work on the cybernetic epistemology as put forth by Gregory Bateson (Boscolo, Cecchin, Hoffman, & Penn, 1987). However, in 1980, the Milan team split with Palazzoli and Prata, maintaining more of the original strategic positioning while Boscolo and Cecchin adopted a more postmodern approach.

The Milan group viewed families as self-regulating systems based upon family rules (Palazzoli, Boscolo, Cecchin & Prata, 1978a). When a couple comes together, they each bring aspects of their families of origin; the overt and covert rules of family functioning. At the beginning of the new family's development, the partners must integrate these different patterns of behavior to create their own homeostasis.

Since all families have problems, problems are not inherently bad. However, when family members display symptoms, it is based upon a family system that has rules that maintain those problems in an effort to preserve the family homeostasis (Palazzoli et al., 1978a). Yet, homeostasis is a twofold process; on the one hand it focuses on the stability of the system. On the other hand, it involves the capacity of change. Like the person who stands up in a canoe, the way to maintain balance (stability) is to slightly rock oneself back and forth (change).

Although the family may come to therapy talking about change, their actions are usually focused around keeping the stability in the family; maintaining the family rules. The therapist then has a choice of whether to focus on the stability (perhaps through some type of symptom prescription) or to push for change. This is what the Milan team talked about in terms of paradox and counterparadox (Palazzoli et al., 1978a). The family comes in with a **paradox** (we want change but do not want to change), which leads the therapist to develop a **counterparadox** (keep doing what you are doing [no change] which will change you).

One of the fundamental issues in family problems is that of control (Boscolo et al., 1987). One person will attempt to unilaterally control the family system. However, this fundamental premise is flawed, as a part of the system cannot control the system. But by operating from this position, one or more members attempt to maintain a superior position over others. This tends to be a violation of the family rules and the other person responds in kind; by attempting to reestablish his or her control. This is where a systemic view comes into play. The therapist understands that power does not happen within an individual but within the rules of the system (Palazzoli et al., 1978a). How the system is currently functioning, with members trying to attain control and usurping one another, becomes the repetitive pattern of the family; what is known as the **family game**. The family game is the rules that distinguish the family transactions around the maintenance of the problem.

One of the difficulties in families is that people view each other through the use of the verb "to be" (Palazzoli et al., 1978a). This captures the person into a position of not being able to change since they "are" a certain way (i.e., he is an angry person or she is a pushover). Instead, the Milan team viewed people through the verbs of "to seem" or "to show." This change in perspective provides a greater sense of maneuverability by people and focuses more on the interactional aspects of relationships rather than a linear perspective. The more family members use "to be" the more they will focus on an identified patient (i.e., "Mark is alcoholic and needs to go to therapy for anger management" or "Hannah is codependent and needs to change"). The label the family puts on a member becomes an operating principle of the family. By shifting the view to "seem" or "show" the therapist is able to highlight transactions (i.e., "Mark seems to be reacting to a change in how the family is engaging each other").

Having an identified patient in a family is both problematic and beneficial. For the non-IP family members, they tend to be more united with one another; usually around a notion of being healthier while the IP is unhealthy (Boscolo et al., 1987). The IP's problematic behavior also shifts the focus of the family from other potentially problematic areas to the IP. Instead of having to deal with a marriage that seems to be drifting apart, the parents can maintain their energy on their child who is not doing well in school.

The family is usually not aware of these potential benefits. They have developed a **family myth**; a way of viewing what is occurring in the system (Boscolo et al., 1987). This is the family's viewpoint on why they are having problems and what needs to happen for things to get better. Usually the family myth centers around the IP; the scapegoat of the family. Given that the family myth maintains the rules around the problem, the therapist attempts to change the rules of the family, which will then most likely lead to a change of the symptom. This is a move from rigidity to flexibility.

The Process of Therapy

Milan Systemic Family Therapy was originally premised on strategic practice. As such, many of its original techniques centered around strategic purposes. Two of these interventions included the positive connotation and family rituals. A **positive connotation**, in its fundamental form, is a reframe. It positively describes the IP's symptomatic behavior as well as the patterns around it as being for the benefit of the family (Boscolo et al., 1987). Through its use, the therapist tells the family that the behavior makes sense within the family context. Positive connotations are counterparadoxes in that they focus on the stability aspect of the family; yet the intention is for some type of change in the problem transactions to occur.

Family rituals are actions that the therapist directs the family to do together to happen outside of the therapy session (Palazzoli, Boscolo, Cecchin, & Prata, 1977). The target of the rituals is on the family games; changing the problematic sequences of interactions. The therapist does not explain the rationale for the ritual, as rituals operate on a different level than explanation. One of the most famous Milan rituals is the **odd days/even days ritual** (Palazzoli, Boscolo, Cecchin, & Prata, 1978b). A therapist would most likely give this ritual to a family when the adults (usually the parents) are undermining one another. One parent is directed to make all decisions for the family on odd days (Monday, Wednesday, and Friday) while the other parent is told to make all decisions on even days (Tuesday, Thursday, and Saturday). On Sunday the parents are told to respond spontaneously. This ritual is intended to block the problematic symmetrical interactions between the parents around childrearing.

In 1980, Palazzoli, Boscolo, Cecchin, and Prata published one of the most important articles in family therapy history, where they proposed three guidelines for the family therapist in conducting a session; hypothesizing, circularity, and neutrality. **Hypothesizing** is when the therapist develops a systemic understanding of what is occurring in the family. This is only a tentative view and not looked at as "truth." The hypothesis is a type of family assessment that is always changing based on the influx of new information. However, it helps to inform the types of questions and/or interventions the therapist makes.

The second guideline has become perhaps the most influential factor; circularity. **Circularity** in this context refers to the therapist taking in feedback from the family while also exploring family process in a reciprocal rather than lineal manner. While it is a way to understand transactions, it has become an interviewing technique in itself. This came through the development of what have become **circular questions**. These are triadic questions, asking one member about the relationship between two or more other members. Circular questions are predicated on the notion of **information**, which, based on Bateson's explications, is a difference that makes a difference. Further, difference is a relationship. Examples of circular questions include: "Who first noticed the problem?", "When your daughter is upset who does she tend to go to for support?", or "When mother and father are fighting, what happens with the children?"

The last guideline that the Milan team put forth is that of **neutrality**. Here, the therapist accepts each family member's viewpoint without judging whether one person's position is more correct than another person's. Neutrality is also about a non-normative way of viewing families. The therapist does not expect the family to be a certain way, but is curious as to how the family will reorganize itself. The therapist attempts to perturb the system in the expectation that the family system can be creative and heal itself. Cecchin (1987) later talked about this notion in terms of curiosity.

The Milan team had several process innovations. The first was working in teams, especially male/female co-therapists. They also developed a five-stage format for operating a session. These parts include the presession, session, intersession, conclusion, and postsession (Boscolo & Cecchin, 1982; Boscolo et al., 1987; Palazzoli et al., 1978a). The **presession** occurs before the therapist(s) meets with the family. Based on previous information (either the intake if a first session or what occurred in previous session(s) if a second or subsequent session), the therapists make some initial hypotheses. These then help to inform the initial interactions in the second stage; the **session**. Here, the therapist utilizes circular questions to help bring forth information. The third stage is the **intersession**, where the therapists in the room take a break and consult with the other team members who have been observing behind a one-way mirror. If there are no team members the intersession is still used as it allows the therapist(s) to take a pause in the action and reevaluate their hypotheses. It further allows the therapist to develop any end-of-session intervention. The **conclusion** of the session is usually the shortest segment, where the

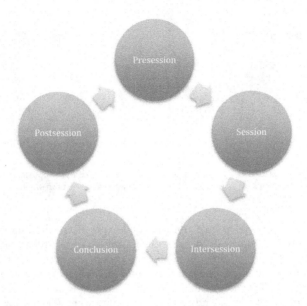

Figure 14.3 The five stages of a Milan Systemic Family Therapy session

therapist delivers the team message and/or intervention. Once the family leaves, the therapists have the **postsession** where they discuss what occurred and come to some final hypotheses about what happened and what might occur during the next session. Figure 14.3 presents a visual of the five stages of a Milan session.

Another innovation made by the Milan team is the spacing of sessions. Instead of having weekly sessions they tended to meet with families once a month (Palazzoli et al., 1978a). This development was serendipitous as they were meeting with families weekly, but some families were traveling long distances in Italy and could only make the several-day trip once a month. The Milan team discovered that the families that had spaced out sessions had more positive gains. The team believed that it took more than a week for some of the interventions to take hold. Similar to the MRI group that they initially consulted with, the Milan therapists tended to contract for a maximum of 10 sessions.

Structural Family Therapy

Structural Family Therapy was primarily developed by Salvador Minuchin, an Argentinian Jewish immigrant, originally trained in psychoanalysis. Working at the Wyltwick School for Boys, he and his colleagues realized the children they were working with might have positive changes while at the institute but reverted back to symptomatic behaviors once they returned to their home environment. They began to bring the families into the treatment room and developed a theory of understanding the family structure and techniques to help reorganize the system. This approach can be seen as the therapist challenging the certainties of the family (Minuchin & Fishman, 1981; Minuchin, Reiter, & Borda, 2014).

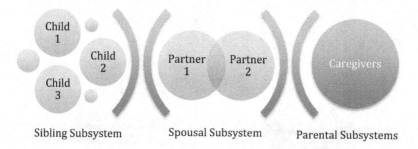

Sibling Subsystem   Spousal Subsystem   Parental Subsystems

Figure 14.4 There are three primary subsystems in families: sibling, spousal, and parental. However, subsystems may be based on age, gender, interest, etc.

Families are organized based on the rules of the system, which comprise its hierarchy. This organization leads to three primary subsystems: parental, sibling, and spousal (Minuchin, 1974). In most families, the adults are usually in the **parental subsystem** and are at a higher position than the children, who are located in the **sibling subsystem**. The third main subsystem in a family is the **spousal subsystem** (see Figure 14.4). Problems tend to form in families when there is some type of organizational imbalance. For instance, if spouses are in conflict and disengaged from one another one of the parties may recruit a child to emotionally replace the partner; thus, the child finds themself in the spousal subsystem.

What distinguishes one subsystem from another are boundaries. Boundaries are the rules that distinguish who and how people can participate in that subsystem (Minuchin, 1974). There are three types of boundaries: rigid, diffuse, and clear. These can be seen on a continuum where the extremes move from less permeability (rigid) to very high permeability (diffuse) with clear boundaries in the middle.

Rigid boundaries prevent much information from moving back and forth. They establish a clear hierarchy with one group holding power over the other. Subsystems with rigid boundaries have a tendency to be disengaged, where there is a separation between members. For instance, a family may be organized where there is a rigid boundary between the parental and sibling subsystem. Here, the parents would develop the rules and the children would not be able to challenge the rules.

Diffuse boundaries are on the other extreme; too much information is passed back and forth. In this family, there is the possibility of enmeshment where members are too close to one another and not able to establish appropriate separation. An example of a family with diffuse boundaries might have the mother going to her 13-year-old daughter and telling her about the conflict that she is having with her substance-abusing husband.

The last type of boundary is a **clear boundary**, where there is an appropriate amount of back and forth between members. This is most likely the normal range of functioning (although, at times, rigid or diffuse boundaries may be more functional to help a family through some type of life situation). Families with clear boundaries have parents who set the rules but the children are able to talk to their parents about the rules with the possibility that they may be adjusted.

Figure 14.5 The Yin-Yang represents complementarity. For white to change, black must also change. For black to change, white must change

People in relationships develop a **complementarity**, where one plays the Yin to the other's Yang (Minuchin & Fishman, 1981) (see Figure 14.5). As one member moves the other moves as well to fill the space just vacated. In a couple, complementarity can be seen as the more one spouse caretakes for the children, the more the other backs off. Reciprocally, as the one backs off of caretaking, the other spouse must fill that role. Since families are tied together in mutual ways of accommodating, a change in one person's functioning changes how the others behave.

Families engage each other through transactions, which involve multiple individuals. Some of these include alliances, coalitions, detouring, and overinvolvement (Minuchin, 1974). **Alliances**, or affiliations, are when two or more family members have a connection to one another. There is nothing problematic in alliances, as families have some members that get along better than others. However, there are times when two members come together against a third member; known as a **coalition**. When the two members in the coalition are from separate subsystems it is known as a **cross-generational coalition**. This is a type of triangulation, where two members involve a third person into the transaction. A dysfunctional type of triangulation, a **detouring conflict**, occurs when two members (usually the parents) are unable to deal with the conflict between themselves and instead shift the focus to a third person (usually the identified patient).

The Process of Therapy

In therapy, the Structural therapist engages in two main processes; joining and restructuring (Minuchin, 1974). This is played out in three steps: joining from a leadership position, distinguishing the family structure, and changing the structure.

Joining operations are what the therapist does to develop the therapeutic system (Minuchin, 1974). This happens from the very first moment of the therapeutic encounter all the way to the last meeting. It is the agar upon which the therapist can challenge the family. One way of joining is through **accommodation**, where the therapist adjusts based on the family's organization. One of the main accommodation techniques is **tracking**, where the therapist follows along with what the family is discussing and gets them to continue. This usually happens as the family explains their view of what they see as the problem. Another joining technique is that of **mimesis**, where the therapist adapts his or her body language and style of speech to be more in line with that of the family. Here, the therapist may speed up their rate of speech with families that are fast talkers, or use more intellectual language with families that do as well.

While therapists join with the family they are also challenging the family's view of the problem. Given that families will most likely present the problem as residing within the IP, therapists must challenge their certainty (Minuchin et al., 2014). This can happen from the very beginning of therapy when the family first explains why they have come to therapy. For instance, if the family states, "We are here because our son, Steve, is disrespectful" the therapist might respond, "Where did he learn that from?" This question moves the problem out of the individual and into the systemic world of transactions.

This challenge to the definition of the problem begins a process of **unbalancing**, where the therapist attempts to change the hierarchical organization in the family (Minuchin & Fishman, 1981). One way of doing this is **boundary making**. This is when the therapist will join with the members of one subsystem to help demarcate that subsystem from another. However, this is a temporary alignment, where some time later in the session or a subsequent session the therapist will align with a different subsystem. As an example, in a family where a grandparent is attempting to take over caretaking responsibilities from the adults in the parental subsystem, the therapist might join with the grandmother and explain, "Rebecca, you've done an excellent job of mothering your children. So good that it is now Pauline's opportunity to do the same for her own children." Another boundary-making action is that of physical proximity. Minuchin became famous for having people switch seating positions to help distinguish one subsystem from another. For instance, if Mark and Hannah are engaging in a detouring conflict by triangulating in Steve, the therapist may ask Steve to move his seat from between the parents. This highlights that husband and wife are in the spousal subsystem and will need to deal with one another rather than bring focus onto the child.

Perhaps the hallmark of Structural work is the technique of enactments. An **enactment** is when the therapist gets the family to engage one another in the session, usually around the dysfunctional transactions (Minuchin & Fishman, 1981). Enactments are multipurposed. They allow the therapist to move from a proximal position, involved in the therapy drama, to a more distal position (see Figure 14.6). This provides the therapist with a chance to sit back and breathe, observe, and think. Enactments are also opportunities for the therapist to then engage in some type of organizational realignment; perhaps through unbalancing or boundary making. In a family where a parent is overwhelmed with their child not following directions, the therapist may ask the two to interact around the parent trying to get the child to do something (i.e., a discussion around not turning in school work). Besides gaining first-hand knowledge of the interactional patterns, the therapist can also intervene. They might, after watching for a while, say to the parent, "Your child is not listening to you. Can you say this in a different way that he can better hear you?" Or if there is a spouse in the room the therapist could say, "Mark, your wife needs your support. What can you do to help her?"

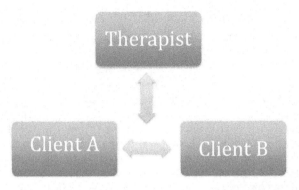

Figure 14.6 A therapeutic enactment occurs when the therapist gets clients to talk with one another around the problem situation to observe family process

The goal of therapy is for the therapist to help realign the family into a more functional hierarchical structure. There is not one set structure that must be in place for the family, yet a movement from rigid or diffuse boundaries to more clear boundaries is usually important to help the family navigate the various life-stage transitions it experiences. Once the family rules and boundaries have been altered, the IP's symptomatic behavior will tend to dissipate.

In families dealing with addiction, the person abusing substances will most likely be presented as the IP. The therapist will then have the difficulty of joining with each member of the family and challenging the notion of the person not being deviant, as not only the family but larger social systems (i.e., courts, law enforcement) view him as the problem. Minuchin and Fishman (1981) explained the importance of therapy in these situations, "Family therapists believe that, given a change in circumstances, people—even people who have been defined as deviant for many years—can experiment with alternatives that are made available to them" (p. 163). This usually entails the therapist challenging the notion that families (and larger systems) have of addiction being an individual problem that needs individual therapy (Minuchin, Nichols, & Lee, 2007).

Postmodern Approaches

Postmodern approaches to therapy focus more on the meanings that people attribute to what occurs in life. This happens through a deconstruction of the person's belief system and a reconstruction of aspects of self that were not highlighted or notated. Thus, change happens by changing the focus of where people look and how they view their lives, as this new understanding of self-in-context shifts people's internal as well as behavioral experience. Postmodern approaches are predicated on constructivist and/or constructionist philosophy where truth is not Truth, but that people develop truth based on how they language their meanings (see Reiter 2019 for a more in-depth explication of constructivist and social constructionist aesthetics and pragmatics).

Solution-Focused Brief Therapy

Solution-Focused Brief Therapy (SFBT) was developed by Steve de Shazer, Insoo Kim Berg, and colleagues in Milwaukee, Wisconsin. The model had its roots in the work of the Brief Therapy of the Mental Research Institute as well as the hypnotic work of Milton Erickson. As opposed to the problem-focused view of the MRI group, where the therapist explores the failed solution attempts that increase the problem, the SFBT therapist examines the non-problem times, as the difficulties that people have are not constant parts of their lives (de Shazer et al., 1986). Solution-Focused Brief Therapy works well with clients from a variety of diverse ethnic, cultural, and religious backgrounds as the therapist honors the client's perspective, bringing forth the client's understandings and ways of doing things rather than having a normative framework (Shafer & Jordan, 2014).

Solution-focused therapists operate from three primary rules (Berg, 1994). The first is *if it is not broken, don't fix it.* Sometimes people try to change something that doesn't need to be changed. For instance, if having a "date night" for a married couple helps them maintain their connection as a couple while also raising children, this should not be changed, although there might be other concerns in the family. The second rule is that *if it doesn't work, don't do it again, do something different.* In the United States, the phrase "If at first you don't succeed try try again" may not always be beneficial. Doing more of the same is similar to our discussion of first-order change; change attempts that are within the existing rule structure (see Chapters 12 & 13). Solution-focused therapists agree that change needs to happen when clients come in with concerns, yet usually the way people have been trying to change is not working because they have been focusing on the "not working" aspect of the problem sequence. This leads to the third rule of SFBT; *once you know what works, do more of it.* This is the most important rule, as the model uses this guideline as the foundation for change. The therapist, during the session, will pay attention to any instance in the client's past where they have experienced a "non-problem" time. These are known as **exceptions**—times when the problem could have happened but did not (de Shazer, 1991). Once exceptions are uncovered, the therapist will help the client to figure out how to engage in more of these non-problem times.

Perhaps out of all of the approaches being covered in this book, SFBT is the one least likely to focus on the past. When it does it is usually because of two reasons. First, it is for the therapist to explore the exceptions that people have experienced. Second, clients may come in expecting to talk about the problem. When clients talk about what is not working in their lives, SFBT refers to this as **problem-talk** (Berg, 1994). Most clients, especially during the first session, will want to discuss what is not right in their lives and what they want to be different. The therapist will stay with the client talking about their concerns as a way to join as well as to see where the non-problem times are occurring. When the therapist shifts the focus from the problem to the non-problem they are engaging in **solution-talk**. In this manner, therapist and client engage in a language game of where each is placing their focus (Reiter & Chenail, 2016) (see Figure 14.7).

Solution-Focused Brief Therapy is an action-oriented approach similar to MRI, Strategic, and Structural Family therapies. Change happens by getting people to do something different from what they have been doing (shifting from a problem

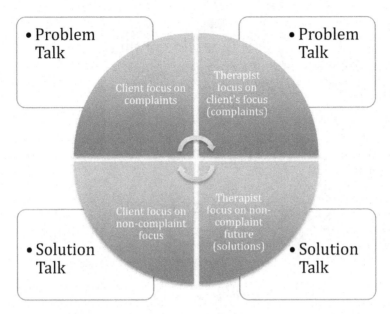

Figure 14.7 Solution-Focused Brief Therapy consists of a language game where client and therapist move back and forth between the focus on problem talk and solution talk

focus to a non-problem focus). A huge transformation is not needed for therapy to be successful. Instead, minimal steps get the process going, which will build upon themselves, like a snowball picking up steam. Once the process of change is started, further changes will be generated by the client.

When exploring the development of problems, SFBT views, in a way similar to the MRI school, that the solutions people are using are the problem, not the presenting problems themselves (de Shazer, 1985). Problems are maintained by clients' rigid adherence to doing more of what they believe will fix the problem. These solutions happen through a focus on the problem sequences rather than the non-problem sequences. Thus, the family pays attention to all the times that alcohol is negatively impacting their lives rather than those times when alcohol has not been present and they have been interacting in ways that they desire. When clients come to therapy, they come with complaints. Complaints are viewed behaviorally at face value. When the clients say that the complaints are gone or have lowered to a level that is no longer a concern for them, therapy has been successful.

Solution-focused therapists tend to classify clients into one of three types: visitors, complainants, and customers (Berg, 1994; de Shazer, 1988). **Visitors** are people who have no overt complaints. Their rationale for being in therapy involves someone telling them to be there. This is someone who may be court ordered to attend therapy or an adolescent whose parents are taking them to therapy because the parents are concerned about the adolescent's behavior.

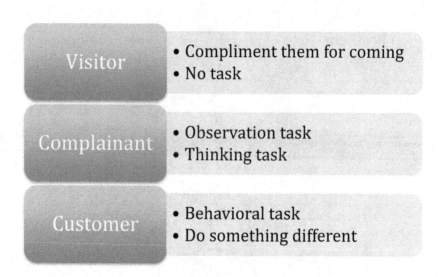

Figure 14.8 Solution-focused therapists will work differently depending on the type of client relationship they are interacting with

The **complainant** is the person who has complaints, yet they are expecting someone else to engage in change to resolve the situation. This would be a spouse of an alcoholic. There are things they want different, but to them it all rests on the other person stopping their drinking. The last type of client is the **customer**; the person who has a complaint and believes that they have a role in changing to make things better.

It is important to determine what type of client is in the room, as therapists do not collaborate with all clients in the same way; they must adapt what they do based on the client-type relationship (Berg, 1994). The therapist promotes cooperation in the relationship by using interventions that correspond with the client's manner of cooperating. For the visitor-type relationship, the therapist will most likely compliment the person for coming but will not give them a task. This is because the person does not see a problem and will not think that they need to change. If the therapist tried to get them to change by giving them a task it would not make sense for the client. With the complainant-type of relationship, the therapist would probably give an observation and/or thinking task. Here, the person recognizes that there is a problem, but believes someone else needs to do something different. By getting the person to do an observational task—centered around viewing interactional processes—the person may come to recognize their own role in the problem sequence patterns. For the customer-type relationship, the therapist will give the client a behavioral task as the person sees a problem and sees their role in it; they are ready to initiate change (see Figure 14.8).

The Process of Therapy

Solution-Focused Brief Therapy is a therapy that is predicated on questions. There are three main types of solution-focused questions; miracle questions, exception questions, and scaling questions (there are also pre-session change, coping, and what's better questions). They are all used in conjunction with one another, all with the goal of helping to uncover the client's preexisting strengths/solutions—which can usually be seen during nonproblem times.

What has perhaps become the hallmark of SFBT is the **miracle question**. This intervention happened by circumstance when Insoo Kim Berg was told by a client that the only thing that would help was a miracle (DeJong & Berg, 2012). Insoo then asked the client what would happen if a miracle did happen. This prompt led to a positive avenue in the therapy. The miracle question goes something like:

> Suppose tonight when you go home and go to sleep a miracle happens. The miracle is that all of the difficulties that you are having are gone. Since you were sleeping you do not know that anything special happened. So what will be the first thing in the morning that will let you know that the miracle happened?

Besides getting clients to shift their focus from an unsatisfactory past to a desired future, it is also one of the first steps in developing goals. Goals in SFBT involve several components: small, measurable, salient, realistic, presence of something, interactional, and inclusive of the client's hard work (Berg, 1994). Figure 14.9 presents a visual depiction of how these components form well-formed goals.

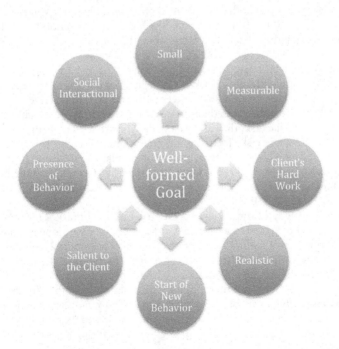

Figure 14.9 Goals in SFBT are designed to be client-centered and bring forth the personal agency of the client

The second main question type involved in SFBT is exception questions. **Exceptions** are times when the problem could have occurred but did not (Berg, 1994; de Shazer, 1991). Since problems do not always happen or at least do not happen at the same level, there are times in the clients' lives when the problem was not there or was at lower levels. Exception questions help to uncover these important points in clients' experiences. When a great deal of attention is paid to the interactional patterns around these periods, it provides clues to what the client needs to do more of. Clients may be asked, "What was happening the last time the two of you were able to get along" or "When was the last time that you hung out with your friends but did not drink."

It is very important to ask exception questions after the miracle picture has been developed to let clients know that what they view as being miraculous are situations that have already existed in their lives. For instance, in the Rothers family, whose miracle picture would most likely include no drinking by Mark, people sitting down to dinner and not arguing, and peace and calm instead of chaos? The therapist can inquire when the last time was that each of these components occurred. Next, the therapist would expand the exception to find out how the clients were able to make the exception happen.

The third type of SFBT questions are **scaling questions**, which help to make abstract concepts concrete. Scaling questions help to define problems in terms of a gradient from more to less (Berg & de Shazer, 1993). They can also be used to develop a baseline and then to chart client progress. Most of us are familiar with scaling questions; especially if you have ever had to go to an emergency room. When interviewing you in the ER, the nurse will most likely ask you to rate your pain on a scale of 0 to 10 with 10 being the higher end. Solution-focused therapists can scale anything, including motivation ("On a scale of 1 to 10 where 1 is none at all and 10 is the most you can have, how motivated are you right now to address this problem"), happiness, or hopefulness.

The exploration of the answers to the miracle question and the exceptions surrounding the various pieces may be interventive in and of themselves. However, since SFBT is an action-oriented approach, some type of task is usually given to clients. Whatever the task, they are usually designed to get the client to do something different. These tasks tended to be generic enough to work with a variety of clients dealing with a variety of problem complaints and came to be called **formula tasks** (de Shazer, 1985). What all SFBT tasks (sometimes called experiments) have in common is the infusion of hope and expectancy of change and difference (Reiter, 2010).

One of the original formula tasks is the **structured fight task**. This is designed for partners who engage in a repetitive type of conflict with one another. The task has four steps: (1) flip a coin to decide who goes first; (2) whoever wins bitches uninterrupted for 10 minutes; (3) after 10 minutes the other person bitches for 10 minutes; and (4) then 10 minutes of silence, after which another round can be begun. Another popular formula task is the **do something different task**, which was originally developed for a family who kept on complaining about one member's behavior and kept trying to fix it in the same way until everyone felt stuck. The therapist giving this formula task might say to the family:

> Between now and next time we meet, I would like each of you
> once to do something different when X (the identified patient)
> does Y (the complained-about behavior). It does not matter
> what you do—which may be silly, crazy, or off-the-wall. The
> important thing is that whatever you do is different than what
> you are now doing when s/he does Y.

Perhaps the most famous of the formula tasks is the **first session formula task**; given at the end of the first session and generic enough to address any type of clients or problem situations (de Shazer, 1985). The task can be worded as:

> Between now and the next time we meet I would like you to
> pay attention to all of the things that are happening in your
> family that you would like to either have continue to happen
> or have happen more often.

This task goes against everything clients think therapy is about—that between sessions you keep a list of all of the things that are bothering you (either about yourself or your family members) so that you can address them the next session. One of the biggest benefits of this task is that it switches family member expectations from looking for problems—and we know that when we look for something we will find it—to looking for exceptions. Whatever the family brings to the next session can be used as the foundation for what to expand on in therapy since these are things they are already doing that are working for them.

Although it is not a task, one of the important interventions in SFBT work is complimenting. **Compliments** are statements from the therapist to the client highlighting things that the client is doing that are good for him (DeJong & Berg, 2012). These are not the typical compliments about hairstyle or clothing choice, but are focused on actions that people make that lead to exceptions. A therapist might say, "Mark, I just wanted to acknowledge that this week instead of going to the bar with your friends you decided to go home to your family to spend time with them. How were you able to make that decision?" We will explore how SFBT has been used around issues of substance abuse in Chapter 15.

Narrative Therapy

Narrative therapy was developed by Michael White and David Epston. While all of the other approaches we've covered, besides Milan Systemic Family Therapy, were developed in the United States, this approach has origins in Australia and New Zealand. Originally working from a cybernetic epistemology based upon the work of Gregory Bateson (White, 1986), White met Epston and both began to shift the foundation of their approach to include narrative and literary metaphors as well as being influenced by the work of the French philosopher, Michel Foucault.

People story their lives, putting segments of their experience into a coherent order, including past, present, and predicted future (White & Epston, 1990). This grouping of events is called a **story** or **self-narrative**. It is created by the individual and creates the individual. We live our stories and are lived by the stories that we develop. Yet we do not do so in isolation. They are grounded in the society in which we are housed. This is where White and Epston borrowed the ideas of Foucault to help explain how the dominant culture influences people based on knowledge and power.

Foucault was interested in the politics of power. He viewed language as an instrument of power. When many people agree to believe in the same ideas, they engage in a "**dominant discourse**," a way of understanding what should or should not be. When individuals do not adhere to the dominant discourse, society implements consequences—usually leading to some type of oppression. For instance, the dominant discourse in the United States is not to engage others outside of one's house when seriously drugged or inebriated. The consequences of doing so are to possibly be arrested.

The dominant discourse comes to be seen as "objective truth" which people internalize. When we internalize the dominant discourse, we begin to self-police ourselves. This may be when we take the labels that others have used about us and act in accord with them (i.e., "I am depressed so I cannot be happy at this party" or "I am the scapegoat in the family so it doesn't matter what I do because I will get in trouble anyway"). Figure 14.10 presents a visual depiction of the impact of the power dynamics associated with dominant discourses.

The dominant discourse helps frame what people's self-narratives will become. It is based on the culture one is raised in, gender orientation, sexual orientation, socioeconomic status, religious orientation, and other national and cultural doctrines. In developing our self-narratives we take in and story those experiences that match the theme we have created—**the dominant story** (White, 2011). Experiences that occur outside of this dominant story are usually excluded from our self-account; we do not pay much attention to them.

The self-narrative, while seemingly an individual process, is actually a relational one. Many of the societal dominant discourses influence the creation and maintenance of people's narratives, as well as the primary relationships in which

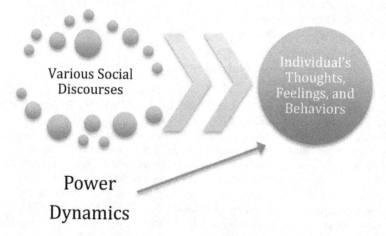

Figure 14.10 Individuals are impacted by the power dynamics associated with various social discourses

we are engaged. For instance, parents in countries where drinking (especially wine) with one's family is acceptable will include their adolescents in family rituals, such as wine at dinner. This would be storied into being a close family. However, families in countries, such as the United States, would have extended family, friends, and the legal system looking down on a family that allowed and encouraged someone under the legal age of drinking to drink alcohol on a regular occurrence.

The dominant story that people develop—housed within cultural/societal expectations as well as more local knowledge—is limiting as it usually provides a restricted range of how people can view themselves and how they can behave. This dominant story is only one of many as people are multistoried; yet they tend to not have the substories of their lives readily available (White, 1995). The difficulty here is that the story that we live our life by lives our life—it gets us to think, feel, and behave in certain ways. When people have problems, it is a sign that the dominant story in their lives is not being useful. The stories they are living by have become **problem-saturated**. As such, people tend to seek therapy when the stories they are living their lives by are not in line with their lived experience (White & Epston, 1990).

Once a problem-saturated story takes hold, it usually inculcates itself into a multitude of avenues (i.e., the individual's view of self, family members' views of the individual, larger systems' expectations of the individual). This process, where family members respond and cooperate with the expectations around the problem, is known as **the life support system of the problem** (White, 1986). When people begin to view the problem as "the truth" as to who someone is, the problem becomes further storied and concretized, leaving little room for the person to establish an identity outside of the problem.

People can have many different identities, yet their dominant story helps to inform which one, at that point in time, takes precedence. Those events that go counter to the dominant story, and are most likely not highlighted and storied, are called **unique outcomes** (White & Epston, 1990) (see Figure 14.11). These events

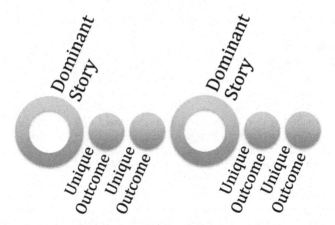

Figure 14.11 Unique outcomes are events that occur outside of the dominant story that is informing people of their identity

most likely are the preferred outcomes that people want for themselves (White, 1995). For instance, Mark may have developed a self-narrative of being a "major disappointment" based on currently engaging in substance abuse, not having a loving marriage, and not being a "good father" by being present and active with his children. However, there were times when he did not drink as much, showed caring for his wife, and spent quality time with his children. Although these times may have been few and far between, they were not placed in the narrative of the Rothers family's narrative, and thus, were not significant.

When people story their lives, two types of landscapes unfold (White, 1993). The first is the **landscape of action**, which is the content of the story. It consists of all of the events that occurred put together in a sequential frame. This then forms the plot of the story. The second landscape is the **landscape of consciousness**, which White (2007) later renamed the **landscape of identity** to highlight how there is a renegotiation of the person's identity. This is the interpretation that the reader of the story has on what the characters in the story did; a focus on their beliefs, values, and motives. In the Rothers family, the landscape of action would include Mark drinking alcohol, having an episode of domestic violence, divorcing his first wife, remarrying his second wife, etc. The landscape of identity would include his perception that he was a bad husband (at least to his first wife), a bad father, and a disappointment to his parents.

In viewing substance abuse through a Narrative Therapy lens, addiction can be viewed as "the addiction to control" (Diamond, 2000, p. 10). Here, there is a push from individuals to try to control their behaviors, feelings, thoughts, as well as trying to control other people. Substances provide a false sense that people have control over what is happening. This process is based on a body of laws and principles that delineate how people should think and act. Diamond explained that many people use substances to not play by the rules but then find out later that not playing by the rules (via substances) has its own rules, which informs how people should be, think, and feel.

The Process of Therapy

Given that the dominant story that people develop and live by does not fit their desired experience, therapy centers around development of new stories with different meanings (White & Epston, 1990). These new stories are called **subordinate storylines** (White, 2007). They are usually filled with unique outcomes; times when the problem could have dominated the person's life but did not.

The hallmark of the Narrative Therapy approach is a process called externalizing. White and Epston (1990) explained that **externalizing** is an objectifying of the problem—personifying it and describing a relational perspective of the person/family to the problem. Whereas MRI therapists stated that "the solution is the problem" Narrative therapists say, "The problem is the problem." Through externalization, there is a shift from an internal state understanding to an intentional state understanding (White, 2007). Mark is no longer "an alcoholic" but has a relationship with alcohol; one where alcohol is taking over and totalizing Mark's identity of who he is as a person, father, husband, and son (as well as impacting each member of the family).

The Narrative therapist focuses on how the problem has recruited the family into how they are currently thinking, feeling, and behaving. However, this does not abdicate the person from responsibility. Clients must take **personal agency** to not allow the problem to recruit them into the problem-saturated experience. The Narrative therapist helps to highlight how the person has stood up to the problem in the past and how they can in the future—shifting their view of themselves from that of victim to that of hero. This happens through a process called **taking responsibility**, where the person connects their actions and the consequences associated with them (White, 2011). In essence, they determine what sort of identity they want for themselves, what type of life they want to live, and what steps they need to take to get there.

In therapy, the Narrative therapist engages the family in various types of conversations that help this process of determining the impact of the dominant story and developing subordinate storylines that are more in line with what people want in their lives. There are six main types of Narrative conversations: externalizing conversations, reauthoring conversations, "re-membering" conversations, definitional ceremonies, conversations that highlight unique outcomes, and scaffolding conversations (White, 2007).

In an **externalizing conversation**, the family's "truth" of the problem (i.e., who the problem is) is deconstructed and an alternative view of the problem develops. This process shifts the location of the problem from internal to a person to housed within the societal constructs that inform people of how they "should" and "should not" be. One of the main aspects of externalizing conversations is when the therapist invites the family to name the problem. In the Rothers family, members might call it "Alcohol," "Anger and Despair," or "The Big Ugly Liquid." This allows a shift in questioning from "When did you become alcoholic" to "When did alcohol enter your life" or "What types of negative things do you do when you are drunk" to "How do you react when alcohol is present."

Reauthoring conversations includes a focus on the subordinate storylines of people's lives rather than the dominant stories. This is usually a shift from deficit-focused views of people to that of people having more personal agency over the problem. These conversations usually surround aspects of self that people desire that they had already engaged in but had not placed into the plot of their lives. In starting to uncover these subordinate plots, the therapist becomes curious as to how they happened, in hopes that the family becomes curious as well. These conversations usually move from a focus on the landscape of action to the landscape of identity.

Because our dominant story is both an internal and relational development, other people are important in the formation of our identity. One way to explore how others have influenced our identity and how they also have a role in shaping our subordinate stories is when Narrative therapists have **"Re-membering" conversations**. There are two lines of inquiry that happen in these conversations (White, 2007). The first is a focus on how the other person (usually someone significant in the client's life) contributed to the person's identity and how that person would view the client. The second line of inquiry is how the client contributed to the other person's identity. These conversations usually revolve around how the other has seen the client stand up to the problem. For instance, Mark may be asked how his parents have seen him not let alcohol get the better of him and how he has contributed to their sense of being good parents.

In **unique outcome conversations,** the therapist talks with the family about the counterplots to the dominant story. These conversations usually entail naming the unique outcome and how those events and experiences are the preferred outcomes (White, 2007). When people give value to these occurrences, they are more likely to become central features in a new plotline.

Given that problems develop based on people internalizing dominant discourses, one way of helping families is to connect them to people who will support the subordinate story that runs counter to the original problem-saturated description. Narrative therapists do this through **definitional ceremonies,** where people are able to tell their newfound stories in front of others who can support this new identity. This process usually happens via outsider witness practices. **Outsider witnesses** are an audience that listens to clients tell their story and then comments on their experience of hearing that story (see Figure 14.12). Usually they are either significant people in the client's life or perhaps other clients who have had similar issues. They may be drawn from a registry where the therapist has asked if they would serve as a support network for others. For instance, a family who overcame addiction in their own lives may serve as outsider witnesses for the Rothers family. They would sit in on a session and observe the conversation between the Rothers and the therapist. The therapist would then interview them about their experience of listening to the story while the Rothers family listened to this telling. The therapist would then talk with the Rothers about what it was like to listen to the outsider witnesses.

Figure 14.12 In outsider witness practices, clients tell their story in front of outsider witnesses, who then discuss what they were drawn to in the discussion, which is then followed by the client discussing what they were drawn to in the outside witness conversation

One of the original aspects of Narrative Therapy was its use of documents in therapy. Once something is written down, people perceive it as having "truth" and it becomes a large part of defining someone. In the mental health realm, these documents would be biopsychosocial assessments and treatment plans. Narrative therapists have developed many **counter documents**, documents that help to provide an alternative identity of the person—one less pathologizing and that exhibit the person's personal agency (White & Epston, 1990). These counter documents can come in the form of certificates, awards, or letter-writing campaigns. For an adolescent who was using marijuana to extremes, the therapist and client may have externalized the problem as "Big Green." Once the client developed personal agency and did not let Big Green rule his life to where he was failing in school, having poor exercise and health, and had disputes with his parents, the therapist might create a certificate called "Escape from Big Green". This document could then be disseminated to his parents, friends, teachers, probation officer, or other significant figures to help support the client's new story.

In discussing substance abuse and addiction, White (1997) examined the notion of a culture of consumption where the therapist has to appreciate how some people utilize drugs and others do not. Questions the therapist might ask the client include, "How, given your situation, have you developed the desire to stop using" or "In what ways have you nurtured your push for an alcohol-free life." When working with people dealing with substance abuse, White recommends the use of the **rite of passage metaphor**. Here, the person goes through three stages: the separation phase, the liminal phase, and the reincorporation phase. The separation phase is the beginning of the ritual where the person separates or breaks from their known life. In the liminal phase, the person experiences disorientation as they are living in ambiguity, not knowing what is happening or will happen. During the reincorporation phase the person recognizes that they've achieved a new way of life.

Termination in Narrative Therapy occurs when family members have not only uncovered new storylines for their lives, but are acting and performing these alternative plots (White, 1995). Their new identity is in line with their preferred outcomes and they are able to distinguish "local knowledge" (their own perspectives) in relation to the dominant discourse.

Case Application

The Strategic therapist of the Rothers family would take responsibility for change in the system. In the assessment of the family, the therapist might hypothesize that the Rothers are having difficulty transitioning from the family with young children stage to the family with adolescent children stage. This may be seen in boundaries that are more on the rigid side where the parents attempt to have greater influence on most aspects of the child's life. Steve is now 14 and is looking for greater levels of independence. The system's homeostasis may be organized around ensuring parental responsibility for children's behaviors. Mark's increased drinking and emotional despair along with Steve's acting out behaviors signal that there is something problematic in the family organization.

Therapy with the Rothers would likely involve all five members of the nuclear family. The first session would find the therapist not only joining with the family, but assessing their interactional rules as well as each member's goals for therapy. The session would end with the therapist giving a directive—a task for the family to do outside of the session. If the Rothers presented with Mark's reduced drinking as the goal, a potential directive would be to give the family a paradoxical technique, and, more specifically, an ordeal. The family could be told that if Mark drank, then during the night, perhaps at 1am, the whole family would have to wake up and Mark would need to help each child with their schoolwork while Hannah oversaw. The thought here is that it would be easier not to have the symptom—drinking—than having to do the ordeal.

A Milan systemic family therapist would develop a systemic hypothesis to understand the Rothers' current homeostasis. The family game holds that Mark distances himself from the family, through both alcohol, time, and emotionality, while Hannah puts more effort into childrearing. Steve's increasing acting out behavior serves as a message that he will not be under the control of his parents. While the family will come in saying that they want change, the change they want is for someone else to do something different (i.e., Steve wants his parents to lay off him, Hannah wants Mark to stop drinking and be more engaged, etc.). They have developed a family myth centered around Mark being an alcoholic and that he needs the support from the rest of the family so he does not become like his father, Ian.

In the Rothers family, a positive connotation may be that Mark's drinking behavior helps to keep his wife from being upset at Steve's problems at school. If the family came in focusing on Steve's acting out behavior, the positive connotation could be that Steve's behaviors are helping the family as father and mother are so focused on him that they do not have to deal with the tension between themselves. Similar to the ritual of ordeals in Strategic therapy, the Milan therapist might prescribe a ritual for the Rothers such as the odd days/even days ritual. This would be in an attempt to disrupt the family game of Mark not taking ownership of child care while Hannah takes full responsibility.

A Structural family therapist working with the Rothers family would likely see all members as this would provide more information to help assess their current family hierarchy. The Structural case conceptualization might focus on understanding the problem, processes, patterns, power dynamics, proximity, and possibilities of the family (Reiter, 2016). There seem to be some disruptions in typical subsystem membership. That is, Steve seems to be on the outside of the sibling subsystem, not really connecting with Kayleigh or Pete. Mark is an infrequent participant of the parental subsystem, having abdicated much of that responsibility to Hannah. While Mark and Hannah are in the spousal subsystem, they are not clearly a unit wherein Hannah is spending more of her emotional energy in her relationships with her children. The symptoms in this family (i.e., Mark's drinking and Steve's acting out) are likely related to the disengagement between spouses and the concomitant adjustment in the family's organization. This is leading to the detouring triangulation occurring between Mark, Hannah, and Steve where Mark and Hannah are focusing more energy on Steve's behaviors than on the dynamics of their marital relationship.

There will likely be many enactments during the Structural session, bringing to light the various interactional processes of the family. Boundary making will also occur, where, depending on seating position, the therapist will ask Mark and Hannah to sit next to each other while they discuss either couple or parental issues. This will demarcate them as a unit in either the spousal or parental subsystems. Another goal of therapy would be to bring Steve closer to Kayleigh and Pete in the sibling subsystem.

A Solution-Focused Brief therapist working with the Rothers will first attempt to determine what type of relationship type of client they are working with, with the understanding that this may change over the course of therapy. Hannah is mainly a complainant, having concerns over Mark's drinking and isolating behaviors as well as Steve's acting out behaviors. Mark is likely a visitor, thinking that he doesn't have a problem. Regarding Steve's behavior, Mark may be a complainant. Steve, as well, is likely a visitor or complainant. He would probably say that he does not have an issue, and would point to Mark's alcohol consumption as the problem. Kayleigh and Pete are likely complainants, with Kayleigh perhaps stating that her father isn't as loving as she wants and that Steve isn't the nicest brother. One goal of therapy would be to see if, during the therapeutic conversation, one or more individuals might see themselves as a customer for change as this would help the motivation of family members to make personal change attempts.

It is likely that during the first session the therapist will ask the miracle question. The technique does not end at the end of asking the question, but, more importantly, in the back-and-forth of developing the various miracle pictures that emerge. For instance, Hannah might say, "Mark wouldn't be drinking any more." The therapist would then want to help language these pictures in terms of qualities of good goals. This might be through questions such as, "And if he wasn't drinking anymore, what would you be doing?" (inclusive of the client's hard work), "What would he be doing instead?" (presence rather than absence of behavior), or "What would be the first thing that you would notice that let you know that path was happening?" (small and measurable).

The SFBT therapist would keep an ear open for various exceptions in the family's life. These might include times when Mark engaged the family in ways all members thought of as pleasant, Steve was engaging in prosocial behaviors, or Mark and Hannah were feeling more loving toward one another. The therapist could then scale a variety of these exceptions, such as, "On a scale of 1 to 10, how hopeful are you of having the type of marriage you want with one another?" The first session will likely end with the therapist giving the family an experiment, the first session formula task, which would help family members switch their lenses from looking for and expecting problems to looking for and expecting things to go right in their lives. The therapist would then help the family members to build on these events so that they occur more often.

A Narrative therapist would not view the Rothers family in isolation, but see them as housed within the ideologies and belief systems of various dominant discourses of who people are. These discourses may be based around gender, age, religion, culture, socioeconomic status, or a variety of other constructs that inform people as to how they should think, feel, and behave. One of these dominant discourses is around gender roles and what men and women should experience in raising children. It seems Mark has internalized more traditional views that women should be the primary caregivers of children as he has accepted that Angelina should be the primary caregiver of Nina and Hannah should be the primary caregiver of Steve, Kayleigh, and Pete. This internalization has led him to act in ways that may go against who he wants to be as a man and a father.

One pathway in therapy would be to help uncover the unique outcomes for the family. This would help bring forth subordinate storylines that were more in line with how the Rothers wanted to be as a family. One means of doing so is by externalizing the problem. Externalizing alcohol would help the family to work together against a common issue rather than viewing Mark as the problem. The therapist might incorporate definitional ceremonies or counter documents to help substantiate the new subordinate plotline the Rothers are developing about who they are as a family.

Summary

This chapter covered five of the most prominent family therapy theories. Strategic Family Therapy showcased how the therapist is responsible for changing a family by developing directives intended to change problematic sequences. The Milan Systemic approach focuses on how a therapist utilizes guidelines such as hypothesizing, circularity, and neutrality to infuse difference into the family system. Structural Family Therapy pays attention to the family organization and gets families to enact new and more functional hierarchies. Solution-Focused Brief Therapy shifts the focus of the therapeutic conversation from problem development to solution development; uncovering times in the family's life when the problem was not present. Narrative Family Therapy explores how individuals and families have become totalized by dominant discourses, internalizing views of who they should be and then working with people to deconstruct these understandings and reconstruct more hopeful storylines.

Key Words

pretend techniques
ordeals
straightforward task
paradoxical ordeal
paradox
counterparadox
family game
family myth
positive connotation
family rituals
odd days/even days ritual
hypothesizing
circularity
circular questions

information
neutrality
presession
session
intersession
conclusion
postsession
parental subsystem
sibling subsystem
spousal subsystem
rigid boundaries
diffuse boundaries
clear boundaries
complementarity

alliances
coalition
cross-generational coalition
detouring conflict
joining
accommodation
tracking
mimesis
unbalancing
boundary making
enactment
exceptions
problem-talk
solution-talk
visitors
complainant
customer
miracle question
exceptions
scaling questions
formula tasks
structured fight task
do something different task
first session formula task

compliments
story/self-narrative
dominant discourse
dominant story
problem saturated
life support system of the
    problem
unique outcomes
landscape of action
landscape of consciousness
landscape of identity
subordinate storylines
externalizing
personal agency
taking responsibility
externalizing conversations
reauthoring conversations
re-membering conversations
unique outcome conversations
definitional ceremonies
outsider witnesses
counter documents
rite of passage metaphor

Discussion Questions

1. Why is the directive so important in Strategic Family Therapy?
2. How does the Strategic Family therapist view one spouse's substance abuse?
3. What is the importance of operating from a stance of hypothesizing, circularity, and neutrality?
4. What is the relationship between the family game in Milan therapy and addiction in a family?
5. How do enactments help the Structural Family therapist work with families in session?
6. How might addiction impact a family's organization? Of what use is this conceptualization for the Structural Family therapist?
7. What role do the three main questions in Solution Focused Brief Therapy hold?
8. How do formula tasks adhere to the three rules of SFBT?
9. How does Narrative Family Therapy conceptualize addictions?
10. Explain the purpose of externalization in Narrative Family Therapy.

FIFTEEN

Family Therapy Application

In the previous two chapters we presented many of the most popular family therapy approaches. While any of them can be used with families who are dealing with a wide range of presenting problems, including substance abuse, this chapter focuses on the specific application of family therapy to the field of addiction. Stevens (2018) explained that family therapy for substance abuse attempts to stop current use while protecting against later multigenerational use. Each model of therapy does so in their own ways based on their unique theories of problem formation and problem resolution (Reiter, 2014).

First, we will explore Multidimensional Family Therapy, a model developed to work with adolescent substance abusers and their families that incorporates family therapy, developmental theory, ecological theory, and risk and protective factors. Next, we will discuss Brief Strategic Family Therapy, an approach developed for families with an adolescent substance abuser that combines Structural and Strategic Family Therapy. Third, we will explore how Solution-Focused Brief Therapy has been applied to substance abuse. Lastly, we explore Behavioral Couples Therapy for addictions. This is not to say that the other models of family therapy previously presented are not appropriate for substance abuse. They all have and can be used effectively with families dealing with addictions. This chapter just provides a slice of how various models can be specifically applied when it comes to this population.

Specific programs for family therapy and addictions are important since alcohol counselors have traditionally avoided the use of family therapy (Lawson & Lawson, 1998). This may be because they believe family therapy goes against the disease model, they do not have training in family therapy, they view family therapy as not in line with 12-step programs, they may not have support from the agency they work for, and they may not have access to the family. However, family-based substance abuse treatment can be both efficacious and cost-effective (Morgan & Crane, 2010).

When using family-based interventions with families dealing with substance abuse, therapists and programs usually have four goals (Thombs & Osborn, 2013). First, they attempt to bring the user, partner, and/or other family members into a collaborative interaction to develop a plan to change the family system. Second, interventions are designed to help clarify and stabilize family rules and roles. Third, given that substance abuse is having a significant negative impact on the family, family-based interventions are usually designed toward

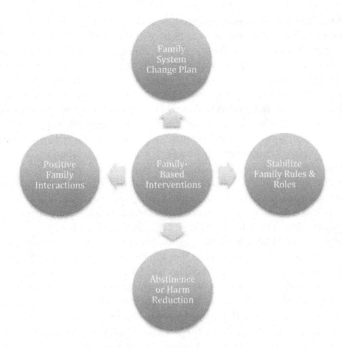

Figure 15.1 Family-based interventions are designed to reduce drinking and increase family stability and positive family interactions

abstinence. However, based on the model of therapy, harm reduction might be the goal rather than abstinence. Lastly, interventions target family interactions in an attempt to improve them and make them more desirable for all members. See Figure 15.1 for a visualization of the four goals of family-based interventions for substance abuse.

Multidimensional Family Therapy

Multidimensional Family Therapy (MDFT) is an empirically validated family-based therapy that was designed to work with adolescent substance abusers and their families (Greenbaum et al., 2015; Liddle, 2002, 2010, 2016; Liddle & Dakof, 2002; Liddle, Dakof, Parker, Diamond, Barrett, & Tejada, 2001). Multidimensional Family Therapy was influenced by Structural Family Therapy and Strategic Family Therapy (Liddle, 1991) as well as Problem-Solving Therapy (Liddle, 2009). The model also incorporates ideas from the risk and protective factor framework, the ecological perspective, as well as a developmental perspective (Liddle, 2010). Multidimensional Family Therapy takes into consideration intra-individual, interpersonal, and intersystem interactions to provide a multicontextual understanding of behavior (Liddle, 2016). It developed with a core understanding that research-based knowledge (regarding adolescents, psychopathology, risk and protective factors, and family therapy) could help treat adolescent substance abuse (Liddle, 1991).

Multidimensional Family Therapy works not only with the adolescent who is abusing substances (or involved in the juvenile justice system) but also their family, as well as the larger systems in which the teen is involved (i.e., school, juvenile justice, and social services). It is an integrative approach that has been manualized to make it functional as well as cost effective (Henderson, Marvel, & Liddle, 2012; Liddle, 2009). Multidimensional Family Therapy can be used as an in-patient, out-patient, or home-based model, and can vary in terms of treatment length, intensity (how much contact between therapist and client), and what other services are used (i.e., drug screening or social services).

The intent behind the approach is that what is needed to help adolescents dealing with substance abuse is to change the adolescent's lifestyle (Liddle & Dakof, 2002). This is because the adolescent's drinking and drug use is based upon a variety of interrelated risk factors (Rowe & Liddle, 2008). Substance abuse is not a healthy or adaptive way of being, especially for adolescents. Multidimensional Family Therapy is designed to help the adolescent develop a more functional developmental pathway (Liddle, Rodriguez, Dakof, Kanzki, & Marvel, 2005). This involves working at multiple levels/dimensions (or what are known as modules), which include the (1) adolescent, (2) parent, (3) interpersonal (the family as a unit), and (4) extrafamilial domains such as school or other social contexts (Liddle et al., 2005). Since the substance abuse is a result of a complex set of factors, treatment and the focus of change targets those multidimensional areas (Rowe & Liddle, 2008). These include a focus on alcohol expectancies, parental substance abuse, and family-based relapse prevention.

Multidimensional Family Therapy rests on 10 therapeutic principles, which help guide the therapist in the pursuit of change. These principles are:

1. Adolescent drug abuse is a multidimensional phenomenon.
2. Family functioning is instrumental in creating new, developmentally adaptive lifestyle alternatives for adolescents.
3. Problem situations provide information and opportunity.
4. Change is multifaceted, multidetermined, and stage oriented.
5. Motivation is malleable but it is not assumed.
6. Multiple therapeutic alliances are required and they create a foundation for change.
7. Individualized interventions foster developmental competencies.
8. Treatment occurs in stages; continuity is stressed.
9. Therapist responsibility is emphasized.
10. Therapist attitude is fundamental to success. (Liddle, 2010, pp. 417–418)

These principles set the stage for a flexible yet targeted approach that focuses change in the four dimensions (adolescent, parent, family, and extrafamilial).

Multidimensional Family Therapy Treatment

Treatment in MDFT follows three stages (Liddle, 2002; Liddle et al., 2005). Stage 1 involves an assessment and joining process. In the adolescent module, incorporating the adolescent's involvement from the very beginning of therapy is key, as their active engagement helps them to get their needs met (Liddle, 1991). The therapist uncovers the problematic areas in the adolescent's life (i.e., perhaps depression, conflict with parents, issues at school—or a combination) as well as the strengths available in the system. During this stage the therapist will procure the adolescent's life story, which allows the therapist to understand the adolescent's connection to various aspects of his or her life, which may include drug use, their belief system, family history, peers, health and lifestyle issues, and possible mental health issues. The adolescent is encouraged to discuss their concerns as well as what they are hoping for from therapy and their hopes and dreams for their life. At this point, the therapist might use drug screening or other assessments to determine whether drug use is continuing. Further, the therapist will assess the possibility of dual diagnosis (see Chapter 8), as this is the norm in this clinical population (Liddle et al., 2005).

The parent assessment focuses on the person as an individual as well as a parent, which explores their psychological and emotional state along with their parenting style. The therapist collects all past solution attempts and determines what worked and what did not work. This helps to highlight problematic patterns but also strengths and competencies (Liddle et al., 2005). Just as work with the adolescent is designed to join with the individual and increase their motivation and cooperation, the therapist needs to recruit the parent to buy in to the idea that therapy is for all family members.

During the familial module assessment, the MDFT therapist focuses on the story and family history. At this point, how the family interacts with one another, especially in the affective area, is key (Liddle et al., 2005). Although it is the assessment phase, the therapist may begin to try to help family members to communicate more productively with one another.

The last part of Stage 1 assessment occurs in the extrafamilial module. Depending on the family and the situation, some larger systems will play a more important role than others. Several areas of exploration include school, court, recreational services for youth, and social services/support for family (Liddle et al., 2005). Based on their connection or disconnection from these extrafamilial systems, the therapist may help connect the family to various services they may find useful. The information obtained in the Stage 1 assessment is used as a therapeutic map, providing the therapist with a framework of where in the adolescent's dimensional world intervention needs to occur (Rowe, 2010). Figure 15.2 presents a visualization of the four modules in Stage 1 of MDFT.

Stage 2 is where change is attempted, focusing within and between dimensions. This is the longest stage of treatment (Dakof, Godley, & Smith, 2010). Treatment takes a variety of forms including working with the adolescent alone, the parent(s) alone, and the family as a whole. This is done as a leveraging to increase the therapeutic alliance and motivation (Liddle, 2010).

Multidimensional Family Therapy targets three primary risk factors: substance expectancies, parental substance abuse, and family-based relapse prevention (Rowe & Liddle, 2008). During this part of treatment, the therapist will challenge the adolescent's motivations for using substances as well as motivation for or ambivalence to change. The discrepancies of what the adolescent wants and what the adolescent is doing help to demonstrate that the individual's drugging

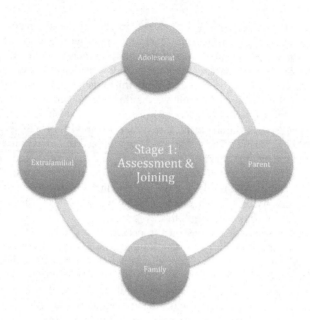

Figure 15.2 Stage 1 of MDFT involves joining and assessing the adolescent, parent, family, and extrafamilial systems

(and problematic) lifestyle (i.e., doing poorly in school or engaging in delinquent behavior) is not in line with their desired lifestyle.

Besides working with the adolescent, MDFT therapists work individually with parents. The rationale behind this is that the adolescent is impacted, on many levels, by what the parent does and how the parent engages the teen. Rowe and Liddle (2008) explained this further, "The therapist motivates parents to take steps to change their own lives by resuscitating their love and commitment for the child, and by highlighting the links between the parent's own functioning, their parenting deficits, and the child's problems" (p. 114). Thus, the therapist may work with the parent to reduce/eliminate their own alcohol/drug use, improve their mental health functioning, and learn more effective parenting skills.

Stage 3 incorporates the changes made and prepares the adolescent and family to utilize what they have learned to maintain the positive changes. Once the individuals in the family have developed a foundation toward positive changes, family sessions can explore the past hurts each member has experienced in the family (Rowe & Liddle, 2008). Family sessions may also focus on relapse prevention, since one aspect of adolescent substance use is based on familial interactions. The goal is that the family, rather than the therapist, becomes the healing agent. One way this occurs is through the Structural technique of enactments (see Chapter 14). During sessions, the MDFT therapist gets the family to discuss issues around substance abuse and then encourages and supports new and more effective responses from and toward one another. See Figure 15.3 for a visual of the three stages of MDFT.

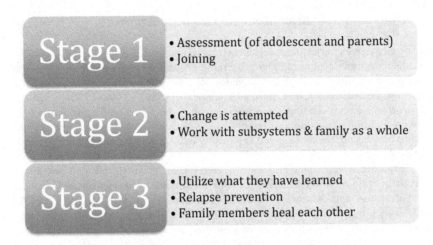

Figure 15.3 Multidimensional Family Therapy is provided in three stages: assessing and
joining; initiating change; and enhancing change and relapse prevention

The change that comes from MDFT is multifaceted. Not only will the adolescent most likely reduce his or her drug use, but family relationships may be
improved, as well as relationships between individuals in the family and larger
systems. These changes can be seen in the behavioral, affective, and cognitive
realms of members of the family (Liddle, 1991).

In today's day and age of evidence-based and empirically-validated treatment approaches, MDFT has had strong support for its efficacy (Dennis et al.,
2004; Greenbaum et al., 2015; Liddle, 2002, 2016; Liddle et al., 2001; van
der Pol et al., 2017). For instance, adolescent substance abusers (marijuana
and alcohol) that received MDFT showed significantly less substance use than
those who received Adolescent Group Therapy or Multifamily Educational
Intervention (Liddle et al., 2001). In another study (Liddle, 2002), MDFT was
compared with Cognitive Behavior Therapy. While both approaches decreased
substance use, only MDFT decreased hard drug use. Further, those who
received MDFT had lower drug use at 6- and 12-month follow-up. Compared
with other empirically supported approaches (Motivational Enhancement
Therapy/Cognitive Behavioral Therapy, Adolescent Community Reinforcement
Approach), MDFT led to similar results, where adolescents reduced their usage
of substances by over 50% from the beginning of the study to the 12-month
follow-up (Dennis et al., 2004). Multidimensional Family Therapy might be
most effective in working with families where the adolescent is dealing with
high severity problems such as severe substance abuse (van der Pol et al., 2017).
Multidimensional Family Therapy works well with adolescents of both genders
and varied ethnicities (Greenbaum et al., 2015). These researchers found that
MDFT was most effective, in relation to comparison treatments, for males,
African Americans, and European Americans, and just as effective for females
and Hispanic clients.

Brief Strategic Family Therapy

For many years the Strategic and Structural models were viewed as one approach, called Strategic-Structural Family Therapy. This was because the founders of the two approaches, Jay Haley and Salvador Minuchin respectively, worked together at the Philadelphia Child Guidance Clinic. During the late 1980s Strategic-Structural Family Therapy was perhaps the primary method by which people were learning about family therapy. In this section we will present an adaptation of these approaches as used specifically with substance abuse; **Brief Strategic Family Therapy (BSFT)**.

Brief Strategic Family Therapy was developed by Szapocznik and colleagues to help families with an adolescent who is engaging in problem behaviors such as drug use and delinquent behavior (Szapocznik, Scopetta, & King, 1978a, 1978b). Originally developed with a Hispanic population, the approach has been expanded to work with all families that are engaging in patterns of functioning that maintain the adolescent's problem behavior. These patterns are the focus of BSFT; where the goal is to change the ways the family interacts so that the family rules change and the problem behavior is no longer acceptable (Szapocznik, Schwartz, Muir, & Brown, 2012). When the family's behavior becomes more adaptive, the adolescent substance abuser will most likely decrease his or her negative behaviors (drugs and/or delinquency).

Since families usually come to therapy with an IP—in this case the drug-abusing adolescent—they may not understand the family dynamics that help to maintain the problem. They have tried to enact change in the IP rather than the relational transactions of the family. This ineffective focus has led to blaming the IP and a sense of hopelessness. The BSFT model is thus designed to use intervention strategies to help get and keep families in treatment as they try to reduce the symptomatic behavior of the adolescent (Szapocznik et al., 2012).

Brief Strategic Family Therapy has been effective in reducing adolescent drug use (Robbins et al., 2008; Robbins et al., 2011a; Robbins et al., 2011b). It has become a manualized intervention (Szapocznik, Hervis, & Schwartz, 2003) and is considered to be an empirically validated intervention (Briones, Robbins, & Szapocznik, 2008). Brief Strategic Family Therapy leads to lower median levels of drug use by adolescents, higher rates of engaging and retaining family members in treatment, and higher family functioning than treatment as usual (Robbins et al., 2011a). An additional benefit of BSFT is that, even though it is designed to reduce adolescent substance use, it also reduces parental substance use (Horigian et al., 2015). This is likely due to improvements in overall family functioning.

Brief Strategic Family Therapy is premised on three core principles: system, structure, and strategy (Briones et al., 2008) (see Figure 15.4). The first principle rests on the notion of family systems—where individual members are interdependent. Children's thoughts, feelings, and behaviors are primarily shaped by their interactions with the family. Here, problem behavior is seen as a symptom of an underlying dynamic within the family. This leads into the second core principle of BSFT; that the family engages in repetitive sequences of behaviors that influence how the various members behave. This is considered to be the family's structure. Families that come to therapy tend to experience a maladaptive family structure; one in which their repetitive ways of being with one

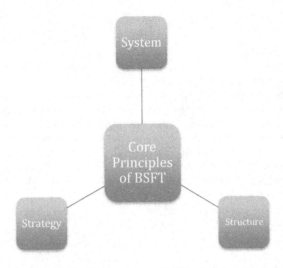

Figure 15.4 Brief Strategic Family Therapy rests on the principles of system, structure, and strategy

another lead to less than desired results. The third core principle of BSFT is more strategic—the therapist designs interventions that target the family's repetitive problem-maintaining sequences. These interventions tend to be practical, problem-focused, and deliberate.

Brief Strategic Family Therapy interventions have been classified into four domains; joining, tracking and diagnostic enactment, reframing, and restructuring (Robbins et al., 2011a). **Joining operations** are designed to develop a therapeutic alliance between the family and the therapist. They occur throughout the whole of the treatment. These techniques include the therapist making a connection with the family. The alliance is extremely important as those families that have a higher alliance with their BSFT therapist are more likely to complete treatment than those with a lower alliance (Robbins et al., 2008).

The second domain of interventions is **tracking and diagnostic enactment**, designed to assess the family's strengths and weaknesses, which help the therapist develop an appropriate treatment plan. The BSFT examines six elements of family interactions (Briones et al., 2008), which include organization, resonance, developmental stages, life context, identified patient, and conflict resolution.

A **family's organization** can be viewed in terms of leadership, subsystem organization, and communication flow. Leadership can also be looked at in terms of authority and hierarchy. Subsystem organization explores the formal (i.e., spousal and sibling) and informal subsystems (i.e., males, females, older kids, those engaged in sports). The last organizational component is communication flow where the therapist observes whether there is direct and specific communication (a sign of being a functional family).

The second element of family interaction is **resonance**, which is the closeness and distance of family members. This is in regards to the emotional and psychological connection family members have with one another. Minuchin (1974) talked about these ideas in terms of enmeshment and disengagement. Enmeshment signifies high resonance while disengagement is a sign of low resonance between people and subsystems.

Brief Strategic Family Therapy explores **developmental stages** in two ways—individual member development and family development. These two aspects are not mutually exclusive. The individual's growth impacts the requirement of the family to transition into a new stage of development (for instance, the move of a child into an adolescent requires the rules of the family to become more permeable). During the assessment of developmental stages, the BSFT therapist focuses on the parenting, marital, sibling, and extended family's tasks and roles.

A fourth element of family interaction that BSFT focuses on is life context. **Life context** regards the interaction between the family system and larger systems such as school, work, extended family, health care, etc. While working with adolescents who are abusing drugs and getting into other types of behavioral problems, their peer system is one of the primary life contexts that impacts them. If the problem behaviors have become severe, the juvenile justice system may also be involved in the family's life.

Family interactions also involve the identified patient. As we know, families usually enter therapy with one member who they provide as being the problem—the **identified patient.** This is the family scapegoat; the symptom bearer that signifies that there is something problematic happening in the family (problematic repetitive patterns of interaction). One important exploration in this area includes the idea that families tend to view the IP through a limited lens, only seeing their substance use rather than other aspects of their behavior.

The last element of exploration is in the area of conflict resolution. The therapist assesses how the family is able to deal with issues that happen around disagreements. Families with drug-abusing adolescents tend to manage conflict in four ineffective ways: denial, avoidance, diffusion, and conflict emergence without resolution. The effective means of handling disagreements is conflict emergence with resolution.

Reframing interventions form the third domain of BSFT. The therapist relabels family behaviors and interactions, deconstructing the view of the IP as "the problem" to a more systemic perspective. This intervention is intended to build hope and motivation in the family.

The fourth domain is **restructuring** where the therapist engages in various techniques (such as redirecting, blocking, unbalancing, and helping the family develop conflict resolution and behavior management skills) to shift the problem-maintaining sequences. These may include detriangulation, working in the present, reframing negativity, working with boundaries and alliances, opening up closed systems, and tasks.

These interventions are put together into an integrated strategy that follows five steps: joining, enactment, interactional diagnosis, treatment plan, and restructuring change (Briones et al., 2008) (see Figure 15.5). Joining involves mutual respect and acceptance while therapist and family develop a therapeutic system. Enactments occur when either the therapist asks family members to interact with one another or the family spontaneously does so. This interaction is usually centered around the presenting complaint. While the family interacts, the therapist is able to sit back and observe the family's process. Third, the therapist makes

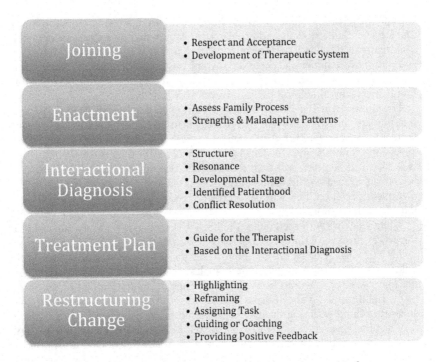

Figure 15.5 Brief Strategic Family Therapy interventions are connected in five steps

an interactional diagnosis, which has five interrelated dimensions (Robbins et al., 2001). These include structure, resonance, developmental stage, identified patienthood, and conflict resolution. The fourth step of BSFT is the development of a treatment plan, which is based upon the interactional diagnosis and informs the therapist on which maladaptive interactional patterns to target and the best means and interactions to do so. Lastly, the therapist engages in restructuring or change-producing interventions. These include highlighting, reframing, assigning tasks, guiding or coaching, and providing positive feedback.

Brief Strategic Family Therapy Treatment

While the assessment and understanding of the family functioning aspect of BSFT is based on Structural Family Therapy, the intervention portion—the strategic aspect of therapy—is based on Strategic Therapy. These interventions can be viewed as the **Three Ps; Practical, Problem-Focused, and Planned** (Briones et al., 2008). The practical aspect of interventions is important because the therapist might use Structural or Strategic techniques, yet may also borrow from other approaches. They are designed to be as efficient as possible, perhaps focused on only one aspect of family restructuring rather than trying to do everything at once. The problem-focused aspect of BSFT is that while families are usually multi-problemed, the therapist specifically keys in to the adolescent substance use issues. Since the way to do this is through changing family rules and structure, other issues and problems the family may be experiencing might also dissipate. The last aspect of interventions is that they are planned. This is a straightforward approach where the therapist assesses the family structure and then deliberately designs interventions, unique for each session, to target the family hierarchy to help properly restructure the family.

The first task the BSFT therapist gives to the client is to get all family members into the session. This is referred to as **engagement** and is perhaps the most important task as most families that are dealing with adolescent drug use problems never enter into therapy. Once the family does come for the first session, the first task they will be given will happen inside the session so that the therapist can help them to identify the family patterns and make constructive changes in the therapist's presence. This will help them to behave similarly when given a task outside of the session.

While working with the family, the BSFT therapist needs to pay attention to the process instead of the content of therapy (Briones et al., 2008). **Content** is the "what" of what is being talked about in session. The **process** is the "how" the talk occurs. For instance, if the family is discussing a fight that they had, what the fight was about would be the content while an understanding of the rules of the fighting (i.e., is the adolescent allowed to defend himself; do the parents support each other during the exchange) would be the process.

When therapists adhere to the BSFT model, families are more likely to engage in and be retained in treatment (Robbins et al., 2011b). Further, family functioning improves as well as a reduction in the adolescent drug use. Brief Strategic Family Therapy lasts for approximately 8 to 24 sessions (Briones et al., 2008). In a 12-month follow-up, those adolescents who went through BSFT had significantly lower levels of arrests, incarceration, and externalizing behaviors (Horigian et al., 2015). However, in these researchers' study, the number of drug-use days was higher than at baseline. This may be due to the frequency of relapse in the adolescent/young adult population as well as these individuals no longer receiving therapy. As of today, BSFT is designed for adolescent rather than adult drug issues. However, it may be effective if the adolescent substance abuser has a parent who moderately abuses drugs. When there is an adult in the family with more severe drug issues, the BSFT therapist can help the adult find an appropriate drug treatment.

Solution-Focused Brief Therapy

As described in the previous chapter, Solution-Focused Brief Therapy (SFBT—not to be confused with BSFT just presented) is an approach that helps clients shift from focusing on the problem times of their lives to those times when the problem was not present or not as severe. This section describes how the solution-focused model has been specifically applied to substance abuse. In this realm it has been effectively utilized in individual, couple, family, and group formats (Pichot, 2001; Smock et al., 2008).

Counter to the disease model of addiction, SFBT views someone dealing with substance abuse as being able to change their lives without the necessity of abstinence. People can alter even the most serious of cases with brief therapeutic interventions (Berg & Miller, 1992). For these authors, brief approaches are extremely important, as their effectiveness enables a multitude of clients who are dealing with addiction to be readily seen, as opposed to a more intensive long-term view of treatment. If both brief and long-term treatments lead to the same outcomes, it would seem the least restrictive treatment would be ideal. Furthermore, SFBT has been shown to be as effective in use with addictions as other evidence-based approaches such as cognitive behavioral therapy and motivation interviewing (Kim, Brook, & Akin, 2018). This supports using a more strength-based approach with clients dealing with addictions, who tend to find others in their social circle taking an oppositional stance toward them. Shaima & Narayanan (2018) supported the importance of having a therapeutic focus on client strengths, which help instill well-being as well as destigmatizing addiction.

Berg and Miller (1992) do not believe in the traditional notion of alcoholism—the progressive, irreversible view of the problem drinker to where the only available option is for them to be abstinent for the rest of their lives. Instead, they believe that there are a multitude of alcoholisms, where a variety of treatment approaches may be useful (or not useful) for that person. Solution-focused therapy is just one of a myriad of approaches that can be applied.

There is also a very different view of the "codependent." Solution-Focused Brief Therapy views people who others would describe as codependent not in a pathological way, but as people who are trying to maintain some type of control and predictability in their lives (Berg & Reuss, 1998). This individual is facing the unpredictability of life with a person dealing with a substance abuse and will try to work extra hard to ensure the other person functions more productively. For instance, in the Rothers family, Hannah may call Mark several times during the day to ensure that he will be home to watch the children and not go to the bar as she needs to attend a work meeting.

The solution-focused approach to addictions starts with the basic premise of exploring mental health rather than mental illness (Berg & Miller, 1992). This is a shift from **pathogenesis** (how diseases develop) to **salutogenesis** (how health develops); a movement from what is going wrong to the resources toward health (Mason, Chandler, & Grasso, 1995). Not much time in session is taken to explore why the problem (the substance abuse) first developed or how it has negatively impacted the person and/or their family. This is considered problem-talk. Perhaps in the first session if the client introduces this information it will be explored, but what is important for the therapist is to focus on the successes of the clients—the non-using times. Thus, client strengths, resiliencies, and resources are explored rather than weaknesses and deficits. This is an important concept since most people, perhaps including the substance user, have been focusing on the unhealthy patterns that exist rather than the healthy patterns, which are present but not highlighted.

One of the key aspects of the SFBT model is the notion of utilization (de Shazer, 1988). The founders of SFBT borrowed this concept from their study of Milton Erickson. One of the hallmarks of Erickson's approach was his **utilization** of whatever the client brought with them to therapy (i.e., their resources). In one of his cases with a retired police officer who was 80 pounds overweight, drank too much, smoked too many cigarettes, had emphysema and high blood pressure, and who had liked to jog but because of his current health could only walk, Erickson gave him the following task (which utilized the client's existing propensity for walking):

> You can do all the smoking you want . . . buy your cigarettes one package at a time by walking to the other side of town to get the package . . . As for your drinking . . . I see no objection to your drinking. There are some excellent bars a mile away. Get your first drink in one bar, your second drink in a bar a mile away. And you'll be in excellent shape before very long. (Gordon & Meyers-Anderson, 1981, p. 112)

In this task Erickson utilized one client strength (walking) to help reduce areas of complaint (smoking and drinking), while also improving desired areas of growth (physical health). Solution-Focused Brief Therapy builds on this process of utilization by exploring client strength areas—things the client has or is doing that is beneficial—to help them move toward their goals. This happens when the therapist understands and can operate within the client's frame of reference (Berg & Miller, 1992).

Solution-Focused Brief Therapy takes a nonnormative view of substance abuse and instead adopts a client-determined perspective (Berg & Miller, 1992). Thus, instead of expecting a substance abuser to exhibit specific characteristics and progression, the therapist attends to how that particular client experiences their own substance abuse and its impact. This shifts the therapist's position from being the expert to a more collaborative position, where the therapist does not teach the client but learns from the client what the substance abuse is like . . . for that particular client.

A premise of the approach is that it operates from the perspective of **parsimony**—trying to operate from the simplest, most efficient, and straightforward way possible. Instead of viewing problems as a signal that there are larger underlying problems, the approach takes the client's statement of complaints at face value and works to, as quickly as possible, address those issues. This is a change from the typical top down view that most people have about addiction—that problem drink/drug use is a sign that there is a progressive and chronic illness or that substance use is a sign of some type of faulty intergenerational patterns. The parsimonious therapist attempts to get the client moving in a positive direction and then lets the client's momentum continue the positive changes; this entails using the simplest and least invasive approach (Miller & Berg, 1995). As such, the therapist does not have to be there from start to finish as the client will be able to maintain and build on the changes they have already made (see Figure 15.6).

In the previous chapter we explained that SFBT proposes that change is constant and inevitable. This notion, in many ways, goes against the philosophy in traditional substance abuse treatment where instead there is a view of constancy and lack of change (Berg & Miller, 1992). These authors explain that in the addictions field, the change that is usually explored is a change for the worse—the person moving toward "rock bottom."

Solution-Focused Brief Therapy is also premised on a present and future orientation rather than an exploration of the past. However, the past is important—as

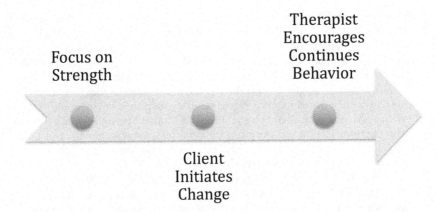

Figure 15.6 Solution-Focused Brief Therapy holds that clients have personal agency to continue to build on previous positive change

it relates to the present. This comes in the exploration of **exceptions** (past events when the problem has not been present). Instead of a traditional view of substance abuse where the future is viewed as an uphill struggle where the person will always be in recovery, SFBT views the future in a hopeful manner where the client will be able to implement whatever past, present, and yet to be uncovered strengths, resources, and solutions to lead a more productive life. One way that this orientation presents itself in therapy is through the therapist's language. Instead of using the word "if," the therapist will use the word "when." This is because "if" provides a possibility that change will not happen whereas "when" presents an expectation that something different will occur. For instance, if a therapist said, "*If* you were not drinking, what would be different" there is an underlying assumption that the person may not stop drinking. However, when the therapist says, "*When* you are not drinking, what will be different in your life" the therapist expects this occurrence to happen, which then will promote this expectation in the client.

Solution-Focused Brief Therapy does not view all clients in the same way. There are three different therapist–client relationships: customer type, complainant type, and visitor type (described in the previous chapter). This view of the relationship between therapist and client differs from the traditional substance abuse model where all addicts are the same (go through the same progression) and thus the therapist treats them all in a similar manner (Berg & Miller, 1992). For traditionally based therapists, those who do not listen to the therapist's directions are considered to be "in denial" or "resistant." However, who is likely more resistant is the therapist, in that they are not understanding where the client is at and adjusting accordingly rather than trying to get the client to adjust to where the therapist wants them to be (de Shazer, 1984).

Therapists, especially addictions counselors, may incorrectly identify the type of client they have. They try to work with a client as if they are a customer instead of recognizing that, at that moment, there is a visitor-type relationship occurring. When there is a visitor-type relationship, the therapist can try to identify the "hidden customer" (Berg & Miller, 1992). This is when a client may not want to address concerns that someone else has for them (i.e., the court or a spouse) but other concerns that are more pertinent for them. For instance, instead of working on the "drinking issues" that their spouse says they have, the person may want to focus on "keeping one's job." This allows therapist and client to work cooperatively rather than in opposition (as the client and the referring body most likely are). As a consequence of focusing on the client's concern the other people's concerns may also dissipate. A correlate of this is the "other" customer—usually the referring person. The therapist can consult with this person/agency to determine what goals they may have for successful outcome. When these are reached, that party is more likely to help reinforce the client's gains.

We can also look at these categories in terms of the stages of readiness for change model (as presented in Chapter 8). Visitors would most likely fall into the precontemplation stage or perhaps the beginning of the contemplation stage. Complainants would likely fall into the contemplation or beginning of the preparation stage. Customers would most likely be in the preparation or action stages (see Figure 15.7).

Most substance abuse therapists spend the beginning portion of treatment engaged in assessment of the client's functioning and severity of addiction. This may come through giving various psychological and behavioral surveys and written assessments, problem checklists, and/or urinalysis. The SFBT therapists also engage in assessment, yet through non-traditional means. Pichot and Smock (2009) explained that substance abuse therapists utilizing SFBT assess through the miracle question, scaling questions, and relational questions. These questions help to assess information about the problem, but also about potential exceptions.

The SFBT model is predicated on a discovery of and expansion of the client's past exceptions—times when the problem could have happened but did not. There are two types of exceptions: deliberate and random (Berg & Miller, 1992). **Deliberate exceptions** are times when the problem did not occur wherein the client actively did something to ensure that it happened and can articulate

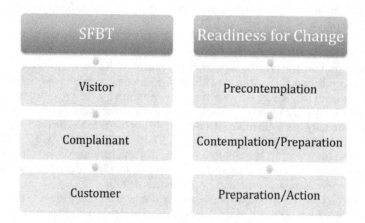

Figure 15.7 Solution-Focused Brief Therapy categorizes the relationship-type of client, which corresponds to the readiness for change model of client motivation

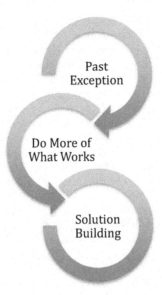

Figure 15.8 Solution building is predicated on getting clients to do more of what works; their past exceptions

this to the therapist. **Random exceptions** are those times when the problem did not occur but the client cannot explain what they did to make it happen. For instance, if Mark Rothers stated, "I knew that if I went to that party that I would be around that wild group and I would end up drinking" would be a deliberate exception, while "I didn't do anything different, but I just came home and never went to the cooler to get a beer" would be a random exception. The goal is to get the client to increase both deliberate and random exceptions, as they are the foundation for solution building (see Figure 15.8).

While exploring for exceptions, there are times when the client may state that there are none. Although the therapist knows that this is not the case, stating this to the client may not connect with where the client is at. Instead, the therapist has several pathways to take. One of these is to get the client to do something different. The therapist might give an observational task of keeping track of what they did when they overcame the urge to drink/drug use (Berg & Miller, 1992).

Another intervention that was developed and applied, particularly to clients dealing with alcohol who cannot uncover past exceptions and are not experiencing hopefulness for change, is **the nightmare question** (Reuss, 1997). This question, in essence, is the flip-side of the coin of the miracle question. It goes something like:

> Suppose tonight when you go home and go to sleep, all of the concerns and problems that brought you here to therapy happen. This would be a nightmare. And since you were sleeping you did not know the nightmare happened during the night. When you woke up, what would be the first thing you would notice that would let you know the nightmare happened?

The nightmare question may best be used after several sessions where the client's miracle and exceptions have been attempted to be explored but without fruition. Once asked, the therapist and client explore the usually negative and painful thoughts and emotions of the client and then develop tasks that would prevent the nightmare from happening (these tasks would be exceptions to the problem). In families, the focus on the problem that comes from exploring the nightmare question helps members stop blaming one another and focus on what they can do together to stop or prevent the nightmare from happening (Berg & Reuss, 1998).

The SFBT therapist provides the client with compliments, highlighting what the client has or is doing that is beneficial. These compliments need to be within the client's frame of reference so that the client is able to accept it as being honest and relatable (Mason et al., 1995). For instance, the therapist might say to the Rothers family, "I am very impressed with the determination that you have as a family to be able to challenge each other."

Most individuals who are dealing with substance abuse relapse at some point in their treatment or post-treatment. Solution-Focused Brief Therapy does not view these incidents as failures but as times when the client can reevaluate what has been useful in the past. Instead of relapses, SFBT therapists call these times **setbacks** (Berg & Miller, 1992). McCollum and Trepper (2001) proposed that when a setback happens, the therapist should assess the setback to determine what specifically happened. Next, in collaboration with the family, they can find partial successes—exceptions in the family, no matter how large or small. The therapist can then help to externalize the problem where there is a focus on the client's personal agency. This would be in the form of asking the client what they specifically did to not let the drinking or drugging take over. After this, the therapist can ask the client what they learned from the relapse so that they can refine their solution attempts and then reinstate them.

Shafer and Jordan (2014) provided five steps to help people who have experienced a relapse (see Figure 15.9). Step one is for the therapist to enter the interaction with the client based on a positive mindset that the client can begin a new future immediately. Step two is a focus on past exceptions; times when the person had stopped drugging or drinking. Step three is based on the notion that clients tend to interact with therapists during times of non-use rather than in the middle of an active relapse. Therapists can then ask about how, since the relapse, the person was able to not use. Step four explores how the current relapse is different than previous relapses. By expecting each relapse to be different, the therapist brings hope into the conversation where the client has more personal agency than they thought previously. Step five in dealing with relapses through an SFBT orientation is talking with the client about what lessons they learned from the relapse situation. Further, the therapist asks about what immediate steps the client will make toward change.

When working with clients who are chronic relapsers, the SFBT therapist will operate from the philosophy of the model but may make some modifications (Berg & Reuss, 1998). These authors "suggest that therapy with the chronic relapser will go better when the therapist spends less time focused on what the client must do differently and more time focused on what she *can* do differently" (p. 94). Further, the therapist may make an active effort to get others involved such as previous professional helpers or significant others.

Figure 15.9 Solution-Focused Brief Therapy therapists use a five-step process when working with clients who have experienced a relapse

Given that many people dealing with substance abuse are mandated into treatment, SFBT therapists approach these clients in a way to enhance effectiveness (Shafer & Jordan, 2014). Based on the notion of "beginning where the client is," the SFBT therapist engages in three steps with mandated substance-abusing clients. First, they assess the person rather than the problem. This entails listening to the client's perspective on how they came to treatment, how they came to their current life situation, and what they value, believe, and want in their life. Second, the therapist takes a not-knowing stance. Anderson and Goolishian (1992) introduced the notion of a therapist's not-knowing posture, where the therapist cannot know another's meanings. As such, the therapist, rather than taking an expert position, helps the client bring forth their own meanings and values. This puts the client in the expert position on themselves—their values, beliefs, understandings, and meanings. Third, the therapist attempts to find ways to cooperate with the client. Shafer and Jordan explained, "The most important contribution a practitioner can make during the initial contact is to shape clients' experience in a way that is different from the negative professional experiences they may have encountered in the past" (p. 212). This entails the ability to view the world from the client's perspective while also holding one's theoretical lens.

Solution-Focused Brief Therapy has been found to be quite effective in working with people dealing with substance abuse. In a group therapy format, level 1 substance abusers who had solution-focused therapy instead of a traditional problem-focused treatment had significantly improved scores on the Beck Depression Inventory and the Outcome Questionnaire (Smock et al., 2008). While clients who received the traditional treatment approach did improve, it was not significant. Solution-Focused Brief Therapy has also been used with alcohol-dependent single mothers and their children with good success (Juhnke &

Coker, 1997). Use of SFBT led to increased parenting confidence, increased parenting satisfaction, and an increase in alcohol abstinence. Solution-Focused Brief Therapy can be used on its own as well as in conjunction with more traditional aspects of substance abuse counseling (Linton, 2005). For instance, Foy (2017) integrates solution-focused therapy and harm reduction since they are both strengths-based, humanistic, empowering of the client, and view the client as expert.

In Bruges, Belgium, Isebaert developed the Bruges Model, which specifically applies SFBT to problem drinking (de Shazer & Isebaert, 2004; Isebaert, 2017). This model holds that substance use is based on choice, where clients learn to make conscious choices between their different habits (various actions, including the use or the non-use of substances). This program, which is both inpatient and outpatient, has shown at four-year follow-up to be quite effective in helping clients reach their goals as 81% of outpatient clients and 84% of inpatient clients maintained their goals of controlled drinking or abstinence (de Shazer & Isebaert, 2004).

Behavioral Couples Therapy

Behavioral Couples Therapy (BCT) is an evidence-based model that has shown to be effective for couples and families where at least one adult is dealing with substance abuse (O'Farrell & Fals-Stewart, 2006). Behavioral Couples Therapy is designed to "build support for abstinence and to improve relationship functioning among married or cohabiting individuals seeking help for alcoholism or drug abuse" (O'Farrell & Fals-Stewart, 2008, p. 196). These two areas of interventions—reduction of substance use and increase in positive couple relationship—are significant since there seems to be a reciprocal causality between relationship distress and substance use where relationship distress is associated with increased substance use and substance use is associated with increased relational distress (see Figure 15.10). Fals-Stewart, O'Farrell, and Birchler (2004) recommended that, for treatment, couples either be married or

Increased Substance Use/Abuse

Increased Couple Distress

Figure 15.10 Behavioral Couples Therapy is premised upon the notion that there is a reciprocal causality between substance use and abuse and couple discord

cohabitating for at least one year. For those partners who are separated, they believed the couple should be in the process of reconciliation.

While not designed to be a 12-step program, BCT aligns very well with 12-step concepts (O'Farrell & Fals-Stewart, 2006). They both have abstinence as a goal and several of the BCT interventions, such as the Recovery Contract, includes 12-step participation. Since most 12-step programs focus on individual programs, the addition of BCT adds an additional element in people's recovery programs. O'Farrell and Fals-Stewart explained, "Patients who have a strong commitment to a 12-step self-help program and make this part of their BCT Recovery Contract may not need individual counseling" (p. 24).

Behavioral Couples Therapy has three primary objectives: abstinence of drug abuse or drinking; increase of the family's support of the substance abuser; and change couple/family interactions for a positive foundation that leads to continued abstinence (O'Farrell & Fals-Stewart, 2006). There are two main intervention pathways to achieve these objectives. First, the therapist begins focusing on substance-focused interventions (O'Farrell & Fals-Stewart, 2008). These interventions occur throughout the whole of therapy to help promote the substance-abusing partner to engage in abstinence. Second, after several weeks where there has been attendance at the therapy sessions along with abstinence, the therapist introduces relationship-focused interventions. These are designed to enhance the partner relationship including better communication and more positive connections between the two. Behavioral Couples Therapy usually lasts for 12–20 sessions over 5 to 6 months (Fals-Stewart et al., 2004; O'Farrell & Fals-Stewart, 2006). Sessions tend to be structured, with the therapist setting the agenda.

One of the primary BCT substance-focused interventions is a daily **recovery contract** (O'Farrell & Fals-Stewart, 2006, 2008). In the spirit of the "one day at a time" ethos, the daily recovery contract specifies the substance abuser's intent to not use that day as well as the partner's intent of support. This is called the **trust discussion**. The contract helps keep both partners focused on the immediate present rather than the disappointment of past use or the fear of future use. The BCT therapist usually gives the couple a calendar where they record the performance of the daily contract. Other aspects of the contract might include attendance at 12-step or self-help meetings, prescribed medication for recovery, as well as drug testing. The couple brings in the calendar to BCT sessions to demonstrate the continued progress in reaching their goals of abstinence and better couple relationship (see Figure 15.11).

During BCT sessions, the therapist will discuss with the substance abuser about thoughts, temptations, cravings, and urges to drink or use drugs (O'Farrell & Fals-Stewart, 2006, 2008). This brings forth potential triggers for use as well as positive coping strategies the individual utilized to not use during the week. Like all approaches in working with substance abuse, slips and relapses do happen. When they do, the therapist works quickly to prevent an extended use of the substance. This might be by contracting with the couple to enter a detoxification unit or engage in alternative solution attempts. The beginning of BCT primarily focuses on abstinence, highlighting triggers and stressors that lead to use and ways to prevent and decrease these potentiates of substance use.

The relationship-focused interventions usually begin once the recovery contract has been in place and working, the abuser has been abstinent, and the

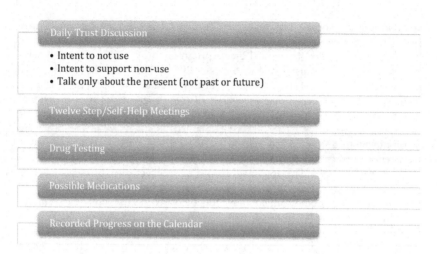

Daily Trust Discussion

- Intent to not use
- Intent to support non-use
- Talk only about the present (not past or future)

Twelve Step/Self-Help Meetings

Drug Testing

Possible Medications

Recorded Progress on the Calendar

Figure 15.11 The components of the BCT recovery contract

couple has been regularly attending sessions (O'Farrell & Fals-Stewart, 2008). Because these couples have usually been dealing with substance abuse for a long time, much disappointment, resentment, and fear of future use is present. This leads to the couple (and family) experiencing a lot of tension. Behavioral Couples Therapy attempts to build goodwill, positive feelings, and a renewed commitment to the relationship (O'Farrell & Fals-Stewart, 2006). Therapy sessions thus focus on how to introduce more positive activities between the couple.

Behavioral Couples Therapy relationship-focused interventions tend to follow four steps (O'Farrell & Fals-Stewart, 2008). These include the therapist instructing and modeling behaviors, the couple practicing these behaviors in front of the therapist, the presentation of homework, and the review of homework that also includes continued practice. Some specific homework activities might include catching the partner doing something nice, planning shared rewarding activities, or having a caring day assignment (where the spouse acts first to show caring to the partner). Behavioral Couples Therapy therapists also teach communication skills to the partners (see Figure 15.12). These include listening skills, expressing feelings directly, communication sessions, negotiating for requests, conflict resolution, and problem solving (O'Farrell & Fals-Stewart 2006, 2008).

Once the BCT therapist has engaged in the appropriate steps and actions for substance and relationship interventions, the final task is continuing recovery. This ending stage of therapy involves five aspects (O'Farrell & Fals-Stewart, 2006): continuing recovery plan, action plan to prevent relapse, check-up visits, relapse prevention sessions, and a focus on couple/family issues to assist in long-term recovery. O'Farrell & Fals-Stewart (2008) suggested that follow-up sessions last for three to five years following stable recovery with an increase in length between these sessions.

While BCT can be a very effective form of therapy for the substance abuser and his or her partner, there are contraindications for its use (O'Farrell & Fals-Stewart,

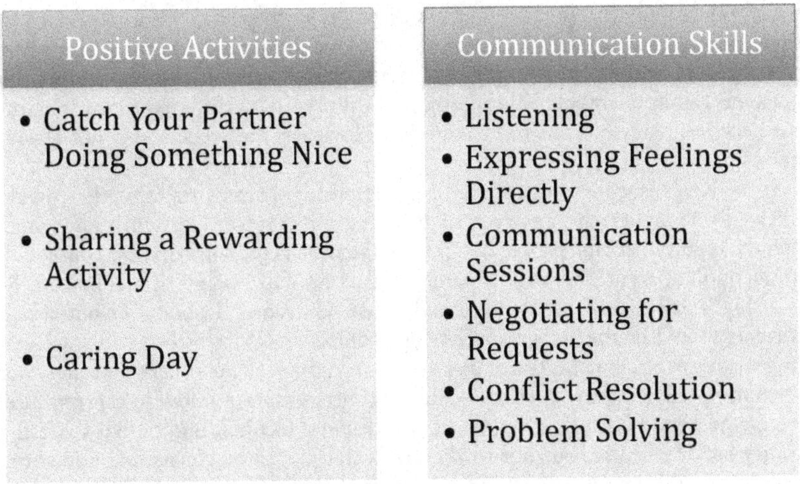

Positive Activities	Communication Skills
• Catch Your Partner Doing Something Nice • Sharing a Rewarding Activity • Caring Day	• Listening • Expressing Feelings Directly • Communication Sessions • Negotiating for Requests • Conflict Resolution • Problem Solving

Figure 15.12 Behavioral Couples Therapy interventions focus on increasing positive activities and communication skills for the couple

2006, 2008). Behavioral Couples Therapy should not be introduced if there is a restraining order of no contact. Once the restraining order is lifted, BCT then becomes a possibility. Further, BCT is not advised for couples when there is severe domestic violence. O'Farrell and Fals-Stewart (2008) described that while many couples dealing with substance abuse have experienced domestic violence, only about 2% of couples have been excluded from BCT because of severe domestic violence (where there were injuries that needed medical attention). Lastly, BCT may not be appropriate if both partners are dealing with substance abuse (Fals-Stewart et al., 2004; O'Farrell & Fals-Stewart, 2006, 2008). However, there is the possibility, with proper client motivation, to work with the couple even if they are both dealing with alcoholism (O'Farrell, & Fals-Stewart, 2006).

Behavioral Couples Therapy is primarily utilized with the substance abuser and his or her partner; whether married or cohabitating. However, it can be used with family members other than the partner, such as parents and/or siblings (Fals-Stewart & O'Farrell, 2003). The research surrounding BCT has shown positive impact of the model (Fals-Stewart, O'Farrell, & Birchler, 2001; McCrady et al., 2009). These benefits include a reduction in substance use, an improvement of the couple's relationship, and a decrease in intimate partner violence (Fals-Stewart et al., 2004).

Case Application

There are various family therapy programs specific to substance abuse that could be quite useful for the Rothers family. If they chose to utilize one, it would be important for the therapist to develop family-based interventions that are likely to help the family through this current difficulty in their life. The goals of any of these programs will be to decrease the use of alcohol and drugs for all members of the family, stabilize the family organization, and increase positive interactions between family members. Each program will do so in different ways, but the Rothers will likely become more cohesive. However, the process may not always be easy.

If the Rothers were to engage in Multidimensional family therapy, they would likely do so under the auspices of working with Steve. Currently his school behaviors have become problematic. Given that he is growing up in a house with an alcoholic parent and with a parental generational history of alcoholism, he is at higher risk for substance use and abuse. Currently, in-home or outpatient formats would be the least restrictive environment, as Steve's behaviors are getting more severe, but he is not at risk for harming self or others and does not seem to be addicted to drugs or alcohol. While we do not know his current use, we might hypothesize that he has tried drugs and alcohol, and perhaps is using somewhat frequently, but not to the levels that could be considered addiction. Stage 1 would include individual and joint sessions so the therapist could join with everyone and assess the various subsystems and how they interact with one another. Stage 2 would target change in multiple subsystems. Not only would Steve's substance use behavior be targeted, but also his delinquent behavior. Further, therapy would likely also focus on reducing Mark's substance use. Areas such as increasing parenting skills and improving mental health would also be a focus of this stage. Stage 3 would be geared around helping the family to ensure that new interactional processes become more ingrained patterns.

Similar to MDFT, the Brief Strategic family therapist will likely come in contact with the Rothers family because of problems being displayed by Steve, such as drug use and disruptive school behaviors. Therapy will focus not on Steve, but on the family's relational patterns, which maintain Steve's problem behaviors. Thus, the rules of the family, such as the emotional distance between Mark and Hannah as well as the children dealing primarily with Hannah rather than Mark, will be targets for intervention. During assessment, the BSFT therapist is likely to see a family in the early stages of a family with an adolescent child where the oldest child is the identified patient. However, the therapist will likely also see a detouring triangulation where Hannah and Mark tend not to have overt conflict with one another and instead focus their energies on the IP, Steve. The therapist might reframe the family's difficulties from "Steve is a problem" to "The family is keeping Steve young." The therapist might then block the coalition of Hannah and the children against Mark and try to strengthen the marital subsystem.

A Solution-Focused Brief therapist would work with whomever the Rothers family chose to attend the session, as the more people that attended, the more possible customers for change. The view of the members of the family would be different as Mark would not be seen as just "an alcoholic" similar to all other alcoholics. Rather, the therapist would attempt to understand the unique way in which he and the other family members engage each other and their context. Similarly, Hannah would not be seen as being codependent but rather that she is trying to do her best in the current situation. Therapy will be focused on exceptions, times when the members were living lives without the problem or with the problem reduced to a point where it was not problematic. For the Rothers, this might be when Mark and Hannah are loving toward one another, where Steve and his parents are getting along, and where the family has Sunday Fun Day together. Focus on these times helps to bring forth patterns of behavior that are desired and that when in place lead to the reduction or cessation of the problematic behaviors.

A Behavioral Couples therapist would likely only see Mark and Hannah, as change in the couple will likely lead to change in other family relationships. One of the goals of BCT would be for Mark to become abstinent from alcohol, marijuana, and other drugs. A second goal would be to increase Mark and Hannah's marital relationship. Behavioral Couples therapy would start by helping Mark become abstinent and then would expand to address the couple's relationship. Toward the beginning of therapy, the therapist would help them develop a recovery contract. The trust discussion would cover Mark's intent to not drink and Hannah's intent to support him in this. This contract would focus on the short-term goals of that day rather than long-term goals. The recovery contract might also include Mark's attendance at AA and Hannah's attendance at Al-Anon. Therapy would focus on increasing Mark and Hannah's communication skills so that they can engage in more positive activities with one another, such as a date night or even just noticing when the other showed a positive sentiment such as bringing home the other's favorite meal from their favorite restaurant.

Summary

Any model of family therapy can be used effectively in working with individuals and families dealing with issues of substance abuse. This chapter presented how four models, Multidimensional Family Therapy, Brief Strategic Family Therapy, Solution-Focused Brief Therapy, and Behavioral Couples Therapy, each understand the process of addiction and what a therapist from that model might do with a family. You are encouraged to take any of the other models of family therapy presented in this book (and those that were not presented) and apply them to addictions. There may be modifications to the techniques and process of the model that may occur, but each, in their own way, can help facilitate change for family members.

Key Words

Multidimensional Family
    Therapy (MDFT)
Brief Strategic Family Therapy
    (BSFT)
triggers
joining operations

tracking and diagnostic
    enactment
family organization
resonance
developmental stages
life context

(continued)

(continued)

identified patient
reframing interventions
restructuring
Three Ps: Practical, Problem-
    Focused, and Planned
engagement
content
process
pathogenesis
salutogenesis

utilization
parsimony
hidden customer
other customer
deliberate exceptions
random exceptions
nightmare questions
setbacks
recovery contract
trust discussion

Discussion Questions

1. Explain how Multidimensional Family Therapy works.
2. What is the process of Brief Strategic Family Therapy?
3. How does Brief Strategic Family Therapy integrate aspects of Strategic and Family Therapy?
4. Discuss how Solution-Focused Brief Therapy's philosophy goes counter to that espoused by the 12-steps.
5. What are the benefits of viewing problem drinking through a behavioral lens? How does Behavioral Couples Therapy help both the substance-abusing and non-abusing partners?

SIXTEEN

Family Recovery

Throughout this book we have seen how what may seem to be one person's problem, in this instance addiction, may actually be viewed as a more systemic process. In Chapter 4 we presented the notion that not only is the addicted individual impacted by the drug use, but the family as a whole can go through a *process of addiction*. In this chapter we discuss how the family goes through the *process of recovery*. Focusing more on the process toward health rather than the process of dysfunction is important since the addictions field has made a major shift from a pathology-oriented perspective to a recovery-oriented perspective (White & Cloud, 2008).

As the substance abuser either reduces or eliminates the drug/alcohol from his or her life, interpersonal relationships change and the family system needs to adjust. Even when the substance abuser becomes sober, family members may have a difficult time adjusting to the change. Some of the relational land mines that family members of the newly sober might experience include monitoring, resentments, and jealousy (Nowinski, 1999) (see Figure 16.1). In **monitoring**, family members have spent a lot of time keeping track of how much the person has been drinking or using drugs. However, how the monitoring comes across tends to be experienced as nagging. Family members also experience **resentments**, both to the drug or alcohol as well as to the person using them. These resentments are associated with feelings of guilt and shame. Lastly, many family members experience feelings of **jealousy** as they had previously lost their loved ones to drugs or alcohol and now that person is spending much of their time and energy in 12-step fellowships. These are some of the possibilities that therapists should keep in mind when helping families who are in recovery.

Recovery here is being used to refer to the process of change when drugs/alcohol are involved so that the drug use is not the organizing principle of the family. This may be through one or more members maintaining **abstinence**—a complete cessation of substance use—or **moderation management**—the use of the substance but at levels that are not problematic. Whichever path is taken, recovery for the family includes a reorganization so that family rules and processes help people engage each other in more honest and open interactions.

This notion of reorganization is an important concept as the family has most likely viewed the cessation of the drug use as the time when everything in the family will go well. However, this is usually not the case. Lewis and Allen-Byrd (2007)

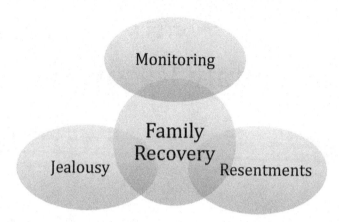

Figure 16.1 The process of family recovery has associated interpersonal difficulties while the family is also improving

explained that "abstinence marks the beginning of a journey that is profoundly difficult for all family members. Without guidance, support, and knowledge of the recovery process, most people will relapse" (p. 106). Therapists can help families by discussing how the family will continue to find new and different challenges even after substances are no longer a daily part of their lives. For any problem that a client initially comes into therapy with, a goal of therapy *should not* be no further problems. Life brings with it difficulties, challenges, and pain. It also brings successes, strengths, and happiness. The family will continue to experience all of these throughout the life span. By developing a new way of being with one another, the family may be able to more easily handle the adversity—as well as the prosperity—that normally happens in life. Yet, one of the key factors to successful recovery is that of hope (Bradshaw et al., 2015). Higher levels of family hope pretreatment is related to later coping skills. This suggests that therapists, from the beginning of treatment, should consider various ways of increasing clients' sense of hope, perhaps through psychoeducation, empirically validated treatment approaches, and positive therapeutic support.

In general, family recovery from substance abuse can be viewed in three stages: attainment of sobriety, adjustment to sobriety, and long-term maintenance of sobriety (Shelton, 2017) (see Figure 16.2). In the attainment of sobriety stage, the substance abuser is likely still using, but there are usually periods of abstinence. The family system at this point is still unbalanced. Therapeutic goals at this stage are to motivate the user to get treatment as well as provide support for family members. During the adjustment to sobriety stage, there has been a sustained period of abstinence from the drug or alcohol. The family system recalibrates itself to develop stronger rules and roles while also being cautious about potential setbacks. During the long-term maintenance of sobriety stage, there has been complete abstinence and the family dynamics have changed to provide more functional ways of being and feeling for family members. Treatment focuses on relapse prevention and further support of positive family interactions.

Figure 16.2 Family recovery can be viewed as three progressive stages

There are various conceptualizations of family recovery. For instance, 12-step programs view family recovery in terms of at least one member of the family beginning the recovery process.

> Specifically, that means taking the first step, which is to acknowledge that one is powerless over another person's addiction (and consequently, not responsible for it) and begins to move from an enabling relationship with the addict toward a relationship characterized by caring detachment. (Nowinski, 1999, p. 10)

Other conceptualizations view family recovery in alternative ways, which we present here in this chapter.

Developmental Model of Family Recovery

Since families are systems, changes in one member impact the other members. As one person become physically and psychologically addicted, their behavior changes and subsequently so does the behavior of the various family members. Concomitantly, as the person decreases their physical and psychological dependence on the substance, their behavior continues to be impacted by and impacts the other family members. If we punctuate this arc in the family's life—from the beginning of the use of the substance to the reduction of the use of the substance and how members operate to create, maintain, and then change their functioning—we can view it as a **developmental model of recovery**. Brown and Lewis (1999) and Schmid and Brown (2008) presented a four-stage developmental model of recovery for those families dealing with alcoholism, which parallels the stages of recovery for individuals. This model can be expanded to fit families in recovery of other types of drugs/addictions.

At each stage there are three domains of experience: the environment, the system, and the individuals within (Brown & Lewis, 1999; Schmid & Brown, 2008). The environment is the daily experiences of family life. It includes the who, what, where, when, and how of family functioning. The system refers to the structure and process of the family. The individual domain focuses on an individual's physiological, behavioral, emotional, cognitive, and intellectual development as well as that person's various attachments, especially to primary caretakers. Figure 16.3

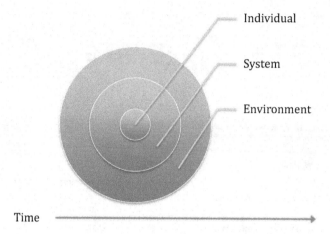

Figure 16.3 Each stage of family recovery involves the individual, system, and environment, and how these change over time

presents a visual of the three interlocking domains of experience for each stage of family recovery.

The first stage of the developmental model is the **Drinking stage.** In this stage there are a lot of double messages family members are telling themselves, telling others, and are experiencing themselves. These include the notions of pretending that there is nothing wrong in the family while also knowing that there is a lot going wrong in the family. Brown and Lewis (1999) described the defensive family focus at this stage:

- To maintain denial of any problem with alcohol.
- To maintain a core belief that there is no alcoholism and no loss of control over drinking.
- To invent explanations for the alcoholic reality.
- To cover up and maintain the family secret. (p. 103)

Family members alter their normal routines, which begin to center around drinking or around trying to show themselves and the world that whatever drinking is occurring is not affecting them. This is the starting point in the arc of family functioning where the tension is beginning to rise, but is most likely not being commented on.

When a family comes to therapy while in the Drinking stage, one of the main keys is for the therapist to develop a strong therapeutic relationship with the various family members. It is from this relationship that the therapist can help members to challenge their denial. This happens when they accept that alcoholism is, at the present moment, a core part of their lives; a part that is harming each individual and the family as a unit. The therapist will also pay attention to and bring forth family members' beliefs about drinking. These are usually based within a framework of denial. As we have seen, these distorted beliefs help to maintain the family's functioning around the addiction. The therapist helps members to see that their beliefs are part of the life-blood of the addiction.

The environment domain is unsafe, and there may be tension, anxiety, and emotional pain (Schmid & Brown, 2008). The system of the family is centered around drinking, yet trying to protect members from the negative effects of the drinking. There tends to be rigid rules and roles where there are impermeable boundaries between the family system and outside systems. Individually, each person in the family finds him or herself conforming to the needs of the drinker. Individual needs tend to be suppressed.

The second stage of family recovery is **Transition**. Based on the previous stage, family members are beginning to recognize how the way they have come to view everyone's role in the family has been problematic. Issues of control have come to the surface, and people realize that they are not able to control one another. Brown and Lewis (1999) operate from an abstinence model, explaining that in the Transition stage one or more family members will begin to become abstinent. However, effective moderation may also be a sign of the family being in the Transition stage.

In the Transition stage family members have a high motivation to push their newfound beliefs that patterns in the family need to change. Brown and Lewis (1999) explained that the family's focus when moving toward abstinence is "to focus intensely on staying dry; to stabilize the out-of-control environment; to allow the system to collapse and remain collapsed; to focus on the individuals" (p. 107). While it may seem non-systemic to focus on the individual, we know that there is a mutuality and complementarity between people. Thus, one person's self-focus will have consequences on others, whether intended or not.

The environment domain is increasingly unsafe as the negative effects of the drinking increase along with the severity of the drinking (Schmid & Brown, 2008). Pressure in the family increases where there is likely more conflict and anxiety. The system of the family is similar to how it was in the Drinking stage, yet it becomes a bit more open to outside influences such as the legal and/or therapeutic systems. Individually, each person in the family finds themselves starting to think about their own role in the substance use.

The family therapist working with the family in the Transition stage will continue to focus on making sure that various members are not in denial. At this point, one or more family members has already taken that step to move toward acceptance of the family's reality, pushing themselves to realize how alcohol has been negatively impacting the family. This helps the other members to move past the dictum of having to keep quiet and pretend that the family is doing well.

Families in the Transition stage begin to accept that the family has been out of control; usually for a longer period of time than they realized. Each time this is discussed or a different member of the family moves past his or her own denial, the core beliefs in the family get challenged and become open for possible change. The family has "hit bottom" and each member shifts from focusing on the family to seeing how the individual can recover.

Family members will most likely begin to utilize some type of outside source for support in the recovery. This might be AA, Al-Anon, or another self-help group (see Chapter 10). This reconnection to self helps the individuals to update their thinking about self; perhaps exploring their own childhood issues, the way in which they currently view their own actions, as well as their hopes and dreams for the future and whether they are on a path to make them happen. In the present, for the adults, there is a reconnection to more positive parenting.

The third stage of family recovery is **Early Recovery**. If we explore our arc of family recovery, we have passed the zenith and are moving on the downward half of the arc. Here, people who were using are now abstinent, or perhaps have learned how to engage in moderation management. The shift in core beliefs that started in previous stages is now prominent and active. Members continue to have a focus on self-recovery, and this is hampered or helped when other members are either not on the same path or are also active in the recovery process.

The environment domain during Early Recovery is usually less conflictual as family members are not spending as much time together as they had previously (Schmid & Brown, 2008). One of the primary emotional impacts is that of fear; fear of isolation, intimacy, emotions, relapse, and the future. For the family system, life still revolves around alcohol, but, rather than around its use, life centers around not drinking. The family is starting to find new rules of interaction. Individually, each person in the family finds themselves primarily in their own recovery.

Families in Early Recovery have several tasks:

- to continue to learn abstinent behaviors and thinking;
- to stabilize individual identities—I am an alcoholic, or I am a co-alcoholic, and I have lost control;
- to continue close contact with 12-step programs and begin working the steps;
- to maintain a focus on individual recovery, seeking supports outside the family;
- to continue detachment and a family focus guided by individual needs;
- To reestablish and maintain attention to children; to maintain parenting responsibilities. (Brown & Lewis, 1999, pp. 111–112)

Here, members may vary in how they engage in growth. While some may find connection in a 12-step group, others may find sports, hobbies, or other means to gain positive connections inside and outside of the house.

While drinking/drug use may go away, this does not mean that everything is fine in the family. In Early Recovery, families tend to not have the coping skills necessary for positive functioning (Higgins, 1998). Thus, abstinence (or moderation) is only one of the goals of family recovery. Other goals include a reconnection to one another—shifting relationships from being problematic to healing.

The final stage of the developmental model of family recovery is **Ongoing Recovery**. This is the culmination of the focus on each individual's recovery and how the family as a whole can reconnect with new patterns of interaction that support one another in more congruent means of engagement. Family members will either be abstinent or have developed a very effective way of managing the moderation of their use of substances. At this point, members are addressing how living in a chaotic alcoholic family has impacted them; yet, they are able to develop newer identities so that they can attain growth. Figure 16.4 represents a visual model of how these stages of family recovery overlap.

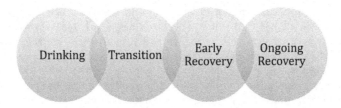

Figure 16.4 A developmental model of family recovery, developed by Brown and Lewis

The environment domain is now based upon peace and order (Schmid & Brown, 2008). Pressure in the family increases where there is likely more conflict and anxiety. The system of the family has likely developed a new family myth, one that involves drinking and recovery. Previously rigid roles and rules are now clear and the family experiences greater openness between itself and outside systems. Individually, each person in the family is able to grow psychologically, emotionally, and interpersonally.

These stages have been supported by qualitative but not quantitative data (Rouhbakhsh, Lewis, & Allen-Byrd, 2004). In these authors' study their quantitative data (MMPI-2, FACES-II, FAM-III, and FILE-C) stayed the same throughout the stages of recovery, thus not showing the breakdown of denial, growth, and learning on the part of family members. However, qualitative data (based on in-depth semi-structured interviews) did demonstrate that the chaos and crisis that families experienced in the early stages of recovery dissipated throughout the recovery process.

There are also differences in how men and women experience the recovery process (Petroni, Allen-Byrd, & Lewis, 2003). Males and females, as well as alcoholics and co-alcoholics, have very different processes in recovery. Male alcoholics tend to have more deviant beliefs than female alcoholics, which may come in the form of various levels of paranoid ideation. This coincides with males' general tendency to **externalize** (blame others) while females tend to **internalize** (blame themselves). Males may also have issues in recovery since they tend to be more self-reliant, which goes against many of the recovery principles espoused by organizations such as AA (such as admitting powerlessness). Recovery may be easier for females as they are more used to open expression of feelings.

One of the most interesting findings of Petroni et al.'s (2003) study were the similarities between alcoholics and co-alcoholics. In males, these two groups only differed in the beginning of the recovery process (0–5 years) on Situational Stress Due to Alcoholism and Mental Confusion. For females in the beginning of recovery, alcoholics had higher scores than non-alcoholics in Anxiety and Tension and Somatic Symptoms. These results help support the notion that addiction impacts more than just the addict and that recovery is a family affair. As recovery continues, the differences seen in the beginning tend to grow smaller.

While the previous developmental model has been useful to view family recovery, it is not the only model. Curtis (1999) provided a six-stage developmental model of family recovery. The pretreatment stage is the beginning of the recovery process when something was significant enough in the family system to lead them into therapy. Next is the stabilization stage where family members take accountability on their own individual roles in the family's functioning and not just focus on the addicted individual. The third stage is early recovery where family members begin to deal with their own issues. Here, they take responsibility for their own actions. In the middle recovery stage, the family begins to readjust family rules while also improving individual self-esteem. The late recovery stage usually encompasses a focus on the resolution of intergenerational patterns that have been problematic. The last stage is maintenance/remission where members continue individual growth as well as not getting caught up in the dysfunctional morass that was there at the beginning of treatment.

Family Recovery Typology

Lewis and Allen-Byrd (2001), based on the framework developed by Brown and Lewis, developed the **Family Recovery Typology Model**, which classifies alcoholic families in recovery into three types. Based on the type of family the therapist is dealing with there are various treatment implications.

Type I families are when both spouses are in recovery. They have both hit bottom and the family system has collapsed. This means that their old pattern, roles, and rules of the system are no longer functional. Both partners have acknowledged that their own drinking contributed to their own and the family's problems. Each person is actively in recovery—perhaps by going to therapy, self-help meetings, or other such activities. Lewis and Allen-Byrd (2001) described the characteristics of Type I families:

> (1) a shift in the balance of power resulting in equality between partners; (2) recovery as the central element of the functioning of the spouses as a system and as individuals; (3) the ability to be open, honest, and direct in the relationship; and (4) a spiritual dimension within the couple's interactions (e.g., they universally feel closer, there is a deeper bond, and there is a "specialness" to their togetherness). (p. 9)

In Type I families, individuals are working on self while reconnecting with others to develop new patterns for a functional family. Family members in this type of family are the most open for intervention and change. They realize that they were part of the problem sequence and are part of the solution. As a unit, Type I families are most likely in the action stage of readiness for change.

Type II families occur when only one spouse is in recovery. This is usually the alcoholic, who finds themselves attempting to change yet being the focal point of other family members who do not trust that the changes they make will be substantive and lasting. Thus, tension in these families occurs between the family system and the individual who is in recovery. Type II families tend to include:

> (1) an imbalance in the power structure such that there is inequality between partners; (2) recovery that pertains only to the alcoholic, thus there is a single IP; (3) denial at the marital/

familial level; (4) tenuous stability at the systems level; and (5) the alcoholic having two identities—recovering alcoholic and practicing (non-recovery) co-alcoholic. (Lewis & Allen-Byrd, 2001, p. 10)

Type II families require an individual and systems approach. For the individual, exploration of what the recovering addict can do to stay in the action or maintenance stages of change is important. For the family, the therapist might explore how the family can change to not only help the substance abuser but to change their own dynamics as well.

Type III families are those in which the substance abuser is now abstinent but does not have a recovery program. In these families, it may seem on the surface that positive changes have been made in the system since the alcoholic is no longer drinking; however, the processes below the surface are still maintained. Here, spouses are still in the Transition stage of recovery, where their thought processes, feelings, and behaviors are the same as they were during the time of drinking. Instead of alcohol being used, the person may transfer their focus and dependence on their spouse (or perhaps a child). Since it seems that the problems have been overcome, Type III families tend not to come to therapy unless they are forced (based on court order or perhaps some issue with a child). Lewis and Allen-Byrd (2001) explained the common characteristics of this type of family:

> (1) an imbalance in the power structure; (2) abstinence only with no developmental recovery process; (3) an attachment with shifts from alcohol to a specific person (typically the spouse); (4) a rigid and closed systems structure with tenuous stability; and (5) split subsystems (lack of integration)—couple and mother–children. (p. 11)

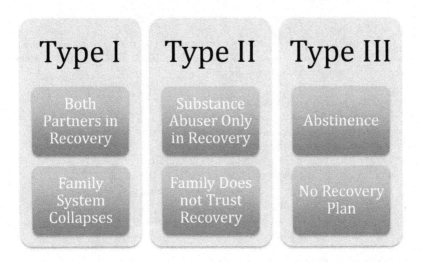

Figure 16.5 Family recovery can be viewed based on a typology of families

Type III families tend to view change as a threat to the person's sobriety. Since the person is no longer drinking, family members do not want to rock the boat, so they maintain the status quo. As a unit, these families may be considered in the contemplation or perhaps preparation stage of readiness. What might be useful for these families is an educational approach where the family recovery process is explored and members may become more open to the possibility that change at this point can be useful and preventative of a breakdown in the system later in the family's life. Figure 16.5 presents a summary of the three types of families in recovery.

Wet and Dry Family Systems

In determining where a family is in recovery and possible courses of action, the therapist needs to understand what role alcohol presently has in the family. Kaufman (1985) distinguished between "wet" and "dry" family systems. **The wet family system** is one in which active alcohol use is present. This use is still being problematic. **A dry family system** occurs when family members either do not drink or do not drink problematically. A family in which the person using alcohol has reduced their use and is currently engaging in moderation management would be considered a dry rather than wet system.

For therapists who come in contact with a wet family system, one of the first goals is to interrupt the problem drinking (Kaufman, 1985). This may come in the form of a discussion with the person using, the family engaging in a form of intervention, or even possible outpatient or inpatient services for the individual. However, not all people using substances will try to reduce their use before the start of family therapy. In this case the therapist can choose to either work with the whole wet family system or see certain subsystems that are more functional. For instance, if Mark Rothers is refusing to reduce his drinking and not wanting to enter therapy, the therapist might work with Hannah and one or more children.

The family therapist will change interventions based on the family moving from a "wet" to a "dry" system (Myers & Salt, 2013). This includes learning sober family living skills. These skills include:

- building healthy communication
- developing sober relationships
- staying in the here and now
- learning appropriate parenting skills
- having the children learn or relearn to be children
- adapting to a personality change of the recovering member
- adapting to a personality change of the recovering codependents
- adapting to a new family structure
- adapting to new activities and relationships of family members
- learning to express anger and sexuality in healthy ways
- letting go
- dealing with the emergence of masked problems
- continuing involvement in new support systems

- stopping "walking on eggs" with the recovering member
- building trust
- abandoning unrealistic expectations. (pp. 192–195)

During recovery, there are many transitions that occur individually and as a family for each member of the family. As one member grows and changes, the family system grows and changes, leading to further aspects of difference and change emanating throughout the whole of the family system.

One of the primary factors leading to successful recovery for families dealing with alcohol is that of resilience. This is because there is a connection between how families access their resilience over their lifespan and the attachment and connectedness to the family (Garrett & Landau, 2007). **Resilience** can be defined as the organism/system to be able to recover from a difficult situation. For a more thorough discussion of resilience, see Chapter 7.

Relapse

When things begin to go well for the family, the therapist might consider introducing the notion that there is a possibility of a relapse. As defined in Chapter 1, a **relapse** is a return to use once an improvement has been made. The relapse might have the person (a) return to their previous use level; (b) use at an increased level; or (c) use but at a reduced level. **Family relapse** might also have family members returning to previous roles and interactional patterns that helped to maintain the substance use. Families play a significant role in whether a relapse occurs as well as the severity of the relapse. For instance, during the early stages of recovery, people are more likely to relapse if they encounter stressful circumstances (Breese et al., 2005). This includes the chaos and stress that might occur in a family exhibiting conflict.

It may seem counterproductive for the therapist to introduce the possibility of a relapse since this is an action the therapist and family are working against. A potential concern is that this could justify the user to use again. However, given that relapses have been such a prevalent part of the process of overcoming an addiction, it would be problematic for the therapist not to. While about 40–60% of people treated for alcohol, opioid, or cocaine abuse remain abstinent for at least one year following discharge, 15–30% may use the substance some, but not to levels that would be considered dependent (McLellan, Lewis, O'Brien, & Kleber, 2000). The remaining individuals may either use at previous levels or possibly even increase their usage. By understanding that relapse may be a normal part of the recovery process (although it does not have to be present), families can maintain higher levels of resilience by not thinking that all of their hard work has gone for naught.

If a relapse occurs, therapists can focus on all of the changes that family members have already made as a new foundation to work from, rather than as a sign that treatment was not successful. When members can return to what they were recently doing that was working, they can more quickly move forward in the recovery process. In this way, they can connect back to the sense of accomplishment and hope that they had before the slip or relapse.

We can also view recovery in terms of the stages of the readiness for change model presented in Chapter 8. To refresh ourselves, these stages move from pre-contemplation, contemplation, preparation, action, and maintenance (where termination is the exit from the cycle). This pathway is a long process that usually does not happen in a linear fashion (DiClemente, 2003). Part of the readiness for change model is a spiraling where the person/family goes through the sequence—perhaps several times—before the termination period. Given that the model was originally developed with substance-abusing clients, there is an understanding that people do not stay at one particular stage but may move more fluidly forward or recursively. With issues of relapse, they will more likely experience slips or relapses during the action stage rather than the maintenance stage. This process of going back through the stages is referred to as **recycling**.

Recovery is based on patterns where the individual has changed their behavior, where the substance does not play a role in their life (or one where problems are not involved) and that these other, more productive, behaviors have become habitual. At this point the person is focused on what is happening well in their life rather than on being worried about a return to the substance use. DiClemente (2003) warns that recovery philosophies such as AA, where there is a focus on *not drinking*, may keep the notion of drinking in the person's life and may lead to the maintenance or reemergence of the habitual drinking—a paradoxical process.

Flemons (1991) discussed this paradoxical notion of how two things are connected in terms of what he calls **completing distinctions**. The notion of not drinking is ultimately tied to the notion of drinking; these two complete each other. When we tell ourselves, "I cannot drink, I cannot drink" what stays with us is "drink, drink." This does not mean that we will drink, but that the thought of drink (even if it is framed as "don't do this") is present. The way out of this dilemma is a focus on a higher order understanding of the connection between the two. In this case, drink/not drink might be viewed as being within the realm of health. So we could view it as: HEALTH/(Not Drink/Drink). When focusing on other aspects of health (such as exercising, positive relationships with others, good nutrition, etc.) we do not focus on "not drinking" and thus do not carry "drinking" with us. When someone has gotten to the termination stage, they will be so focused on these other aspects of health that drug use is not an active part of their thoughts.

If we expand this from an individual recovery to a family recovery, we can see that the family would not be focused on keeping secrets surrounding substance use and trying not to upset the fragile balance in the house, where they were once afraid of upsetting the addicted individual and having a situation that spiraled into conflict. Instead, they are able to explore areas of family health; times, situations, or rituals that they engage in where they are actively enjoying one another's company.

As we have seen, the development of addiction happens within a family environment that helps to maintain the problematic functions within the whole system. Conversely, the development and maintenance of recovery also happens within the family context. As the rules of the family change, so do the roles that members adopt, shifting the boundaries between subsystems as well as between the family and the larger systems. These new interactions, which do not include the use of the substance or the emotional dynamics associated with it, become habitual; they become the patterned interactions that set the family's homeostasis. Their new ways of being are most likely more desired than when alcohol and/or drugs were a central focus.

Recovery Capital

One of the main factors that lead to recovery is what is known as recovery capital (Davidson et al., 2010; White & Cloud, 2008). **Recovery capital** are the internal and external resources that someone has to start and maintain change. There are three types of capital; personal, family/social, and community (White & Cloud, 2008). **Personal recovery capital** are the individual factors that help support and sustain the person. These can be divided into two forms: physical and human capital. **Physical capital** can be things such as the necessities for people to live; food, shelter, clothing, as well as being financially functional. **Human capital** are aspects of the person that help them cope. These include, among other things, having a sense of humor, intelligence, self-esteem, hopefulness, and having a developed sense of self. Human capital can be thought of as extratherapeutic factors (Lambert, 1992).

Family/social recovery capital contains the various interpersonal relationships that help people overcome the challenges of their lives. These may include family relationships as well as friends or other individuals who help them maintain sobriety. Examples of family/social recovery capital may be that friends or family attend treatment with the person, be empathetic, or may spend time with the person away from drugs or alcohol.

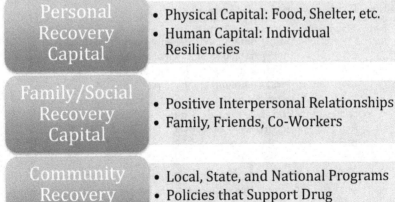

Figure 16.6 Recovery capital are the resources that help people to start and maintain change

The last type of recovery capital is **community recovery capital**. This category includes the local, state, and national programs, policies, and opportunities that support the reduction of drugs and alcohol. Examples of this include various drug treatment programs, programs that are designed to reduce the stigma of addictions, drug courts, and various self-help organizations. Figure 16.6 summarizes the three types of recovery capital.

Every person has some level of recovery capital, in personal, family/social, and community. White and Cloud (2008) provide several suggestions of how therapists can work with clients to enhance their recovery capital:

1. Support screening and brief intervention programs.
2. Engage people with low recovery capital through aggressive programs of community outreach.
3. Assess recovery capital on an ongoing basis.
4. Use recovery capital levels to help determine level of care placement decisions.
5. Target all three spheres of recovery capital within professionally-directed treatment plans and client-directed recovery plans.
6. Support recovery-linked cultural revitalization and community development models.
7. Use changes in levels of recovery capital to evaluate your program and your own professional performance. (pp. 5–8)

The more resources, strengths, and support individuals and families have, the greater the motivation, hope, and pathways they have toward changing the patterns of problematic behaviors.

Therapists working from this perspective engage in recovery support services where they try to enhance the addicted individual's recovery capital. The person may be coached or mentored to address basic needs such as food, finances, and housing. Recovery support services are designed to:

> (1) establish and maintain environments supportive of recovery; (2) remove personal and environmental obstacles to recovery; (3) enhance linkage to, identification with, and participation in local communities of recovery; and (4) increase the hope, inspiration, motivation, confidence, efficacy, social connections, and skills needed to initiate and maintain the difficult and prolonged work of recovery. (Davidson et al., 2010, p. 398)

The more people who are involved and supportive of the various changes that the individual and the family make, the better chance there is that these changes will last.

There are many possibilities for families to engage in a productive recovery. The National Council on Alcoholism and Drug Dependence (NCADD) provides several recommendations for family recovery, including having the family stop isolating itself from larger systems. This would be a shift from the rigid boundaries that cut-off individuals and the family system from possible outside support.

This might come in the form of educational or support groups. Another related aspect of recovery is educational. When family members understand the addiction process—both for the addicted individual and the family as a whole—they are better able to act consciously rather than being swept up in the emotional system that is currently organized around the substance abuse. Once family members are aware of the addiction process, they are then better able to develop alternative communication skills. Their previous communication has most likely been inundated with secrets, hesitancy, and deception. All of these have negatively impacted each member's self-esteem.

The NCADD also suggests that members stop focusing so much on others and take more responsibility for their own well-being. This skill will likely be most difficult for the codependent and others in the family who engage in enabling. To do this, individuals will need to stop old behaviors that have created the dysfunctional patterns which shaped the family's current homeostasis. These behaviors include denial, lying, blaming, and enabling. Instead of these problematic behaviors, there are several things families can do to heal, including engaging the children in the recovery process, building on resilience, engaging in personal and family activities, and preparing for relapse.

Family-Based Substance Abuse Prevention: Paul J. Kiser

Frequently lost in the discussion of interventions and treatments of substance use and abuse is the concept of the prevention of the initiation of substance use altogether (see Figure 16.7). The World Health Organization broadly describes

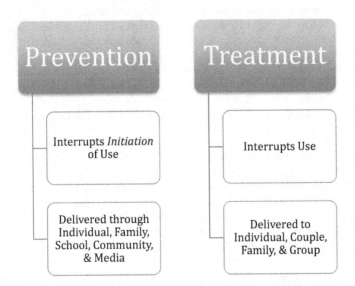

Figure 16.7 Substance abuse prevention targets people before use while substance abuse treatment targets people who are already using

the field of prevention as a combination of disease prevention and health promotion. Disease prevention is "understood as specific, population-based and individual-based interventions for primary and secondary (early detection) prevention, aiming to minimize the burden of diseases and associated risk factors." Accordingly, health promotion is "the process of empowering people to increase control over their health and its determinants . . . and usually addresses behavioral risk factors such as tobacco use, obesity, diet and physical inactivity, drug abuse control, alcohol control, and sexual health," among others (WHO EMRO, 2018). As the field of prevention further develops and more research and longitudinal-based studies continue, novel and effective evidence-based practices continue to be developed and refined to reduce the numbers of substance abusers/addicts in society.

In any consideration of the onset of substance abuse issues, a preliminary acknowledgment of the two main factors influencing that condition is essential. Both genetic ("nature") and environmental ("nurture") elements play significant roles in the adverse transition from the use of addictive substances to abuse and subsequent addiction. Certainly one of these concerns is beyond the influence or control of the clinician or therapist, save for yet-to-be-developed gene therapies or genetic counseling practices based on the identification of genetic and epigenetic markers that indicate higher risk of addiction upon use of these substances (Dick & Agrawal, 2008; Xu, Wang, Kranzler, Gelernter, & Zhang, 2017). However, multiple environmental factors have been identified that have been shown to be modifiable and doing so can have significant impact in the effort to influence and reduce behaviors that ultimately lead to substance abuse and addiction. The US Substance Abuse and Mental Health Services Administration recognizes prevention as a continuum that extends from the deterrence of diseases and the behaviors that promote them to the delaying of onset and reduction of severity of illnesses when they do occur. They promote the systemic use of scientifically proven, effective strategies to decrease risk factors and enhance protective factors to help shield individuals from the negative consequences of engaging in high-risk behaviors (SAMHSA, Rev. 2017).

The following narrative is frequently told in prevention circles to concisely describe the differences between treatment, intervention, and prevention. A group of well-intentioned individuals were standing by a river when they saw a person floating downstream struggling for their life. Thinking quickly they acted together to rescue the drowning man. Not a moment after they rescued the one person another was found fighting to stay afloat in the current. Upon saving that one, another was needing help, and the urgency was increasing. A few members of the group left the scene, much to the chagrin of those rescuing people in the current, and headed up-stream. There they found people falling off a high cliff into the river. Thinking quickly they acted hastily to place a net across the river and caught most of the individuals falling into the water. Quite pleased with themselves some of the rescuers remained puzzled while a smaller group started climbing the cliff to reach the top. When the climbers were questioned by those manning the nets as to where they were going they simply replied, "To build a fence."

Prevention initiatives generally make use of the three-pronged public health model emphasizing the interactions between an agent—i.e., alcohol, addictive drugs, high risk sexual activity; a host—the individual/user and the environment; and a setting—social, cultural, and physical settings in which the activity takes place (see Figure 16.8). Effective prevention programs and initiatives work "upstream" of the potential problem to address all three components of the model to reduce, or even avoid all together, the initiation and engagement of the individual in high-risk activities.

In general, treatment of the disease of substance abuse and addiction is targeted at "fixing" the problem or "curing" the individual by helping them to break the cycle of addiction, understand the consequences of continued use, and develop coping skills to avoid engagement in high-risk situations and behaviors to prevent future use and abuse of the addictive drug. Effective treatment programs work to not only include the individual user but also support systems around them including partners, families, and groups. All of these therapeutic practices, however, are focused on creating a localized environment supportive of individuals impacted by the addiction to assist them with the skills they are developing to improve quality of life and reduce the likelihood of future negative consequences.

Prevention approaches are not only targeted at individuals and selective populations but also work to change the societal environment in which the individuals exist on a daily basis. In an effort to prevent initiation of high-risk behaviors, obviously the approaches are most effective when they are delivered prior to any interaction with the addictive drug or high-risk behavior. Education, messaging, and policy change work together in a spectrum of prevention strategies developed in the mid-1980s to impact all three facets of the public health model. At the most basic level this spectrum emphasized strengthening individual knowledge and skills through classes, counseling, and curricula presented directly to the target audience. In ever-broadening levels of impact the spectrum then expands to include promoting community education through presentations and

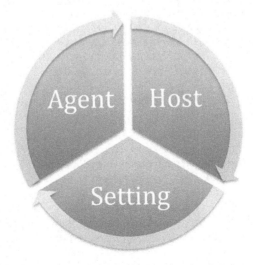

Figure 16.8 Prevention initiatives target the agent, host, and setting

media messages, educating healthcare providers to promote prevention strategies in their practices, fostering coalition and network development to increase the strength of the message delivery system and encourage action, changing organizational practices to establish new health-promoting norms, and improve safety and utilizing all of the previous levels for influencing community policies through legislation to gain population-based outcomes (Cohen & Satterwhite, 2002; Cohen & Swift, 1999).

These strategies have been used very successfully in the public health battle against cigarette manufacturers. At the individual level, evidence-based curricula such as *Life Skills Training* and *Project Towards No Tobacco Use* were implemented with fidelity in middle and high schools across the country (Cowell, Farrelly, Chou, & Vallone, 2009; Farrelly, Davis, Duke, & Messeri, 2009; Farrelly, Nonnemaker, Davis, & Hussin, 2009; Johnston et al., 2016; Thrasher et al., 2004). There were nationwide efforts to have doctors specifically monitor smoking habits of patients as a part of their basic intake interviews and to encourage those who do smoke to quit. Nationwide anti-smoking coalitions flourished with development support from The National Center for Tobacco-Free Kids and the Robert Woods Johnson Foundation, and even funding from the Master Settlement Agreement punitively collected from the tobacco industry itself. These national and community coalitions worked tirelessly to promote individual businesses and organizations to adopt smoke-free policies in the workplace, increase health insurance rates for smokers vs non-smokers, and encourage organizations to reduce their roles in tobacco-use promotion to children including product placement in retail establishments or depictions of tobacco use in movies. At the highest level, national legal advice was provided by groups like the Tobacco Control Legal Consortium and the American Nonsmokers' Rights Foundation supporting organized local, state, and national policy initiatives to increase tobacco tax rates, restrict youth exposure to tobacco advertising and youth access to tobacco products, remove flavorings from cigarettes and enact laws to prohibit indoor consumption of tobacco products in public places. The combined results of all of these efforts dropped the national percentage of daily smoking by high school seniors from 24.6% in 1997 to 5.5% in 2015, more than a 75% decline (Johnston et al., 2016).

Pathways of Prevention

Perhaps one of the most important things to be aware of in the understanding and implementation of prevention strategies and programs at every level of the prevention spectrum is that in order to truly be effective they must be based in well-researched, documented, and reviewed methods. No matter the level of conviction, sincerity of intent, or masterfulness of content delivery, a one-time prevention presentation or event is unlikely to result in any long-term effect in altering perceptions or changing behaviors. Neither will scare tactics, heartfelt testimonials, or moralistic messages have any significant impact (Tobler, Lessard, Marshall, Ochshorn, & Roona, 1999). Effective prevention campaigns and programs are based in evidence-supported strategies and concepts developed through extensive research from decades of previous successful and failed initiatives. The current foundational approaches of successful programs and campaigns focus on interactive strategies for building resilience and coping skills in the target population, changing societal norms to increase accurate and healthy perceptions of substance use, and policy changes to both limit access to drugs and mitigate harm to users and others from their consumption.

There are numerous credible private and governmental agencies tracking, evaluating, and monitoring substance abuse and addiction that serve as reliable resources to assist in the development of comprehensive prevention programs and initiatives at multiple levels. The US Department of Health and Human Services Substance Abuse and Mental Health Services Administration (SAMHSA), the National Institutes of Health National Institute on Drug Abuse (NIDA), Community Anti-Drug Coalitions of America (CADCA), the Centers for Disease Control and Prevention (CDC), the Search Institute, the National Social Norms Center, scores of state and local coalitions, private foundations, and many more agencies are all excellent resources for both funding and evidence-based development of targeted and comprehensive prevention efforts.

Although the prevention spectrum outlines the tiered levels of prevention initiatives involved in a comprehensive prevention campaign with large population-based health improvement objectives, individual components of specific activities and initiatives within that spectrum can also be viewed as key elements of a protective ring of prevention for very specific sub-populations or even individuals. As comprehensive prevention curricula are implemented in schools and delivered to individuals through mentoring and peer-to-peer relationships they should be tied into consistent messaging, skill development, monitoring, and support from family close to the target audience. When combined with community standards, policies, and social norms messaging consistent with what is being taught at school and in homes, the overall protective value increases. Every aspect of this preventive web of protection should ultimately be supported by local, state, and federal legislative action to not only limit access to illicit substances through legislative action but also to provide funding and other forms of support for all of the other pieces of a comprehensive prevention puzzle (see Figure 16.9).

Adolescent Prevention

By necessity, the overwhelming majority of prevention efforts are focused on the adolescent years, when individuals are at greatest risk for initiating and engaging in high-risk behaviors that could ultimately lead to substance abuse and behavior problems. An inordinate amount of research conducted over decades has repeatedly shown that if an individual successfully navigates their adolescent years without initiating the use of addictive drugs, the likelihood of them ever becoming addicted diminishes significantly (Chen, Storr, & Anthony, 2009; Dawson, Goldstein, Chou, Ruan, & Grant, 2008; Lopez-Quintero et al., 2011). There is extensive evidence correlating age of initiation of substance use with significantly greater risks of subsequent substance abuse and dependence. That is not to say that there are not specific instances and examples of individuals that did not initiate substance use until adulthood and became addicted, just that the incidence of those occurrences is significantly less than in individuals that initiate use as an adolescent. Likewise, as the population increases in average age, there is a growing incidence of seniors who become addicted to prescription pain medications

Figure 16.9 Prevention programs are focused on individual, family, school, community, and legislative initiatives

and are as equally dependent upon them as the heroin addict strung-out in an abandoned apartment. While programs and policies addressing the senior addict are important and necessitate research and subsequent action, the vast majority of prevention programs designed to be as effective as possible and provide the greatest cost/benefit ratio are targeted at impacting the most vulnerable population; youth.

In 2016 The US Surgeon General released the report *Facing Addiction in America: The Surgeon General's Report on Alcohol, Drugs, and Health* that called for a public health approach to substance use, misuse, and abuse. Five major recommendations were offered to address alcohol and drug misuse and substance use as a society. These included: (1) the implementation of effective prevention strategies and policies to reduce the injuries, disabilities, and deaths caused by substance misuse; (2) implementation of comprehensive, evidence-based community prevention programs that are sustained over time; (3) full integration of the continuum of services for substance use disorders with the rest of health care; (4) coordination and implementation of recent health reform and parity laws to help ensure increased access to services for people with substance use disorders; and (5) future research to guide the new public health approach to substance misuse and substance use disorders (U.S. Department of Health and Human Services (HHS), 2016).

It is with those recommendations in mind that we consider evidence-based practices currently in use to reduce substance use and abuse, particularly among youth and adolescents. These evidence-based strategies for reducing substance use, specifically alcohol since it is the most widely used substance, include limiting availability of alcohol, attempts to make it illegal for those under 21 to drive after consuming alcohol, and developing ways to identify early problem drinkers (Harding et al., 2016). Numerous empirically effective school-based prevention programs have been developed over the past several decades that significantly reduce the likelihood that participants who complete the programs will engage in high-risk behaviors (Dent et al., 1995; Hansen, Johnson, Flay, Graham, & Sobel, 1988; Pentz et al., 1989; Thomas & Perera, 2006; Zollinger et al., 2009). Sadly these multi-session programs, while undeniably effective when properly presented and attended, are fairly expensive and are far too often not implemented with fidelity compromising the integrity and the beneficial effects that would otherwise be gained. To quote the 2016 Surgeon General's Report, "Prevention programs and interventions can have a strong impact and be cost-effective, but only if evidence-based components are used and if those components are delivered in a coordinated and consistent fashion throughout the at-risk period" (U.S Department of Health and Human Services (HHS), 2016, p. 74).

Family-Based Prevention

While the vast majority of these preventive programs, policies, and practices focus their efforts on the target individual, there are numerous evidence-based programs and effective strategies designed with a specific approach to work through families and family dynamics. An active and involved family can have a preventive impact in reducing substance use (and subsequent abuse) through the monitoring and prevention of high-risk behaviors and development of individual resiliency factors that is as significant as any role they might play in helping interventions and treatments to break the cycle of addiction once it has taken hold.

Numerous studies have evaluated family-based prevention programs and have derived a set of core components that have been found to be effective in reducing adolescent substance abuse and high-risk behaviors (Bailey, Hill, Meacham, Young, & Hawkins, 2011; Kumpfer, 2014; Lochman & van den Steenhoven, 2002; Van Ryzin, Roseth, Fosco, Lee, & Chen, 2016). Kumpfer (2014) stated, "Standardized family-based interventions are the most effective way of preventing or treating adolescent substance abuse and delinquency" (p. 1). Perhaps not surprisingly, with the abundance of evidence that shows that delayed initiation of substance use significantly reduces the likelihood of long-term addictions and problems, many family-based prevention programs place an emphasis on directly and indirectly achieving that goal. The Search Institute has initiated more recent efforts to create and evaluate the impact of a Developmental Relationships framework that identifies 20 key components of powerful relationships adolescents encounter across different parts of their lives. With youth in the study identifying parent–youth relationships as the strongest of categories identified, the importance of the role of parents (and families) in prevention efforts becomes even more apparent (Roehlkepartain, Syvertsen, & Wu, 2017).

Distinctions are often made in these studies between specific parent-focused components of prevention programs such as monitoring, involvement, behavior management, and problem solving, and those youth-focused components to build life skills, resiliency, and positive family relations. Family-based prevention programs tend to include psychoeducation components surrounding substance use etiology, parents as role models, importance of anti-drug values, positive family engagement and relationships, and proactive monitoring and supervision of children. However, the largest and most current meta-analysis of family-based prevention programs found that the addition of two specific components delivered to the youth themselves will likely add significant impact to program effectiveness (Van Ryzin et al., 2016). These are: content related to encouraging more positive family relationships and the encouragement of concrete thinking about/planning for the future. Inclusion of family-based prevention is significantly important as family-based approaches have effect sizes two to nine times larger than prevention programs working only with the child (Kumpfer, Alvarado, & Whiteside, 2003).

Historically, prevention efforts and studies have not had ethnic and racial minorities as the primary focus (Blume, 2016). However, in recent years, prevention (and treatment) programs have been targeting a wider range of populations, becoming more inclusive and sensitive to the various contextual factors that various racial, ethnic, gender, and sexual minorities experience. As Blume explained,

> Culturally relevant prevention programs that focus on the family rather than on individuals have been successful, because they acknowledge beliefs held by many minority cultures concerning the importance of the family (rather than the individual) as the principal unit of function. (p. 50)

Case Application

The Rothers family has been going through the process of addiction. While Mark is the person who drinks (although Hannah may occasionally consume alcohol and Steve may be beginning to experiment with drugs and alcohol), the whole family has developed rules and interactional patterns that are maintaining and even increasing their misery. The Rothers will also be going through family recovery. Each individual must adjust in their intrapersonal and interpersonal functioning in order to develop new rules, roles, and patterns that are more amenable to the family's desires. For example, Hannah will likely have difficulty not monitoring Mark's behaviors, especially as to the possibility of whether he will drink and what type of mood he is in. Her change in monitoring is related to Mark not feeling like she is overseeing his behaviors. All members of the family have developed resentments; some toward alcohol, but likely most toward Mark and his isolating or angry behaviors. However, Mark has developed resentments toward various family members; most likely Hannah for trying to get him to change and Steve for his acting out behaviors.

As family recovery is a process, there may be relapses along the way. Mark may take a drink or even get drunk. The family may also relapse in that they engage in negative patterns that were present during the time of active drinking. The therapist working with the family might engage in psychoeducation so the family knows that one slip or relapse does not mean that individuals, but mainly the family, are not improving. Further, the family can develop greater levels of hope when they can hold on to and build on their past successes.

The Rothers are currently in the Drinking Stage of Developmental Recovery. At this point, they would need to be made aware of their own beliefs about drinking and how they may be experiencing aspects of denial. The Rothers have rigid roles that are restricting the family from being able to grow. We can hypothesize that the Rothers will, when entering the Transition stage, experience a lot more conflict in their relationships as the pressure in the family is increasing as people are recognizing that change needs to happen but do not know how that is going to happen. In Early Recovery, their relationships will shift so that there are more positive relationships occurring. This will help to diminish the monitoring, resentments, and jealousy that are prevalent in recovering families.

The Rothers can be classified as being a Type II family in Lewis and Allen-Byrd's (2001) family recovery typology model. Mark is likely to be the only individual in recovery. He is the focal point of the family, where most members probably see his drinking and negative attitude and behaviors as the primary problem in the family. Looking at the characteristics of Type II families, the Rothers match them quite well in that there is inequality between partners, with Hannah having an overwhelming difference in power, where she is the center point of family stability. Mark is the sole IP. Even though Steve's behaviors are starting to become problematic, he has not been expelled, arrested, or found to be doing drugs or alcohol. The family is currently in some types of denial. Mark's drinking is seen as inconvenient and non-desired, but the family has not yet talked about alcoholism or realized that they have organized around the alcohol. There are stability issues in the family, with tension between Mark and Hannah as well as between Steve and his parents. Therapy with the Rothers would focus on how to help all members get to and remain in the action stage, until such time that abstinence or moderation has occurred and there are positive transactional relationships. At that point, the therapist would work with them as they transition to the maintenance stage of change.

The Rothers are a wet family system. That is, alcohol is currently being consumed and its use is leading to problems in the family. The therapist working with them would likely have abstinence or a reduction in drinking as one of the primary goals of therapy. Once Mark either stopped drinking or drank in moderation, the therapist would likely focus more on sober family living skills, which would include helping Mark and Hannah to more effectively co-parent, supporting positive communication between all members, and developing a more effective family structure where Mark is not an outsider but has positive influence as a parent.

The Rothers family has a range of different recovery capital available for them. Mark and Hannah are both maintaining occupations and are able to provide for the family all of the basic necessities of life. Each person in the family has individual resiliencies, such as Kayleigh's intelligence, Hannah's caring, Steve's independence, Pete's sense of humor, and Mark's enjoyment of video games. Each person has interpersonal relationships that provide support such as Mark's friends, Hannah's siblings, and school friends for the children. Lastly, community recovery capital includes many self-help groups for substance abuse that are located in their community.

Summary

Recovery from drugs or alcohol abuse is a process, where not only the cessation of the use occurs, but the interactions of family members change. Therapists working with families may assess where in the family recovery process the family is in order to adapt and tailor their treatment to match how the family is functioning. One avenue of treatment is a focus on relapse, as people tend to view slips or relapses as a sign that nothing has changed. However, by viewing recovery in a more recursive way, where treatment spirals back and forth, the family can understand the gains they have made and may more readily build on these changes. A significant source of change is recovery capital—the elements in people's lives that help them to change and maintain those changes. Therapists can help clients to access as wide variety of recovery capital to push forward the change process and increase the possibility of the changes holding.

Key Words

monitoring
resentments
jealousy
recovery
abstinence
moderation management
developmental model of
   recovery
Drinking Stage
Transition
Early Recovery
Ongoing Recovery
externalize
internalize
Family Recovery Typology
   Model

Type I families
Type II families
Type III families
wet family system
dry family system
resilience
relapse
family relapse
recycling
completing distinctions
recovery capital
personal recovery capital
physical capital
human capital
family/social recovery capital
community recovery capital

Discussion Questions

1. What is the process of family recovery?
2. How might family recovery be enhanced by viewing families through different family types?
3. Discuss recovery capital and the role it plays in people reaching their goals.
4. How might relapse be viewed in a positive way?
5. What are some strategies of enhancing family recovery?

SEVENTEEN

The Self of the Family Therapist

Regardless of one's choice of model, understanding oneself, one's relationship to the model chosen, and one's relationship to clients are perhaps the most important aspects of being a family therapist; or a therapist of any modality. *You* are the most important treatment tool that you have available at any moment. More than a specific theory, empirically-based treatment, or type of intervention, the most significant aspect that you bring to therapy is you. Understanding yourself and your role in the therapeutic system is perhaps the key factor for effective treatment.

I have saved this topic for the end of the book because of the integral position it holds in effective therapy, and I want you to be able to think about everything you have learned in this book and let it all settle in to how you view people, therapy, and yourself. If the therapist is not aware of who they are, including values, belief about people, belief about how problems develop, and how they have been impacted in life to have developed their personal style, therapy will most likely be stilted. While understanding and being able to apply various therapy theories is very important, it does not mean much if the therapist utilizing it is ineffective.

In most training programs a majority of the time is spent on understanding diagnostic categories, counseling theories, and various assessment techniques. However, what is usually missing is a focus on one of the main players in the therapeutic system. While we learn about psychopathology and addiction—using various personality and counseling theories to understand why the client/family does what he/she/they do—we tend to overlook that the therapist is a human being who brings themself into the therapy room.

Further, when therapists contact a client, not only is their personality in play, but also their skills of being a therapist. These are intertwined in their personhood. When therapists are unaware of self, they do not realize how techniques may be coming across. For instance, two therapists may engage in the same technique, but one may do it with a dominant one-up style while the other operates from a more deferential one-down position. While it will be the connection of the therapist's style with the client's preferences, the therapist should be aware of this dynamic.

Skills for the Family Therapist

Similar to a therapist that works with groups or individuals, the family therapist has certain characteristics to help them be effective. These include the abilities/

core conditions that Carl Rogers (1961) put forth; accurate empathetic understanding, unconditional positive regard, and congruence. However, the family therapist must also be able to move beyond the content of what the client is saying and be able to observe, in the moment, the transactional patterns between the various family members, as well as between the family and the therapist (i.e., if a couple tries to triangulate the therapist into who between them is right).

In 2004, the American Association of Marriage and Family Therapy (AAMFT) put forth the Marriage and Family Therapy **Core Competencies**. This consisted of 128 competencies organized into six primary domains and five secondary domains (see Figure 17.1). The primary domains are admission to treatment, clinical assessment and diagnosis, treatment planning and case management, therapeutic interventions, legal issues, ethics, and standards and, lastly, research and program evaluation. The five secondary domains pertain to conceptual, perceptual, executive, evaluative, and professional skills and knowledge.

Besides developing these Core Competencies, therapists working in the substance abuse field may also need to be able to set limits and boundaries (Myers & Salt, 2013). Many individuals who are involved with addictions may try to push boundaries, such as inquiring into the therapist's past use. Here, it is important for the therapist to develop **boundary rules**, which distinguish what each person's role is in the therapeutic relationship and what is and is not accepted. These expectations try to define how each person should be with one another. This may be difficult when working with an addicted family, as they are most likely engaging one another through boundary violations (such as the codependent trying to take over for the dependent). Family therapists will need to distinguish

Figure 17.1 The AAMFT divides the Core Competencies of Family Therapists into primary and secondary domains

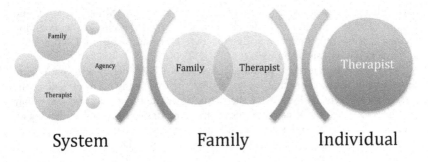

System   Family   Individual

Figure 17.2 Therapists must develop boundaries that allow them to engage in self-reflection while interacting with clients and larger systems

themselves when they are alone, in session with a family, or navigating the various systems of therapy such as the family, agency, and larger systems (i.e., school, legal) (see Figure 17.2)

Common Factors of Therapy

Over the last 25 years or so of therapy, there has been a push away from specific theoretical models of therapy toward an understanding of the **common factors of therapy** (Davis & Piercy, 2007; Grencavage & Norcross, 1990; Lambert, 1992). These are the aspects that all models utilize, in their own way, that lead toward positive client change. One of the main people in the area of common factors is Michael Lambert. Lambert, through doing meta-analyses of prior studies into

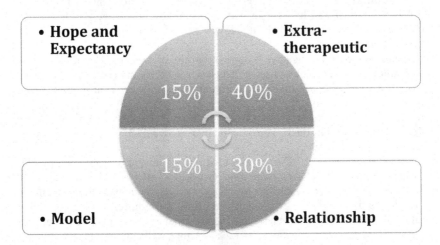

Figure 17.3 Lambert's model of common factors

psychotherapy outcomes, delineated four common factors. Miller, Duncan, and Hubble (1997) adjusted this understanding and provided the following common factors: extratherapeutic factors, therapeutic relationship, hope and expectancy, and model factors (see Figure 17.3).

Extratherapeutic factors, which account for 40% of therapeutic change, are those aspects of the client that lead to change. These usually occur outside of the session and do not really involve the therapist or the therapeutic process. They may be issues such as the client maturing and overcoming the problem, having an epiphany, or other learning situations. We can look at extratherapeutic factors in terms of the resiliencies we discussed in Chapter 7 and the recovery capital you read about in Chapter 16.

The **therapeutic relationship** accounts for 30% of positive change. This factor addresses the connection between therapist and client and how the therapeutic relationship acts as the agar for positive change to happen. One of the most important things that you can do to ensure that your clients reach their goals is to focus on, as quickly as possible, developing a positive alliance.

Hope and expectancy, accounting for 15% of change, highlights how, when people expect to change, they tend to change. This can be found in just making an appointment for therapy. Usually, between the time when the client calls to make a first session and when they get to that first session, there has already been some positive movement. This is why Solution-Focused therapists have developed the pretreatment change question (Weiner-Davis, de Shazer, & Gingerich, 1987), which asks clients what they noticed that is better between the time they made the appointment and the actual appointment.

The last common factor Lambert proposed, accounting for 15% of change, is that of **model factors.** Here, the aspects of the specific models make a difference for change. For instance, the use of enactments in Structural Therapy, helping a client to decrease anxiety in Natural Systems Theory, exploring the pieces to the miracle question in Solution-Focused Therapy, or providing a directive in Strategic Therapy helps lead toward change. The model one uses is important (even if it is an integrative model) as the more the therapist can utilize the model and believes in it, the greater the hope they will have that change will happen for the client. However, we know that one model is not better than another.

Other therapy theorists have proposed that the therapist should be viewed as a common factor (Sprenkle, Davis, & Lebow, 2009; Wampold & Imel, 2015). Therapists, regardless of model, are differentially effective. That is, two therapists may operate from the same therapy model but one will consistently get better results than the other. This may be based on the therapist's ability to develop and maintain the therapeutic alliance as well as maintaining fidelity to the treatment paradigm.

Miller and Moyers (2015) recommended that, in substance abuse therapy, the variables of therapist effects, client effects, relational effects, and basic processes are candidates to be studied to ensure effectiveness of treatment. **Therapist effects** include the therapist's ability to empathize, their warmth, reflection-to-question ratio, and their ability to engage in motivational interviewing. **Client effects** include change-talk-to-sustain-talk ratio, change talk strength, self-efficacy, readiness for change, and experiencing. **Relational effects** focus on the working alliance, client feedback, discourse analysis, and talk time. **Basic processes** include therapeutic model interventions as well as sequential analysis of therapist and client discourse.

In this book we have very briefly covered some of the most prominent family therapy theories. Knowing that one approach is not better than any other, but that having an approach (including the possibility of an integrative approach) is paramount to effective work, which theory should you operate from? To answer this question you have to know yourself and determine which approach fits your value system.

Matching the Approach to the Therapist

As we have just covered, there are common factors that cut across all therapeutic models. In the field of family therapy there may be more particular common factors, which include a relational conceptualization, the expanded direct treatment system, and the expanded therapeutic alliance (Sprenkle & Blow, 2004). There are also philosophical issues that help to determine which approach is a good fit for the therapist; let alone a good fit with the client. Before an approach can be useful for the client, it needs to be useful for the therapist. This means that there is a harmony between the philosophical tenets of the model and the value system of the therapist. Simon (2003) presented five issues that help to determine this fit: individual/group; freedom from/freedom for; good/evil; mind/body; and being/becoming.

The dialectic of **individual/group** is whether an approach highlights individual change or is more collectivist—exploring how the individual changes based on change in the group. Individualist therapies, such as Bowen Natural Systems Theory, Symbolic-Experiential Family Therapy, Human Process Validation Movement, and Narrative Therapy understand problems as internal processes that occur in reaction to others. Collectivist therapies, such as Structural, Strategic, and MRI: Brief Therapy conceptualize problems at the group level.

The distinction of **freedom from** and **freedom for** are housed within an ethical dimension. They focus on the notion of whether the person gives up self for others or maintains the individual as opposed to the group. Therapies that focus on the welfare of the larger system rather than the individual would be considered operating from a freedom for perspective. They are freedom for the group. These would be the Contextual, Strategic and Structural approaches. Freedom from approaches highlight how the individual can become protected from the forces of the relationships they are housed in. These models include Bowen Therapy, Narrative Therapy and Solution-Focused Therapy.

A therapist, in determining where they stand on the **good/evil dynamic**, examines whether they view people as naturally moving toward good based on intellect or whether they are ruled by will. For the former, therapy is geared toward highlighting what the person is doing that is problematic so that they can choose to engage self and others differently. Approaches from this orientation would include Bowen Therapy, Solution-Focused Therapy, and Narrative Therapy. Therapies based on the latter, where people are ruled more by will, include the psychoanalytic family therapies, Structural, Strategic, and Symbolic-Experiential therapies.

The **mind–body problem** explores how internal processes are related to external events. Questions the therapist might ask include how much does changing environmental factors influence internal psychological processes. Idealist therapies put minimal emphasis on the external and much more on internal meaning-making. Narrative Therapy is an example of this orientation. Aristotelian therapies place less importance on the power of words and more on actions that put those words into effect. Approaches such as Symbolic-Experiential, Bowen Therapy, Strategic and Structural family therapies fall under this category.

The last area of value exploration for the family therapist that Simon presents is that of **To Be or To Become**. Therapies that focus on "To Be" are more "in-the-moment" type therapies. They attempt to get clients to become aware of themselves in the moment. Alternatively, "To Become" therapies view change as a process. Here, what happens in one session of therapy makes sense within the whole of the therapeutic encounter. Being therapies include Symbolic-Experiential and Human Process Validation Movement. Becoming therapies include the Strategic and Structural therapies, Bowen Therapy, and the postmodern approaches.

I know that this is a very brief overview of these types of concepts, but hopefully you will begin to explore the underlying philosophical principles that each approach of therapy is structured around. Once you have explored your own value system you will be able to better determine which approaches fit your sensibilities. For instance, if you believe in the moral model of addiction, where the person chooses to engage in substance abuse, working from a model that highlights personal autonomy might make sense.

While Simon (2006) holds that it is the therapist that is the bridge between the common-factors perspective and model-specific factors perspective, Sprenkle and Blow (2007) argue that therapist expertise and effectiveness vary, even for those who operate from a specified model. They also argue that therapeutic alliance is not given enough importance in Simon's position. This leads to therapists needing to balance their own worldview with that of the client's, as well as what is happening in the therapeutic process. Sprenkle and Blow explained, "If a focus on the therapist's worldview leads to therapeutic rigidity, it could be iatrogenic" (p. 111). Thus, they hold that the link between therapy model and common factors is a skillful/competent/expert therapist.

What Makes a Good Addictions Therapist?

As we talked about above, not all therapists are equal in their skill and effectiveness. Why would some therapists be better than others? And, further, why are some therapists better at working with individuals and families dealing with addiction? The following section explores what we know about the characteristics of effective substance abuse therapists.

In 1995, the Center for Substance Abuse Treatment (CSAT) organized the Task Force on the Characteristics of Effective Addictions Counselors. The task force developed the following characteristics that good addictions therapists should espouse:

- the mental health and personal adjustment of the individual counselor;
- therapeutic optimism;
- organizational ability;
- the ability to recognize and maintain appropriate boundaries and balance client and counselor needs;
- positive experience and convictions about recovery;
- investment in personal and professional growth;
- appropriate ethics and values;
- sense of humor.

The task force recommended that further research occur on these characteristics and whether and how they can be taught.

The task force then provided a list of skills the general therapist should develop to be able to work effectively with clients dealing with substance abuse. These new skills included:

- develop appropriate conceptualizations of addiction;
- examine the effects of alcohol and other drugs in their own lives and the lives of their families;
- be prepared to deal with challenges around personal boundaries;
- view themselves as role models;
- become familiar with 12-step work;
- conceptualize the meaning of "powerlessness;"
- understand the effects of group processes on recovery;
- Learn to be direct if needed.

These skills, in conjunction with the therapist's model of therapy, help them to better make sense of how addiction develops and is maintained as well as the dynamics that occur in the therapy process between client/family and therapist.

While mental health professionals have their perspective of what a substance abuse therapist should be, so do clients. Rohrer, Thomas, and Yasenchak (1992) surveyed substance abuse clients to determine the characteristics that they viewed were important for their therapists to have (and not to have). The top 10 positive and negative traits substance abuse clients wanted/did not want in a therapist were:

Positive Trait	Negative Trait
1. Understanding	1. Asshole
2. Concerned	2. Can't relate
3. Caring	3. Dishonest
4. Experienced	4. Treat like children
5. Honest	5. Uneducated
6. Certified	6. Bull-shitter
7. Good listener	7. Rude
8. Streetwise	8. Foul mouth
9. Easy to talk to	9. Show favorites
10. Direct	10. Unfair

Grosenick and Hatmaker (2000) found that female substance abuse clients perceived the following therapist characteristics as being influential in obtaining treatment goals: knowledge and experience, supportiveness, nonthreatening behaviors, and availability. As can be seen, there are some differences between these various characteristics and those that the CSAT Task Force developed. It seems that clients also hold that Carl Rogers' understanding that an open and honest therapeutic relationship is extremely important for productive therapeutic work to occur.

There are so many factors that lead to the development of a positive therapeutic relationship. These come in the form of how the characteristics of not only the therapist but those of the client come together. Some of these may be age, gender, past addictions experience, religion, ethnicity, and sexual orientation. For instance, Lawson (1982) found that addictions clients experienced higher levels of unconditionality with therapists who were older than they were. The results may have interacted with past personal addiction history and therapist experience. This is something that the therapist cannot control (you cannot determine that the client will not react to your gender, attractiveness level, accent, race, etc.). But you do have influence on determining whether any of these factors is impacting the therapeutic alliance and then discussing them with the client. One way of doing this is to frequently utilize formal client feedback about the process and outcome of what is happening in the therapy room (Miller et al., 2006).

One's Relationship to Addiction

Doukas and Cullen (2010) provided several issues for therapists going into the substance abuse field. These included their motivation to enter the field, relationship to self-help groups, potential over-involvement with clients, potential over-involvement with work, potential over-identification with clients, risk of relapse through work-related cue exposure, and the repercussions of relapse. Many substance abuse therapists find themselves in the addiction field because they want to give back to others having had the experience of being helped themselves. Others enter to maintain their sobriety and continue to work on their own growth. In relationship to self-help groups, substance abuse therapists must navigate both their clinical work as well as their personal work in the self-help group. If other group members know the person's clinical expertise, the therapist needs to keep these two areas separate to avoid dual relationships. Given that some substance abuse therapists have personal experience with addictions, they may be more prone to want to help the addictions client avoid pain, which may lead to the therapist becoming over-involved with the client. Further, therapists in recovery who work in the addictions field place themselves into a context in which they are consistently around substance use cues. This may heighten the risk of relapse, which would have significant repercussions. This is why all therapists, but especially therapists in recovery, are encouraged to ensure their own self-care and maintain their recovery.

In most therapy situations clients do not ask the therapist whether they have experienced a similar situation as what they are experiencing. Occasionally, a client going through a divorce, a death of a close family member, or depression may inquire as to the therapist's personal familiarity with that type of situation. But these times are not frequent. In the substance abuse realm, the situation is reversed. In most situations the client, from the beginning of therapy, delves into the personal experience of the therapist in dealing with their own addiction. A person's desire for their own self-disclosure as well as the person they are in contact with may be related to their exposure to 12-step programs. Mallow (1998) explained that programs such as AA have a basic premise that growth comes from opening up to others. If the therapist says that they have never dealt with addiction personally, the client may seek out another therapist or not put faith in the therapist being able to help. This is a common thought in the substance abuse arena; however, it is not accurate.

In looking at the research literature regarding substance abuse therapists with or without past addiction history, Culbreth (2000) found that client perceptions of effectiveness of treatment did not change based on whether the therapist was in recovery or not. These results differ from Lawson (1982) where clients of therapists in recovery had higher scores on a therapy relationship inventory than clients of therapists with no past alcohol experience. While there are not differing treatment outcomes based on therapist recovery status, there are different treatment methods and attitude differences. For instance, therapists in recovery were found to be more concrete and rigid. Therapists in recovery may also exhibit lower levels of conscientiousness and emotional stability (Saarnio, 2010).

It is a myth that the therapist has to have experienced addiction and be in active recovery to help the person who is currently abusing substances. This is not an expectation in any other area of mental health. The client dealing with obsessive thoughts and behaviors does not demand that the therapist has been obsessive at some point in their life. The client dealing with schizophrenia does not expect the therapist to be in remission from schizophrenia. The couple dealing with domestic violence issues does not seek out a therapist who was either an abuser of their partner or had been abused.

While many therapists who work in the substance abuse field have experienced some type of substance abuse in their own life (either their own addiction or a family member's), it is *not* a necessary criteria. It actually may make therapy more difficult in some cases. One of the most important skills a therapist can have is that of being able to be empathetic toward one's client. The more the therapist's personal life is similar to a client's, the more potential there is for both understanding *and* misunderstanding.

Empathy is the ability to be able to feel what another person is feeling. When we have experienced a similar situation to the person we are in conversation with, we are able to use our past feelings and understandings as a template to what the other person is probably experiencing. For instance, if I had been addicted to cocaine for two years and during that span went through getting fired, a divorce, and being homeless, I can understand the sadness and desperation of my client who is now in that type of predicament.

However, although there are similarities, people deal with situations idiosyncratically. There is a danger of misunderstanding and disengagement if I use my experience as the template for my client's experience. Perhaps my divorce was pretty nasty with my partner serving me with restraining orders, attempting to get sole custody of the children, and hiring lawyers to ensure that they come out on top of the process. Yet my client's divorce may be much more amiable. If they tell me they are having a rough time and I say, "This sounds like one of the worst experiences of your life" I may be overstating the client's experience. Here, I am not trying to feel what *they* feel but get them to feel what *I* felt in the similar circumstance, or at least using my own experience as a heuristic for understanding others. One way to overcome this possible bias is to engage with clients in a "not-knowing" manner, where the therapist is an expert on engaging in a therapeutic discourse with the client but the client is the expert on his or her own experiences and meanings (Anderson & Goolishian, 1992).

Given that overcoming an addiction, especially for those people whose brains have been altered physiologically (see Chapter 2), is difficult, the non-addictive addictions counselor might consider trying to change some type of habit they have which they want to change (Miller, 2005). This prevents the therapist from telling the client how they changed or what they changed, but may enable them to be more empathetic to the difficulty of changing a long-standing pattern.

Another potential problem with being in recovery and working with substance abusers is that your day is filled with talk and focus on substances. If you are newly in recovery this may be too stressful for you. Therapy as a profession, regardless of what types of clients and client problems you work with, is stressful. Add a frequent focus on the issue that you are trying to get over and you may experience more stress than you can handle.

If a client knows that you are in recovery, they may look to you to tell them how you overcame your addiction. While it is potentially useful for the client to realize that there is hope—if you were able to move away from substances and into recovery then they should be able to—there are also potential problems here. Your path to recovery may not be the same as the client's. In systems theory there is a concept called **equifinality**. In essence, there are many paths to the same outcome. If we use a baseball analogy this might help to understand this. Take a second to think about how many different ways there are for an offensive player to get to first base.

There are six ways (see Figure 17.4). The first is that the batter swings the bat and makes contact with the ball. The batter may get on first because of getting a single, a fielder's choice, an error, or a fielder or umpire obstruction, but they swung and hit the ball and is at first base. Second, they may be walked (issued four balls). Third, they might strike out, but on the third strike the catcher did not cleanly catch the ball and the batter ran to first before the catcher threw the ball to the first baseman. Fourth, the pitcher might hit the batter with the ball. Fifth, they could be used as a pinch runner for an existing player on first base. Lastly, the batter might get on by catcher interference—this is when the batter swings and the bat hits the catcher's glove. In using this analogy, hopefully you can see that if either the therapist or the client expects the other to change based on the way the therapist did they may be missing out on other potential pathways toward reaching the client's goals.

Thus, the substance abuse therapist will almost surely face the dilemma of **self-disclosure** and whether to talk about whether or not addictions were a part of their past. If the client asks the therapist about whether they are in recovery, the therapist can first inquire with the client as to their worldview of asking that question (Mallow, 1998; Nerenberg, 2009). This should be done in a nonjudgmental

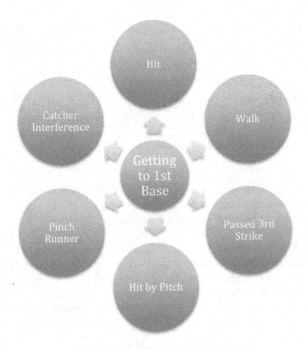

Figure 17.4 Equifinality holds that there are multiple pathways to the same outcome, such as the variety of ways for a baseball player to get to first base

manner so that it is based on a curiosity of the therapist into how the client understands what they are going through as well as their desire for a positive therapeutic relationship. It is important to work from a position of curiosity about the client rather than defensiveness, as the former helps promote the therapeutic relationship while the latter hampers it. Demonstrating to clients that you have an understanding of the addiction process can be important, allowing the client to know that you will be able to work with them. Diamond (2000) explained, "Most clients are seeking reassurance that you have some frame of reference for understanding their plight and are familiar with the language and customs of AA or other 12-step groups" (p. 318).

When a therapist self-discloses, the boundaries shift between therapist and client from somewhere more on the rigid side (as more strict psychoanalytic therapists would be) to clearer boundaries. However, given that the substance abuse field—especially those who are steeped in the 12-steps—have an expectation of self-disclosure, there is the possibility that the boundaries can move too far toward the diffuse side (see Figure 17.5). Given that many clients dealing with addictions have poor boundaries (Nerenberg, 2009), it is important for the therapist to be conscientious about what gets disclosed and the impact that it will have on the therapeutic relationship.

Another reason to potentially withhold information about one's own recovery status is that it can lead to the client worrying whether the therapist will, during

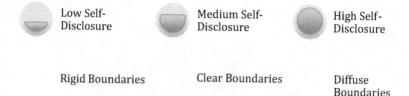

Low Self-
Disclosure

Medium Self-
Disclosure

High Self-
Disclosure

Rigid Boundaries   Clear Boundaries   Diffuse
Boundaries

Figure 17.5 Substance abuse therapists must determine how much they want to self-disclose and the impact on the therapeutic boundaries

the course of the therapy, relapse (Mallow, 1998). While this may not always be the case, any time a therapist self-discloses they impact the therapeutic relationship. You become more of a person to the client, which changes their focus from themselves to you.

Whether to self-disclose about one's relationship to addiction may be based on the therapist's orientation as well as the therapist's belief on the impact that the disclosure or non-disclosure will have on the client and the dynamic between therapist and client. Perhaps the deciding factor for the therapist is whether the disclosure will enhance or detract from the therapeutic relationship.

Therapists in Recovery

For those therapists who happen to be in recovery, depending on the size of the city that you live in, there may be times when you run into your clients at self-help meetings. If this happens it is important to separate your working relationship from what happens in the self-help meetings. Nerenberg (2009) provided several suggestions for when therapist and client might attend the same 12-step meeting. It is better for the therapist to attend a different meeting since this will allow them a safe place to open up and be vulnerable, rather than thinking about how what they say may impact their client and the therapeutic relationship during future sessions with that client. As such, it would be up to the therapist to attend a different meeting. Several possibilities would be to attend an online meeting or to find or develop a therapist-only meeting.

Therapy for the Therapist

When the field of psychotherapy began it was expected that therapists would go through their own therapy. Given that psychoanalysis was the predominant approach during the first half of the 20th century, psychoanalysts had to go through their own analysis, usually consisting of many sessions over many years. As psychotherapy started to be taught at universities, having a requirement of one's own therapy was a standard part of the training. However, in the last quarter century, this is no longer the case. Most training programs do not require therapy of their therapists-in-training, but might just suggest it as an overarching benefit for all students.

Should you go for your own therapy while you are training to become a therapist? The answer to this is individualistic. There are advantages to having experienced therapy. You can better understand the position that clients are in when they first go to therapy. For instance, there is an expectation that during the first session clients will divulge some of their most personal experiences. This is not a common thing that we do when we meet people in other contexts, but it happens in therapy. By going through the therapy experience and recognizing this issue of immediate self-disclosure, you may be more hesitant to label a client "resistant" who is hesitant to open up in the beginning phases of therapy.

As the field of family therapy developed, many of the founders thought it was important for therapists-in-training to experience therapy for the purposes of growing as a person. Bowen (1992) believed it was imperative that therapists be able to differentiate from their own family so as not to experience anxiety during what will inevitably be conflictual and stressful periods in the therapy room. Minuchin, at the beginning of his career, engaged in his own psychoanalysis (Minuchin et al., 2014). This allowed him to explore aspects of himself which, when conducting therapy, helped him to develop a homunculus to be more effective in the room—a **homunculus** is a little you (metaphorically) that sits atop your shoulder and provides you with a perspective of you in the situation. It is the ability for you to be reflective and self-aware, in the moment.

Similar to this is the ability to be mindful while engaging clients. **Mindfulness** has become an important concept in the field of therapy during this last decade. Keane (2013) suggested that a therapist who practices mindfulness may more readily develop and espouse the core skills necessary for effective therapeutic relationships. These skills include the ability to stay attentive in the therapy room as well as engaging in quality empathic contact. Another potential benefit of mindfulness is that it heightens therapists' awareness of self-care needs and the possibility of addressing them. Although mindfulness is a mode of being, rather than just a technique (Brito, 2013), just doing five minutes of mindfulness centering before a session leads to the therapist believing they are more present in the session and the client believing the session is more effective (Dunn, Callahan, Swift, & Ivanovic, 2013).

All therapists have the potential of experiencing **burnout**. Corey et al. (2019) explained, "Burnout is a state of physical, emotional, intellectual, and spiritual depletion characterized by feelings of helplessness and hopelessness" (p. 60). Elman and Dowd (1997) found the following to be correlates of burnout for substance abuse therapists: occupational stress, psychological strain, personal stress, emotional exhaustion, role conflicts, poor attitude toward work, lack of occupational recognition, emotional distress, excessive job demands, and frequent physical symptoms. Substance abuse counselors are perhaps more at risk of burnout than other therapists since they work with quite challenging clients who tend to not fully engage in therapy and have frequent relapses (Baldwin-White, 2016). This leads to the possibility of substance abuse therapists leaving their jobs, leading to high turnover rates at many substance abuse facilities, which is one of the most significant issues in the field (Young, 2015).

If you do experience distress in your personal life, then it is imperative that you seek out help for yourself as there is too much risk that your own problems can impact your ability to help others. This is also an ethical mandate. For instance,

Principal 3.3 of the American Association of Marriage and Family Therapy code of ethics states, "Marriage and family therapists seek appropriate professional assistance for their personal problems or conflicts that may impair work performance or clinical judgment."

Case Application

As the therapist for the Rothers family, you will need to decide what type of therapy you think will be most beneficial for them. You will also need to decide on what level of treatment to provide, such as inpatient, outpatient, individual, group, or family. Further, you will need to negotiate your views of what will be most effective with the various family member views. These decisions will be based upon the setting that you are working at, who in the family initiates therapy, and your beliefs as a therapist. You will need to be able to navigate the waters of family relationships, where members will likely try to triangulate you to take their side against someone else in the family. To be able to make all of these therapeutic decisions, you will need to be self-aware of yourself before, during, and after the session so that you do not get swept away in the process.

Summary

This chapter highlights perhaps the most important instrument in all of therapy—the therapist. In this book, we have presented many different models of family therapy and ways to conceptualize clients and families and the various issues they are dealing with. However, if you are not aware of yourself, your therapeutic style, and actively work to recognize how and when you are or are not being effective, you will not be tapping into one of the most important resources in the therapy room, you—the therapist (Keeney & Keeney, 2013).

Being a family therapist utilizes the skills of the individual therapist as well as other skills of being able to contextualize problems within their social contexts. Being an addictions therapist requires the therapist to understand how substance use and abuse impacts not only individual functioning, but the familial and relational interchanges that promote and maintain those symptoms as well.

My hope for you in reading this book is that you will have a more expansive view of people and problems. So the next time an individual client comes into your office stating that they are dealing with addictions (or any other symptom), not only can you view them through an individualistic lens, but that you will have more resources available to you—that you can understand how their behavior makes sense within a systemic perspective. This will provide you with more possibilities of working with them, either individually or relationally. I wish you good luck on your continued journey through the field of substance abuse and the family.

Key Words

Core Competencies
boundary rules
common factors of therapy
extratherapeutic factors
therapeutic relationship
hope and expectancy
model factors
therapist effects
client effects
relational effects
basic processes

individual/group
freedom from/freedom for
good/evil
mind–body problem
To Be/To Become
empathy
equifinality
self-disclosure
homunculus
mindfulness
burnout

Discussion Questions

1. How might an understanding of the common factors of therapy be useful when first engaging a family where there is addiction present?
2. Review Simon's five philosophical dimensions and determine where you fall in the various dialectics.
3. Where is the line in working with a client of self-disclosing too much?
4. Why is it important to focus on the self of the therapist, especially in addictions counseling?
5. What are the pros and cons of having an experience that is closely related to the client's experience?

References

Abel, E. L. (1998). *Fetal alcohol abuse syndrome*. New York: Plenum Press.

Aboujaoude, E., Koran, L., Gamel, N., Large, M., & Serpe, R. (2006). Potential markers for problematic internet use: A telephone survey of 2,513 adults. *CNS Spectrums, 11*(10), 750–755.

Adam, M., & Gutierrez, V. (2011). Working with gay men and lesbian women with addiction concerns. In G. W. Lawson & A. W. Lawson (Eds), *Alcoholism and substance abuse in diverse populations* (2nd Ed.) (pp. 213–225). Austin, TX: Pro-ed.

Adinoff, B. (2004). Neurobiologic processes in drug reward and addiction. *Harvard Review of Psychiatry, 12* (6), 305–320.

Agrawal, A., Sartor, C., Lynskey, M., Grant. J., Pergadia, M., Grucza, R., Bucholz, K., Nelson, E., Madden, P., Martin, N., & Heath, A. (2009). Evidence for an interaction between age at first drink and genetic influences on DSM-IV alcohol dependence symptoms. *Alcoholism, Clinical, and Experimental Research, 33*, 2047–2056.

Alegría, M., Canino, G., & Stinson, F. S. (2006). Nativity and *DSM–IV* psychiatric disorders among Puerto Ricans, Cuban Americans, and Non-Latino whites in the United States: Results from the National Epidemiologic Survey on alcohol and related conditions. *Journal of Clinical Psychiatry, 67*, 56–65.

Alford, K. M. (1998). Family roles, alcoholism, and family dysfunction. *Journal of Mental Health Counseling, 20*(3), 250–260.

Alghazo, R., Upton, T. D., & Cioe, N. (2011). Duty to warn versus duty to protect confidentiality: Ethical and legal considerations relative to individuals with AIDS/HIV. *Journal of Applied Rehabilitation Counseling, 42*(1), 43–49.

Allem, J.-P., Sussman, S., Soto, D. W., Baezconde-Garbanati, L., & Unger, J. B. (2016). Role transitions and substance use among Hispanic emerging adults: A longitudinal study using coarsened exact matching. *Addictive Behaviors, 58*, 95–99.

Amaro, H., Arévalo, S., Gonzalez, G., Szapocznik, J., & Iguchi, M. Y. (2006). Needs and scientific opportunities for research on substance abuse treatment among Hispanic adults. *Drug and Alcohol Dependence, 84*, 64–75.

Ambermoon, P., Carter, A., Hall, W. D., Dissanayaka, N. N., & O'Sullivan, J. D. (2011). Impulse control disorders in patients with Parkinson's disease receiving dopamine replacement therapy: Evidence and implications for the addictions field. *Addiction, 106*(2), 283–293.

American Association of Marriage and Family Therapy (2004). Marriage and family therapy core competencies. Retrieved from www.aamft.org February 15, 2014.

American Psychiatric Association (APA) (2013). *Diagnostic and statistical manual of mental disorders* (5th Ed.). Washington, DC: Author.

American Society of Addiction Medicine (2014, March 17). *Public policy statement: Definition of addiction.* Retrieved from www.asam.org.

Amourette, C., Lamproglou, I., Barbier, L., Fauquette, W., Zoppe, A., Viret, R., & Diserbo, M. (2009). Gulf War illness: Effects of repeated stress and pyridostigmine treatment on blood–brain barrier permeability and cholinesterase activity in rat brain. *Behavioral Brain Research, 203*, 207–214.

Anderson, H., & Goolishian, H. (1992). The client is the expert: A not-knowing approach to therapy. In S. McNamee & K. J. Gergen (Eds), *Therapy as social construction* (pp. 25–39). London: Sage.

Anderson, S. C. (2009). *Substance use disorders in lesbian, gay, bisexual, and transgender clients.* New York: Columbia University Press.

Andrews C. (2000). Simplicity circles and the compulsive shopper. In A. Benson (Ed.), *I shop, therefore I am – compulsive buying and the search for self* (pp. 484–496). New York: Aronson.

Anton, R., Oroszi, G., O'Malley, S., Couper, D., Swift, R., Pettinati, H., & Goldman, D. (2008). An evaluation of μ-opioid receptor (OPRM1) as a predictor of naltrexone response in the treatment of alcohol dependence: Results from the Combined Pharmacotherapies and Behavioral Interventions for Alcohol Dependence (COMBINE) study. *Archives of General Psychiatry, 65*, 135–144.

Aponte, H. J., & Nelson, G. (2018). "I matter, too". *Journal of Family Psychotherapy, 29*(1), 30–42.

Applewhite, S. R., Mendez-Luck, C. A., Kao, D., Torres, L. R., Scinta, A., Villarreal, Y. R., Haider, A., & Bordnick, P. S. (2017). The perceived role of family in heroin use behaviors of Mexican-American men. *Journal of Immigrant and Minority Health, 19*(5), 1207–1215.

Arenson, G. (1991). *Born to spend: How to overcome compulsive spending.* Blue Ridge Summit, PA: Tab Books.

Armstrong, E. M. (2003). *Conceiving risk, bearing responsibility: Fetal alcohol syndrome & the diagnosis of moral disorder.* Baltimore, MD: The Johns Hopkins University Press.

Augustine Fellowship (1986). *Sex and love addicts anonymous.* Augustine Fellowship. Retrieved from https://slaafws.org/english.

Bailey, J. A., Hill, K. G., Meacham, M. C., Young, S. E., & Hawkins, J. D. (2011). Strategies for characterizing complex phenotypes and environments: General and specific family environmental predictors of young adult tobacco dependence, alcohol use disorder, and co-occurring problems. *Drug and Alcohol Dependence, 118*(2–3), 444–451.

Baker, A., Moschis, G., Rigdon, E. & Mathur, A. (2011). Effects of family structure on compulsive buying: A life course perspective. *Advances in Consumer Research, 39*, 422.

Bakken, I. J., Wenzel, H. G., Götestam, K. G., Johansson, A., & Øren, A. (2009). Internet addiction among Norwegian adults: A stratified probability sample study. *Scandinavian Journal of Psychology, 50*(2), 121–127.

Baldwin-White, A. (2016). Psychological distress and substance abuse counselors: An exploratory pilot study of multiple dimensions of burnout. *Journal of Substance Use, 21*(1), 29–34.

Barr, A. M., Panenka, W. J., MacEwan, G. W., Thornton, A. E., Lang, D. J., Honer, W. G., & Lecomte, T. (2006). The need for speed: An update on methamphetamine addiction. *Journal of Psychiatry and Neuroscience, 31*, 301–313.

Bateson, G. (1972). *Steps to an ecology of mind.* Chicago, IL: University of Chicago Press.

Baudry, A., Mouillet-Richard, S., Schneider, B., Launay, J.-M., & Kellermann, O. (2010). miR-16 targets the serotonin transporter: A new facet for adaptive responses to antidepressants. *Science, 329*(5998), 1537–1541.

Baumrind, D. (1967). Child care practices anteceding three patterns of preschool behavior. *Genetic Psychology Monographs, 75*, 43–88.

Beauvais, F., Jumper-Thurman, P., & Burnside, M. (2008). The changing patterns of drug use among American Indian students over the past 30 years. *American Indian and Alaska Native Mental Health Research*, 15, 15–24.

Becvar, D. S. (2008). From the editor: The legacy of Michael White. *Contemporary Family Therapy: An International Journal*, 30(3), 139–140.

Beesley, D., & Stoltenberg, C. D. (2002). Control, attachment style, and relationship satisfaction among adult children of alcoholics. *Journal of Mental Health Counseling*, 24, 281–298.

Belgrave, F. (2002). Relational theory and cultural enhancement interventions for African American adolescent girls. *Public Health Reports*, 117, 76–81.

Bell, S., Carter, A., Matthews, R., Gartner, C., Lucke, J., & Hall, W. (2014). Views of addiction neuroscientists and clinicians on the clinical impact of a "brain disease model of addiction". *Neuroethics*, 7(1), 19–27.

Belmontes, K. C. (2018). When family gets in the way of recovery: Motivational interviewing with families. *The Family Journal*, 26(1), 99–104.

Benotsch, E. G., Kalichman, S. C., & Kelly, J. A. (1999). Sexual compulsivity and substance use in HIV-seropositive men who have sex with men: Prevalence and predictors of high-risk behaviors. *Addictive Behaviors*, 24(6), 857–868.

Benson, A. (2006). *Stopping overshopping – A comprehensive program to help eliminate overshopping*. New York: April Benson. Retrieved from www.stoppingovershopping.com.

Benson, A., & Eisenach, D. (2013). Stopping overshopping: An approach to the treatment of compulsive-buying disorder. *Journal of Groups in Addiction & Recovery*, 8, 3–24.

Berg, I. K. (1994). *Family based services: A solution focused approach*. New York: W. W. Norton & Company, Inc.

Berg, I. K., & de Shazer, S. (1993). Making numbers talk: Language in therapy. In S. Friedman (Ed.), *The new language of change: Constructive collaboration in psychotherapy* (pp. 5–24). New York: Guilford Press.

Berg, I. K., & Miller, S. D. (1992). *Working with the problem drinker: A solution-focused approach*. New York: W. W. Norton & Company.

Berg, I. K., & Reuss, N. H. (1998). *Solutions step by step: A substance abuse treatment manual*. New York: W. W. Norton & Company.

Berman, E. (1999). Gender, sexuality, and romantic love genograms. In R. DeMaria, G. R. Weeks, & L. Hof (Eds), *Focused genograms: Intergenerational assessment of individuals, couples and families* (pp. 145–176). Philadelphia: Brunner/Mazel.

Bernschneider-Reif, S., Oxler, F., & Freudenmann, R. W. (2006). The origin of MDMA ("ecstasy")—separating the facts from the myth. *Pharmazie*, 61, 966–972.

Berridge, K. C., & Robinson, T. E. (1998). What is the role of dopamine in reward: Hedonic impact, reward learning, or incentive salience? *Brain Research Reviews*, 28 (3), 309–369.

Bersamira, C. S., Lin, Y.-A., Park, K., & Marsh, J. C. (2017). Drug use among Asian Americans: Differentiating use by acculturation status and gender. *Journal of Substance Abuse Treatment*, 79, 76–81.

Bien, T. H., Miller, W. R., & Tonigan, J. S. (1993). Brief interventions for alcohol problems: A review. *Addiction*, 88, 315–336.

Bischof, G., Iwen, J., Freyer-Adam, J., & Rumpf, H.-J. (2016). Efficacy of the community reinforcement and family training for concerned significant others of treatment-refusing individuals with alcohol dependence: A randomized controlled trial. *Drug and Alcohol Dependence*, 163, 179–185.

Bissell, L. C., & Royce, J. E. (1994). *Ethics for addiction professionals* (2nd Ed.). Center City, MN: Hazelden.

Black, C. (2001). *It will never happen to me: Children of alcoholics as youngsters, adolescents, adults*. Denver, CO: M.A.C.

Black, D. W. (2007). A review of compulsive buying disorder. *World Psychiatry, 6,* 14–18.

Black, D. W. (2012). Epidemiology and phenomenology of compulsive buying disorder. In J. E. Grant & M. N. Potenza (Eds), *The Oxford handbook of impulse control disorders.* Oxford, UK: Oxford University Press.

Black, D. W., Kehrberg, L. L. D., Flumerfelt, D. L., & Schlosser, S. S. (1997). Characteristics of 36 subjects reporting compulsive sexual behavior. *American Journal of Psychiatry, 154,* 243–249.

Black, D. W., Monahan, P. O., Temkit, M., & Shaw, M. (2006). A family study of pathological gambling. *Psychiatry Research, 141*(3), 295–303.

Black, D. W., Repertinger, S., Gaffney, G., & Gabel, J. (1998). Family history and psychiatric comorbidity in persons with compulsive buying: Preliminary findings. *The American Journal of Psychiatry, 155,* 960–963.

Blakey, J. M. (2016). The role of spirituality in helping African American women with histories of trauma and substance abuse heal and recover. *Social Work and Christianity, 43*(1), 40–59.

Blum, K., Chen, T. J., Chen, A. L., Madigan, M., Downs, B. W., Waite, R. L., Braverman, E. R., Kerner, M., Bowirrat, A., Giordano, J., Henshaw, H., & Gold, M. S. (2010). Do dopaminergic gene polymorphisms affect mesolimbic reward activation of music listening response? Therapeutic impact on Reward Deficiency Syndrome (RDS). *Medical Hypotheses, 74,* 513–520.

Blume, A. W. (2016). Advances in substance abuse prevention and treatment interventions among racial, ethnic, and sexual minority populations. *Alcohol Research: Current Reviews, 38*(1), 47–54.

Bohnert, A. S. B., Roeder, K. M., & Ilgen, M. A. (2011). Suicide attempts and overdoses among adults entering addictions treatment: Comparing correlates in a U.S. national study. *Drug and Alcohol Dependence, 119*(1–2), 106–112.

Bohnert, K. M., Ilgen, M. A., Louzon, S., McCarthy, J. F., & Katz, I. R. (2017). Substance use disorders and the risk of suicide mortality among men and women in the US Veterans Health Administration. *Addiction, 112*(7), 1193–1201.

Bond, C., LaForge, K. S., Tian, M., Melia, D., Zhang, S., Borg, L., Gong, J., Schluger, J., Strong, J. A., Leal, S. M., Tischfield, J. A., Kreek, M. J., & Yu, L. (1998). Single-nucleotide polymorphism in the human mu opioid receptor gene alters beta-endorphin binding and activity: Possible implications for opiate addiction. *Proceedings of the National Academy of Sciences USA, 95,* 9608–9613.

Boscolo, L., & Cecchin, G. (1982). Training in systemic therapy at the Milan centre. In R. Whiffen & J. Byng-Hall (Eds), *Family therapy supervision: Recent developments in practice* (pp. 153–165). London: Academic Press.

Boscolo, L., Cecchin, G., Hoffman, L., & Penn, P. (1987). *Milan systemic family therapy.* New York: BasicBooks.

Boszormenyi-Nagy, I. (1987). *Foundations of contextual therapy: Collected papers of Ivan Boszormenyi-Nagy, M.D.* New York: Brunner/Mazel.

Boszormenyi-Nagy, I., & Krasner, B. (1986). *Between give and take.* New York: Brunner/Mazel.

Bourke, E., Magill, M., & Apodaca, T. R. (2016). The in-session and long-term role of a significant other in motivational enhancement therapy for alcohol use disorders. *Journal of Substance Abuse Treatment, 64,* 35–43.

Bowen, M. (1992). *Family therapy in clinical practice.* Lanham, MD: Jason Aronson.

Boyd-Franklin, N. (2003). *Black families in therapy* (2nd Ed.). New York: Guilford Press.

Bradshaw, S., Shumway, S. T., Wang, E. W., Harris, K. S., Smith, D. B., & Austin-Robillard, H. (2015). Hope, readiness, and coping in family recovery from addiction. *Journal of Groups in Addiction & Recovery, 10*(4), 313–336.

Braitman, A. L., Kelley, M. L., Ladage, J., Schroeder, V., Gumienny, L. A., Morrow, J. A., & Klostermann, K. (2009). Alcohol and drug use among college student adult children of alcoholics. *Journal of Alcohol and Drug Education, 53*, 69–88.

Breese, G. R., Chu, K., Dayas, C. V., Funk, D., Knapp, D. J., Koob, G. F., Le, D. A., O'Dell, L. E. Overstreet, D. H., Roberts, A. J., Sinha, R., Valdez, G. R., & Weiss, F. (2005). Stress enhancement of craving during sobriety: A risk for relapse. *Alcoholism: Clinical and Experimental Research, 29*, 185–195.

Briones, E., Robbins, M. S., & Szapocznik, J. (2008). Brief strategic family therapy: Engagement and treatment. *Alcoholism Treatment Quarterly, 26*, 81–193.

Brito, G. (2013). Rethinking mindfulness in the therapeutic relationship. *Mindfulness, 5*(4), 1–9.

Bronfenbrenner, U. (1979). *The ecology of human development: Experiments by nature and design.* Cambridge, MA: Harvard University Press.

Brown, R. A., Dickerson, D. L., & D'Amico, E. J. (2016). Cultural identity among urban American Indian/Alaska Native youth: Implications for alcohol and drug use. *Prevention Science, 17*, 852–861.

Brown, S., & Lewis, V. (1999). *The alcoholic family in recovery: A developmental model.* New York: Guilford Press.

Buelow, G. D., & Buelow, S. A. (1998). *Psychotherapy in chemical dependence treatment.* Pacific Grove, CA: Brooks/Cole Publishing Company.

Burke, B. L., Vassilev, G., Kantchelov, A., & Zweben, A. (2002). Motivational interviewing with couples. In W. R. Miller & S. Rollnick (Eds), *Motivational interviewing: Preparing people for change* (2nd Ed.) (pp. 347–361). New York: Guilford Press.

Burkemper, E. M. (2002). Family therapists' ethical decision-making processes in two duty-to-warn situations. *Journal of Marital and Family Therapy, 28*(2), 203–211.

Burnett, G., Jones, R. A., Bliwise, N. G., & Ross, L. T. (2006). Family unpredictability, parental alcoholism, and the development of parentification. *The American Journal of Family Therapy, 34*, 181–189.

Butler, M. H., Rodriguez, M.-K. A., Roper, S. O., & Feinauer, L. L. (2010). Infidelity secrets in couple therapy: Therapists' views on the collision of competing ethics around relationship-relevant secrets. *Sexual Addiction & Compulsivity, 17*(2), 82–105.

Butt, O. I., Buehler, P. W., & D'Agnillo, F. (2011). Blood-brain barrier disruption and oxidative stress in guinea pig after systemic exposure to modified cell-free hemoglobin. *The American Journal of Pathology, 178*, 1316–1328.

Button, T., Stallings, M., Rhee, S., Corley, R., Boardman, J., & Hewitt, J. (2009). Perceived peer delinquency and the genetic predisposition for substance dependence vulnerability. *Drug and Alcohol Dependence, 100*(1–2), 1–8.

Button, T., Stallings, M., Rhee, S., Corley, R., & Hewitt, J. (2011). The etiology of stability and change in religious values and religious attendance. *Behavior Genetics, 41*, 201–210.

Cable, L. C. (2000). Kaleidoscopes and epic talks: Diverse narratives of adult children of alcoholics. In J.-A. Krestan (Ed.), *Bridges to recovery* (pp. 45–76). New York: The Free Press.

Cafferky, B. M., Mendez, M., Anderson, J. R., & Stith, S. M. (2018). Substance use and intimate partner violence: A meta-analytic review. *Psychology of Violence, 8*(1), 110–131.

Caldwell, B. E., & Stone, D. J. (2016). Using scaling to facilitate ethical decision-making in family therapy. *American Journal of Family Therapy, 44*(4), 198–210.

Caldwell, C., Sellers, R., Bernat, D., & Zimmerman, M. (2006). Racial identity, parental support and alcohol use in a sample of at-risk African American high school students. *American Journal of Community Psychology, 34*, 71–82.

Campbell, R., & Morris, M. (2017). Complicating narratives: Defining and deconstructing ethical challenges in community psychology. *American Journal of Community Psychology, 60*(3–4), 491–501.

Campbell-Meiklejohn, D., Wakeley, J., Herbert, V., Cook, J., Scollo, P., Ray, M. K., Selvaraj, S., Passingham, R. E., Cowen, P., & Rogers, R. D. (2011). Serotonin and dopamine play complementary roles in gambling to recover losses. *Neuropsychopharmacology: Official publication of the American College of Neuropsychopharmacology, 36*(2), 402–410.

Cardoso, J. B., Goldback, J. T., Cervantes, R. C., & Swank, P. (2016). Stress and multiple substance use behaviors among Hispanic adolescents. *Prevention Science, 17*(2), 208–217.

Carlezon, W. A. Jr., & Chartoff, E. H. (2007). Intracranial self-stimulation (ICSS) in rodents to study the neurobiology of motivation. *Nature Protocols, 2,* 2987–2995.

Carmel, A., Ries, R., West, I. I., Bumgardner, K., & Roy-Byrne, P. (2016). Suicide risk and associated demographic and clinical correlates among primary care patients with recent drug use. *The American Journal of Drug and Alcohol Abuse, 42*(3), 351–357.

Carnes, P. (1991). *Don't call it love.* New York: Bantam.

Carroll, K. M., Ball, S. A., Nich, C., Martino, S., Frankforter, T. L., Farentinos, C., & Woody, G. E. (2006). Motivational interviewing to improve treatment engagement and outcome in individuals seeking treatment for substance abuse: A multisite effectiveness study. *Drug and Alcohol Dependence, 81,* 301–312.

Carter, B., & McGoldrick, M. (1999). Overview: The expanded family life cycle. In B. Carter & M. McGoldrick (Eds), *The expanded family life cycle: Individual, family, and social perspectives* (3rd Ed.) (pp. 1–26). Boston, MA: Allyn & Bacon.

Carvajal, S. & Young, R. (2009). Culturally based substance abuse treatment for American Indians/Alaska Natives and Latinos. *Journal of Ethnicity in Substance Abuse, 8,* 207–222.

Catalano, E. M., & Sonenberg, N. (1993). *Consuming passions – help for compulsive shoppers.* Oakland, CA: New Harbinger Publications.

Cecchin, G. (1987). Hypothesizing, circularity, and neutrality revisited: An invitation to curiosity. *Family Process, 26,* 405–413.

Center for Behavioral Health Statistics and Quality (2016). *2015 national survey on drug use and health: Detailed tables.* Rockville, MD: Substance Abuse and Mental Health Services Administration.

Centers for Disease Control and Prevention (www.cdc.gov). Retrieved September 14, 2013.

Centers for Disease Control (2003). WISQARS Fatal injuries: Leading causes of death reports. National Center for Injury Prevention and Control. Retrived from www.cdc.gov.

Center for Substance Abuse Treatment (2004). *Substance abuse treatment and family therapy.* Treatment Improvement Protocol (TIP) Series, No. 39. HHS Publication No. (SMA) 15-4219. North Bethesda, MD: Substance Abuse and Mental Health Services Administration.

Chadwick, B., Miller, M. L., & Hurd, Y. L. (2013). Cannabis use during adolescent development: Susceptibility to psychiatric illness. *Frontiers in Psychiatry, 4,* 129.

Chaffin, M., Chenoweth, S., & Letourneau, E. J. (2016). Same-sex and race-based disparities in statutory rape arrests. *Journal of Interpersonal Violence, 31*(1), 26–48.

Chapman, C. (1997). Dual relationships in substance abuse treatment. *Alcoholism Treatment Quarterly, 15*(2), 73–79.

Charlet, K., Rosenthal, A., Lohoff, F. W., Heinz, A., & Beck, A. (2018). Imaging resilience and recovery in alcohol dependence. *Addiction, 113* (10), 1933–1950.

Chase-Lansdale, P. L., Cherlin, A. J., & Kiernan, K. E. (1995). The long-term effects of parental divorce on the mental health of young adults: A developmental perspective. *Child Development, 66,* 1614–1634.

Chavous, T., Bernat, D., Schmeelk-Cone, K., Cadwell, C., Kohn-Wood, L., & Zimmerman, M. (2003). Racial identity and academic attainment among African American adolescents. *Child Deviance, 74,* 1076–1090.

Chen, C. Y., Storr, C. L., & Anthony, J. C. (2009). Early-onset drug use and risk for drug dependence problems. *Addictive Behavior, 34*(3), 319–322.

Chen, H.-J., Balan, S., & Price, R. K. (2012). Association of contextual factors with drug use and binge drinking among White, Native American, and mixed-race adolescents in the general population. *Journal of Youth and Adolescence, 41*(11), 1426–1441.

Chen, J., Paredes, W., Lowinson, J. H., & Gardner, E. L. (1990). Delta 9-tetrahydrocannabinol enhances presynaptic dopamine efflux in medial prefrontal cortex. *European Journal of Pharmacology, 6*, 259–262.

Cheney, A. M., Booth, B. M., Borders, T. F., & Curran, G. M. (2016). The role of social capital in African Americans' attempts to reduce and quit cocaine use. *Substance Use & Misuse, 51*(6), 777–787.

Chiamulera, C., Epping-Jordan, M. P., Zocchi, A., Marcon, C., Cottiny, C., et al., ... Conquet, F. (2001). Reinforcing and locomotor stimulant effects of cocaine are absent in mGluR5 null mutant mice. *Nature Neuroscience, 4*(9), 873–874.

Cho, J., & Kogan, S. M. (2016). Risk and protective processes predicting rural African American young men's substance abuse. *American Journal of Community Psychology, 58*(3–4), 422–433.

Christakis, D., Moreno, M. G., Jelenchick, L., Myaing, M. T., & Zhou, C. H. (2011). Problematic internet usage in US college students: A pilot study. *BMC Medicine, 9*(77), 1–6.

Christenson, G. A., Faber, J. R., & de Zwann, M. (1994). Compulsive buying: Descriptive characteristics and psychiatric comorbidity. *Journal of Clinical Psychiatry, 55*, 5–11.

Chrzastowski, S. K. (2011). A narrative perspective on genograms: Revisiting classical family therapy methods. *Clinical Child Psychology and Psychiatry, 16*, 635–644.

Chuang, S., & Su, Y. (2009). Do we see eye to eye? Chinese mothers' and fathers' parenting beliefs and values for toddlers in Canada and China. *Journal of Family Psychology, 23*, 331–341.

Chung, T., Ye, F., Hipwell, A. E., Stepp, S. D., Miller, E., Borrero, S., & Hawk, M. (2017). Alcohol and marijuana use in pathways of risk for sexually transmitted infection in white and black adolescent females. *Substance Abuse, 38*(1), 77–81.

Clark, L., Averbeck, B., Payer, D., Sescousse, G., Winstanley, C. A., & Xue, G. (2013). Pathological choice: The neuroscience of gambling and gambling addiction. *The Journal of Neuroscience: The Official Journal of the Society for Neuroscience, 33*(45), 17617–17623.

Clark, T. T., Nguyen, A. B., & Belgrave, F. Z. (2011). Risk and protective factors for alcohol and marijuana use among African-American rural and urban adolescents. *Journal of Child & Adolescent Substance Abuse, 20*, 205–220.

Cohen, L. B. N., & Satterwhite P. (2002). Developing effective coalitions: An eight step guide. In M. E. Wurzbach (Ed.), *Community Health Education and Promotion: A Guide to Program Design and Evaluation* (pp. 144–161). Gaithersburg, MD: Aspen Publishers, Inc.

Cohen, L., & Swift, S. (1999). The spectrum of prevention: Developing a comprehensive approach to injury prevention. *Injury Prevention, 5*(3), 203–207.

Colombo, G., Agabio, R., Fà, M., Guano, L., Lobina, C., Loche, A., Reali, R., & Gessa, G. L. (1998). Reduction of voluntary ethanol intake in ethanol-preferring sP rats by the cannabinoid antagonist SR-141716. *Alcohol and Alcoholism, 33*, 126–130.

Connors, G. J., Donovan, D. M., & DiClemente, C. C. (2001). *Substance abuse treatment and the stages of change.* New York: Guilford Press.

Cooke, C. G., Kelley, M. L., Fals-Stewart, W., & Golden, J. (2004). A comparison of the psychosocial functioning of children with drug- versus alcohol-dependent fathers. *The American Journal of Drug and Alcohol Abuse, 30*, 695–710.

Corey, G., Corey, M. S., & Callanan, P. (2007). *Issues and ethics in the helping professions* (7th Ed.). Belmont, CA: Brooks/Cole.

Corey, G., Corey, M. S., & Corey, C. (2019). *Issues and ethics in the helping professions* (10th Ed.). Boston, MA: Cengage.

Cotton, N. (1979). The familial incidence of alcoholism: A review. *Journal of Studies on Alcohol, 40,* 89–116.

Cowell, A. J., Farrelly, M. C., Chou, R., & Vallone, D. M. (2009). Assessing the impact of the national 'truth' antismoking campaign on beliefs, attitudes, and intent to smoke by race/ethnicity. *Ethnicity & Health, 14*(1), 75–91.

Crisp, C. L., & DiNitto, D. M. (2012). Substance abuse treatment with sexual minorities. In C. A. McNeece & D. M. DiNitto (Eds), *Chemical dependency: A systems approach* (4th Ed.) (pp. 336–353). New York: Pearson.

Croff, R. L., Rieckmann, T. R., & Spence, J. D. (2014). Provider and state perspectives on implementing cultural-based models of care for American Indian and Alaska Native patients with substance use disorders. *Journal of Behavioral Health Services & Research, 41*(1), 64–79.

Culbreth, J. R. (2000). Substance abuse counselors with and without a personal history of chemical dependency. *Alcoholism Treatment Quarterly, 18,* 67–82.

Curtis, O. (1999). *Chemical dependency: A family affair.* Belmont, CA: Brooks/Cole.

Dakof, G. A., Godley, S. H., & Smith, J. (2010). Multidimensional Family Therapy (MDFT) and Adolescent Community Reinforcement (A-CRA): Addressing relapse during treatment. In Y. Kaminer & K. Winters (Eds), *Clinical manual of adolescent substance abuse treatment* (pp. 299–333). New York: American Psychiatric Publishing, Inc.

Daley, D. C., Salloum, I. M., & Thase, M. E. (2003). Integrated treatment using a recovery-oriented approach. In J. J. Westermeyer, R. D. Weiss, & D. M. Ziedonis (Eds), *Integrated treatment for mood and substance use disorders* (pp. 68–89). Baltimore, MD: Johns Hopkins University Press.

Danovitch, I., & Gorelick, D. A. (2012). State of the art treatments for cannabis dependence. *Psychiatric Clinics of North America, 35,* 309–326.

D'Arrigo-Patrick, J., Hoff, C., Knudson-Martin, C., & Tuttle, A. (2017). Navigating critical theory and postmodernism: Social justice and therapist power in family therapy. *Family Process, 56*(3), 574–588.

Dauria, E. F., McWilliams, M. A., & Tolou-Shams, M. (2018). Substance use prevention and treatment interventions for court-involved, non-incarcerated youth. In P. M. Monti, S. M. Colby, & T. O. Tevyaw (Eds), *Brief interventions for adolescent alcohol and substance abuse* (pp. 213–241). New York: Guilford Press.

Davidson, D., Swift, R. & Fitz, E. (1996). Naltrexone increases the latency to drink alcohol in social drinkers. *Alcoholism: Clinical and Experimental Research, 20,* 732–739.

Davidson, L., White, W., Sells, D., Schmutte, T., O'Connell, M., Bellamy, C., & Rowe, M. (2010). Enabling or engaging? The role of recovery support services in addiction recovery. *Alcoholism Treatment Quarterly, 28,* 391–416.

Davila, J., & Safren, S. A. (2017). Introduction to the special section on sexual and gender minority health. *Journal of Consulting and Clinical Psychology, 85*(12), 1109–1110.

Davis, S. D., & Piercy, F. P. (2007). What clients of couple therapy model developers and their former students say about change, Part II: Model-independent common factors and an integrative framework. *Journal of Marital and Family Therapy, 33,* 344–363.

Dawson, D. A., Goldstein, R. B., Chou, S. P., Ruan, W. J., & Grant, B. F. (2008). Age at first drink and the first incidence of adult-onset DSM-IV alcohol use disorders. *Alcoholism, Clinical and Experimental Research, 32*(12), 2149–2160.

Dei, K. A. (2002). *Ties that bind: Youth and drugs in a black community.* Prospect Heights, IL: Waveland Press.

DeJong, P., & Berg, I. K. (2012). *Interviewing for solutions* (4th Ed.). Belmont, CA: Brooks/Cole.

De La Rosa, M., Holleran, L., Rugh, D., & MacMaster, S. (2005). Substance abuse among U.S. Latinos: A review of the literature. *Journal of Social Work Practice in the Addictions, 5,* 1–20.

Dell'Osso, B., Allen, A., Altamura, C., Buoli, M., & Hollander, E. (2008). Impulsive-compulsive buying disorder: Clinical overview. *Australian and New Zealand Journal of Psychiatry*, 42(4), 259–266.

Delva, J., Wallace, J., O'Malley, P., Bachman, J., Johnston, L., & Schulenberg, J. (2005). The epidemiology of alcohol, marijuana, and cocaine use among Mexican American, Puerto Rican, Cuban American and other Latin American eighth-grade students in the United States: 1991–2002. *American Journal of Public Health*, 95, 696–702.

Dennis, M. L., Godley, S. H., Diamond, G. S., Tims, F. M., Babor, T., Donaldson, J., Liddle, H. A., Titus, J. C., Kaminer, Y., Webb, C., Hamilton, N., & Funk, R. R. (2004). The Cannabis Youth Treatment (CYT) study: Main findings from two randomized trials. *Journal of Substance Abuse Treatment*, 27, 197–213.

Dent, C. W., Sussman, S., Stacy, A. W., Craig, S., Burton, D., & Flay, B. R. (1995). Two-year behavior outcomes of project towards no tobacco use. *Journal of Consulting and Clinical Psychology*, 63(4), 676–677.

de Shazer, S. (1984). The death of resistance. *Family Process*, 23, 79–93.

de Shazer, S. (1985). *Keys to solution in brief therapy*. New York: W. W. Norton & Company.

de Shazer, S. (1988). *Clues: Investigating solutions in brief therapy*. New York: W. W. Norton & Company, Inc.

de Shazer, S. (1991). *Putting difference to work*. New York: W. W. Norton & Company, Inc.

de Shazer, S., Berg, I. K., Lipchik, E., Nunnally, E., Molnar, A., Gingerich, W., & Weiner-Davis, M. (1986). Brief therapy: Focused solution development. *Family Process*, 25, 207–222.

de Shazer, S., & Isebaert, L. (2004). The Bruges model: A solution-focused approach to problem drinking. *Journal of Family Psychotherapy*, 14(4), 43–52.

Devine, C., & Braithwaite, V. (1993). The survival roles of children of alcoholics: Their measurement and validity. *Addiction*, 88, 69–78.

Diamond, J. (2000). *Narrative means to sober ends*. New York: Guilford Press.

Dick, D. M., & Agrawal, A. (2008). The genetics of alcohol and other drug dependence. *Alcohol Research & Health: The Journal of the National Institute on Alcohol Abuse and Alcoholism*, 31(2), 111–118.

Dick, D. M., & Kendler, K. S. (2012). The impact of gene–environment interaction on alcohol use disorders. *Alcohol Research: Current Reviews*, 34(3), 318.

DiClemente, C. C. (2003). *Addiction and change*. New York: Guilford Press.

DiClemente, C. C., Corno, C. M., Graydon, M. M., Wiprovnick, A. E., & Knoblach, D. J. (2017). Motivational interviewing, enhancement, and brief interventions over the last decade: A review of reviews of efficacy and effectiveness. *Psychology of Addictive Behaviors*, 31(8), 862–887.

Diehl, A., Pillon, S. C., dos Santos, M. A., Rassool, G. H., & Laranjeira, R. (2016). Criminality and sexual behaviours in substance dependents seeking treatment. *Journal of Psychoactive Drugs*, 48(2), 124–134.

Dopp, A. R., Coen, A. S., Smith, A. B., Reno, J., Bernstein, D. H., Kerns, S. E. U., & Altschul, D. (2018). Economic impact of the statewide implementation of an evidence-based treatment: Multisystemic therapy in New Mexico. *Behavior Therapy*, 49(4), 551–566.

Doukas, N., & Cullen, J. (2010). Recovered addicts working in the addiction field: Pitfalls to substance abuse relapse. *Drugs: Education, Prevention and Policy*, 17(3), 216–231.

Doukas, N., & Cullen, J. (2011). Addiction counselors in recovery: Perceived barriers in the workplace. *Journal of Addiction Research & Therapy*, 2(3), 1–7.

Doyle, K. (1997). Substance abuse counselors in recovery: Implications for the ethical issue of dual relationships. *Journal of Counseling & Development*, 75(6), 428–432.

Dreyer, J. (2010). New insights into the roles of microRNAs in drug addiction and neuro-plasticity. *Genome Medicine*, 2, 92.

Duba, J. D., Graham, M. A., Britzman, M., & Minatrea, N. (2009). Introducing the "basic needs genogram" in reality therapy-based marriage and family counseling. *International Journal of Reality Therapy, 28*, 15–19.

Ducommon-Nagy, C., & Reiter, M. D. (2014). Contextual therapy. In M. D. Reiter (Ed.), *Case conceptualization in family therapy* (pp. 55–81). Boston, MA: Pearson.

Dunn, R., Callahan, J. L., Swift, J. K., & Ivanovic, M. (2013). Effects of pre-session centering for therapists on session presence and effectiveness. *Psychotherapy Research, 23*, 78–85.

Dyck, E. (2005). Flashback: Psychiatric experimentation with LSD in historical perspective. *Canadian Journal of Psychiatry, 50*, 381–388.

Ehlers, C. L., & Gizer, I. R. (2013). Evidence for a genetic component for substance dependence in Native Americans. *The American Journal of Psychiatry, 170*(2), 154–164.

Ehlers, C. L., Gizer, I. R., Gilder, D. A., Ellingson, J. M., & Yehuda, R. (2013). Measuring historical trauma in an American Indian community sample: Contributions of substance dependence, affective disorder, conduct disorder and PTSD. *Drug and Alcohol Dependence, 133*(1), 180–187.

Eiden, R. D., Molnar, D. S., Colder, C., Edwards, E. P., & Leonard, K. E. (2009). A conceptual model predicting internalizing problems in middle childhood among children of alcoholic and nonalcoholic fathers: The role of marital aggression. *Journal of Studies on Alcohol and Drugs, 70*, 741–750.

Eipper-Mains, J., Kiraly, D., Palakodeti, D., Mains, R., Eipper, B., & Graveley, B. (2011). microRNA-Seq reveals cocaine-regulated expression of striatal microRNAs. *RNA, 17*, 1529–1543.

Elliott, D. S., Huizinga, D., & Ageton, S. S. (1985). *Explaining delinquency and drug use*. Beverly Hills, CA: Sage.

Elman, B. D., & Dowd, E. T. (1997). Correlates of burnout in inpatient substance abuse treatment therapists. *Journal of Addictions & Offender Counseling, 17*(2), 56–65.

Enoch, M., & Goldman, D. (1999). Genetics of alcoholism and substance abuse. *Psychiatric Clinics of North America, 22*, 289–299.

Epstein, J., Williams, C. & Botvin, G. (2002). How universal are social influences to drink and problem behaviors for alcohol use? A test comparing urban African American and Caribbean American adolescents. *Addictive Behaviors, 27*, 75–86.

Escobedo, P., Allem, J.-P., Baezconde-Garbanati, L., & Unger, J. B. (2018). Cultural values associated with substance use among Hispanic emerging adults in Southern California. *Addictive Behaviors, 77*, 267–271.

Eshleman, J. R., & Bulcroft, R. A. (2010). *The family* (12th Ed.). Boston, MA: Allyn & Bacon.

Espinosa, E. M., Sorensen, J. R., & Lopez, M. A. (2013). Youth pathways to placement: The influence of gender, mental health need and trauma on confinement in the juvenile justice system. *Journal of Youth and Adolescence, 42*(12), 1824–1836.

Falicov, C. J. (2014). *Latino families in therapy* (2nd Ed.). New York: Guilford Press.

Falk, D., Yi, H., & Hiller-Sturmhofel, S. (2008). An epidemiologic analysis of co-occurring alcohol and other drug use and disorders. *Alcohol Research: Current Reviews, 31*, 155–167.

Fall, K. A., & Lyons, C. (2003). Ethical considerations of family secret disclosure and post-session safety management. *The Family Journal, 11*(3), 281–285.

Fals-Stewart, W., & O'Farrell, T. J. (2003). Behavioral family counseling and naltrexone for male opioid dependent patients. *Journal of Consulting and Clinical Psychology, 71*, 432–442.

Fals-Stewart, W., O'Farrell, T. J., & Birchler, G. R. (2001). Behavioral couples therapy for male methadone maintenance patients: Effects on drug-using behavior and relationship adjustment. *Behavior Therapy, 32*(2), 391–411.

Fals-Stewart, W., O'Farrell, T. J., & Birchler, G. R. (2004). Behavioral couples therapy for substance abuse: Rationale, methods, and findings. *Addiction Science & Clinical Practice, 2*(2), 30–41.

Fang, L., & Schinke, S. P. (2011). Alcohol use among Asian American adolescent girls: The impact of immigrant generation status and family relationships. *Journal of Ethnicity in Substance Abuse, 10,* 275–294.

Farrell, A. D., & Danish, S. J. (1993). Peer drug associations and emotional restraint: Causes or consequences of adolescents' drug use? *Journal of Consulting and Clinical Psychology, 61*(2), 327–334.

Farrelly, M. C., Davis, K. C., Duke, J., & Messeri, P. (2009). Sustaining 'truth': Changes in youth tobacco attitudes and smoking intentions after 3 years of a national antismoking campaign. *Health Education Research, 24*(1), 42–48.

Farrelly, M. C., Nonnemaker, J., Davis, K. C., & Hussin, A. (2009). The influence of the national truth campaign on smoking initiation. *American Journal of Preventive Medicine, 36*(5), 379–384.

Feduccia, A. A., & Mithoefer, M. C. (2018). MDMA-assisted psychotherapy for PTSD: Are memory reconsolidation and fear extinction underlying mechanisms? *Progress in Neuro-Psychopharmacology and Biological Psychiatry, 84* (Part B), 221–228.

Fernandez, A. C., Begley, E. A., & Marlatt, G. A. (2006). Family and peer interventions for adults: Past approaches and future direction. *Psychology of Addictive Behaviors, 20,* 207–213.

Fisch, R., Weakland, J. H., & Segal, L. (1982). *The tactics of change: Doing therapy briefly.* San Francisco, CA: Jossey-Bass Publishers.

Fischer, J. L., Pidcock, B. W., Munsch, J., & Forthun, L. (2005). Parental abusive drinking and sibling role differences. *Alcoholism Treatment Quarterly, 23*(1), 79–97.

Fischer, J. L., & Wampler, R. S. (1994). Abusive drinking in young adults: Personality type and family role as moderators of family-of-origin influences. *Journal of Marriage and the Family, 56*(2), 469–479.

Fish, J., Osberg, T. M., & Syed, M. (2017). "This is the way we were raised": Alcohol beliefs and acculturation in relation to alcohol consumption among Native Americans. *Journal of Ethnicity in Substance Abuse, 16*(2), 219–245.

Fisher, G. L. (2011). *Understanding why addicts are not all alike: Recognizing the types and how their differences affect intervention and treatment.* Santa Barbara, CA: Praeger.

Fisher, G. L., & Harrison, T. C. (2018). *Substance abuse: Information for school counselors, social workers, therapists, and counselors* (6th Ed.). New York: Pearson.

Fitzgerald, H. E., Puttler, L. I., Refior, S., & Zucker, R. A. (2007). Family response to children and alcohol. In J. L. Fischer, M. Mulsow, & A. W. Korinek (Eds), *Familial responses to alcohol problems* (pp. 11–25). New York: The Haworth Press.

Flanzer, J. P. (2005). Alcohol and other drugs are key causal agents of violence. In D. R. Loseke, R. J. Gelles, & M. M. Cavanaugh (Eds), *Current controversies on family violence* (2nd Ed.) (pp. 163–173). Thousand Oaks, CA: Sage.

Flemons, D. G. (1991). *Completing distinctions.* Boston, MA: Shambala.

Flemons, D., & Gralnik, L. M. (2013). *Relational suicide assessment.* New York: Norton.

Foroud, T., Bice, P., Castelluccio, P., Bo, R., Miller, L., Ritchotte, A., Lumeng, L., Li, T., & Carr, L. (2000). Identification of quantitative trait loci influencing alcohol consumption in the high alcohol drinking and low alcohol drinking rat lines. *Behavior Genetics, 30,* 131–140.

Foy, S. (2017). *Solution focused harm reduction.* Cham, Switzerland: Palgrave Macmillan.

Frey, W. H. (2018). The US will become 'minority white' in 2045, Census projects. Retrieved from www.brookings.edu/blog/the-avenue/2018/03/14/the-us-will-become-minority-white-in-2045-census-projects.

Friedman, A., Kaufer, D., Shemer, J., Hendler, I., Soreq, H., & Tur-Kaspa, I. (1996). Pyridostigmine brain penetration under stress enhances neuronal excitability and induces early immediate transcriptional response. *Nature Medicine, 2,* 1382–1385.

Friese, B., Grube, J. W., & Seninger, S. (2015). Drinking among Native American and White youths: The role of perceived neighborhood and school environment. *Journal of Ethnicity in Substance Abuse*, *14*(3), 287–307.

Gallagher, S. N. (2014). Treatment strategies for forensic psychologists working with clients dealing with substance abuse, legal charges, and enabling parents. *Journal of Forensic Psychology Practice*, *14*(2), 158–168.

Garavan, H., Pankiewicz, J., Bloom, A., Cho, J.-K., Sperry, L., Ross, T. J., Salmeron, B. J., Risinger, R., Kelley, D., & Stein, E. A. (2000). Cue-induced cocaine craving: Neuroanatomical specificity for drug users and drug stimuli. *American Journal of Psychiatry*, *157* (11), 1789–1798.

Garrett, J., & Landau, J. (2007). Family motivation to change: A major factor in engaging alcoholics in treatment. *Alcoholism Treatment Quarterly*, *25*, 65–83.

Garrett, J., Landau-Stanton, J., Stanton, M. D., Stellato-Kabat, J., & Stellato-Kabat, D. (1997). ARISE: A method for engaging reluctant alcohol- and drug-dependent individuals in treatment. *Journal of Substance Abuse Treatment*, *14*, 235–248.

Gearing, R. E., Schwalbe, C. S., & Short, K. D. (2012). Adolescent adherence to psychosocial treatment: Mental health clinicians' perspectives on barriers and promoters. *Psychotherapy Research*, *22*(3), 317–326.

Ghasemzadeh, M. B., Nelson, L. C., Lu, X. Y., & Kalivas, P. W. (1999). Neuroadaptations in ionotropic and metabotropic glutamate receptor mRNA produced by cocaine treatment. *Journal of Neurochemistry*, *72*(1), 157–165.

Gil, A., Wagner, E., & Vega, W. (2000). Acculturation, familism, and alcohol use among Latino adolescent males: Longitudinal relations. *Journal of Community Psychology*, *28*, 443–458.

Glover, G. J. (1994). The hero child in the alcoholic home: Recommendations for counselors. *School Counselor*, *41*, 185–190.

Goldbach, J. T., Mereish, E. H., & Burgess, C. (2017). Sexual orientation disparities in the use of emerging drugs. *Substance Use and Misuse*, *52*(2), 265–271.

Gooding, P., & Tarrier, N. (2009). A systematic review and meta-analysis of cognitive-behavioural interventions to reduce problem gambling: Hedging our bets? *Behaviour Research and Therapy*, *47*, 592–607.

Gordon, D., & Meyers-Anderson, M. (1981). *Phoenix: Therapeutic patterns of Milton H. Erickson*. Cupertino, CA: Meta Publications.

Gouzoulis-Mayfrank, E., & Daumann, J. (2009). Neurotoxicity of drugs of abuse—the case of methylenedioxyamphetamines (MDMA, ecstasy), and amphetamines. *Dialogues in Clinical Neuroscience*, *11*, 305–317.

Grant, J. D., Heath, A., Bucholz, K., Madden, P., Agrawal, A., Statham, D., & Martin, N. (2007). Spousal concordance for alcohol dependence: Evidence for assortative mating or spousal interaction effects? *Alcoholism, Clinical, and Experimental Research*, *31*, 717–728.

Grant J. E. (2003). Three cases of compulsive buying treated with naltrexone. *International Journal of Psychiatry in Clinical Practice*, *7*, 223–225.

Grant, J. E., Kim, S. W., & Hartman, B. K. (2008). A double-blind, placebo-controlled study of the opiate antagonist naltrexone in the treatment of pathological gambling urges. *The Journal of Clinical Psychiatry*, *69*, 783–789.

Gray, J. S., & McCullagh, J. A. (2014). Suicide in Indian country: The continuing epidemic in rural Native American communities. *Journal of Rural Mental Health*, *38*(2), 79–86.

Greenbaum, P. E., Wang, W., Henderson, C. E., Kan, L., Hall, K., Dakof, G. A., & Liddle, H. A. (2015). Gender and ethnicity as moderators: Integrative data analysis of multidimensional family therapy randomized clinical trials. *Journal of Family Psychology*, *29*(6), 919–930.

Greene, K., & Bogo, M. (2002). The different faces of intimate violence: Implications for assessment and treatment. *Journal of Marital and Family Therapy*, *28*, 455–466.

Greene, K. M., Eitle, T. M., & Eitle, D. (2014). Adult social roles and alcohol use among American Indians. *Addictive Behaviors, 39*(9), 1357–1360.

Grencavage, L. M., & Norcross, J. (1990). Where are the commonalities among the therapeutic common factors? *Professional Psychology: Research and Practice, 21,* 372–378.

Griffin, K. W., Botvin, G. J., Scheier, L. M., Diaz, T., & Miller, N. L. (2000). Parenting practices as predictors of substance use, delinquency, and aggression among urban minority youth: Moderation effects on family structure and gender. *Psychology of Addictive Behaviors, 14,* 174–184.

Griffiths, M. (2014, July 6). Term warfare: 'Problem gambling' and 'gambling addiction' are not the same. Retrieved from https://drmarkgriffiths.wordpress.com/2014/07/06/term-warfare-problem-gambling-and-gambling-addiction-are-not-the-same.

Grosenick, J. K., & Hatmaker, C. M. (2000). Perceptions of staff attributes in substance abuse treatment. *Journal of Substance Abuse Treatment, 19*(3), 272–284.

Gruber, K. J., & Taylor, M. F. (2006). A family perspective for substance abuse: Implications from the literature. In S. L. A. Straussner & C. H. Fewell (Eds), *Impact of substance abuse on children and families: Research and practice implications* (pp. 1–29). New York: The Haworth Press.

Hahm, H. C., Lahiff, M., & Guterman, N. B. (2003). Acculturation and parental attachment in Asian-American adolescents' alcohol use. *Journal of Adolescent Health, 33,* 119–129.

Haley, J. (1984). *Ordeal therapy.* San Francisco, CA: Jossey-Bass Publishers.

Haley, J. (1987). *Problem-solving therapy* (2nd Ed.). San Francisco, CA: Jossey-Bass Publishers.

Haley, J. (1993). *Uncommon therapy.* New York: W. W. Norton & Company.

Haley, J., & Richeport-Haley, M. (2007). *Directive family therapy.* New York: The Haworth Press.

Hall, G. W., Carriero, N. J., Takushi, R. Y., Montoya, I. D., Preston, K. L., & Gorelick, D. A. (2000). Pathological gambling among cocaine-dependent outpatients. *American Journal of Psychiatry, 157,* 1127–1133.

Han, D. H., Hwang, J. W., & Renshaw, P. F. (2011). Bupropion sustained release treatment decreases craving for video games and cue-induced brain activity in patients with internet video game addiction. *Psychology of Popular Media Culture, 1*(S), 108–117.

Han, Y., Lin, V., Wu, F., & Hser, Y.-I. (2016). Gender comparisons among Asian American and Pacific Islander patients in drug dependency treatment. *Substance Use & Misuse, 51*(6), 752–762.

Hansen, W. B., Johnson, C. A., Flay, B. R., Graham, J. W., & Sobel, J. (1988). Affective and social influences approaches to the prevention of multiple substance abuse among seventh grade students: Results from project SMART. *Preventive Medicine, 17*(2), 135–154.

Hanson, M., & El-Bassel, N. (2014). Motivating clients with substance use disorders through the helping process. In S. L. A. Straussner (Ed.), *Clinical work with substance-abusing clients* (3rd Ed.) (pp. 141–164). New York: Guilford Press.

HapMap data release #27, International HapMap Project. Retrieved from http://hapmap.ncbi.nlm.nih.gov/index.html.en.

HapMap data release #28, International HapMap Project. Retrieved from http://hapmap.ncbi.nlm.nih.gov/index.html.en.

Harding, F. M., Hingson, R. W., Klitzner, M., Mosher, J. F., Brown, J. et al., . . . Cannon, C. L. (2016). Underage drinking: A review of trends and prevention strategies. *American Journal of Prevention Medicine, 51*(4S2), 2148–S157.

Hardoon, K. K., Gupta, R., & Derevensky, J. L. (2004). Psychosocial variables associated with adolescent gambling. *Psychology of Addictive Behaviors, 18*(2), 170–179.

Hardy, K., & Laszloffy, T. (1995). The cultural genogram: Key to training culturally competent family therapists. *Journal of Marital and Family Therapy, 21,* 227–237.

Hartshorn, K. J. S., Whitbeck, L. B., & Prentice, P. (2015). Substance use disorders, comorbidity, and arrest among indigenous adolescents. *Crime & Delinquency, 61*(10), 1311–1332.

Hartston, H. (2012). The case for compulsive shopping as an addiction. *Journal of Psychoactive Drugs, 44*(1), 64–67.

Hastings, A. S. (2000). *Discovering sexuality that will satisfy you both*. Gretna, LA: Wellness Institute.

Hatzenbuehler, M. L., McLaughlin, K. A., & Xuan, Z. (2015). Social networks and sexual orientation disparities in tobacco and alcohol use. *Journal of Studies on Alcohol and Drug, 76*(1), 117–126.

Haugland, B. S. M. (2005). Recurrent disruptions of rituals and routines in families with paternal alcohol abuse. *Family Relations, 54*, 225–241.

Haverfield, M. C., & Theiss, J. A. (2016). Parent's alcoholism severity and family topic avoidance about alcohol as predictors of perceived stigma among adult children of alcoholics: Implications for emotional and psychological resilience. *Health Communication, 31*(5), 606–616.

Hawkins, C. A., & Hawkins, R. C. (2012). Family systems and chemical dependency. In C. A. McNeece & D. DiNitto (Eds), *Chemical dependency: A systems approach* (4th Ed.) (pp. 256–284). New York: Pearson.

Hayakawa, K., Mishima, K., Hazekawa, M., Sano, K., Irie, K., Orito, K., Egawa, T., Kitamura, Y., Uchida, N., Nishimura, R., Egashira, N., & Fujiwara, M. (2008). Cannabidiol potentiates pharmacological effects of Δ9-tetrahydrocannabinol via CB1 receptor-dependent mechanism. *Brain Research, 1188*, 157–164.

Heath, A., Jardine, R., & Martin, N. (1989). Interactive effects of genotype and social environment on alcohol consumption in female twins. *Journal of Studies on Alcohol, 50*, 38–48.

Hecksher, D. (2007). Former substance users working as counselors: A dual relationship. *Substance Use & Misuse, 42*(8), 1253–1268.

Heilig, M., Goldman, D., Berrettini, W., & O'Brien, C. (2011). Pharmacogenetic approaches to the treatment of alcohol addiction. *Nature Reviews Neuroscience, 12*, 670–684.

Henderson, C. E., Marvel, F., & Liddle, H. A. (2012). Multidimensional Family Therapy: An evidence-based treatment for juvenile justice involved and substance abusing adolescents. In N. Jainchill (Ed.), *Understanding and treating adolescent substance use disorders* (pp. 11–1 to 11–13). Kingston, NJ: Civic Research Institute.

Henggeler, S. W., Clingempeel, W. G., Brondino, M. J., & Pickrel, S. G. (2002). Four-year follow-up of multisystemic therapy with substance-abusing and substance-dependent juvenile offenders. *Journal of the American Academy of Child and Adolescent Psychiatry, 41*, 868–876.

Henggeler, S. W., Halliday-Boykins, C. A., Cunningham, P. B., Randall, J., Shapiro, S. B., & Chapman, J. E. (2006). Juvenile drug court: Enhancing outcomes by integrating evidence-based treatments. *Journal of Consulting and Clinical Psychology, 74*, 42–54.

Henggeler, S. W., Rowland, M. D., Randall, J., Ward, D. M., Pickrel, S. G., Cunningham, P. B., Miller, S. L., Edwards, J., Zealberg, J. J., Hand, L. D., & Santos, A. B. (1999). Home based multisystemic therapy as an alternative to the hospitalization of youths in psychiatric crisis: Clinical outcomes. *Journal of the American Academy of Child and Adolescent Psychiatry, 38*, 1331–1339.

Henggeler, S. W., & Schaeffer, C. M. (2016). Multisystemic therapy: Clinical overview, outcomes, and implementation research. *Family Process, 55*, 514–528.

Henggeler, S. W., & Schaeffer, C. M. (2017). Treating serious antisocial behavior using multisystemic therapy. In J. R. Weisz & A. E. Kazdin (Eds), *Evidence-based psychotherapies for children and adolescents* (3rd ed.) (pp. 197–214). New York: Guilford Press.

Henggeler, S. W., Schoenwald, S. K., Borduin, C. M., Rowland, M. D., & Cunningham, P. B. (2009). *Multisystemic therapy for antisocial behavior in children and adolescents* (2nd Ed.). New York: Guilford Press.

Henggeler, S. W., Schoenwald, S. K., Rowland, M. D., & Cunningham, P. B. (2002). *Serious emotional disturbance in children and adolescents: Multisystem therapy*. New York: Guilford Press.

Henggeler, S. W., Sheidow, A. J., Cunningham, P. B., Donohue, B. C., & Ford, J. D. (2008). Promoting the implementation of an evidence-based intervention for adolescent marijuana abuse in community settings: Testing the use of intensive quality assurance. *Journal of Clinical Child and Adolescent Psychology, 37*, 682–689.

Hernandez, L., & Moreno, O. (2018). Latino youth, acculturation, and parenting. In P. M. Monti, S. M. Colby, & T. O. Tevyaw (Eds), *Brief interventions for adolescent alcohol and substance abuse* (pp. 262–283). New York: Guilford Press.

Hesselbrock, V., & Hesselbrock, M. (1990). Behavioral/social factors that may enhance or attenuate genetic effects. In C. Cloninger & H. Begleiter (Eds) (1991), *Genetics and biology of alcoholism (banbury report 33)* (pp. 75–85). New York: Cold Spring Harbor Laboratory Press.

Hicks, D. (2000). The importance of specialized treatment programs for lesbian and gay patients. *Journal of Gay & Lesbian Psychotherapy, 3*(3/4), 81–94.

Higgins, M. P. (1998). Alcoholic families: The crisis of early recovery. *Family Therapy, 253*, 203–219.

Higgins, S. T., Silverman, K., & Heil, S. H. (2008). *Contingency management in substance abuse treatment*. New York: Guilford Press.

Higuchi, S., Matsushita, S., Masaki, T., Yokoyama, A., Kimura, M., Suzuki, G., & Mochizuki, H. (2004). Influence of genetic variations of ethanol-metabolizing enzymes on phenotypes of alcohol-related disorders. *Annals of the New York Academy of Sciences, 1025*, 472–480.

Hong, J., Huang, H., Sabri, B., & Kim, J. (2011). Substance abuse among Asian American youth: An ecological review of the literature. *Children and Youth Services Review, 33*, 669–677.

Hook, J. N., Hook, J. P. & Hines, S. (2008). Reach out or act out: Long-term group therapy for sexual addiction. *Sexual Addiction & Compulsivity, 15*(3), 217–232.

Horigian, V. E., Feaster, D. J., Brincks, A., Robbins, M. S., Perez, M. A., & Szapocznik, J. (2015). The effects of Brief Strategic Family Therapy (BSFT) on parent substance use and the association between parent and adolescent substance use. *Addictive Behaviors, 42*, 44–50.

Horigian, V. E., Feaster, D. J., Robbins, M. S., Brincks, A. M., Ucha, J., Rohrbaugh, M. J., Shoham, V., Bachrach, K., Miller, M., Burlew, K. A., Hodgkins, C. C., Carrion, I. S., Siverstein, M., Werstlein, R., & Szapocznik, J. (2015). A cross-sectional assessment of the long term effects of brief strategic family therapy for adolescent substance use. *American Journal of Addictions, 24*(7), 637–645.

Hudak, J., Krestan, J. A., & Bepko, C. (1999). Alcohol problems and the family life cycle. In B. Carter & M. McGoldrick (Eds), *The expanded family life cycle* (3rd Ed.) (pp. 455–469). Boston, MA: Allyn & Bacon.

Hughes, J. R. (2009). Alcohol withdrawal seizures. *Epilepsy Behavior, 15*, 92–97.

Hughes, T. L., Wilsnack, S. C., & Kantor, L. W. (2016). The influence of gender and sexual orientation on alcohol use and alcohol-related problems: Toward a global perspective. *Alcohol Research: Current Reviews, 38*(1), 121–132.

Hui, M., & Gang, Z. (2014). The dopamine system and alcohol dependence. *Shanghai Archives of Psychiatry, 26* (2), 61–68.

Humphreys, K., Blodgett, J. C., & Wagner, T. H. (2014). Estimating the efficacy of Alcoholics Anonymous without self-selection bias: An instrumental variable re-analysis of randomized clinical trials. *Alcoholism: Clinical and Experimental Research, 38*(11), 2688–2694.

Hur, M. H. (2006). Demographic, habitual, and socioeconomic determinants of Internet Addiction Disorder: An empirical study of Korean teenagers. *Cyberpsychology & Behavior, 9*(5), 514–525.

Hussong, A. M., Huang, W., Curran, P. J., Chassin, L., & Zucker, R. A. (2010). Parent alcoholism impacts the severity and timing of children's externalizing symptoms. *Journal of Abnormal Child Psychology, 38*, 367–380.

Hussong, A. M., Huang, W., Serrano, D., Curran, P. J., & Chassin, L. (2012). Testing whether and when parent alcoholism uniquely affects various forms of adolescent substance use. *Journal of Abnormal Child Psychology, 40*, 1265–1276.

Isebaert, L. (2017). *Solution-focused cognitive and systemic therapy: The Bruges model.* New York: Routledge.

Iwamoto, D. K., Grivel, M. M., Cheng, A. W., & Zamboanga, B. L. (2016a). Asian American and White college students' heavy episodic drinking and alcohol-related problems. *Substance Use & Misuse, 51*(10), 1384–1392.

Iwamoto, D. K., Kaya, A., Grivel, M., & Clinton, L. (2016b). Under-researched demographics: Heavy episodic drinking and alcohol-related problems among Asian Americans. *Alcohol Research: Current Reviews, 38*(1), 17–25.

Jaffe, P., Wolfe, D. A., & Campbell, M. (2012). *Growing up with domestic violence.* Cambridge, MA: Hogrefe.

Jellinek, E. M. (1983). *The disease concept of alcoholism.* New Haven, CT: College and University Press.

Jensen, C. D., Cushing, C. C., Aylward, B. S., Craig, J. T., Sorell, D. M., & Steele, R. G. (2011). Effectiveness of motivational interviewing interventions for adolescent substance use behavior change: A meta-analytic review. *Journal of Consulting and Clinical Psychology, 79*(4), 433–440.

John, R. (2012). The Native American family. In R. Wright, Jr., C. H. Mindel, T. V. Tran, & R. W. Habenstein (Eds), *Ethnic families in America: Patterns and variations* (5th Ed.) (pp. 361–410). Boston, MA: Pearson.

Johnides, B. D., Borduin, C. M., Wagner, D. V., & Dopp, A. R. (2017). Effects of multisystemic therapy on caregivers of serious juvenile offenders: A 20-year follow-up to a randomized clinical trial. *Journal of Consulting and Clinical Psychology, 85*(4), 323–334.

Johnson, M. W., & Griffiths, R. R. (2017). Potential therapeutic effects of psilocybin. *Neurotherapeutics, 14* (3), 734–740.

Johnson, V. E. (1986). *Intervention: How to help someone who doesn't want help.* Minneapolis, MN: Johnson Institute Books.

Johnston, L. D., Miech, R. A., O'Malley, P. M., Backman, J. G., Schulenberg, J. E., & Patrick, M. E. (2018). 2017 overview: Key findings on adolescent drug use. Retrieved from National Institute on Drug Abuse website: www.monitoringthefuture.org/pubs/monographs/mtf-overview2017.pdf.

Johnston, L. D., O'Malley, P. M., Miech, R. A., Bachman, J. G., & Schulenberg, J. E. (2016). *Monitoring the Future national survey results on drug use, 1975–2015: Overview, key findings on adolescent drug use.* Ann Arbor, MI: Institute for Social Research, The University of Michigan.

Jonkman, S., & Kenny, P. (2013). Molecular, cellular, and structural mechanisms of cocaine addiction: A key role for microRNAs. *Neuropsychopharmacology, 38*, 198–211.

Joutsa, J., Johansson, J., Niemelä, S., Ollikainen, A., Hirvonen, M. M., Piepponen, P., Arponen, E., Alho, H., Voon, V., Rinne, J., Hietala, J., & Kaasinen, V. (2012). Mesolimbic dopamine release is linked to symptom severity in pathological gambling. *NeuroImage, 60*, 1992–1999.

Juhnke, G. A., & Coker, J. K. (1997). A solution-focused intervention with recovering, alcohol-dependent, single parent mothers and their children. *Journal of Addictions & Offender Counseling, 17*, 77–88.

Kafka, M. (2010). Hypersexual disorder: A proposed diagnosis for DSM-V. *Archives of Sexual Behavior, 39*, 377–400.

Kandel, D., Chen, K., Warner, L. A., Kessler, R. C., & Grant, B. (1997). Prevalence and demographic correlates of symptoms of last year dependence on alcohol, nicotine, marijuana and cocaine in the U.S. population. *Drug and Alcohol Dependence, 44*, 11–29.

Kasl, C. D. (1989). *Women, sex, and addiction: A search for love and power.* New York: Ticknor & Fields.

Kaufman, E. (1984). Family system variables in alcoholism. *Alcoholism: Clinical and Experimental Research, 8*(1), 4–8.

Kaufman, E. (1985). Family therapy in the treatment of alcoholism. In T. E. Bratter & G. G. Forrest (Eds), *Alcoholism and substance abuse: Strategies for clinical intervention* (pp. 376–397). New York: The Free Press.

Keane, A. (2013). The influence of therapist mindfulness practice on psychotherapeutic work: A mixed-methods study. *Mindfulness, 5*(6), 689–703.

Keeney, B. P. (1983). *Aesthetics of change.* New York: Guilford Press.

Keeney, H., & Keeney, B. (2013). *Creative therapeutic technique.* Phoenix, AZ: Zeig, Tucker, & Thiesen.

Kelley, A. E., & Berridge, K. C. (2002). The neuroscience of natural rewards: relevance to addictive drugs. *Journal of Neuroscience, 22*(9), 3306–3311.

Kelley, A., Bingham, D., Brown, E., & Pepion, L. (2017). Assessing the impact of American Indian peer recovery support on substance use and health. *Journal of Groups in Addiction & Recovery, 12*(4), 296–308.

Kelley, M. L., Braitman, A., Henson, J. M., Schroeder, V., Ladage, J., & Gumienny, L. (2010). Relationships among depressive mood symptoms and parent and peer relations in collegiate children of alcoholics. *American Journal of Orthopsychiatry, 80*, 204–212.

Kelly, S., & Hudson, B. N. (2017). African American couples and families and the context of structural oppression. In S. Kelly (Ed.), *Diversity in couple and family therapy* (pp. 3–32). Santa Barbara, CA: Praeger.

Kendler, K., Gardner, C., & Dick, D. (2011). Predicting alcohol consumption in adolescence from alcohol-specific and general externalizing genetic risk factors, key environmental exposures and their interaction. *Psychological Medicine, 41*, 1507–1516.

Kennedy, P., Feng, J., Robison, A., Maze, I., Badimon, A., Mouzon, E., Chaudhury, D., Damez-Werno, D., Haggarty, S., Han, M., Bassel-Duby, R., Olson, E., & Nestler, E. (2013). Class I HDAC inhibition blocks cocaine-induced plasticity by targeted changes in histone methylation. *Nature Neuroscience, 16*, 434–440.

Kerr, M. E., & Bowen, M. (1988). *Family evaluation: An approach based on Bowen theory.* New York: W. W. Norton & Company.

Kessler, R. C., Hwang, I., LaBrie, R. L., Petukhova, M., Sampson, N. A., Winters, K. C., & Shaffer, H. J. (2008). DSM-IV pathological gambling in the National Comorbidity Survey Replication. *Psychological Medicine, 38*(9), 1351–1360.

Kim, J. S., Brook, J., & Akin, B. A. (2018). Solution-focused brief therapy with substance-using individuals: A randomized controlled trial study. *Research on Social Work Practice, 28*(4), 452–462.

Kim, S. W. (1998). Opioid antagonists in the treatment of impulse-control disorders. *Journal of Clinical Psychiatry, 59*, 159–164.

King, K. A., Vidourek, R. A., & Hill, M. K. (2014). Recent alcohol use and episodic heavy drinking among American Indian youths. *Journal of Child & Adolescent Substance Abuse, 23*(5), 334–346.

King, K. A., Vidourek, R. A., Merianos, A. L., & Bartsch, L. A. (2017). Psychosocial factors associated with alcohol use among Hispanic youth. *Journal of Immigrant and Minority Health, 19*(5), 1035–1041.

Kishline, A. (1994). *Moderate drinking: The moderation management guide for people who want to reduce their drinking.* New York: Crown Trade Paperbacks.

Kleinig, J. (2008). The ethics of harm reduction. *Substance Use & Misuse, 43*(1), 1–16.

Knapp, S. J., Gottlieb, M. C., & Handelsman, M. M. (2015). The ethical decision-making model. In S. J. Knapp, S. J. Gottlieb, & M. M. Handelsman (Eds), *Ethical dilemmas in psychotherapy: Positive approaches to decision making* (pp. 25–45). Washington, DC: American Psychological Association.

Knapp, S. J., & VandeCreek, L. D. (2012). *Practical ethics for psychologists: A positive approach* (2nd Ed.). Washington DC: American Psychological Association.

Knapp, S. J., VandeCreek, L. D., & Fingerhut, R. (2017). *Practical ethics for psychologists: A positive approach* (3rd Ed.). Washington DC: American Psychological Association.

Ko, C., Liu, G., Hsiao, S., Yen, J., Yang, M., Lin, W., Yen, C., & Chen, C. (2009). Brain activities associated with gaming urge of online gaming addiction. *Journal of Psychiatric Research, 43*(7), 739–747.

Ko, C.-H., Yen, J.-Y., Chen, C.-C., Chen, S.-H., Wu, K., & Yen, C.-F. (2006). Tridimensional personality of adolescents with internet addiction and substance use experience. *The Canadian Journal of Psychiatry, 51*(14), 887–894.

Kohler, D. (2014). A monetary valuation of the quality of life loss associated with pathological gambling: An application using a health utility index. *Journal of Gambling Issues, 29*, 1–23.

Kõlves, K., Draper, B. M., Snowdon, J., & De Leo, D. (2017). Alcohol-use disorders and suicide: Results from a psychological autopsy study in Australia. *Alcohol, 64*, 29–35.

Koob, G. F., & Volkow, N. D. (2010). Neurocircuitry of addiction. *Neuropsychopharmacology, 35*, 217–238.

Koopmans, J., Slutske, W., van Baal, G., & Boomsma, D. (1999). The influence of religion on alcohol use initiation: Evidence for genotype X environment interaction. *Behavior Genetics, 29*, 445–453.

Kopak, A. M., Hurt, S., Proctor, S. L., & Hoffman, N. G. (2016). Clinical indicators of successful substance use treatment among adults in the criminal justice system. *International Journal of Mental Health and Addiction, 14*(5), 831–843.

Koran, L., Faber, R., Aboujaoude, M. A., Large, M., & Serpe, R. (2006). Estimated prevalence of compulsive buying behavior in the United States. *American Journal of Psychiatry, 21*, 109–142.

Kosok, A. (2006) Moderation Management programme in 2004: What type of drinker seeks controlled drinking? *International Journal of Drug Policy, 17*, 295–303.

Kosten, T., Rounsaville, B., Kosten, T., & Merikangas, K. (1991). Gender differences in the specificity of alcoholism transmission among the relatives of opioid addicts. *The Journal of Nervous and Mental Disorders, 179*, 392–400.

Kosutic, I., & McDowell, T. (2008). Diversity and social justice issues in family therapy literature: A decade review. *Journal of Feminist Family Therapy: An International Forum, 20*(2), 142–165.

Kress, V. E., Protivnak, J. J., & Sadlak, L. (2008). Counseling clients involved with violent intimate partners: The mental health counselor's role in promoting client safety. *Journal of Mental Health Counseling, 30*(3), 200–210.

Krestan, J.-A. (2000). Addiction, power, and powerlessness. In J.-A. Krestan (Ed.), *Bridges to recovery* (pp. 15–44). New York: The Free Press.

Kuehl, B. P. (1996). The use of genograms with solution-based and narrative therapies. *The Family Journal, 4*, 5–11.

Kulis, S., Hodge, D. R., Ayers, S. L., Brown, E. F., & Marsiglia, F. F. (2012). Spirituality and religion: Intertwined protective factors for substance use among urban American Indian youth. *The American Journal of Drug and Alcohol Abuse, 38*(5), 444–449.

Kumpf, C. I. (2013). Frameworks and models in ethical decision making. In C. M. Jungers & J. Gregoire (Eds), *Counseling ethics: Philosophical and professional foundations* (pp. 47–70). New York: Springer.

Kumpfer, K. L. (2014). Family-based interventions for the prevention of substance abuse and other impulse control disorders in girls. *ISRN Addict*, March 3, 308789.

Kumpfer, K. L., Alvarado, R., & Whiteside, H. O. (2003). Family-based interventions for substance use and misuse prevention. *Substance Use & Misuse, 38*(11–13), 1759–1787.

Kunos, G., & Bátkai, S. (2001). Novel physiologic functions of endocannabinoids as revealed through the use of mutant mice. *Neurochemical Research, 26*, 1015–1021.

Kuzma, J. M., & Black, D. W. (2008). Epidemiology, prevalence, and natural history of compulsive sexual behavior. *Psychiatric Clinics of North America*, *31*(4), 603–611.

Lacey, K. K., Mouzon, D. M., Govia, I. O., Matusko, N., Forsythe-Brown, I., Abelson, J. M., & Jackson, J. S. (2016). Substance abuse among Blacks across the diaspora. *Substance Use & Misuse*, *51*(9), 1147–1158.

Ladd, G. T., & Petry, N. M. (2003). A comparison of pathological gamblers with and without substance abuse treatment histories. *Experimental and Clinical Psychopharmacology*, *11*(3), 202–209.

Lambert, M. J. (1992). Psychotherapy outcome research: Implications for integrative and eclectic therapists. In J. C. Norcross & M. R. Goldfried (Eds), *Handbook of psychotherapy integration* (pp. 94–129). New York: BasicBooks.

Lambert, M. J., & Bergin, A. E. (1994). The effectiveness of psychotherapy. In A. E. Bergin & S. L. Garfield (Eds), *Handbook of psychotherapy and behavior change* (4th Ed.) (pp. 143–189). New York: Wiley.

Landau, J., & Garrett, J. (2008). Invitational intervention: The ARISE model for engaging reluctant alcohol and other drug abusers in treatment. In O. J. Morgan & C. H. Litzke (Eds), *Family intervention in substance abuse: Current best practices* (pp. 147–168). New York: The Haworth Press.

Landau, J., Garrett, J., Shea, R. R., Stanton, M. D., Brinkman-Sull, D., & Baciewicz, G. (2000). Strength in numbers: The ARISE method for mobilizing family and network to engage substance abusers in treatment. *American Journal of Drug and Alcohol Abuse*, *26*, 379–398.

Landau, J., Garrett, J., & Webb, R. (2008). Assisting a concerned person to motivate someone experiencing cybersex into treatment. *Journal of Marital and Family Therapy*, *34*(4), 498–511.

Landau, J., Stanton, M. D., Brinkman-Sull, D., Ikle, D., McCormick, D., Garrett, J., Baciewicz, G., Shea, R. R., Browning, A., & Wamboldt, F. (2004). Outcomes with the ARISE approach to engaging reluctant drug- and alcohol-dependent individuals in treatment. *The American Journal of Drug and Alcohol Abuse*, *30*, 711–748.

Lawson, A. W. (2011). Children of alcoholics and adult children of alcoholics. In G. W. Lawson & A. W. Lawson (Eds), *Alcoholism and substance abuse in diverse populations* (2nd Ed.) (pp. 171–212). Austin, TX: Pro.ed.

Lawson, A., & Lawson, G. (1998). *Alcoholism and the family* (2nd Ed.). Gaithersburg, MD: Aspen Publishers, Inc.

Lawson, G. (1982). Relation of counselor traits to evaluation of the counseling relationship of alcoholics. *Journal of Studies on Alcohol*, *43*, 834–838.

Leavitt, R. A., Ertl, A., Sheats, K., Petrosky, E., Ivey-Stephenson, A., & Fowler, K. A. (2018). Suicides among American Indian/Alaska Natives—National violent death reporting system, 18 states, 2003–2014. *Morbidity and Mortality Weekly Report*, *67*(8), 237–242.

Le Foll, B., Gallo, A., Le Strat, Y., Lu, L., & Gorwood, P. (2009). Genetics of dopamine receptors and drug addiction: A comprehensive review. *Behavioral Pharmacology*, *20*, 1–17.

Le, T., Goebert, D., & Wallen, J. (2009). Acculturation factors and substance use among Asian American youth. *Journal of Primary Prevent*, *30*, 453–473.

Lee, Y. S., Han, D. H., Kim, S. M., & Renshaw, P. F. (2013). Substance abuse precedes Internet addiction. *Addictive Behaviors*, *38*(4), 2022–2025.

Legha, R., Raleigh-Cohn, A., Fickenscher, A., & Novins, D. (2014). Challenges to providing quality substance abuse treatment services for American Indian and Alaska native communities: Perspectives of staff from 18 treatment centers. *BMC Psychiatry*, *14*, 181.

Lejoyeux, M., & Weinstein, A. (2010). Compulsive buying. *The American Journal of Drug and Alcohol Abuse*, *36*(5), 248–253.

Lemieux, C. M. (2009). *Offenders and substance abuse: Bringing the family into focus*. Alexandria, VA: American Correctional Association.

Lemieux, C. M. (2014). Family treatment of individuals with substance use disorders. In S. L. A. Straussner (Ed.), *Clinical work with substance-abusing clients* (3rd Ed.) (pp. 303–325). New York: Guilford Press.

Lenz, A. S., Rosenbaum, L., & Sheperis, D. (2016). Meta-analysis of randomized controlled trials of motivational enhancement therapy for reducing substance use. *Journal of Addictions & Offender Counseling, 37*(2), 66–86.

Leonard, K. E., & Quigley, B. M. (2017). Thirty years of research show alcohol to be a cause of intimate partner violence: Future research needs to identify who to treat and how to treat them. *Drug and Alcohol Review, 36*(1), 7–9.

Lewis, M. E., & Myhra, L. L. (2017). Integrated care with indigenous populations: A systematic review of the literature. *American Indian and Alaska Native Mental Health Research, 24*(3), 88–110.

Lewis, V., & Allen-Byrd, L. (2001). The alcoholic family typology. *Alcoholism Treatment Quarterly, 19,* 1–17.

Lewis, V., & Allen-Byrd, L. (2007). Coping strategies for the stages of family recovery. In J. L. Fischer, M. Mulsow, & A. W. Korinek (Eds), *Familial responses to alcohol problems* (pp. 105–124). New York: The Haworth Press.

Li, Y., Kantelip, J. P., Gerritsen-van Schieveen, P., & Davani, S. (2008). Interindividual variability of methadone response: Impact of genetic polymorphism. *Molecular Diagnosis & Therapy, 12*(2), 109–124.

Liddle, H. A. (1991). A multidimensional model for treating the adolescent who is abusing alcohol and other drugs. In W. Snyder & T. Ooms (Eds), *Empowering families, helping adolescents: Family-centered treatment of adolescents with alcohol, drug abuse and other mental health problems* (pp. 91–100). Washington, DC: United States Public Health Service.

Liddle, H. A. (2002). *Multidimensional family therapy for adolescent cannabis users, cannabis youth treatment (CYT) series,* Volume 5. Rockville, MD: Center for Substance Abuse Treatment, Substance Abuse and Mental Health Services Administration.

Liddle, H. A. (2009). *Multidimensional family therapy for adolescent drug abuse: Clinician's manual.* Center City, MN: Hazelden Publishing Co.

Liddle, H. A. (2010). Multidimensional family therapy: A science-based treatment system. *The Australian and New Zealand Journal of Family Therapy, 31,* 133–148.

Liddle, H. A. (2016). Multidimensional family therapy: Evidence base for transdiagnostic treatment outcomes, change mechanisms, and implementation in community settings. *Family Process, 55*(3), 558–576.

Liddle, H. A., & Dakof, G. A. (2002). A randomized controlled trial of intensive outpatient, family based therapy versus residential drug treatment for comorbid adolescent drug abusers. *Drug and Alcohol Dependence, 66,* S2–S202 (#385), S103.

Liddle, H. A., Dakof, G. A., Parker, K., Diamond, G. S., Barrett, K., & Tejada, M. (2001). Multidimensional family therapy for adolescent substance abuse: Results of a randomized clinical trial. *American Journal of Drug and Alcohol Abuse, 27,* 651–687.

Liddle, H. A., Rodriguez, R. A., Dakof, G. A., Kanzki, E., & Marvel, F. A. (2005). Multidimensional family therapy: A science-based treatment for adolescent drug abuse. In J. Lebow (Ed.), *Handbook of clinical family therapy* (pp. 128–163). New York: John Wiley and Sons.

Lidz, C. W., Appelbaum, P. S., & Meisel, A. (1988). Two models of implementing informed consent. *Archives of Internal Medicine, 148,* 1385–1389.

Lieb, R., Merikangas, K., Hofler, M., Pfister, H., Isensee, B., & Wittchen, H. (2002). Parental alcohol use disorders and alcohol use and disorders in offspring: A community study. *Psychological Medicine, 32,* 63–78.

Linnet, J., Møller, A., Peterson, E., Gjedde, A., & Doudet, D. (2011). Dopamine release in ventral striatum during Iowa Gambling Task performance is associated with increased excitement levels in pathological gambling. *Addiction, 106*(2), 383–390.

Linton, J. M. (2005). Mental health counselors and substance abuse treatment: Advantages, difficulties, and practical issues to solution-focused interventions. *Journal of Mental Health Counseling, 27*(4), 297–310.

Lippi, G., Steinert, J., Marczylo, E., D'Oro, S., Fiore, R., Forsythe, I., Schratt, G., Zoli, M., Nicotera, P., & Young, K. (2011). Targeting of the Arpc3 actin nucleation factor by miR-29a/b regulates dendritic spine morphology. *The Journal of Cell Biology, 194,* 889–904.

Liu, W., & Iwamoto, D. (2007). Conformity to masculine norms, Asian values, coping strategies, peer group influences and substance use among Asian American men. *Psychology of Men and Masculinity, 8,* 25–39.

Livingston, J. A., Eiden, R. D., Lessard, J., Casey, M., Henrie, J., & Leonard, K. E. (2018). Etiology of teen dating violence among adolescent children of alcoholics. *Journal of Youth and Adolescence, 47*(3), 515–533.

Lloyd-Hazlett, J., Honderich, E. M., & Heyward, K. J. (2016). Fa-MI-ly: Experiential techniques to integrate motivational interviewing and family counseling. *The Family Journal, 24*(1), 31–37.

Lo, C., & Cheng, T. (2012). Discriminations role in minority group's rates of substance-use disorder. *The American Journal on Addictions, 21,* 150–156.

Lochman, J. E., & van den Steenhoven, A. J. J. o. P. P. (2002). Family-based approaches to substance abuse prevention. *Journal of Primary Prevention, 23*(1), 49–114.

Loneck, B., Garrett, J. A., & Banks, S. M. (1996a). A comparison of the Johnson Intervention with four other methods of referral to outpatient treatment. *American Journal of Drug and Alcohol Abuse, 22,* 233–246.

Loneck, B., Garrett, J. A., & Banks, S. M. (1996b). The Johnson Intervention and relapse during outpatient treatment. *American Journal of Drug and Alcohol Abuse, 22,* 363–375.

Lopez-Quintero, C., Pérez de los Cobos, J., Hasin, D. S., Okuda, M., Wang, S., Grant, B. F., & Blanco, C. (2011). Probability and predictors of transition from first use to dependence on nicotine, alcohol, cannabis, and cocaine: results of the National Epidemiologic Survey on Alcohol and Related Conditions (NESARC). *Drug and Alcohol Dependence, 115,* 120–130.

Lowe, J., Liang, H., Riggs, C., & Henson, J. (2012). Community partnership to affect substance abuse among Native American adolescents. *The American Journal of Drug and Alcohol Abuse, 38*(5), 450–455.

Lui, C. K., & Mulia, N. (2018). A life course approach to understanding racial/ethnic differences in transitions into and out of alcohol problems. *Alcohol and Alcoholism, 53*(4), 487–496.

Luk, J., Emery, R., Karyadi, K., Patock-Peckham, J., & King, K. (2013). Religiosity and substance use among Asian American college students: Moderated effects of race and acculturation. *Drug and Alcohol Dependence, 130,* 142–149.

Luk, J. W., Patock-Peckham, J. A., & King, K. M. (2015). Are dimensions of parenting differentially linked to substance use across Caucasian and Asian American college students? *Substance Use & Misuse, 50*(10), 1360–1369.

Ma, M., Malcolm, L. R., Diaz-Albertini, K., Sanchez, J. C., Simpson, B., Cortes, L., & Kibler, J. L. (2017). Cultural assets and substance use among Hispanic adolescents. *Health Education & Behavior, 44*(2), 326–331.

Maag, J., & Irvin, D. (2005). Alcohol use and depression among African-American and Caucasian adolescents. *Adolescence, 40,* 87–101.

Maccallum, F., & Blaszczynski, A. (2002). Pathological gambling and comorbid substance use. *Australian and New Zealand Journal of Psychiatry, 36*(3), 411–415.

Madanes, C. (1981). *Strategic family therapy.* San Francisco, CA: Jossey-Bass Publishers.

Madanes, C. (1991). Strategic family therapy. In A. S. Gurman & D. P. Kniskern (Eds), *Handbook of family therapy: Vol. II* (pp. 396–416). New York: Brunner/Mazel.

Mahabee-Gittens, E. M., Khoury, J. C., Huang, B., Dorn, L. D., Ammerman, R. T., & Gordon, J. S. (2011). The protective influence of family bonding on smoking initiation in adolescents by racial/ethnic and age subgroups. *Journal of Child & Adolescent Substance Abuse*, *20*, 270–287.

Makarchuk, K., Hodgins, D. C., & Peden, N. (2002). Development of a brief intervention for concerned significant others of problem gamblers. *Addictive Disorders & Their Treatment*, *1*(4), 126–134.

Mallow, A. J. (1998). Self-disclosure: Reconciling psychoanalytic psychotherapy and alcoholics anonymous philosophy. *Journal of Substance Abuse Treatment*, *15*, 493–498.

Manual, J. K., Austin, J. L., Miller, W. R., McCrady, B. S., Tonigan, J. S., Meyers, R. J., Smith, J. E., & Bogenschutz, M. P. (2012). Community Reinforcement and Family Training: A pilot comparison of group and self-directed delivery. *Journal of Substance Abuse Treatment*, *43*, 129–136.

Marano, M. R., & Roman, E. (2017). Latino couples and families. In S. Kelly (Ed.), *Diversity in couple and family therapy* (pp. 63–90). Santa Barbara, CA: Praeger.

Marjot, D. (2006). Problem drinking is not a synonym with gambling addiction: A comment on Blaszczynski (2005). *Addiction*, *101*(3), 450.

Markowitz, R. (2014). Dynamics and treatment issues with children of individuals with substance use disorders. In S. L. A. Straussner (Ed.), *Clinical work with substance-abusing clients* (3rd Ed.) (pp. 348–368). New York: Guilford Press.

Marshal, M. P., Friedman, M. S., Stall, R., King, K. M., Miles, J., Gold, M. A., Bukstein, O. G., & Morse, J. Q. (2008). Sexual orientation and adolescent substance use: A meta-analysis and methodological review. *Addiction*, *103*, 546–556.

Martinez, M. J., Ayers, S. L., Kulis, S., & Brown, E. (2015). The relationship between peer, parent, and grandparent norms and intentions to use substances for urban American Indian youths. *Journal of Child & Adolescent Substance Abuse*, *24*(4), 220–227.

Martinez, M. J., Huang, S., Estrada, Y., Sutton, M. Y., & Prado, G. (2017). The relationship between acculturation, ecodevelopment, and substance use among Hispanic adolescents. *Journal of Early Adolescence*, *37*(7), 948–974.

Marzell, M., Sahker, E., Pro, G., & Arndt, S. (2017). A brief report on Hispanic youth marijuana use: Trends in substance abuse treatment admissions in the United States. *Journal of Ethnicity in Substance Abuse*, *16*(2), 155–164.

Mason, M. J., Aplasca, A., Morales-Theodore, R., Zaharakis, N., & Linker, J. (2016). Psychiatric comorbidity and complications. *Child and Adolescent Psychiatric Clinics of North America*, *25*(3), 521–532.

Mason, W. H., Chandler, M. C., & Grasso, B. C. (1995). Solution based techniques applied to addictions: A clinic's experience in shifting paradigms. *Alcoholism Treatment Quarterly*, *13*, 39–49.

Masson, C. L., Shopshire, M. S., Sen, S., Hoffman, K. A., Hengl, N. S., Bartolome, J., McCarty, D., Sorensen, J. L., & Iguchi, M. Y. (2013). Possible barriers to enrollment in substance treatment among a diverse sample of Asian Americans and Pacific Islanders: Opinions of treatment clients. *Journal of Substance Abuse Treatment*, *44*(3), 309–315.

Matthes, H. W., Maldonado, R., Simonin, F., Valverde, O., Slowe, S., Kitchen, I., Befort, K., Dierich, A., LeMeur, M., Dolle, P., Tzavara, E., Hanoune, J., Roquest, B. P., & Kieffer, B. L. (1996). Loss of morphine-induced analgesia, reward effect and withdrawal symptoms in mice lacking the mu-opioid-receptor gene. *Nature*, *383*, 819–823.

Mays, V. M., Jones, A. L., Delany-Brumsey, A., Coles, C., & Cochran, S. D. (2017). Perceived discrimination in health care and mental health/substance abuse treatment among blacks, latinos, and whites. *Medical Care*, *55*(2), 173–181.

McCabe, S. E., Morales, M., Cranford, J. A., Delva, J., McPherson, M. D., & Boyd, C. J. (2007). Race/ethnicity and gender differences in drug use and abuse among college students. *Journal of Ethnicity in Substance Abuse*, *6*, 75–95.

McCall, K. (2000). Financial recovery counseling. In A. Benson (Ed.), *I shop, therefore I am – compulsive buying and the search for self* (pp. 457–483). New York: Aronson.

McCollum, E. E., & Trepper, T. S. (2001). *Family solutions for substance abuse.* New York: The Haworth Clinical Practice Press.

McConnell, E. A., Birkett, M. A., & Mustanski, B. (2015). Typologies of social support and associations with mental health outcomes among LGBT youth. *LGBT Health, 2*(1), 55–61.

McCoy, T. P., & Dunlop, W. L. (2017). Down on the upside: Redemption, contamination, and agency in the lives of adult children of alcoholics. *Memory, 25*(5), 586–594.

McCrady, B. S., Epstein, E. E., Cook, S., Hildbrandt, T., & Jensen, N. (2009). A randomized trial of individual and couple behavioral alcohol treatment for women. *Journal of Consulting and Clinical Psychology, 77*(2), 243–256.

McCrady, B. S., Ladd, B. O., & Hallgren, K. A. (2012). Theoretical bases of family approaches to substance abuse treatment. In S. T. Walters & F. Rotgers (Eds), *Treating substance abuse: Theory and technique* (3rd Ed.) (pp. 224–255). New York: Guilford Press.

McGoldrick, M., Gerson, R., & Petry, S. (2008). *Genograms: Assessment and intervention* (3rd Ed.). New York: W. W. Norton & Company.

McKnight, A. S. (1998). Family systems with alcoholism: A case study. In P. Titelman (Ed.), *Clinical applications of Bowen family systems theory* (pp. 263–298). New York: The Haworth Press.

McLaughlin, K. D. (2017). Ethical considerations for clinicians treating victims and perpetrators of intimate violence. *Ethics & Behavior, 27*(1), 43–52.

McLellan, A. T., Lewis, D. C., O'Brien, C. P., & Kleber, H. D. (2000). Drug dependence, a chronic medical illness: Implications for treatment, insurance, and outcome evaluation. *Journal of the American Medical Association, 284*, 1689–1695.

Mellan, O. (2000). Overcoming overspending in couples. In A. Benson (Ed.), *I shop, therefore I am – compulsive buying and the search for self* (pp. 341–366). New York: Aronson.

Mennis, J., & Stahler, G. J. (2016). Racial and ethnic disparities in outpatient substance use disorder treatment episode completion for different substances. *Journal of Substance Abuse Treatment, 63*, 25–33.

Mereish, E. H., Gamarel, K. E., & Operario, D. (2018). Understanding and addressing alcohol and substance use in sexual and gender minority youth. In P. M. Monti, S. M. Colby, & T. O. Tevyaw (Eds), *Brief interventions for adolescent alcohol and substance abuse* (pp. 305–327). New York: Guilford Press.

Mereish, E. H., O'Cleirigh, C., & Bradford, J. B. (2014). Interrelationships between LGBT-based victimization, suicide, and substance use problems in a diverse sample of sexual and gender minorities. *Psychology, Health & Medicine, 19*(1), 1–13.

Merikangas, K. (1990). The genetic epidemiology of alcoholism. *Psychological Medicine, 20*, 11–22.

Meyers, R. J., Miller, W. M., Smith, J. E., & Tonigan, J. S. (2002). A randomized trial of two methods for engaging treatment-refusing drug users through concerned significant others. *Journal of Consulting and Clinical Psychology, 70*, 1182–1185.

Meyers, R. J., Roozen, H. G., & Smith, J. E. (2011). The community reinforcement approach: An update of the evidence. *Alcohol Research and Health, 33*, 380–388.

Middleton-Moz, J., & Dwinell, L. (2010). *After the tears: Helping adult children of alcoholics heal their childhood trauma* (Revised and Expanded). Deerfield Beach, FL: Health Communications, Inc.

Mignon, S. I., Faiia, M. M., Myers, P. L., & Rubington, E. (2009). *Substance use & abuse: Exploring alcohol & drug issues.* Boulder, CO: Lynne Rienner Publishers.

Mignon, S. I., & Holmes, W. M. (2013). Substance abuse and mental health issues within Native American grandparenting families. *Journal of Ethnicity in Substance Abuse, 12*, 210–227.

Miles, D., Silberg, J., Pickens, R., & Eaves, L. (2005). Familial influences on alcohol use in adolescent female twins: Testing for genetic and environmental interactions. *The Journal of Studies on Alcohol, 66,* 445–451.

Miller, G. (2005). *Learning the language of addiction counseling* (2nd Ed.). Hoboken, NJ: John Wiley & Sons, Inc.

Miller, H. V., & Miller, J. M. (2016). Substance abuse treatment in criminal justice: Issue introduction. *American Journal of Criminal Justice, 41*(1), 1–2.

Miller, S. D., & Berg, I. K. (1995). *The miracle method.* New York: W. W. Norton & Company.

Miller, S. D., Duncan, B. L., Brown, J., Sorrell, R., & Chalk, M. B. (2006). Using formal client feedback to improve retention and outcome: Making ongoing, real-time assessment feasible. *Journal of Brief Therapy, 5,* 5–22.

Miller, S. D., Duncan, B. L., & Hubble, M. A. (1997). *Escape from babel.* New York: W. W. Norton & Company.

Miller, W. R., Meyers, R. J., & Tonigan, J. S. (1999). Engaging the unmotivated in treatment for alcohol problems: A comparison of three strategies for intervention through family members. *Journal of Consulting and Clinical Psychology, 67,* 688–697.

Miller, W. R., & Moyers, T. B. (2015). The forest and the trees: Relational and specific factors in addiction treatment. *Addiction, 110*(3), 401–413.

Miller, W. R., & Rollnick, S. (2012). *Motivational interviewing: Helping people change* (3rd Ed.). New York: Guilford Press.

Miller, W. R., & Sanchez, V. C. (1994). Motivating young adults for treatment and lifestyle change. In G. Howard (Ed.), *Issues in alcohol use and misuse by young adults* (pp. 55–82). Notre Dame, IN: University of Notre Dame Press.

Minuchin, S. (1974). *Families & family therapy.* Cambridge, MA: Harvard University Press.

Minuchin, S., & Fishman, H. C. (1981). *Family therapy techniques.* Cambridge, MA: Harvard University Press.

Minuchin, S., Nichols, M. P., & Lee, W.-L. (2007). *Assessing families and couples.* Boston, MA: Allyn & Bacon.

Minuchin, S., Reiter, M. D., & Borda, C. (2014). *The craft of family therapy.* New York: Routledge.

Misouridou, E., & Papadatou, D. (2017). Challenges in engaging parents in the drug and alcohol treatment: The professionals' perspective. *Qualitative Health Research, 27*(13), 1948–1958.

Mohammad, A. (2016). *The anatomy of addiction.* New York: Penguin Random House.

Moilanen, K. L., Markstrom, C. A., & Jones, E. (2014). Extracurricular activity availability and participation and substance use among American Indian adolescents. *Journal of Youth and Adolescence, 43*(3), 454–469.

Montgomery, K. L., & Springer, D. W. (2012). Treating substance-abusing youth. In C. A. McNeece & D. M. DiNitto (Eds), *Chemical dependency: A systems approach* (4th Ed.) (pp. 235–255). Boston, MA: Pearson.

Montgomery, L., Burlew, A. K., & Korte, J. E. (2017). Does change in readiness influence retention among African American women and men in substance abuse treatment? *Journal of Ethnicity in Substance Abuse, 16*(4), 420–431.

Morgan, T. B., & Crane, D. R. (2010). Cost-effectiveness of family based substance abuse treatment. *Journal of Marital and Family Therapy, 36*(4), 486–498.

Morrell, H. E. R., Hilton, B. T., & Rugless, K. L. (2018). Correlates of substance use among American Indian/Alaska Native adolescents. *International Journal of Mental Health and Addiction,* Advance online publication: doi.org/10.1007/s11469-018-9971-z.

Morrison, J. K., Layton, D., & Newman, J. (1982). Ethical conflict in decision making. In J. C. Hansen & L. L'Abate (Eds), *Values, ethics, legalities, and the family therapist* (pp. 75–86). Rockville, MD: Aspen.

Moyer, R. A., Wang, D., Papp, A. C., Smith, R. M., Duque, L., Mash, D. C., & Sadee, W. (2011). Intronic polymorphisms affecting alternative splicing of human dopamine D2 receptor are associated with cocaine abuse. *Neuropsychopharmacology, 36,* 753–762.

Mueller, A., Claes, L., Mitchell, J. E., Faber, R. J., Fischer, J., & de Zwaan, M. (2011). Does compulsive buying differ between male and female students? *Personality and Individual Differences, 50*(8), 1309–1312.

Mukamal, K. J. (2010). A 42-year-old man considering whether to drink alcohol for his health. *JAMA: Journal of the American Medical Association, 303,* 2065–2073.

Mulsow, M. (2007). Treatment of comorbidity in families. *Alcoholism Treatment Quarterly, 25,* 125–140.

Munafò, M. R., Matheson, I. J., & Flint, J. (2007). Association of the DRD2 gene Taq1A polymorphism and alcoholism: A meta-analysis of case-control studies and evidence of publication bias. *Molecular Psychiatry, 12,* 454–461.

Muñoz, R. E., & Tonigan, J. S. (2017). Alcoholics Anonymous-related benefit for urban Native Americans: Does urban Native American gender moderate AA engagement and outcomes? *Alcoholism Treatment Quarterly, 35*(1), 34–45.

Murphy, J., & Hardaway, R. (2017). LGBTQ adolescents of color: Considerations for working with youth and their families. *Journal of Gay & Lesbian Mental Health, 21*(3), 221–227.

Myers, P. L., & Salt, N. R. (2013). *Becoming an addictions counselor.* Burlington, MA: Jones & Bartlett Learning.

Myhra, L. L., & Wieling, E. (2014). Intergenerational patterns of substance abuse among urban American Indian families. *Journal of Ethnicity in Substance Abuse, 13*(1), 1–22.

Myhra, L. L., Wieling, E., & Grant, H. (2015). Substance use in American Indian family relationships: Linking past, present, and future. *American Journal of Family Therapy, 43*(5), 413–424.

Nam, E., Matejkowski, J., & Lee, S. (2016). Criminal justice contact and treatment utilization among people with mental illness and substance use disorders. *Psychiatric Services, 67*(10), 1149–1151.

Nasim, A., Belgrave, F., Jagers, R., Wilson, K., & Owens, K. (2007). The moderating effects of culture on peer deviance and alcohol use among high-risk African- American adolescents. *Journal of Drug Education, 37,* 335–363.

Nasim, A., Fernander, A., Townsend, T. G., Corona, R., & Belgrave, F. Z. (2011). Cultural protective factors for community risks and substance use among rural African American adolescents. *Journal of Ethnicity in Substance Abuse, 10,* 316–336.

National Coalition Against Domestic Violence (2014). *Domestic violence fact sheet.* Retrieved from www.ncadv.org/files/DomesticViolenceFactSheet(National).pdf.

National Council on Alcoholism and Drug Dependence (n.d.). Retrieved from www.ncadd.org.

National Institute on Drug Abuse (2014). Retrieved from www.drugabuse.gov. Retrieved 3/06/14.

Negash, S. M., & Hecker, L. L. (2010). Ethical issues endemic to couple and family therapy. In L. Hecker (Ed.), *Ethics and professional issues in couple and family therapy* (pp. 225–241). New York: Routledge.

Nehlig, A., Armspach, J. P., & Namer, I. J. (2010). SPECT assessment of brain activation induced by caffeine: No effect on areas involved in dependence. *Dialogues in Clinical Neuroscience, 12,* 255–263.

Neill, J. R., & Kniskern, D. P. (Eds) (1982). *From psyche to system: The evolving therapy of Carl Whitaker.* New York: Guilford Press.

Nerenberg, A. (2009). Treating addictions: A balanced approach to boundaries and therapist self-disclosure. In A. Bloomgarden & R. B. Mennuti (Eds), *Psychotherapist revealed* (pp. 135–148). New York: Routledge.

Newbury-Birch, D., McGovern, R., Birch, J., O'Neill, G., Kaner, H., Sondhi, A., & Lynch, K. (2016). A rapid systematic review of what we know about alcohol use disorders and brief interventions in the criminal justice system. *International Journal of Prisoner Health*, 12(1), 57–70.

Ng, S. K., Hauser, W. A., Brust, J. C., & Susser, M. (1988). Alcohol consumption and withdrawal in new-onset seizures. *New England Journal of Medicine, 319*, 666–673.

Nguyen, T. T., Levy, S. S., Riley, E. P., Thomas, J. D., & Simmons, R. W. (2012). Children with heavy prenatal alcohol exposure experience reduced control of isotonic force. *Alcoholism: Clinical and Experimental Research, 37*, 315–324.

Nicosia, N., MacDonald, J. M., & Pacula, R. L. (2017). Does mandatory diversion to drug treatment eliminate racial disparities in the incarceration of drug offenders? An examination of California's proposition 36. *Journal of Quantitative Criminology, 33*(1), 179–205.

Nielsen, M., Hansen, E. H., & Gotzsche, P. C. (2012). What is the difference between dependence and withdrawal reactions? A comparison of benzodiazepines and selective serotonin re-uptake inhibitors, *Addiction, 107*, 900–908.

Noble, E. P., Blum, K., Ritchie, T., Montgomery, A., & Sheridan, P. J. (1991). Allelic association of the D2 dopamine receptor gene with receptor-binding characteristics in alcoholism. *Archives of General Psychiatry, 48*, 648–654.

Nowinski, J. K. (1999). *Family recovery and substance abuse.* Thousand Oaks, CA: Sage.

Nowinski, J. (2006). *The twelve step facilitation outpatient program.* Center City, MN: Hazelden.

Nowinski, J. (2012). Facilitating 12-step recovery from substance abuse. In S. T. Walters & F. Rotgers (Eds), *Treating substance abuse: Theory and technique* (3rd Ed.) (pp. 191–223). New York: Guilford Press.

Nowinski, J. (2015). *If you work it it works!* Center City, MN: Hazelden.

Nowinski, J., & Baker, S. (2018). *The twelve-step facilitation handbook: A systematic approach to recovery from alcoholism and addiction* (2nd Ed., Revised). Center City, MN: Hazelden.

O'Connell, L. A., & Hofmann, H. A. (2011). Genes, hormones, and circuits: An integrative approach to study the evolution of social behavior. *Frontiers in Neuroendocrinology, 32*, 320–335.

O'Farrell, T. J., & Clements, K. (2012). Review of outcome research on marital and family therapy in treatment for alcoholism. *Journal of Marital and Family Therapy, 38*, 122–144.

O'Farrell, T. J., & Fals-Stewart, W. (2003). Alcohol abuse. *Journal of Marital and Family Therapy, 29*, 121–146.

O'Farrell, T. J., & Fals-Stewart, W. (2006). *Behavioral couples therapy for alcoholism and drug abuse.* New York: Guilford Press.

O'Farrell, T. J., & Fals-Stewart, W. (2008). Behavioral couples therapy for alcoholism and other drug abuse. In O. J. Morgan & C. H. Litzke (Eds), *Family intervention in substance abuse: Current best practices* (pp. 195–219). New York: The Haworth Press.

Olds, J. (1958). Self-stimulation in the brain. *Science, 127*, 315–324.

Olsen, R. W., & DeLorey, T. M. (1999). GABA and Glycine. In G. J. Siegel, B. W. Agranoff, S. K. Fisher, R. W. Albers, & M. D. Uhler (Eds), *Basic neurochemistry: molecular, cellular, and medical aspects* (6th Ed., Chapter 16). Philadelphia, PA: Lippincott-Raven.

Padilla-Walker, L., Nelson, L., Carroll, J., & Jensen, A. (2010). More than just a game: Video game and internet use during emerging adulthood. *Journal of Youth and Adolescence, 39*, 103–113.

Pagliaro, L. A., & Pagliaro, A. M. (2012). *Handbook of child and adolescent drug and substance abuse.* Hoboken, NJ: John Wiley & Sons.

Palazzoli, M. S., Boscolo, L., Cecchin, G., & Prata, G. (1977). Family rituals: A powerful tool in family therapy. *Family Process, 16*, 445–453.

Palazzoli, M. S., Boscolo, L., Cecchin, G., & Prata, G. (1978a). *Paradox and counterparadox.* New York: Jason Aronson.

Palazzoli, M. S., Boscolo, L., Cecchin, G., & Prata, G. (1978b). A ritualized prescription in family therapy: Odd days and even days. *Journal of Marriage and Family Counseling*, 4, 3–9.

Palazzoli, M. S., Boscolo, L., Cecchin, G., & Prata, G. (1980). Hypothesizing-Circularity-Neutrality: Three guidelines for the conductor of the session. *Family Process*, 19, 3–12.

Park, S. K., Kim, J. Y., & Cho, C. B. (2009). Prevalence of internet addiction and correlations with family factors among South Korean adolescents. *Family Therapy*, 36, 163–177.

Patterson, J., Williams, L., Edwards, T. M., Chamow, L., & Grauf-Grounds, C. (2009). *Essential skills in family therapy* (2nd Ed.). New York: Guilford Press.

Paul, T. M., Lusk, S. L., Becton, A. B., & Glade, R. (2017). Exploring the impact of substance use, culture, and trauma on American Indian adolescents. *Journal of Applied Rehabilitation Counseling*, 48(1), 31–39.

Pellebon, D. A. (2012). The African American family. In R. Wright, Jr., C. H. Mindel, T. V. Tran, & R. W. Habenstein (Eds), *Ethnic families in America: Patterns and variations* (5th Ed.) (pp. 326–360). Boston, MA: Pearson.

Pentz, M. A., MacKinnon, D. P., Dwyer, J. H., Wang, E. Y., Hansen, W. B., Flay, B. R., & Johnson, C. A. (1989). Longitudinal effects of the midwestern prevention project on regular and experimental smoking in adolescents. *Preventive Medicine*, 18(2), 304–321.

Peters, R. H., Wexler, H. K., & Lurigio, A. J. (2015). Co-occurring substance use and mental disorders in the criminal justice system: A new frontier of clinical practice research. *Psychiatric Rehabilitation Journal*, 38(1), 1–6.

Petroni, D. C., Allen-Byrd, L., & Lewis, V. M. (2003). Indicators of the alcohol recovery process: Critical items from Koss-Butcher and Lachar-Wrobel analysis of the MMPI-2. *Alcoholism Treatment Quarterly*, 21, 41–56.

Petry N. M. (2000). Gambling problems in substance abusers are associated with increased sexual risk behaviors. *Addiction*, 95, 1089–1100.

Petry, N. M. (2007). Gambling and substance use disorders: Current status and future directions. *The American Journal on Addictions*, 16(1), 1–9.

Petry, N. M., Stinson, F. S., & Grant, B. F. (2005). Comorbidity of DSM-IV pathological gambling and other psychiatric disorders: Results from the National Epidemiologic Survey on Alcohol and Related Conditions. *The Journal of Clinical Psychiatry*, 66(5), 564–574.

Pichot, T. (2001). Co-creating solutions for substance abuse. *Journal of Systemic Therapies*, 20(2), 1–23.

Pichot, T., & Smock, S. A. (2009). *Solution-focused substance abuse treatment*. New York: Routledge.

Pietrzykowski, A. (2010). The role of microRNAs in drug addiction: A big lesson from tiny molecules. *International Review of Neurobiology*, 91, 1–24.

Pinderup, P. (2017). Training changes professionals' attitudes towards dual diagnosis. *International Journal of Mental Health and Addiction*, 15(1), 53–62.

Poduska, B. E. & Allred, G. H. (1990). Family finances: The missing link in MFT training. *The American Journal of Family Therapy*, 18(2), 161–168.

Porter, M., & Nuntavisit, L. (2016). An evaluation of multisystemic therapy with Australian families. *Australian and New Zealand Journal of Family Therapy*, 37(4), 443–462.

Pos, A. E., Greenberg, L. S., & Elliot, R. (2008). Experiential therapy. In J. L. Lebow (Ed.), *Twenty-first century psychotherapies* (pp. 80–122). Hoboken, NJ: John Wiley & Sons.

Potenza, M. N. (2008). Review. The neurobiology of pathological gambling and drug addiction: an overview and new findings. *Philosophical Transactions of the Royal Society of London. Series B, Biological Sciences*, 363(1507), 3181–3189.

Potenza, M. N., Koran, L. M., & Pallanti, S. (2009). The relationship between impulse-control disorders and obsessive-compulsive disorder: A current understanding and future research directions. *Psychiatry Research*, 170(1), 22–31.

Potter, A. E., & Williams, D. E. (1991). Development of a measure examining children's roles in alcoholic families. *Journal of Studies on Alcohol, 52*, 70–77.

Prochaska, J. O., & DiClemente, C. C. (1986). Toward a comprehensive model of change. In W. R. Miller & N. Heather (Eds), *Treating addictive behaviors: Process of change* (pp. 3–27). New York: Plenum Press.

Prochaska, J. O., DiClemente, C. C., & Norcross, J. C. (1992). In search of how people change: Applications to addictive behaviors. *American Psychologist, 47*, 1102–1114.

Project MATCH Research Group (1993). Project MATCH: Rationale and methods for a multisite clinical trial matching patients to alcoholism treatment. *Alcoholism: Clinical and Experimental Research, 17*, 1130–1145.

Puttler, L. I., Zucker, R. A., Fitzgerald, H. E., & Bingham, C. R. (1998). Behavioral outcomes among children of alcoholics during the early and middle childhood years: Familial subtype variations. *Alcoholism: Clinical and Experimental Research, 22*, 1962–1972.

Raab, G., Elger, C. E., Neuner, M., & Weber, B. (2011). A neurological study of compulsive buying behaviour. *Journal of Consumer Policy, 34*, 401–413.

Ramirez, R., & De la Cruz, G. (2002). *The Hispanic population in the United States: March current population reports.* Washington, DC: U.S. Census Bureau.

Ransome, Y., & Gilman, S. E. (2016). The role of religious involvement in Black-White differences in alcohol use disorders. *Journal of Studies on Alcohol and Drugs, 77*(5), 792–801.

Rawson, R. A., Washton, A. M., Domier, C. P., & Reiber, C. (2002). Drugs and sexual effects: Role of drug type and gender. *Journal of Substance Abuse Treatment, 22*, 103–108.

Ray, W., & Brasher, C. (2010). Legends, lessons, & practical magic: Rediscovering the contributions of the MRI Brief Therapy Center. *Journal of Systemic Therapies, 29*(Special Section), 17–73.

Raymond, N. C., Coleman, E., & Miner, M. H. (2003). Psychiatric comorbidity and compulsive/impulsive traits in compulsive sexual behavior. *Comprehensive Psychiatry, 44*(5), 370–380.

Reid, N., Dawe, S., Harnett, P., Shelton, D., Hutton, L., & O'Callaghan, F. (2017). Feasibility study of a family-focused intervention to improve outcomes for children with FASD. *Research in Developmental Disabilities, 67*, 34–46.

Reid, R. C., Carpenter, B. N., Hook, J. N., Garos, S., Manning, J. C., Gilliand, R., Cooper, E. B., McKittrick, H., Davtian, M., & Fong, T. (2012). Report of findings in a DSM-5 field trial for hypersexual disorder. *The Journal of Sexual Medicine, 9*(11), 2868–2877.

Reilly, D. M. (1985). Drug-abusing families: Intrafamilial dynamics and brief triphasic treatment (pp. 105–119). In E. Kaufman & P. Kaufman (Eds), *Family therapy of drug and alcohol abuse* (2nd Ed.). Boston, MA: Allyn & Bacon.

Reiter, M. D. (2010). The use of hope and expectancy in solution-focused therapy. *Journal of Family Psychotherapy, 21*, 132–148.

Reiter, M. D. (2014). *Case conceptualization in family therapy.* Boston, MA: Pearson.

Reiter, M. D. (2016). A quick guide to case conceptualization in Structural family therapy. *Journal of Systemic Therapies, 35*(2), 25–37.

Reiter, M. D. (2018). *Family therapy: An introduction to process, practice, and theory.* New York: Routledge.

Reiter, M. D. (2019). *Systems theories for psychotherapists.* New York: Routledge.

Reiter, M. D., & Chenail, R. J. (2016). Defining the focus in solution-focused brief therapy. *International Journal of Solution-Focused Practices, 4*(1), 1–9.

Reuss, N. H. (1997). The nightmare question. *Journal of Family Psychotherapy, 8*, 71–76.

Reuter, J., Raedler, T., Rose, M., Hand, I., Gläscher, J., & Büchel, C. (2005). Pathological gambling is linked to reduced activation of the mesolimbic reward system. *Nature Neuroscience, 8*, 147–148.

Rhodes, J., & Blackham, G. J. (1987). Differences in character roles between adolescents from alcoholic and nonalcoholic homes. *American Journal of Drug and Alcohol Abuse, 13*, 145–155.

Richeport-Haley, M., & Carlson, J. (Eds) (2010). *Jay Haley revisited.* New York: Routledge.

Rindfleisch, A., Burroughs, J. E., & Denton, F. (1997). Family structure, materialism and compulsive consumption. *Journal of Consumer Research, 23*, 312–325.

Ritchie, T., & Noble, E. P. (2003). Association of seven polymorphisms of the D2 dopamine receptor gene with brain receptor-binding characteristics. *Neurochemical Research, 28*, 73–82.

Robbins, M. S., Feaster, D. J., Horigian, V. E., Bachrach, K., Burlew, K. A., Carrion, I., Schindler, E., Rohrbaugh, M., Shoham, V., Miller, M., Hodgkins, C., Vandermark, N., Werstlein, R., & Szapocznik, J. (2011a). Brief strategic family therapy versus treatment as usual: Results of a multisite randomized trial for substance using adolescent. *Journal of Consulting and Clinical Psychology, 79*, 713–727.

Robbins, M. S., Feaster, D. J., Horigian, V. E., Puccinelli, M. J., Henderson, C., & Szapocznik, J. (2011b). Therapist adherence in brief strategic family therapy for adolescent drug abusers. *Journal of Consulting and Clinical Psychology, 79*, 42–53.

Robbins, M. S., Hervis, O. E., Mitrani, V. B., & Szapocznik, J. (2001). Assessing changes in family interaction: The Structural Family Systems Ratings. In P. K. Kerig & M. Lindahl (Eds), *Family observational coding systems: Resources for systemic research* (pp. 207–224). Mahwah, NJ: Erlbaum.

Robbins, M. S., Mayorga, C. C., Mitrani, V. B., Szapocznik, J., Turner, C. W., & Alexander, J. F. (2008). Adolescent and parent alliances with therapists in brief strategic family therapy with drug-using Hispanic adolescents. *Journal of Marital and Family Therapy, 34*, 316–328.

Robbins, R., Ryland-Neal, T., Murphy, S., & Geis, C. (2017). Challenges faced by Native American couples and families and a place-focused approach to treatment. In S. Kelly (Ed.), *Diversity in couple and family therapy* (pp. 91–120). Santa Barbara, CA: Praeger.

Rober, P., Walravens, G., & Versteynen, L. (2012). "In search of a tale they can live with": About loss, family secrets, and selective disclosure. *Journal of Marital and Family Therapy, 38*(3), 529–541.

Roberts, J., Manolis, C., & Tanner, J. (2003). Family structure, materialism, and compulsive buying: A reinquiry and extension. *Journal of the Academy of Marketing Science, 31*, 300–311.

Roberts, J. A., & Tanner, J. F. Jr. (2000). Compulsive buying and risky behavior among adolescents. *Psychological Reports, 86*, 763–770.

Robinson, T. E. & Berridge, K. C. (2003). Addiction. *Annual Review of Psychology, 54*, 25–53.

Robison, A., & Nestler, E. (2011). Transcriptional and epigenetic mechanisms of addiction. *Nature Reviews Neuroscience, 12*, 623–637.

Roehlkepartain, E. C., Syvertsen, A. K., & Wu, C.-Y. (2017). *A snapshot of developmental relationships between parents and youth.* Minneapolis, MN: Search Institute. Retrieved from www.search-institute.org/wp-content/uploads/2017/12/Snapshot-of-Parent-Youth-Relationships-2017-final.pdf.

Rogers, C. (1961). *On becoming a person.* London: Constable.

Rohrer, G. E., Thomas, M., & Yasenchak, A. B. (1992). Client perceptions of the ideal addictions counselor. *The International Journal of the Addictions, 27*, 727–733.

Roozen, H. G., de Waart, R., & van der Kroft, P. (2010). Community reinforcement and family training: An effective option to engage treatment-resistant substance-abusing individuals in treatment. *Addiction, 105*, 1729–1738.

Rosenberg, K. P., & Feder, L. C. (2014). *Behavioral addictions: Criteria, evidence, and treatment.* Boston, MA: Academic Press.

Rouhbakhsh, P., Lewis, V., & Allen-Byrd, L. (2004). Recovering alcoholic families. *Alcoholism Treatment Quarterly, 22*, 35–53.

Rounsaville, B., Kosten, T., Weissman, M., Prusoff, B., Pauls, D., Anton, S., & Merikangas, K. (1991). Psychiatric disorders in relatives of probands with opiate addiction. *Archives of General Psychiatry, 48,* 33–42.

Rowe, C. L. (2010). Multidimensional family therapy: Addressing co-occurring substance abuse and other problems among adolescents with comprehensive family-based treatment. *Child and Adolescent Psychiatric Clinics of North America, 19,* 563–576.

Rowe, C. L., & Liddle, H. A. (2008). Multidimensional family therapy for adolescent alcohol abusers. *Alcoholism Treatment Quarterly, 26,* 105–123.

Rowland, M. D., Chapman, J. E., & Henggeler, S. W. (2008). Sibling outcomes from a randomized trial of evidence-based treatments with substance abusing juvenile offenders. *Journal of Child & Adolescent Substance Abuse, 17,* 11–26.

Ruiz, P., & Strain, E. C. (2014). *The substance abuse handbook* (2nd Ed.). Philadelphia, PA: Lippincott Williams & Wilkins.

Ruiz, P., Strain, E. C., & Langrod, J. G. (2007). *The substance abuse handbook.* Pennsylvania, PA: Lippincott Williams & Wilkins.

Ryabov, I. (2015). Relation of peer effects and school climate to substance use among Asian American adolescents. *Journal of Adolescence, 42,* 115–127.

Ryan, C., Huebner, D., Diaz, R. M., & Sanchez, J. (2009). Family rejection as a predictor of negative health outcomes in white and Latino lesbian, gay, and bisexual young adults. *Pediatrics, 123,* 346–352.

Saarnio, P. (2010). Personality traits and interpersonal functioning in substance abuse therapists with and without personal recovery status. *Alcoholism Treatment Quarterly, 28,* 451–463.

Sabato, T. (2016). Breaking the model minority stereotype: An exploration of Asian American and Pacific Islander student substance abuse. *College Student Journal, 50*(4), 477–488.

Sahker, E., Yeung, C. W., Garrison, Y. L., Park, S., & Arndt, S. (2017). Asian American and Pacific Islander substance use treatment admission trends. *Drug and Alcohol Dependence, 171,* 1–8.

SAMSHA (2009). *Children living with substance-dependent or substance-abusing parents: 2002 to 2007.* The NSDUH Report. National Survey on Drug Use and Health. Rockville, MD: U.S. Department of Health and Human Services, Substance Abuse and Mental Health Services Administration (SAMHSA), Center for Substance Abuse Prevention. Retrieved August 31, 2013.

SAMHSA (Rev. 2017). *Focus on prevention.* Retrieved from Rockville, MD: U.S. Department of Health and Human Services, Substance Abuse and Mental Health Services Administration (SAMHSA), Center for Substance Abuse Prevention https://store.samhsa.gov/system/files/sma10-4120.pdf.

Samson, H. H., Hodge, C. W., Tolliver, G. A., & Haraguchi, M. (1993). Effect of dopamine agonists and antagonists on ethanol-reinforced behavior: The involvement of the nucleus accumbens. *Brain Research Bulletin, 30,* 133–141.

Sanchez-Craig, M., Wilkinson, D. A., & Davila, R. (1995). Empirically based guidelines for moderate drinking: 1-year results from three studies with problem drinkers. *American Journal of Public Health, 85,* 823–828.

Sartor, C. E., Agrawal, A., McCutcheon, V. V., Duncan, A. E., & Lynskey, M. T. (2008). Disentangling the complex association between childhood sexual abuse and alcohol-related problems: A review of methodological issues and approaches. *Journal of Studies on Alcohol and Drugs, 69,* 718–727.

Sartor, C. E., Waldron, M., Duncan, A. E., Grant, J. D., McCutcheon, V. V., Nelson, E. C., Madden, P. A. F., Bucholz, K. K., & Heath, A. C. (2013). Childhood sexual abuse and early substance use in adolescent girls: The role of familial influence. *Addiction, 108,* 993–1000.

Satir, V. (1983). *Conjoint family therapy* (3rd Ed.). Palo Alto, CA: Science and Behavior Books, Inc.

Satir, V., & Baldwin, M. (1983). *Satir step by step*. Palo Alto, CA: Science and Behavior Books, Inc.

Satir, V., Banmen, J., Gerber, J., & Gomori, M. (1991). *The Satir model: Family therapy and beyond*. Palo Alto, CA: Science and Behavior Books, Inc.

Savage, J. E., & Mezuk, B. (2014). Psychosocial and contextual determinants of alcohol and drug use disorders in the National Latino and Asian American Study. *Drug and Alcohol Dependence, 139*, 71–78.

Schaefer, R. T. (2010). *Racial and ethnic groups* (12th Ed.). Upper Saddle River, NJ: Prentice Hall.

Schaeffer, C. M., Saldana, L., Rowland, M. D., Henggeler, S. W., & Swenson, C. C. (2008). New initiatives in improving youth and family outcomes by importing evidence-based practices. *Journal of Child and Adolescent Substance Abuse, 17*, 27–45.

Scheffler, S. (2014). Assessment and treatment of clients with co-occurring psychiatric and substance use disorders. In S. L. A. Straussner (Ed.), *Clinical work with substance-abusing clients* (3rd Ed.) (pp. 371–394). New York: Guilford Press.

Schmid, J., & Brown, S. (2008). Beyond "happily ever after": Family recovery from alcohol problems. In O. J. Morgan & C. H. Litzke (Eds), *Family intervention in substance abuse: Current best practices* (pp. 31–58). New York: The Haworth Press.

Schoenwald, S. K., Heiblum, N., Saldana, L., & Henggeler, S. W. (2008). The international implementation of multisystemic therapy. *Evaluation & the Health Professions, 31*(2), 211–225.

Scott, C. G., Cox-Romain, L. A., & Stanley, J. B. (2011). Issues of addiction and abuse among African Americans. In G. W. Lawson & A. W. Lason (Eds), *Alcoholism and substance abuse in diverse populations* (2nd Ed.) (pp. 125–148). Austin, TX: Pro-ed.

Segal, L. (1991). Brief therapy: The MRI approach. In A. S. Gurman & D. P. Kniskern (Eds), *Handbook of family therapy* (Vol. 2) (pp. 171–199). New York: Brunner/Mazel.

Senreich, E., & Vairo, E. (2014). Assessment and treatment of lesbian, gay, and bisexual clients with substance use disorders. In S. L. A. Straussner (Ed.), *Clinical work with substance-abusing clients* (3rd Ed.) (pp. 466–494). New York: Guilford Press.

Serec, M., Svab, I., Kolsek, M., Svab, V., Moesgen, D., & Klein, M. (2012). Health-related lifestyle, physical and mental health in children of alcoholic parents. *Drug and Alcohol Review, 31*, 861–870.

Shafer, K. C., & Jordan, S. A. S. (2014). Working with mandated clients with substance use disorders: A solution-focused approach. In S. L. A. Straussner (Ed.), *Clinical work with substance-abusing clients* (3rd Ed.) (pp. 202–224). New York: Guilford Press.

Shaffer, H. J., Hall, M. N., & Vander Bilt, J. (1999). Estimating the prevalence of disordered gambling behavior in the United States and Canada: A research synthesis. *American Journal of Public Health, 89*(9), 1369–1376.

Shaima, N., & Narayanan, G. (2018). A glass half full not empty: Strength-based practice in persons with substance use disorders. *Psychological Studies, 63*(1), 19–24.

Shaw, M., & Black, D. W. (2008). Internet addiction: Definition, assessment, epidemiology and clinical management. *CNS Drugs, 22*, 353–365.

Sheidow, A. J., & Henggeler, S. W. (2008). Multisystemic therapy for alcohol and other drug abuse in delinquent adolescents. In O. J. Morgan & C. H. Litzke (Eds), *Family intervention in substance abuse: Current best practices* (pp. 125–145). Binghamton, NY: Haworth Press.

Sheidow, A. J., & Henggeler, S. W. (2012). Multisystemic therapy with substance using adolescents: A synthesis of the research. In N. Jainchill (Ed.), *Understanding and treating adolescent substance use disorders* (pp. 9-1–9-13). Kingston, NJ: Civic Research Institute.

Sheidow, A. J., & Houston, J. L. (2013). Multisystemic therapy for adolescent substance abuse. In P. M. Miller, S. A. Ball, M. E. Bates, A. W. Blume, & K. M. Kampman (Eds), *Comprehensive addictive behaviors and disorders, Vol 3: Interventions for addiction* (pp. 77–86). San Diego, CA: Elsevier Academic Press.

Shelton, M. (2017). *Fundamentals of LGBT substance use disorders.* New York: Harrington Park Press.

Simon, G. M. (2003). *Beyond technique in family therapy: Finding your therapeutic voice.* Boston, MA: Allyn & Bacon.

Simon, G. M. (2006). The heart of the matter: A proposal for placing the self of the therapist at the center of family therapy research and training. *Family Process, 45,* 331–344.

Skultétyová, I., Tokarev, D., & Jezová, D. (1998). Stress-induced increase in blood-brain barrier permeability in control and monosodium glutamate-treated rats. *Brain Research Bulletin, 45,* 75–178.

Smith, D. E. (2012). The process addictions and the new ASAM definition of addiction. *Journal of Psychoactive Drugs, 44*(1), 1–4.

Smith, J. E., & Meyers, R. J. (2004). *Motivating substance abusers to enter treatment.* New York: Guilford Press.

Smith, J. E., Meyers, R. J., & Austin, J. L. (2008). Working with family members to engage treatment-refusing drinkers: The CRAFT program. In O. J. Morgan & C. H. Litzke (Eds), *Family intervention in substance abuse: Current best practices* (pp. 169–193). New York: The Haworth Press.

Smock, S. A., Trepper, T. S., Wetchler, J. L., McCollum, E. E., Ray, R., & Pierce, K. (2008). Solution-focused group therapy for level 1 substance abusers. *Journal of Marital and Family Therapy, 34,* 107–120.

Snyder, D. K., Castellani, A. M., & Whisman, M. A. (2006). Current status and future directions in couple therapy. *Annual Review of Psychology, 57,* 317–344.

Söderpalm, B., & Ericson, M. (2013). Neurocircuitry involved in the development of alcohol addiction: The dopamine system and its access points. *Current Topics in Behavioral Neuroscience, 13,* 127–161.

Sohn, S. H., & Choi, Y. J. (2014). Phases of shopping addiction evidenced by experiences of compulsive buyers. *International Journal of Mental Health and Addiction, 12,* 243–254.

Song, M., & Omar, H. A. (2009). Discovering the complexities of adolescent compliance to treatment. *International Journal of Adolescent Medicine and Health, 21*(1), 3–8.

Southern, S. (2013). Relational ethics: Ethical decision making in couple, marriage, and family counseling and therapy. In C. M. Jungers & J. Gregoire (Eds), *Counseling ethics: Philosophical and professional foundations* (pp. 245–261). New York: Springer.

Sparks, S. N., Tisch, R., & Gardner, M. (2013). Family-centered interventions for substance abuse in Hispanic communities. *Journal of Ethnicity in Substance Abuse, 12*(1), 68–81.

Spillane, N. S., & Venner, K. (2018). Cultural considerations and recommendations for implementing brief interventions with American Indian adolescents. In P. M. Monti, S. M. Colby, & T. O. Tevyaw (Eds), *Brief interventions for adolescent alcohol and substance abuse* (pp. 284–304). New York: Guilford Press.

Sprenkle, D. H., & Blow, A. J. (2004). Common factors and our sacred models. *Journal of Marital and Family Therapy, 30,* 113–129.

Sprenkle, D. H., & Blow, A. J. (2007). The role of the therapist as the bridge between common factors and therapeutic change: More complex than congruency with a worldview. *Journal of Family Therapy, 29*(2), 109–113.

Sprenkle, D. H., Davis, S. D., & Lebow, J. L. (2009). *Common factors in couple and family therapy.* New York: Guilford Press.

Squeglia, L. M., Jacobus, J., & Tapert, S. F. (2009). The influence of substance use on adolescent brain development. *Clinical EEG and Neuroscience, 40*(1), 31–39.

Stanley, L. R., Miller, K. A., Beauvais, F., Walker, P. S., & Walker, R. D. (2014). Predicting an alcohol use disorder in urban American Indian youths. *Journal of Child & Adolescent Substance Abuse, 23*(2), 101–108.

Stanton, M. D. (1985). The family and drug abuse: Concepts and rationale. In T. E. Bratter & G. G. Forrest (Eds), *Alcoholism and substance abuse* (pp. 398–430). New York: The Free Press.

Stanton, M. D., & Shadish, W. W. (1997). Outcome, attrition, and family-couples treatment for drug abuse: A meta-analysis and review of the controlled, comparative studies. *Psychological Bulletin, 122*(2), 170–191.

Steinberg, M. A. (1993). Couples treatment issues for recovering male compulsive gamblers and their partners. *Journal of Gambling Studies, 9*(2), 153–167.

Steinglass, P. (1985). Family systems approaches to alcoholism. *Journal of Substance Abuse Treatment, 2,* 161–167.

Steinglass, P. (2008). Family systems and motivational interviewing: A systemic-motivational model for treatment of alcohol and other drug problems. In O. J. Morgan & C. H. Litzke (Eds), *Family intervention in substance abuse: Current best practices* (pp. 9–29). New York: Haworth Press.

Steinglass, P., Bennett, L. A., Wolin, S. J., & Reiss, D. (1987). *The alcoholic family.* New York: Basic Books, Inc.

Stevens, P. W. (2018). Family counseling with individuals diagnosed with substance use disorder. In P. W. Stevens & R. L. Smith (Eds), *Substance use counseling: Theory and practice* (6th Ed.) (pp. 208–227). New York: Pearson.

Stevens, P. W., & Smith, R. L. (2018). *Substance use counseling: Theory and practice* (6th Ed.). New York: Pearson.

Stevenson, L., Faucher, Y., Hewlett, S., Klemm, K., & Nelson, D. (2004). Chronic hepatitis C virus and the Hispanic community: Cultural factors impacting care. *Gastroenterology Nursing, 27,* 230–238.

Stewart, C., Koeske, G. F., & Pringle, J. L. (2017). The relationship between spirituality and overall health in African American substance abuse clients. *Social Work and Christianity, 44*(3), 39–59.

Strong, T. (2015). Diagnoses, relational processes and resourceful dialogs: Tensions for families and family therapy. *Family Process, 54*(3), 518–532.

Substance Abuse and Mental Health Services Administration (SAMHSA) (2005). *Results from the 2004 National Survey on Drug Use and Health: National findings.* Office of Applied Studies, NSDUH Series H-28, DHHS Publication No. SMA 05-4062. Rockville, MD: Author.

Substance Abuse and Mental Health Services Administration (SAMHSA) (2009). *The NSDUH report: Concurrent illicit drug and alcohol use.* Office of Applied Studies. Rockville, MD: Author.

Substance Abuse and Mental Health Services Administration (SAMHSA) (2012). *Results from the 2011 National Survey on Drug Use and Health: Mental health findings.* NSDUH Series H-45, HHS Publication No. (SMA) 12-4725. Rockville, MD: Author.

Sullivan R. J., & Hagen E. H. (2002). Psychotropic substance-seeking: Evolutionary pathology or adaptation? *Addiction, 97,* 389–400.

Sutherland, O., Couture, S., Silva, J. G., Strong, T., Lamarre, A., & Hardt, L. (2015). Social justice oriented diagnostic discussions: A discursive perspective. *Journal of Feminist Family Therapy: An International Forum, 28*(2–3), 76–99.

Suzuki, L. A., Wong, G., Mori, M., & Toyama, K. M. (2017). Asian American couples and families. In S. Kelly (Ed.), *Diversity in couple and family therapy* (pp. 33–62). Santa Barbara, CA: Praeger.

Sylwestrzak, A., Overholt, C. E., Ristau, K. I., & Coker, K. L. (2015). Self-reported barriers to treatment engagement: Adolescent perspectives from the National Comorbidity Survey-Adolescent Supplement (NCS-A). *Community Mental Health Journal, 51,* 775–781.

Szapocznik, J., Hervis, U., & Schwartz, S. (2003). *Brief strategic family therapy for adolescent drug abuse.* NIH Publication No. 03-4751. Bethesda, MD: National Institute on Drug Abuse.

Szapocznik, J., Prado, G., Burlew, A. K., Williams, R. A., & Santisteban, D. A. (2007). Drug abuse in African American and Hispanic adolescents: Culture, development, and behavior. *Annual Review of Clinical Psychology, 3,* 77–105.

Szapocznik, J., Schwartz, S. J., Muir, J. A., & Brown, C. H. (2012). Brief strategic family therapy: An intervention to reduce adolescent risk behavior. *Couple and Family Psychology: Research and Practice, 1*, 134–145.

Szapocznik, J., Scopetta, M. A., & King, O. E. (1978a). The effect and degree of treatment comprehensiveness with a Latino drug abusing population. In D. E. Smith, S. M. Anderson, M. Burton, N. Gotlieb, W. Harvey, & T. Chung (Eds), *A multicultural view of drug abuse* (pp. 563–573). Cambridge, MA: G. K. Hall.

Szapocznik, J., Scopetta, M. A., & King, O. E. (1978b). Theory and practice in matching treatment to the special characteristics and problems of Cuban immigrants. *Journal of Community Psychology, 6*, 112–122.

Tallaksen-Greene, S. J., Kaatz, K. W., Romano, C., & Albin, R. L. (1998). Localization of mGluR1a-like immunoreactivity and mGluR5-like immunoreactivity in identified populations of striatal neurons. *Brain Research, 780*(2), 210–217.

Tan, E. C., Tan. C. H., Karupathivan, U., & Yap, E. P. (2003). Mu opioid receptor gene polymorphisms and heroin dependence in Asian populations. *Neuroreport, 14*, 569–572.

Task Force on the Characteristics of Effective Addictions Counselors (1995, April). *Task force on the characteristics of effective addictions counselors progress review.* Washington, DC: Center for Substance Abuse Treatment.

Templeton, A. R. (1998). Human races: A genetic and evolutionary perspective. *American Anthropologist, 100*, 632–650.

Thai, N., Connell, C., & Tebes, J. (2010). Substance use among Asian American adolescents: Influence of race, ethnicity, and acculturation in the context of key risk and protective factors. *Asian American Journal of Psychology, 1*, 261–274.

Thomas, E. J., & Santa, C. A. (1982). Unilateral family therapy for alcohol abuse: A working conception. *American Journal of Family Therapy, 10*, 49–58.

Thomas, R., & Perera, R. (2006). School-based programmes for preventing smoking. *Cochrane Database of Systematic Reviews, 3*, Cd001293.

Thombs, D. L. (1999). *Introduction to addictive behaviors* (2nd Ed.). New York: Guilford Press.

Thombs, D. L., & Osborn, C. J. (2013). *Introduction to addictive behaviors* (4th Ed.). New York: Guilford Press.

Thompson, A. B., Goodman, M. S., & Kwate, N. O. A. (2016). Does learning about race prevent substance abuse? Racial discrimination, racial socialization and substance use among African Americans. *Addictive Behaviors, 61*, 1–7.

Thrasher, J. F., Niederdeppe, J., Farrelly, M. C., Davis, K. C., Ribisl, K. M., & Haviland, M. L. (2004). The impact of anti-tobacco industry prevention messages in tobacco producing regions: Evidence from the US truth campaign. *Tobacco Control, 13*(3), 283–288.

Tingey, L., Cwik, M., Chambers, R., Goklish, N., Larzelere-Hinton, F., Suttle, R., Lee, A., Alchesay, M., Parker, A., & Barlow, A. (2017). Motivators and influences on American Indian adolescent alcohol use and binge behavior: A qualitative exploration. *Journal of Child & Adolescent Substance Abuse, 26*(1), 75–85.

Tinnfalt, A., Eriksson, C., & Brunnberg, E. (2011). Adolescent children of alcoholics on disclosure, support, and assessment of trustworthy adults. *Child and Adolescent Social Work Journal, 28*, 133–151.

Tobler, N. S., Lessard, T., Marshall, D., Ochshorn, P., & Roona, M. (1999). Effectiveness of school-based drug prevention programs for marijuana use. *School Psychology International, 20*(1), 105–137.

Tooley, E. M., & Moyers, E. M. (2012). Motivational interviewing in practice. In S. T. Walters & F. Rotgers (Eds), *Treating substance abuse: Theory and technique* (3rd Ed.) (pp. 28–47). New York: Guilford Press.

Topf, J. L., Yip, S. W., & Potenza, M. N. (2009). Pathological gambling: Biological and clinical considerations. *Journal of Addiction Medicine, 3*(3), 111–119.

Tosto, G., Talarico, G., Luigi Lenzi, G., & Bruno, G. (2008). Effect of citalopram in treating hypersexuality in an Alzheimer's Disease case. *Neurological Sciences: Official Journal of the Italian Neurological Society and of the Italian Society of Clinical Neurophysiology, 29*, 269–270.

Tupala, E., & Tiihonen, J. (2004). Dopamine and alcoholism: Neurobiological basis of ethanol abuse. *Progress in Neuro-Psychopharmacology and Biological Psychiatry, 28*(8), 1221–1247.

Turner, J., Lloyd, D., & Taylor, L. (2006). Stress burden, drug dependence and the nativity paradox among U.S. Hispanics. *Drug & Alcohol Dependence, 28*, 79–89.

Turner, M. (2009). Uncovering and treating sex addiction in couples therapy. *Journal of Family Psychotherapy, 20*(2–3), 283–302.

Uhl, G. (2004). Molecular genetics of substance abuse vulnerability: Remarkable recent convergence of genome scan results. *Annals of the New York Academy of Sciences, 1025*, 1–13.

Unger, J. B., Ritt-Olson, A., Wagner, K. D., Soto, D. W., & Baezconde-Garbanati, L. (2009). Parent-child acculturation patterns and substance use among Hispanic adolescents: A longitudinal analysis. *Journal of Primary Prevention, 30*(3–4), 293–313.

Unger, J. B., Soto, D. W., & Baezconde-Garbanati, L. (2016). Trajectories of perceived discrimination from adolescence to emerging adulthood and substance use among Hispanic youth in Los Angeles. *Addictive Behaviors, 53*, 108–112.

United Nations Office on Drugs and Crime (2013). *Drug statistics and trends*. Vienna: Author. Retrieved from www.unodc.org/documents/wdr/WDR_2010/2.0_Drug_statistics_andTrends.pdf.

U.S. Census (2010). *Decennial census of population and housing*. Washington, DC: Author. Retrieved from www.census.gov/2010census.

U.S. Census (2012). *American Indian and Alaska Native Heritage Month: November 2012*. Washington, DC: Author. Retrieved from www.census.gov/newsroom/releases/archives/facts_for_features_special_editions/cb12-ff22.html.

U. S. Department of Health and Human Services. Washington, DC: Author.

U.S Department of Health and Human Services (HHS), Office of the Surgeon General (2016). *Facing addiction in America: The Surgeon General's report on alcohol, drugs, and health*. Washington, DC: Author. Retrieved from www.surgeongeneral.gov/library/2016alcoholdrugshealth/index.html.

Vaccarino, A. L., & Kastin, A. J. (2000). Endogenous opiates: 2000. *Peptides, 22*, 2257–2328.

Vachon, J., Vitaro, F., Wanner, B., & Tremblay, R. E. (2004). Adolescent gambling: Relationships with parent gambling and parenting practices. *Psychology of Addictive Behaviors, 18*(4), 398–401.

VanDeMark, N. R., Russell, L. A., O'Keefe, M., Findelstein, M., Noether, C. D., & Gampel, J. C. (2005). Children of mothers with histories of substance abuse, mental illness, and trauma. *Journal of Community Psychology, 33*, 445–459.

Van den Wildenberg, E., Wiers, R. W., Dessers, J., Janssen, R. G. J. H., Lambrichs, E. H., Smeets, H. J. M., & van Breukelen, G. J. P. (2007). A functional polymorphism of the mu-opioid receptor gene (OPRM1) influences cue-induced craving for alcohol in male heavy drinkers. *Alcoholism: Clinical and Experimental Research, 31*, 1–10.

Van der Pol, T. M., Hoeve, M., Noom, M. J., Stams, G. J. J. M., Doreleijers, T. A. H., van Domburgh, L., & Vermeiren, R. R. J. M. (2017). Research review: The effectiveness of multidimensional family therapy in treating adolescents with multiple behavior problems—a meta-analysis. *Journal of Child Psychology and Psychiatry, 58*(5), 532–545.

Van der Stouwe, T., Asscher, J. J., Stams, G. J. J. M., Deković, M., & van der Laan, P. H. (2014). Effectiveness of multisystemic therapy (MST): A meta-analysis. *Clinical Psychology Review, 34*(6), 468–481.

Van Ryzin, M. J., Roseth, C. J., Fosco, G. M., Lee, Y. K., & Chen, I. C. (2016). A component-centered meta-analysis of family-based prevention programs for adolescent substance use. *Clinical Psychology Review, 45*, 72–80.

Van Wormer, K., & Davis, D. R. (2013). *Addiction treatment: A strengths perspective* (3rd Ed.). Belmont, CA: Brooks/Cole.

Vaught, E. L., & Wittman, P. P. (2011). A phenomenological study of the occupational choices of individuals who self identify as adult children of alcoholics. *Journal of Occupational Science, 18*, 356–365.

Vega, W. A., Aguilar-Gaxiola, S., Andrade, L., Bijl, R., Borges, G., Caraveio- Anduaga, J. J., DeWit, D. J., Heeringa, S. G., Kessler, R. C., Kolody, B., Merikangas, K. R., Molnar, B. E., Walters, E. E., Warner, L. A., & Wittchen, H.-U. (2002). Prevalence and age of onset for drug use in seven international sites: Results from the international consortium of psychiatric epidemiology. *Drug and Alcohol Dependence, 68*, 285–297.

Vernig, P. M. (2011). Family roles in homes with alcohol-dependent parents: An evidence-based review. *Substance Use & Misuse, 46*, 535–542.

Veronie, L., & Fruehstorfer, D. B. (2001). Gender, birth order and family role identification among adult children of alcoholics. *Current Psychology, 20*, 53–67.

Vidourek, R. A., King, K. A., Burbage, M., & Okuley, B. (2018). Impact of parenting behaviors on recent alcohol use among African American students. *Child & Adolescent Social Work Journal, 35*, 271–282.

Volkow, N. D., Koob, G. F., & McLellan, A. T. (2016). Neurobiological advances from the brain disease model of addiction. *The New England Journal of Medicine, 374*(4), 363–371.

Wade, J., & Peralta, R. L. (2017). Perceived racial discrimination, heavy episodic drinking, and alcohol abstinence among African American and White college students. *Journal of Ethnicity in Substance Abuse, 16*(2), 165–180.

Wallace, J. (2012). Theory of 12-step-oriented treatment. In S. T. Walters & F. Rotgers (Eds), *Treating substance abuse: Theory and technique* (3rd Ed.) (pp. 167–190). New York: Guilford Press.

Walther, B., Morgenstern, M., & Hanewinkel, R. (2012). Co-occurrence of addictive behaviours: Personality factors related to substance use, gambling and computer gaming. *European Addiction Research, 18*(4), 167–174.

Wampold, B. E., & Imel, Z. E. (2015). *The great psychotherapy debate* (2nd Ed.). New York: Routledge.

Wang, M., Kviz, F. J., & Miller, A. M. (2012). The mediating role of parent–child bonding to prevent adolescent alcohol abuse among Asian American families. *Journal of Immigrant and Minority Health, 14*, 831–840.

Washton, A. M. (1989). *Cocaine addiction: Treatment, recovery, and relapse prevention.* New York: Norton.

Washton, A. M. (1990). *Quitting cocaine.* Center City, MN: Hazelden.

Washton, A. M., & Stone-Washton, N. (1990). Abstinence and relapse in outpatient cocaine addicts. *Journal of Psychoactive Drugs, 22*(2), 135–147.

Washton, A. M., & Zweben, J. E. (2006). *Treating alcohol and drug problems in psychotherapy practice: Doing what works.* New York: Guilford Press.

Watkins, T. R., Lewellen, A., & Barrett, M. C. (2001). *Dual diagnosis: An integrated approach to treatment.* Thousand Oaks, CA: Sage Publications, Inc.

Watts-Jones, T. D. (2010). Location of self: Opening the door to dialogue on intersectionality in the therapy process. *Family Process, 49*, 405–420.

Watzlawick, P., Bavelas, J. B., & Jackson, D. D. (1967). *Pragmatics of human communication.* New York: W. W. Norton & Company.

Watzlawick, P., Weakland, J., & Fisch, R. (1974). *Change: Principles of problem formation and problem resolution.* New York: W. W. Norton & Company.

Weakland, J. H., Fisch, R., Watzlawick, P., & Bodin, A. M. (1974). Brief therapy: Focused problem resolution. *Family Process, 13*(2), 141–168.

Wegscheider-Cruse, S. (1989). *Another chance: Hope and health for the alcoholic family* (2nd Ed.). Palo Alto, CA: Science and Behavior Books.

Wegscheider-Cruse, S., & Cruse, J. (2012). *Understanding codependency, updated and expanded: The science behind it and how to break the cycle.* Deerfield Beach, FL: Health Communications, Inc.

Weiner-Davis, M., de Shazer, S., & Gingerich, W. J. (1987). Using pretreatment change to construct a therapeutic solution: A clinical note. *Journal of Marital and Family Therapy, 13,* 359–363.

Weiss, R. (2004). Treating sex addiction. In R. H. Coombs (Ed.), *Handbook of addictive disorders: A practical guide to diagnosis and treatment* (pp. 233–272). Hoboken, NJ: Wiley.

Wells, C., Adhyaru, J., Cannon, J., Lamond, M., & Baruch, G. (2010). Multisystemic therapy (MST) for youth offending, psychiatric disorder and substance abuse: Case examples from a UK MST team. *Child and Adolescent Mental Health, 15* (3), 142–149.

Welte, J., Barnes, G., Wieczorek, W., Tidwell, M.-C., & Parker, J. (2001). Alcohol and gambling pathology among U. S. adults: Prevalence, demographic patterns and comorbidity. *Journal of Studies on Alcohol, 62*(5), 706–712.

Whitaker, C. (1975). Psychotherapy of the absurd: With a special emphasis on the psychotherapy of aggression. *Family Process, 14,* 1–16.

Whitaker, C. A., & Bumberry, W. M. (1988). *Dancing with the family: A symbolic-experiential approach.* New York: Brunner/Mazel.

White, M. (1986). Negative explanation, restraint and double description: A template for family therapy. *Family Process, 25,* 169–184.

White, M. (1993). Deconstruction and therapy. In S. Gilligan & R. Price (Eds), *Therapeutic conversations* (pp. 22–61). New York: W. W. Norton.

White, M. (1995). *Re-authoring lives: Interviews & essays.* Adelaide: Dulwich Centre Publications.

White, M. (1997). Challenging the culture of consumption: Rites of passage and communities of acknowledgement. *Dulwich Centre Newsletter, 2 & 3,* 38–47.

White, M. (2007). *Maps of narrative practice.* New York: W. W. Norton & Company.

White, M. (2011). *Narrative practice: Continuing the conversation.* New York: W. W. Norton & Company.

White, M., & Epston, D. (1990). *Narrative means to therapeutic ends.* New York: W. W. Norton & Company.

White, W. L., & Cloud, W. (2008). Recovery capital: A primer for addictions professionals. *Counselor, 9,* 22–27.

Whitesell, N. R., Asdigian, N. L., Kaufman, C. E., Crow, C. B., Shangreau, C., Keane, E. M., Mousseau, A. C., & Mitchell, C. M. (2014). Trajectories of substance use among young American Indian adolescents: Patterns and predictors. *Journal of Youth and Adolescence, 43*(3), 437–453.

Wilbanks, W. (1989). The danger in viewing addicts as victims: A critique of the disease model of addiction. *Criminal Justice Policy Review, 3,* 407–422.

Wilcoxon, S. A., Remley, T. P., Jr., & Gladding, S. T. (2013). *Ethical, legal, and professional issues in the practice of marriage and family therapy* (updated 5th Ed.). Boston, MA: Pearson.

Wilhoit, L. F., Scott, D. A., & Simecka, B. A. (2017). Fetal alcohol spectrum disorders: Characteristics, complications, and treatment. *Community Mental Health Journal, 53*(6), 711–718.

Williams, I. L. (2016). The intersection of structurally traumatized communities and substance use treatment: Dominant discourses and hidden themes. *Journal of Ethnicity in Substance Abuse, 15*(2), 95–126.

Willoughby, T., Good, M., Adachi, P. J. C., Hamza, C., & Tavernier, R. (2014). Examining the link between adolescent brain development and risk taking from a social-developmental perspective. *Brain and Cognition, 89,* 70–78.

Wise, R. A. (1989). Opiate reward: Sites and substrates. *Neuroscience and Biobehavioral Reviews, 13,* 129–133.

Wlodarczyk, O., Schwarze, M., Rumpf, H.-J., Metzner, F., & Pawils, S. (2017). Protective mental health factors in children of parents with alcohol and drug use disorders: A systematic review. *Plos One, 12*(6), 1–15.

Wolin, S. J., & Wolin, S. (1993). *The resilient self.* New York: Villard Books.

Woo, B., Wang, K., & Tran, T. (2017). Racial and ethnic differences in associations between psychological distress and the presence of binge drinking: Results from the California health interview survey. *Addictive Behaviors, 65*, 1–6.

World Health Organization (WHO) (2018). *Global status report on alcohol and health 2018.* Retrieved from http://apps.who.int/iris/bitstream/handle/10665/274603/97892 41565639-eng.pdf?ua=1.

World Health Organization, Eastern Mediterranean Regional Office (WHO EMRO) (2018). *Health promotion and disease prevention through population-based interventions, including action to address social determinants and health inequity.* Cairo: Author. Retrieved from www.emro.who.int/about-who/public-health-functions/health-promotion-disease-prevention.html.

Wrase, J., Schlagenhauf, F., Kienast, T., Wüstenberg, T., Bermpohl, F., Kahnt, T., & Heinz, A. (2007). Dysfunction of reward processing correlates with alcohol craving in detoxified alcoholics. *NeuroImage, 35*(2), 787–794.

Wright, E. M. (2001). Substance abuse in African American communities. In S. L. A. Straussner (Ed.), *Ethnocultural factors in substance abuse treatment* (pp. 31–51). New York: Guilford Press.

Xu, H., Wang, F., Kranzler, H. R., Gelernter, J., & Zhang, H. (2017). Alcohol and nicotine codependence-associated DNA methylation changes in promoter regions of addiction-related genes. *Scientific Reports, 7*, 41816.

Yalom, I. D., & Leszcz, M. (2005). *Theory and practice of group psychotherapy* (5th Ed.). New York: Basic Books.

Yamamoto, B. K., Moszczynska, A., & Gudelsky, G. A. (2010). Amphetamine toxicities: Classical and emerging mechanisms. *Annals of the New York Academy of Sciences, 1187*, 101–121.

Yang, Y., Li, H., Chen, X., Zhang, L., Huang, B., & Zhu, T. (2017). Electro-acupuncture treatment for internet addiction: Evidence of normalization of impulse control disorder in adolescents. *Chinese Journal of Integrative Medicine, 23*(11), 837–844.

Yen, J. Y., Ko, C. H., Yen, C. F., Chen, S. H., Chung, W. L., & Chen, C. C. (2008). Psychiatric symptoms in adolescents with Internet addiction: Comparison with substance use. *Psychiatry and Clinical Neurosciences, 62*, 9–16.

Yen, J., Yen, C., Chen, C., Chen, S., & Ko, C. (2007). Family factors of internet addiction and substance use experience in Taiwanese adolescents. *Cyberpsychology & Behavior, 10*, 323–329.

Yoo, H., Gee, G., & Lowthrop, C. (2010). Self- reported racial discrimination and substance use among Asian Americans in Arizona. *Journal of Immigrant Minority Health, 12*, 683–690.

Young, K. S. (1996). Internet addiction: The emergence of a new clinical disorder. Paper presented at the 104th annual meeting of the American Psychological Association, August 11, Toronto, Canada.

Young, K. S. (1999). Internet addiction: Symptoms, evaluation, and treatment. In L. VandeCreek & T. L. Jackson (Eds), *Innovations in clinical practice* (Vol. 17) (pp. 1–17). Sarasota, FL: Professional Resource Press.

Young, K. S. (2011). CBT-IA: The first treatment model for internet addiction. *Journal of Cognitive Psychotherapy, 25*, 304–312.

Young, L. B., & Timko, C. (2015). Benefits and costs of alcoholic relationships and recovery through Al-Anon. *Substance Use & Misuse, 50*(1), 62–71.

Young, S. (2015). Understanding substance abuse counselor turnover due to burnout: A theoretical perspective. *Journal of Human Behavior in the Social Environment, 25*, 675–686.

Yu, M., & Stiffman, A. (2007). Culture and environment as predictors of alcohol abuse/dependence symptoms in American Indian youths. *Addictive Behaviors, 32*, 2253–2259.

Yuan, N., Eaves, E., Koss, M., Polacca, M., Bletzer, K., & Goldman, D. (2010). "Alcohol is something that been with us like a common cold": Community perceptions of American Indian drinking. *Substance Use and Misuse, 45*, 1909–1929.

Yuodelis-Flores, C., & Ries, R. K. (2015). Addiction and suicide: A review. *The American Journal on Addictions, 24*(2), 98–104.

Zelvin, E. (2014). Treating the partners of individuals with substance use disorders. In S. L. A. Straussner (Ed.), *Clinical work with substance-abusing clients* (3rd Ed.) (pp. 326–347). New York: Guilford Press.

Zemore, S. E., Ye, Y., Mulia, N., Martinez, P., Jones-Webb, R., & Karriker-Jaffe, K. (2016). Poor, persecuted, young, and alone: Toward explaining the elevated risk of alcohol problems among Black and Latino men who drink. *Drug and Alcohol Dependence, 163*, 31–39.

Zhang, C., Brook, J. S., Leukefeld, C. G., & Brook, D. W. (2016). Associations between compulsive buying and substance dependence/abuse, major depressive episodes, and generalized anxiety disorder among men and women. *Journal of Addictive Diseases, 35*(4), 298–304.

Zhang, L., Amos, C., & McDowell, W. (2008). A comparative study of internet addiction between the United States and China. *Cyberpsychology, Behavior, and Social Networking, 11*, 727–729.

Zhang, R., Miao, Q., Wang, C., Zhao, R., Li, W., Haile, C., Hao, W., & Zhang, X. (2013). Genome-wide DNA methylation analysis in alcohol dependence. *Addiction Biology, 18*, 392–403.

Zlebnik, N. E., & Cheer, J. F. (2016). Beyond the CB1 receptor: Is cannabidiol the answer for disorders of motivation? *Annual Review of Neuroscience, 39*, 1–17.

Zollinger, T. W., Saywell, R. M., Muegge, C. M., Wooldridge, J. S., Cummings, S. F., & Caine, V. A. (2009). Impact of the Life Skills Training Curriculum on middle school students tobacco use in Marion County, Indiana, 1997–2000. *Journal of School Health, 73*(9), 338–346.

Index

absent family system 61–62
abstinence 6, 190, 345, 346, 347
accommodation 301
acculturation 72, 76–78, 84, 86
addiction (definition of) 4–8
adult children of alcoholics 128–130
affiliation 244
African American families 79–83; risk
    and protective factors 81–82; and
    substance abuse 79–80; youth 81
Africentrism 82
agonist drug 27
Al-Anon 185–186
alcohol dehydrogenases (ADHs) 49
alcoholic family types 61–63
Alcoholic Anonymous 182–185
alleles 42
alliances 244–245, 301
American Indian families 87–92; risk and
    protective factors 90–91; substance
    abuse 88–89; youth 89–90
amino acids 41
antagonistic drug 27
antianxiety and sedative hypnotics 32–34
anxiolytic 32
ARISE 190–192; level 1 191–192; level 2
    192; level 3 192
assent 216
Asian American families 83–87; risk and
    protective factors 86; and substance
    abuse 84–85; youth 85
attachment 125–126, 266
autonomy 215
authoritarian parents 244
authoritative parents 244

Bateson, G. 240, 284, 292–293, 296
battle for initiative 281–282
battle for structure 281–282
behavioral addiction 165
benders 13
beneficence 212–213
benevolent sabotage 287
bioecological systems theory 16–17;
    exosystem 16; macrosystem 16;
    mesosystem 16; microsystem 16
Black, C. 104, 108
blackouts 13
Black's family roles 104–108; the acting-
    out child 107; the adjuster 106;
    codependent 105; the placater
    106–107; the responsible child
    105–106
blood-brain barrier 42
boundaries 55, 57, 63, 65, 120, 137,
    243–244, 300, 379–381; clear 120,
    243–244, 300, 380; diffuse 243–244,
    300, 379–380; rigid 300, 349,
    379–380
boundary making 302
boundary rules 370
brief strategic family therapy (BSFT)
    326–330
BSFT elements of family interactions
    328–329; conflict resolution 327;
    developmental stages 328; family
    organization 327; identified
    patient 328; life context 328;
    resonance 327
BSFT intervention 329–330; planned 329;
    practical 329; problem-focused 329

423